Major Problems in

AMERICAN DIPLOMATIC HISTORY

MAJOR PROBLEMS IN

American *DIPLOMATIC* HISTORY

Documents and Readings

EDITED BY *Daniel M. Smith*
UNIVERSITY OF COLORADO

D. C. HEATH AND COMPANY BOSTON

Library of Congress Catalog Card Number: 63–22521 (6 L 3)

PRINTED IN THE UNITED STATES OF AMERICA

PREFACE

It seemed to the editor, in reflecting on his experiences as student and teacher, that a need existed for a volume on American diplomatic history based on a sharply defined problems approach. Much of the interest and value in the study of American foreign relations is found in the asking and answering of the "great questions" of the causes and consequences of decisions for war, peacemaking, and the declaration of major policies.

With the exception of the first introductory chapter, the emphasis has been placed on the debates among historians and statesmen concerning 20 specific events or policies. A few selected documents precede the secondary accounts in the chapters, in part because of the conviction that the student should be exposed to the raw material of history, but primarily in order to illustrate the depth and range of the problem under study. It is hoped that this approach will broaden the student's appreciation of American diplomatic history and will not only give him some basis for evaluating the past but will facilitate an understanding of the nature of the historical craft.

Although the editor alone is responsible for the materials in this volume—and is aware that many will ask why certain documents and secondary readings were either included or omitted—he wishes to express gratitude for wisdom and guidance received in the past from Professor Armin Rappaport at the University of California, Berkeley, and Professor Thomas A. Bailey of Stanford University.

MAPS

CONTENTS

PART I:

The Expansion of the United States, 1776–1889

PART I

The Expansion of the United States

1776–1889

INTRODUCTION

In the period prior to 1889, the United States successfully established its independence and expanded the national domain. Certain basic foreign policies and attitudes were formed and were followed with a degree of consistency. The naval historian, A. T. Mahan, summed up 19th-century policies, with much accuracy, as abstention in Europe, cooperation in the Far East, and dominance in Latin America. Toward Europe, American policy was one of avoidance of its politics and wars, expressed in the form of neutrality proclamations and the Washington Farewell Address, and in an insistence on observance in wartime of a liberal concept of neutral rights. In Latin America, at least in areas of interest to the United States, it was a policy of hegemony, implied by the Monroe Doctrine and American territorial expansion. In the Far East, it was largely commercial expansion based on cooperation with other powers interested in Oriental trade, and eventually to be expressed as the Commercial Open Door policy. The story of American foreign relations is how these basic policies were formulated and applied in the 19th century, and the changes wrought by the dramatically different challenges of the present century.

I PUBLIC OPINION AND AMERICAN FOREIGN RELATIONS

Some knowledge of how American foreign policy is formulated and administered and the role of public opinion in that process is prerequisite to the study of major problems in American diplomatic history.

The foreign relations power of the national government is derived from two main sources: the existence of the nation as a sovereign state, and the constitutional provisions. As a sovereign state in a world of independent states, the United States necessarily has to conduct relations of war, peace, and trade with the other powers. Consequently, from the viewpoint of the international community, the American government possesses the powers, privileges, and responsibilities of a member of the world family of nations. The Constitution grants certain powers over foreign affairs to the central government and these have been supplemented and extended by Supreme Court rulings, congressional legislation, and practice. The President is vested with the general executive power, is commander-in-chief of the armed forces, can receive foreign diplomatic representatives, and with the approval of the Senate makes treaties and appointments. Though its powers are less imposing, the Congress also has an important role. Senatorial approval of treaties and appointments is required, the House of Representatives initiates all money appropriations, and both houses together have the power to declare war and regulate commerce and immigration. Article VI of the Constitution contains the supremacy clause that the Federal Constitution, laws of Congress, and treaties are the supreme law of the land. These provisions, with court rulings (*Missouri vs. Holland,* 1920), leave no residuum of powers over foreign relations to the several states of the union. In practice, however, a state may so handle local matters as to impinge on the foreign relations power.

Apart from question of the machinery, and without examining the built-in conflicts between the President and the Congress in the field of foreign affairs, the student of American diplomatic history is necessarily concerned with the role of public opinion. A democratic republic, as Thomas Jefferson long ago commented, presupposes the existence of an informed and interested electorate. The President and his appointees, together with members of Congress, are periodically held accountable for their conduct by the mass of citizens and must therefore be constantly preoccupied with the mood and desires of the public. This fact raises several important questions: what is public opinion, how does it influence foreign policy and diplomacy, what defects does it have, and what can be done to improve it and make it more effective within the democratic context? The following readings are selected to examine aspects of the problems and to suggest possible solutions.

1. The Case for More Education

Thomas A. Bailey, a prominent American diplomatic historian at Stanford University and the author of numerous studies and articles, in the following selection examines the nature and function of public opinion in relation to foreign affairs through an analysis of the historical record. Public opinion, he concludes, determines the outer limits within which foreign policy formulators work, and elected officials often are severely limited or are even forced by public pressures to adopt courses which they regard as unfortunate. Although he acknowledges the many defects of public opinion, and especially those resulting from ignorance and prejudice, Bailey is optimistic that great improvement can be achieved through more intensive educational efforts.

The Man in the Street

THOMAS A. BAILEY

The Sovereign Citizen

1

Nero murdered his mother and his divorced wife and did many other diabolical deeds with complete impunity, but he was forced to give up his ambition to become an actor when the Roman populace reacted unfavorably to his efforts. The Pharisees attempted to lay unfriendly hands on the Apostles, but they were compelled to desist when an angry murmur rose from the multitude. These are but two early examples, and by no means the earliest ones, of the sovereign power of an aroused public. . . .

All governments, whatever their nature, rest on the foundation stone of public opinion. The Scottish philosopher David Hume observed as long ago as 1741: "As force is always on the side of the governed, the governors have nothing to support them but opinion." The yellowing scroll of history reveals few if any instances when a ruler flagrantly and persistently defied the will of his subjects without courting disaster. Even dictators are keenly aware of their servitude to public opinion, and this explains why they are at such pains to propagandize their people into supporting arbitrary rule. Hitler had to deceive the German nation through Dr. Goebbels' lie factory, and Mussolini and Stalin and other dictators of recent vintage had to employ similar chicanery. Censorship and propaganda are the unconscious compliments that despots pay to the potency of public opinion.

All this seems like an attempt to prove the obvious, but the truth is that millions of people are still unconvinced. Public opinion is so apathetic and preoccupied, so changeful and impulsive, so ill-informed and misinformed, that critics are apt to sneer at its power. Yet a giant who is fickle and ignorant still has a giant's strength, and may use it with frightful effect.

Another source of skepticism is that public opinion is awkward to

Thomas A. Bailey, *The Man in the street; the Impact of American Public Opinion on Foreign Policy* (New York: The Macmillan Company, 1948), 1–13, 130–139, 318–319. Reprinted with the permission of Thomas A. Bailey.

describe, elusive to define, difficult to measure, and impossible to see, even though it may be felt. James Russell Lowell once remarked that popular sentiment was like the pressure of the atmosphere: one could not see it but "all the same, it is sixteen pounds to the square inch." The British Foreign Secretary Sir Samuel Hoare had never seen public opinion when, in 1935, he plotted with the French premier to sacrifice Ethiopia on the altar of Italy's imperial ambitions. But when the backfire of public resentment blew him out of office, he could not deny its force. An angered electorate is an awesome thing.

In a dictatorship, the masses must be deceived; in a democracy, they must be educated. In either case, they must be courted if public programs are to be carried through. If Mr. Average American wants to get a glimpse at the power behind the officeholder's chair, all he has to do is pick up a mirror and look into it.

2

The most powerful nation in the world today is the United States, and consequently the most powerful body of public opinion in existence is formed by the American people. What the government in Washington does or fails to do in the field of foreign affairs will depend largely on the wishes of our citizens, and what our citizens demand or fail to demand will affect mightily the destiny of this planet.

A vexatious problem here at home, such as housing or unemployment, touches the Man in the Street more immediately than one abroad. For this reason there is normally much more popular pressure on Washington for action regarding internal affairs than foreign affairs.

The sovereign American people may influence their government either positively or negatively. The classic example of positive action may be found in 1898, when the masses rose and cried out for war against Spain with such overwhelming insistence that the amiable McKinley dared not deny their demands.

Negative pressure is much less obvious but no less potent. Fear as to how the people may react has often caused the President and the State Department to recoil from a contemplated course. When the United States minister in Mexico City, James Gadsden, was negotiating in 1853 for the strip of southwestern territory that bears his name, he suggested that the State Department supply him with money for bribing certain Mexican officials. He was informed from Washington that such funds could be provided only by Congressional action, and that the resulting stench would be undesirable. Similarly, the ingrained distrust of the average American for entangling alliances, combined with his hereditary dislike of England, has repeatedly caused the State Department to draw back from a closer understanding with Downing Street, lest the news leak out and recoil disastrously upon the administration.

The Harding landslide of 1920 was falsely interpreted as a tremendous mandate against the League of Nations, and Republican administrations for the next decade, paralyzed by their prodigious plurality of 7,000,000 votes, shunned the League as they would a leper. The cautious Republican politician would invite no similar rebuke from a presumably wrathful electorate.

By the early 1930's it was clear to all discerning students of finance that the debts owed us by our associates in World War I were uncollectible. The alternatives were cancellation or just not getting the money. But the almighty taxpayer, knowing that he would have to foot the bill in either case, bristled up at the slightest suggestion of cancellation. The officials in Washington had to keep crying for the moon, many of them knowing perfectly well they were crying uselessly, except in so far as they were usefully placating the public.

3

How does the citizen actually exert pressure on his government? He may send letters, telegrams, and petitions to his congressman, his senator, or his President, but his most formidable bludgeon is the ballot. As Oliver Wendell Holmes put it,

> The freeman, casting with unpurchased hand
> The vote that shakes the turret of the land.

The President fears the electorate, although he may not respect it. He is the head of a great political party first; the director of foreign affairs second or perhaps third. With a natural desire for the endorsement of reelection, he is bedeviled by his eligibility for a second term and, in the days of Franklin Roosevelt, for a third and a fourth. If he offends or defies the voter, he may be repudiated at the polls.

A war with France in 1800 would have been good for the party but bad for the country, and President John Adams, courageously ignoring the clamor of the crowd for blood, patched up existing disputes and gave the nation peace. He suspected that he was committing political suicide when he boldly put patriotism above party, and the event proved him correct. He was defeated for reelection in 1800, and never thereafter held public office. A century later, in 1898, war with Spain over Cuba was good for the party but bad for the country. President McKinley, yielding to the clamor of the crowd for blood, gave the country war. He was triumphantly reelected in 1900. In all fairness it must be added that the two cases are only roughly parallel, but in each instance there was tremendous pressure from the mob and an awareness in the White House of the political penalties and preferments involved. Someone has urged that we award medals to public servants who show courage above and beyond the call of politics.

Even if the President does not care about his own personal fortunes, as Cleveland notoriously did not, he cannot without the basest ingratitude be indifferent to the fortunes of the party that gave him immortality. Scores of Congressmen and other elected officials ride into office on the coattails of a popular President, and their careers are jeopardized if their titular leader needlessly antagonizes the ballot casters.

The Chief Executive is usually more exposed to public pressure regarding major issues of foreign policy than is the Congress and the

State Department. He is one; they are many, and some of them are entrenched behind bureaucratic barriers. His name and White House residence are well known, and the ordinary voter can easily send him a postal card, a letter, or a telegram. The names of the bureaucrats may not be known, and their addresses present difficulties. The President is elected every four years; the bureaucrats often have life tenure under civil service. The pressure may therefore converge upon the Executive Mansion with fearful force, as was notably true when McKinley had to take sleeping powders while pondering the fateful decision of war or peace with Spain.

A Frenchman in the days of the Revolution is supposed to have dashed to his window, when he heard the mob go roaring by, and to have cried: "There go my followers. I must follow them. I am their leader." Like this legendary Frenchman, the President must seem to follow public opinion, or at least not get too far out in front of it, for he will then be sniped at from the rear. Franklin Roosevelt's Quarantine Speech of 1937, defiantly delivered in the isolationist capital of America (Chicago), evoked such an uproar from the noninterventionist camp as to force a hasty retreat.

One British statesman, so it is said, would have made fewer political blunders "if he had only ridden more in omnibuses." The President does not ride the busses at all, and if the people have not indicated their desires, he must anticipate their reaction to his moves. His touch must be sure, for if he guesses wrong, his political life may be forfeited. Franklin Roosevelt had no directive from the American public when in 1938 he boldly declared at Kingston, Ontario, that the United States would help defend Canada against foreign invasion; nor when in the pre-Pearl Harbor days of 1941 he dramatically took over the defense of Iceland from Great Britain. But both of these strokes were aimed at the security of the United States, and the President assumed that the American people would support him, as the Gallup polls later revealed that they did in overwhelming measure. Roosevelt was a successful leader because he was generally clever enough to lead in a direction where the masses were willing to go.

4

The State Department likewise fears the hands that cast the ballots. If it blunders, the administration may be swept out, including the Secretary of State and other top men in the Department.

William H. Seward, who served with distinction during the Civil War, was the first Secretary of State to conduct foreign relations with a keen eye to the necessity of informing and placating public opinion. He published diplomatic papers with unusual frequency, and inaugurated the annual series of official documents which for recency and completeness far surpasses anything put out by other foreign offices. His master stroke came in 1861 with the handling of the *Trent* affair. The United States naval officer who seized two Confederate commissioners from the British mail steamer *Trent* was clearly in the wrong, but his bold wrenching of the lion's tail was ecstatically popular in the North. The Lincoln administration dared not keep the prisoners, lest England declare war; it was unwilling to turn them loose, lest the populace get out of hand. But after passions had cooled, the Confederate envoys could be released, and public opinion was to some extent mollified when in a clever note Seward congratulated the British on having finally accepted the principles for which we had vainly fought them in 1812. Seward's specious discourse was clearly more of a sop to public opinion than a contribution to international law. . . .

The average citizen, instead of complaining that the State Department has no policy, could better say: "Let's give the Department a policy." Public pressure can force a policy upon an unwilling administration, as was true of the neutrality legislation of the 1930's, but the administration can hardly force a major policy upon an unwilling people, as Franklin Roosevelt attempted to do in his Quarantine Speech. When there is a strong and articulate public opinion, the Department may move with the assurance that it will not be left out on the end of a limb. When opinion is confused, or when the issue is minor and no public opinion exists regarding it, the Department must make its decisions more or less blindly, and on a guess-and-pray basis. These are the occasions when it has the greatest latitude, and some seemingly minor decisions, regarding which the people were apathetic, have drawn us deeper and deeper into the international quicksands. Commitments in the 1940's to support the Nationalist government of China against the Communists, while fraught with grave dangers, passed virtually unnoticed in the United States.

Congressmen fear the electorate even more than the President does, for they have only two sure years of political life as compared with his four. If President McKinley kept his ear to the ground for rumblings from the grassroots, Congressman Claghorn keeps his political antennae spread for every current from his constituents. The late Senator Norris records that in 1917 a number of his colleagues told him they did not favor the war resolution against Germany, but they dared not vote against it, so strong was the pressure from their districts. "The conscience of Congress," as one writer puts it, "is peculiarly responsive to large numbers." In more recent years it has also become markedly responsive to Gallup polls.

The national opinion surveys reveal that in the pre-1941 era the people were many months in advance of Congress on such burning issues as lifting the arms embargo and instituting compulsory military training. With the air of a discoverer, one recent writer concludes that during the years from 1935 to 1943 "public opinion was, on the average, between one and two years ahead of Congress." More than fifty years earlier, and without benefit of Gallup polls, Lord Bryce observed that public opinion "leads" the politicians, not vice versa. A Washington publisher has defined a politician as one who is only six months behind popular sentiment. . . .

The caution of the average congressman is quite understandable. He is badgered and confused by lobbyists, and he is often unable to distinguish public opinion from pressure opinion. When in doubt he had better play safe. He is also a candidate for reelection; the Gallup pollee is not. He must stand up and be counted when the votes are taken in Congress; the Gallup pollee remains anonymous, and for this reason can enjoy the luxury of a more unselfish or more moral attitude. As Francis Bacon long ago observed: "Do not wonder if the common people speak more truly than those of higher rank; for they speak with more safety."

A United States senator is in a much more comfortable position than his colleague in the House. He is elected for six years, and only one third of the entire membership of the Senate comes up for reelection every two years. The individual voters have notoriously short memories; it is difficult for them to hold a grudge against a senator for some vote on foreign policy, especially if they do not know his name, which often they do not. Domestic affairs are normally more important than foreign affairs to the ordinary American, and even if he dislikes the record of his senators on foreign policy, he may still vote for them if they are sound on free silver or the tariff on lemons. Sometimes the senator rises high enough in state politics (like Hiram W. Johnson of California) or serves long enough in the Senate (like William E. Borah of Idaho) to become an "institution," in which case the voters are apt to overlook his idiosyncrasies regarding such minor matters as foreign affairs, and keep him on for the good he has done. Many of the senators are from Southern poll tax districts, where less than the ordinary amount of interest is shown in foreign policy.

Ensconced behind the six-year term, the Senate has to a surprising degree been deaf to the voice of public opinion. "God made the world in seven days," remarked a South Carolina newspaper at the height of the League of Nations struggle in 1919, "but he didn't have a senate to deal with." Yet when an aroused citizenry speaks in stentorian tones, even the proud Solons come to heel. Although one senator sneered at the Kellogg-Briand pact of 1928 as an "international kiss," and another spoke of "throwing peace paper wads at the dogs of war," so great was the tidal wave of public approval that the treaty was passed with only one dissenting vote and with no formal reservations. When the American people in 1945 arose as almost one man to demand the United Nations Charter, isolationist senators grew quiet or clambered onto the bandwagon, and the much-feared opposition melted away before the hot breath of public opinion.

6

A purposeful public has on numerous occasions actually forced the President and the State Department to move, sometimes against their better judgment.

In 1803 a rising tide of Western resentment over the closure of the Mississippi prodded President Jefferson into a course that led to the purchase of Louisiana. In 1809, with public opinion so hostile that the very foundations of government trembled, Jefferson was forced to bring about a repeal of the embargo on shipping. In 1854 an enraged North halted the pro-Southern President Pierce in his design to wrest Cuba from the palsied grasp of Spain. In 1893 an aroused nation compelled Cleveland to abandon his plans to restore the dusky Hawaiian queen to her throne. In 1898 the war-mad masses forced the nation into an unnecessary clash with Spain, in spite of McKinley, Mark Hanna, and Big Business. (It was a victory for Main Street rather than Wall Street.) In 1921 a determined citizenry insisted upon the Washington Disarmament Conference, for which a lackadaisical President Harding received more than his just share of praise. In 1928 an organized and inspired public kicked Secretary Kellogg into immortality by forcing him to negotiate the Kellogg-Briand pact, for which at the outset he revealed little enthusiasm but for which he ultimately received the Nobel Peace Prize. . . .

The sovereign voter may not only compel his elected servants to do his bidding, but by defying his own government he may turn laws and treaties into dead letters, with consequent international friction.

Certain parts of the treaty of peace with England in 1783, specifically those having to do with debts and loyalists, were so unpopular in some sections of the country that they were openly nullified. During the Texas revolution of 1835–1836, the Canadian rebellion of 1837, and the Irish-Fenian invasions of Canada in the 1860's and 1870's, public sympathy was so overwhelmingly favorable to the rebels that the federal officials found it difficult or impossible to enforce the neutrality laws. In some instances government agents brazenly joined with the revolutionists in violating the statutes which they had sworn to uphold. The mid-century American filibustering expeditions, notably those of López in Cuba and Walker in Central America, were warmly applauded in the expansionist and slave-holding South, so much so that the federal officials were unable to secure juries that would convict even the most flagrant violators of our national laws. A half-century later the people of the Pacific Coast, determined to hold the dike against an Oriental inundation, deliberately flouted the treaties and statutes of the United States so as to compel the Washington government to adopt exclusion.

The force of American opinion is felt not only at home but abroad. Foreign statesmen study our national crosscurrents with meticulous care, and not infrequently shorten sail rather than risk shipwreck.

The explosive rising of the Westerners in 1803 against the Spanish and French was not lost on Paris when Napoleon sold us Louisiana. American wrath in 1844 over British machinations in Texas was a clear storm warning that Downing Street had better go more slowly. The swelling demand to throw the French out of Mexico in 1867 presumably hastened their going; and the uproar against German brutality during the Venezuela intervention of 1902 certainly had a similar result. The British whitened their blacklist of American firms in 1916 when they saw how offensive it was to us, and they came to terms with Ireland in 1921 partly, although not primarily, out of a desire to reduce the chronic inflammation of Anglo-American relations resulting from the Irish problem. . . .

7

The President and the State Department have on occasion disregarded or even defied a strong majority opinion, but not frequently, and then not too openly. Such defiance is easier in war time, for the government can then hide behind the shield of secrecy. During World War II our continued relations with Fascist-tainted Vichy France, to say nothing of other dubious dealings, were highly unpopular among American liberals. But Washington apologized for these disturbing bedfellows by pleading military necessity, and as a consequence our people were more tolerant than they otherwise would have been.

If the public is rather evenly divided on a given issue, the government may occasionally support what appears to be a minority group. When President Washington angered the pro-French faction in America by issuing his neutrality proclamation in 1793, and when he infuriated the same partisans by sponsoring John Jay's unpopular treaty with Britain in 1795, he may have sided with the minority, but in any event the issue was close and the clatter great. The earlier incident, so Mark Sullivan surmises, inspired Kipling's immortal "If."

When the American people favor a proposed step by a large majority, but with only weak intensity, they may be disregarded by the State Department with relative impunity. After the Sino-Japanese "incident" flared forth in 1937, American sentiment promptly sided with underdog China, although there was a vast amount of indifference. But by 1939, when the issues had sharpened, the opinion polls showed that our people were only 2 per cent pro-Japanese while 74 per cent were pro-Chinese. By 1940 the nation was 90 per cent favorable to an embargo on munitions for the Japanese aggressors.

This overwhelming display of solicitude did not stampede the Roosevelt administration, which stubbornly declined to halt the flow of war materials to Japan until three full years after the Marco Polo Bridge incident. The President reasoned that an invocation of the Neutrality Act of 1937 would cut off munitions from both Japan and China, and we wanted China to get her trickle. Also, as was later revealed, Roosevelt feared that strong measures against Japan would drive her into a premature descent upon the Dutch East Indies.

No democratic government on earth can long resist a 90 per cent public opinion, provided it is unified and intense. American sympathy for China was widespread but not intense; we sympathized but we sympathized lukewarmly. The Far East was far away and the Great Depression was close at hand. The Roosevelt administration was fully aware of these facts, and consequently felt free to pursue what it regarded as a farsighted program. . . .

8

The dangers of flying in the face of public opinion are so apparent that in time of crisis the administration is strongly tempted to resort to deception rather than to defiance.

Some deception is comparatively harmless. When President Madison, in his message to Congress in 1815, congratulated the nation (and incidentally his own administration) on its glorious prosecution of the inglorious War of 1812, he was merely glossing over one of the most disgraceful episodes in our history. When Secretary Marcy in 1855 deliberately deleted damaging passages from his published correspondence describing the attempt to grab Cuba, he was merely trying to whiten his name with posterity, which he succeeded in doing until 1928, at which time a lynx-eyed scholar sharply blackened it. When President Wilson told an inquisitorial Senate committee in 1919 that he had never heard of the notorious secret treaties before reaching the Paris conference, he was presumably trying to smooth the path for the ratification of the Treaty of Versailles. Presidents have claimed achievements for themselves, such as the results of disarmament conferences, which a candid examination of the facts would not support. Theodore Roosevelt was a past master at leading and misleading public opinion by magnifying minor issues and minifying major ones. But such episodes were usually political gestures, designed to make or at least to save votes.

More serious was the deception practiced by President Polk in 1846. He ordered an armed detachment into an area in southern Texas to which the Texans had a highly debatable claim. The Mexicans were provoked into an attack, as Polk expected and rather hoped they would be, and then he triumphantly announced that "American blood" had been shed on "American soil." The people of the United States, even those of the opposition Whig party, arose to avenge this wanton assault, and we were off for the Halls of the Montezumas. Crude young Representative Abraham Lincoln repeatedly taunted the President for this fraud; he wanted to know the exact spot on *American* soil where blood had been shed. If Polk had been writing history instead of making it, he would have said that the Mexican troops were goaded into shedding the blood of those whom they regarded as invaders of their soil. This would have been a good deal nearer the truth than his wordy misrepresentation.

Franklin Roosevelt repeatedly deceived the American people during the period before Pearl Harbor. When he warned them against the aggressors, he was branded a sensationalist. When he pointed to the perils of storm-cellar neutrality, he was branded an interventionist. When he urged adequate armaments, he was branded a warmonger. He was faced with a terrible trilemma. If he let the people slumber in a fog of isolation, they might well fall prey to Hitler. If he came out unequivocally for intervention, he would be defeated in 1940, or shelved for a candidate more willing to let the masses enjoy their fool's paradise. If he was going to induce the people to move at all, he would have to trick them into acting for their best interests, or what he conceived to be their best interests. He was like the physician who must tell the patient lies for the patient's own good. Congresswoman Clare Boothe Luce missed the point entirely when she violently charged, in the campaign of 1944, that Roosevelt "lied us into a war because he did not have the political courage to lead us into it." The latter course would have been foolhardy rather than courageous. The country was overwhelmingly noninterventionist to the very day of Pearl Harbor, and an overt attempt to lead the people into war would have resulted in certain failure and an almost certain ousting of Roosevelt in 1940, with a consequent defeat for his ultimate aims.

9

The embattled democracies in 1939 needed our munitions, and it was to our interests as well as theirs to lift the arms embargo. In a memorable message to the special session of Congress, Franklin Roosevelt urged that we return to international law, though actually we had never abandoned it: the arms embargo was purely domestic legislation. He dramatically declared that the embargo policy of Jefferson's day had resulted in the burning of the predecessor of the Capitol building from which he was then speaking, though actually the embargo-nonintercourse policy of that time came within a few days of preventing war. Like Polk in 1846, Roosevelt was making history rather than writing it, and he was doing it effectively. Dr. Gallup found a sharp increase of five points in the majority sentiment for lifting the arms embargo following the President's appearance before Congress.

Roosevelt's spectacular transfer of fifty overage United States destroyers to the British, in September, 1940, was difficult to defend on any legal grounds, but Attorney General Jackson dutifully built up a case, much of which hinged on the placement of a comma in the relevant federal statute. The destroyer deal, to say nothing of other acts of unneutrality, was further defended by a shyster-like appeal to an international law that had largely been trampled to death under the hobnailed boots of the belligerents. When the Lend-Lease Act was being debated in 1941, its foes insisted that the munitions would have to be convoyed and convoy would mean war. But the specter of convoy was then unpopular, and administration spokesmen brushed it aside: one thing at a time. Thus sympathy for the democracies led to Lend-Lease, Lend-Lease led to convoy, convoy led to shooting, and shooting led to war.

The noninterventionists cried out against war, and because they were in a strong majority some color of legality had to be found for every questionable step that was taken. Lend-Lease almost certainly would not have been passed, at least not as it was and when it was, if the people could have foreseen that the scheme would lead so inexorably to hostilities. After the bill was safely approved, Roosevelt himself quietly issued the orders to convoy.

The President was also anxious to make it appear, again with the isolationist masses in view, that the aggression was coming from Germany. After a U-boat had fired two torpedoes at the United States destroyer *Greer*, Roosevelt went on the air and declared that henceforth the Navy would repel the piratical acts of these seagoing "rattlesnakes" and defend freedom of the seas by firing first. (Actually, freedom of the seas in the American tradition was not involved at all.) Again Roosevelt's dramatic methods brought results; Dr. Gallup found a strong majority in favor of shoot-at-sight. Yet more than a month after the event the Navy Department revealed that the *Greer* had been trailing the U-boat for three and one-half hours and broadcasting the latter's position to nearby British destroyers when the submarine turned and attacked.

Roosevelt either knew these facts or he did not know them. If he knew them, he deliberately deceived the American people; if he did not, he handled a critical situation with inexcusable precipitancy.

A president who cannot entrust the people with the truth betrays a certain lack of faith in the basic tenets of democracy. But because the masses are notoriously shortsighted, and generally cannot see danger until it is at their throats, our statesmen are forced to deceive them into an awareness of their own long-run interests. This is clearly what Roosevelt [felt he] had to do, and who shall say that posterity will not thank him for it?*

Deception of the people may in fact become increasingly necessary, unless we are willing to give our leaders in Washington a freer hand. In the days of the horse and buggy we could jog along behind our billowy barriers with relative impunity, but in the days of the atomic bomb we may have to move more rapidly than a lumbering public opinion will permit. Just as the yielding of some of our national sovereignty is the price that we must pay for effective international organization, so the yielding of some of our democratic control of foreign affairs is the price that we may have to pay for greater physical security. . . .

The Incubus of Ignorance

1

An appalling ignorance of foreign affairs is one of the most striking and dangerous defects of American public opinion. This is not to say that we are thick-witted; there is a world of difference between a stupid person and an uninformed one. Even the most brilliant scholars must necessarily be ignorant of a vast body of knowledge.

The American people have informed themselves very creditably on a number of complex questions, *once their interest was aroused.* The heated nation-wide debates on imperialism in the 1890's, on the League of Nations in 1919–1920, on the neutrality issues of the 1930's, on the repeal of the arms embargo in 1939, and on Lend-Lease in 1941, while bringing out specious as well as valid arguments, on the whole gave encouragement to those who have faith in the democratic ideal. But we seldom become aroused to this high pitch, and largely because we are uninterested we lack information. The journalist Raymond Clapper used to say: "Never overestimate the people's knowledge, nor underestimate their intelligence."

As a nation we may be reasonably well informed, yet we are not well enough informed to exercise understandingly our present direct and hence dangerous control of foreign affairs. For many years the average citizen has passed judgment on, and exercised pressure regarding, knotty

* Professor Bailey wrote the editor of this volume that in a revised edition, he would have inserted the bracketed words to clarify his meaning.

problems of international law upon which not even the ablest international lawyers could agree. Questions of blockade and maritime rights, which figured so prominently in our history during the nineteenth century, baffled both the jurists of that time and the historians of a later generation. But this did not prevent the layman from expressing his judgment with great vigor, often substituting emotion for reason. A true patriot has been aptly defined as one who is unable to wait for the facts. Sanity indeed receives a setback when interpretations of treaty obligations and international law fall into the hands of the mob. . . .

Lord Bryce, who was as sympathetic a critic of American democracy as one could hope to find among foreigners, wrote regarding control of foreign policy: "Not one in a thousand of the citizens, not one in ten of the representatives, may have enough knowledge to enable him to form a sound opinion." If this was true in the horse-and-buggy era, it is even more true today. In the nineteenth century, when the Atlantic was a tremendous barrier, the American people could better afford the luxury of being ignorant or apathetic or wrong or late, but even then they had some narrow escapes. Those happy days of blessed ignorance are gone forever; we shall continue in some degree to be ignorant, but in a perilous rather than in a blissful state. Facts cannot be ignored out of existence.

The average American is a self-reliant individual; his forefathers rolled back a wilderness with their own muscular arms and backs. He is too prone to rely on himself for an opinion, whether he is in possession of the facts or not—a not uncommon failing. "Nothing is so firmly believed as that which we least know," wrote the French philosopher Montaigne in the sixteenth century. The ordinary citizen is also inclined to believe most readily that which he hopes for most earnestly, and he is all too often most easily persuaded by arguments which he cannot understand. All these human shortcomings are to be found in a despotism, but in a democracy they are more dangerous, for a democracy is the one system in which the ignorant have the most influence and where they are listened to with the most respect.

2

In the midst of the Roosevelt-Dewey campaign of 1944, one opinion poll revealed that 14 per cent of the people did not know the name of the Republican candidate then running (Dewey), though many of this group no doubt were going to vote for him. If the American citizen is not better informed than this about political campaigns being waged under his very window, how can he be well informed about controversies on the other side of two wide oceans? The answer is that he is not.

The opinion polls from 1940 to 1945 turned up some almost incredible information as to our general ignorance.

In 1940, when the debate over renewing the Reciprocal Trade Agreements Act was at its height, only one voter in ten understood what the law was designed to accomplish. The informed one tenth were overwhelmingly favorable to renewal.

In 1941, when the Good Neighbor Policy was being actively pushed, nearly two in ten did not know that Latin America is rich in natural resources. Such ignorance of foreign countries is more or less typical of Americans.

In 1942, several months after the Atlantic Charter had been dramatically drawn up by Roosevelt and Churchill, and the results had been heralded in the headlines, nearly eight in ten admitted that they had neither read nor heard about the Charter. . . .

In 1944, when "unconditional surrender" was a vital part of our military policy, only half of our citizens could give a reasonably satisfactory explanation of the term.

In 1944, when there was strong popular agitation to amend the Constitution so as to deprive the Senate of the one-third veto voice on treaties, nearly seven Americans in ten did not even know that the Senate has to approve treaties by a two-thirds vote. This explains in a nutshell why the Constitution was not amended. Nothing short of a veritable tidal wave of public sentiment can drive an amendment through two thirds of both Houses of Congress and through three fourths of the states, and no such tidal wave arises from an ocean of ignorance and apathy.

In 1944, when a new League of Nations was being widely discussed, more than half of our citizens did not know that we had never joined the old League of Nations. Perhaps some of the ill-informed were suffering from a guilt complex growing out of the breakdown of the League and the coming of World War II, and they were wishfully thinking that we had joined. . . .

In 1945, when delegates from the United Nations were assembling in San Francisco to frame a world charter, only two voters in three had ever heard of the conference, and most of these had either no ideas or erroneous ideas as to why it was meeting.

In 1945, when Japan was collapsing and our future security depended on the fate of her government, only slightly more than half of our citizens could name the Japanese emperor (Hirohito). Some guesses were as far afield as Tito, Yokohama, Fujiyama, and Hara-Kiri. . . .

4

The following table, taken from the census of 1940, tells its own shocking story:

Persons in the U.S. 25 years of age or over	74,775,836
Persons who never completed one school year	2,799,923
Persons who completed grades 1 to 4	7,304,689
Persons who completed grades 5 to 6	8,515,111
Persons who completed grades 7 to 8	25,897,953
Persons who completed high school years 1 to 3	11,181,995
Persons who completed 4th year of high school	10,551,680
Persons who completed 1 to 3 years of college	4,075,184
Persons who completed 4 or more years of college	3,407,331
Not reported	1,041,970
Median school years completed	8.4

About six adult Americans in ten—hereafter referred to as "graders"—have never gone beyond the eighth grade. Hundreds of thousands have never attended school at all, and several million are completely illiterate.

This huge mass of the educationally underprivileged is a great abscess on our body politic. . . .

The more ignorant the citizen, the more bellicose and jingoistic he was, the more certain that he could knock the stuffings out of any or all other nations. After Pearl Harbor the uninformed group was most confident that we would whip the Japanese in short order.

The grader was by far the most chauvinistic and imperialistic. He was much more willing than his less ignorant fellows to take on the task of running the world alone, and more inclined to say that we should grab all the new territory we could get, not merely island bases for military purposes. He was the most reluctant to turn American conquests over to a trusteeship of the United Nations; he was most favorable to starting an atomic war against Russia on mere suspicion.

The poorly educated citizen was the most militaristic of all, possibly because he felt the most insecure. He was more disposed to spend money for armaments rather than for education, and he was more willing to rely upon a powerful United States Army than on any international police force. He was also more favorable to conscripting young men for the army in time of peace.

The grader operated on the principle of "our country right or wrong," but our country has never been wrong. Of all groups he was the most favorable to highly nationalistic textbooks, and he was the least willing to have them examined and revised by an outside agency in the interests of balance and fairness. Naturally he was attached to the sacred cow of sovereignty, and he was not at all enthusiastic about giving up the control of anything to foreigners, whom he distrusted on general principles, especially Japanese, Russians, Germans, and British imperialists.

The grader was the most provincial, the least interested in other countries, and the most preoccupied with local trivia and the comic-strip doings of Dick Tracy and Orphan Annie. He was the least concerned about the opinions of the outside world regarding us, and he was the least favorable to broadcasting informational programs to foreign lands. He was the least farsighted, and the most eager to grasp the present short-run gain to the exclusion of the more important long-run advantage.

Rather than undergo the mental sweat of thinking complex issues through, the grader much preferred to personalize foreign affairs. He was inclined to blame World War I on the Kaiser, and our participation in it on J. P. Morgan and the Du Ponts. He was disposed to attribute World War II solely to Hitler, and commonly believed that the deranged house-painter had ordered the Japanese to attack Pearl Harbor.

Prejudice is the child of ignorance. The grader betrayed the largest amount of anti-Semitism, and during the war he was the most bitter against the Japanese, who had not only humbled his pride but had done so by delivering a sneak punch below the belt. He approved less humane treatment of the Germans than did his better educated brothers, and he was the most favorable to using poison gas on the Japanese. He most begrudged relief for our devastated Allies, and he was the least willing to rehabilitate the prostrate nations of Europe.

Generally more gullible, the grader group was the most satisfied with the war news printed in the press, and the least critical of information received over the radio. More than his fellows the ill-educated citizen was stampeded by Orson Welles's realistic broadcast in 1938 of the invasion from Mars. Ignorance has a numerous brood, but one of her least lovely sucklings is mass hysteria.

5

In certain other categories the grader sticks out like a sore thumb. He was the most opposed to reciprocal trade agreements, though generally he did not know what they meant. He showed the least enthusiasm for the proposition that we must buy abroad in order to sell. He was the most favorable to tariff walls and other weapons of economic noncollaboration, presumably because he was a laboring man who had suffered from unemployment and hence was easily swayed by the argument about cheap coolie labor. . . .

The grader was the backbone of American isolationism. He was the most hostile in 1939 to lifting the arms embargo in favor of the Allies, and he was the least willing to send aid to Britain in 1940. Throughout 1941 he was most determined not to risk war in helping England, even though she was in danger of sinking. He was the least worried about Hitler's winning, and to the very end was the least favorable to declaring war on the Axis, though no group was prepared to do so.

After Pearl Harbor the grader was the least agreeable to ties of close alliance with other nations, and he was the most disposed to say that it was not our job to help keep world peace. He was the least concerned about war prevention, the most reluctant to begin peace planning in the midst of the war, and the most fatalistic about the coming of future conflicts. He was the least clear as to why he was fighting, and the most antagonistic to even an embryonic world government in which foreigners might outvote the United States. He was the least enthusiastic about a new League of Nations; he was more favorable to American control of the new world organization than equal control with other nations; he was less willing that we should share the costs of the new organization; and he was the most unfriendly to a powerful world government, especially one commanding military forces. Yet when the United Nations was actually started, the graders were more complacently pleased with its halting progress than any other group.

The most poorly educated citizens were the least happy about a united military command in 1945, and more inclined to be satisfied with our war effort. They were also more inclined to believe that the "secret" of the atomic bomb could be kept, and that foreign observers should be barred from the Bikini atom bomb tests.

6

The attitude of the grader toward specific outside nations was most revealing.

He was the backbone of Anglophobia and xenophobia. He was more predisposed to annex Canada than other groups, and most hostile to world union with Britain and Russia. He was the least favorable to the British loan of 1946, presumably because he felt that "the slick British diplomats" would cheat us out of our money, as they had allegedly done after World War I.

Regarding Germany, the grader was inclined to believe that we had not treated the Reich too harshly in the past, and that we were in no way responsible for the conditions that spawned Naziism. He was the most certain that the Germans would always want war, and he was all for knocking them down and stamping on them so hard that they would never want to fight again. He was the most eager to punish Germany by dividing her into small states and by reducing her to a potato patch through the destruction of her industry. Yet after having ruined her economically, he was the most anxious to drain heavy reparations from her, as though one could get both milk and beefsteak from the same cow.

The prejudices against Russia, discussed earlier in this chapter, were most deeply rooted in the lowest educational group. If you scratched an ignoramus you often found not only an isolationist but an Anglophobe and an anti-communist as well. Curiously enough, the poorer classes in America, to whom communism is supposed to appeal, were much more distrustful of Russia than the more well-to-do classes, which are supposed to be in mortal fear of a communistic redistribution of their wealth. The basic answer appears to be that the American masses, which are relatively poor and ignorant, were still being frightened by the Bolshevist bogies of the 1920's, while the wealthier and hence better informed classes were able to discount some of these exaggerations. . . .

7

Glancing backward at this disquieting picture, the reader cannot escape one fundamental conclusion. On practically every public question where the respondents were classified by education, the lowest bracket revealed itself to be the most narrow, short-sighted, and unenlightened.

Yet one highly important qualification must be made. A *majority* of the graders *with opinions* were not to be found in these illiberal camps on every public question. If a strong majority were consistently there, our democracy would have cut its own throat long ago. *On most public issues the grader was on the same side as the high school and college groups, but almost invariably by a smaller percentage,* ranging from a negligible figure to a substantial one. On practically every question the strongest trend toward unenlightenment came from the graders, and this is a fact of disturbing significance.

The educationally underprivileged constitute the largest single group in the United States. They are prone to think with their emotions rather than their brains, especially in a crisis, or not to think at all, which may be almost as bad. The distressingly large number of "Don't knows" or "Undecideds" or "No opinions" in the various polls is concentrated in this group. The graders are apt to have the wrong opinion or the myopic opinion on problems of grave public import. Sometimes it is a confused opinion, as when an earnest citizen, possibly suffering from back trouble, wrote his congressman at the time of the repeal of the arms embargo in 1939: "Keep the lumbargo."...

Conclusions

When Emerson said that the Man in the Street does not know a star in the sky, he uttered a profound truth. But it is comforting to realize that our ignorance of the firmament can in no way affect the movements of the heavenly bodies. The same reassuring thought unfortunately cannot be used to excuse our ignorance of public affairs.

Enough has been said to demonstrate that every American citizen is a sovereign, whether he chooses to exercise his sovereignty or not. The question is whether we shall be good or bad sovereigns, alert or apathetic ones, intelligent or stupid ones. "The problem of democracy is not the problem of getting rid of kings," wrote F. C. Morehouse. "It is the problem of clothing the whole people with the elements of kingship."

Many Americans, through sheer indifference or incapacity, have abdicated their kingship. We have set up a representative government, and then all too often have failed to indicate in what way we wish to be represented. In 1776 we needed the consent of the governed; today we need direction from the governed.

One of the most encouraging aspects of American public opinion is that in the last quarter of a century or so we have developed much greater maturity in our approach to international relations. But the increasing complexity of world affairs makes it imperative that we rise more effectively to our responsibilities. With this end in view, and by way of summary and conclusion, the following suggestions are offered.

We should attract our best brains into government service. Leadership of the highest quality is urgently needed.

We should exercise extreme care in the election of our public servants, and in particular give thought to their capacity for a broad approach to foreign affairs. It is much better to vote for the right senator than later to write to the wrong senator.

We should delegate more responsibility to our public officials, after we have gone to pains to select the ablest ones. In a sense we have neither a representative nor a delegate government: not representative, because too many of us are inarticulate; not delegate, because too many of us delegate authority by default.

We should educate for statesmanship at the same time we are educating for citizenship. If we pick out our ablest men, train them from the beginning, and delegate more authority to them, we shall get a relatively quick return on our investment. But even this is only a partial answer.

We should, above all, undertake the Gargantuan task of raising the educational and apperceptive level of our entire population. Elihu Root once said that when foreign affairs were handled by despots, the danger was in sinister purposes; when they are handled by the people, the danger lies in mistaken beliefs.

We should rip away the prejudice-encrusted legends about the past of foreign peoples, and for this purpose we need more critical textbooks, more critical teachers, and a more critical public.

We should develop more tolerance, and realize that in a complicated international situation one side has never had a complete monopoly of the right, and the other side a complete monopoly of the wrong.

We should learn in our thinking to put ourselves in the other fellow's sandals, and view the common problem as he would see it through the lenses of his racial psychology and national bias. To this end we should encourage foreign travel, and the widespread exchange of students and professors.

We should train ourselves to keep our heads in time of crisis, as we definitely failed to do on the eve of the Spanish-American War. The mob is always wrong. Even when it hangs the guilty man, it also hangs Justice.

We should keep vigilant and demand of our government that in so far as possible it take us into its confidence.

We should remember that in unity there is strength. A common complaint of the "little fellow" is that his views do not count. But if he would pool his voice with that of countless other "little fellows," it would count for a great deal. If he does not do this, the purposeful minority will.

Upon every citizen in our democracy rests a solemn obligation to inform himself so that he can direct our foreign policy—*his* foreign policy—along intelligent and far-visioned lines.

2. *Needed: Greater Public Tolerance*

Gabriel A. Almond is much less hopeful than T. A. Bailey in the previous selection about remedying the defects in public opinion through more intensive mass education. A Professor of Political Science at Yale University, Almond envisions the public as divided into the great masses of people, who have little information about foreign affairs and usually have little interest as well, and the elites. In the latter class he includes the "attentive public" of the more interested and informed citizens and the "effective public" of those few who help shape mass opinion and who often have direct access to policymakers. Mass public opinion obviously has serious defects and it often affects adversely the shaping of policy. The remedy, Almond concludes, lies less in improving substantially the level of knowledge of the mass of citizens and more in promoting a tolerant public attitude with a concentration on improving the quality of the smaller groups or elites.

The American People and Foreign Policy

GABRIEL A. ALMOND

World Leadership and Human Material

An estimate of our capacity for intelligent foreign policy decisions also requires an understanding of the policy-making apparatus—popular attitudes toward politics which are conditioned by the "national character"

Gabriel A. Almond, *The American People and Foreign Policy* (New York: Frederick A. Praeger, 1960 edition), 4–8, 53–68. Reprinted with permission.

and its regional and class variants, the system of indoctrination, education and information, the influential interest and pressure associations, the party system and the electoral process, and finally, the legislative and administrative establishments. In the American democracy control over policy is highly decentralized. But while power is widely distributed, a mass democracy obviously precludes the possibility of a direct and literal control of public policy by public opinion.

The treatment of problems of public opinion and foreign policy in the United States has been obscured and distorted by ethical bias and inhibition. All political systems have their myths, and democracies are not exceptions in this regard. The democratic myth is that the people are inherently wise and just, and that they are the real rulers of the republic. These propositions do have meaning; but if they become, as they do even among scholars, matters of faith, then scientific progress has been sacrificed in the interest of a morally satisfying demagogy.

A scientifically adequate approach to the problems of public opinion and public policy must begin with knowledge of psychic, social, and political structure and processes. This is the beginning of realism in the analysis of a democratic policy-making process. Opinions must be placed in their subjective matrices of values and basic attitudes if we are to gain an impression of their stability, ramifications, and possible future development. Opinions must be sociologically placed if we are to speculate intelligently about the potential political behavior of large social aggregations and their sub-groupings. Opinions and attitudes must be located in the political structure if there is to be any possibility at all of predicting policy developments from public opinion data. Finally, opinions have to be evaluated from the point of view of the objective problems to which they are a response.

If we examine any problem of public opinion and public policy with this type of structural analysis, the shortcomings of the democratic myth immediately become apparent. For example, can any people in the mass grasp with justice and wisdom the complex issues and strategies of foreign policy in the present era? Can any people in the mass and in the modern era make foreign policy in the specific sense of that term? The objectives which underlie such assumptions are inherently unrealizable, and by concentrating our attention on them we lose sight of the kind of popular control over public policy which is possible today.

There are inherent limitations in modern society on the capacity of the public to understand the issues and grasp the significance of the most important problems of public policy. This is particularly the case with foreign policy where the issues are especially complex and remote. The function of the public in a democratic policy-making process is to set certain policy criteria in the form of widely held values and expectations. It evaluates the results of policies from the point of view of their conformity to these basic values and expectations. The policies themselves, however, are the products of leadership groups ("elites") who carry on the specific work of policy formulation and policy advocacy. The public share in policy decisions may be compared, with important qualifications, to a market. It buys or refuses to buy the "policy products" offered by competing elites. However, the policy market is not as simple as an economic market. There is, unfortunately, no simple policy currency in which the costs of alternative policies can be computed. The policy products cannot be felt, tasted, or weighed. They are predictions of consequences of action, hardly a tangible product with regard to which consumer preferences can easily be registered.

In view of these considerations many of the moralistic exhortations to the public to inform itself and to play an active role in policy-making, particularly in foreign policy, have the virtues and failings of evangelism. This approach spreads the apocalyptic vision of a public, resolute and courageous, intelligent and informed, doing battle with vested interests, minority groups, or the power-hungry bureaucracy. But the resolution collapses with the next edition of the morning paper when the fall of another French government dramatizes the incapacity of the average man to understand the details of the distant world which shapes and conditions his fate. Such an approach as this fails to give due weight to the complicated structure of the policy-making process in a mass democracy, and attempts to impose a type of burden on the layman which he in most cases and in good sense rejects.

Public education ought never to attempt to make experts and specialists of laymen. Not expertness but improved understanding is the target which the public should be urged to set for itself, if progress is to be made in dispelling the fog of apathy and ignorance which facilitates the misrepresentation of the national interest. But such a program would have to start with more modest expectations and a more rigorous conception of social and political structure. It would recognize the awful proportions of a task which attempts to modify basic cultural, and perhaps human, predispositions and frailties. It would also have to place great emphasis on the training of specialized personnel, as well as on mass enlightenment.

Thus more advantage may be gained by the training of a few specialists in foreign affairs to serve on the staffs of the great interest associations such as the Chamber of Commerce or the American Federation of Labor, than by a half dozen short-lived experiments in community participation in world affairs. A well-trained specialist, able to devote full time to his particular field of policy interest, is in a position to inform and moderate the views of the leadership of his interest group, undertake the training and education of local officials, and institute informational programs under relatively favorable conditions.

Far greater returns may be expected from efforts to broaden the curricula of teachers colleges, theological seminaries, and schools of journalism to include sober studies of international economics and politics than from the more spectacular efforts of the "forums of the air." The problem is to introduce information and critical intelligence into the stream of communication at key points in the political process and in channels which conform to the "social terrain," at points where trust and intimacy open the minds of men to new thoughts and recognitions.

The layman inevitably turns to his leaders for guidance on public questions. He can draw sound inferences and arrive at sober conclusions if he can trust his specialists to formulate the issues and alternatives in such a manner that a reasoned choice becomes possible. This is the task and the responsibility of the opinion and policy elites in a mass democracy. The layman ordinarily cannot formulate alternatives so that he can see how and in what way his interests are engaged. If his feelings are manipulated or his interests misrepresented, if he is continually shocked and terrorized, a sense of distrust of the entire policy-making apparatus develops. In some measure the problem of public apathy and ignorance might be solved if the political, bureaucratic, pressure group, and communications elites were governed by codes of conduct which minimized these elements of distortion and panic in the stream of communication. But to state this problem is not to suggest that deeply rooted cultural tendencies such as these can be remedied by short-run or spectacular measures. Given the bedlam which actually obtains, it is hardly an evasion of public duty if the ordinary human being shuts his ears and keeps a close hand on the wallet of his short-run interests.

From this viewpoint no sudden cultural maturation is to be anticipated in the United States which will be proportionate to the gravity and power of its newly acquired international status. The objective challenge of American primacy in world affairs will have to be met by present-day Americans with existing institutions and culturally imposed qualities of character. . . .

Mood Versus Policy

Since Americans tend to exhaust their emotional and intellectual energies in private pursuits, the typical approach to problems of public policy is perfunctory. Where public policy impinges directly on their interest, as in questions of local improvements, taxation, or social security policy, they are more likely to develop views and opinions resting on some kind of intellectual structure. But on questions of a more remote nature, such as foreign policy, they tend to react in more undifferentiated ways, with formless and plastic moods which undergo frequent alteration in response to changes in events. The characteristic response to questions of foreign policy is one of indifference. A foreign policy crisis, short of the immediate threat of war, may transform indifference to vague apprehension, to fatalism, to anger; but the reaction is still a mood, a superficial and fluctuating response. To some extent American political apathy is a consequence of the compulsive absorption of energy in private competitiveness. To inform oneself on public issues, to form policies on the basis of careful thought-taking, is hardly a task that is beyond the intellectual competence of a large proportion of the population. The intellectual demands of business life are in some respects as complicated as those of foreign policy. But the American has a powerful cultural incentive to develop policies and strategies relating to his business and professional career, and little incentive, if any, to develop strategies for foreign policy.

The orientation of most Americans toward foreign policy is one of mood, and mood is essentially an unstable phenomenon. But this instability is not arbitrary and unpredictable. American moods are affected by two variables: (1) changes in the domestic and foreign political-economic situation involving the presence or absence of threat in varying degrees, (2) the characterological predispositions of the population. Our knowledge of American character tendencies, meager as it may be, makes it possible to suggest potential movements of opinion and mood which may have significant effects on foreign policy.

1. Withdrawal-Intervention

Given the intense involvement of most Americans with private interests and pursuits, the normal attitude toward a relatively stable world political situation is one of comparative indifference and withdrawal. This was the case throughout the greater part of the nineteenth century, in the period between World War I and II, and as we shall show in a later chapter, in the period immediately following World War II. The existence of this cyclical withdrawal-intervention problem suggests at least two serious dangers for foreign policy decision-making: (1) possible overreactions to threat; (2) possible overreactions to temporary equilibria in world politics. Under ordinary circumstances American emotion and action are directed with considerable pressure in the normal orbits of private competition. However, when threats from abroad become grave and immediate, Americans tend to break out of their private orbits, and tremendous energies become available for foreign policy. Thus, we see the explosions of American energy in World Wars I and II when, after periods of indifference and withdrawal, exceptional feats of swift mobilization were achieved. There is some evidence to suggest that the Russian threat may, if carelessly handled, produce dangerous overreactions. Thus the press conference of Secretary of State Marshall in the spring of 1947, in which he urged the American people to "keep calm," produced what amounted to a war scare. The volatility and potential explosiveness of American opinion must be constantly kept in mind if panic reactions to threat are to be avoided.

The danger of overreaction to threat is only one aspect of this withdrawal-intervention tendency of American opinion. Equally serious is the prospect of overreaction to temporary stabilizations in the world crisis. Because of the superficial character of American attitudes toward world politics, American opinion tends to react to the external aspects of situations. A temporary Russian tactical withdrawal may produce strong tendencies toward demobilization and the reassertion of the primacy of private and domestic values. The pull of "privatism" in America creates a strong inclination to self-deception. And while this is less characteristic of the informed and policy-making levels, it undoubtedly plays an important role here as well. The great American demobilization of 1945, both in the military establishment and in the civilian bureaucracy, and the hasty dismantling of war agencies and controls reflected the overwhelming eagerness to withdraw to private values and normal conditions.

This movement was not based on a sober evaluation of the foreign situation and what this might require in military and political terms, but was a response to the overwhelming urge to have done with alarms and external interruptions and get back to the essential and important values.

2. Mood-Simplification

Closely connected with the withdrawal-intervention pattern is a tendency which has to do with characteristic changes in the internal structure of American foreign policy moods. It has already been pointed out that under conditions of political equilibrium American attitudes toward world politics tend to be formless and lacking in intellectual structure. We define policy, as distinguished from mood, as consisting of a relatively stable intellectual structure including (1) explicit assumptions as to the values involved in domestic or international political conflict, (2) explicit evaluations of the relative costs and efficiency of alternative means of maximizing the value position of one's own country or political group. From the point of view of this criterion, American attitudes tend to range from unstructured moods in periods of equilibrium to simplification in periods of crisis. So long as there is no immediate, sharply defined threat, the attitude is vague and indefinite—e.g., apathetic, mildly apprehensive, euphoric, skeptical. When the crisis becomes sharpened American responses become more specific. Here American distrust of intellectualism and subtlety, the faith in "common sense," and the belief in simple answers lead to oversimplifications of the threat and the methods of coping with it.

While these tendencies are more characteristic of the "uninformed" general run of the population, they affect policy-makers as well. Thus during World War II, the Roosevelt shift from "Dr. New Deal" to "Dr. Win-the-War" reflected this need at the very highest level of policy-making to reduce the issues to simplified proportions. The "unconditional surrender" policy was a similarly oversimplified resolution of the moral and political problems of the war. The journalists and writers who directed American propaganda efforts in World War II solved their complex policy problems by the slogan of "the strategy of truth," which left to the lower-level, competitive policy-making process practically all of the important decisions of propaganda policy during the war. The policy of "non-fraternization" with Germans which was imposed on the American army of occupation similarly was understandable as a gratification of a need for moral simplism, but it bore only a slight relation to the complex and uncomfortable realities on which it was imposed. The entire sequence of American policies toward Germany had this character of mixed moral-expediential improvisations. At first these improvisations were motivated primarily by anti-German reactions; more recently the tendency is toward more pro-German improvisations. At the present time this tendency to oversimplify seems to be taking the form of reducing all the problems of world politics to a simple "East-West" conflict. There is considerable pressure to take as an ally any country or movement which is anti-Communist and anti-Russian.

It would, of course, be an exaggeration to attribute the same degree of "simplism" to policy-makers as might be expected of the "man in the street." But there can be little doubt that the process of foreign policy-making is strongly influenced by this common-sense, improvisational tendency. Faith in policy-planning (which means in simple terms, taking the "long view," acquiring sufficient reliable information on which sound policy can be based, weighing and balancing the potential value of military, political, diplomatic, and psychological means in relation to proposed courses of action) has hardly taken root in the American policy-making process.

3. *Optimism-Pessimism*

The problem of shifts in mood from euphoric to dysphoric expectations is clearly related to those aspects of American opinion already described. The involvement in private concerns, coupled with an optimistic faith in good will, common sense, and simple answers, renders the American public vulnerable to failure. This reaction tends to result from the frustration of successive improvisations, none of which have been adapted to the complex character of the problem. Under these circumstances there are two possible dangers: (1) withdrawal reactions; (2) hasty measures motivated by irritation and impatience. The development of American attitudes toward Russia since the end of the war is an excellent illustration of this problem. During the war and in the period immediately following its termination there was a widely shared belief among Americans and among American policy-makers that the Russian problem could be readily solved by good will and the "man-to-man" approach. The continued thwarting of American overtures and concessions to the Russians now seems to have produced an attitude of hopeless pessimism. Pessimism certainly seems to be justifiable on the basis of the facts, but the negativism which has resulted may possibly constitute a danger if negotiation and bargaining with the Russians in principle is interdicted. The objective problem would seem to be one of choosing the time, the occasion, and the conditions when negotiation might lead to advantage. There is a similar danger of excessive pessimism in relation to potential allies. Perhaps there is a tendency toward a premature "writing off" of peoples whose social and political structures are unstable, countries which don't react with "American speed" to American proposals or which are not ready to commit themselves to the American "side" in as whole-hearted a fashion as we might desire.

4. *Tolerance-Intolerance*

The point has already been made that the American attitude toward authority, toward moral and ideological norms, contains conflicting elements. On the one hand, the American is not hemmed in by the mores and morals of "the horse and buggy days," and at the same time he is a conformist, a value-imitator. He is ready to try new things and new methods, but not if they make him look "different" or "peculiar." The truth of the matter would seem to be that, while he has loosened himself from the bonds of earlier moral standards and beliefs, he has not replaced these guides for conduct with any other set of principles. The autonomous conscience of Puritanism has been replaced by the "radar-directed" conduct of the "marketer." He tends to take his judgments as to what is right and wrong, proper and improper, from the changing culture as it impinges on him through the various social institutions and media of communication. This makes for a certain flexibility in attitudes toward other cultures and ideologies. But the flexibility is negative rather than positive. That is, the American has moved away from older moral and traditional norms without acquiring new bases of judgment. His toleration of difference therefore is unstable, and there is a substratum of ideological fundamentalism which frequently breaks through the surface and has an important impact on foreign policy. Thus in our efforts to stabilize the weakened and chaotic areas of Western Europe we have been prepared to go a long way in aiding "Socialist Great Britain" and the left-inclined powers of Western Europe. But there is a continual sabotage of this tolerance, frequent efforts at ideological imperialism, even occasional interferences at the administrative level, which are motivated by ideological fundamentalism.

In general, this intolerance of difference is more clearly expressed in periods of normalcy. Thus, even though the possibility appears to be remote, the prospect of a recrudescence of isolationism cannot be excluded. A tactical cessation of Russian pressure might produce just this kind of demobilization and withdrawal reaction and the reassertion of older principles of conduct. This is not to say that such a reaction would be decisive so far as policy is concerned; but it is a prospect which sound policy-planning should anticipate.

5. *Idealism-Cynicism*

In still another respect American moral predispositions may have consequences for foreign policy. The annoyance and irritation of the peoples of foreign countries over American self-righteousness is, on the whole, a relatively minor source of difficulty. Americans would appear to be happiest when they can cloak an action motivated by self-interest with an aura of New Testament selflessness, when an action which is "good business," or "good security" can be made to "look good" too. Similarly there is resistance among Americans over the straightforward expression of conscience-motivated behavior. What is "good" has to be represented as satisfying the criteria of self-interest. They are happiest when they can allay the Christian conscience at the same time that they satisfy self-interested criteria. In this regard the peoples of foreign countries are well protected, perhaps overprotected, by their own cynicism.

But there are a number of respects in which this moral dualism may produce more serious problems for the policy-maker. There would appear to be a certain cyclical trend in American moral attitudes. The great wave of idealism in the first world war gave way to the cynicism about foreign countries of the 1920's. The friendliness for our British and French allies of World War I gave way to bitterness over their defaults on their indebtedness. A little more than a decade ago the little country of Finland had a place at the very center of the American heart because she had kept up her payments on her war debts, while the European powers which had defaulted, and on the fate of which our security rested, were prevented from borrowing money in the American capital market. The chiliastic faith in the reasonableness of the Russians has now been supplanted by deep resentment over their base ingratitude.

American generosity and humanitarianism is a tentative phenomenon. Along with impulses toward good will and generosity, there is a deep-seated suspicion that smart people don't act that way, that "only suckers are a soft touch." In this connection a recent study which appeared in a popular magazine is of considerable interest. This investigation, claiming to have been based on "reliable sampling procedures," reflected a degree of religious piety among Americans considerably greater than had previously been estimated. Of greatest interest was its description of American attitudes toward ethics. It would appear that almost half of the sample was sharply aware of the conflict between what was "right" and the demands of secular life. A somewhat smaller proportion considered that religion influenced their activities in business, political and social life. Considerably more than half felt that their conduct toward neighbors was governed by the golden rule; but more than 80 per cent felt that their neighbors fell considerably short of the golden rule in their conduct toward their fellowmen.

Quite aside from the question of the full reliability of a study asking such "loaded" and personal questions, there seems to be confirmation here for the proposition regarding the moral dualism in the American character. The aspiration to conform to Christian ethical ideals is clearly present among most members of the culture, but there would appear to be a strong apprehension that such standards of conduct are inapplicable because the outside world does not behave that way. Hence any impulse toward ethically motivated generosity is impaired not only by the feeling that it will go unrequited, but that one's neighbors will ridicule it or attribute it to some concealed, self-interested motive.

It would appear to be a reasonable speculation from the foregoing findings that any action involving the giving or loaning of American wealth to foreign peoples, even though it be motivated by calculations of self-interest, activates this fear that "only a sucker is a soft touch." Under conditions of threat, such as those of the present, these doubts and suspicions about "giving things away" have been kept within manageable proportions. But in a period of temporary stabilization when the superficial aspect of the foreign situation encourages withdrawal reactions, these feelings may play a role of some significance.

6. *Superiority-Inferiority*

In a sense America is a nation of parvenus. A historically unique rate of immigration, social, and geographic mobility has produced a people which has not had an opportunity to "set," to acquire the security and stability which come from familiar ties, associations, rights, and obligations. It is perhaps not accidental that in the vulgarization of psychoanalytic hypotheses in America in the last decades one of the first to acquire popular currency was the "superiority-inferiority" complex. In more stably stratified societies the individual tends to have a greater sense of "location," a broader and deeper identification with his social surroundings. He has not *made* his own identity, while in America a large proportion of each generation is *self-made*. Being self-made produces a certain buoyancy, a sense of mastery, but it leaves the individual somewhat doubtful as to his social legitimacy. This sense of insecurity and uncertainty may add a strident note to American claims for recognition. This may explain the stereotype of the American abroad, confronted with complex and ancient cultures, taking alcoholic refuge in assertions of American moral, political, and technical virtue. It may also account for a feeling in the United States that American diplomats are no match for the wiliness and cunning of Old World negotiators. In other words, Americans typically overreact in their self-evaluations. They over- and under-estimate their skills and virtues, just as they over- and under-estimate the skills and virtues of other cultures and nations.

It is perhaps this quality among Americans—and among the American elites—which strongly militates against a balanced and empathic appreciation of cultural and national differences so essential to the development of an effective diplomacy. One may entertain the hypothesis that Americans tend to judge other nations and cultures according to a strictly American scoreboard, on the basis of which America is bound to win. It is difficult for Americans to accept a humane conception of cultural and national differences. Somehow, other cultural values must be transmuted into an American currency so that it becomes possible in a competition of national cultures to rate the United States as the "best all-around culture of the year."

There is a noticeable sensitivity among Americans on the score of cultural and intellectual inferiority. Only recently the American press cited the throngs of visitors to art museums exhibiting the Habsburg collection of paintings as effectively refuting European claims of American cultural inferiority. Feelings of crudeness and inferiority are not only expressed in the form of direct refutation by citing such evidence as the above; they also are frequently expressed in the tendency to equate esthetic and intellectual subtlety with lack of manliness—artists and intellectuals are "queers."

This superiority-inferiority ambivalence may manifest itself in policy-making in a number of ways. It may take the direct and perhaps more typical form of cultural arrogance—assertions of the superiority of the American way in politics, in economics, in social relations, in morality, or in the physical amenities of life. In this case the psychological mechanism involved is a reaction-formation; unconscious feelings of inferiority lead to the assertion of superiority. Or it may take the form of an admission of inferiority and an attribution of superiority to other cultures or elite groups. In either case there is an alienation from the real character and potentialities of the self. One either becomes an ideal and non-existent

American—a *persona* American—or one rejects one's Americanism entirely and attempts to "pass," for example, into English or French culture. These formulations, of course, state the problem in the extreme for purposes of clarity.

These reactions have a selective appeal among the various elite groups. Thus American artists, writers, and intellectuals have historically tended to manifest inferiority feelings in the form of imitativeness, or in expatriation. It has been asserted that members of the American foreign service have tended to assimilate themselves too readily to foreign cultures and aristocratic "sets," perhaps at the expense of their American perspective. The tendency for American families of wealth and prestige to ape the English and Continental aristocracies is too well known to call for detailed comment. All of these groups have in common the quality of having differentiated themselves from the American pattern through extraordinary wealth, through artistic or intellectual deviation, or through long residence abroad. The more "representative" American—the Congressman for example—tends to manifest the simpler form of cultural arrogance.

Either inferiority or superiority feelings in relation to other cultures may have a negative effect on the national interest. Cultural arrogance may alienate other peoples, impair confidence in the United States among actual and potential allies, or aid in some measure in the mobilization of hostile sentiment among neutrals and potential enemies. Cultural subservience, particularly if manifested by American diplomats and negotiators, may result in real and unnecessary sacrifices of the national interest.

The hypothesis may also be advanced that there is a certain periodicity of national moods of confidence and lack of confidence. These have perhaps been associated in the United States with the fluctuations of the business cycle. One may speculate that not least among the catastrophic foreign policy consequences of a serious depression in the United States would be an impairment of national self-confidence, a sudden welling to the surface of underlying doubt, which might result in a weakening of foreign policy resolution, a feeling of being overextended, a need for contraction, for consolidation, for withdrawal.

Conclusion: The Many Faces of America

It would be unfortunate if the preceding analysis conveyed the impression of a neat periodicity of American foreign policy moods. Actually the American approach to foreign policy problems at any given time is a historically unique phenomenon. It is influenced not only by these (and other) ambivalences in the American character, but by the immediate historical background and the specific content of the foreign policy problem. While it is useful analytically to talk about the alternation of "normalcy" and "crisis" moods, it must be recognized that crises differ from one another, just as do periods of normalcy, and that the American character is undergoing continual change. Thus from one era to the next, both the subjective and objective components of foreign policy moods may greatly change.

In the period before World War II, the dominant and overt foreign policy mood was a composite of withdrawal impulses, cynicism about power politics, intolerance of foreign peoples and cultures, and pessimism about the prospects of idealistic internationalism. Many experiences had combined to produce this state of mind. The development of a power structure in Europe which did not immediately and overtly threaten the United States provided a plausible justification for isolationism. Disillusionment over the collapse of the high moral purposes of the Allies in World War I provoked a cynical and pessimistic reaction which strengthened the withdrawal trend. The default on Allied war debts contributed to American arrogance with regard to the inefficiency and lack of integrity of foreign governments.

The growing threat to American security began to undermine this withdrawal mood in the late 1930's. But it took the catastrophe of Pearl Harbor to produce a broad interventionist consensus. American intolerance of foreign countries and social systems was supplanted by a tolerance of actual and potential allies. Cynicism and pessimism about international power politics were supplanted by moderately idealistic aspirations and somewhat optimistic expectations of peace and international amity.

This mood pattern lasted through the latter years of the war and the brief period of Allied amity which followed it. But as specific conflicts with the Soviet Union broadened into the general impasse of the Cold War, the American foreign policy mood changed again. Optimism about the future of peace gave way to pessimism. Idealist internationalism faded into "security realism." Overtones of impatience and intolerance began to emerge in public reactions to our relations with the Soviet Union, England, China; but the continuance of threat precluded an unequivocal expression of these reactions.

There is some value for the purposes of foreign policy planning in recognizing that an overtly interventionist and "responsible" United States hides a covertly isolationist longing, that an overtly tolerant America is at the same time barely stifling intolerance reactions, that an idealistic America is muttering *sotto voce* cynicisms, that a surface optimism in America conceals a dread of the future. Understanding of these ambivalences might save statesmen periodic shocks at the sequences of American moods. One must always take into account the fact that Americans in this period of their development are both responsible and irresponsible. A momentary rift in the clouds brings the irresponsible trends to the surface; an intensification of threat brings out a sober readiness to sacrifice.

America's contemporary role in world politics is hardly more than a decade old. Other nations have had generations to assimilate their great political lessons. That America has begun to assimilate some of its political lessons is suggested by the widespread resolution that it can no longer tolerate the degree of economic instability which has characterized the past. This rejection of the inevitability of the severe shocks of the business cycle is matched in the political sphere by a growing acceptance of our foreign policy status and the sacrifices it imposes. But with regard to the foreign policy cycle, as well as the business cycle, a confident sense of self-mastery is still lacking. . . .

Additional Reading

Max Beloff, *Foreign Policy and the Democratic Process* (1955).
W. Y. Elliott, *et al., United States Foreign Policy: Its Organization and Control* (1952).
G. L. Grassmuck, *Sectional Biases in Congress on Foreign Policy* (1951).
Ernest Lefever, *Ethics and United States Foreign Policy* (1957).
Hans J. Morgenthau, *In Defense of the National Interest* (1951).
R. E. Osgood, *Ideals and Self-Interest in America's Foreign Relations* (1953).
Dexter Perkins, *The American Approach to Foreign Policy* (1952).
H. M. Wriston, *Diplomacy in a Democracy* (1956).

2 *JEFFERSON AND HAMILTON: Which One Was the Realist?*

The United States achieved independence in a world war and at the price of a permanent defensive military alliance with a major European power. Smarting from defeat in the Seven Years War and determined to diminish British power, the ministers of Louis XVI of France first gave secret aid to the American patriots in their struggle against the mother country and then concluded in 1778 an alliance with the nascent United States. Spain, with reasons of its own for disliking Great Britain, entered the war as an ally of France in 1779 and the Netherlands was involved in the following year. By 1781, Britain was at war with three European states and was threatened by an Armed League of neutrals. War weary and hoping to dissolve the hostile coalition, the British government in 1782 accepted the inevitable and recognized the independence of the thirteen rebellious North American colonies.

Although the Peace of 1783 granted generous boundaries to the American republic, difficulties were soon experienced in persuading Great Britain to observe the terms. From 1783 to 1794, the Americans sought in vain to persuade the British government to withdraw from the military posts it continued to occupy on American soil. Additional trouble ensued over the absence of a commercial arrangement between the two countries. The United States wanted to retain trading privileges formerly enjoyed as colonies within the empire. The British, however, were soon satisfied that Americans by force of habit and credit would continue to buy and sell most of their goods in England, and so felt little compulsion to accede. Removal of the British from the northern posts and negotiation of a satisfactory commercial treaty were serious problems to the federal government established under the new Constitution in 1789.

The French Alliance created still another disturbing problem. The 1778 Alliance became an encumbrance when the French Revolution entered a radical stage in 1792–1793, marked by overthrow of the monarchy, execution of Louis XVI, and the inauguration of a bloody reign of terror. Conservative sentiment in Europe and America denounced the violent excesses as the inevitable results of democracy and liberalism. The Federalist party, which formed around the Washington Administration and whose chief architect was Alexander Hamilton, Secretary of the Treasury, deplored events in France and sympathized with Great Britain as a bulwark of sane and conservative constitutionalism. In contrast, the opposition Republican party, led by James Madison and Secretary of State Thomas Jefferson, defended the French Revolution as a glorious victory for freedom and advocated more democratization of government in America.

When war began in 1793 between republican France and monarchical Europe, factionalism within the United States was sharpened. Serious issues for the young nation were raised: Should the United States recognize the French republic by receiving its minister? Was the Treaty of Alliance still valid and operative? What should be the American response if France invoked the treaty and requested aid in defense of the French West Indies? Sharp differences over these questions developed between President Washington's two advisers, Hamilton and Jefferson. The basic issue was whether American policy should favor the British or the French, since events and ties to Europe rendered absolute impartiality virtually impossible. Eventually, Hamilton scored a victory over Jefferson and American policy acquired an orientation reserved toward France and benevolent toward Great Britain. In the interval, basic policies relating to recognition of new *de facto* governments and neutrality during European wars were established.

DOCUMENTS

1. The French Treaties

The treaty of commerce with France in 1778 was noteworthy for its statement of liberal neutral rights. The Continental Congress adopted a model treaty scheme, known as the "Plan of 1776," which incorporated provisions protecting private and neutral property on the high seas against arbitrary belligerent interferences and seizures. As the United States was interested in expanding its trade and expected to remain neutral in future European wars, it sought to conclude treaties with other states which recognized a wide latitude of neutral rights on the high seas during wartime. France, similarly interested in curbing such arrogant sea powers as Great Britain, concurred.

Excerpts from the Treaty of Amity and Commerce between the United States and France, signed February 6, 1778

Article 16 [*14*]. On the contrary it is agreed, that whatever shall be found to be laden by the Subjects and Inhabitants of either Party on any Ship belonging to the Enemys of the other or to their Subjects, the whole although it be not of the Sort of prohibited Goods may be confiscated in the same manner, as if it belonged to the Enemy, except such Goods and Merchandizes as were put on board such Ship before the Declaration of War, or even after such Declaration, if so be it were done without knowledge of such Declaration. So that the Goods of the Subjects and People of either Party, whether they be of the Nature of such as are prohibited or otherwise, which, as is aforesaid were put on board any Ship belonging to an Enemy before the War, or after the Declaration of the same, without the Knowledge of it, shall no ways be liable to confiscation, but shall well and truely be restored without Delay to the proprietors demanding the same; but so as that, if the said Merchandizes be contraband, it shall not be any Ways lawful to carry them afterwards to any Ports belonging to the Enemy. The two contracting Parties agree, that the Term of two Months being passed after the Declaration of War, their respective Subjects, from whatever Part of the World they come, shall not plead the Ignorance mentioned in this Article.

Article 19 [*17*]. It shall be lawful for the Ships of War of either Party & Privateers freely to carry whithersoever they please the Ships and Goods taken from their Enemies, without being obliged to pay any Duty to the Officers of the Admiralty or any other Judges; nor shall such Prizes be arrested or seized, when they come to and enter the Ports of either Party; nor shall the Searchers or other Officers of those Places search the same or make examination concerning the Lawfulness of such Prizes, but they may hoist Sail at any time and depart and carry their Prizes to the Places express'd in their Commissions, which the Commanders of such Ships of War shall be obliged to shew: On the contrary no Shelter or Refuge shall be given in their Ports to such as shall have made Prize of the Subjects, People or Property of either of the Parties; but if such shall come in, being forced by Stress of Weather or the Danger of the Sea, all proper means shall be vigorously used that they go out and retire from thence as soon as possible. . . .

Article 24 [22]. It shall not be lawful for any foreign Privateers, not belonging to Subjects of the most Christian King nor Citizens of the said United States, who have Commissions from any other Prince or State in enmity with either Nation to fit their Ships in the Ports of either the one or the other of the aforesaid Parties, to sell what they have taken or in any other manner whatsoever to exchange their Ships, Merchandizes or any other lading; neither shall they be allowed even to purchase victuals except such as shall be necessary for their going to the next Port of that Prince or State from which they have Commissions.

Article 25 [23]. It shall be lawful for all and singular the Subjects of the most Christian King and the Citizens People and Inhabitants of the said United States to sail with their Ships with all manner of Liberty and Security; no distinction being made, who are the Proprietors of the Merchandizes laden thereon, from any Port to the places of those who now are or hereafter shall be at Enmity with the most Christian King or the United States. It shall likewise be Lawful for the Subjects and Inhabitants aforesaid to sail with the Ships and Merchandizes aforementioned and to trade with the same Liberty and security from the Places, Ports and Havens of those who are Enemies of both or either Party without any Opposition or disturbance whatsoever, not only directly from the Places of the Enemy afore mentioned to neutral Places; but also from one Place belonging to an Enemy to another place belonging to an Enemy, whether they be under the Jurisdiction of the same Prince or under several; And it is hereby stipulated that free Ships shall also give a freedom to Goods, and that every thing shall be deemed to be free and exempt, which shall be found on board the Ships belonging to the Subjects of either of the Confederates, although the whole lading or any Part thereof should appertain to the Enemies of either, contraband Goods being always excepted. It is also agreed in like manner that the same Liberty be extended to Persons, who are on board a free Ship, with this Effect, that although they be Enemies to both or either Party, they are not to be taken out of that free Ship, unless they are Soldiers and in actual Service of the Enemies.

Article 26 [*24*]. This Liberty of Navigation and Commerce shall extend to all kinds of Merchandizes, excepting those only which are distinguished by the name of contraband; And under this Name of Contraband or prohibited Goods shall be comprehended, Arms, great Guns, Bombs with the fuzes, and other things belonging to them, Cannon Ball, Gun powder, Match, Pikes, Swords, Lances, Spears, halberds, Mortars, Petards, Granades, Salt Petre, Muskets, Musket Ball, Bucklers, Helmets, breast Plates, Coats of Mail and the like kinds of Arms proper for arming Soldiers, Musket rests, belts, Horses with their Furniture, and all other Warlike Instruments whatever. These Merchandizes which follow shall not be reckoned among Contraband or prohibited Goods, that is to say, all sorts of Cloths, and all other Manufactures woven of any wool, Flax, Silk, Cotton or any other Materials whatever; all kinds of wearing Apparel together with the Species, whereof they are used to be made; gold & Silver as well coined as uncoin'd, Tin, Iron, Latten, Copper, Brass Coals, as also Wheat and Barley and any other kind of Corn and pulse; Tobacco and likewise all manner of Spices; salted and smoked Flesh, salted Fish, Cheese and Butter, Beer, Oils, Wines, Sugars and all sorts of Salts; & in general all Provisions, which serve for the nourishment of Mankind and the sustenance of Life; furthermore all kinds of Cotton, hemp, Flax, Tar, Pitch, Ropes, Cables, Sails, Sail Cloths, Anchors and any Parts of Anchors; also Ships Masts, Planks, Boards and Beams of what Trees soever; and all other Things proper either for building or repairing Ships, and all other Goods whatever, which have not been worked into the form of any Instrument or thing prepared for War by Land or by Sea, shall not be reputed Contraband, much less such as have been already wrought and made up for any other Use; all which shall be wholly reckoned among free Goods: as likewise all other Merchandizes and things, which are not comprehended and particularly mentioned in the foregoing enumeration of contrabrand Goods: so that they may be transported and carried in the freest manner by the Subjects of both Confederates even to Places belonging to an Enemy such Towns or Places being only excepted as are at that time besieged, blocked up or invested. . . .

Excerpts from the Treaty of Alliance between the United States and France, February 6, 1778

Article 1. If War should break out betwan France and Great Britain, during the continuence of the present War betwan the United States and England, his Majesty and the said United States, shall make it a common cause, and aid each other mutually with their good Offices, their Counsels, and their forces, according to the exigence of Conjunctures as becomes good & faithful Allies.

Article 2. The essential and direct End of the present defensive alliance is to maintain effectually the liberty, Sovereignty, and independance absolute and unlimited of the said united States, as well in Matters of Gouvernement as of commerce. . . .

Article 5. If the united States should think fit to attempt the Reduction of the British Power remaining in the Northern Parts of America, or the Islands of Bermudas, those Contries or Islands in case of Success, shall be confederated with or dependent upon the said United States.

Article 6. The Most Christian King renounces for ever the possession of the Islands of Bermudas as well as of any part of the continent of North america which before the treaty of Paris in 1763, or in virtue of that Treaty, were acknowledged to belong to the Crown of Great Britain, or to the united States heretofore called British Colonies, or which are at this Time or have lately been under the Power of The King and Crown of Great Britain.

Article 7. If his Most Christian Majesty shall think proper to attack any of the Islands situated in the Gulph of Mexico, or near that Gulph, which are at present under the Power of Great Britain, all the said Isles, in case of success, shall appertain to the Crown of France.

Article 8. Neither of the two Parties shall conclude either Truce or Peace with Great Britain, without the formal consent of the other first obtain'd; and they mutually engage not to lay down their arms, until the Independence of the united states shall have been formally or tacitly assured by the Treaty or Treaties that shall terminate the War. . . .

Article 11. The two Parties guarantee mutually from the present time and forever, against all other powers, to wit, the United States to his most Christian Majesty the present Possessions of the Crown of France in America as well as those which it may acquire by the future Treaty of peace: and his most Christian Majesty guarantees on his part to the united states, their liberty, Sovereignty, and Independence absolute, and unlimited, as well in Matters of Government as commerce and also thair Possessions, and the additions or conquests that their Confedération may obtain during the war, from any of the Dominions now or heretofore possessed by Great Britain in North America, conformable to the 5th & 6th articles above written, the whole as their Possessions shall be fixed and assured to the said States at the moment of the cessation of their present War with England. . . .

2. The Paris Peace Treaty

The preliminary peace treaty was signed by British and American emissaries on November 30, 1782. The definitive peace treaty awaited the conclusion of a general peace at Paris and was signed on September 3, 1783; ratifications were exchanged on May 12, 1784.

Definitive Treaty of Peace between Great Britain and the United States

Article 1st. His Britannic Majesty acknowledges the said United States, viz. New-Hampshire Massachusetts Bay, Rhode-Island & Providence Plantations, Connecticut, New York, New Jersey, Pennsylvania, Delaware, Maryland, Virginia, North Carolina, South Carolina & Georgia, to be free sovereign & Independent States; that he treats with them as such, and for himself his Heirs & Successors, relinquishes all Claims to the Government Propriety & Territorial Rights of the same & every Part thereof.

Article 2d. [boundaries]

Article 3d. It is agreed that the People of the United States shall continue to enjoy unmolested the Right to take Fish of every kind on the Grand Bank and on all the other Banks of New-foundland, also in the Gulph of St. Lawrence, and at all other Places in the Sea where the Inhabitants of both Countries used at any time heretofore to fish. And also that the Inhabitants of the United States shall have Liberty to take Fish of every Kind on such Part of the Coast of New-foundland as British Fishermen shall use, (but not to dry or cure the same on that Island) And also on the Coasts Bays & Creeks of all other of his Britannic Majesty's Dominions in America, and that the American Fishermen shall have Liberty to dry and cure Fish in any of the unsettled Bays Harbours and Creeks of Nova Scotia, Magdalen Islands, and Labrador, so long as the same shall remain unsettled but so soon as the same or either of them shall be settled, it shall not be lawful for the said Fishermen to dry or cure Fish at such Settlement, without a previous Agreement for that purpose with the Inhabitants, Proprietors or Possessors of the Ground.

Article 4th. It is agreed that Creditors on either Side shall meet with no lawful Impediment to the Recovery of the full Value in Sterling Money of all bona fide Debts heretofore contracted.

Article 5th. It is agreed that the Congress shall earnestly recommend it to the Legislatures of the respective States to provide for the Restitution of all Estates, Rights and Properties which have been confiscated belonging to real British Subjects. . . . And that Persons of any other Description shall have free Liberty to go to any Part or Parts of any of the thirteen United States and therein to remain twelve Months unmolested in their Endeavours to obtain the Restitution of such of their Estates Rights & Properties as may have been confiscated. . . .

And it is agreed that all Persons who have any Interest in confiscated Lands, either by Debts, Marriage Settlements, or otherwise, shall meet with no lawful Impediment in the Prosecution of their just Rights.

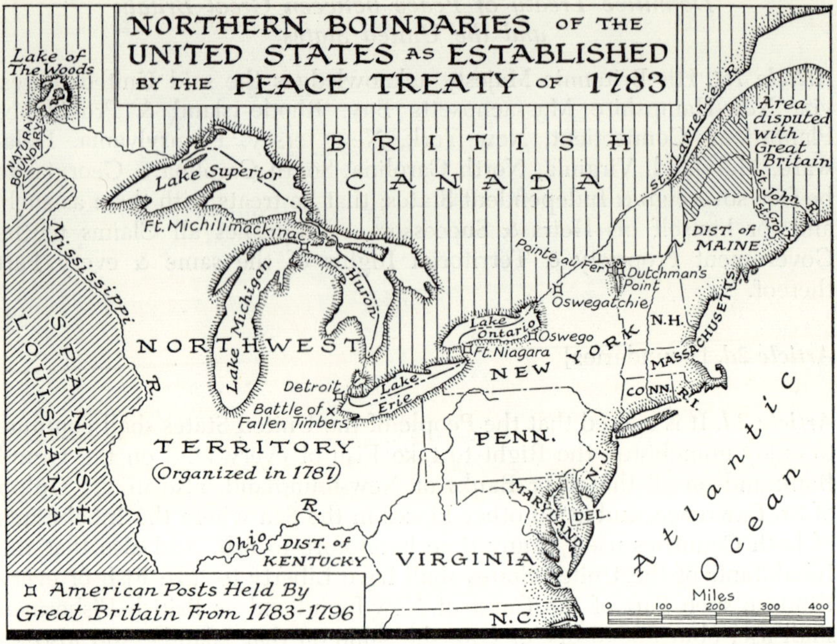

Article 6th. That there shall be no future Confiscations made nor any Prosecutions commenc'd against any Person or Persons for or by Reason of the Part, which he or they may have taken in the present War, and that no Person shall on that Account suffer any future Loss or Damage, either in his Person Liberty or Property; and that those who may be in Confinement on such Charges at the Time of the Ratification of the Treaty in America shall be immediately set at Liberty, and the Prosecutions so commenced be discontinued.

Article 7th. There shall be a firm and perpetual Peace between his Britannic Majesty and the said States and between the Subjects of the one, and the Citizens of the other, wherefore all Hostilities both by Sea and Land shall from henceforth cease: All Prisoners on both Sides shall be set at Liberty, and his Britannic Majesty shall with all convenient speed, and without causing any Destruction, or carrying away any Negroes or other Property of the American Inhabitants, withdraw all his Armies, Garrisons & Fleets from the said United States, and from every Port, Place and Harbour within the same; leaving in all Fortifications the American Artillery that may be therein: And shall also Order & cause all Archives, Records, Deeds & Papers belonging to any of the said States, or their Citizens, which in the Course of the War may have fallen into the Hands of his Officers, to be forthwith restored and deliver'd to the proper States and Persons to whom they belong.

Article 8th. The Navigation of the River Mississippi, from its source to the Ocean shall for ever remain free and open to the Subjects of Great Britain and the Citizens of the United States. . . .

3. *Nootka Sound and the Neutrality Issue*

In 1789, Spanish naval vessels seized as interlopers several English merchant ships in Nootka Sound on Vancouver Island, off the northwest coast of North America. Great Britain denied the Spanish claims to exclusive control of the area and threatened war if reparations and apologies were not forthcoming. The resulting war scare raised the question of American neutrality and caused President Washington to seek the advice of the cabinet on the problem. Specifically, Washington asked what the American response should be if British authorities requested permission to cross United States territory in order to attack Spanish possessions. Anxious to avoid even a remote possibility of trouble with Britain, Hamilton advised assent; Jefferson, pro-French but also eager to bargain with American neutrality and thereby perhaps to win concessions from the contending powers, counseled an evasive reply. The crisis subsided when Spain capitulated to the British demands.

Hamilton to Washington, September 15, 1790

It is not to be forgotten that we received from France, in our late revolution, essential succor, and from Spain valuable countenance and some direct aid. It is also to be remembered that France is the intimate ally of Spain, and there subsists a connection by treaty between the former power and the United States.

It might thence be alleged that obligations of gratitude towards those powers require that we should run some risk, rather than concur in a thing prejudicial to either of them, and particularly in favor of that very nation against which they assisted us. And the natural impulse of every good heart will second the proposition, till reason has taught it that refinements of this kind are to be indulged with caution in the affairs of nations.

Gratitude is a word, the very sound of which imposes something like respect. Where there is even an appearance upon which the claim to it can be founded, it can seldom be a pleasing task to dispute that claim. But where a word may become the basis of a political system, affecting the essential interests of the state, it is incumbent upon those who have any concern in the public administration, to appreciate its true import and application.

It is necessary, then, to reflect, however painful the reflection, that gratitude is a duty, a sentiment, which between nations can rarely have any solid foundation. Gratitude is only due to a kindness or service, the predominant object of which is the interest or benefit of the party to whom it is performed. Where the interest or benefit of the party performing is the predominant cause of it, however there may result a debt, in cases in which there is not an immediate adequate and reciprocal advantage, there can be no room for the sentiment of gratitude. Where there is such an advantage, there is then not even a debt. If the motive of the act, instead of being the benefit of the party to whom it was done, should be a compound of the interest of the party doing it and of detriment to some other, of whom he is the enemy and the rival, there is still less room for so noble and refined a sentiment. This analysis will serve as a test of our true situation in regard both to France and Spain.

It is not to be doubted, that the part which the courts of France and Spain took in our quarrel with Great Britain, is to be attributed, not to an attachment to our independence or liberty, but to a desire of diminishing the power of Great Britain by severing the British Empire. This they considered as an interest of very great magnitude to them. In this their calculations and their passions conspired. For this they united their arms with ours, and encountered the expenses and perils of war. This has been accomplished; the advantages of it are mutual; and so far the account is balanced. . . .

Let it be added to this, that the conduct of France in the manner of affording her aid, bore the marks of a liberal policy. She did not endeavor to extort from us, as the price of it, any disadvantageous or humiliating concessions. In this respect, however, she may have been influenced by an enlightened view of her own interest. She entitled herself to our esteem and good-will. These dispositions towards her ought to be cherished and cultivated; but they are very distinct from a spirit of romantic gratitude, calling for sacrifices of our substantial interests, preferences inconsistent with sound policy, or complaisances incompatible with our safety.

The conduct of Spain towards us presents a picture far less favorable. The direct aid we received from her during the war was inconsiderable in itself, and still more inconsiderable compared with her faculty of aiding us. She refrained from acknowledging our independence; has never acceded to the treaty of commerce made with France,—though a right of doing it was reserved to her,—nor made any other treaty with us; she has maintained possessions within our acknowledged limits without our consent; she perseveringly obstructs our sharing in the navigation of the Mississippi, though it is a privilege essential to us, and to which we consider ourselves as having an indisputable title. And perhaps it might be added upon good ground, that she has not scrupled to intrigue with leading individuals in the western country, to seduce them from our interests, and to attach them to her own.

Spain therefore must be regarded, upon the whole, as having slender claims to peculiar good-will from us. There is certainly nothing that authorizes her to expect we should expose ourselves to any extraordinary jeopardy for her sake. . . .

This is so true, that if a war should really ensue between Great Britain and Spain, and if the latter should persist in excluding us from the Mississippi (taking it for granted our claim to share in its navigation is well founded), there can be no reasonable ground of doubt that we should be at liberty, if we thought it our interest, consistently with our present engagements with France, to join Britain against Spain. . . .

Now, it is manifest, that a government scarcely ever had stronger motives to avoid war, than that of the United States at the present juncture. They have much to dread from war; much to expect from peace; something to hope from negotiation, in case of a rupture between Britain and Spain.

We are but just recovering from the effects of a long, arduous, and exhausting war. The people but just begin to realize the sweets of repose. We are vulnerable both by water and land; without either fleet or army. We have a considerable debt in proportion to the resources which the state of things permits the government to command. Measures have been recently entered upon for the restoration of credit, which a war could hardly fail to disconcert, and which, if disturbed, would be fatal to the means of prosecuting it. Our national government is in its infancy. . . .

It ought also to be taken into the account, that by placing ourselves at this time in a situation to go to war against Great Britain, we embark with the weakest party—with a total uncertainty what accession of strength may be gained—and without making any terms with regard either to succor, indemnity, or compensation. . . .

These considerations are additional admonitions to avoid, as far as possible, any step that may embroil us with Great Britain. It seems evidently our true policy to cultivate neutrality. This, at least, is the ground on which we ought to stand, until we can see more of the scene, and can have secured the means of changing it with advantage. . . .

Jefferson to Washington, August 28, 1790

Opinion upon the question what the answer of the President should be in case Lord Dorchester should apply for permission to march troops through the territory of the United States, from Detroit to the Mississippi.

I am so deeply impressed with the magnitude of the dangers which will attend our government, if Louisiana and the Floridas be added to the British empire, that, in my opinion, we ought to make ourselves parties in the *general war* expected to take place, should this be the only means of preventing the calamity.

But I think we should defer this step as long as possible; because war is full of chances, which may relieve us from the necessity of interfering; and if necessary, still the later we interfere, the better we shall be prepared.

It is often indeed more easy to prevent the capture of a place, than to retake it. Should it be so in the case in question, the difference between the two operations of preventing and retaking, will not be so costly as two, three, or four years more of war.

So that I am for preserving neutrality as long, and entering into the war as late, as possible.

If this be the best course, it decides, in a good degree, what should be our conduct, if the British ask leave to march troops through our territory, or march them without leave.

It is well enough agreed, in the laws of nations, that for a neutral power to give or refuse permission to the troops of either belligerent party to pass through their territory, is no breach of neutrality, provided the same refusal or permission be extended to the other party.

If we give leave of passage then to the British troops, Spain will have no just cause of complaint against us, provided we extend the same leave to her when demanded.

If we refuse, (as indeed we have a right to do,) and the troops should pass notwithstanding, of which there can be little doubt, we shall stand committed. For either we must enter immediately into the war, or pocket an acknowledged insult in the face of the world; and one insult pocketed soon produces another.

There is indeed a middle course, which I should be inclined to prefer; that is, to avoid giving any answer. They will proceed notwithstanding, but to do this under our silence, will admit of palliation, and produce apologies, from military necessity; and will leave us free to pass it over without dishonor, or to make it a handle of quarrel hereafter, if we should have use for it as such. But, if we are obliged to give an answer, I think the occasion not such as should induce us to hazard that answer which might commit us to the war at so early a stage of it; and therefore that the passage should be permitted.

If they should pass without having asked leave, I should be for expressing our dissatisfaction to the British court, and keeping alive an altercation on the subject, till events should decide whether it is most expedient to accept their apologies, or profit of the aggression as a cause of war.

4. The Incubus of the French Alliance

Upon receipt of news that France had declared war on Great Britain, President Washington wrote his department heads on April 18, 1793, and raised a number of policy questions for discussion at a cabinet meeting on the following day: Should the United States proclaim formal neutrality? Should a minister from republican France be received? Was the United States still bound by the 1778 Alliance? Again, Jefferson and Hamilton held sharply contrasted views, although both were agreed that the United States should not become actively involved in the war. Most historians view Jefferson's argument on the continued validity of the 1778 treaty, despite the revolution in France, as sound and in accordance with international law and practice.

Hamilton to Washington

Are the United States bound, by the principles of the laws of nations, to consider the treaties heretofore made with France as in present force and operation between them and the actual governing powers of the French nation? or may they elect to consider their operation as suspended, reserving also a right to judge finally whether any such changes have happened in the political affairs of France as may justify a renunciation of those treaties?

It is believed that they have an option to consider the operation of those treaties as suspended, and will have eventually a right to renounce them, if such changes shall take place as can *bona fide* be pronounced to render a continuance of the connections which result from them disadvantageous or dangerous.

There are two general propositions which may be opposed to this opinion: 1st. That a nation has a right, in its own discretion, to change its form of government—to abolish one, and substitute another. 2d. That *real* treaties (of which description those in question are) bind the NATIONS whose governments contract, and continue in force notwithstanding any changes which happen in the forms of their government.

The truth of the first proposition ought to be admitted in its fullest latitude. But it will by no means follow, that, because a nation has a right to manage its own concerns as it thinks fit, and to make such changes in its political institutions as itself judges best calculated to promote its interests, it has therefore a right to involve other nations, with whom it may have had connections, *absolutely* and *unconditionally,* in the consequences of the changes which it may think proper to make. This would be to give to a nation or society not only a power over its own happiness, but a power over the happiness of other nations or societies. It would be to extend the operation of the maxim much beyond the *reason* of it, which is simply, that every nation ought to have a right to provide for its own happiness. . . .

All general rules are to be construed with certain reasonable limitations. That which has been just mentioned must be understood in this sense, that changes in forms of government do not of course abrogate *real* treaties; that they continue absolutely binding on the party which makes the change, and will bind the other party, unless, in due time and for just cause, he declares his election to renounce them; that in good faith he ought not to renounce them, unless the change which happened does really render them useless, or materially less advantageous, or more dangerous than before. But for good and sufficient cause he may renounce them.

Nothing can be more evident than that the existing forms of government of two nations may enter far into the motives of a real treaty. . . .

Two nations may form an alliance because each has confidence in the energy and efficacy of the government of the other. A revolution may subject one of them to a different form of government—feeble, fluctuating, and turbulent, liable to provoke wars, and very little fitted to repel them. Even the connections of a nation with other foreign powers may enter into the motives of an alliance with it. If a dissolution of ancient connections shall have been a consequence of a revolution of government, the external political relations of the parties may have become so varied as to occasion an incompatibility of the alliance with the Power which had changed its constitution with the other connections of its ally—connections perhaps essential to its welfare.

In such cases, reason, which is the touchstone of all similar maxims, would dictate that the party whose government had remained stationary would have a right, under a *bona-fide* conviction that the change in the situation of the other party would render a future connection detrimental or dangerous, to declare the connection dissolved.

Contracts between nations as between individuals must lose their force where the considerations fail.

A treaty pernicious to the state is of itself void, where no change in the situation of either of the parties takes place. By a much stronger reason it must become *voidable* at the option of the other party, when the voluntary act of one of the allies has made so material a change in the condition of things as is always implied in a radical revolution of government. . . .

Jefferson to Washington

I proceed, in compliance with the requisition of the President, to give an opinion in writing on the general Question, Whether the U.S. have a right to renounce their treaties with France, or to hold them suspended till the government of that country shall be established? . . .

I consider the people who constitute a society or nation as the source of all authority in that nation, as free to transact their common concerns by any agents they think proper, to change these agents individually, or the organisation of them in form or function whenever they please: that all the acts done by those agents under the authority of the nation, are the acts of the nation, are obligatory on them, & enure to their use, & can in no wise be annulled or affected by any change in the form of the government, or of the persons administering it. Consequently the Treaties between the U.S. and France, were not treaties between the U.S. & Louis Capet, but between the two nations of America & France, and the nations remaining in existence, tho' both of them have since changed their forms of government, the treaties are not annulled by these changes. . . .

. . . Compacts then between nation & nation are obligatory on them by the same moral law which obliges individuals to observe their compacts. There are circumstances however which sometimes excuse the non-performance of contracts between man & man: so are there also between nation & nation. When performance, for instance, becomes *impossible,* non-performance is not immoral. So if performance becomes *self-destructive* to the party, the law of self-preservation overrules the laws of obligation to others. . . .

But Reason, which gives this right of self-liberation from a contract in certain cases, has subjected it to certain just limitations.

The danger which absolves us must be great, inevitable & imminent. Is such the character of that now apprehended from our treaties with France? What is that danger. . . . Obligation is not suspended, till the danger is become real, & the moment of it so imminent, that we can no longer avoid decision without forever losing the opportunity to do it. . . .

The danger apprehended, is it that, the treaties remaining valid, the clause guarantying their West India islands will engage us in the war? But Does the Guarantee engage us to enter into the war in any event?

Are we to enter into it before we are called on by our allies? Have we been called on by them?—shall we ever be called on? Is it their interest to call on us?

Can they call on us before their islands are invaded, or imminently threatened?

If they can save them themselves, have they a right to call on us?

Are we obliged to go to war at once, without trying peaceable negotiations with their enemy?

If all these questions be against us, there are still others behind.

Are we in a condition to go to war?

Can we be expected to begin before we are in condition?

Will the islands be lost if we do not save them? Have we the means of saving them?

If we cannot save them are we bound to go to war for a desperate object?

Will not a 10 years forbearance in us to call them into the guarantee of our posts, entitle us to some indulgence?

Many, if not most of these questions offer grounds of doubt whether the clause of guarantee will draw us into the war. Consequently if this be the danger apprehended, it is not yet certain enough to authorize us in sound morality to declare, at this moment, the treaties null. . . .

Is the danger apprehended from the 22nd Art. of our treaty of commerce, which prohibits the enemies of France from fitting out privateers in our ports, or selling their prizes here. But we are free to refuse the same thing to France, there being no stipulation to the contrary, and we ought to refuse it on principles of fair neutrality.

But the reception of a Minister from the Republic of France, without qualifications, it is thought will bring us into danger: because this, it is said, will determine the continuance of the treaty, and take from us the right of self-liberation when at any time hereafter our safety would require us to use it. The reception of the Minister at all (in favor of which Col. Hamilton has given his opinion, tho reluctantly as he confessed) is an acknolegement of the legitimacy of their government: and if the qualifications meditated are to deny that legitimacy, it will be a curious compound which is to admit & deny the same thing. But I deny that the reception of a Minister has any thing to do with the treaties. There is not a word, in either of them, about sending ministers. This has been done between us under the common usage of nations, & can have no effect either to continue or annul the treaties.

But how can any act of election have the effect to continue a treaty which is acknoleged to be going on still? For it was not pretended the treaty was void, but only voidable if we chuse to declare it so. To make it void would require an act of election, but to let it go on requires only that we should do nothing, and doing nothing can hardly be an infraction of peace or neutrality.

But I go further & deny that the most explicit declaration made at this moment that we acknolege the obligation of the treaties could take from us the right of non-compliance at any future time when compliance would involve us in great & inevitable danger.

I conclude then that few of these sources threaten any danger at all; and from none of them is it inevitable: & consequently none of them give us the right at this moment of releasing ourselves from our treaties. . . .

READINGS

1. Hamilton: Far-sighted Statesman

Alexander Hamilton has been portrayed by the majority of historians as a conservatively inclined realist in foreign policy and politics. According to this view, Hamilton realized that the weak nation required peace to establish firmly the new government under the constitution and for the nation to flourish and prosper. In particular, Hamilton was determined not to risk hostilities with Great Britain, lest trade be interrupted and with it the tariff revenues upon which the Hamiltonian fiscal system depended. Jefferson, on the other hand, has usually been depicted as a pro-French visionary and idealist, whose policy views if adopted might well have led to war against England. The first selection, by the eminent diplomatic historian Samuel Flagg Bemis, author of a number of studies on the early national period, envisions Hamilton as a realistic statesman concerned with the national interest in peace and prosperity.

Hamilton and the French Alliance

SAMUEL FLAGG BEMIS

. . . There remained the question of what attitude to take if Great Britain in any invasion of Spanish Louisiana should demand a passage across the Northwest Territory. As a matter of fact, the British plans of attack on Louisiana appear to have been based on naval operations; the researches for this essay have revealed no idea of a descent in 1790 on that province from Canada; really the Ministry feared an American attack on the posts during the Spanish crisis as much as the President apprehended an advance through the territory of the United States. But Washington imagined such an invasion to be imminent, as Dorchester [Governor General of Canada] fancied an attack on the posts to be dangerously near, and the President dreaded the British encirclement

Samuel Flagg Bemis, *Jay's Treaty: A Study in Commerce and Diplomacy* (New Haven, Conn.: Yale University Press, 1962 revised edition), 98–105, 122, 140–145, 188–194. Reprinted with permission.

of American territory which the conquest of Louisiana would mean. So much did he fear this that he made to his Cabinet officers the well-known request for written opinions on what answer to make in case Dorchester should ask permission to send troops across American soil.

The advice which Washington received shows much confusion of opinion and no determination to resist such an aggression. Jefferson appreciated the fatal results of a conquest of Louisiana but had in mind no resolute course of action. He would refuse to answer any such demand. If the passage were then made, nevertheless, he would keep alive an altercation on the subject until events should decide whether it were more expedient to accept apologies or to profit by the incident as a cause for war. [Vice President] Adams would refuse passage; in case the refusal should be overridden he recommended an energetic negotiation as the utmost action for redress. Jay [Chief Justice of the Supreme Court], whose opinion was also requested, would not go to war if the passage were forced; he thus practically agreed with Adams. Knox, Secretary of War, gave an indefinite answer counseling strict neutrality and yet speaking of the possibility of sufficient inducements which might be accepted to enter the war on the more profitable side. Hamilton took much time and molded his answer into a long state paper. There was a right by international law to refuse or to consent to such a passage; the choice should be made solely according to the interests of the United States. A middle course, that of withholding an answer, was timidly evasive, he believed, undignified and impolitic. Refusal would involve the nation in either war or disgrace; if it could not be backed effectively by force it ought not to be made. All things considered, he believed it would be best to grant the request; there was more to be gained by cultivating the friendship of England than of Spain.

Fortunately these opinions, which would have been so interesting to the Foreign Office during the Nootka crisis, remained unknown to Beckwith [British Agent in the United States].

While the general tenor of Jefferson's counsel dictated neutrality in case of a European war, he characteristically attempted to exploit the situation for the interests of the United States, in order to secure from Great Britain evacuation of the posts and from Spain opening of the Mississippi. In instructions to Morris,* written after receiving the latter's account of the notable interview of May 21 with Leeds and Pitt, the Secretary of State declared that if England should formally propose an exchange of diplomatic representatives the United States would appoint a minister. It was the wish of the United States to be neutral, and it would be so if Great Britain would execute the treaty fairly and attempt no conquest adjoining its territory. Simultaneously instructions, also based on the assumption of war, were dispatched to the American *chargés* in Spain and France. In case of hostilities Carmichael, in Madrid, was to press firmly for the opening of the Mississippi and to magnify the unrest of the Western citizens whom the United States was endeavoring to quiet

* Gouverneur Morris, on an unofficial mission in England, conferred with Prime Minister William Pitt and the Foreign Minister, the Duke of Leeds. [EDITOR'S NOTE]

with expectations of attaining their object by peaceful means. Short, in Paris, was instructed that in case France should join her ally, she might reasonably be expected to do everything to diminish the number of Spain's enemies: "she cannot doubt that we will be among them if she does not yield our right to navigate the Mississippi." Through the influence of Lafayette, Short was to induce France to urge Spain to open the river. Thus Jefferson, in the event of war being declared, would have threatened Spain with a rush on New Orleans of irate western citizens; to France he would have spoken openly of placing the United States among Spain's enemies; but to England, the enemy of France and Spain, he would have promised neutrality upon conditions. "Peace and profit" would be the aim of the neutral United States in case of war in Europe, he caused it to be made known to the British Government through a private correspondent of his own, Benjamin Vaughan of London: "A high price and sure market for our productions, and no want of carrying business will I hope enable my countrymen to pay off both their private and public debts."

The question also came up at this time of the expediency of apprising Lord Dorchester of the purpose of the proposed campaign against the Indians. Jefferson's writings contain an opinion against giving such notice.

> For, if the notification be early, he [Dorchester] will get the Indians out of the way, and defeat our object. If it be so late as not to leave him time to withdraw them before our stroke be struck, it will then be so late also as not to leave him time to withdraw any secret aids he may have sent them. And the notification will betray to him that he may go on without fear in his expedition against the Spaniards, and for which he may yet have sufficient time after our expedition is over.

Nevertheless the British commandant at Detroit was informed officially by General St. Clair, under whose command the American frontier troops were placed, that the President desired assurances to be given of the peaceful disposition of the United States toward Great Britain and that the military expedition was not against Detroit or any other post in possession of the British: the sole object was to chastise savage tribes, perpetrators of outrages on the American people and humanity in general. The President trusted, therefore, that the savages would receive no assistance nor encouragement and that traders would be restrained from inciting them. Hamilton already had told Beckwith that an expedition was under way against the western Indians, which, said Beckwith, had been mentioned in order "to prevent any alarm at our Posts, although he relied on my not speaking of it here."

This confidence illustrates the diplomatic intimacy which had grown up between Hamilton and Beckwith. Until the arrival in October, 1791, of a regularly accredited British Minister, Beckwith kept constantly in close touch with the Secretary of the Treasury. If it was not possible, for lack of proper credentials, to establish any official contact with the Secretary of State, it was easy to communicate informally with the influential Federalist leader who had frankly declared and who continued to declare himself an advocate of a political as well as a commercial connection with England.

In a case of a European war Hamilton would have chosen the side of England if it proved impossible to get both the posts and the Mississippi navigation in return for American neutrality. He had advised Washington that the continued possession of New Orleans by Spain meant in the near future "infallibly . . . a war with Spain, or separation of the Western Country." But

> in regard to the possessions of Great Britain on our left [east] it is at least problematical, whether the acquisition of them will ever be desirable to the United States. It is certain that they are in no shape essential to our prosperity. Except, therefore, the detention of our Western posts, (an object, too, of far less consequence than the navigation of the Mississippi,) there appears no necessary source of future collision with that power.

It was his prime object of foreign policy to adjust as soon as possible all differences with Great Britain and he was impatient at anything or anybody who stood in the way of such an adjustment. To communicate his idea to the British Government he made use of Beckwith, and these communications, always oral and confidential, were frequent, full, and free. After winter closed the river route to Quebec, Beckwith, on whose letters we rely for the revelation of these secret efforts for an Anglo-American *rapprochement,* sent his dispatches direct to England as well as to Quebec, and continued to do so during the remainder of his sojourn in America. Hamilton thus got a quick and ready hearing in London. It is safe to say that this informal diplomacy was far more effective in securing an eventual exchange of regular diplomatic representatives than was the negotiation of Gouverneur Morris. The Secretary of the Treasury early explained to Beckwith that any minister regularly appointed as resident in America would have to negotiate directly with the Secretary of State, who would then become the channel of communication to the President:

> in the turn of such affairs the most minute circumstances, mere trifles, give a favorable bias or otherwise to the whole.
>
> The President's mind I can declare to be perfectly dispassionate on this subject. Mr. Jefferson . . . is a gentleman of honor and zealously desirous of promoting . . . the interests of his country . . . but from some opinions which he has given respecting your Government, and possible predilections elsewhere, there may be difficulties which may possibly frustrate the whole, and which might be readily explained away.

In case such difficulties should occur, Hamilton, who had constant access to the President, wished to know of them, in order that they might be "clearly understood and candidly examined.". . .

The person selected for the appointment to America was George Hammond, a young diplomat of twenty-seven years, who was possessed of some experience in minor positions at several of the European courts. At Paris in 1783 when secretary to David Hartley during the peace negotiations he had made the acquaintance of Jefferson. Endowed with a fairly keen mind and a fluent pen, Hammond was an assiduous worker who devoted himself unflaggingly to his duty during his stay in the United States and followed his instructions with a diligence which uniformly met the approbation of his superiors. Upon his return to England in 1795 he was made Undersecretary for Foreign Affairs, a post at which he spent a life which was long and serviceable but never brilliant. . . .

Hamilton continued with the officially accredited British Minister the same relations which he had held with the informal agent Beckwith. Hammond, too, fully aware of the opposite policies of the two American Secretaries and of the different political and economic systems with which they were identified, zealously cultivated Hamilton. The Englishman divined with considerable accuracy Hamilton's motive for not wishing to upset good relations with Great Britain. "Of this gentleman's sincerity," he wrote, "I have the surest pledge in the knowledge that any event which might endanger the tranquillity of the United States would be as fatal to the systems he has formed for the benefit of his country as to his present personal reputation and to his future projects of ambition." In 1793 Hammond stated that he preferred to make most of his communications privately to Hamilton and to have relations with Jefferson only when absolutely necessary.

Hammond's first "long and confidential conversation" with Hamilton, which confirmed his previous impressions of "that Gentleman's just and liberal way of thinking," had been on the subject of Indian hostilities and foreign relations of the United States in general. Hamilton then had hinted that the affairs of the country were in an important crisis from which would issue the complexion of its political as well as of its foreign relations, and he allowed it to be understood that France in a proposed treaty had offered additional advantages to American navigation. This, he said, had led him to prepare a report on the actual state of the navigation and commerce of the United States to show that French laws were more favorable to American shipping than British, but that England presented the better opportunities for American commerce generally; balancing the two systems the scales would incline decidedly in favor of the commercial advantages of Great Britain.

This intimacy between the two men existed throughout Hammond's stay in the United States. During all of his official negotiation with Jefferson he was in constant communication with the Federalist leader. When the Secretary of State began the negotiation with an enumeration of American charges against Great Britain, which led to the preparation of Hammond's abstract, the British Minister discussed confidentially with Hamilton the actual weight of those charges. Hamilton at once admitted that there had been contraventions of the treaty in the United States, some of them of great magnitude, which were not to be excused on any other principle than the inefficiency of the former Congress to enforce respect for its own regulations; but he stated the federal courts could now do full justice. If the posts should be evacuated he thought some arrangement might be made to secure the interests of British fur traders. He believed some settlement could be effected for other infractions by the United States and that the Government would consent to any reasonable and practicable means of doing so. British trade was important to the United States: he hoped that commercial questions could be adjusted amicably and that the West Indian Islands could be opened to American vessels of limited tonnage. Hammond listened attentively, letting fall no hint that Great Britain would retreat from her system in the West Indies. He then asked when Jefferson's anticipated report on commercial restrictions might be expected. Hamilton believed that the report had been abandoned now that a British Minister had arrived and negotiations had been started.

Before Jefferson delivered his reply to Hammond's abstract he had submitted it to the Secretary of the Treasury with a request for advice, something which a man of the Virginian's acumen certainly never would have done had he known that practically every argument so strongly made therein had already been neutralized by his colleague in confidential oral negotiations with the British Minister. Upon reading the document Hamilton concluded that much strong ground had been taken and strongly held, especially as to the recommendatory clauses of the treaty and the lodging of the burden of prior infraction with Great Britain. He thought that the question of interest, and the suggestions of the British Minister touching particular acts and adjudications, were met satisfactorily but doubted strongly the expediency of the argument of retaliation and the soundness of the doctrine that all acts prior to proclamation of the preliminary articles of peace were cut off from discussion. He considered it better to extenuate than to vindicate the action of the states. He added a few minor and technical and rhetorical suggestions. Jefferson accepted the latter but left unaltered the main principles of his case. He submitted a copy of Hamilton's criticism to Washington together with a summary of his own views. The President sanctioned Jefferson's statement as it stood, being especially convinced that the charges as to recovery of debts should be vindicated rather than extenuated.

Upon delivery of Jefferson's stunning reply the British Minister, greatly aroused by what he termed an "extraordinary performance," immediately went to Hamilton. On being told in astonished tones of the note, the latter lamented the "intemperate violence of his colleague," saying that it was far from a faithful exposition of the true sentiments of the United States Government, that the President had had no opportunity of reading it and had relied on Jefferson's assurances that it was conformable to the opinions of the other members of the Cabinet. "Notwithstanding this explanation," writes Hammond, "which in reality I could esteem only a decided proof of personal confidence, I thought it my duty to take some immediate notice of this paper to Mr. Jefferson himself."

An interview with the Secretary of State followed, from which Hammond gathered that there was a total disagreement as to the facts of his case, since the accuracy was questioned of his statements made on the basis of evidence collected by the consuls.

> Though I presumed there might exist some errors in my statement, I still imagined that the general evidence of the infractions imputed to this country [i.e., the United States] was not materially invalidated by his counter-representation. . . . But that even admitting for an instant the whole force of his argument, there were other matters to be settled exclusive of an arrangement on the subject of the posts and the satisfaction of the claims of the Loyalists and the British creditors.

He therefore determined to refer the whole matter to his superiors for consideration.

Jefferson retired from the same interview strengthened in his set conviction that Great Britain had no intention whatsoever to give up the posts, and that, from mention Hammond had made about the disputed sources of the Mississippi (a question which now for the first time had been brought forth as one of the "other matters" which were to be adjusted), there was not only a disinclination to evacuate the parts of American soil already held but a desire to slice off a part of our Northwest Territory. . . .

During the controversy between the United States and Great Britain over British occupation of the posts, France had made no move to implement or execute her territorial guaranty, and the United States had not invoked it. Secretary of State Jefferson studiously refrained from doing so lest it should inspire France to invoke the American guaranty of her West Indian islands in some future war with Great Britain and thus jeopardize the neutrality of the United States. When France did declare war on Great Britain in 1793, both Jefferson and Hamilton agreed that neutrality was the proper policy for the United States. Jefferson's proclivities for France were well known, and his properly stiff attitude during the Hammond negotiations had shown him to be entirely untouched by the "British interest." His European experience had been almost wholly French. His sympathies instinctively went out to the revolutionary party. A man who professed to believe a revolution every thirty years was a purgative greatly to be desired in the life of any nation, he looked with complacence on the decentralizing tendencies of the French Revolutionary Government. With the agility of the doctrinaire his philosophy leaped over the bloody actualities of revolution to the Utopian democracy he thought he saw beyond. Feeling toward those unfortunate human beings who perished in the upheaval the same resigned grief which he had for men fallen in battle, he declared: "My own affections have been deeply wounded by some of the martyrs to this cause, but rather than it should have failed, I would have seen half the earth desolated. Were there but an Adam and an Eve left in every country, and left free, it would be better than as it now is."

There slept fitfully in Jefferson's mind a dread of monarchy and "monocrats," and he believed the Hamiltonian policy was directed toward these monsters. He had little use and less trust for the genius of his colleague. He had but a feeble comprehension of that sound financial policy which had made a reality of independence by supporting the Government with the strong arm of national credit. The very force of the new Government which Jefferson had been applying to claim execution of the treaty was, really, the fresh product of Hamilton's genius. If one cannot wholeheartedly commend the policy of Hamilton in reaching out of his own department to tamper with the Secretary of State's diplomacy, none the more can one excuse the conduct of Jefferson, who was now secretly engineering the notorious attack in Congress on Hamilton's financial administration, one of the gravest charges of which was the absurd accusation that two specific foreign loans for more efficient stewardship had been lumped into one, that sums had been taken from the lump to pay creditors abroad instead of making those payments from one specific loan allocated strictly to those particular creditors. Politically and personally the two men had come to distrust each other.

Despite his stiff attitude toward Great Britain, Jefferson never desired war with any nation under any circumstances. He often spoke loudly of it, but his real pull was for peace. He had inveterate confidence in his ability to play upon the commercial fears of Great Britain and upon the embarrassments of that country in the face of European upheaval. Possessed in 1793, as later when President, with a passion for peace, Jefferson meant in the last extremities to go no further than an embargo. He never prepared for war, and this ought to be conclusive proof that he never expected to encounter it. He trusted rather to his political ingenuity and to the chances of the unknown future.

The sympathies of Hamilton were wholly with Great Britain but for no sentimental or even philosophical reason. He admired the working of the British Constitution and a strong central government conducive to "law and order." He had little sympathy for democratic movements and abhorred reform by violence. The excesses of the French excited profound disgust in his mind. His was an intellect of realism. He had no philosophic bent that helped him to see a silver lining in the clouds beyond the horizon so darkly shadowing the French National Convention. "It cannot be without danger and inconvenience to our interests," he wrote, "to impress on the nations of Europe an idea that we are actuated by the *same spirit* which has for some time past fatally misguided the measures of those who conduct the affairs of France, and sullied a cause once glorious, and that might have been triumphant." To Hamilton, too, the most important fact of American foreign policy was the certain prostration of the new national government which would follow a break with England.

The three most eminent figures in American public life were for peace when in March, 1793, news of the critical relations between France and Great Britain reached the United States. Washington ardently hoped that nothing would force his country into war. With great satisfaction he viewed the recent progress of the nation and foresaw that all which was necessary to "be ranked, not only among the most respectable, but among the happiest people on this globe" was to enjoy uninterrupted for a few years the great natural advantages at hand. Early in April he received letters from Hamilton and Jefferson transmitting unofficial reports of the outbreak of the war, and he hurried from Mount Vernon to Philadelphia to take immediate steps for strict neutrality. A long list of questions, thirteen in number, he submitted to the two Secretaries and to the other members of the Cabinet as to proper attitude toward the belligerents. Everybody in the Administration favored neutrality. Jefferson, who on April 7 had written Washington that every justifiable means should be taken for preserving neutrality and who had doubted the authority of the executive to proclaim it, now assented to a proclamation in which the word neutrality as applying to the *attitude* of the Government would be studiously avoided in order that its absence might lead Great Britain to offer broad concessions for satisfactory assurance as to the ultimate action of the United States. The wording was changed in accordance with this opinion, but no bid was afterward made by Great Britain, which power much to Jefferson's disappointment considered the form of the proclamation satisfactory. The official correspondence soon began to refer to the "proclamation of neutrality." Jefferson himself quickly lapsed into use of the term.

The famous proclamation, drafted by Attorney General Edmund Randolph, was brief. It admonished Americans to refrain from all acts inconsistent with friendly and impartial conduct. Those who committed or abetted hostilities against any of the belligerent powers would be "liable to punishment or forfeiture under the laws of nations," and American citizens were warned of the danger of carrying "articles which are deemed contraband by the *modern* usage of nations." The public was informed that instructions had been given to the proper officials to prosecute all persons committing with respect to the powers at war "offenses against the laws of nations, within the cognizance of the courts of the United States." Thus the law of nations, all too vaguely defined, was by executive proclamation made to supply the deficiency of the domestic law. The Foreign Enlistment Act was not passed until the spring of the following year.

The proclamation itself disposed of the first three questions which the President had directed to the Cabinet. The others concerned the official attitude to be taken toward the new French Government and the new French plenipotentiary, who had landed at Charleston coincidentally with the news of war; and the question of what force the American treaties with the former King of France should have with the national Convention. A lively discussion, supplemented by long written papers, ensued in the Cabinet.

Hamilton saw danger in the guaranty of the French West Indian Islands. He believed that circumstances had become favorable for getting rid of this and other embarrassing stipulations. The treaties of 1778 had been made with Louis Capet, he stated, a monarch who had been illegally executed by a body of persons who could in no way claim the political heritage of the Bourbon King. Hence the obligations of those treaties should be regarded as having ceased, just as the National Convention had considered the Family Compact with Spain to have lapsed after the death of Louis XVI. He feared that to receive the French Minister without qualifying his reception would be to recognize the continuance of the embarrassing clauses. But the filaments which Hamilton spun from Vattel, Grotius, and Puffendorf to support this legal opinion were very weak.

Jefferson contended that the treaties continued binding notwithstanding the change in the French Government, the means of effecting which no outsider had a right to criticize. He argued that there had been no question as to continuing force of the treaties when a change had been made in the American Government in 1788, that none the more should such a question arise at this time, that reception of the new French Minister should not be qualified, that nothing should be said about treaties or guaranties, that reception of a minister did not concern the matter of a treaty, which could be reserved for consideration; that there had been as yet no demand from France to execute that guaranty. Jefferson's view was adopted. Citizen Genet was received as the Minister Plenipotentiary of the French Republic on May 17, 1793. . . .

2. *Jefferson: A Realist in Foreign Policy*

The following article by A. H. Bowman, a foreign affairs specialist for the federal government, reflects the view of several recent writers who have attempted to show that Hamilton often was guided by emotion and conservative philosophical inclinations, while Jefferson was more practical than usually portrayed. It was Jefferson's belief that European troubles eventually would give the United States an advantageous bargaining position. Time was to prove the correctness of his approach.

Jefferson, Hamilton and American Foreign Policy

ALBERT H. BOWMAN

In a recent book on American foreign policy, Professor Hans J. Morgenthau finds "two opposing conceptions of foreign policy . . . at the very beginning of the history of the United States": a "realistic position," ascribed to Alexander Hamilton and his followers, and a "moralistic illusion," allegedly adhered to by Thomas Jefferson and his supporters. The issue of realism versus moralism, according to the author, was first joined in 1793 over the question of an American proclamation of neutrality after Britain had entered the First Coalition's war against revolutionary France.* To illustrate this thesis Hamilton is assumed to represent neutrality, while Jefferson stood for American intervention on the side of France. This is a plausible enough assumption if, like Professor Morgen-

Albert H. Bowman, "Jefferson, Hamilton and American Foreign Policy," *Political Science Quarterly*, LXXI (1956), 18–41. Reprinted with permission.

* Hans J. Morgenthau, Jr., *In Defense of the National Interest* (New York, 1951), pp.14–19. The same thesis was advanced in Hans J. Morgenthau, Jr., and Kenneth W. Thompson, eds., *Principles & Problems of International Politics: Selected Readings* (New York, 1950), p. 37.

thau, one relies exclusively on the testimony of Hamilton. The historical facts suggest quite a different interpretation.

Professor Morgenthau has taken a set of historical circumstances which seem to support his general thesis, and Hamilton has led him into the same trap which historians have fallen into for well over a hundred years.** The purpose of this paper is to examine the question of realism versus idealism in American foreign policy in relation to Jefferson and Hamilton.

A reconsideration of the Jefferson-Hamilton contest over American foreign policy suggests that Jefferson, not Hamilton, did "unswervingly apply as standard the national interest of the United States." Hamilton's foreign policy was based constantly upon what he wanted the United States to become, not upon what it was or was likely to be. In short, Hamilton acted "unswervingly" to transform the United States into a George III-type oligarchy. Even in the formative years of the Republic this was a gross misreading of the American tradition, of the American spirit and of the American promise. It was not realism.

I

The issue between Hamiltonian and Jeffersonian concepts of United States foreign policy was first joined, not in 1793, but in the Nootka Sound controversy between Britain and Spain three years earlier. That episode clearly revealed Secretary of State Jefferson as a daring and knowing champion of American interests, and as a skillful diplomatic strategist as well. It demonstrated that Secretary of the Treasury Hamilton preferred to submit to humiliating British demands rather than to incur a hypothetical risk of war with that country. British trade was the main support of Hamilton's controversial fiscal system, and his devotion to that system blinded him to the importance to the United States of a

** Historians generally have accepted the Hamiltonian view of American foreign policy during the administrations of George Washington. George Bancroft, writing in the mid-nineteenth century, might have been an early exception, but his *History* ends with the adoption of the Federal Constitution. Richard Hildreth (1851) frankly presented the Hamiltonian viewpoint. John Bach McMaster's account (1885) favors Hamilton's position, Woodrow Wilson (1902) admired it, and John S. Bassett (*The Federalist System,* New York and London, 1906) endorsed it, although without enthusiasm.

Charles A. Beard (*The Economic Origins of Jeffersonian Democracy,* New York, 1915) viewed Hamiltonian foreign policy harshly, but he backhandedly approved it nevertheless. Edward Channing's rather noncommittal narrative (1917) leans toward the Hamiltonian interpretation, while Claude G. Bowers' scathing indictment of Hamiltonianism in general (*Jefferson and Hamilton,* Boston, 1925) for the most part ignores the international implications of the foreign policy issues of the times.

Nathan Schachner's treatment of Federalist foreign policy (*The Founding Fathers,* New York, 1954) was more impartial than the standard Federalist accounts, but it challenged none of the traditional interpretations. Among diplomatic historians, Samuel Flagg Bemis explicitly upholds Hamilton as the "*realpolitiker*" (*Jay's Treaty,* New York, 1924) who "saved American nationality" (*A Diplomatic History of the United States,* New York 1936 and 1942). Thomas A. Bailey (*A Diplomatic History of the American People,* New York, 1940) and Julius W. Pratt (*A History of United States Foreign Policy,* New York, 1955) less confidently arrive at similar conclusions.

Two important biographies, however, have challenged the traditional view. Irving Brant (*James Madison,* 4 vols., in process, Indianapolis and New York, 1941–53) presents a narrative highly critical of Hamilton's foreign policy, and Dumas Malone (*Jefferson and His Time,* 2 vols., in process, Boston, 1948–51) takes direct issue with the usual interpretation.

balance of European interests in America. This consideration was always the cornerstone of Jefferson's policy.

In the summer of 1790, when Spain and Britain reached the verge of war over possession of a remote harbor on the Northwest coast of North America, Jefferson immediately perceived an opportunity to extract American advantage from the expected conflict. The neutrality of the United States, lying between the American empires of the two antagonists, would become a matter of interest to both in case of war. If the United States should guarantee not to support Spain, Britain might be induced to evacuate the Northwest posts, which she still held in violation of the peace treaty of 1783. Conversely, Spain might be persuaded to yield the free navigation of the Mississippi River, which she controlled through possession of its left bank and its delta. These were then the two overriding problems of American foreign policy. Through a fortuitous confrontation of opposing European interests, both might be resolved at no cost to the United States.

So spectacular a diplomatic triumph at the beginning of the great American experiment in republican government was not to be gained, but the fault was not Jefferson's. He moved at once to exert pressure upon Spain through France, her partner in the Family Compact. William Short, American chargé d'affaires at Paris, was instructed to solicit French intervention at Madrid. Jefferson assumed that France had an interest in reducing the number of her ally's enemies: "She cannot doubt that we will be of that number if she does not yield our right to the common use of the Mississippi, and the means of using and securing it."

This was diplomatic bluster. Jefferson believed, with the others comprising Washington's official family, that the only possible danger to the United States from Nootka Sound was war with Britain. This possibility so concerned the President that he asked his advisers to consider an answer to an anticipated British demand for the passage of troops through American territory to attack Spanish Louisiana. The answers of Jefferson and Hamilton in 1790 delineated the conflict between realism and a perverse idealism. Hamilton's position foreshadowed the repeated surrenders of the Federalist administrations to British requirements.

Blunt John Adams recommended refusal of such a British demand, but his advice was never taken seriously. The significant opinions were those of Jefferson and Hamilton. Jefferson thought the best answer would be none at all, because evasion was most likely to prolong the neutrality which was America's real interest and would leave her free to act as later developments dictated. Hamilton balanced his patriotism against his reverence for British institutions; after a tortured consideration of all the pros and cons, he finally concluded that submission to Britain would pose the least danger to the United States.

In substance, Hamilton conceived the interest of the United States exclusively in terms of a close connection with England, while Jefferson's dedication to a balance of European power in America would have led him to accept war with Britain to preserve it. Both men recognized the value of neutrality, but Hamilton would have surrendered it on Britain's demand, thus risking war with Spain and France, while Jefferson would have used it as a diplomatic weapon against all Europe. It is difficult to find here Jefferson's "moralism," and even more elusive is any Hamiltonian monopoly on the national interest of the United States. The tough-minded champion of American interests was Jefferson; the apparition of British power unnerved Hamilton.

The threatened storm passed in 1790 when Spain, lacking firm French support, gave way before a British ultimatum. Neither the diplomatic opportunities hoped for by Jefferson nor the dangers foreseen by Hamilton materialized, for no British summons was received. When the subject assumed paramount importance again early in 1793, opposing attitudes had been hardened and brought into sharper focus by the progress of the French Revolution. From this time at least until the advent of Napoleon, American foreign policy depended on the great European struggle between the Rights of Man and legitimist reaction; it was determined in the context of a domestic political struggle between the "natural rights" philosophy of the American Revolution and the oligarchism of the Hamiltonians.

II

The neutrality proclamation of April 22, 1793, is usually described as "a notable document" which declared diplomatic independence and signaled the withdrawal of the United States from Old World embroilments. But the proclamation was really irrelevant to the national interest at that time. The real issue was not neutrality, but whether the United States could maintain freedom of action—diplomatic independence. Rather than asserting that independence, the much-admired proclamation resolved the issue by surrendering it.

The traditional view of the neutrality proclamation evades the fundamental question: Who benefited from such a pronouncement? France was in amity with the United States, bound to her by a defensive treaty of alliance. England was hostile, occupying American territory in violation of the peace treaty of 1783, giving aid and comfort to marauding savages on the American frontier and refusing to regularize trade relations by a treaty of commerce. The British emphasized their condescension by reminding Americans that their trade depended on the sufferance of George III.

The circumstances surrounding the adoption of the proclamation shed some light on the campaign in England's interest. When President Washington heard of the outbreak of war in Europe, he commanded his cabinet to consider means "for the United States to maintain a strict neutrality between the powers at war," for he had learned that American vessels were preparing to sail as privateers. He hurried back to Philadelphia from his Mount Vernon home and addressed to his official advisers the famous thirteen questions on the enforcement of neutrality.

The President's questions have been described thus: "whether to issue a proclamation of neutrality, already decided in Washington's mind and speedily supported by his advisers, was the first. . . . The other twelve concerned the French alliance." But the adviser most immediately concerned, the Secretary of State, did not speedily support the issuance of a neutrality proclamation. Jefferson favored neutrality wholeheartedly, but he opposed a formal declaration on the ground that it would severely restrict the government's freedom of action.

The other twelve questions not only betrayed their real author, they also exposed his aim of re-orienting American foreign policy toward an intimate connection with Great Britain. Jefferson recognized the questions at once as "not the President's, that they were raised upon a prepared chain of argument, in short, that the language was Hamilton's, and the doubts his alone. They led to a declaration of the executive, that our treaty with France is void." The President himself confirmed Jefferson's conclusion; he had never doubted the validity of the treaties, he said, but it had seemed proper to discuss the question once it had been raised.

Hamilton meant to use the occasion to break the legal and moral bonds between France and the United States, and this was tacitly acknowledged in the written answers submitted to Washington by Jefferson, Attorney-General Edmund Randolph, and Hamilton himself. Hamilton's argument could only be sustained by a denial of a people's right of revolution, the very premise upon which the independence of his own country rested. If Washington did not take this natural right seriously, Jefferson did. "Would you suppose it possible," he demanded of Madison, "that it should have been seriously proposed to declare our treaties with France void . . . and that it should be necessary to discuss it?"

Outvoted on the question of issuing a proclamation, Jefferson reluctantly acquiesced in the publication of a declaration defining the duties of American citizens toward the European belligerents. He managed to keep the word "neutrality" out of the document Randolph drafted, however, in deference to the constitutional provision giving to Congress the power to declare war. That power, Jefferson reasoned, logically included the power *not* to declare war, and the Hamiltonian strategy of aggrandizing the executive by encroachments upon the prerogatives of the legislature had already assumed a familiar pattern.

But more immediately important, Jefferson continued to hope that some American advantage might be extracted from Europe's adversities. England continued to negate the treaty of 1783 and Spain still withheld the navigation of the Mississippi. At the least, Jefferson thought the United States might gain the belligerents' recognition of the broadest neutral rights in return for a formal guarantee of neutrality. But events were moving swiftly. Jefferson could not have foreseen the alacrity with which the French consul at Charleston acted upon his own interpretation of the treaties of 1778. Events precipitated by French official agents and their extreme sympathizers, as well as the machinations of Hamilton and Britain's friends, militated against an effective diplomacy in the national interest.

Jefferson had not forgotten that America's real interest lay in avoiding involvement in the war. He expressed his own views, as well as those of his countrymen, in a letter of April 20, 1793 to Gouverneur Morris, American minister at Paris. "No country perhaps was ever so thoroughly against war as ours. These dispositions pervade every description of its citizens whether in or out of office. They cannot perhaps suppress their affections, nor their wishes. But they will suppress the effects of them so as to preserve a fair neutrality." The Pinckney treaty with Spain in 1795 and the Louisiana Purchase in 1803 proved the soundness of the Jeffersonian policy of manipulating the European balance of power for the benefit of the United States.

Jefferson's hope of American gain from Europe's embroilment was doomed to disappointment, for already "Hamilton . . . had triumphed in Jefferson's own domain." The proclamation deprived Jefferson of room for diplomatic maneuver and, thanks to the intimacy between the Secretary of the Treasury and the British minister, George Hammond, His Majesty's Government already had Hamilton's pledge that America's French connections need cause it no concern. Partly because Hamilton had been plotting with Hammond for more than a month to scuttle the Franco-American treaties, the British government was soon demanding that America pay for the privilege of remaining neutral.

Under these circumstances, it would indeed have been unrealistic for Jefferson to attempt a diplomatic *tour de force,* if only because he had already been sabotaged by Hamilton. The latter has been chided by his most recent biographer for his "surprising freedom" in sharing the secrets of his government with the agent of a foreign Power. This "freedom" might well deserve an uglier name.

III

Jefferson realized that "a fair neutrality will prove a disagreeable pill to our friends [the French], though necessary to keep out of the calamities of war." He was soon hard put in Washington's cabinet to uphold even a "sneaking neutrality." For that much the President's vote was responsible, for Jefferson was always outvoted by his fellow cabinet members "2½ against 1½." Secretary of War Henry Knox habitually echoed Hamilton, and Randolph's congenital ambivalence accounted for the split vote. Hamilton, according to Jefferson, was "panic-struck if we refuse our breach to every kick which Gr. Brit. may chuse to give it."

James Madison was shocked at the "anglified complexion" of executive policies which the presidential proclamation of neutrality announced. His reasons for calling the proclamation a "most unfortunate error" deserve quotation:

> It wounds the national honor, by seeming to disregard the stipulated duties to France. It wounds the popular feeling by a seeming indifference to the cause of liberty. And it seems to violate the forms & spirit of the Constitution by making the executive Magistrate the organ of the disposition, the duty & the interest of the Nation in relation to War and peace, subjects appropriated to other departments of the Government.

Madison astutely perceived that Hamilton aimed to "shuffle off" the treaty of alliance with France—a trick he considered "equally contemptible for the meanness and folly of it." If a change of government absolved a nation from foreign engagements, would not such a change abrogate domestic obligations as well? Hamilton's fiscal system was based on an opposite doctrine. Madison described with alarm its ultimate effect: "In fact, the doctrine would perpetuate every existing Despotism, by involving in a reform of the Govt a destruction of the social pact, an annihilation of property, and a compleat establishment of the state of Nature." Here was no "filthy democrat" yearning for a Rousseauan idyll; Madison understood the principles of public order better than Hamilton.

The public outcry against the Washington administration's evident tenderness toward England alarmed Hamilton almost as much as it misled the volatile Genet, the first minister of the French Republic to the United States. Fuming at a neutrality which he continually flouted, Genet mistook the war cries of the Francophile lunatic fringe for the authentic voice of a nation which wanted only a fair neutrality fulfilling America's international obligations and interests. Genet arrogated to himself proconsular powers in order to instruct Americans in the principles of freedom. A Girondist revolutionary democrat in theory, he was an autocrat in practice. He soon became Hamilton's foil and the worst enemy of his cause.

It was the recklessness of Genet which lent an aura of plausibility to the arguments of "Pacificus" (Hamilton). Against the background of the reaction Genet aroused and the Federalists cultivated, he painted the bogey of a suicidal war with England, slyly tarring the great mass of Republicans with the brush of Genet's extremism. The interest of the United States was opposed to the straw man of a purported Republican desire for war which, as Hamilton knew from his cabinet disputations with Jefferson, was a hoax.

Hamilton's defense of the neutrality proclamation tended directly to a denunciation of the treaties with France. It also imputed treason to the proclamation's critics. Both were calculated to produce a sharp reaction among Republican leaders. Jefferson lamented to Madison: "Nobody answers him, & his doctrines will therefore be taken for confessed. For God's sake, my dear Sir, take up your pen, select the most striking heresies and cut him to pieces in the face of the public." The "Helvidius" articles, which Madison wrote in answer to his friend's plea, have been belittled as "tiresome" pieces dealing "exclusively with the constitutional question." They were neither. Through Madison's argument runs the thread of the danger to republicanism contained in Hamilton's tendentious assertions. There was nothing legalistic about his opening sentence. "Several pieces with the signature of Pacificus were lately published, which have been read with singular pleasure and applause by the foreigners and degenerate citizens among us, who hate our republican government and the French Revolution."

Madison's attack centered on "a secret Anglomany" hiding behind "the mask of Neutrality." Hamilton's case rested upon an interpretation of constitutional powers concerning war and peace which all but excluded the legislative branch of the government. But this Congressional power over war and peace was the heart of the matter and Madison, the most authoritative expounder of the Constitution, attacked Hamilton's unsupportable assertion of executive primacy. Where, he demanded, had "Pacificus" borrowed this foreign doctrine? "There is but one answer to this question. The power of making treaties and the power of declaring war, are *royal prerogatives* in the *British government*, and are accordingly treated as *executive prerogatives* by *British commentators*."

Madison's five letters all assailed Hamilton's constitutional misinterpretations and his contention that a change in government suspended the operation of treaties, an assumption which denied "the only lawful tenure by which the United States hold their existence as a nation." Madison's analytical rebuttal demolished Hamilton's basic premises, but even before it was published Genet's indiscretions were accomplishing what no amount of Hamiltonian argumentation could do. Genet's foolish attacks on the President enabled the Hamiltonians to use Washington's prestige and popularity to counter the popular sympathy for France.

Hamilton designated Jefferson in later years as a "contemptible hypocrite," a comment more revealing of its author than descriptive of Jefferson. Nowhere was Hamilton's hypocrisy more evident than in his defense of Washington's neutrality proclamation. Hamilton wanted to place Britain in the favored place France had won by her services and treaties; he admitted only to a desire for an impartial neutrality. He aimed at the repudiation of treaties which presented no immediate and present danger to his country; he rationalized this with a spurious appeal to the national interest. He was unable to refute the Jeffersonian logic, so he denounced it as warmongering.

In his zeal to remake the United States on an un-American and unpopular British model, Hamilton lost touch with reality. He would have forced upon his country a course carrying the stain of international faithlessness—a course which, moreover, was juridically untenable. He was a captive of his own misconceived "idealism."

IV

Secretary of State Jefferson, on the eve of his retirement at the end of 1793, made a final attempt to arrest the trend of American policy toward open support of Britain and an unnecessary war with France which might have fragmented the American Union. Three years earlier, the Hamiltonian phalanx in Congress had defeated James Madison's program for a system of commercial discrimination against nations refusing to negotiate commercial treaties. At the same time, however, Congress ordered Jefferson to prepare a report on foreign commercial restrictions, and Jefferson began the collection of materials from overseas while Madison made domestic tonnage studies with the help of Tench Coxe, one of Hamilton's subordinates in the Treasury.

But the European war which began in 1793 aggravated America's commercial grievances. While Washington's hard-pressed government sought to work out a policy of neutrality, Britain vastly augmented her maritime provocations. Reinvoking the doctrine of the *Consolato del mare*, which repudiated the more recent and liberal "free ships, free goods" principle, was a serious irritation, but the "provision order" of June 8, 1793 resulted in widespread seizures of American ships carrying grain to France.

Jefferson's Report on Commerce was sent to Congress on December 16, 1793, a few days before news reached Philadelphia of wholesale seizures of American vessels in the West Indies. This resulted from a November order-in-council broadening the provision order to include the produce and supply of the colonies of France—an order which, according to a student of British policy, "headed Britain straight for war with the United States." The ensuing debate in the House of Representatives was further enlivened by "the letting loose the Algerines upon us," which was accomplished through a British-arranged treaty between Portugal and the piratical Dey of Algiers.

Jefferson's report, dealing with the situation as it existed before the belligerents enacted war measures, showed that American commerce was well treated by France, Spain and Holland, but was severely restricted by Great Britain. On January 3, 1794, Madison reintroduced in the House his 1791 commercial resolutions, in order to translate Jefferson's conclusions into legislative action. The resolutions called for exact commercial reciprocity, restrictions on foreign commerce to match those placed on American trade and American favors in return for those granted the United States.

Jefferson retired to his Virginia home confident that Congress would do its duty: "if this should produce war tho' not wished for, it seems not to be feared." The interests and honor of the United States could not be protected by supinely turning the other cheek, and Britain's excesses were now causing even the High Federalists to view the British attitude with a new realism.

> I believe we shall endeavour to do ourselves justice in a peaceable and rightful way. We wish to have nothing to do in the present war; but if it is to be forced upon us, I am happy to see in the countenances of all but our paper men a mind ready made up to meet it, unwillingly, indeed, but perfectly without fear. No nation has strove more than we have done to merit the peace of all by the most rigorous impartiality to all. . . .

Britain feared the consequences of the violent outburst of anger in the United States because, as a London newspaper warned, "her situation renders her formidable against [us] on account of the English West India commerce." Hamilton too was fearful. Probably after hurried conferences with Hammond, he rallied his Congressional forces to a reluctant defense of England. William Smith of South Carolina led the counterattack on Madison's proposals with a speech which Jefferson recognized immediately as "every tittle of it . . . Hamilton's except the introduction." The speech was a naked appeal to the fears of merchants and mercantile speculators whose profits would be the first casualties of war. Quite bluntly, Smith predicted that Madison's program would lead the United States into a disastrous war with Britain. Hamilton's editor comments approvingly that Smith's speech placed the "question on business and commercial principles, and [lifted] it above national prejudices and resentments."

This is exactly the way Hamilton would have explained the second surrender to the phantom of a British war.

It is at least debatable whether Britain, as sorely in need of American provisions as France, would have forced the United States into the war. British merchants were as jealous of a most profitable branch of their commerce as their government was ruthless in extending and protecting it. Because prevailing winds required shipping to beat up the American coast before standing off for Europe, American privateers might in effect have canceled out the British command of the North Atlantic. And certainly Britain and her allies, whose forces were reeling across the Rhine before the victorious armies of Republican France, could not have supported a land war in America.

The Hamiltonian argument against Madison's commercial program was based not on realism but on demagoguery. Hamilton and his supporters were motivated by devotion to the revenue-producing commercial connection with England and to the cause England represented, rather than by a concern with America's real interests.

V

Britain herself nullified Hamilton's defense, for accumulating reports of British West Indian depredations infuriated even the staunchest Federalists. A New England correspondent of Secretary Knox wrote in March that "most of our cool good men think war inevitable," and Madison had to inform Jefferson that his resolutions had been set aside because "the evils which they were to remedy . . . called for more active medicine." Madison, however, believed that war with England would be avoided: "War would turn the arrangement against her by breaking up the trade with her, and forcing that with her enemies. I conclude therefore that she will push her aggressions just so far and no farther, than she imagines we will tolerate."

Few of Madison's colleagues shared his calm. In March 1794, Congress overwhelmingly enacted a thirty-day embargo on all foreign commerce and considered more drastic measures, including a prohibition of English imports and the sequestration of British debts. In desperation, Hamilton turned all his persuasiveness upon President Washington, in effect proposing his own appointment as special envoy to London to obtain redress of America's grievances.

It was neither the first nor the last time that Hamilton used Washington's prestige for his own purposes. Intimations of Hamilton's appointment, however, promised to cause such a sensation that Washington quickly dropped him and named Chief Justice John Jay in his stead. As Madison lamented, "the influence of the Executive on events, the use made of them, and the public confidence in the President are an overmatch for all the efforts Republicanism can make." Madison was vindicated nevertheless; for Britain, alarmed at the public outcry in America, had already rescinded the obnoxious November order-in-council.

John Jay was as experienced a diplomat as America then boasted, for the incomparable Benjamin Franklin had died four years earlier. But Jay, like Hamilton, was "perfectly British in his affections," as a Virginia Republican remarked. The suspicion of France which had led him to initiate separate peace negotiations with Britain in 1782 turned to antipathy in the French Revolution. An aristocrat with a seaboard outlook, Jay had earned the hatred of the American West and South for his abortive attempt in 1785 to surrender American claims to the navigation of the Mississippi in return for Spanish commercial benefits. Jay's defects of personality made him similarly vulnerable to British blandishments. His exaggerated vanity and self-esteem were well known at Whitehall, which had been advised that "Mr. Jay's weak side is Mr. Jay." The British government flattered and entertained Jay till his head spun.

Jay's negotiations with the adroit British Foreign Secretary, Lord Grenville, resulted in a treaty amounting to a virtual alliance with England against France. Jay not only surrendered the American definition of neutral rights, but he explicitly committed the United States to acquiescence in Britain's arbitrary maritime practices. He deprived the United States of a potent weapon which caused real concern in the British mercantile community by agreeing to a permanent prohibition, even in time of war, of the sequestration or confiscation of debts. Instead of "strenuously pressing" for compensation for all injuries and captures sustained by American commerce, as he had been instructed, Jay contracted to refer all American spoliation claims, boundary disputes, and American private debts incurred before the peace of 1783, to mixed arbitral commissions. The treaty said nothing of the slaves carried off by the British during the Revolution, of England's bloody incitements of the Indians along the American frontier, or of other equally important American grievances.

In return for Jay's pliability, Grenville agreed to surrender the Northwestern posts, which had already been American territory under the international law of treaties since 1783. He also conceded to the United States the niggardly right of trading with the British West Indies in vessels of a maximum seventy-tons cargo capacity for the duration of the war and for two years after its termination. This privilege, however, included a prohibition of American imports of such staples as sugar and cotton, and even the Hamiltonians considered it unacceptable.

But the treaty was not wholly the fault of Jay. Its provisions bore closer resemblance to Hamilton's stated views than to the virtually ignored instructions of Secretary of State Edmund Randolph. Hamilton later described Randolph's instructions as "a crude mass" which only "a great confidence in the person to be sent" had prevented him from attempting to remedy.

Jay's hint of possible American participation in a new League of Armed Neutrality produced British concessions at one stage of the negotiations, but these were soon withdrawn. Hamilton's gratuitous assurance to Hammond that the United States would have nothing to do with such a system reached Grenville in time to erase Jay's advantage. Apparently neither Jay nor Hamilton considered Madison's program of commercial discrimination useful, even as a diplomatic bargaining weapon.

Hamilton's interference with the Jay mission demonstrated an ideological rigidity which was the opposite of realism. It was a particularly damaging instance of the incorrigible meddling which repeatedly saved the British ministry the trouble of giving serious thought to American grievances.

VI

Despite his own responsibility for Jay's Treaty, Hamilton insolently denounced it in private as an "execrable one" made by "an old woman." Then, with the aid of Hammond's financial resources and influence, he proceeded to whip the Senate's overwhelming Federalist majority into line for approval. French Minister Fauchet, appreciating the treaty's significance, was beside himself when approval was obtained on June 24, 1795, without a single vote to spare. He later offered a blunt explanation of this culminating failure of his mission—Hammond had reached two wavering senators with "*Res non verba.*"

Senate approval of the Jay Treaty, minus the West Indian article, opened the floodgates of public indignation. With "Damn John Jay" ringing in every city in the land, even so impeccable a patriot as John Rutledge of South Carolina, recently appointed Chief Justice of the United States, denounced the treaty as a betrayal of American interests and an insult to American manhood. The indefatigable Hamilton rushed into print with thirty-eight articles signed "Camillus," but he was stoned in New York when he attempted an oral defense of the treaty.

The arrogance of England's maritime policy toward the United States was matched only by her determination that Jay's Treaty be ratified. The harsh provision order of June 1793, which had pushed America to the brink of war, was secretly renewed in April 1795. When Randolph discovered this, he persuaded President Washington that the order's repeal should be a prerequisite to ratification of the treaty. Randolph's belated opposition, however, had already been foreseen in London, and a malicious plot to destroy him was already taking shape.

Although Fauchet always believed that Randolph was the treaty's most ardent champion, Foreign Secretary Grenville had long thought otherwise. As early as November 1794 Grenville had become thoroughly displeased with Randolph. He instructed Hammond to "converse confidentially" with England's powerful friends (that is, Hamilton and company) with a view to Randolph's removal. The Secretary's personal sentiments, Grenville observed, might endanger the "permanent Union" which he regarded as established by Jay's Treaty.

The following April, Grenville confessed to "a great degree of uneasiness" concerning the success of the treaty. Encouraged by Hammond's groundless presumption that Randolph was treasonably corrupt, "which the pecuniary embarrassments and general character of Mr. Randolph render far from improbable," Grenville seized upon some vague intercepted despatches of Fauchet and ordered Hammond to "communicate such Parts of them as you may deem expedient to well disposed Persons in

America." Hammond had no difficulty in selecting two strategically placed "well disposed Persons": the slippery and slavish follower of Hamilton, Oliver Wolcott, principal assistant and now his successor as head of the Treasury, and the fanatic and malevolent Federalist hack, Timothy Pickering, recently transferred from the office of postmaster-general to the secretaryship of war.

Despite, or perhaps because of, the close personal relationship between Randolph and the President, Pickering and Wolcott were able to contrive an unmerited disgrace for Randolph which remains unparalleled in cabinet history for sheer malice. The participation of the intensely virtuous Washington in Randolph's frame-up can be explained only in terms of advanced physical and mental deterioration. Thereafter, the High Federalist clique brazenly manipulated Washington for its own partisan advantage.

Even before the star-chamber proceedings which accomplished the unhappy Randolph's ruin, Washington ratified the treaty with England, in complete disregard of his own previous ultimatum to Hammond. Britain's diplomatic triumph, thanks to her unscrupulous partisans in Washington's administration, was complete. The fiction of American neutrality in the desperate struggle between France and Britain was, for practical purposes, ended. Ironically, it was the pen of Washington, whose name has become indissolubly linked with American neutrality, which put a period to neutrality in 1795.

By aligning itself with England in the economic phase of the European war, the United States had in effect declared war on France. So it seemed to the new French government of the Directory. It soon decided to send a special envoy to Philadelphia to protest what it regarded as "the equivalent of an intimate alliance with our cruelest enemy." To James Monroe, American minister to France, the Directory added that it preferred an open enemy to a treacherous friend. Although France spent several months seeking a way out of this dilemma, subsequent acts of the Federalist government and the logic of events propelled the two countries toward open, if undeclared, war.

The Jay Treaty was foisted upon the American people in the name of peace; instead, it made war inevitable. Although preferring peace with profits, the Hamiltonians were not averse to war with France if the eradication of French (and American) Republican ideals required it. Standard historical treatments of the Jay Treaty assume that its failure would have meant inevitable war with Britain, but this view relies mainly on Federalist propaganda for the treaty. The logical corrollary—that the treaty's success pointed equally to war with France—is curiously ignored. The traditional premise, moreover, failed to take into account the indications of British disinclination to war with the United States, which Madison had perceived from the very outset. The general British awareness of their vulnerability to American sea forays, the British government's concern over Armed Neutrality proposals, Grenville's anxiety over the delay in ratification of the treaty, and the unscrupulous measures he and Hammond employed for the treaty's adoption, all suggest that its rejection might instead have made possible a more just and equitable Anglo-American accommodation. They certainly indicate that Jay (and Hamilton) could have made a much better treaty.

VII

As Grayson L. Kirk recently remarked, it is "*de rigueur* to expatiate on the prescient wisdom of the Founding Fathers." Alexander Hamilton has received more than his share of the credit for the founding of the American nation. Historians writing in the Darwinian economic and social climate of the late nineteenth century tended to exalt him as the preëminent Founding Father, the creator of American nationality. This tendency was climaxed in Henry Cabot Lodge's edition of Hamilton's writings and it spilled over into the twentieth century in a spate of eulogistic biographies. It has remained for Professor Morgenthau's school, however, to formulate a conception of the history of American foreign policy which places Hamilton at the pinnacle of American wisdom, in original and exclusive possession of the true understanding of the national interest of the United States.

Hamilton's concept of the national interest, in fact, was grossly in error. The distinctly American vision which Republicans and Adams Federalists shared was entirely foreign to him. Hamilton was a philosophical monarchist and a practical mercantilist. But for his genius at dissimulation, he must have appeared the most incongruous public figure of a generation whose spirit was devoted to republicanism and the spirit of the Enlightenment. To further his retrogressive, Hobbesian system, Hamilton consciously and cynically sought to transfer to America what Professor R. R. Palmer calls the vicious practice and the virtuous theory of the eighteenth-century British Constitution. Or, as Jefferson explained it, Hamilton was "so bewitched & perverted by the British example, as to be under thoro' conviction that corruption was essential to the government of a nation." Hamiltonian foreign policy was necessarily based on Hamilton's unreal vision of the United States as another seventeenth-century British Leviathan. So archaic and non-American a frame of reference could not produce realism.

Jeffersonian foreign policy, on the other hand, flowed from a sympathetic understanding of the uniqueness of the American political experiment—that uniqueness which Jefferson and his colleagues sought to preserve in the main stream of American development. Jefferson was a nationalist who knew and loved his country as Hamilton never did. Jefferson's view of the interest of the United States has been vindicated by American history. It represented the future of America and of the Western World.

Additional Reading

Joseph Charles, "The Jay Treaty: The Origins of the American Party System," *William and Mary Quarterly*, XII (1955), 581–630.

Alexander DeConde, *Entangling Alliances: Politics and Diplomacy under George Washington* (1958).
Charles S. Hyneman, *The First American Neutrality* (1934).
Dumas Malone, *Jefferson and the Ordeal of Liberty* (1962).
John C. Miller, *Alexander Hamilton* (1959).
Charles M. Thomas, *American Neutrality in 1793* (1931).

3 *THE JAY AND PINCKNEY TREATIES: Europe's Distresses or American Power?*

The United States received title to an empire in the 1783 peace treaty, with boundaries extending to the Mississippi River on the west and the 31st parallel on the south. The question, however, was could the American government redeem in fact the promise of 1783. In addition to British retention of military posts south of the international frontier, which the Jay Treaty finally ended, the Spanish government rejected American claims in the southwest.

Spain's case was good, both in point of international law and on the basis of actual physical occupancy. At the general peace made in 1783, Great Britain returned the Floridas to Spain but without reference to the southern boundary granted the Americans. Spain assumed that Florida was re-ceded with the boundary it had had in Britain's possession, approximately along the parallel of 32° 30″ or the Yazoo River line. Furthermore, based on military operations in the recent war, the Spanish government claimed territorial jurisdiction to the north as far as the Ohio River. Spain also maintained that Britain had no right to grant the Americans free navigation of the Mississippi River from its source to the Gulf, because both banks of the lower river were indisputably under Spanish control. Consequently, Spanish authorities closed that section of the river to foreign navigation in 1784. In addition the Madrid government attempted to protect the vulnerable provinces of Louisiana and the Floridas against aggressive Yankee frontiersmen by fomenting separatist intrigue among discontented American settlers in the Kentucky and Tennessee areas, and through use of the Indian tribes in the southwest as buffers and allies against the United States.

Although there was some sentiment in the United States for compromise with Spain, the issues were too vital for retreat. Settlers flooding across the Appalachian mountain barrier depended of necessity on the Mississippi River for transportation of goods and agricultural produce to eastern and European markets. If Spain achieved its goals, either the American West would wither economically or resort to violence for a solution. Negotiations for a compromise with Spain failed in 1785–1786 and the Washington Administration continued to maintain the full American claims.

After years of fruitless diplomacy, a satisfactory treaty was concluded with dramatic suddenness in the fall of 1795. The American commissioner William Short and Minister Thomas Pinckney negotiated a treaty with Prime Minister Manuel de Godoy which resolved the boundary and navigation issues in accordance with American desires. The question of interest to historians has been how to explain the Spanish capitulation. Was it because of the growing power of the United States or was the explanation to be found in the tangled skein of European diplomacy?

DOCUMENTS

1. An Unpopular "Peace" with England

The treaty which John Jay concluded with Great Britain in 1794 in many ways failed to meet American desires. Although it made satisfactory commercial arrangements for trade with the British Isles and India, Canada remained closed to American shipping and the provisions in regard to the West Indies were so objectionable that the Senate rejected all of Article 12. The treaty also failed to incorporate the American concept of neutral rights. In fact, France was to complain that the Jay terms relating to contraband categories and privateers violated the Franco-American commercial treaty of 1778 (see Chapter 2). It was understandable, therefore, that Jay and his handiwork were roundly denounced by many in America as "truckling" to British arrogance and Jay was burned repeatedly in effigy. Yet he had probably secured all that circumstances permitted and by achieving British withdrawal from the northern posts averted an unfortunate war between the two nations.

Jay's Treaty between the United States and Great Britain, November 19, 1794

Article 2. His Majesty will withdraw all His Troops and Garrisons from all Posts and Places within the Boundary Lines assigned by the Treaty of Peace to the United States. This Evacuation shall take place on or before the first Day of June One thousand seven hundred and ninety six. . . .

Article 3. It is agreed that it shall at all Times be free to His Majesty's Subjects, and to the Citizens of the United States, and also to the Indians dwelling on either side of the said Boundary Line freely to pass and repass by Land, or Inland Navigation, into the respective Territories and Countries of the Two Parties on the Continent of America (the Country within the Limits of the Hudson's Bay Company only excepted) and to navigate all the Lakes, Rivers, and waters thereof, and freely to carry on trade and commerce with each other. . . .

All Goods and Merchandize whose Importation into His Majesty's said Territories in America, shall not be entirely prohibited, may freely, for the purposes of Commerce, be carried into the same in the manner aforesaid, by the Citizens of the United States, and such Goods and Merchandize shall be subject to no higher or other Duties than would be payable by His Majesty's Subjects on the Importation of the same from Europe into the said Territories. And in like manner, all Goods and Merchandize whose Importation into the United States shall not be wholly prohibited, may freely, for the purposes of Commerce, be carried into the same, in the manner aforesaid, by His Majesty's Subjects, and such Goods and Merchandize shall be subject to no higher or other Duties than would be payable by the Citizens of the United States on the Importation of the same in American Vessels into the Atlantic Ports of the said States. And all Goods not prohibited to be exported from the said Territories respectively, may in like manner be carried out of the same by the Two Parties respectively, paying Duty as aforesaid. . . .

Article 4. Whereas it is uncertain whether the River Mississippi extends so far to the Northward as to be intersected by a Line to be drawn due West from the Lake of the woods in the manner mentioned in the Treaty of Peace between His Majesty and the United States, it is agreed, that measures shall be taken in Concert between His Majesty's Government in America, and the Government of the United States, for making a joint Survey of the said River, from one Degree of Latitude below the falls of St. Anthony to the principal Source or Sources of the said River, and also of the parts adjacent thereto, And that if on the result of such Survey it should appear that the said River would not be intersected by such a Line as is above mentioned; The two Parties will thereupon proceed by amicable negotiation to regulate the Boundary Line in that quarter as well as all other Points to be adjusted between the said Parties, according to Justice and mutual Convenience, and in Conformity, to the Intent of the said Treaty.

Article 5. Whereas doubts have arisen what River was truly intended under the name of the River St. Croix mentioned in the said Treaty of Peace and forming a part of the boundary therein described, that question shall be referred to the final Decision of Commissioners to be appointed. . . .

Article 6. Whereas it is alleged by divers British Merchants and others His Majesty's Subjects, that Debts to a considerable amount which were bonâ fide contracted before the Peace, still remain owing to them by Citizens or Inhabitants of the United States, and that by the operation of various lawful Impediments since the Peace, not only the full recovery of the said Debts has been delayed, but also the Value and Security thereof, have been in several instances impaired and lessened, so that by the ordinary course of Judicial proceedings the British Creditors, cannot now obtain and actually have and receive full and adequate Compensation for the losses and damages which they have thereby sustained: It is agreed that in all such Cases where full Compensation for such losses and damages cannot, for whatever reason, be actually obtained had and received by the said Creditors in the ordinary course of Justice. The United States will make full and complete Compensation for the same to the said Creditors; . . .

For the purpose of ascertaining the amount of any such losses and damages, Five Commissioners shall be appointed and authorized to meet and act. . . .

Article 7. Whereas Complaints have been made by divers Merchants and others, Citizens of the United States, that during the course of the War in which His Majesty is now engaged they have sustained considerable losses and damage by reason of irregular or illegal Captures or Condemnations of their vessels and other property under Colour of authority or Commissions from His Majesty, and that from various Circumstances belonging to the said Cases adequate Compensation for the losses and damages so sustained cannot now be actually obtained, had and received by the ordinary Course of Judicial proceedings; It is agreed that in all such Cases where adequate Compensation cannot for whatever reason be now actually obtained, had and received by the said Merchants and others in the ordinary course of Justice, full and Complete Compensation for the same will be made by the British Government to the said Complainants. . . .

Article 10. Neither the Debts due from Individuals of the one Nation, to Individuals of the other, nor shares nor monies, which they may have in the public Funds, or in the public or private Banks shall ever, in any Event of war, or national differences, be sequestered, or confiscated, it being unjust and impolitick that Debts and Engagements contracted and made by Individuals having confidence in each other, and in their respective Governments, should ever be destroyed or impaired by national authority, on account of national Differences and Discontents.

Article 12. His Majesty Consents that it shall and may be lawful, during the time hereinafter Limited, for the Citizens of the United States, to carry to any of His Majesty's Islands and Ports in the West Indies from the United States in their own Vessels, not being above the burthen of Seventy Tons, any Goods or Merchandizes, being of the Growth, Manufacture, or Produce of the said States. . . .

And His Majesty also consents that it shall be lawful for the said American Citizens to purchase, load and carry away, in their said vessels to the United States from the said Islands and Ports, all such articles being the Growth, Manufacture or Produce of the said Islands, as may now by Law be carried from thence to the said States in British Vessels, and subject only to the same Duties and Charges on Exportation to which British Vessels and their Cargoes are or shall be subject in similar circumstances.

Provided always that the said American vessels do carry and land their Cargoes in the United States only, it being expressly agreed and declared that during the Continuance of this article, the United States will prohibit and restrain the carrying any Molasses, Sugar, Coffee, Cocoa or Cotton in American vessels, either from His Majesty's Islands or from the United States, to any part of the World, except the United States, reasonable Sea Stores excepted. Provided also, that it shall and may be lawful during the same period for British vessels to import from the said Islands into the United States, and to export from the United States to the said Islands, all Articles whatever being of the Growth, Produce or Manufacture of the said Islands, or of the United States respectively, which now may, by the Laws of the said States, be so imported and exported. And that the Cargoes of the said British vessels, shall be subject at no other or higher Duties or Charges, than shall be payable on the same articles if so imported or exported in American Vessels.

It is agreed that this Article, and every Matter and Thing therein contained, shall continue to be in Force, during the Continuance of the war in which His Majesty is now engaged; and also for Two years from and after the Day of the signature of the Preliminary or other Articles of Peace by which the same may be terminated. . . .

Article 13. His Majesty consents that the Vessels belonging to the Citizens of the United States of America, shall be admitted and Hospitably received in all the Sea Ports and Harbours of the British Territories in the East Indies: and that the Citizens of the said United States, may freely carry on a Trade between the said Territories and the said United States, in all articles of which the Importation or Exportation respectively to or from the said Territories, shall not be entirely prohibited. . . .

Article 14. There shall be between all the Dominions of His Majesty in Europe, and the Territories of the United States, a reciprocal and perfect liberty of Commerce and Navigation. . . .

Article 17. It is agreed that, in all Cases where Vessels shall be captured or detained on just suspicion of having on board Enemy's property or of carrying to the Enemy, any of the articles which are Contraband of war; The said Vessel shall be brought to the nearest or most convenient Port, and if any property of an Enemy, should be found on board such Vessel, that part only which belongs to the Enemy shall be made prize, and the Vessel shall be at liberty to proceed with the remainder without any Impediment. . . .

Article 18. In order to regulate what is in future to be esteemed Contraband of war, it is agreed that under the said Denomination shall be comprized all Arms and Implements serving for the purposes of war by Land or Sea; such as Cannon, Muskets, Mortars, Petards, Bombs, Grenades, Carcasses, Saucisses, Carriages for Cannon, Musket rests, Bandoliers, Gunpowder, Match, Saltpetre, Ball, Pikes, Swords, Headpieces Cuirasses Halberts Lances Javelins, Horsefurniture, Holsters, Belts and, generally all other Implements of war, as also Timber for Ship building, Tar or Rosin, Copper in Sheets, Sails, Hemp, and Cordage, and generally whatever may serve directly to the equipment of Vessels, unwrought Iron and Fir planks only excepted, and all the above articles are hereby declared to be just objects of Confiscation, whenever they are attempted to be carried to an Enemy. . . .

Article 24. It shall not be lawful for any Foreign Privateers (not being Subjects or Citizens of either of the said Parties) who have Commissions from any other Prince or State in Enmity with either Nation, to arm their Ships in the Ports of either of the said Parties, nor to sell what they have taken, nor in any other manner to exchange the same, nor shall they be allowed to purchase more provisions than shall be necessary for their going to the nearest Port of that Prince or State from whom they obtained their Commissions.

Article 25. It shall be lawful for the Ships of war and Privateers belonging to the said Parties respectively to carry whithersoever they please the Ships and Goods taken from their Enemies without being obliged to pay any Fee to the Officers of the Admiralty, or to any Judges whatever; nor shall the said Prizes when they arrive at, and enter the Ports of the said Parties be detained or seized. . . . No Shelter or Refuge shall be given in their Ports to such as have made a Prize upon the Subjects or Citizens of either of the said Parties. . . . Nothing in this Treaty contained shall however be construed or operate contrary to former and existing Public Treaties with other Sovereigns or States. But the Two parties agree, that while they continue in amity neither of them will in future make any Treaty that shall be inconsistent with this or the preceding article. . . .

2. *The Spanish Treaty*

In striking contrast with the Jay Treaty, Pinckney's treaty with Spain in the following year was probably the most popular and satisfactory in the annals of American diplomacy. Note its provisions relating to neutral rights, which embodied the substance of the "Plan of 1776."

Pinckney's Treaty with Spain, October 27, 1795

Article II. To prevent all disputes on the subject of the boundaries which separate the territories of the two High contracting Parties, it is hereby declared and agreed as follows: to wit: The Southern boundary of the United States which divides their territory from the Spanish Colonies of East and West Florida, shall be designated by a line beginning on the River Mississipi at the Northermost part of the thirty first degree of latitude North of the Equator, which from thence shall be drawn due East to the middle of the River Apalachicola or Catahouche, thence along the middle thereof to its junction with the Flint, thence straight to the head of St. Mary's River, and thence down the middle thereof to the Atlantic Ocean. And it is agreed that if there should be any troops, Garrisons or settlements of either Party in the territory of the other according to the above mentioned boundaries, they shall be withdrawn from the said territory within the term of six months after the ratification of this treaty or sooner if it be possible and that they shall be permitted to take with them all the goods and effects which they possess.

Article IV. It is likewise agreed that the Western boundary of the United States which separates them from the Spanish Colony of Louissiana, is in the middle of the channel or bed of the River Mississipi from the Northern boundary of the said States to the completion of the thirty first degree of latitude North of the Equator; and his Catholic Majesty has likewise agreed that the navigation of the said River in its whole breadth from its source to the Ocean shall be free only to his Subjects, and the Citizens of

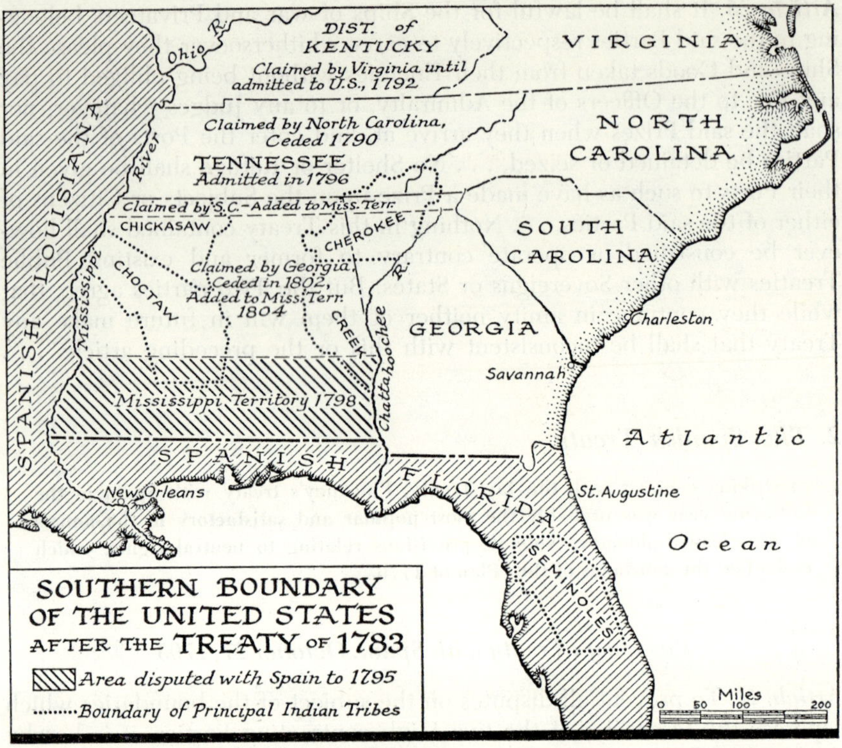

SOUTHERN BOUNDARY OF THE UNITED STATES AFTER THE TREATY OF 1783

the United States, unless he should extend this privilege to the Subjects of other Powers by special convention.

Article V. The two High contracting Parties shall by all the means in their power maintain peace and harmony among the several Indian Nations who inhabit the country adjacent to the lines and Rivers which by the preceeding Articles form the boundaries of the two Floridas; and the beter to obtain this effect both Parties oblige themselves expressly to restrain by force all hostilities on the part of the Indian Nations living within their boundaries: so that Spain will not suffer her Indians to attack the Citizens of the United States, nor the Indians inhabiting their territory; nor will the United States permit these last mentioned Indians to commence hostilities against the Subjects of his Catholic Majesty, or his Indians in any manner whatever. . . .

Article XV. It shall be lawful for all and singular the Subjects of his Catholic Majesty, and the Citizens People, and inhabitants of the said United States to sail with their Ships with all manner of liberty and security, no distinction being made who are the proprietors of the merchandizes laden thereon from any Port to the Places of those who now are or hereafter shall be at enmity with his Catholic Majesty or the United States. . . . and it is hereby stipulated that Free Ships shall also give freedom to goods, and that every thing shall be deemed free and exempt which shall be found on board the Ships belonging to the Subjects of either of the contracting Parties although the whole lading or any part thereof should appartain to the Enemies of either; contraband goods being always excepted. . . .

Article XVI. This liberty of navigation and commerce shall extend to all kinds of merchandizes excepting those only which are distinguished by the name of contraband; and under this name of contraband or prohibited goods shall be comprehended arms, great guns, bombs, with the fusees, and other things belonging to them, cannon ball, gun powder, match, pikes, swords, lances, speards, halberds, mortars, petards, granades, salpetre, muskets, musket ball bucklers, helmets, breast plates, coats of mail, and the like kind of arms proper for arming soldiers, musket rests, belts, horses with their furniture and all other warlike instruments whatever. These merchandizes which follows shall not be reckoned among contraband or prohibited goods; that is to say, all sorts of cloths and all other manufactures woven of any wool, flax, silk, cotton, or any other materials whatever, all kinds of wearing aparel together with all species whereof they are used to be made, gold and silver as well coined as uncoined, tin, iron, latton, copper, brass, coals, as also wheat, barley, oats, and any other kind of corn and pulse: tobacco and likewise all manner of spices, salted and smoked flesh, salted fish, cheese and butter, beer, oils, wines, sugars, and all sorts of salts, and in general all provisions which serve for the sustenance of life. Furthermore all kinds of cotton, hemp, flax, tar, pitch, ropes, cables, sails, sail cloths, anchors, and any parts of anchors, also ships masts, planks, wood of all kind, and all other things proper either for building or repairing ships, and all other goods whatever which have not been worked into the form of any instrument prepared for war by land or by sea, shall not be reputed contraband, much less such as have been already wrought and made up for any other use: all which shall be wholly reckoned among free goods, as likewise all other merchandizes and things which are not comprehended and particularly mentioned in the foregoing enumeration of contraband goods: so that they may be transported and carried in the freest manner by the subjects of both parties, even to Places belonging to an Enemy, such towns or Places being only expected as are at that time besieged, blocked up, or infested. . . .

READINGS

1. Spanish Fears and an Unearned American Diplomatic Victory

The Jay Treaty was signed in London almost a year prior to conclusion of the treaty with Spain. European diplomacy was in flux, with Spain in the Peace of Basle withdrawing from the war against revolutionary France and most fearful that its former ally Great Britain would retaliate against Spain and its colonies. Did news of the signing of the Jay Treaty influence the Spanish government to placate the United States by conceding its claims in America?

Samuel F. Bemis answers affirmatively in the following selection. He is convinced that Godoy feared an Anglo-American alliance and a joint assault on Spanish possessions in the new world. As Godoy probably did not know in time the full terms of Jay's Treaty and in any case could not be positive that secret clauses of alliance did not exist, the Spanish leader persuaded his government to capitulate to the Americans in order to avoid that peril. Fear of British retaliation in Europe and possible Anglo-American operations against Spain overseas thus explain the American diplomatic triumph.

Jay's Treaty and its Effect

SAMUEL FLAGG BEMIS

I

Interesting intrigues of Jaudenes [Spanish agent in America] with the western separatists, which had led to his delay in delivering Godoy's propositions for the President, did not change the new-born desire of that Spanish Minister for an alliance with the United States in return for recognition of American claims to the navigation of the Mississippi and the boundary line of 31°. The notorious propositions for the President, drafted on July 26, 1794, had been despatched to Jaudenes on the 31st of the same month only after another meeting of the Council of State, in which had occurred a thorough canvass of the whole situation as based on a *précis* of the most recent reports of Governor Carondelet, of Louisiana, including the latter's correspondence with Wilkinson.* Nothing therein elucidated had caused any modification in the recently adopted policy of conciliation and alliance with the United States, as decided by the Council so promptly after the arrival in Madrid of news from Jaudenes and Viar of the Anglo-American crisis of March, 1794, and the departure of Jay for London. When it became known in Madrid, in December, 1794, that a treaty had been signed by Jay with Great Britain, the Spanish Court —this means Godoy—became still more confirmed in this policy and genuinely anxious for a treaty of alliance at the cost of conceding the principal American demands. The separate peace of Basle, between Spain and the French Republic, which followed on July 22, 1795, with the resulting end of the Anglo-Spanish alliance and the imagined danger of revenge from Great Britain on a deserting ally, made Godoy even more anxious for the most cordial understanding with the United States, for fear of a combination of that country with Great Britain to the damage of Spanish possessions in America. . . .

The Jay negotiation, as we have already pointed out in mentioning the decision of the Spanish Council of State, had assumed primary significance in the Spanish-American negotiations. Short had reflected abundantly on the good that might result for his own situation if a satisfactory

Samuel Flagg Bemis, *Pinckney's Treaty: America's Advantage from Europe's Distress*, 1783–1800 (New Haven: Yale University Press, 1960 revised edition), 218–219, 227–234, 267–268, 272–282, 284. Reprinted with permission.

* James Wilkinson, a Revolutionary War general, Kentucky separatist, and later the American military commander in the southwest. [EDITOR'S NOTE]

treaty should be signed by Jay in London, but he was absolutely uninformed by his own Government as to the parallel negotiation then proceeding in England, despite the fact that it was of utmost importance for him to know it. In vain he had appealed to Pinckney, the regular minister there, for information, and to John Trumbull, the secretary of Jay. These persons hesitated to interfere in Jay's business or to trust any information to the mails. December 22, 1794, the day after the conference above described between Gardoqui and Short, an English mail arrived with a letter from Jay of November 24, 1794, telling of the signature of a treaty between the United States and Great Britain, and another from Pinckney, of November 27, conveying in cipher a digest of the terms. The Spanish Ambassador in London at the same time notified Godoy of the settlement of disputes between the United States and Great Britain, stating that the British had agreed to evacuate the frontier posts in eighteen months, and that the treaty also contained articles of advantage to the Americans in matters of commerce and navigation between the United States and the British West Indian islands. Presumably it arrived in the same mail.

Realizing the significance of this treaty in suggesting to Spain that the United States might now have British support in its demand for the Mississippi and other claims based on the Anglo-American peace treaty of 1783, Short saw that events were beginning to break nicely for the advantage of the United States. He felt that the time had come to clinch the claim to the navigation of the Mississippi, to secure recognition of the boundary contended for by the United States, and, more than that, to break into Spain's commercial monopoly in her colonies of North and South America. Spain, he thought, particularly in case of a separate peace with France, which Short was so assiduously attempting to engineer, would be in a position, after deserting from Great Britain and in face of an imagined Anglo-American rapprochement, to yield almost anything the United States might demand.

II

The special courier Blake at last was about to depart as the news arrived in Madrid of the signature of Jay's Treaty. Carmichael was too ill by now to attempt the journey home to Maryland. Short, who had been exasperated beyond measure by the repeated delays of Blake's departure, due to Carmichael's desire to keep him for a traveling companion, now himself held the courier a few more days, in order to be able to inform the Government of the Spanish reaction to Jay's Treaty. Without directly seeking a conference with Gardoqui, which might betray undue eagerness, Short managed to throw himself in the way of that Minister in order to give him a chance to continue the subject of the former conversations in regard to a separate peace with France and to see how he was affected by this new American treaty.

> With him [wrote Short in his despatch of December 29, 1794,] I had only vague and general conversation in the same old way but evidently more reserved in respect to pacification with France, probably wishing

first to see whether this new arrangement with England might not have rendered it less safe to communicate to me his wishes as to France. On the subject of our treaty he said little, pretended it was a fortunate circumstance to have been able to have settled such differences in a manner that would avoid the misfortune of war, and expressed his satisfaction at it from his regard and attachment to the United States. When I observed to him how much more fortunate Mr. Jay had been in his mission, which was certainly a more difficult and less hopeful one, than we had been here, he brought forth a shower of protestations at his personal regret at the delay which had taken place here, of all his personal efforts to have had the business long ago concluded, and of his full persuasion that there would not be a moment's delay after the President's answer should be received, which might be now expected every day, his expressions of friendship for the United States, and of his desire to see the closest ties formed between them and Spain, were if possible warmer than ever, but all this of course led to nothing.

Short waited to meet Godoy in his regular audience with him as Foreign Minister. The younger Spaniard proved not so hackneyed as Gardoqui in the ways of dissimulation. He registered mortification and disappointment. Short recalled to him the delay which he had met in trying to settle affairs between the United States and Spain. The Duke held off. As soon as the answer should arrive from the President, he declared, Spain would hasten to negotiate a treaty, and it would not be a treaty which would stipulate *eighteen years,* as did that of Great Britain, for evacuation of the frontier posts. Short, without divulging the terms of the treaty, corrected Godoy on the item of eighteen years.

The Duke enquired [wrote Short] with seeming anxiety as to the time when the treaty with England would have arrived in America, and comparing the dates was much pleased with the consideration that the propositions made from hence [i.e., the proposals for alliance, of July, 1794], would have been received and decided on long before. He said more than once that if the treaty were to be postponed, as he understood, being completely executed for some time to come, he still had hope that we should make one and fulfill it yet sooner, than that with England would be, as the King did not intend to ask for any further delay as England had done.

The announcement in Spain of an adjustment between the United States and Great Britain achieved by John Jay in London had prompt results in Spanish official conclaves. The very next day after Short's above-described interview with Godoy there occurred an important meeting of the Council of State. Already the British, observing the apathy of their ally in prosecuting the war outside of Spain proper, had been demanding more effective cooperation in naval affairs and specifically assistance in a campaign then under way for the suppression of the revolt in the French half of the island of Santo Domingo. The activity of the British in that island could not but be prejudicial to the interests of Spain in the New World. In the Council Godoy declared that Spain, rather than deliberating on the means of making with Great Britain joint conquests in the island of Santo Domingo or elsewhere, as requested by the British, ought to do all in her power to prevent the British from making them, and to endeavor to keep her own possessions in order and tranquillity, immune from the contagion of insurrection. England, said he, soon would have only Austria left with her in the Coalition. Deserted on all quarters she would seek a reconciliation with America. He did not mention the existence of Jay's Treaty, which must have been in the thought of the Council, since it was known to both Godoy and Gardoqui; but he declared that Spain should endeavor to forestall such a dire event as an Anglo-American *entente*, by concluding as soon as possible, as the Council had already agreed in policy, an arrangement with the United States.

Although Godoy had now turned with unusual alacrity to the idea of an American alliance and settlement accordingly of the Mississippi Question and boundary issue, he did not lose sight of the intrigues of Carondelet and Jaudenes with the Kentucky conspirators and the possibility offered by them as an alternate policy in case he should be anticipated by the British in winning the support, even the alliance of the Americans. Splitting off the western settlements from the union of the United States seemed, particularly at that time, to afford too good a prospect of success to be abandoned altogether. In answering, February 15, 1795, the pleas which had come from Jaudenes for powers to deal with the western separatist intrigues, Godoy resorted to fine ambiguity. His Majesty approved, said the Duke, of the means which Jaudenes had taken, through the representative of the western people, to destroy the false ideas which the English were trying to instill to the prejudice of Spain:

> In order to block those ideas and to weaken the influence of the British Government among the inhabitants of Kentucky, His Majesty desires you, in accordance with what I advised you in my letter of July 26 [1794], to continue to assure them of the good faith with which we proceed; and that we may the more confirm them in this concept, you will set up with the greatest secrecy direct negotiations with them, to hold them off until we can settle the question of the important points on which we are now treating with the [United] States. This will serve to keep them devoted to us in case the States do not accept the just propositions which we are making to them.

Similar instructions at the same time went out to Carondelet, who in fact had been responsible, through Wilkinson, for the resurrection of this old plot which dated back to Wilkinson's first visit to New Orleans in 1787.

It is apparent that a primary aim of Spanish policy was now alliance with the United States, with a mutual guaranty of territory, which would act as an estoppel to all further American aggression on adjacent Spanish dominions and which would counteract the menace of the unknown terms of Jay's Treaty, terms which were feared by the Spanish to contain an agreement by the United States and Great Britain to support each other in maintaining, perhaps by force, the free navigation of the Mississippi as guaranteed in the treaty of 1783. That the full terms of Jay's Treaty do not appear to have been known to Godoy until after the signature of Pinckney's Treaty, traditionally known as the treaty of San Lorenzo, on October 27, 1795, is a significant supposition in our study of these highly complicated negotiations. It is further apparent that Godoy, now contemplating a desertion of the British alliance, wished to support himself as much as possible for encountering the indignation of Great Britain in the case of a separate peace between France and Spain. This could be accomplished partially by an alliance with the United States, purchased, he conceived, by yielding to the well-known American demands. Such would relieve Spain from embarrassment in Louisiana and the Floridas. It could be accomplished still more fully if he could bring the United States into a triple alliance with Spain and France, to be negotiated simultaneously and secretly with the proposed French separate peace. As the separate peace negotiations with France took more tangible shape during the clandestine conversations which the Duke began to hold through more than one channel with that republic, the idea of coupling a Franco-Spanish peace and alliance with such a triple alliance became more and more attractive. . . .

III

If Godoy had known the full, precise terms of Jay's Treaty during negotiations with Pinckney, we suggest, it would have injured rather than helped American interests; because that Minister imagined there was something in the treaty tantamount to alliance, dangerous to Spanish interests in America, whereas actually it contained nothing so portentous. Luckily Pinckney's delay in London did not damage his chances in Madrid, for one reason because notwithstanding Jay's and Pinckney's desires, the full terms of Jay's Treaty do not appear to have been known in Madrid until after Pinckney had concluded his business there and departed from Spain, and for another reason because, through no foresight of his own, the long wait in London caused him to arrive in Madrid, June 28, 1795, at the proper psychological moment.

The situation at that date could not have been more favorable for the success of his mission. Prussia and the Netherlands had already left the Coalition against France. French armies in increased strength were pressing through the Pyrenees into the heart of Spain. Godoy was now anxiously and directly negotiating through several separate channels, with the French, and the terms of peace were rapidly assuming shape. His proposal at Basle for an alliance with France was not fulfilled in these negotiations, though it was to be consummated, to the devastating ruin of Spain, a few months later. On July 22, 1795, the Peace of Basle was signed secretly in Switzerland, but the courier bearing the document did not reach the Spanish capital until the third of August. It was ratified in Paris on July 29. . . .

Now the great news was publicly known. On August 3 a copy of the secret treaty with France arrived at Court. It was immediately ratified and sent back to Paris. Four days later the end of the French war was announced in Madrid. In the streets of the city sedate old men embraced each other with joy. The populace was delirious with happiness. Godoy received from a grateful, supine monarch the title of Principe de la Paz. But it was necessary to face the English.

Godoy hastened to prepare the Spanish Ambassador at London to encounter the protests of that Government. The motives for continuing the war no longer existed, he explained; no advantages had come to Spain since hostilities had been declared; the country had been overwhelmed with disasters; the King must now look to the welfare of his own subjects. Standing before the imagined vengeance of Great Britain, Godoy hastened to clinch the friendship of the United States.

The day following the public announcement of the peace, Godoy told Pinckney that their business would be settled speedily to their joint satisfaction, since His Majesty was determined to sacrifice something of what he considered his right, in order to testify his good will to the United States. At a meeting of the Council of State of August 14, 1795, it was decided to proceed with the United States on the basis of conceding the right of navigation of the Mississippi and yielding the boundary of 31°, and this without an accompanying alliance or mutual guaranty of territory. "His Majesty would have left in those and other parts of America," said Godoy, "possessions, peoples and rights of great importance and sufficient for our commerce and navigation."

The nervous Prince of the Peace was cowering before the anticipated vengeance of a deserted ally which already had contracted with the United States a mysterious treaty that had all the earmarks of a definite understanding which might be used against Spain in America, possibly to force open the navigation of the Mississippi and to wrest away her vast and vacant provinces north of Mexico. "Everything is to be feared," the Spanish Ambassador at London reported September 18, after noting England's reaction to the Peace of Basle and her great preparations for launching a campaign in America. This confirmed Godoy's own fears. Far more than at any previous time it appeared to him necessary for the sake of Spain's overseas possessions, stripped bare by the recent European war of effective military defense, to conciliate the American republic. More troops than ever would be needed at home after the peace, he had some time previously prophesied to the Council, in order to defend the peninsula itself and to insure protection against possible risings of Spanish radicals. The costly reinforcements for which Carondelet had been pleading for the defense of Louisiana and the Floridas could not be spared.

Pinckney now began to see the light. "My present opinion is, that the new position of Spain with respect to England will induce them to come to a decision with us," he wrote to Randolph.

The Prince of the Peace actively and earnestly began to negotiate. With the Mississippi Question and the boundary conceded by Spain, the biggest difficulties had disappeared. Pinckney pressed Godoy at first for a treaty of commerce with reciprocal rights of nationals in all the domains of each party. It was soon evident that Spain would make no concessions here; by virtue of her existing treaties, to open up her colonial ports to the United States would be to open them up *ipso facto* to all European nations who enjoyed most-favored-nation privileges. Pinckney therefore forbore to push this point further. The two principal issues which remained were the adjustment of spoliations and the arrangement of the article for fixing the free navigation of the Mississippi. We have seen that Pinckney had instructions to get an agreement on principles for reparation for spoliations and then to set up a mixed commission to adjudicate them. Concerning the navigation question, his instructions, like those of his predecessors, cautioned him to avoid, if possible, accepting the navigation of the Mississippi as a *grant* from Spain rather than an acknowledgement of a right, and to procure the cession of a port or at least a landing place in Spanish territory near the mouth of the river for transshipment of goods from river boats to ocean-going vessels.

On the question of the spoliations Pinckney, taking advantage of the fact that Godoy in his verbal concessions to Short had accepted the definition of neutral rights in the Franco-American treaty of 1778, urged the Prince to accept the principle of the Armed Neutrality of 1780 as the basis of assessing damages to American neutral shipping by Spanish armed vessels. Godoy absolutely refused to do this or even to admit that his declaration to Short had any retroactive force applying to spoliations occurring before the date of that declaration, April 6, 1795. On this point he would not yield. This was not settled until the final conference of the two men preceding signature of the treaty. On the Mississippi Question Pinckney held out for a right of deposit at the mouth of the river and tried to write the whole navigation article in such a way as to imply a recognition of American right. On August 15 Pinckney presented the sketch of a proposed treaty of friendship, commerce, and navigation, with a separate article on the navigation of the Mississippi, which it is desirable to quote, in its English translation from the French:

> That the navigation of the Mississippi be recognized as free to both nations, and all facilities for its use [*pour la rendre utile*] be mutually accorded.

Godoy asked for a full-length draft of a treaty. Negotiations on the details of the draft consumed the next four weeks. On September 18 Godoy returned a counterdraft which left out the articles of commerce, omitted mention of a deposit, and rejected Pinckney's wording of the navigation article. In return Pinckney let go the commercial articles, at first proposing that the matter of a treaty of commerce be left to be drafted later by a mixed commission, each government enjoying, reciprocally, most-favored-nation privileges meanwhile. Eventually he relinquished even this, but he insisted on the right of deposit, and objected strenuously to Godoy's wording of the navigation article. He said:

> The words *solo et exclusivamente* (alone and exclusively) should be omitted, for Spain could scarcely confide in the good faith of the United States, nor in this convention, which she is about to conclude with them, if they agreed to an article which would be an infraction of another treaty, previously made. Now, by the treaty of peace between the United

> States and Great Britain, concluded in 1783, it is stipulated that the navigation of the River Mississippi shall continue free to the subjects of Great Britain and the citizens of the United States. It appears that the following provision would have all the desired effect: "It is nevertheless agreed, that nothing contained in this article shall be construed or interpreted, to communicate the right of navigating this river, to other nations or persons, than to the subjects of His Catholic Majesty and the citizens of the United States."

It is highly important to notice that this qualification, desired by Pinckney to remove a contravention of the Mississippi article of the treaty of peace between the United States and Great Britain of 1783, was not written into the final treaty with Spain.

In reply to Godoy's neglect to include an article providing for the right of deposit, Pinckney, demanding such a stipulation, argued that the United States was entitled to more than that; he asked for an outright cession of a plot of ground on the lower river. He maintained that the right to the navigation of the Mississippi had now been accepted as incontestably proven. Without a right to land and transship goods within Spanish territory at the mouth of the river, the acknowledged right, he asserted, would be "illusory, without utility, and without effect." If the port of deposit were granted, he intimated, his Government would not press its perfectly good claim for large damages already sustained by the twelve years' interruption of that navigation right.

Godoy sent Pinckney a brief note October 7, assuming that, as a result of their discussions, the treaty was closed, and asked that it be signed forthwith. Pinckney refused to sign without securing what he termed "one of the principal objects of his mission," the right of deposit, and he suggested some other small revisions in the articles of the treaty draft which had been already accepted by both in principle. It was at this time, too, that he made a last attempt to get Godoy to accept the principles of the Franco-American treaty of 1778, or the Armed Neutrality of 1780, as the rules for adjudication of spoliation cases. As to the right of deposit, Pinckney had offered to accept, pending a future agreement on the place of such a depot, that citizens of the United States should have the right of depositing their goods, free of duty charge, in the New Orleans custom house, to which the owners of the deposited goods were to have a key, with another key for the proper Spanish official. Godoy offered to allow this, without granting a key for the American owners of the deposited goods. The question of deposit and the rules for adjudication of spoliation still remained the only issues which prevented the completion of the negotiation. Godoy refused any cession of a place of deposit, or even to mention the matter of deposit in the main body of the treaty. His furthest concession was to promise to propose to His Majesty that, in a separate convention, the United States be given a facility of deposit at New Orleans pending further arrangements. Pinckney refused this. Godoy answered, October 20, that he could not vary in the least what he had already said concerning the deposit, observing that His Majesty would look into the means by which the navigation of the Mississippi could increase the commerce of his subjects and of the citizens of the United States. Pinckney still refused to budge.

Short had been called by Pinckney to San Ildefonso from Madrid, for consultation on points brought up in the draft projects. In October, the Court moved to San Lorenzo, its autumnal residence, and Short retired to Madrid, close at hand, where he was kept informed by Pinckney to take some vigorous and decisive step on the question of deposit, which would reveal the real intentions of the Spanish Government. Pinckney decided to do this and to make the right of deposit a *sine qua non.* On October 24, 1795, he therefore asked for his passports, on the assumption that the negotiation had failed. It was no bluff. His correspondence with Short shows he was determined to leave if they had been handed to him. He resolved to stake everything to get the right of deposit. It was a bold and daring move, and successful. Godoy capitulated. Another conference was held the next day at which an agreement was reached. Pinckney accepted a mixed commission, without prior agreement on rules of international law, for adjudication of the spoliations. Godoy on his side consented to the principle of *permitting* the *privilege* of deposit for three years at New Orleans with the liberty of continuing it at the expiration of that period, if another equal establishment should not be granted elsewhere on the river upon the expiration of that period.

The treaty was signed on October 27, 1795, at San Lorenzo, the village which nestles at the foot of the southern slopes of the Guadarramas, where the cathedral and palace of the Escorial rise against the somber background of the mountains and stand gloomy guard over the tombs of the Kings of Spain. A mighty ruler of empire built it. Could the great Philip II, seated there by his palace on his chair of stone and gazing as was his wont of a summer evening out across the baked and sterile plains to the distant spires of his capital—could that powerful monarch, ruling in three continents, with his galleons ranging seven seas, ever have imagined that at this very place one day an upstart court adventurer, rising by his amorous intrigues with a Queen of Spain over the ruin of able ministers, would sign such a fateful treaty? That proud King slept mercifully on in the still depths of the royal sepulchre beneath the heavy pile of the Escorial. A new state, also undreamed of by him, had arisen across the Atlantic. Thanks to Europe's convulsions it was able to declare and secure its independence and to achieve its territorial integrity—more than that, to take that first step in a career of expansion which was to witness, in our own times, the extinction of the last American vestige of that vast colonial empire over which the son of the Emperor Charles V once held sway.

A few days before Pinckney had brought the negotiation to a head by asking for his passports, that is on October 19, he was informed by the Spanish Government of the occupation of Barrancas de Margot (Chickasaw Bluffs, present Memphis, Tenn.) by a Spanish detachment following a rumor that American settlers had designed to occupy Muscle Shoals on the Tennessee. After the treaty was signed Godoy delivered a note to the American envoy stating that this place, "comprehended within our ancient limits," had been occupied at the order of the Governor of Natchez, after having heard of the intention of inhabitants of Kentucky and neighboring states to occupy Muscle Shoals, and that as a consequence of the new treaty of friendship, limits, and navigation having now been signed, orders had been sent out to the Governor of Natchez to suspend all hostilities, in case any should have occurred between him and the citizens of the United States, "leaving matters in the situation in which they may be on the receipt of the order until the ratification of the treaty." Further, the Governors of the two Floridas (Louisiana was not mentioned) had been enjoined to maintain the most complete harmony with the commanders of the troops of the United States on their frontiers; and it was hoped that the President of the United States would expedite the issue of similar orders on his part. . . .

. . . But the investigator, in following the negotiation as it is preserved in the sources which have come down to us, cannot help but feel a sense of almost dramatic suspense. What if the actual text of Jay's Treaty had arrived in Spain before Pinckney signed with Godoy! What if Godoy, before setting his name to a document which marks the initial disaster in a career which was to be full of great mistakes, had discovered that after all the articles of Jay's Treaty were not so formidable as he had imagined! Would he then have been alarmed at the conception of an Anglo-American understanding and a possible military combination directed at Louisiana and the Floridas? Would he have made the enormous concessions which he made? If Jay's Treaty had been known *in its full text* in Spain would Pinckney's triumph have been possible?

2. *Frontier Pressures and Spain's Retreat*

A. P. Whitaker disagrees with Professor Bemis. A specialist in interhemispheric relations, his study leads him to conclude that Godoy in all probability had received a full copy of the text of the Jay Treaty from his minister in Philadelphia, where it was published in July of 1795, and therefore realized that there was no danger from that quarter. The decision to concede the American claims reflected instead frontier realities in the new world: the pressure of growing American strength and western population, failure of the separatist intrigue, and the unreliability of the Indian buffers. Spain recognized the facts of the situation and chose to retreat lest it imperil its lightly defended and sparsely populated provinces.

San Lorenzo: A Frontier Treaty

ARTHUR P. WHITAKER

On October 27, 1795, at the palace-monastery of San Lorenzo a treaty was signed whereby Spain surrendered its dispute with the American republic. It was a crucial document that was signed on that day by Manuel de Godoy, the handsome guardsman of Badajoz, and Thomas Pinckney, South Carolina gentleman; for the treaty of San Lorenzo marks the begin-

Arthur Preston Whitaker, *The Spanish-American Frontier, 1783–1795* (Boston & New York: Houghton-Mifflin Company, 1927), 201–222. Reprinted with permission.

ning of the disintegration of the Spanish empire as well as the first stage in the territorial expansion of the United States. The following pages will show how the concatenation of events in a Swiss town, on royal Spanish backstairs, and in the backwoods of North America forced this portentous surrender.

It was in November, 1794, that Thomas Pinckney, minister to Great Britain, was directed by his government to undertake a special commission to the Spanish court. . . .

The period from July 26, 1794 . . . to June 29, 1795, the date of Pinckney's arrival at the Spanish court, was marked by the almost complete suspension of the negotiation between the two governments. The same period, it may be remarked by way of anticipation, was one of intense activity on the Mississippi Valley frontier, where Spanish officials and American frontiersmen ploughed an independent furrow, with little knowledge of the plans of their respective governments and with little regard for their wishes.

The length of this diplomatic hiatus of eleven months was due to Pinckney's delay in reaching Spain; and his delay is in turn explained by various causes. In the first place, one of the considerations that led to his appointment seems to have been Washington's desire to placate the Kentuckians. There was little hope in administration circles that a new minister would succeed where Short had failed; but the whole American West was in a ferment, many Kentuckians angrily demanding that the Mississippi be seized while Spain was engaged in war at home. Something must be done to quiet the clamor on the Ohio; and it is significant that at the same time that Colonel James Innes was sent to Kentucky to convince its governor of Washington's determination to open the Mississippi, the President resolved to accept Godoy's invitation of May, 1794, and send a new and more distinguished envoy to Spain.

Maladroit Diplomacy

In view of the origin of his mission, there seemed to be no reason why Pinckney should proceed post-haste to Spain; and the maladroit policy of the United States government actually delayed his departure from London. So long indeed was it delayed that he lost all the immense benefit that he might have derived from Jay's mission to England (1794). The American government's policy has been called maladroit because it relied on the worst and neglected the best means of extorting the desired terms from Spain. Reliance was placed in the good offices of France, which, it was hoped, would utilize its victories over Spain to secure the terms desired by the United States. This fatuous optimism found its best expression in the letters of James Monroe, American minister at Paris, who wrote in 1795 that France was giving us material aid in the Spanish negotiations. As a matter of fact, the French government was engaged at that very time in a determined effort to secure from Spain the retrocession of Louisiana, and in order to carry its point was exciting Spain's fear of the ambitious Americans and was promising to keep the Mississippi River closed in order to check their westward expansion.

The opportunity neglected by Washington's government was afforded by Jay's mission. The hindsight test is often unfair, and yet it seems strange that Randolph, Jay and Pinckney, the three best-informed persons in the diplomatic service of the United States at that juncture, should all have failed so utterly to perceive the real relation of Jay's mission to the negotiation between their government and Spain. They either knew or should have known by the winter of 1794–95 that the Anglo-Spanish alliance was in danger of dissolution, that the secrecy surrounding Jay's mission and his treaty with Grenville had created great alarm in Spain, and that this Spanish fear of an Anglo-American alliance would be the most effective means of extorting a treaty favorable to the United States. Since, as these three diplomats knew, Jay's treaty did not in fact provide for an alliance between England and the United States, it would seem as plain as day that Pinckney should have hastened to Spain before the veil of secrecy was lifted from Jay's treaty and while Godoy was still haunted by the spectre of Anglo-American union.

Instead, the American diplomats followed the opposite course. On the advice of Jay and with the approval of Randolph, Pinckney deliberately awaited in London news of the ratification of Jay's treaty by the United States Senate; and it was only when he learned that there would be a long delay in the consideration of the treaty that he proceeded to Spain. This maladroit diplomacy secured its immediate object, for Jay's treaty was ratified while Pinckney was in Spain and news of the ratification and the text of the treaty reached Spain a full month before the conclusion of the treaty with Godoy. As might have been foreseen, and as Pinckney now frankly admitted, this news was prejudicial to his negotiation. It might indeed have wrecked it but for an abrupt change in the European situation which the American diplomats could not have foreseen.

Godoy Deserts England

This abrupt change was brought about by the treaty of Bâle (July, 1795) whereby Spain deserted England and made peace with the victorious French Republic. The negotiation was kept even more profoundly secret than Jay's with Grenville, for Godoy feared to face British resentment until the treaty with France was a *fait accompli*. . . .

It was while negotiations at Bâle were in progress that Thomas Pinckney arrived at court (June 29, 1795); and of course he was unable to make the slightest progress until that affair was terminated. Once the French treaty was concluded, Godoy gave the North American situation his immediate attention. On August 4, 1795, King Charles IV ratified the French treaty. Ten days later (August 14) the Spanish Council of State completed the diplomatic retreat begun in the time of Floridablanca and decided to surrender the dispute with the United States. In the first stage of the controversy (1780–87), Spain had refused to concede on any terms the navigation and boundary demanded by the United States. In 1787, under the combined pressure of a frontier menace and European complications, Floridablanca had offered boundary concessions in return for an alliance with the United States. In 1791, he was apparently ready to include the navigation of the Mississippi in the bargain; and in the despatch to Jáudenes of July 26, 1794, Godoy had virtually declared Spain's willingness to concede both points in return for a defensive alliance and territorial guarantee. Now in August, 1795, the Council of State decided to surrender both points without exacting the equivalent alliance. What were the considerations that led it to make this momentous decision?

Ever since the publication of Godoy's *Memoirs,* most American historians have been content to repeat his statement that the surrender was due to the secrecy surrounding Jay's treaty and the consequent fear that the treaty included an alliance between Great Britain and the United States. We now know, however, that this product of the blurred memory of an old man in exile is not supported by the facts; for, far from being ignorant of the terms of Jay's treaty, Godoy had a copy of it in his possession a full month before he signed the treaty with Pinckney, and far from facilitating, Jay's treaty actually rendered more difficult Pinckney's negotiation. Even before the publication of its terms Jay's treaty had ceased to be a decisive factor in shaping Spanish policy. It was not even mentioned in the lengthy minutes of the Council of State of August 14, 1795, when the surrender to the United States was agreed upon.

It was not Jay's treaty with England but Godoy's treaty with France that made possible Pinckney's triumph at San Lorenzo. By concluding a separate peace with France at Bâle, Godoy violated Spain's treaty of 1793 with England and he knew that as soon as he had made peace with the former he would have to face the angry resentment of the latter. . . . The blow might fall in Santo Domingo, or in Mexico, or somewhere else; but in any case it appeared certain that Great Britain was about to assail some colony of Spain in the neighborhood of the Gulf of Mexico. In that case the attitude of the United States would be of the utmost importance. An alliance with the Americans would be of great value; their neutrality at least was indispensable, and Thomas Pinckney could not be suffered to leave Spain unsatisfied. Hence it was that only ten days elapsed between the Spanish ratification of the treaty of Bâle and the decision of the Council of State to yield to the United States in the matter of the boundary and the navigation of the Mississippi. Six months after San Lorenzo, Godoy himself gave this explanation of its terms. In a conversation (May, 1796) with Earle Bute, the British ambassador, Godoy complained that Britain's hostile preparations against Mexico in 1795 had forced him to make extensive concessions to the United States.

Backstairs Intrigue

It was not only Spain's insecurity in Europe and America, but also Godoy's insecurity in Spain that led to the capitulation at San Lorenzo. Most precarious was the royal favorite's situation in the summer and early fall of 1795. Heavy taxation had created intense discontent, and military reverses had done much to discredit the youthful minister's conduct of affairs. So cordially was he hated at this time that he rarely showed his face in public; and on one occasion, when the court was moving from one royal estate to another, the danger of popular violence was so great that he deserted his own carriage and took refuge with the king and queen.

One result of this widespread discontent was the Malaspina plot, a typical backstairs episode of the old régime. In it were implicated Antonio Valdés, one of the most influential, though the laziest, of Godoy's colleagues in the ministry; the confessors of the king and queen; and the naval officer and explorer, Malaspina, an Italian by birth. The object of the conspirators was simply to persuade the king to get rid of Godoy, who they said was endangering the monarchy by his incompetence; but to the favorite their intrigue seemed nothing less than treason. To meet the crisis, he first set to work to remove the chief grievances, which were military reverses and heavy taxation. Clearly the only way to remove both grievances at once was to make peace. Peace was accordingly made with France, and, to avert war with the United States, the treaty of San Lorenzo was signed. Having thus strengthened his position, Godoy proceeded to crush the conspiracy, imprisoning the confessors, exiling Malaspina, and forcing the resignation of Valdés. . . .

From Spanish backstairs to the backwoods of North America may seem a far cry, and yet backwoods as well as backstairs played an important part at San Lorenzo. Had not Spain's frontier policy proved a failure by 1795, and had not Godoy been acutely conscious of the failure, it hardly seems probable that he would have made so complete a surrender of the Mississippi Valley controversy. . . .

Carondelet Courts the Kentuckians

While diplomacy drifted in the doldrums from the summer of 1794 to the summer of 1795, Carondelet fought the Americans tooth and nail on the frontier. His object was twofold: To defend Louisiana, and to aid Spanish diplomacy by tightening Spain's grip on the Mississippi Valley. In Miró's time, this object had been pursued through Floridablanca's immigration policy, with the Kentucky intrigue playing a distinctly subordinate part, since the court considered it a remote possibility. Upon Carondelet's arrival in Louisiana (1792), he had modified the immigration policy beyond recognition, and since the Western intrigue gave but faint promise of success, he had devoted all his energies to the elaboration of an aggressive Indian policy. Baffled in this effort by his unsympathetic superiors and the intractable Indians, and threatened with invasion from Georgia and Kentucky, he had welcomed with open arms the treasonable overtures of General James Wilkinson and Judge Harry Innes in the early months of 1794. At the same time, the Baron began to execute a plan that he had long had in contemplation: the military occupation of the east bank of the Mississippi River up to its junction with the Ohio.

The Kentucky intrigue was nothing new, as we have already had abundant occasion to see; but it was now given a decidedly novel character by Carondelet. Hitherto, according to various orders of the court, the revolutionizing of Kentucky had been neither the immediate nor the sole object of the intrigue. Floridablanca's purpose in cultivating it had been to use the Kentucky conspirators as propagandists and information agents for Spain; the revolutionizing of the American West was regarded as a remote possibility; and Spain was to have no open dealings with the conspirators until after they had set up a separate government. Now Carondelet's avowed object was to foment an immediate insurrection in Kentucky, to bring Wilkinson and other leading conspirators into Spanish territory and conclude an alliance with them, and, by supplying them liberally with munitions and money, to aid them in establishing their independence. Thus divided into rival powers, he said, the United States would no longer be a serious menace to Spain in North America. We have already discussed, in connection with Spanish diplomacy and the royal order of July 26, 1794, his despatches of that year to Godoy on the subject of the conspiracy; but to Wilkinson also, without waiting to receive the court's reply, he began to communicate his designs.

We have no space here to trace the sinuosities of the intrigue, but it may be pointed out that despite the lukewarmness of the American frontiersmen as well as his own government, the Baron continued the intrigue to the bitter end. Already, early in 1795, he had received a disconcerting proof of the indifference to Spain of even the most discontented frontiersmen. . . .

Nevertheless, the Baron went doggedly ahead with his plans. On July 16, 1795, he wrote Wilkinson a letter that was designed to bring the intrigue to a head at once. "My letter of the first instant," he wrote, "was already signed when I received orders from his Majesty very satisfactory to the Western states: since his Majesty being very desirous of giving them a commerce reciprocaly advantageous to both parties has authorized me to treat privately with the Agents chosen & sent by the State of Kentucky to New Madrid on that purpose. Consequently I send to Colonel Gayoso the necessary instructions, & sufficient powers to agree privately with the aforesaid Agents upon every point and object of this momentous plan. . . ." The letter concluded with the following: "G. W. [General Wilkinson] can aspire to the same dignity in the western states that P. W. [President Washington] has in the eastern." Carondelet knew his man.

This letter was sent to Gayoso with an order directing him to proceed at once to New Madrid, forward it to Wilkinson, and negotiate with the Kentucky envoys who should come down in response to the invitation. His powers were narrowly limited, as he was instructed to conclude only a commercial convention, and even that was to be kept secret at first from all but the "notables" of Kentucky; but we learn from Carondelet's other correspondence that in his shallow optimism he expected this proof of Spain's generosity to effect the separation of Kentucky from the Union. Thereupon it was the Baron's plan to conclude an offensive and defensive alliance with Kentucky and to aid their revolution with ammunition, twenty field guns and ten thousand rifles.

Gayoso ascended the Mississippi to New Madrid, as he had been directed, and from September to December, 1795, he was engaged in correspondence with Wilkinson, Lacassagne and Innes. Wilkinson displayed little enthusiasm at the opportunity of embracing his dear friend, Gayoso, to whom he had once written that he would willingly sacrifice one arm if he might embrace Gayoso with the other. Now he protested that he had a difficult game to play, as he was suspected by both his commander-in-chief, Wayne, and by Washington, and that the ground had not yet been sufficiently prepared in Kentucky. Nevertheless, though he could not visit Gayoso himself, had not consulted Innes, and did not trust Lacassagne, he finally sent a delegate, Benjamin Sebastian, to confer with the Spaniard, adding that, while Sebastian had no power to make a treaty, the conference would undoubtedly forward Spain's interest in Kentucky. In order to prepare the ground in Kentucky and oil the wheels of intrigue, he urgently requested the immediate remittance of twenty thousand dollars and an increase in the amount of his pension. In December, 1795, Sebastian actually descended the Ohio and conferred with Gayoso; but the powers of both were so limited that it was soon decided to adjourn the discussion to New Orleans and, under Carondelet's guidance, concert a plan of action. Arriving at the capital early in January, they were busily engaged in hatching a scheme when, to their consternation, despatches from Havana brought news of the treaty of San Lorenzo. . . .

Fort San Fernando: Fur Trader and Land Speculator

The extension of Spain's military frontier was, as we have seen, Carondelet's second device for gaining the upper hand in the controversy with the United States. As early as his first year in Louisiana (1792), he had persuaded the Cherokee to request the establishment of Spanish posts at Muscle Shoals and Chickasaw Bluffs (the Barrancas de Margot, or Ecores à Margot, the site of the present Memphis, Tennessee), both of which localities, by the way, were outside of the Cherokee hunting grounds. Various circumstances had prevented his granting this complaisant request; but in 1794 a step in that direction was taken when, under circumstances already described, Fort Confederation was built on the Tombigbie River, well within the territory claimed by the United States.

Just as the designs of the South Carolina Yazoo Company had led Miró to occupy Walnut Hills (Los Nogales) in 1791, so in 1795 the activities of the Georgia land companies were immediately responsible for the erection of Fort San Fernando de las Barrancas at Chickasaw Bluffs. Towards the end of 1794, land speculators interested in the Yazoo country began to bestir themselves, perhaps encouraged by the federal government's assurance that it was at last going to force a settlement of the dispute with Spain. Gentle pressure was brought to bear on the Georgia legislature, and once more in the history of the American frontier political power was exploited in the interest of land speculation. Their pockets bulging with shares and banknotes, the legislators deeded away principalities for a pittance. Millions of acres of Georgia's western territory were conveyed to three companies, two of the grants lying on the Mississippi between Natchez and Chickasaw Bluffs, and one on the Tennessee River around Muscle Shoals.

As soon as Gayoso heard of the designs of the companies he hastily forwarded a detachment up the Mississippi to hold the Bluffs until his arrival with well-armed reinforcements, for he was much disturbed by a visit that Cumberland settlers had paid to the Bluffs in 1794, and by their influence among the Chickasaw. Carondelet, when advised of Gayoso's action, gave his approval, took command of the situation, and despatched instructions, reinforcements and supplies. Most important of all, he persuaded Panton, Leslie and Company to send one of its partners, John Forbes, with a boatload of goods to open a store at the new fort. Again the American land speculator and frontiersman found the Anglo-Spanish fur trader in their path.

As the Chickasaw Bluffs extend for many miles along the Mississippi, the site of the fort was not chosen until after Gayoso's arrival. That done, a review of the troops was held and the construction of the fort begun on May 30, 1795; and since that was the name-day of the Prince of Asturias, Fernando, the fort was called San Fernando de las Barrancas, St. Ferdinand of the Bluffs. Thus the last outpost of Spanish advance in the Mississippi Valley received the ill-omened name of that prince who later, as the notorious Ferdinand VII, lost the bulk of Spain's empire in America. . . .

Godoy Looks at the Mississippi Valley

In despatches that still glow with pride and tremble with eager hope, Carondelet informed Godoy of his achievements in Kentucky and at Chickasaw Bluffs. In a despatch of June 10, 1795, he reported the establishment of Fort San Fernando, which, he declared, forestalled the Americans, strengthened Spain's hold on the Mississippi, and would promote Panton's trade and Spain's influence among the Chickasaw and Choctaw, at the same time that it advanced the Western intrigue by facilitating communications with Kentucky. This conspiracy was the subject of a despatch of July 1, and the burden of the Baron's song was a plea for funds, more funds, and still more funds. The plan to revolutionize Kentucky was feasible, he declared, and such a revolution was almost essential to the safety of Spanish North America; but tens of thousands of dollars must be made available at once for propaganda, bribery and aid to the insurgents. Whether this were done or not, he continued, still larger sums must be placed at his disposal to consolidate his recent gains on the frontier. Forts San Fernando and Confederation as well as the older forts must be strengthened, their garrisons reinforced, Panton subsidized and the annual Indian presents increased to meet the competition of the United States government. Otherwise, he concluded, Spain must face the necessity of surrender in the controversy with the United States, and all the dire consequences that would flow from the surrender; but such a calamity need never occur, since, thanks to Carondelet's Kentucky intrigue, Indian alliances and string of forts, His Majesty held the fate of the Mississippi Valley in the hollow of his hand.

These despatches Godoy received more than a week before he signed the treaty of San Lorenzo and almost a week before Pinckney brought the negotiation to a crisis by demanding his passport. Had Godoy been convinced by the Baron's eager optimism, he would have issued the passport that Pinckney had requested but did not expect or desire to receive. The situation thus created was similar in many respects to that of July, 1794. On both occasions the Council of State, on Godoy's advice, had decided to make concessions to the United States in the frontier controversy, and on both occasions, after the decision had been made but before its execution, despatches had been received from Louisiana urging continued resistance and giving positive assurance of success. The parallel was completed when, on October 27, 1795, as on July 25, 1794, Godoy turned a deaf ear to the Baron's rhetoric and consummated the surrender. This time there was no miscarriage. Pinckney was on hand, the treaty was signed, and both the disputed territory and the control of the Mississippi were irrevocably lost to Spain.

We have already intimated that the treaty of San Lorenzo was essentially a frontier treaty. It is of course true that, as we have seen, the European situation was one of Godoy's reasons for concluding the treaty, and that it contained provisions of no little significance in the history of neutral rights on the high seas in time of war. At the same time, it is equally true that by far the most important terms of the treaty related to the Spanish-American frontier: the disputed territory, the navigation of the Mississippi, the right of deposit at New Orleans; and that one of the chief reasons why the Spanish government agreed to these terms was that it had failed, and knew that it had failed, in its frontier conflict with the United States.

That the most important terms of the treaty related to the frontier is so obvious that the mere statement of the fact would be sufficient, since that fact requires not proof but emphasis. It may, however, be well to remind the reader that the navigation of the Mississippi was an essential element in the frontier controversy, for while the exclusive control of the river was still prized by Spain as a means of suppressing contraband trade, it was prized still more as a means of checking the growth of the American West, separating it from the United States, and stimulating immigration into Louisiana and West Florida.

That the fact as well as the terms of the Spanish surrender was conditioned by Spanish failure in the frontier conflict stands more in need of proof; for historians, relying on Godoy's *Memoirs,* have generally explained his course at San Lorenzo by the existing diplomatic situation. These *Memoirs,* however, were written nearly forty years after the event, and contemporary records tell a different story, a story in which the frontier plays a prominent part.

On August 14, 1795, occurred a meeting of the Council of State to which reference has already been made. Two official accounts of the deliberations of the Council have been preserved, each relating to a separate aspect of the subject under discussion. The first of these documents possesses great interest for us, since it throws a flood of light on the reasons for Spain's surrender to the United States and since it has never been utilized by any previous writer on this subject. According to this record, Godoy carefully explained the nature of the controversy to the Council with the aid of documents and maps, and in his exegesis he established two "capital facts." The first of these was that Spain's failure to protest against the Anglo-American treaty of 1783 was taken by the Americans as the silence of consent. The second "capital fact" was the small importance of the disputed territory and the forts contained within its limits; the unsatisfactory state of relations with the "barbarous, voluble and perfidious nations of Indians" of that region, who were incessantly menacing the possessions of Spain; and the undesirability of continuing a very uncertain and very expensive dispute. Godoy concluded with the observation that, even if this controversy were settled according to the "moderate ideas" of the United States, Spain would still have "possessions, peoples and rights quite sufficient, and important to our navigation and commerce in those and other principal parts of the two Americas."

There are many omissions from this document and there are some distortions in it. For example, the "moderate ideas" of the United States had long been regarded as "absurd pretensions" by the Spanish government, and Godoy's novel characterization was simply a sugar-coating to render palatable the bitter pill of defeat. Our interest, however, lies in the second of his two "capital facts," for it shows that the treaty of San Lorenzo was not signed until the Council had canvassed the situation on the Spanish-American frontier and had decided that the chances of success did not justify the continuance of the struggle. From the second report of the Council's deliberations on August 14, and from other documents, we learn that at this time the government was much alarmed at two other developments in the Mississippi Valley, namely, by the activity of British fur traders in the upper Missouri Valley, and by the efforts of Americans to establish settlements at Muscle Shoals and Chickasaw Bluffs.

It may be observed that neither of these reports of the Council's deliberations mentioned the Kentucky conspiracy. Other sources show that Spain did not trust Wilkinson, and was unwilling to incur the expense of revolutionizing Kentucky or the danger of war with the United States. Hence it was that Godoy was unmoved when, on October 18, 1795, he read Carondolet's perfervid despatches about the progress of the western conspiracy. Like Floridablanca, he had no stomach for dealing with the American frontiersmen. His first object was to check their progress through Spain's frontier, and since that appeared impossible he preferred a treaty with the established government of the United States to an intrigue with its irresponsible frontiersmen.

Stripping for Action

Our task is now done, for we are not concerned either with the details of the Pinckney-Godoy negotiation, or with the execution of the treaty. Pinckney conducted himself most becomingly and quite creditably; but in no essential respect did he get more than Godoy was ready to concede when their conferences began, and he failed to secure either a commercial treaty or a satisfactory article on the right of deposit. His rôle was very much like that of Monroe and Livingston at Paris in 1803, when Napoleon tossed Louisiana into their laps. As for the long delay in the treaty's execution, we must content ourselves with pointing out that a frontier event, William Blount's conspiracy, provided Spain with its chief pretext for postponing compliance with its terms. When Natchez, the chief post in the disputed territory, was at last evacuated (1798), it was no less a person than General James Wilkinson who took possession of it in the name of the United States government.

From what has been said, it should be apparent that the treaty of San Lorenzo did not so much change the situation in the Mississippi Valley as accord recognition to changes that had taken place there since 1783. Even before the treaty was signed, citizens of the United States were enjoying the navigation of the Mississippi River from its headwaters to its mouth. From Kentucky down to New Orleans, their commerce had been legalized by a royal order; from the mouth of the Mississippi up to New Orleans, it was connived at by the governor of Louisiana, who informed his government that no other course was possible. As for the disputed territory, Spain was still in actual possession of it in 1795; but it was by that time apparent that this territory as well as upper Louisiana would fall an easy prey to the United States in case of war. For Spain indeed the treaty of San Lorenzo was one of momentous significance, for it was in effect an admission of failure of Floridablanca's attempt to make of the Mississippi Valley another Mexico. The admission of failure on the east bank of the Mississippi involved the tacit admission of failure on the west bank as well. The treaty of San Lorenzo of 1795 found its fitting, its inevitable complement in the treaty of San Ildefonso of 1800, whereby Spain retroceded Louisiana to France.

For the United States as well this treaty was one of great significance. It was a victory not only for the United States over Spain, but also for expansionists in the United States over particularists, both Eastern and Western. It appeased frontier discontent, gave a mortal blow to separatism, and secured the Union from a serious menace to its integrity. It completed the work begun by Jay's treaty and established the frontiers claimed by the United States at the end of the Revolution; and yet it did more than Jay's treaty for the rights that it established had hitherto rested on a dubious legal basis. By terminating a dangerous controversy and by securing the American government's terms without the formation of the alliance which Spain had long required as the price of concession, the treaty carried one step further the government's policy of cutting loose from the European state system; a policy which, in retrospect, seems a kind of stripping for action in the western hemisphere. Finally, by confirming the United States in the possession of virtually the whole east bank of the Mississippi and by validating the Americans' claim to the free navigation of that river, the treaty laid a substantial foundation for the further extension of the new republic in North America.

Additional Reading

Samuel Flagg Bemis, *Jay's Treaty: A Study in Commerce and Diplomacy* (1923).
Arthur B. Darling, *Our Rising Empire, 1763–1803* (1940).
R. W. Van Alstyne, *The Rising American Empire* (1960).

4 *WASHINGTON'S FAREWELL ADDRESS: Timeless Wisdom or Politics?*

In the years after 1796, the Farewell Address of President Washington acquired a nearly sacred place in history and tradition. It was generally believed that the first president, upon retiring from office, had chosen to utter sage, timeless, and unbiased words of advice to Americans of all generations to avoid entanglements with Europe. His valedictory counsel was regarded as valid not only in 1796 but in 1896 or 1936 as well. Whatever Washington had initially sought to accomplish, the Address became a founding stone for the policy of American political isolation from Europe and it was repeatedly invoked in the years thereafter to prohibit almost any type of foreign involvement and obligation.

American isolationism was actually a "myth" in several important ways. The United States had never been totally isolated from Europe. Geographically, the Atlantic was always more of an ocean highway than a forbidding moat, and with modern technological and economic developments it has become a busy avenue of communication and transportation. Politically, America has been unable to avoid involvement in Europe's major wars, as 1812, 1917, and 1941 aptly attest. The century of peace and prosperity, from 1815 to 1914, was the result of the general peace which prevailed in Europe, and not of the isolationist policies followed by the United States. Unfortunately, most Americans, at least until the 1930's, failed to understand that fact. The term "myth" is also justified because recent studies reveal that Washington did not condemn all alliances, but only permanent ones; his remarks were addressed to the still weak and small nation whose independence had only been recently established; and the message was by no means divorced from the domestic politics of his own era.

DOCUMENT

The Farewell Address

The Farewell Address was not delivered as a formal speech but was released to the public through the pages of a Philadelphia Federalist newspaper. In reading Washington's comments on the banefulness of political parties, it should be remembered that Hamilton and administration supporters denied that they comprised a political party and attributed factionalism solely to the opposition led by Jefferson and Madison.

Washington's Farewell Address

The period for a new election of a citizen to administer the Executive Government of the United States being not far distant, and the time actually arrived when your thoughts must be employed in designating the person who is to be clothed with that important trust, it appears to me proper, especially as it may conduce to a more distinct expression of the public voice, that I should now apprise you of the resolution I have formed to decline being considered among the number of those out of whom a choice is to be made. . . .

I have already intimated to you the danger of parties in the State, with particular reference to the founding of them on geographical discriminations. Let me now take a more comprehensive view, and warn you in the most solemn manner against the baneful effects of the spirit of party generally.

This spirit, unfortunately, is inseparable from our nature, having its root in the strongest passions of the human mind. It exists under different shapes in all governments, more or less stifled, controlled, or repressed; but in those of the popular form it is seen in its greatest rankness and is truly their worst enemy.

The alternate domination of one faction over another, sharpened by the spirit of revenge natural to party dissension, which in different ages and countries has perpetrated the most horrid enormities, is itself a frightful despotism. But this leads at length to a more formal and permanent despotism. The disorders and miseries which result gradually incline the minds of men to seek security and repose in the absolute power of an individual, and sooner or later the chief of some prevailing faction, more able or more fortunate than his competitors, turns this disposition to the purposes of his own elevation on the ruins of public liberty.

Without looking forward to an extremity of this kind (which nevertheless ought not to be entirely out of sight), the common and continual mischiefs of the spirit of party are sufficient to make it the interest and duty of a wise people to discourage and restrain it.

It serves always to distract the public councils and enfeeble the public administration. It agitates the community with ill-founded jealousies and false alarms; kindles the animosity of one part against another; foments occasionally riot and insurrection. It opens the door to foreign influence and corruption, which find a facilitated access to the government itself through the channels of party passion. Thus the policy and the will of one country are subjected to the policy and will of another. . . .

Observe good faith and justice toward all nations. Cultivate peace and harmony with all. Religion and morality enjoin this conduct. And can it be that good policy does not equally enjoin it? It will be worthy of a free, enlightened, and at no distant period a great nation to give to mankind the magnanimous and too novel example of a people always guided by an exalted justice and benevolence. Who can doubt that in the course of time and things the fruits of such a plan would richly repay any temporary advantages which might be lost by a steady adherence to it? Can it be that Providence has not connected the permanent felicity of a nation with its virtue? The experiment, at least, is recommended by every sentiment which ennobles human nature. Alas! is it rendered impossible by its vices?

In the execution of such a plan nothing is more essential than that permanent, inveterate antipathies against particular nations and passionate attachments for others should be excluded, and that in place of them just and amicable feelings toward all should be cultivated. The nation which indulges toward another an habitual hatred or an habitual fondness is in some degree a slave. It is a slave to its animosity or to its affection, either of which is sufficient to lead it astray from its duty and its interest. Antipathy in one nation against another disposes each more readily to offer insult and injury, to lay hold of slight causes of umbrage, and to be haughty and intractable when accidental or trifling occasions of dispute occur.

Hence frequent collisions, obstinate, envenomed, and bloody contests. The nation prompted by ill will and resentment sometimes impels to war the government contrary to the best calculations of policy. The government sometimes participates in the national propensity, and adopts through passion what reason would reject. At other times it makes the animosity of the nation subservient to projects of hostility, instigated by pride, ambition, and other sinister and pernicious motives. The peace often, sometimes perhaps the liberty, of nations has been the victim.

So, likewise, a passionate attachment of one nation for another produces a variety of evils. Sympathy for the favorite nation, facilitating the illusion of an imaginary common interest in cases where no real common interest exists, and infusing into one the enmities of the other, betrays the former into a participation in the quarrels and wars of the latter without adequate inducement or justification. It leads also to concessions to the favorite nation of privileges denied to others, which is apt doubly to injure the nation making the concessions by unnecessarily parting with what ought to have been retained, and by exciting jealousy, ill will, and a disposition to retaliate in the parties from whom equal privileges are withheld; and it gives to ambitious, corrupted, or deluded citizens (who devote themselves to the favorite nation) facility to betray or sacrifice the interests of their own country without odium, sometimes even with popularity, gilding with the appearances of a virtuous sense of obligation, a commendable deference for public opinion, or a laudable zeal for public good the base or foolish compliances of ambition, corruption, or infatuation.

As avenues to foreign influence in innumerable ways, such attachments are particularly alarming to the truly enlightened and independent patriot. How many opportunities do they afford to tamper with domestic factions, to practice the arts of seduction, to mislead public opinion, to influence or awe the public councils! Such an attachment of a small or weak toward a great and powerful nation dooms the former to be the satellite of the latter. Against the insidious wiles of foreign influence (I conjure you to believe me, fellow-citizens) the jealousy of a free people ought to be *constantly* awake, since history and experience prove that foreign influence is one of the most baneful foes of republican government. But that jealousy, to be useful, must be impartial, else it becomes the instrument of the very influence to be avoided, instead of a defense against it. Excessive partiality for one foreign nation and excessive dislike of another cause those whom they actuate to see danger only on one side, and serve to veil and even second the arts of influence on the other. Real patriots who may resist the intrigues of the favorite are liable to become suspected and odious, while its tools and dupes usurp the applause and confidence of the people to surrender their interests.

The great rule of conduct for us in regard to foreign nations is, in extending our commercial relations to have with them as little *political* connection as possible. So far as we have already formed engagements let them be fulfilled with perfect good faith. Here let us stop.

Europe has a set of primary interests which to us have none or a very remote relation. Hence she must be engaged in frequent controversies, the causes of which are essentially foreign to our concerns. Hence, therefore, it must be unwise in us to implicate ourselves by artificial ties in the ordinary vicissitudes of her politics or the ordinary combinations and collisions of her friendships or enmities.

Our detached and distant situation invites and enables us to pursue a different course. If we remain one people, under an efficient government, the period is not far off when we may defy material injury from external annoyance; when we may take such an attitude as will cause the neutrality we may at any time resolve upon to be scrupulously respected; when belligerent nations, under the impossibility of making acquisitions upon us, will not lightly hazard the giving us provocation; when we may choose peace or war, as our interest, guided by justice, shall counsel.

Why forego the advantages of so peculiar a situation? Why quit our own to stand upon foreign ground? Why, by interweaving our destiny with that of any part of Europe, entangle our peace and prosperity in the toils of European ambition, rivalship, interest, humor, or caprice?

It is our true policy to steer clear of permanent alliances with any portion of the foreign world, so far, I mean, as we are now at liberty to do it; for let me not be understood as capable of patronizing infidelity to existing engagements. I hold the maxim no less applicable to public than to private affairs that honesty is always the best policy. I repeat, therefore, let those engagements be observed in their genuine sense. But in my opinion it is unnecessary and would be unwise to extend them.

Taking care always to keep ourselves by suitable establishments on a respectable defensive posture, we may safely trust to temporary alliances for extraordinary emergencies.

Harmony, liberal intercourse with all nations are recommended by policy, humanity, and interest. But even our commercial policy should hold an equal and impartial hand, neither seeking nor granting exclusive favors or preferences; consulting the natural course of things; diffusing and diversifying by gentle means the streams of commerce, but forcing nothing; establishing with powers so disposed, in order to give trade a stable course, to define the rights of our merchants, and to enable the Government to support them, conventional rules of intercourse, the best that present circumstances and mutual opinion will permit, but temporary and liable to be from time to time abandoned or varied as experience and circumstances shall dictate; constantly keeping in view that it is folly in one nation to look for disinterested favors from another; that it must pay with a portion of its independence for whatever it may accept under that character; that by such acceptance it may place itself in the condition of having given equivalents for nominal favors, and yet of being reproached with ingratitude for not giving more. There can be no greater error than to expect or calculate upon real favors from nation to nation. It is an illusion which experience must cure, which a just pride ought to discard. . . .

READINGS

1. A Second Declaration of Independence

Professor Samuel F. Bemis challenges the older interpretation of the Address as intended primarily for future generations. His article describes the problems presented by the 1778 French Alliance and depicts the interference of French diplomats in American domestic politics. In sharp reaction to Jay's Treaty, which was viewed as a virtual alliance of the United States with hated England, the French ministers sought to defeat the Federalists and to ensure a Jeffersonian victory in the 1796 presidential election. It was understandable, then, that President Washington came to view the French Alliance as a dangerous entanglement and sought to warn his countrymen against permanent alliances in the future.

Washington's Farewell Address: A Foreign Policy of Independence

SAMUEL F. BEMIS

The Farewell Address is often thought of as an expression of abstract ideas of policy looking toward the future, but with little reference to the events of 1796. Its fundamental ideas were, on the contrary, suggested by experience, and very recent and painful experience. To comprehend Washington's point of view and feel the weight of his advice, it is necessary to consider the historical setting, and, for that, to go back to the outbreak of a general European war in February and March, 1793.

In the desperate conflict with the allied monarchies of the First Coalition the French Republic expected to find a valuable counterweight in the independent United States, separated from Great Britain by French

Samuel Flagg Bemis, "Washington's Farewell Address: A Foreign Policy of Independence," *American Historical Review*, XXXIX (1934), 250–268. Reprinted with permission.

diplomacy and arms in the previous war. Thoroughly conscious of the naval impotence of the new American nation, France had preferred not to invoke the *casus fœderis* of the treaty of alliance of 1778—the defense of the French West India Islands. A neutral United States promised greater advantages: (1) as a possible transatlantic base of operations against enemy colonies and commerce, (2) as the largest remaining neutral supply of provisions and naval stores, commodities that perhaps might be passed through the British navy under cover of the neutral flag. To finance both of these objects there was the gradually maturing American debt.

President Washington's proclamation of neutrality and the refusal of his government to lend itself to Genêt's projects soon showed France that her ally did not intend to involve itself in the European war by becoming such a base of belligerent naval and military operations. France perforce acquiesced in that decision, being still unwilling to invoke the letter of the alliance. This was because the actual belligerency of the United States which had no navy was worth nothing in itself and had the really great disadvantage of making American shipping immediately liable to capture and confiscation as enemy property. The neutrality of the United States, even though it could not serve as a base for such projects as Genêt attempted, was far more serviceable than American military assistance. The principal object of France was to secure from neutral America provisions for her beleaguered homeland and colonies, imported in American ships under protection of the principles of the commercial treaty of 1778: free ships free goods; provisions and naval stores not contraband; neutral right to trade in non-contraband goods to and between unblockaded enemy ports.

This Franco-American treaty did not bind France's enemy, Great Britain, the principal maritime belligerent. The British had never admitted these "novel" principles. They considered them as exceptional articles in particular treaties binding only between the signatory parties. When hostilities commenced in 1793 Great Britain began seizing enemy property right and left wherever it could be found outside neutral territorial waters, whether in enemy or neutral bottoms. British prize courts under orders in council began to apply the Rule of 1756, itself an innovation as late as the Seven Years' War. Secretary of State Thomas Jefferson protested in the name of the United States against this practice, which was contrary to the articles written into the Franco-American treaty and all the other European treaties of the United States. But Great Britain was not bound by those treaties. The United States was powerless to challenge the British navy. American credit, newly established, depended primarily on tariff revenue, and tariff revenue depended principally on imports from Great Britain. The collapse of credit at this time would have meant the collapse of the newly established nationality of the United States. Rather than go to war with Great Britain President Washington took Alexander Hamilton's advice and ratified Jay's Treaty with England which acquiesced in British naval practice for the next twelve years, in effect for the duration of the war. That treaty did not violate the treaties of the United States with France. It recognized a condition which already existed, namely, that the United States could not compel Great Britain to observe the terms of the Franco-American treaty. In 1793 the other maritime powers, which in the War for American Independence had followed principles similar to those of the Franco-American treaty, made treaties with Great Britain agreeing to harass the commerce of France in every possible way. These powers included the old Armed Neutrals of 1780, except Sweden and Denmark. A group of ardent, hateful enemies ringed France about by land and sea to close her frontiers, to sweep her commerce from the seas, to take her colonies from her, and to deprive her of naval supplies and of foodstuffs. The neutral United States, the ally of yesteryear, which France herself had brought into the world, stood aloof and acquiesced in this British naval-diplomatic system of strangulation. Thus were frustrated the advantages of neutral carriage which France had relied on from the American treaty of amity and commerce of 1778.

This situation was aggravated in the eyes of French statesmen by Jay's Treaty. If in the face of that document and of British practice the French were still to adhere to the terms of the American treaty, they would have to stand quietly by and watch British cruisers take French property from neutral American ships, confiscate American-owned naval stores as contraband when *en route* in American vessels to France, and preëmpt (as was the British practice) foodstuffs under similar conditions. Deprived thus by belligerent action of naval stores, foodstuffs, and of the advantages of neutral carriage they would find themselves obliged to abstain from following the British practice; they would have to watch these same goods go unchallenged by French warships into British harbors to feed and strengthen the might of the enemy.

It is not difficult to understand that this seemed unfair to France, and that Jay's Treaty seemed an outrageous, even a treacherous document, made by an ungrateful nation. But one would be more ready to sympathize with France if her own hands were clean. We must remember that when John Jay signed his famous treaty with Lord Grenville on November 19, 1794, France herself was pursuing and had been pursuing, off and on, since May 9, 1793, a maritime policy of retaliation in practice identical with that of Great Britain in the treatment of neutral shipping, and had been applying it to American ships and cargoes, and that notwithstanding her obligations under her treaty with the United States. As in later European wars (1803–1812, and 1914–1917) the force of these belligerent retaliations fell heavily on the neutral United States and developed grave diplomatic problems. Unlike the later wars, in this case the United States was protected by the paper and ink of a treaty against such practice on the part of one belligerent. Nevertheless, French spoliations on American shipping rivaled those of Great Britain. French privateers and naval vessels also vied with the British in violence and outrages against neutral crews and passengers.

The French diplomatic commission, headed by Joseph Fauchet, which in 1794 had succeeded the ruined Genêt in Philadelphia, did not even pretend to reconcile French maritime policy with the obligations of the treaty of commerce of 1778. Nevertheless it claimed for France all the articles of the treaty which were of advantage to her, and requested benevolent interpretations of them. The committee of public safety, in drawing up instructions for these commissioners, anticipated that there would be objections in the United States to the retaliatory French decrees. Admitting deviations from the treaty it became the task of the commissioners to extenuate French policy on the ground of altered circumstances.

Washington and his advisers had foreseen the possible further effect on France of the intended treaty between the United States and Great Britain when John Jay, the Federalist, pro-British diplomatist departed on his famous mission to London. To mask this mission they sent to France the pro-French Republican senator from Virginia, James Monroe, an old opponent of Jay's diplomacy since 1786, who considered Jay's mission as mischievous and in the Senate voted against his confirmation. Monroe never saw Jay's instructions, possibly was not aware of their real scope.

Like an apostle of the rights of man, Monroe set to work to persuade the French government to observe the treaty of amity and commerce of 1778. The restrictions on private trade in French harbors, the embargoes, the delays in payment for purchased cargoes, had already so jeopardized the American provision supply that the Convention admitted the force of the American remonstrances on every point except free ships free goods. The envoy now argued for the full and entire enforcement of the articles of the treaty. He appealed to old friendship and present interest. He contended that it would be good policy for France to repeal her obnoxious decrees before Great Britain should repeal hers. If she did so, it would combine all America in condemnation of the conduct of the British; if she did not, any later repeal would appear merely to be forced by her enemy. At just this time news arrived of the setting aside, by an order in council of August 6, 1794, of the British provision order of June 8, 1793—this had been a means in London of easing the English negotiations with Jay. It reënforced Monroe's argument in Paris. The French law of May 9, 1793, had made the duration of the "retaliatory" maritime measures contingent upon the repeal by the enemy of his illegal procedure. The Convention now (January 2, 1795) availed itself of this provision to yield to the importunities of the ingratiating James Monroe. "As a grand act of honesty and justice," it wiped out at one stroke all the offensive decrees and enjoined the strict observance of the provisions of the treaty of 1778. Orders were immediately given for the adjudication of all claims arising out of violations of that treaty.

Monroe's triumph was short-lived. Before anything very effective could actually be done about the relief of the claimants the significance of Jay's Treaty began to be suspected in Paris. In August, 1795, the text arrived from Philadelphia. It completely undid Monroe's successes. In 1796 Washington recalled the unhappy minister for not having defended with sufficient vigor the new English treaty. In truth Monroe had repeated to the French government the arguments and defenses sent to him by Secretaries of State Randolph and Pickering. They read well, but one may doubt that his heart was in his words. He thought Jay's Treaty a shameful document. There is evidence suggesting that he had confidential conversations with the French Revolutionary leaders about "the real dispositions of his countrymen," conversations which he did not reveal to his own government. He kept up an intimate correspondence with Madison, and other friends of Jefferson, who opposed Jay's Treaty and favored a pro-French policy. He certainly led the French government to believe that any treaty of amity between the United States and Great Britain would never be ratified. When it was known that a treaty had been signed, Monroe repeated this assurance. When Jay's Treaty went through Congress he tried rather lamely to explain its success, and still argued that it would be good policy for the French Republic to observe loyally the terms of its American treaties; the example of that loyalty and the contrasting attitude of the British government would win the good will of the American *people,* from whose eyes the scales of British deception must eventually fall. He led them in Paris to believe that the people would overthrow the administration of President Washington as a result of the treaty, that better things might be expected after the election of 1796. This supposition was reënforced by advice from the French diplomatic representative in the United States, Fauchet, and his successor Adet, and by Americans in Paris like Monroe's friend, Tom Paine.

After Jay's departure from New York Fauchet had become increasingly nervous about the object of the new mission. He sent one of his colleagues to Paris to warn the committee of public safety that something was in the air, and to say that the other two members of the commission, La Forest and Petry, could not be trusted because they hobnobbed with Alexander Hamilton and other Federalists. When news of the signature of the treaty and rumors of its contents began to leak out, the French minister became very much exasperated. His notes of protest against fancied violations of neutral obligations under the treaty of 1778 took on a more rasping tone, full of intimations of American disloyalty. Fauchet tried by fair means and foul, but in vain, to block the ratification of the treaty by the Senate. He hoped with Secretary Randolph that the President might not sign the ratification, even though the Senate had so advised and consented. His successor Adet, encouraged by the widespread popular protests, labored with the House of Representatives to refuse the appropriations necessary to carry it into effect. When the treaty passed unscathed through the House, Adet's last hope was that the people would overthrow the administration of President Washington in the forthcoming election of 1796. Through the agency of organs of the Republican press which he manipulated and inspired to the extent of his limited financial resources, and by means of the democratic societies which had arisen at the wave of Genêt's wand to applaud the French Revolution, the French minister was working with might and main to that end. He did not know, of course, of the President's determination, long since fixed and presently to be announced, to refuse a third term.

In Paris, American affairs had received less attention than they merited. Before the reorganization of the French government under the constitution of the Year III, (1795) the rapidly changing administration of the foreign office failed to give methodical attention. French diplomatists at Philadelphia complained bitterly that their dispatches went unanswered. For months they waited without instructions. None of them had been told what to do about Jay's Treaty. Fauchet, and his successor Adet, had acted on their own responsibility in their protests against that instrument. The new Directory put the conduct of foreign affairs on a more businesslike basis, under a single minister, Charles Delacroix. He straightway brought in a report concerning the United States. Washington must go, he said. "A friend of France must succeed him in that eminent office." He continued:

> We must raise up the people and at the same time conceal the lever by which we do so . . . I propose to the Executive Directory to authorize me to send orders and instructions to our minister plenipotentiary at Philadelphia to use all the means in his power in the United States to bring about the right kind of revolution (*l'heureuse Révolution*) and Washington's replacement, which, assuring to the Americans their independence, will break off treaties [*sic*] made with England and maintain those which unite them to the French Republic.

As in the case of the Netherlands at that time, France and French agents regarded that political party in the United States which was most useful to their purposes as the "patriot" party. Jefferson, Madison, Monroe, Robert R. Livingston, Senator Tazewell of Virginia, Governor Clinton of New York, and Governor Mifflin of Pennsylvania were patriots. Washington, Hamilton, Jay, Rufus King, and John Adams were aristocrats unfriendly to real liberty. The French foreign office looked on the United States as "the Holland of the New World." It hoped for and expected a popular revolution there, on French models, such as did take place in Holland in 1795, to overturn the existing régime of ordered liberty, to cast off the formidable ascendency of President Washington and his Federalist advisers who themselves were esteemed to be beyond the reach of French influence and purpose.

At first the Directory decided on a more positive step to offset Jay's Treaty: to send a special envoy extraordinary to Philadelphia to recall Adet and to announce the end of the Franco-American treaties and then himself to withdraw. Monroe confidentially urged Delacroix against such action: it would please the enemies of both countries. "Left to ourselves," he hinted, "everything will I think be satisfactorily arranged and *perhaps in the course of the present year:* and it is always more grateful to make such arrangements ourselves than to be pressed to it."

Delacroix and the Directory took the advice of President Washington's minister to await the President's overthrow. They blamed Washington, Hamilton, and the Federalist Senate, in short the elected government of the people of the United States, against which, according to French agents and correspondents (including Americans in Paris), the people were now in an uproar, from Boston to Savannah. Well they knew that Monroe's hint referred to the approaching presidential election of 1796.

of the document, and his previous expression of some of the ideas, we may be sure that in the final text the two men were thinking together in absolute unison. The Address was as directly pointed to the diplomatic problems of the time of the French Revolution as were Woodrow Wilson's Fourteen Points to the intricate diplomacy of the World War. President Wilson and Colonel House worked no more intimately together on that document in 1918, drafting and redrafting its clauses, than did President Washington and Colonel Hamilton in 1796, composing and recomposing the paragraphs of the Farewell Address.

The immortal document, ever since a polestar of American foreign policy, represented the crystallization of the experience of remarkably clear-headed men with foreign affairs since the Declaration of Independence. It was given forthwith to the public in a newspaper. It spoke directly to the great and simple audience of the American people. "The name of AMERICAN," it said to them, putting the word into bold type, "which belongs to you in your national capacity, must always exalt the just pride of Patriotism, more than any appelation derived from local discriminations."

We must keep in mind the involvement of the French alliance in American diplomacy and domestic politics as we read the Farewell Address, even as the authors of the document had that constantly before them.

It began thus with an appeal to support the *National Union*. The orthodox phrase Federal Union does not occur in the document, a very significant omission. It continued with a counsel against the practice of party politics, lest the new nation be undermined by internal dissension assisted by foreign intrigue. The first President and his adviser Alexander Hamilton believed that, with the system of checks and balances in the new government, party politics was unnecessary for the preservation of ordered liberty. The rise of an opposition they identified with a faction opposed not only to the policies of the administration but to the new national government itself. They connected this faction with the French government and its agents.

Turning to the subject of foreign affairs, the Address admonished his fellow citizens to steer clear of European alliances and wars. It justified American neutrality whilst the nation, assisted by the advantages of so peculiar a situation, might grow strong enough to command its own fortune. In these words and these counsels the authors of the Address had continually before them the apparition of the life-giving, but the entangling French alliance, and the distant scene of the great wars engulfing Europe. They had behind them the problems solved by Jay's Treaty and by Pinckney's Treaty, thanks to the occupation of Britain and Spain with those troubles in Europe.

The immediate purpose of the Address was to strike a powerful blow against French intermeddling in American affairs. After the victory of Jay's Treaty in the House of Representatives it had been Adet's advice, and this was also recommended by the returned Fauchet, that some strong and positive action ought to be taken to make the American ally more amenable to French interests. The people, both of those agents had reported—and reported most voluminously—were in favor of France and opposed to their government, but if France did not call Washington's government to terms, and thus support the action of the "good" people to overthrow it, nothing could be hoped from them. Adet advocated that the French Republic proceed to treat American ships precisely as the United States government allowed its flag to be treated by Great Britain, that is, according to the principles of Jay's Treaty. This was, indeed, what France had been doing up to January 3, 1795, when Monroe secured from the Convention the full and entire recognition of the treaty of 1778. But that "grand act of honesty and justice" had not been enforced since the nature of Jay's Treaty had become suspected in France. Nor was it ever to be. It was to be the United States government itself which was finally to pay—throughout a century of litigation—most of the damages to its citizens wrought by the French spoliations in this war.

Jay's Treaty at last having gone into effect, the French Directory prepared its denunciation of the treachery of Washington's government. As a warning to the American people of worse things to follow if President Washington were continued in office it decided to suspend Adet's functions, and with them formal diplomatic relations with the United States. Characterizing Jay's Treaty as equivalent to an alliance between France's principal enemy and her old, ungrateful ally, it proceeded to invoke against American shipping, as a reprisal for that perfidious treaty, the maritime principles of that document itself. If Jefferson should be elected the plan was to restore relations on the old basis, hoping that a new treaty with France might undo Jay's.

To his great satisfaction Adet was able to communicate to the United States government, on October 27, 1796, the text of a decree of the Directory announcing that "All neutral or allied Powers shall, without delay, be notified that the flag of the French republic will treat neutral vessels, either as to confiscation, as to searches, or capture, in the same manner as they shall suffer the English to treat them."

A few weeks later (November 15) he announced the definite suspension of his functions, not, indeed, to indicate a formal rupture between the United States and France, "but as a mark of just discontent, which is to last until the government of the United States returns to sentiments, and to measures, more conformable to the interests of the alliance, and the sworn friendship of the two nations."

It was now the eve of the presidential election of 1796. The several states were choosing their electors. They still had to meet and cast their votes. The precedent had not yet become set which allows the electors no canvass or deliberation among themselves. The French move was studiously calculated to influence the electors to choose Jefferson instead of John Adams. With this in mind, according to his instructions, Adet accompanied his announcement of suspension of his functions with a long and *ex-parte* review (with documents) of the whole quarrel between France and the United States over American neutrality. He included a passionate indictment of Jay's Treaty, all under cover of a fervid manifesto to the American people. A summary in English of the contents of this note appeared in the newspapers before the translation of the French original could be prepared in the Department of State. "Let your Government return to itself," wrote Adet, addressing the people rather than the government to which his note was delivered, "and you will still find in Frenchmen faithful friends and generous allies."

To that uncompromising Federalist, Timothy Pickering, old soldier, negotiator of Indian treaties, professional and capable officeholder, and general utility man in Washington's cabinet, now fell the task of defending the foreign policy laid down in the Farewell Address. Four others had declined the proffered appointment of Secretary of State, with its meager emolument, before he took it. Though Pickering had no special training for the office, he was a facile penman and a sharp-minded debater. These were the qualifications principally in demand from 1795 to 1800.

Space only forbids us to describe and to analyze Pickering's defense of American neutrality, of Jay's Treaty with England, in short of the foreign policy of George Washington. We may be sure that it was inspired by Alexander Hamilton, the man who inspired Jay's Treaty, and who phrased the Farewell Address. The remarkable public disputation took the form of instructions to Charles C. Pinckney, dated January 16, 1797, who had already sailed to France as successor to the recalled Monroe; but its real purpose, as shown by its immediate release to the press on January 19, 1797, was to serve as a counter-manifesto to Adet's passionate attacks on the administration and his undercover efforts to secure the election of Thomas Jefferson rather than John Adams, the champion of Washington's policies. The historian to-day who is privileged to read the archives of France and of the United States can have no serious quarrel with Pickering's eloquent rebuttal of French charges of American ingratitude directed against Washington's government, nor with his blunt conclusion after a long review that France owed fully as much to the United States as the United States to France in the way of service rendered. The day for finesse had passed. It was time that some one put the truth in this way to the American people, at a moment when foreign diplomacy was again trying to reach over the heads of their government to whip them into European complications. Even then in 1795 and 1796 while French diplomatists were accusing the United States of ingratitude and treachery, they themselves were plotting to reëstablish control and tutelage over the American republic by getting Louisiana and West Florida back from Spain, allying France with the southwestern Indians, and tempting the allegiance to the Union of the new western states, to build up thereby a new colonial empire that would be the preponderant power in the New World.

The instructions to C. C. Pinckney, embodying these arguments, rank with Jefferson's rejoinder to Hammond of 1792, with John Quincy Adams's defense of General Jackson's execution of Arbuthnot and Ambrister in 1818, and with Lansing's reply to Austria in 1915 on the question of contraband, as one of the greatest defensive documents in the diplomatic history of the United States. Pickering's paper clinched the case for President Washington's foreign policy.

Before the document was printed the presidential electors had elected John Adams President by a majority of one vote and margin of three votes over Thomas Jefferson, who became Vice President according to the original constitutional provision. Washington's successor fully recognized that the significance of his election lay in the question whether the American people were to govern themselves or be governed by foreign nations. As President he took over Washington's policies, and, to his later vexation, his entire cabinet.

We cannot conclude that Pickering's instructions to Pinckney decided the election. It had been won already. The dispatch was published after the votes of the electors had been announced on the first Wednesday in January, but before they were formally counted on the first Wednesday in February. The document was rather an appeal to the people to support the foreign policy of Washington—and of Hamilton—and an argument to open the door to an escape from the French alliance, by proving, as Hamilton suggested, that the United States had maintained good faith with its engagements; that if the conduct of the other party released it, the release should not be refused, so far as possible without compromising peace. "This idea is very important," Hamilton wrote to Wolcott, of course for Pickering's benefit.

Despite the high hopes which France had placed on Jefferson's election, both John Adams and his close contestant, the new Vice President, Thomas Jefferson, were equally good Americans (albeit of different political philosophy), and, incidentally, almost equally good friends of France. Nor were they unfriendly to each other. Jefferson had gone so far as to authorize his friend Madison to advise electors, in case of a tie, to vote for Adams as a statesman of senior claims to the presidency. Adet came to sense this relationship before he left. He wrote:

> Mr. Jefferson likes us because he detests England; he seeks to draw near to us because he fears us less than England; but tomorrow he might change his opinion about us if England should cease to inspire his fear. Although Jefferson is the friend of liberty and of science, although he is an admirer of the efforts we have made to cast off our shackles and to clear away the cloud of ignorance which weighs down the human race, Jefferson, I say, is an American, and as such, he cannot sincerely be our friend. An American is the born enemy of all the peoples of Europe.

Such was the historical setting of the famous Farewell Address. Such were the reasons for its pronouncement in 1796, so different a pronouncement from what it would have been if given to the people in 1792. Such was its victory over foreign intrigue within our own country. It did not disown the French alliance, but it taught a patronizing ally that we were an independent and a sovereign nation, and that the French Republic could not use in America the tool that had been so successful with the border satellite states in Europe, the lever of a political opposition to overthrow any government that stood in the way of French policy, purpose, and interest. In Washington's time avoidance of foreign alliances and of foreign entanglement was a question of independence and national sovereignty. What we have generally construed as a policy of "isolation" we ought really to interpret as a policy of vigilant defense and maintenance of sovereign national independence against foreign meddling in our own intimate domestic concerns.

2. *A Hamiltonian-Inspired Campaign Document*

Alexander DeConde, whose writings range from the Washington era to Herbert Hoover's Latin American policies, has also evaluated the Farewell Address in terms of the contemporary political context. Contrary to others, however, he views Hamilton as the directing mind behind most Washington policies, determined to dissolve the French connection and draw closer to Britain. Consulted by the retiring President, Hamilton drafted a farewell message which in effect bitterly scored the opposition Jeffersonians and the French Alliance. The Farewell Address was a partisan campaign document intended to promote a Federalist victory in the next presidential election.

Washington's Farewell, the French Alliance, and the Election of 1796

ALEXANDER DECONDE

When in 1789 George Washington became the nation's first president the French alliance was the cornerstone of American foreign policy. It largely had made possible American independence and had established American foreign policy orientation. At the end of Washington's second term, in fact as he prepared his farewell to public life, the life-giving alliance was practically dead and the United States was virtually at war with France. Why, in eight formative years, did such a drastic reversal in foreign policy take place? A full answer to this question would be long and complex; yet by looking closely at the election of 1796 and by reviewing the Farewell Address in its political context we may find a partial answer as to how the alliance received its mortal wound. We may also find additional reason for revising the traditional interpretation of the Farewell Address as a wise, timeless, and unbiased warning to the nation.

The blow from which the alliance never recovered was the Jay Treaty of 1794. While this Federalist-negotiated treaty averted a war with England, a war which Federalists feared, the major objectives which John Jay had been expected to win were not realized. Because it failed to obtain specific concessions on impressments, ship seizures, and Indian raids on the frontier, the treaty infuriated Republicans and others who still nurtured a Revolution-bred hatred of England. At the same time it blighted Franco-American relations. Successive French revolutionary governments were convinced that the Jay Treaty violated the Franco-

Alexander DeConde, "Washington's Farewell, the French Alliance, and the Election of 1796," *Mississippi Valley Historical Review*, XLIII (1956–57), 641–658. Reprinted with permission.

American treaties of 1778 and that the American government had accepted it against the will of an overwhelming public sentiment. Believing that the bulk of the American people were pro-French even though Washington's Federalist government was pro-English, the French sought to arouse their allies, the American people, to their true interest. This true interest was alliance with France and disassociation with England, America's natural enemy and France's major antagonist in war since February, 1793.

To arouse the American people in defense of the 1778 alliance the French Directory in June, 1795, sent to the United States a new minister, a young man in his early thirties, Pierre Auguste Adet. To the French the Jay Treaty created an intimate alliance between the United States and France's worst enemy. In Adet's instructions, therefore, the idea that the treaty violated the French alliance stood out as the foremost grievance against the Washington administration.

Despite French anger, and despite Adet's attempts to prevent ratification, the Senate approved the Jay Treaty eleven days after Adet had landed in Philadelphia. Two months later, while Adet continued his efforts to kill it, Washington ratified the treaty. England accepted the ratified treaty and in April, 1796, after a long, last-ditch battle in which Adet used all the influence he could muster against the treaty, the House of Representatives voted funds to implement it. To Adet as to other Frenchmen this meant the end of the 1778 alliance and another triumph for England and English gold.

Not knowing that Washington already had decided to retire from the presidency, Adet now saw the overthrow of Washington and his Federalist administration as the only salvation for the 1778 alliance. Adet and the French Directory viewed the Washington administration as the captive of English policy; to save the alliance it had to be replaced by a pro-French Republican administration. Charles Delacroix, French foreign minister, advocated inciting an uprising against Washington to break the Jay Treaty and to invigorate the alliance. Thomas Jefferson, he believed, would replace Washington and thus France would command the influence in the United States which she deserved. Prospects for the defeat of Washington were good, he believed, since the President, once the idol of the American people, had become to some an object of scorn and even hatred as the result of the Jay Treaty; already the journals attacked him, his principles, and his conduct.

Taking into account what it conceived to be the temper of American popular opinion, and with the objective of destroying English influence in the United States and salvaging the 1778 alliance, the French government intervened actively in the presidential election of 1796. Through Adet and other French officials in the United States the Directory openly supported the Republican party and wherever possible attacked the Federalist party. French intervention in the election became, therefore, one of the main issues in the campaign of 1796. The fate of the alliance hung on the outcome of the election.

The decision of the Directory to intervene in the 1796 election, while a decisive factor, contributed but one element to the complex politics of the election. Domestic issues and the Jay Treaty itself contributed others. Final acceptance of the treaty plunged Franco-American relations to their lowest depths since independence and marked a great political triumph for Federalists. Yet to Republicans all hope of ultimately defeating the treaty did not appear lost. Seeing the extent of the Jay Treaty's unpopularity, Republican leaders believed that it would make an excellent campaign issue in the 1796 election as an unrivaled party rallying point for national sentiment. Thomas Jefferson, James Madison, and other party leaders believed that popular opinion remained still largely pro-French and anti-British. Being politicians they reacted logically. Their party had ready-made national issues; they had only to exploit them properly and victory would be theirs. Republicans, consequently, carried over into the election of 1796 their campaign against the Jay Treaty and the pro-British "system" of Alexander Hamilton.

Granted the logic and appeal of the Republican campaign plan, a towering obstacle—the person and prestige of George Washington—stood in the way of success, as was clear to the French. So deep was the impression Washington had made on fellow Americans that to attack him would be to risk injuring the attacker. Twice he had been chosen president without a dissenting vote. Had he so desired he could undoubtedly have held office for a third term, for, as a foreign observer remarked, "there is a Magic in his name more powerful in this Country than the Abilities of any other man." No man, moreover, was better aware of this than Jefferson. "Republicanism," he advised, "must lie on it's [*sic*] oars, resign the vessel to it's pilot [Washington], and themselves to the course he thinks best for them."

Despite Washington's great political strength the situation in 1796 was far different from 1789 and 1792; Washington probably could have had a third term, but not by unanimous choice. In political battles over neutrality, the Jay Treaty, and other issues, he had divested himself of nonpartisanship. To Republicans and Francophiles the guise of being above party and of working for the welfare of the nation as a whole, in view of his intimate connections with his Federalist subordinates and his consistent practice of acting in accord with their principles, appeared the sheerest hypocrisy. In town and country some men now spat at the mention of his name, denounced him as a monocrat and an Anglomaniac, and prayed for his removal from office. Washington in 1796 had become a central figure in emerging party politics; he was a principal target for the violent personal politics of the time; and to the French he was the main barrier to reactivation of the 1778 alliance.

So bitter was feeling between English and French partisans that domestic issues drifted into relative insignificance. In their conviction that the Federalist administration did not truly represent the American people, the French were encouraged by pro-French partisans among Republicans who indicated that the Federalist government would topple if only France were to take a strong stand. As the election year of 1796 opened, Republicans intensified their attacks against the Federalist administration.

The Jay Treaty and the loud cry of aristocracy, monarchy, and plutocracy aroused deep popular emotions. Mutual hatred characterized the two large political segments of the American public.

With his government under fire on both domestic and foreign policy and with himself the target of unrestrained scurrility, Washington found the demands of his office increasingly difficult to endure. Publicly he maintained a dignified silence, but privately he revealed the strain. Even he had come to see that the myth of nonpartisanship was shattered, and that his concept of an administration above party and the tumult of politics had been illusory. Foreign relations had exploded the myth while serving as a catalyst in the formation of national political parties. This was an issue capable of transforming the opposing local alliances of Federalist and anti-Federalist into integrated national parties—an emotional foreign policy issue capable of capturing public imagination in a way which abstruse problems of finance could not.

Despite his increasing distaste for the office and the increasing speculation about his not wishing to be a candidate for a third term, the President remained silent as to future plans. Leaders of both political parties, however, had little doubt that he would not run. "He gave me intimations enough," asserted John Adams, "that his reign would be very short." Early in 1796, and even before, both parties had laid tentative plans which did not include Washington as a candidate.

The attacks on Washington grew increasingly bitter during the year. Opponents charged that he had betrayed a solemn pledge to France by destroying the French alliance. Personal attacks accused him of taking more salary than was allotted him. His mail was tampered with for political advantage, and forged letters of 1777 were refurbished and printed as genuine. Particularly cutting was Tom Paine's bitter attack from Paris, which city was the source, Federalists were convinced, of the anti-Washington campaign. Jefferson, too, had lost patience with the exalted role of Washington. The President, he wrote, like Samson had had his head "shorn by the harlot England."

Despite pressures to stay and ride out the storm, Washington disclosed in May, 1796, that he intended definitely to retire. If he had nurtured at all the desire to seek a third term it was killed by the acid criticism to which he had been subjected. The President decided not to seek a third term not only because he sought retirement in his old age but also because he was disgusted with the abuse from political opponents. "The true cause of the general's retiring," declared one of his staunchest supporters, "was . . . the *loss of popularity* which he had experienced, and the further loss which he apprehended from the rupture with France, which he looked upon as inevitable."

Once the decision to retire was made, Washington turned to Hamilton, as usual, for advice. When, he asked, would be the best time for publication of his farewell to the nation? Hamilton, with his eye on the coming election, advised that the public announcement be held off as long as possible. "The proper period now for your declaration," wrote Hamilton, "seems to be *Two months* before the time for the Meeting of the Electors.

This will be sufficient. The parties will in the meantime electioneer conditionally, that is to say, *if you decline;* for a serious opposition to you will I think hardly be risked."

Three months before the gathering of electors Washington announced to the nation his intention to retire. Although in 1792 he had planned a valedictory to the nation and James Madison had drafted one, the September, 1796, version, in which Hamilton's hand was prominent, became a piece of partisan politics directed specifically against Republicans and Francophiles who had made Washington's last years miserable. At the time, it was recognized for what it was: a political manifesto, a campaign document. The 1792 version, drawn up before popular passions had been stirred by war in Europe, did not, for example, stress politics nor did it touch on foreign affairs. In the 1796 version partisan politics and foreign affairs were central.

Washington's specific target in foreign affairs, heartily seconded by Hamilton, was the alliance with France. He struck at Adet's partisan activities, at French meddling in American politics (while passing over British meddling), and at the allegedly dangerous implications of the French alliance. Washington told Hamilton that had it not been for the status of "party disputes" and of foreign affairs he would not have considered it necessary to revise his valedictory. He was convinced that a warning to the nation was necessary to combat foreign (French) intrigue "in the internal concerns of our country." It is indeed easy "to foresee," he warned, "that it may involve us in disputes and finally in War, to fulfill political alliances." This was the crux of the matter; Washington believed that the French alliance was no longer an asset to the country.

Washington's valedictory trumpeted the Federalist answer to Republican accusations that the administration had sold the country to the British; it countered the anti-administration furor over the Jay Treaty; it was a justification and defense of his policies. As such it was designed and as such it became the opening blast in the presidential campaign, contrived to prevent the election of Thomas Jefferson. The Farewell laid the basis for Federalist strategy of using Washington's great prestige to appeal to patriotism, as against the evil of foreign machinations, to make "Federalist" and "patriot" synonyms in the minds of the electorate. Under the banner of patriotism the Farewell spearheaded the attack on the opposition party and on French diplomacy.

In the address Washington opened with the announcement that he would not be a candidate for a third term and then stressed the advantages of union and the evils of political parties. Having in mind, undoubtedly, the French Republic, he advised against "a passionate attachment of one Nation for another." Such "sympathy for the favourite nation," he warned, leads to wars and quarrels "without adequate inducement or justification." Then followed the oft-quoted "Great rule of conduct" that with foreign nations we should have "as little *political* connection as possible." While stressing fidelity to "already formed engagements," he announced that "'tis our true policy to steer clear of permanent Alliances with any portion of the foreign world." Washington deplored the growth of political opposition, chastised the public for its attachment to France, and concluded with a defense of his foreign policy, particularly his much criticized policy of neutrality which was based on the Proclamation of April 22, 1793. He called this the "index" to his plan or policy.

Although cloaked in phrases of universal or timeless application, the objectives of the address were practical, immediate, and partisan. Men often attempt to rationalize their partisan political views in pronouncements studded with timeless patriotic appeals; so it was with Washington and Hamilton. The valedictory bore directly on the coming election, on the French alliance, and on the status of Franco-American relations in general.

While expressed cogently and linked forever with Washington's name, the main ideas and foreign policy principles of the Farewell were not unique with either Hamilton or Washington. They were prevalent Federalist ideas on current foreign policy and politics, and can be found expressed in various ways in the polemical literature of the time. The concept of no entanglement with Europe, for instance, was a common one among Federalists and others. More often than not it was a universalized reaction against a specific annoyance—the French alliance. Stated as non-involvement with Europe an attack against the alliance had great psychological appeal. In time this specific meaning was lost and only the generalization remained.

As partisans had expected, Washington's words stoked an already hot political situation. "It will serve as a signal," exclaimed New England Federalist Fisher Ames, "like dropping a hat, for the party racers to start." The Farewell was indeed soon under partisan attack. Washington's advice for the future, taunted William Duane, "is but a defence for the past." Referring to the warning against "permanent alliances," he exclaimed, "this extraordinary advice is fully exemplified in your departure from the spirit and principle of the treaty with France, which was declared to be permanent, and exhibits this very infidelity you reprobate in a most striking and lamentable light." The President had not, Duane continued, "adhered to that rigid and neutral justice which you profess—every concession to Britain in prejudice of France was a deviation from neutrality." Much of the evil which Washington attributed to faction, he claimed, came from the Federalist party. "Your examples of party influence are uniformly drawn from occasions wherein your personal opinions, your pride and passions, have been involved." As to Washington's advice to steer clear of permanent alliances, why, critics asked, was it unwise to extend the nation's political engagements? Was not the Jay Treaty a political connection, practically an alliance with England?

To James Madison—who earlier had feared that under Hamilton's influence the address would become a campaign document—the valedictory confirmed his assumptions; it was all politics. Under the complete influence of the British faction, Madison wrote, Washington obviously sought to destroy the French alliance. "It has been known," he continued, "that every channel has been latterly opened that could convey to his mind a rancor against that country [France] and suspicion of all who are thought to sympathize with its revolution and who support the policy of extending our commerce and in general of standing well with it. But it was not easy to suppose his mind wrought up to the tone that could dictate or rather adopt some parts of the performance."

Minister Adet believed wrongly that the address would arouse the indignation of pro-French "patriots" and would not have the effect on the people that the British faction hoped it would. He consequently plunged into the campaign to see to it that the address would not have its intended effect. Looking upon John Adams as an enemy of France and a friend of England, he electioneered brazenly for Jefferson. The future conduct of France toward America, he made clear to Americans, would be governed by the election's outcome.

Beginning at the end of October and timing himself carefully, Adet began publication of a series of public manifestoes designed to influence the electorate. He conjured up the prospect of war with France, stressing that Jefferson's election would eliminate such a possibility. With the Quakers of Pennsylvania, Federalists lamented, Adet's strategy of fear worked. Fearing a Federalist-sponsored war against France, Quakers cast their votes for Republicans. "French influence never appeared so open and unmasked as at this city [Philadelphia] election," cried William Loughton Smith, Hamilton's congressional mouthpiece. "French flags, french cockades were displayed by the Jefferson party and there is no doubt that french money was not spared. . . . In short there never was so barefaced and disgraceful an interference of a foreign power in any free country."

Adet's procedure was to write an official note to the Secretary of State and then to send a copy for publication to Benjamin Bache's Philadelphia *Aurora*. In his note of October 27, for example, he protested against American foreign policy and appealed to the people to renew their friendship with France by disavowing the Jay Treaty and honoring the French alliance. A few days later (November 5) the pages of the *Aurora* carried Adet's second manifesto, dubbed by Federalists the "cockade proclamation." In the name of the Directory it called on all Frenchmen in the United States—in the land of an ally—to mount the tricolored cockade, symbol of liberty. Those who did not so give public evidence of their support of the French Republic were to be denied the services of French consuls and the protection of the French flag. Immediately the tricolored cockade blossomed in the streets. Americans as well as Frenchmen wore it as a badge of devotion to the French cause. It became, in short, a symbol of republicanism.

Ten days later Adet followed the "cockade proclamation" with his last and most florid note, which he again sent simultaneously to the Secretary of State and to Bache's *Aurora*. In it he announced that as a result of the Jay Treaty his function as minister had been suspended and that he was returning to France. Adet had timed his announcement so that it might have a maximum political influence, particularly on the electors who were soon to meet to choose Washington's successor.

Adet's notes and Secretary of State Timothy Pickering's replies were used as campaign ammunition by both sides. Federalists, of course, were furious. They denounced Adet's pronouncements for what they were—brazen electioneering maneuvers by a foreign agent. John Adams, against whom the last note was directed, found "it an instrument well calculated to reconcile me to private life. It will purify me from all envy of Mr. Jefferson, or Mr. Pinckney, or Mr. Burr, or Mr. any body who may be chosen President or Vice President." William Cobbett, violent Francophobe and anti-Jeffersonian, published Adet's note under the title of *The Gros Mousqueton Diplomatique; or Diplomatic Blunderbuss.* He ran with it, of course, an adverse commentary.

Friends of France, according to Adet, were delighted. Republican leaders were willing and even eager to use the issue of the French alliance to gain votes. But, contrary to Adet's opinion, they were not happy with the French minister's personal interference. Madison, for instance, maintained that Adet's note announcing his return to France worked "all the evil with which it is pregnant." Its indiscretions, he added, gave comfort to Federalists who had the "impudence" to point out that it was "an electioneering maneuver," and that "the French government had been led into it by the opponents of the British treaty."

Adet did not realize that his activities worked mainly to injure the cause he sought to aid. French popularity, according to competent observers, decreased as a result. Disgusted by Adet's conduct, Washington drew even closer to the British. One piqued New England writer went so far as to declare that since Adet's electioneering on behalf of Jefferson "there is not an elector on this side of the Delaware that would not be sooner shot than vote for him." And Philip Key maintained that Adet's meddling "irretrievably diminished that good will felt for his Government & the people of France by most people here."

Unaware of any adverse reaction, Adet and his intimates believed that his actions and the Directory's measures would influence the presidential electors decisively in favor of Jefferson. What Adet and the Directory had not taken into account was that invariably when a foreign diplomat takes sides openly in the domestic politics of the nation to which he is accredited he makes the party leader he seeks to aid appear to be the pawn of a foreign government. Such a charge, whether or not true, gives the opposition the opportunity of patriotically denouncing foreign interference and of posing as the defender of national honor against foreign subversives. So it was with the Adet case. His activities seemed to confirm the very warnings of foreign interference that were stressed in Washington's Farewell Address.

Sensing the opportunity, Federalists attacked the French alliance, denounced French domestic interference, and pitted the patriotism of Washington and Adams against the Jacobin-tainted Republican campaign. Voters were importuned to beware of foreign influence; to "decide between the address of the President and the [French]"; to follow Washington's counsel. Adet and the Directory, they were told, wished to draw the nation into war and to sever the Western from the Atlantic states. No doubt clouded the Federalist mind; the Union was in danger.

Federalist warnings, persistent though they were, did not stop French interference in American politics; nor did the interference end with the choosing of electors in November. Few of the electors were pledged to a specific candidate, so the campaign continued with increasing tumult until December 7, when the electors cast their ballots. Adet, having suspended his diplomatic functions, remained in Philadelphia to continue his anti-administration campaign. He and the Republicans hammered at similar themes, stressing that if Adams were elected the errors of the Washington administration would be continued, since Adams was committed to Washington's tragic policies; and that such policies would lead to war with France.

Candidate Adams, on the other hand, believed that only time would tell whether "the French Directory have only been drawn in to favor the election of a favorite, or whether in their trances and delirium of victory they think to terrify America, or whether in their sallies they may not venture on hostilities." He advised that under the circumstances "Americans must be cool and steady if they can."

But Americans were not cool and steady. In newspapers and elsewhere they debated the French alliance, the mounting crisis with France, and the possibility of war. Hamilton, as was his practice in time of crisis, wrote articles for the press to reply to Adet's manifestoes, to defend administration foreign policy, and to attack the French alliance. Another prominent Federalist, Noah Webster, editor of the *American Minerva*, wrote a series of articles in which he also attacked the alliance. His articles were reprinted and widely circulated. In the Federalist press, in fact, attacks on the alliance now became common. Webster in his articles stressed that France had equated the term ally with that of vassal; "an *open* enemy," he declared, "is less dangerous than an *insidious friend.*" Although the British, too, had injured the United States, Webster maintained that the American connection with Great Britain was stronger than the French alliance because "our connection with her is solely *an alliance of interest.* This is the true basis of all national connections. We are therefore in no danger from Great Britain."

In the first week of February, 1797, the American people finally learned the results of the election. Although the Federalist victory was narrow, it was enough to sink French hopes for a revived alliance. By "three votes" John Adams, who wisely had perceived that he was "not enough of an Englishman, nor little enough of a Frenchman, for some people," was elected second president of the United States.

Jefferson, however, captured the second highest electoral total and became vice-president. America's first contested presidential election therefore, although a clear-cut Federalist victory, gave some comfort to Republicans and struck fear into Federalist ranks. But Republican strength had not been sufficient to overturn the government and hence to reverse the course of Franco-American relations. To staunch Hamiltonian Federalists this aspect of the election was indeed sweet. In various election post-mortems, in New England in particular, such Federalists rejoiced that the "French party is fallen," and that the French alliance was at last valueless. Even Adet, one of them pointed out, "avows, and it is rather a tough point to avow, that our treaty is disadvantageous." Now he might inform the Directory that it has "been deceived by the revolutionary Americans in Paris; that we (at least the Yankees) have not been traitors, and have ceased to be dupes."

With the Federalist victory, narrow though it was, the Farewell Address had done its work. The French alliance which had been drawn to last "forever" and which had been the core of American foreign policy when Washington launched the federal government was practically dead as he prepared to leave office. Despite French and Republican efforts to the contrary, and in large part because of the impact of Washington's Farewell, the basic foreign policy orientation of the United States remained pro-British. The Farewell Address now belonged to posterity and posterity has given it meanings to fit its own problems.

Additional Reading

Gilbert Chinard, *Honest John Adams* (1933).

Alexander DeConde, *Entangling Alliances: Politics and Diplomacy under George Washington* (1958).

Felix Gilbert, *To the Farewell Address: Ideas of Early American Foreign Policy* (1961).

Bradford Perkins, *The First Rapprochement; England and the United States, 1795–1805* (1955).

Albert K. Weinberg, "Washington's 'Great Rule' in Its Historical Evolution," in Eric F. Goldman, ed., *Historiography and Urbanization* (1941), pp. 109–138.

5 THE WAR OF 1812: Western Grievances or National Causes?

In the initial phase of the French Revolutionary and Napoleonic Wars (1793–1801), the United States was able to preserve neutrality and to settle important boundary disputes with Great Britain and Spain. After the renewal of the great European struggle in 1803, America was less fortunate. England and France, the two mighty antagonists, each supreme in its own element and unable to directly engage the other, resorted to economic warfare which inevitably affected the neutral United States. Napoleon decreed the Continental System to close all Europe to British goods and to compel neutrals to cease trade with the British Isles. In retaliation, the British government issued a series of Orders in Council which instituted a counter blockade and sought to control neutral commerce with Europe. Both belligerents trampled on American rights and interests, but as mistress of the seas Britain's interferences were more numerous and onerous. When the efforts of Jefferson and Madison to protect the national interests by economic pressure—embargo and non-intercourse acts—failed, war with England ensued in 1812.

There has been a "swinging pendulum" of historical explanations of the causes of the War of 1812.[1] The older interpretation emphasized issues of violated national honor and legal neutral rights: the British impressment of American seamen, and the interferences and seizures of American shipping en route to Europe. In the first quarter of the twentieth century, scholars became more aware of the role of the West in demanding war in 1812, motivated by expansionist interests in Canada and the desire to eradicate the Indian danger by expulsion of the British from North America. In recent years, historians have partly returned to the older version and once more view maritime factors as the causes for war—but with the emphasis less on rights and honor and more on the economic grounds that the British blockade system strangled American commerce and agriculture in all sections of the nation and thereby created a desire for relief through war on the oppressor.

DOCUMENTS

Madison's Reasons for War

In despair at the failure of economic coercion and under increasing pressure from the War Hawks within his own party, who were eager for war and conquest, President Madison in effect requested Congress to declare war against Great Britain in June, 1812. Among the grievances he listed to justify such a

[1] W. H. Goodman, "The Origins of the War of 1812: A Survey of Changing Interpretations," *Mississippi Valley Historical Review,* XXVIII (1941), 171–186.

step were the impressment of seamen, the hovering of British warships off the American coasts, British violations of neutral rights and seizures of American ships and cargoes, and Indian outrages on the northwestern frontier.

Madison's War Message

I communicate to Congress certain documents, being a continuation of those heretofore laid before them on the subject of our affairs with Great Britain.

Without going back beyond the renewal in 1803 of the war in which Great Britain is engaged, and omitting unrepaired wrongs of inferior magnitude, the conduct of her Government presents a series of acts hostile to the United States as an independent and neutral nation.

British cruisers have been in the continued practice of violating the American flag on the great highway of nations, and of seizing and carrying off persons sailing under it, not in the exercise of a belligerent right founded on the law of nations against an enemy, but of a municipal prerogative over British subjects. British jurisdiction is thus extended to neutral vessels in a situation where no laws can operate but the law of nations and the laws of the country to which the vessels belong. . . .

The practice, hence, is so far from affecting British subjects alone that, under the pretext of searching for these, thousands of American citizens, under the safeguard of public law and of their national flag, have been torn from their country and from everything dear to them; have been dragged on board ships of war of a foreign nation and exposed, under the severities of their discipline, to be exiled to the most distant and deadly climes, to risk their lives in the battles of their oppressors, and to be the melancholy instruments of taking away those of their own brethren.

Against this crying enormity, which Great Britain would be so prompt to avenge if committed against herself, the United States have in vain exhausted remonstrances and expostulations, and that no proof might be wanting of their conciliatory dispositions, and no pretext left for a continuance of the practice, the British Government was formally assured of the readiness of the United States to enter into arrangements such as could not be rejected if the recovery of British subjects were the real and the sole object. The communication passed without effect.

British cruisers have been in the practice also of violating the rights and the peace of our coasts. They hover over and harass our entering and departing commerce. To the most insulting pretensions they have added the most lawless proceedings in our very harbors, and have wantonly spilt American blood within the sanctuary of our territorial jurisdiction. The principles and rules enforced by that nation, when a neutral nation, against armed vessels of belligerents hovering near her coasts and disturbing her commerce are well known. When called on, nevertheless, by the United States to punish the greater offenses committed by her own vessels, her Government has bestowed on their commanders additional marks of honor and confidence.

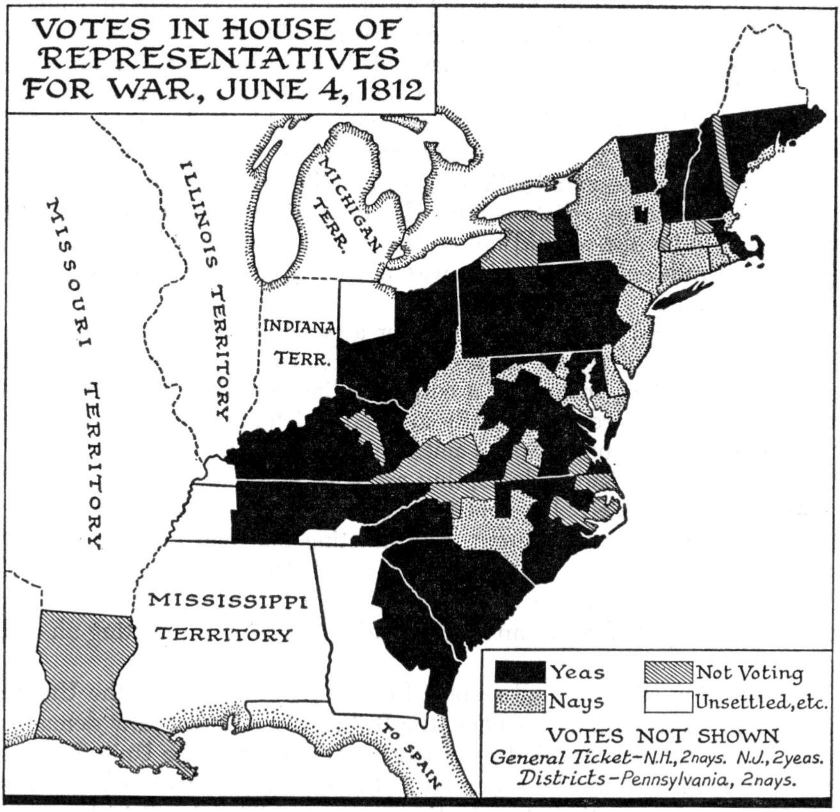

Under pretended blockades, without the presence of an adequate force and sometimes without the practicability of applying one, our commerce has been plundered in every sea, the great staples of our country have been cut off from their legitimate markets, and a destructive blow aimed at our agricultural and maritime interests. In aggravation of these predatory measures they have been considered as in force from the dates of their notification, a retrospective effect being thus added, as has been done in other important cases, to the unlawfulness of the course pursued. And to render the outrage the more signal these mock blockades have been reiterated and enforced in the face of official communications from the British Government declaring as the true definition of a legal blockade "that particular ports must be actually invested and previous warning given to vessels bound to them not to enter."

Not content with these occasional expedients for laying waste our neutral trade, the cabinet of Britain resorted at length to the sweeping system of blockades, under the name of orders in council, which has been molded and managed as might best suit its political views, its commercial jealousies, or the avidity of British cruisers.

To our remonstrances against the complicated and transcendent injustice of this innovation the first reply was that the orders were reluctantly adopted by Great Britain as a necessary retaliation on decrees of her enemy proclaiming a general blockade of the British Isles at a time when the naval force of that enemy dared not issue from his own ports. She was reminded without effect that her own prior blockades, unsupported by an adequate naval force actually applied and continued, were a bar to this plea; that executed edicts against millions of our property could not be retaliation on edicts confessedly impossible to be executed; that retaliation, to be just, should fall on the party setting the guilty example, not on an innocent party which was not even chargeable with an acquiescence in it.

When deprived of this flimsy veil for a prohibition of our trade with her enemy by the repeal of his prohibition of our trade with Great Britain, her cabinet, instead of a corresponding repeal or a practical discontinuance of its orders, formally avowed a determination to persist in them against the United States until the markets of her enemy should be laid open to British products, thus asserting an obligation on a neutral power to require one belligerent to encourage by its internal regulations the trade of another belligerent, contradicting her own practice toward all nations, in peace as well as in war, and betraying the insincerity of those professions which inculcated a belief that, having resorted to her orders with regret, she was anxious to find an occasion for putting an end to them.

Abandoning still more all respect for the neutral rights of the United States and for its own consistency, the British Government now demands as prerequisites to a repeal of its orders as they relate to the United States that a formality should be observed in the repeal of the French decrees nowise necessary to their termination nor exemplified by British usage, and that the French repeal, besides including that portion of the decrees which operates within a territorial jurisdiction, as well as that which operates on the high seas, against the commerce of the United States should not be a single and special repeal in relation to the United States, but should be extended to whatever other neutral nations unconnected with them may be affected by those decrees. . . .

It has become, indeed, sufficiently certain that the commerce of the United States is to be sacrificed, not as interfering with the belligerent rights of Great Britain; not as supplying the wants of her enemies, which she herself supplies; but as interfering with the monopoly which she covets for her own commerce and navigation. She carries on a war against the lawful commerce of a friend that she may the better carry on a commerce with an enemy—a commerce polluted by the forgeries and perjuries which are for the most part the only passports by which it can succeed.

Anxious to make every experiment short of the last resort of injured nations, the United States have withheld from Great Britain, under successive modifications, the benefits of a free intercourse with their market, the loss of which could not but outweigh the profits accruing from her restrictions of our commerce with other nations. And to entitle these experiments to the more favorable consideration they were so framed as to enable her to place her adversary under the exclusive operation of them. To these appeals her Government has been equally inflexible, as if willing to make sacrifices of every sort rather than yield to the claims of justice or renounce the errors of a false pride. Nay, so far were the attempts carried to overcome the attachment of the British cabinet to its unjust edicts that it received every encouragement within the competency of the executive branch of our Government to expect that a repeal of them would be followed by a war between the United States and France, unless the French edicts should also be repealed. Even this communication, although silencing forever the plea of a disposition in the United States to acquiesce in those edicts originally the sole plea for them, received no attention. . . .

In reviewing the conduct of Great Britain toward the United States our attention is necessarily drawn to the warfare just renewed by the savages on one of our extensive frontiers—a warfare which is known to spare neither age nor sex and to be distinguished by features peculiarly shocking to humanity. It is difficult to account for the activity and combinations which have for some time been developing themselves among tribes in constant intercourse with British traders and garrisons without connecting their hostility with that influence and without recollecting the authenticated examples of such interpositions heretofore furnished by the officers and agents of that Government.

Such is the spectacle of injuries and indignities which have been heaped on our country, and such the crisis which its unexampled forbearance and conciliatory efforts have not been able to avert. It might at least have been expected that an enlightened nation, if less urged by moral obligations or invited by friendly dispositions on the part of the United States, would have found in its true interest alone a sufficient motive to respect their rights and their tranquillity on the high seas; that an enlarged policy would have favored that free and general circulation of commerce in which the British nation is at all times interested, and which in times of war is the best alleviation of its calamities to herself as well as to other belligerents; and more especially that the British cabinet would not, for the sake of a precarious and surreptitious intercourse with hostile markets, have persevered in a course of measures which necessarily put at hazard the invaluable market of a great and growing country, disposed to cultivate the mutual advantages of an active commerce.

Other counsels have prevailed. Our moderation and conciliation have had no other effect than to encourage perseverance and to enlarge pretensions. We behold our seafaring citizens, still the daily victims of lawless violence, committed on the great common and highway of nations, even within sight of the country which owes them protection. We behold our vessels, freighted with the products of our soil and industry, or returning with the honest proceeds of them, wrested from their lawful destinations, confiscated by prize courts no longer the organs of public law but the instruments of arbitrary edicts, and their unfortunate crews dispersed and lost, or forced or inveigled in British ports into British fleets, whilst arguments are employed in support of these aggressions which have no foundation but in a principle equally supporting a claim to regulate our external commerce in all cases whatsoever.

We behold, in fine, on the side of Great Britain a state of war against the United States, and on the side of the United States a state of peace toward Great Britain.

Whether the United States shall continue passive under these progressive usurpations and these accumulating wrongs, or, opposing force to force in defense of their national rights, shall commit a just cause into the hands of the Almighty Disposer of Events, avoiding all connections which might entangle it in the contest or views of other powers, and preserving a constant readiness to concur in an honorable reestablishment of peace and friendship, is a solemn question which the Constitution wisely confides to the legislative department of the Government. In recommending it to their early deliberations I am happy in the assurance that the decision will be worthy the enlightened and patriotic councils of a virtuous, a free, and a powerful nation.

Having presented this view of the relations of the United States with Great Britain and of the solemn alternative growing out of them, I proceed to remark that the communications last made to Congress on the subject of our relations with France will have shewn that since the revocation of her decrees, as they violated the neutral rights of the United States, her Government has authorized illegal captures by its privateers and public ships, and that other outrages have been practiced on our vessels and our citizens. It will have been seen also that no indemnity had been provided or satisfactorily pledged for the extensive spoliations committed under the violent and retrospective orders of the French Government against the property of our citizens seized within the jurisdiction of France. I abstain at this time from recommending to the consideration of Congress definitive measures with respect to that nation, in the expectation that the result of unclosed discussions between our minister plenipotentiary at Paris and the French Government will speedily enable Congress to decide with greater advantage on the course due to the rights, the interests, and the honor of our country.

READINGS

1. Honor and Neutral Rights

Admiral A. T. Mahan, the eminent historian of sea power and expansionism, followed the nineteenth-century historical tradition in emphasizing British affronts to American honor and legal rights through arbitrary impressment and maritime restrictions on commerce.

Antecedents of the War

A. T. MAHAN

. . . The two principal immediate causes of the War of 1812 were the impressment of seamen from American merchant ships, upon the high seas, to serve in the British Navy, and the interference with the carrying trade of the United States by the naval power of Great Britain. For a long time this interference was confined by the British Ministry to methods which they thought themselves able to defend—as they did the practice of impressment—upon the ground of rights, prescriptive and established, natural or belligerent; although the American Government contended that in several specific measures no such right existed—that the action was illegal as well as oppressive. As the war with Napoleon increased in intensity, however, the exigencies of the struggle induced the British cabinet to formulate and enforce against neutrals a restriction of trade which it confessed to be without sanction in law, and justified only upon the plea of necessary retaliation, imposed by the unwarrantable course of the French Emperor. These later proceedings, known historically as the Orders in Council, by their enormity dwarfed all previous causes of complaint, and with the question of impressment constituted the vital and irreconcilable body of dissent which dragged the two states into armed collision. Undoubtedly, other matters of difficulty arose from time to time, and were productive of dispute; but either they were of comparatively trivial importance, easily settled by ordinary diplomatic methods, or there was not at bottom any vital difference as to principle, but only as to the method of adjustment. For instance, in the flagrant and unpardonable outrage of taking men by force from the United States frigate "Chesapeake," the British Government, although permitted by the American to spin out discussion over a period of four years, did not pretend to sustain the act itself; the act, that is, of searching a neutral ship of war. Whatever the motive of the Ministry in postponing redress, their pretexts turned upon points of detail, accessory to the main transaction, or upon the subsequent course of the United States Government, which showed conscious weakness by taking hasty, pettish half-measures; instead of abstaining from immediate action, and instructing its minister to present an ultimatum, if satisfaction were shirked.

In the two causes of the war which have been specified, the difference was fundamental. Whichever was right, the question at stake was in each case one of principle, and of necessity. Great Britain never claimed to impress American seamen; but she did assert that her native-born subjects could never change their allegiance, that she had an inalienable right to their service, and to seize them wherever found, except within foreign territory. From an admitted premise, that the open sea is common to all nations, she deduced a common jurisdiction, in virtue of which she arrested her vagrant seamen. This argument of right was reinforced by a paramount necessity. In a life and death struggle with an implacable

Alfred Thayer Mahan, *Sea Power in Its Relations to the War of 1812* (Boston, 1905), I, 2–8.

enemy, Great Britain with difficulty could keep her fleet manned at all; even with indifferent material. The deterioration in quality of her ships' companies was notorious; and it was notorious also that numerous British seamen sought employment in American merchant ships, hoping there to find refuge from the protracted confinement of a now dreary maritime war. Resort to impressment was not merely the act of a high-handed Government, but the demand of both parties in the state, coerced by the sentiment of the people, whose will is ultimately irresistible. No ministry could hope to retain power if it surrendered the claim to take seamen found under a neutral flag. This fact was thoroughly established in a long discussion with United States plenipotentiaries, five years before the war broke out.

On the other hand, the United States maintained that on the sea common the only jurisdiction over a ship was that of its own nation. She could not admit that American vessels there should be searched, for other purposes than those conceded to the belligerent by international law; that is, in order to determine the nature of the voyage, to ascertain whether, by destination, by cargo, or by persons carried, the obligations of neutrality were being infringed. If there was reasonable cause for suspicion, the vessel, by accepted law and precedent, might be sent to a port of the belligerent, where the question was adjudicated by legal process; but the actual captor could not decide it on the spot. On the contrary, he was bound, to the utmost possible, to preserve from molestation everything on board the seized vessel; in order that, if cleared, the owner might undergo no damage beyond the detention. So deliberate a course was not suited to the summary methods of impressment, nor to the urgent needs of the British Navy. The boarding officer, who had no authority to take away a bale of goods, decided then and there whether a man was subject to impressment, and carried him off at once, if he so willed.

It is to the credit of the American Government under Jefferson, that, though weak in its methods of seeking redress, it went straight back of the individual sufferer, and rested its case unswervingly on the broad principle. That impressment, thus practised, swept in American seamen, was an incident only, although it grievously aggravated the injury. Whatever the native allegiance of individuals on board any vessel on the open ocean, their rights were not to be regulated by the municipal law of the belligerent, but by that of the nation to which the ship belonged, of whose territory she was constructively a part, and whose flag therefore was dishonored, if acquiescence were yielded to an infringement of personal liberty, except as conceded by obligations of treaty, or by the general law of nations. Within British waters, the United States suffered no wrong by the impressment of British subjects—the enforcement of local municipal law—on board American vessels; and although it was suggested that such visits should not be made, and that an arriving crew should be considered to have the nationality of their ship, this concession, if granted, would have been a friendly limitation by Great Britain of her own municipal jurisdiction. It therefore could not be urged upon the British Government by a nation which took its stand resolutely upon the supremacy of its own municipal rights, on board its merchant shipping on the high seas.

It is to be noted, furthermore, that the voice of the people in the United States, the pressure of influence upon the Government, was not as unanimous as that exerted upon the British Ministry. The feeling of the country was divided; and, while none denied the grievous wrong done when an American was impressed, a class, strong at least in intellectual power, limited its demands to precautions against such mistakes and to redress when they occurred. The British claim to search, with the object of impressing British subjects, was considered by these men to be valid. Thus Gouverneur Morris, who on a semi-official visit to London in 1790 had had occasion to remonstrate upon the impressment of Americans in British ports, and who, as a pamphleteer, had taken strong ground against the measures of the British Government injurious to American commerce, wrote as follows in 1808 about the practice of seizing British subjects in American ships: "That we, the people of America, should engage in ruinous warfare to support a rash opinion, that foreign sailors in our merchant ships are to be protected against the power of their sovereign, is downright madness." "Why not," he wrote again in 1813, while the war was raging, "waiving flippant debate, lay down the broad principle of national right, on which Great Britain takes her native seamen from our merchant ships? Let those who deny the right pay, suffer, and fight, to compel an abandonment of the claim. Men of sound mind will see, and men of sound principle will acknowledge, its existence." In his opinion, there was but one consistent course to be pursued by those who favored the war with Great Britain, which was to insist that she should, without compensation, surrender her claim. "If that ground be taken," he wrote, "the war [on our part] will be confessedly, as it is now impliedly, unjust." Morris was a man honorably distinguished in our troubled national history—a member of the Congress of the Revolution and of the Constitutional Convention, a trained lawyer, a practised financier, and an experienced diplomatist; one who throughout his public life stood high in the estimation of Washington, with whom he was in constant official and personal correspondence. It is to be added that those to whom he wrote were evidently in sympathy with his opinions.

So again Representative Gaston, of North Carolina, a member of the same political party as Morris, speaking from his seat in the House in February, 1814, maintained the British doctrine of inalienable allegiance. "Naturalization granted in another country has no effect whatever to destroy the original primary allegiance." Even Administration speakers did not deny this, but they maintained that the native allegiance could be enforced only within its territorial limits, not on the high seas. While perfectly firm and explicit as to the defence of American seamen—even to the point of war, if needful—Gaston spoke of the British practice as a right. "If you cannot by substitute obtain an abandonment of the right, or practice, to search our vessels, regulate it so as to prevent its abuse; waiving for the present, not relinquishing, your objections to it." He expressed sympathy, too, for the desperate straits in which Great Britain found herself. "At a time when her floating bulwarks were her whole safeguard against slavery, she could not view without alarm and resentment the warriors who should have manned those bulwarks pursuing a more gainful occupation in American vessels. Our merchant ships were crowded with British seamen, most of them deserters from their ships of war, and all furnished with fraudulent protections to prove them Americans. To us they were not necessary." On the contrary, "they ate the bread and bid down the wages of native seamen, whom it was our first duty to foster and encourage." This competition with native seamen was one of the pleas likewise of the New England opposition, too much of which was obstinately and reprehensibly factious. "Many thousands of British seamen," said Governor Strong of Massachusetts, in addressing the Legislature, May 28, 1813, "deserted that service for a more safe and lucrative employment in ours." Had they not, "the high price for that species of labor would soon have induced a sufficient number of Americans to become seamen. It appears, therefore, that British seamen have been patronized at the expense of our own; and should Great Britain now consent to relinquish the *right of taking her own subjects*, it would be no advantage to our native seamen; it would only tend to reduce their wages by increasing the numbers of that class of men." Gaston further said, that North Carolina, though not a commercial state, had many native seamen; but, "at the moment war was declared, though inquiry was made, I could not hear of a single native seaman detained by British impressment."

It is desirable, especially in these days, when everything is to be arbitrated, that men should recognize both sides of this question, and realize how impossible it was for either party to acquiesce in any other authority than their own deciding between them. "As I never had a doubt," said Morris, "so I thought it a duty to express my conviction that British ministers would not, *dared not*, submit to mediation a question of essential right." "The way to peace is open and clear," he said the following year. "Let the right of search and impressment be acknowledged as maxims of public law."...

2. *The Indian Menace and the West*

Other historians before Julius W. Pratt had noted the desire of the Western states and territories for war against Great Britain in 1812. While some explained it on the grounds of wasteful pioneer agriculture and the resultant land hunger of settlers for the virgin soil of Canada, Professor Pratt places the emphasis on the Indian danger and the desire of Americans to end it by conquest of Canada and expulsion of the British fur trappers and agents whom it was believed had instigated Indian outrages. Pratt, who has specialized in studies of American expansionism and colonial administration, does not deny that other causes of hostilities were operative in 1812—impressment and maritime seizures—but he does conclude that there would not have been a declaration of war without Western grievances. Within that context, he develops the theory of a "sectional bargain" between the Northwest, which sought Canada, and the Southwest which wanted to acquire Spanish Florida.

The Expansionists of 1812

JULIUS W. PRATT

Introduction

That the United States went to war with Great Britain in 1812 at the insistence of western and southern men, and over the opposition of the Northeast, is a fact about which there has never been any doubt. There was a paradox here which apparently gave little concern to the older historians. If the real grievances which caused the war were interference by Great Britain with American commerce and the rights of American sailors, why was war to redress those grievances opposed by the maritime section of the nation and urged by the inland section, which they scarcely affected? The old answers, that New England was Anglophile, and that the West and South had developed a more aggressive and martial spirit, which felt the humiliation if not the pecuniary loss occasioned by the British measures, were in a measure true, but hardly sufficient. For some years past, historians have been turning to new explanations.

In this field, as in almost every other in American history, it is easy to see the profound influence of Professor F. J. Turner. Before the publication in 1893 of his essay, "The Significance of the Frontier in American History," the frontier had been regarded as little more than a picturesque phase in the national development. Since that event, the frontier—the "West"—has come to be recognized as the source of many aspects of American character and the determining factor in many American policies. It was natural, therefore, that students of the War of 1812 should come to view the West—particularly the Northwest—with more careful scrutiny. The result of such examination has been the placing of new emphasis upon the western demand for the annexation of Canada, which is seen to have arisen in large part from the conviction that the British were in league with the northwestern Indians and that only by destroying that alliance could the Northwest continue its career of expansion.

The war found its sponsors, however, not only in the Northwest but along the whole frontier from New Hampshire round about to Georgia. For the states south of Kentucky, there was little to be gained by the conquest of Canada, and, since the divergence of interests between North and South was already evident, there was reason for southern states to fear the political effect of a large addition to northern territory. Why, then, did the Southwest support the war? The answer to this question has been suggested, but has never been worked out with anything approaching completeness. The examination made in the course of this study reveals an ardent expansionist sentiment already at work along the whole southern and southwestern border, varying in scope from the relatively modest proposal for the annexation of the Floridas to the more visionary idea of seizing all the Spanish possessions on the continent of North America. The link between the designs of the Southwest and those of the Northwest was

From *The Expansionists of 1812* by Julius W. Pratt, pp. 9–14, 42–59, 120–125. Reprinted with permission of the publisher.

the existence of the alliance between Great Britain and Spain. It was widely assumed that war with Great Britain would mean war with Spain, and that thus expansion at the north and at the south would proceed *pari passu.*

The purposes of the present study have been: to examine the development in the Northwest of the demand for the conquest and annexation of Canada; to trace the rise in the South and Southwest of the plan to annex the Floridas and possibly Mexico; to discover the relations of these two proposals to each other and to the question of war with Great Britain; to determine the position of the executive branch of the United States government (especially of Madison and his Secretary of State, Monroe) toward the plans for expansion, north and south; and finally, to determine the causes for the failure, all along the line, of the expansionist hopes with which the war began.

The principal conclusions arrived at may be summarized as follows:

I. The belief that the United States would one day annex Canada had a continuous existence from the early days of the War of Independence to the War of 1812. From 1783 to about 1810 such annexation was thought of only as a matter for an indefinite future, the nation during those years having neither the strength, nor any sufficient motive, for taking Canada by force. The rise of Tecumseh, backed, as was universally believed, by the British, produced an urgent demand in the Northwest that the British be expelled from Canada. This demand was a factor of primary importance in bringing on the war.

II. The South was almost unanimous in its demand for the Floridas, for agrarian, commercial, and strategic reasons, and in the spring of 1812 appeared to be in a fair way to accomplish its purpose. In the Southwest, at the same time, there was a lively interest in Mexico and a widely prevalent opinion that it was ready to fall into American hands.

III. Even within the Republican party, there was already a distinct sectional rift between North and South, and neither section was anxious to see the other increase its territory and population. But if both could gain at the same time, and in something like equal proportion, such objections would be obviated on both sides. There is good evidence that, before the declaration of war, northern and southern Republicans came to a definite understanding that the acquisition of Canada on the north was to be balanced by the annexation of the Floridas on the south. Thus the war began with a double-barrelled scheme of territorial aggrandizement.

IV. Both Madison and Monroe, especially the latter as Secretary of State, were wholly in sympathy with the proposal for annexing Florida. The invasion of East Florida by General Mathews in March and April, 1812, was effected with the full knowledge of the administration. Special circumstances forced the government to repudiate Mathews, but the territory he had taken from the Spanish was held for over a year, until Congress had twice refused to sanction the occupation. At the same time, Monroe's official correspondence shows that he never really desired or expected the annexation of Canada.

V. It appears that in the all round failure of the expansionist plans, sectional feeling played a larger part than is commonly supposed. The sectional bargain with which the war had begun broke down. Opposition from northern Republicans combined with Federalists forced the abandonment of East Florida. On the other hand, it is evident that in the utter failure of the efforts to take Canada, not only want of skill and preparation, but also a lack of enthusiasm on the part of the administration and of certain southern men in Congress played a part.

VI. Finally, in the expansionist program with which the war opened, we have the first general appearance of the idea which later received the name of "Manifest Destiny." Although enthusiasts like Jefferson had dreamed years before of a nation destined to embrace the continent, the date usually given for the dawn of "Manifest Destiny" is about 1830. Yet both in the Congressional debates of 1812 and in the contemporary press, particularly that of the Southwest, we find the idea repeatedly expressed. "Where is it written in the book of fate," asked the editor of the Nashville *Clarion* (April 28, 1812), "that the American republic shall not stretch her limits from the Capes of the Chesapeake to Nootka sound, from the isthmus of Panama to Hudson bay?"

Two explanations are due, with respect to the scope and proportions of this study. First, it makes no effort to give a full account of the causes of the War of 1812, but deals with one set of causes only. The exclusion from all but briefest mention of the maritime grievances against Great Britain is with no wish to belittle them. Without them, it is safe to say, there would have been no war, just as the writer feels safe in saying that without the peculiar grievances and ambitions of the West there would have been no war. One set of causes was perhaps as essential as the other. . . .

The Northwest and Canada

. . . Throughout the year 1811, alarm at the menace of Tecumseh's confederacy and conviction that the British were instrumental in its formation and support grew rapidly among government officials and the people of the West. Governor Harrison wrote in February to the Secretary of War: "If the intentions of the British Government are pacific, the Indian department of Upper Canada have not been made acquainted with them: for they have very lately said every thing to the Indians, who visited them, to excite them against us."

In July a group of citizens of Knox County, Indiana, met at Vincennes and adopted resolutions demanding that the Indian settlement at Tippecanoe—one hundred and fifty miles up the Wabash—be broken up. The wish was natural, in view of the serious menace which the Prophet's town held over the heads of the Knox County settlers; but it was significant that the British were charged with responsibility for the whole situation. "We are fully convinced," said the resolutions, "that the formation of the combination, headed by the Shawanee prophet, is a British scheme, and that the agents of that power are constantly exciting the Indians to hostilities against the United States." Similar views were reflected in resolutions adopted by residents of St. Clair County, Illinois, which mentioned "the seditious village of Peoria, the great nursery of hostile Indians and traitorous British Indian traders."

Meanwhile the *Kentucky Gazette* was warning its readers of the British-Indian menace in outspoken language:

"It would seem from the attitude of the Indians—the combination of the Northern and Southern tribes—the conference at Malden—the circumstances attendant on the mission of *Foster*—the late arrival of regular troops in Canada, that the British ministry were planning *'another expedition.'* . . .

"From the friendly course pursued by Mr. Jefferson, towards our red neighbors, and which has been followed by Mr. Madison, we had supposed the Indians would never more treat us otherwise than as brethren. But we have been mistaken—British intrigue and British gold, it seems, has greater influence with them of late than American justice and benevolence. . . . We have in our possession information which proves beyond doubt, the late disturbances to be owing to the too successful intrigues of British emissaries with the Indians."

Governor Harrison, representative of "American justice and benevolence" toward the Indians, was at this time planning to open the way to a military career by an attack on the Indian village at Tippecanoe. But he knew that war with England was probable, and suspected that the regiment of regular troops now on their way to him from Pittsburgh, were destined "to our frontiers bordering on Upper Canada." More important than his own ideas on the subject was his estimate of the spirit of the western people, whom he knew if any one knew them. "The people of this Territory [Indiana] and Kentucky," he wrote, "are extremely pressing in offers of their service for an expedition into the Indian Country. Any number of men might be obtained for this purpose or for a march into Canada."

Early in September it was reported to Harrison "that defection is evidenced amongst all the Tribes from the Wabash to the Mississippi and the Lakes. That the Indians of the Wabash, Illinois, etc., have recently visited the British agent at Malden. That they are now returning from thence with a larger supply of goods than is ever known to have been distributed to them before. That rifles or fusees are given to those who are unarmed and powder and lead to all. And that the language and measures of the Indians indicate nothing but war." Harrison passed on the information to the War Department a few days later (September 17, 1811), with additional details of the extent of British subsidies: "A trader of this country was lately in the King's store at Malden, and was told that the quantity of goods for the Indian department, which has been sent out this year, exceeded that of common years by £20,000 sterling. It is impossible to ascribe this profusion to any other motive than that of instigating the Indians to take up the tomahawk; it cannot be to secure their trade, for all the peltries collected on the waters of the Wabash, in one year, if sold in the London market, would not pay the freight of the goods which have been given the Indians."

Harrison, however, went on to say that, "although I am decidedly of opinion that the tendency of the British measures is hostility to us, candor obliges me to inform you, that, from two Indians of different tribes, I have received information that the British agent absolutely dissuaded them from going to war against the United States." That the compulsion of candor was necessary to bring the governor to pass on this last bit of information is an interesting commentary on his state of mind; but the information itself is perfectly consistent with the other facts of the situation. General Brock wrote, after Harrison's battle with the Indians, that the latter had been "implicitly told not to look for assistance from us," but the phrase occurs in a letter whose main purpose was to point out how the effective aid of the Indians was to be secured and used against the Americans. Throughout the period of the rise of Tecumseh, the British had dissuaded the Indians from beginning a war against the United States; but the purpose of this policy was to allow time for the consolidation of the confederacy, that the aid of the Indians might be the more effective when needed.

Early in November came Harrison's badly managed campaign ending in the battle of Tippecanoe. From the facts already presented it is clear that the blood there shed would be added to the grievances already existing against the British and would bring the West to an eagerness for war without precedent in the entire controversy. "*The blood of our murdered countrymen must be revenged,*" wrote Andrew Jackson to Harrison. "I do hope that Government will see that it is necessary to act efficiently and that this hostile band which must be excited to war by the secret agents of Great Britain must be destroyed." The battle of Tippecanoe gave inestimable support to the war party in the Twelfth Congress, now assembled in Washington for its first session.

The war party, composed of western men and "radical, expansionist, malcontent politicians of the east," which had existed in Congress since 1810 at least, found itself in full control when the Twelfth Congress met. Clay, the most prominent of the "war hawks," came now to the House of Representatives, where he was at once chosen speaker. He was supported in his warlike policy by members from the frontier sections of the northern states, such as Peter B. Porter of New York and John A. Harper of New Hampshire; by almost the entire delegation of the western states—Worthington of Ohio and Pope of Kentucky, both in the Senate, were the only important exceptions—by a fair proportion of the members from Pennsylvania, Virginia, and North Carolina; and by a very able and aggressive group of young men from South Carolina and Georgia—Calhoun, Cheves, Lowndes, Crawford, Troup, and others—men who had reasons of their own for promoting a war of expansion.

It was soon apparent that the war to which this party was committed was to be no such purely defensive war as the Tenth Congress had contemplated, but that it was to be waged aggressively and with the conquest of Canada as a major object. Some Easterners might agree with Monroe that Canada might be invaded, "not as an object of the war but as a means to bring it to a satisfactory conclusion," but the West was more of the mind of a correspondent of the Philadelphia *Aurora*, "who wrote that if England were to restore all impressed seamen and make compensation for all her depredations we should listen to no terms that did not include Upper Canada."

President Madison's annual message, delivered to Congress on November 5, contained language that could plainly be interpreted as meaning war. After touching upon the obdurate persistence of Great Britain in attacking American commerce, he went on to say: "With this evidence of hostile inflexibility, in trampling on rights which no independent nation can relinquish, Congress will feel the duty of putting the United States into an armor and an attitude demanded by the crisis, and corresponding with the national spirit and expectations." To deal with that part of the message concerned with foreign relations, Speaker Clay appointed a select committee, upon which he placed a group of the most reliable war men—Porter, Calhoun, Grundy, Harper, and Desha. The committee reported on November 29 a set of six resolutions recommending an increase of ten thousand men for the regular army, a levy of fifty thousand volunteers, the outfitting of all vessels of war not in active service, and the arming of merchant vessels.

It was in the House debate on these resolutions that the war party frankly revealed their designs upon Canada. Mr. Porter, chairman of the committee, speaking on December 6, explained that in addition to the injury which American privateers could inflict upon British commerce, "there was another point where we could attack her, and where she would feel our power still more sensibly. We could deprive her of her extensive provinces lying along our borders to the north. These provinces were not only immensely valuable in themselves, but almost indispensable to the existence of Great Britain, cut off as she now in a great measure is from the north of Europe. He had been credibly informed that the exports from Quebec alone amounted during the last year, to near six millions of dollars, and most of these too in articles of the first necessity—in ship timber and in provisions for the support of her fleets and armies. By carrying on such a war as he had described . . . we should be able in a short time to remunerate ourselves tenfold for all the spoliations she had committed on our commerce."

Grundy of Tennessee, three days later, dwelt upon the peculiar advantage to the Westerner to be derived from war. "We shall drive the British from our Continent—they will no longer have an opportunity of intriguing with our Indian neighbors, and setting on the ruthless savage to tomahawk our women and children. That nation will lose her Canadian trade, and, by having no resting place in this country, her means of annoying us will be diminished." Rhea of Tennessee was equally explicit upon the object of the war—"That all that part of North America which joins the United States on the Northeast, North, and Northwest, shall be provided for in a mode which will forever thereafter put it out of the power of Great Britain, or of any British agent, trader, or factor, or company of British traders to supply Indian tribes with arms or ammunition;

to instigate and incite Indians to disturb and harass our frontiers, and to murder and scalp helpless women and children."

Two members of the House, one from Kentucky and one from New Hampshire, expounded the doctrine of Manifest Destiny. "I shall never die contented," announced R. M. Johnson, "until I see her [Great Britain's] expulsion from North America, and her territories incorporated with the United States. . . . In point of territorial limit, the map will improve its importance. The waters of the St. Lawrence and the Mississippi interlock in a number of places, and the great Disposer of Human Events intended those two rivers should belong to the same people." "The northern provinces of Britain are to us great and valuable objects," proclaimed Harper of New Hampshire. "Once secured to this Republic, and the St. Lawrence and the Lakes become the Baltic, and more than the Baltic to America; north of them a population of four millions may easily be supported; and this great outlet of the northern world should be at our command for our convenience and future security. To me, sir, it appears that the Author of Nature has marked our limits in the south, by the Gulf of Mexico; and on the north, by the regions of eternal frost."

While Congress debated, reports continued to come in of British agents at work among the Indians. As a matter of fact, it would appear that presents to the Indians, and particularly ammunition, were less at this time than previously. Claus wrote General Brock from Amherstburg in June, 1812, that during the last six months the Indians had received only 1211 pounds of powder—"nineteen hundred and twenty-one pounds less than at former periods—of lead, not one ounce has been issued to them since last December." But a letter from Fort Wayne in February stated that two British emissaries had recently passed that way on a mission to the Prophet, and that "their business was to invite all the Indians to meet at Malden very early in the spring." Any event of this kind would of course receive the most unfavorable interpretation. The same letter gave other disturbing reports: "The Pottawatomy chief, Marpack, has been in the neighborhood of Malden since August last. . . . He has about one hundred and twenty of the best warriors in this country with him. . . . I know this chief is hostile inclined towards the United States, and have no hesitation in saying, that he is kept at that place by the British agents at Malden."

If their relations with the Indians constituted a standing reason for driving the British from Canada, a special reason was furnished by the publication of the Henry Letters, for Henry had been in the employ of the Governor-General of Canada. "Can any American, after this discovery," wrote Congressman Desha to a friend in Kentucky, "doubt the propriety of ousting the British from the continent, or hesitate in contributing his proportionable part of the expense which will necessarily be incurred in the laudable undertaking."

The West no longer needed any such prompting from its representatives in Washington. The rise of Tecumseh and the Prophet, the battle of Tippecanoe, the outspoken position of their congressmen together with the current belief that the British were behind all their Indian troubles, had resulted in an insistent demand from the Westerners for the conquest of Canada. The Lexington *Reporter* published in January a "*Franklinian Prescription—To cure Indian hostilities, and to prevent their recurrence:* Interpose the American arm between the hands of the English and their savage allies. This done, the occupation of the Canadas, New Brunswick and Nova-Scotia, would give us perpetual concord with the Indians; who would be obliged *to depend upon us* for supplies of Blankets, knives, gunpowder, etc."

The Kentucky Legislature, which in the crisis of 1807–1808 had made no official mention of the border question, in its resolutions of February, 1812, added to Great Britain's violations of American rights at sea her practice of "inciting the savages (as we have strong reasons to believe) to murder the inhabitants of our defenseless frontiers—furnishing them with arms and ammunition lately, to attack our forces; to the loss of a number of our brave men."

Another indication of public opinion in Kentucky is the character of the toasts proposed at a Washington's Birthday dinner in Lexington. The banqueters drank to such toasts as "*Great Britain, when she comes to her senses*—If she continues lunatic, *Canada* and our arms!" or "*The American Congress*—If they barter the nation's honor under the false idea of temporary popularity, may they meet with the just scorn of an indignant people!"

Public opinion in Ohio paralleled closely that of Kentucky. The Circleville *Fredonian* declared the "indignant spirits" of Americans could be appeased only "by the restoration of our rights, or the conquest of Canada." Correspondents of Senator Thomas Worthington believed that if war came, "we would attack [and] conquer Cannady & humble their overbearing pride," or hoped that American troops would "sever Upper Canada from the British without delay."

As the year advanced, the tone of the press grew even more determined. The *Fredonian* saw no hope of peace and security from the savages until "another WAYNE shall force *them* to become our friends, and another WASHINGTON exterminates from the Canadas, the base remains of royal perfidy." The British "must be for ever driven from all their possessions in America." The same paper professed itself eager to undertake a war against both France and Great Britain when it appeared that neither nation was willing to recognize American rights. In April the *Kentucky Gazette* stated: "Great Britain has determined not to recede, and Congress seem at last to have got in earnest, and appear disposed to prepare for war. . . . The recruiting service has been actually commenced in various places, and large bodies of militia are to be raised to march for Detroit and other parts of our frontier. This is all preparatory to the invasion of Canada, now more than ever necessary, as presenting whilst in the possession of Britain, a never failing source of Indian hostility. Until those civilized allies of our Savage neighbors, are expelled from our continent, we must expect the frequent recurrence of the late scenes on the Wabash."

The same paper could not suppress its wrath when the *National Intel-*

ligencer, reputed to be the administration organ, hinted that war might yet be avoided. "Notwithstanding a mass of evidence of this kind [i.e. as to captures, impressment, Henry plots, etc.], the Intelligencer may talk of *negociation* and *'honorable accommodation'* with England; but when we view the effects of her policy in the *West*—when we hear of the tragic scenes that are now acting on our frontiers, after the slaughter of Tippecanoe, it is really surprising to hear that there is any doubt about the *'active preparations for warlike operations'* . . . We will only add, at this time, that we should much like to know the price which the 'Intelligencer' would receive as a compromise for the scalps of *Western Farmers*."

On May 26, three weeks before the declaration of war, the *Gazette* gave what appears like a parting injunction to Congress: "Can it be expected that those savage butcheries will have an end until we take possession of Malden and other British forts on the Lakes? And must the settlements in our territories be entirely destroyed, and the blood of the women and children drench the soil before this can be done? . . . What will our Congress say?" In similar tone the *Reporter* of May 30 declared: "Britain has commenced war in the Western Country, equally so as France would have done, was she to burn New York. The citizens of the Eastern States, and members in Congress, may abandon 7,000 seamen—they may term it, a *trifling impropriety* on the part of England, but the old Revolutionary Heroes here are not to be deceived by the misrepresentations of any man whatever. The Government MUST not abandon the Western Country to the British."

Thus by the end of the spring of 1812, the whole frontier country from New Hampshire to Kentucky was insisting that the British must be expelled from Canada. The demand had been of slow growth. Taking its origin from the ideas of Revolutionary statesmen, it was fed from various sources—from jealousy of the British fur trade, from exasperation at British contempt for the American flag at sea, from the alluring vision of a continent destined to recognize a single sovereignty—but unquestionably most of all from the conviction that the British in Canada were in unholy alliance with the western Indians, and that only by cutting off the Indians from British support could the West gain peace and security. Only thus could the Westerner be free to continue that policy of "justice and benevolence" toward the Indians, which consisted in pushing the boundaries of the white settlements ever farther into the Indian country. Other motives—commercial, political, punitive—played a part; but the overmastering desire of the people of the Northwest was to feel free to develop their country without peril from those Indian conspiracies which were universally believed to have their origin in British Canada.

Lure of the Spanish Provinces

. . . If the frontiersman of the Northwest demanded war with Great Britain as indispensable, his kinsman of the southern border at least saw in it a means of fulfilling his expansionist dreams. The past two years had done much to give him what he thought his territorial rights, but much remained to be gained. The Spanish still held Mobile and Pensacola, St. Mark's and St. Augustine, and the American troops that held the country between the St. John's and the St. Mary's rivers were, it was supposed, about to be withdrawn.

The demand for the annexation of all Florida was more insistent than ever. Georgians like Floyd, Mitchell, Troup, and Crawford—the last two influential members of the war party in Congress—held the acquisition of East Florida essential to the prosperity, to the very safety, of their state. The Augusta *Chronicle,* cited on a previous page, hoped for "some new measures for the purpose of placing the whole of that colony under the control of the United States." Out in Mississippi Territory, the news of the occupation of East Florida aroused a lively hope of similar action farther west. "There is no doubt," wrote a recent settler at St. Stephens, to a friend in the East, "but Mobille and Pensacola will share the same fate in a few weeks, which no doubt will occation considerable action in this quarter during this summer, and all the citizens in this part of the country are much gratified at the Idea of the United States getting Possession of this Southern Coast, as it is certainly of all importance to the citizens of this country." The Nashville *Clarion,* quoting at length from the Congressional Report of 1803 on the navigation of the southern rivers, and explaining in detail how Tennessee's transportation difficulties would be solved by the opening of the Alabama and Tombigbee, declared that "No part of the union can be so much interested in the acquisition of West Florida as the State of Tennessee. . . . The Floridas will soon be occupied by American troops."

But if the whole southern border was eager to take what remained of Florida, war with England seemed to afford a perfectly clear occasion for doing so. Spain was England's ally in the European war, and it was safe to assume that Spanish harbors in America would be open to British fleets and armies. As a simple measure of self-defense, the occupation of Florida seemed to many indispensable, and it was commonly assumed at the South that war with England meant war with Spain, or at least the forcible occupation of all Florida.

The notion of a war at once against England and Spain had been broached by Jefferson in 1807, in which case, he declared, "our southern defensive force can take the Floridas." Mathews had alluded to a similar connection when he instructed the "discontents" of East Florida "not to expect that prompt and efficient aid from the United States, if our negotiation with the British Minister terminates auspiciously for us, that they might in the other event expect." Expansionists like Clay and Harper, when they hurled defiance at Great Britain, had spoken in one breath of the nation's prospective conquests on the St. Lawrence and the Gulf of Mexico. Grundy of Tennessee, in the war debate in December, 1811, stated that he felt anxious "not only to add the Floridas to the South, but the Canadas to the North of this empire." and he wrote to Jackson that in case of war "the Canadas & Floridas will be the Theatres of our offensive operations."

Jackson himself, when shortly after the declaration of war he called upon his division of Tennessee militia to be in readiness, assured them that it was in West Florida that their arms should find employment. Jefferson, writing of the mustering of the militia in his Virginia county in June, 1812, said that "the only inquiry they make is whether they are to go to Canada or Florida."

In Georgia it was generally assumed that war with Great Britain would mean the certain seizure of all of Florida that remained unoccupied. "Had we no other claim on Florida or Spain," said the Augusta *Chronicle* in May, "sound policy would dictate the propriety as well as necessity of retaining possession of it till the close of the war we are now on the eve of commencing with an ally of that country." On the day preceding the declaration of war, the Republican citizens of Milledgeville passed resolutions approving the war measures against Great Britain, and declaring their belief that with war in prospect the occupancy of East Florida was "essential to the interests of the country and the safety of our southern frontier." A letter from Milledgeville dated July 8, 1812, reported that Governor Mitchell, who was at St. Mary's, had received news of the declaration of war, and, "considering that the Spaniards and British are in alliance both offensive and defensive, and that the vital interests of this state and the honor of the United States are implicated and will be hazarded by suffering the occupancy of East Florida by the banditti now in possession"—not the "patriots" evidently, to whom the term might have been applied, but the Spanish governor and his negro and Indian auxiliaries—"he will be detained until the reinforcements he has sent for and which are now assembling on the Oconee River, are received." Mitchell himself explained later to the Georgia legislature the light in which, prior to the declaration of war, he had viewed the situation. "The confidence with which I anticipated the declaration of war against Great Britain," said the governor, "led me with equal confidence to anticipate an enlargement of the powers of the President, by congress, as the necessary consequence, having for its object the entire occupancy of East and West Florida."

War with Great Britain, then, meant, to the average Southerner, war also with Spain, and the completion of the annexation of the Floridas. To the people of the Southwest it meant the possibility of even greater things. The old dream of revolutionizing Mexico and, if not actually annexing it to the United States, at least profiting by its agricultural, mineral, and commercial wealth, revived with new vigor. The Southwest tried to persuade itself that the Federal government favored such plans, quoting cryptic passages from "prints known to be in the interest of the administration," and citing the promotion of Colonel Pike, an avowed annexationist, and his position then in command of the troops on the border, as evidence that an invasion was contemplated. A writer signing himself "Americus" contributed to the Nashville *Clarion* of April 28 a long article in which "Manifest Destiny" ran riot.

"The Canadas," wrote Americus, "freed from the chains of an European master, shall take the rank of an independent state; or, too weak for sovereignty, shall hover under the wings of the American eagle. . . . The Floridas will sink into the confederation of American states. . . . Whilst our eastern and southern brethren are purchasing renown in arms, and extending the limits of the republic, are we condemned to remain inactive . . . ? No, citizens of the West! a destiny still more splendid is reserved for you. Behold the empire of Mexico, a celestial region, whose valiant sons are now struggling for their liberties as we struggled for ours thirty years ago. . . . Here it is that the statesman shall see an accession of Territory sufficient to double the extent of the republic; where the merchant shall see commercial resources unrivalled in other countries; the farmer, a luxuriant soil and delicious climate, where the financier shall be dazzled with gold and silver mines; while the ardent and generous mind, in the idea of establishing a new republic . . . shall deliver himself up to an enthusiasm of glory. . . . Besides, where is it written in the book of fate that the American republic shall not stretch her limits from the capes of the Chesapeake to Nootka sound, from the isthmus of Panama to Hudson bay?"

Thus while the Northwesterner expected to take Canada as a result of war with Great Britain, southern men generally expected to complete the seizure of Florida from Great Britain's ally, Spain, while the more ambitious expansionists of the Southwest dreamed of further aggressions upon the Spanish territories, which should end in making the United States coextensive with the continent of North America. . . .

3. *Economic Depression and War*

A. L. Burt, an authority on Canadian-American relations, rejects the concept of special Western causes for the War of 1812. His study reveals that the vote for war in Congress necessarily had support in Eastern areas as well and that purely Western grievances have been exaggerated. There was still much good agricultural land available in the old Northwest without seizure of Canada and the Indian danger was not a major cause of Western discontent. Instead, all sections of the country and especially the agricultural areas were in an economic decline as a result of British interferences with American trade. War was seen as the only release from an intolerable situation.

The War of 1812: An Analysis of Issues

A. L. BURT

In 1812 the United States made war on Canada, having declared it on Britain, for Canada was the only part of the British Empire vulnerable to American attack. This statement may seem open to challenge for ignoring a recent tendency to regard the declaration against Britain as an excuse for the attack against Canada; but, as will be explained, further examination makes the traditional view appear sounder than the revision.

A. L. Burt, *The United States, Great Britain and British North America* (New Haven: Yale University Press for the Carnegie Endowment for International Peace, 1940), 207–224, 305–310. Reprinted with permission of the Carnegie Endowment for International Peace.

As Canada was caught between the United States and Britain, so was the United States caught between Britain and France. These two powers were the principals in the mightiest war the modern world had yet seen, and the United States was the greatest neutral. What happened seems almost, if not quite, inevitable. The remarkable thing is that it was delayed so long. Of the two periods into which the long war was divided by the short Peace of Amiens, the first passed and the second was nearly over before the United States was drawn in to fight Britain—nineteen years after Republican France had declared war on the island empire.

Why did not the American war come in the first period of the European conflict? As we have already seen, it very nearly did come at the beginning. The blow which Britain dealt at France also hit the United States so hard that it almost knocked the American Republic into the war on the side of the French Republic. The desperate mission of Jay averted the impending catastrophe by the narrowest margin. By reaction, however, it produced another tragedy which, though it drew the United States and Britain closer together for a while, throws an interesting light on the fundamental cause of the ultimate breach between them. . . .

That neutrality was a counsel of perfection appears clearly in this first period of the great struggle in Europe. Neither Britain nor France would tolerate seeing the United States aiding its enemy by sharing in its trade, for belligerents are no respecters of neutrals, particularly weak ones. Lacking sufficient strength to resist, the United States was bound to be squeezed by both powers when they became locked in their deadly conflict. For two reasons, the international position of the American Republic was then essentially unstable: it was intolerable; and the pressure from both sides could not be equal. Some escape had to be found, and the inequality of pressure made for war with one and an accommodation with the other.

If Jay had failed, his country could hardly have avoided falling into the arms of France and plunging into war with Britain. This was what the Anti-Federalists wanted when they fought to block his mission and later to reject its fruit. They pinned their faith on the Paris mission of Monroe, one of their leading members, and he was very frank in his correspondence with the Secretary of State. Writing in September, 1795, while still hoping that "the most shameful transaction" would not be ratified, he urged cordial coöperation with France, then "willing to give us the fortune of its arms, in support of our claims against a common enemy." Only by compulsion, he said, would Britain be persuaded to acknowledge the just rights of the United States.

> To secure success, by embarking this Government with full zeal in our behalf, and striking terror into England, it will be necessary to lay hold of her property within the United States, take the posts, and even invade Canada. This would not only secure to us completely our claims upon Britain, and especially if we likewise cut up her trade by privateers; but, by making a decisive and powerful diversion in favor of France, promote, and very essentially, a general peace.

Here was the war of 1812, advocated seventeen years earlier by the spokesman of the party which was to bring on that war and the very man who was Secretary of State in 1812.

Jay's Treaty, though barely sufficient to prevent the threatened outbreak of hostilities with Britain, led to hostilities with France; and the growing quarrel between the two republics thrust into the background the serious Anglo-American differences which the maritime war had raised and the treaty had not removed. The Royal Navy did not need to bear so heavily upon American commerce, now that the irate French were driving it away from their shores, and the United States drew even closer to Britain. The mouths of the Republicans were effectively stopped, and the minds of the Federalists began to cherish wild dreams of British sea power's being used in a combined onslaught of Britain and the United States upon the French and Spanish empires in the New World.

The key to the international position of the American Republic was in France. French folly had pushed things to this pass; French wisdom might pull them back. On the receipt of definite suggestions from Paris that a reconciliation was possible, President John Adams sent over a delegation which achieved it in a treaty signed on September 30, 1800. The conclusion of this agreement reversed the direction in which the United States had been traveling. Escaping from the quarrel with France meant getting tangled up once more in the quarrel with Britain over her maritime conduct. Moreover, the wily Bonaparte saw to it that the treaty contained articles postulating maritime principles which were acceptable to the Americans but repugnant to the British. The logical consequence, however, did not follow, because the operation of the new treaty was suspended until after it could do its work. A hitch over the French payment of American claims delayed final ratification until December, 1801, nearly three months after the signature of the preliminaries which restored peace between Britain and France. Thus did the first period of the European struggle come to a close just as the United States was headed back toward war with Britain. It was the natural course from which, during the greater part of this period, France had compelled her to retreat.

The second period of the European war, which opened with the rupture of the Peace of Amiens in May, 1803, presents a striking parallel. Again the United States found that the equilibrium of neutrality was essentially unstable. Again the pressure from both sides was so intolerable that she sought an escape by accommodation with either, which of course meant the abandonment of neutrality. . . . This time it was a fight to the finish between the powerful belligerents. Both scorned her potential resistance and resorted to more violent measures, thereby making it more difficult for her to find any basis of accommodation with either. Neither would yield to her demands even to win her alliance, which was offered in the vain hope of playing off one against the other. She had an abundance of provocation for making war on both, but that was utterly impossible. Finally, so it has been said, Napoleon tricked her into declaring it against Britain. But we can see this end coming independently of his deception: for Britain, being in command of the sea, pressed much harder than France upon American neutral rights under international law; and France, having no foothold on the continent of North America, was much less vulnerable.

Before following in detail the evolution just outlined, it may be well to clarify the issues in the quarrel between the United States and Britain arising out of the latter's conflict with France. To accomplish this purpose, it will first be advisable to make some comments upon international law; for the quarrel was embedded in it, each side seeking to uphold its own "rights" under that law.

The nature of international law is perhaps the most important thing of all to remember in this connection. As a human institution, law implies some legislator and some tribunal capable of interpreting it and commanding its enforcement; but the sovereignty of the state has denied these conditions for international law, and therefore many careful authorities have insisted that it is not law at all. Strictly speaking, it has been a body of rules derived from common custom and consent. Private individuals, such as Grotius and Vattel, analyzed and expounded it in scholarly texts which became classics but nothing more. The principles thus set forth, being based on precedents which were by no means uniform, were necessarily very general and always open to conflicting interpretations to cover conflicting interests. Then the only solution was the superior force of one side. The whole structure was made more uncertain still by one principle, that of reprisal, which might undo any other principle, and by the insoluble problem of change. Consent is necessary for change, but consent becomes most impossible when change becomes most imperative —when war reveals new circumstances that undermine and destroy the old law governing the conduct of hostilities. . . .

Impressment was the most baffling issue between the two countries. Though thrust forward by the war, it was not a question of the laws of war which define the balance between belligerent and neutral rights. It concerned something more permanent, more deep-seated—sovereignty. It was raised by the attraction of British seamen to the American service. They deserted the navy, where life was too much like a floating hell; and they left the British mercantile marine, whence they were liable at any time to be impressed into the navy. There was only one place where they could go, and it was an inviting heaven where they would be at home right away. The merchant marine of the United States was hungry for sailors. Under the stimulus of the war, it was expanding so rapidly that it required four or five thousand additional hands every year. The increased demand tripled American wages afloat. This salvation of the British tar, however, threatened the destruction of Britain by draining the lifeblood of her sea power, the one thing that stood between her and downfall. To check this vital loss, British warships searched American vessels and removed British fugitives.

Necessity overrides law, and Britain was impelled by necessity. But she insisted that her action was not illegal. Though this may seem strange now, it was not then, for important developments in international law and usage have since taken place. One is in our concept of nationality. We have become accustomed to think of people changing their national status almost as readily as they change their shirts. Then nationality was commonly considered to be about as impossible to change as one's skin. It is the phenomenal growth of the United States by immigration that has made the difference, and even yet the new American-born principle has not gained universal acceptance. This principle, however, played no part in the quarrel over impressment. The American government did not pretend to throw the protecting cloak of American naturalization around the bodies of these British fugitives. The quarrel over impressment turned on the right of search for deserters, and on the abuses which inevitably accompanied the practice.

The right of search was the main point in the dispute, and here the clash between the past and the future stands out clearly. The British position rested on the prerogative of sovereignty to pursue fugitive nationals anywhere up to a line where another sovereignty barred the pursuit. The United States claimed no right to protect American vessels from search in British territorial waters; nor, on the other hand, did Britain claim the right of search within territorial waters of the United States. It was a question of jurisdiction on the high seas, over which there was of course no sovereignty, and there the difference was not over the immunity of government vessels. Though the *Chesapeake* incident has at times led people to suppose the contrary, Britain never asserted the right to search units of the United States Navy. What she did assert, and the United States deny, was the right to search private vessels because this involved no invasion of another sovereignty. Both sides were right, Britain by the old usage, and the United States by a new doctrine then only beginning to take shape: that a country's ships at sea are detached portions of its soil and therefore covered by its sovereignty. Though already admitted for public vessels, it was not yet really established for private ones. Even today this sovereignty is not as complete as that which exists on land or within the limits of territorial waters, and the United States admitted qualification then. The American government recognized, for example, the British right to stop and search private American ships for contraband in time of war.

It was the abuses which accompanied the practice of search for deserters that inflamed the quarrel, and these abuses occurred on both sides. The British never claimed the right to impress American seamen, but they did impress them as British subjects. It was often impossible to tell the difference between the American and the British members of a crew, for there was no national distinction of language, physical appearance, dress, or manners. British deserters sailing under the Stars and Stripes would insist that they belonged to that flag; and the officers under whom they were serving, loath to lose valuable hands, would support their contention. A boarding officer in search of men whom he badly needed was judge in his own cause, and there was no real check upon his arbitrary decisions. No officer who seized goods as contraband could touch his share of the prize until it was brought into port and there condemned after a legal trial of the seizure, but there was no such procedure to protect human beings seized on the wide ocean. The only way to rescue an American thus carried off was to prove to the Admiralty that he was an American, and then an order for his release would be issued; but this was a difficult business and painfully slow. Early in the first period of the war the American government thought to check the abuse by what were known as "protections." These were certificates of American citizenship issued by magistrates at home and consuls abroad. But the granting of these papers was not hedged about by proper restrictions. It was all too easy for a British tar to get one. They were often given out indiscriminately; sailors lost them and sold them; they were cheap. So notorious did the traffic become that the device made things worse instead of better. British officers naturally came to have nothing but scorn for these official documents of the United States. As the years passed, the number of kidnaped Americans serving in the Royal Navy mounted until it was several thousand. This right of search and practice of impressment was the British counterpart of the unrestricted submarine campaign conducted by Germany a century later, for it touched American lives, and lives are more precious than goods.

Interference with American trade, the other great issue which the French war raised between the United States and Britain, was a complicated question. Though some references have previously been made to this problem, a fuller analysis is necessary here. The trouble springs from the very nature of war. It is a triangular affair. In addition to the clash of arms between belligerents, it precipitates a clash of interest between belligerent and neutral over intercourse with the enemy. The one would like to stop it completely and the other to continue it without any interruption. Long experience has tended to work out a rough compromise between them, for both have felt the restraint of prudence, the belligerent fearing to push the neutral to the point of open hostility, and the neutral shrinking from resistance that would mean fighting. Hence it came to be generally recognized that a belligerent could seize and condemn as legal prize any neutral vessel and cargo containing contraband being sent to the enemy country; and also, under the same penalty, could prohibit any neutral vessel, no matter what her cargo, from entering or leaving a blockaded port of the enemy.

All governments admitted that arms and accouterments of war constituted contraband, but there was no common agreement upon the further definition of the term. The textbook writers offered confusing advice. From the conflicting precedents which they recorded, they could deduce only the general principle that other things which might be used by the fighting forces could be treated as contraband when particular circumstances warranted such procedure. A few treaties gave greater precision to the meaning of the word; but there was conflict between them, and each had only limited application. Thus the original clash of interest survived. Belligerents sought to expand the definition of the term, and neutrals to contract it. Both dressed up selfish interests as legal rights, and the decision between them was left as before to force tempered by prudence. Because the British soon chased the French from the sea, it was the interest of the latter to uphold the narrowest neutral view, and of the former to maintain the opposite, so that over this question the United States became embroiled with Britain and not with France. As we have already seen, however, prudential considerations moved Britain to qualify her seizure of provisions as contraband by purchasing them and paying demurrage. . . .

More exasperating difficulties grew out of the application of the other principle mentioned above. When was a blockade not a blockade? It was commonly conceded that a blockade had to be officially declared and had to be effective, but there was absolutely no consensus of opinion on what was "effective." . . .

From the ancient and undoubted right of a belligerent to capture private ships and goods of the enemy at sea, sprang other issues between the United States and Britain. One was the principle of "free ships, free goods," which would limit this right by giving immunity to enemy goods, other than contraband, on board neutral vessels. The limitation was so severe that, if enforced, it would have largely destroyed the value of the right, for an enemy could then trade with impunity under the protection of neutral flags. It was a doctrine made by neutrals in the interest of neutrals, to whom it would hand over the carrying trade of belligerents. Its advocates gave it a specious appearance of justice by coupling it with the converse, "enemy ships, enemy goods," which would likewise benefit neutrals by discouraging neutral use of belligerent bottoms. Free ships, free goods, was another of the principles laid down in the Declaration of Paris in 1856. At the time of the French Revolutionary wars, it was a subject of rather violent disagreement. It was already well on the way to establishment, for it had been written into a number of specific treaties. Even Britain had signed an odd treaty embodying it, but she had never admitted its general application, and she could not do so then without playing into the hands of France. For this very reason, France had lined up with the neutral powers; and she tried to use them, particularly her American protégé and ally, in forcing it upon Britain. It was the official doctrine of the United States government. . . .

Of more serious consequence was the disputed right of neutrals in time of war to enter a trade that was shut to them in time of peace. This likewise threatened to destroy the value of the belligerent right to capture enemy property at sea. No compromise principle of any kind had arisen to regulate this issue. It involved two important branches of trade—coasting and colonial. Both were almost universally preserved as strict national monopolies in the period with which we are concerned. If a belligerent, exercising the clear right of capturing enemy ships and cargoes, could drive the enemy from the sea, the enemy would naturally seek relief by temporarily opening its monopoly to neutrals. If they took advantage of this indulgence they would certainly be bringing succor to the distressed enemy. Could neutrals do it and yet remain neutrals?

It was the colonial side of the question which first thrust itself forward, and therefore the first to get any answer. That was in the Seven Years' War, during which the British Empire devoured most of the French

Empire overseas. Hard pressed by British maritime superiority, France was unable to supply her West Indies or to bring their produce to Europe under her own flag; and therefore she resorted to the expedient of relaxing her colonial monopoly in favor of neutrals. To counter this novel action, the British prize courts promulgated the novel doctrine which came to be known as "the Rule of the War of 1756," and later simply "the Rule of 1756," to which reference has already been made in a previous chapter. It was naturally a categorical negative to the question just stated. Made in Britain to support the interest of Britain, it was another illustration of law being the declared will of superior force. But there was justice in the contention that a trade prohibited by municipal law during peace should be prohibited by international law during war. It deprived neutrals of no right which they enjoyed prior to the outbreak of war, and it was necessary to preserve the value of an unquestioned belligerent right. It was a new rule called forth by new conditions, and it was promulgated in the only way possible. Yet, however just it might be, it ran counter to the interests of neutrals and of belligerents that suffered from naval impotence; and they would not recognize the validity of this fiat of a single power.

The first American collision with this rule, as we have already seen, nearly precipitated the United States into a declaration of war in the spring of 1794. Indeed Britain had overstepped her own mark by ordering the indiscriminate capture of American vessels trafficking in the French West Indies, for a limited trade in American vessels of small burthen had been legalized before the war; and she drew back just in time. She then contented herself with only a partial application of the rule, ordering the capture of vessels laden in the French West Indies with produce of those islands and sailing thence for Europe. The fruits of the naval superiority of the belligerent were being shared with a neutral. . . .

American action, both public and private, was responsible for destroying the foundation of the British prize-court decisions favorable to the American interest. The doctrine of the broken voyage rested on the assumption that the goods in question were legally imported for use in the United States before they were reëxported. Importation meant the payment of customs duties, and the performance of such operations as unloading, checking, weighing, and storing, all of which involved time and expense. The corresponding operations attendant upon exportation of course added more to the cost. Here were hardships which the trade winds could not blow away, but American ingenuity might remove.

In 1799, Congress passed an act authorizing drawbacks which reduced to a nominal rate the duties paid on certain articles. These, it was observed, were "the ordinary and peculiar subjects of trade between Europe and the West-India colonies." This piece of legislation, which would go far to mend what had been broken, remained unnoticed in England for some time, probably because the hostile relations then subsisting between the United States and France blocked its effect upon the operation of the Rule of 1756. But it could not escape attention after the rupture of the Peace of Amiens, when its effect was bound to be felt because Franco-

American relations were once more friendly. This effect was enhanced by another mending process which, by contrast, was quite illegal and therefore conducted less openly. There was a constant temptation to cut corners with cargoes in port. Why go through all the motions of importing and reëxporting, when the same freight was put back in the same hold? Why should Americans suffer this absurd handicap for the benefit of British competitors? Patriotism pulled with profits, private shippers conspired with public officials, and proper papers covered improper performance. Some vessels even cleared with untouched cargoes. What was pious fraud in American ports became plain fraud under British questioning elsewhere. Thus, by congressional enactment and by official connivance, the Rule of 1756 was circumvented in the United States. But it was impossible to mend the broken voyage without ending it. That this was what Americans were doing, the British began to see when the war with France was resumed in the spring of 1803. Almost immediately the modern doctrine of the continuous voyage raised its head in the British prize courts, though it was not until the spring of 1805 that it was finally established by a judgment on appeal. Its establishment doomed American ships and cargoes to capture and condemnation, thereby ruining a lucrative American trade.

Whether neutrals could engage in the coasting trade of an enemy—the other part of the question which had evoked the Rule of 1756—remained in the background much longer than the problem of colonial trade. Though it had not yet pressed for an answer, Bonaparte's treaty with the United States in 1800 supplied one inferentially. The definition of commercial rights mentioned above stipulated the freedom of a neutral to navigate between enemy ports. Not until some little time after the renewal of hostilities in 1803 did this issue thrust itself forward, and then it was soon obscured by other issues. As Napoleon's power spread on land and Britain's grew on the sea, he was relieved and she was frustrated by neutrals' taking over the coasting trade of his empire. Sooner or later she was bound to strike at their interference in this new sphere as she had struck at their interference in colonial trade during the Seven Years' War. She held her hand until January, 1807, when, finding a plausible excuse in Napoleon's recent Berlin Decree which was still little more than an empty threat, she outlawed all commerce between ports under his control. Apparently this extension of the Rule of 1756 was directed at northern Europeans, chiefly the Danes, rather than the Americans, but it was plainly recognized that they would feel the blow too. The American government promptly protested that the British action was illegal unless based on "actual blockades," and pointed out that it would ruin a trade which Britain herself recognized as wholly legitimate. The profits of a voyage commonly depended on dropping some cargo here and some there, and on picking up a return cargo in the same way. If an American merchantman had to make the whole exchange in one place, it might as well not go to France at all.

Thus did the issue over the enemy's coasting trade come into the open when the issue over the enemy's colonial trade was finally chased out of its hole by the doctrine of the continuous voyage. Together they were capable of doing great damage to Anglo-American relations, and therefore it is easy to imagine the havoc wrought by the quarrel which soon swallowed them up along with all the other particular issues concerning trade—the quarrel over Napoleon's Berlin and Milan decrees and Britain's equally famous orders-in-council.

To understand these decrees and orders, we should remember that they accompanied the approach of the supreme crisis in the life-and-death struggle between the two powers which were then by far the greatest on earth. Napoleon had come to realize that his position in Europe would never be secure until he subdued Britain, and she that her freedom depended on his downfall. Having had to abandon his projected invasion of the island kingdom because British sea power effectively barred the way, he perforce fell back upon the use of his land power to accomplish by slow strangulation what was impossible by quick assault. Taking advantage of the fact that Britain had stretched her declaration of blockade to cover a considerable length of his northern coast line, he stretched his declaration still farther and justified his action as a proper reprisal. He proclaimed the blockade of the whole of the British Isles.

This was a sort of fantastic and inverted blockade. Napoleon had no navy to enforce it, and his object was not so much to keep goods from reaching Britain as it was to prevent them from leaving. Because of this inversion, however, and also because of the wide extent of his power upon the Continent, he could undertake to enforce the blockade without a navy. This was what he was doing when he ordered the confiscation of all British goods and also, under pain of confiscation, the exclusion of every ship that touched at a British port. By depriving Britain of access to the European market upon which her economic life depended, he calculated that he could soon reduce the nation of traders and manufacturers to cry for mercy. Such, in short, was his Continental System which he began to enforce vigorously in the late summer of 1807. Britain saw that, if he carried it through, she was done. The orders-in-council were her desperate reply. She extended her blockade to every port from which he excluded her ships; and she turned back upon him provisions of his own decrees, declaring that she would treat as an enemy any ship which, without first going to Britain, sought to enter any port controlled by him.

The position of neutrals became impossible. It would have been much easier for them if they could have chosen to trade either with Britain or with the Napoleonic empire, but this was not the alternative that was forced upon them. The real issue was the Continental System. Would they coöperate with Napoleon in upholding it, or with Britain in undermining it? The question presented a perfect dilemma. A neutral vessel could not approach any European port that was under Napoleon's sway without being liable to seizure, either outside by a ship of the Royal Navy or inside by Napoleon's officials; inside, if it had touched at a British port, or had procured British papers; outside, if it had not. It was a choice between the devil and the deep sea.

Each belligerent was coercing neutrals to serve its own end; and as neutral rights disappeared under the combined pressure, each belligerent defended its departures from the traditional law of nations by accusing the other of prior violations and by blaming neutrals for their non-resistance to these violations. Neutrals, however, could not accept the self-justification of either without shedding their neutrality, nor could they offer resistance to either without running the same risk. Resistance to both was unthinkable. It was then more terribly true than ever that law is what those who can and will enforce it say that it is; and that the principle of reprisal, once let loose, may destroy the other principles of the laws of war. Indeed, the "laws of war" is a contradiction in terms.

Both belligerents this time flouted the United States, and both professed eagerness to resume conformity to traditional law; but each insisted that the other should do it first, or that the Americans should resist with force the coercion of the other. Theoretically, the two belligerents were equally oppressive; but practically, legally, and psychologically they were not. Britain's control of the sea, being greater than Napoleon's control of the land, gave her greater power of enforcement. Much more important was the legal difference. Her seizures were made at sea and therefore, according to her own admission, were a violation of neutral rights under international law, her justification being that it was a necessary reprisal against Napoleon. His seizures, except an occasional capture by a fugitive French frigate or privateer at sea, were all made in port and therefore within the undoubted jurisdiction of his own or a subordinate government. Strictly speaking, his only violation of neutral rights under international law was confined to the occasional captures just mentioned. Napoleon also struck a responsive chord in the United States when he denounced the orders-in-council as designed to establish the economic supremacy of England upon the ruins of the industry and commerce of European countries. Here we approach another fundamental factor in the growing Anglo-American bitterness.

Between Britain and the United States there was a mutual suspicion mounting to a settled conviction that each was using the war to cheat the other out of its rights. The British were exasperated by the paradox of their position. Never had they possessed such complete control of the sea, yet more than ever the sea-borne trade of the enemy was escaping from their grasp. As already suggested, neutrals were running off with it and giving it their protection. They were climbing up on the back of the British navy, whose supremacy persuaded the enemy to hand over this trade; and they were throwing dust in the eyes of British judges, causing them to release as neutral what was really enemy property. By such means not only were they expanding their merchant marine while that of Britain shrank; they were actually robbing her of the profitable prizes of war and also of the crowning prize of a victorious end to the war. In other words, their cupidity had leagued them with the enemy and drawn them into an underhand war against Britain. The tricks by which they performed the daily miracle of transforming enemy into neutral commerce were publicly exposed, and a new British policy was demanded, by James Stephen in his *War in Disguise, or the Frauds of the Neutral Flags,* a pamphlet of more than two hundred pages which appeared in the fall of 1805. The author knew whereof he spoke, for he was perhaps the leading practitioner in the prize appeal court and he had earlier followed his profession in the West Indies. He probably shared the responsibility for the adoption of the principle of the continuous voyage, but this did not satisfy him. He was positive that there was only one cure for the evil, and that was a rigorous application of the Rule of 1756. Even if it drove neutrals into open hostilities, that would be preferable to this covert war. Britain would then be free to use her strength to strike down those who were injuring her. . . .

As British people believed that Americans were abusing their neutral rights to the vital injury of Britain, so were Americans convinced that Britain was abusing her temporary belligerent rights to serve her permanent economic interests and that in doing so she was furtively dealing a dangerous blow at their country. They saw her trying, under cover of the war, to monopolize the commerce of the world. This may seem absurd when we remember that their mercantile marine had enjoyed a phenomenal expansion through the war while hers had suffered a contraction; but we should not overlook some other important considerations. Britain was in a position to do this very thing, international law being what it was and the Royal Navy being virtually supreme upon the sea; and there was no gainsaying the fact that measures which she took to win the war also tended to benefit her own carrying trade and commerce at the expense of others. In the United States this further effect was bound to be regarded as intentional and not just incidental. The adoption of the doctrine of the continuous voyage contained the suggestion that Britain would destroy what she could not appropriate; and the orders-in-council seemed to prove it.

The American reaction appears all the more natural when viewed in the light of the past. Britain had laid herself open to this suspicion by a policy which she, and she alone, had followed for generations. It was the policy of her navigation laws, by which she excluded foreigners from all but a corner of her carrying trade. This application of the monopolistic principle was purposely made to stimulate the growth of the country's merchant marine, and was commonly credited, both at home and abroad, with having made it what it was—the greatest in the world. Another object of the exclusion of foreigners was to deprive them, particularly the Dutch, of their function as middlemen in international trade, and to transfer this function and its profits to England. Not unconsciously had she become the chief storehouse and clearinghouse of the world's commerce, or, to use the language of the day, the great entrepot. She had attained a position where she held the world in fee. It is not surprising, therefore, that non-British eyes saw in the orders-in-council a new and ruthless projection of the old and selfish design. To Americans, of all people, these orders-in-council were particularly offensive. The reason for their peculiar sensitiveness lay in their own history: they were being forced back into the dependence of colonial days. Once more Britain was insisting that they should have no trade of their own, that all their foreign commerce must be under her control. American Independence was at stake!

. . . According to a thesis which has been widely accepted in recent years, we cannot understand why there was a War of 1812 unless we look inland. This thesis may be summarized as follows. The quarrel over neutral rights on the sea brought the United States to the verge of war with Britain but did not do more than that, for the maritime constituencies voted against war. The force that induced the last fatal step was largely, though not wholly, an urge to conquer Canada. This urge was chiefly inspired by the determination to uproot the British-Indian evil but was also compounded of the old jealousy of the British fur trade and a new lust for territorial expansion that anticipated "Manifest Destiny"; and it found abundant "righteous pretexts" in the maritime quarrel. "By the end of the spring of 1812, the whole frontier country from New Hampshire to Kentucky was insisting that the British must be expelled from Canada." But the people of the Northwest might have clamored in vain for war if they had not found fortuitous allies in the people of the South, who were likewise impatient to take Florida from Spain, the weak ally of Britain. This combination, which promised to preserve the balance between North and South by adding territory and population to both, brought on the war. . . . Confirmation has also been found in the division of Congress on the war issue, "most of the navigating interests voting nay, and the interior, particularly the whole frontier in a great crescent from Vermont to Louisiana, voting aye," with "only a small majority for war."

There is more than one *non sequitur* in this argument. Does the voting of the maritime constituencies prove that neutral rights alone could not have produced the war? Their votes were divided, as a glance at the map shows; and the division would have been more equal if it had truly reflected the opinions of the people. Nor should it be forgotten that this was the part of the country that stood to suffer most in a trial of strength with British sea power. Much more serious is another consideration which we have already seen. The American government had to champion the maritime interests not only in spite of their opposition but also because of their opposition. The commercial and shipping elements had been betraying the national honor. They would have sold neutral rights and the country's independence for selfish profit and sectional welfare.

The southern pressure for war is also misconstrued. Why should Americans want war with Britain in order to seize Florida? Part had already been taken without it, and the obstacle that seemed to stand in the way of getting the rest was the possibility of British intervention. Britain ruled the waves, and the waves nearly surrounded Florida. Moreover the administration's schemes for acquiring this weakly held Spanish possession were well under way long before the "War Hawks" flocked to the Twelfth Congress. The one reason why the South should welcome war with Britain to aid in getting Florida was to buy off sectional opposition within the United States by letting the North have its *quid pro quo* in Canada; but, as already suggested, this meant running the obvious danger of the means' defeating the end. The reports of the debates in the *Annals of Congress* contain no suggestion of Florida's being a motive for war; but they do reveal another material motive which has attracted too little attention. It was a strong one.

The planters were being badly pinched. "Our cotton is reduced to seven cents, and our tobacco to nothing," cried old Robert Wright of Maryland in the House. He denied Randolph's assertion "that our own restrictive system has undone us," pointing out that restrictions on the export of these articles had ceased and if they had been the cause the effect should have ceased too. "The price of cotton depends on the demand for the manufactures of that article; the English-made cottons depended on the continental markets, from which the British manufactures are excluded. The price of tobacco never was materially varied by the consumption in England, but depended on the foreign demand from Great Britain, which, by their exclusion from the continent, is almost entirely arrested." The retaliatory system of the two great belligerents, he said, had ruined the market for these American staples, and since Napoleon had revoked his decrees the blame now rested on the British orders-in-council. Wright put his finger on the sore spot of the South. This was the one section of the country that was vitally dependent upon the markets controlled by Napoleon. It was not a commercial region; but its very life was tied up with commerce. Here was a further reason for championing the maritime interests in their own despite. Maritime New England would have deserted the planter South; and the rural North would have done the same thing, for it was attracted by the fabulous price of wheat in England and the market for provisions created by the Peninsular War.

The voting of the frontier constituencies from Kentucky to New Hampshire also calls for more careful analysis. Another glance at the map shows that the unanimity was broken in Vermont and more particularly in New York. But if there had been no such break, the attitude of the members from the interior would be quite understandable without any reference to Canada. Practically all the members of Congress, no matter what part of the country they represented or how they voted in the end, admitted that the United States had just grounds for declaring war on Britain. This being so, it stands to reason that those who came from the interior were least inhibited by the fear of consequences. Their electors had little direct interest in the sea-borne commerce which would be disrupted; they had no settlements which might be bombarded by British naval guns; and, if we except inhabitants of New York and Vermont, they were about as secure from a British military attack. This immunity was the common contemporary explanation of the pronounced bellicose attitude of the interior. It was also said that the western members saw in a war a lever to raise the price of hemp and of other produce which their people wished to sell but could not.

Though the Indian menace, which was played up by the Republican press, haunted the minds of some members of Congress, there is a good reason for doubting if it had any appreciable influence in bringing on the war with Britain. The sea of the native strife lay off in a remote corner. Relatively few whites lived anywhere near it, and they had no representatives in Congress. There it was openly said that Americans had stirred up the hornets' nest, and the aggressive character of Harrison's advance on Tippecanoe was so obvious that it was difficult to deny. A close study of all the debates from the opening of the session until the declaration of war shows that very few members, and they only very occasionally, pointed to the red peril or accused Britain of instigating it. If the old nightmare turned any vote from peace to war, there is no evidence for it in the *Annals of Congress.* In the President's historic message of June 1, 1812, recommending a declaration of war, Britain is charged most positively with "a series of acts, hostile to the United States as an independent and neutral nation," and after the enumeration of these acts, which are a catalogue of the maritime grievances, a short paragraph insinuating that there was some connection between the hostility of the savages and their intercourse with the British is inserted as a sort of afterthought. This is the only reference to the Indian troubles and it makes no definite charge. Apparently the administration did not consider the native hostilities to be a cause of war any more than did the majority in Congress.

The conquest of Canada was frequently mentioned in the debates, but the suggestion that it was desirable for its own sake was made so rarely that a reader of the debates might miss it if he did not look for it. Randolph's words which have been quoted above should not be taken at their face value. This Virginian stood out from among his fellow members of the House as the most persistent opponent of war. He denounced it eloquently, at great length, and often. If he really believed that the effective cause of the pressure for war was agrarian cupidity, rather than maritime grievances, we might expect to find that he directed his invective at this dishonorable motive again and again. But he did not. His words which have been so aptly used to support this thesis constitute only a short passage in a long speech delivered six months before the war, and there is hardly an echo of them in the records of his many other speeches during these six months. In the reports of what was said by all the other speakers who opposed war, there is equally little to support the startling charge he flung at the warmongers in December, 1811. Evidently it was not considered to have much point.

This conclusion is confirmed by a careful reading of Foster's letters. They reveal him not only as most interested in whatever was going on but also as one of the best-informed men in the country, and they do not even suggest that an urge for the conquest of Canada was a cause of war. At the very end, during the secret session in which Congress passed the act declaring war, the idea did creep into one of his dispatches. He wrote that Harper of New Hampshire, a member of the committee on foreign relations, was reported as saying that "it would be advisable to go to war for Canada alone" and "he would be for never laying down arms until Canada should be taken." The British minister's only comment was, "It is supposed that this was a manoeuvre by which to get rid of the question of war altogether, as it would be impossible ever to get the House to agree to so great an absurdity." He was perfectly familiar with the talk of an attack on Canada, but he saw war coming as a consequence of what had happened at sea and not because of what was expected to happen on land.

This concept of the war dominated the discussions in Congress, and it was not the product of the "War Hawks." Erskine had described it before their party was hatched. It was simple, logical, and honorable. Britain had injured the United States on the high seas, where she was invincible. To challenge her there would be to court defeat. Britain had a thousand warships; the United States had not a single ship-of-the-line and only a half dozen frigates. A swarm of American privateers might prey upon British commerce, but a few heavy vessels of the Royal Navy might bombard American cities and even capture American ports. The only way to make Britain submit was to strike her where she was vulnerable—in the provinces adjoining on the north. Quebec might be too hard a nut to crack, but the United States could easily overrun the two Canadas right down to that fortress, and Quebec without the country back of it would be of little value to Britain. The small attention paid to Halifax is explained by the plain fact that it was beyond the American reach. The prevailing thought was that the United States was potentially supreme on land, as Britain was actually supreme on the sea. Each country had its own element, though only one had used it; and Britain would cease from her oppression at sea rather than lose her share of the land. If the worst came to the worst and, as one senator pointed out, Britain should get possession of New York and New Orleans, they could be recovered by an exchange of conquests. The conquest of Canada was anticipated as the seizure of a hostage rather than as the capture of a prize. . . .

Additional Reading

Irving Brant, *James Madison: Secretary of State, 1800–1809* (1953).

———, *James Madison: Commander in Chief, 1812–1836* (1961).

Albert Z. Carr, *The Coming of War* (1960).

Louis M. Hacker, "Western Land Hunger and the War of 1812," *Mississippi Valley Historical Review*, X (1924), 365–395.

Margaret K. Latimer, "South Carolina—a Protagonist of the War of 1812," *American Historical Review*, LXI (1956), 914–929.

Bradford Perkins, *Prologue to War: England and the United States, 1805–1812* (1961).

Julius W. Pratt, "Western Aims in the War of 1812," *Mississippi Valley Historical Review*, XII (1925), 36–50.

G. R. Taylor, "Agrarian Discontent in the Mississippi Valley preceding the War of 1812," *Journal of Political Economy*, XXXIX (1931), 471–505.

6 THE MONROE DOCTRINE: *Altruism or Self-interest?*

President Monroe's Seventh Annual Message to Congress on December 2, 1823 contained, in widely separated passages, three important statements on foreign policy. Although the initial impact was fleeting, this portion of the address was to be revived and reapplied in the 1840's as *the* Monroe Doctrine. In the course of time, as the United States waxed in power and came to play a predominant role in the international affairs of the Western Hemisphere, the Monroe Doctrine, together with the Farewell Address, became virtually sacrosanct in American foreign policy. What Monroe stated in 1823 was that the Western Hemisphere was no longer open to European colonization schemes—the noncolonization clause; that the new world comprised a separate sphere from the old and therefore that it was sound American policy to abstain from involvement in purely European wars—the two-spheres concept; and that, in return, the United States would view as an unfriendly act any effort by European states to use force to suppress the independence of states in the two Americas—the nonintervention clause. Monroe's fame resulted not from originality in formulating a new foreign policy, but in stating forcibly and succinctly views which most Americans then and later accepted as profoundly wise and true. Monroe had capsulized truths derived from American experiences since the founding of the colonies.

The immediate prelude to Monroe's action was the efforts of the Quadruple Alliance, popularly if misleadingly known in America as the Holy Alliance, to suppress liberalism and revolutionary movements in Europe. France, again respectable after the Bourbon restoration, sought to atone for its revolutionary past by acting as the agent for monarchical and conservative Europe and used armed intervention in Spain to destroy a liberal constitution and return Ferdinand VII to absolute power. The Great Powers then became interested in the problem of restoring Spanish rule over the rebellious colonies in the Americas, and understandably aroused fears in the United States that an armed intervention was planned for the Western Hemisphere. Both England and the United States had benefited commercially from the independence movements in Latin America which had destroyed the old closed Spanish mercantilist system and neither of these powers wished to see that system restored. In addition, many Americans sympathized with the independence movements in Latin America and were apprehensive that a successful Holy Alliance intervention there might subsequently be turned against the United States.

On August 20, 1823, British Foreign Secretary George Canning suggested to the American minister, Richard Rush, that since the interests of the two nations were similar a joint declaration against possible European intervention would be wise. Canning's overtures, when transmitted to Washington, D.C., precipitated policy discussions within the Monroe Administration from which resulted the warnings contained in the annual message to Congress in December, Scholars have debated several aspects of the formulation of the Monroe Doctrine, including that of authorship of its several clauses. The following documents and readings are focused on the problem of American motives and purposes.

DOCUMENTS

1. Cooperation versus Separate Action

Upon receipt of information about Canning's proposal, President Monroe consulted his cabinet and the two Republican ex-presidents for advice on the policy to be adopted. Madison and Jefferson agreed that despite the dangers of entanglement, the United States should cope with the peril in cooperation with Great Britain. Secretary of State John Quincy Adams dissented. Convinced that there actually was little danger and that if it did materialize Great Britain would have to act in any case, he advised an independent American statement against Holy Alliance intervention. His diary account of the cabinet meeting where the decision, in effect, was made for separate action indicates his reasons.

Jefferson Advises Monroe to Accept British Cooperation

Dear Sir, The question presented by the letters you have sent me, is the most momentous which has ever been offered to my contemplation since that of Independence. That made us a nation, this sets our compass and points the course which we are to steer through the ocean of time opening on us. And never could we embark on it under circumstances more auspicious. Our first and fundamental maxim should be, never to entangle ourselves in the broils of Europe. Our second, never to suffer Europe to intermeddle with cis-Atlantic affairs. America, North and South, has a set of interests distinct from those of Europe, and peculiarly her own. She should therefore have a system of her own, separate and apart from that of Europe. While the last is laboring to become the domicile of despotism, our endeavor should surely be to make our hemisphere that of freedom. One nation, most of all, could disturb us in this pursuit; she now offers to lead, aid, and accompany us in it. By acceding to her proposition, we detach her from the bands, bring her mighty weight into the scale of free government, and emancipate a continent at one stroke, which might otherwise linger long in doubt and difficulty. Great Britain is the nation which can do us the most harm of any one, or all on earth; and with her on our side we need not fear the whole world. With her then, we should most sedulously cherish a cordial friendship; and nothing would tend more to knit our affections than to be fighting once more, side by side, in the same cause. . . .

But we have first to ask ourselves a question. Do we wish to acquire to our own confederacy any one or more of the Spanish provinces? I candidly confess, that I have ever looked on Cuba as the most interesting addition which could ever be made to our system of States. The control which, with Florida Point, this island would give us over the Gulf of Mexico, and the countries and isthmus bordering on it, as well as all those whose waters flow into it, would fill up the measures of our political well-being. Yet, as I am sensible that this can never be obtained, even with her own consent, but by war; and its independence, which is our second interest, (and especially its independence of England,) can be secured without it, I have no hesitation in abandoning my first wish to future chances, and accepting its independence, with peace and the friendship of England, rather than its association, at the expense of war and her enmity.

I could honestly, therefore, join in the declaration proposed, that we aim not at the acquisition of any of those possessions, that we will not stand in the way of any amicable arrangement between them and the Mother country; but that we will oppose, with all our means, the forcible interposition of any other power, as auxiliary, stipendiary, or under any other form or pretext, and most especially, their transfer to any power by conquest, cession, or acquisition in any other way. I should think it, therefore, advisable, that the Executive should encourage the British government to a continuance in the dispositions expressed in these letters, by an assurance of his concurrence with them as far as his authority goes; and that as it may lead to war, the declaration of which requires an act of Congress, the case shall be laid before them for consideration at their first meeting, and under the reasonable aspect in which it is seen by himself. . . .

John Quincy Adams' Account of the Cabinet Meeting On November 7, 1823

Washington, *November* 7th.—Cabinet meeting at the President's from half-past one till four. Mr. Calhoun, Secretary of War, and Mr. Southard, Secretary of the Navy, present. The subject for consideration was, the confidential proposals of the British Secretary of State, George Canning, to R. Rush, and the correspondence between them relating to the projects of the Holy Alliance upon South America. There was much conversation, without coming to any definite point. The object of Canning appears to have been to obtain some public pledge from the Government of the United States, ostensibly against the forcible interference of the Holy Alliance between Spain and South America; but really or especially against the acquisition to the United States themselves of any part of the Spanish-American possessions.

Mr. Calhoun inclined to giving a discretionary power to Mr. Rush to join in a declaration against the interference of the Holy Allies, if necessary, even if it should pledge us not to take Cuba or the province of Texas; because the power of Great Britain being greater than ours to *seize* upon them, we should get the advantage of obtaining from her the same declaration we should make ourselves.

I thought the cases not parallel. We have no intention of seizing either Texas or Cuba. But the inhabitants of either or both may exercise their primitive rights, and solicit a union with us. They will certainly do no such thing to Great Britain. By joining with her, therefore, in her proposed declaration, we give her a substantial and perhaps inconvenient pledge against ourselves, and really obtain nothing in return. Without entering now into the enquiry of the expediency of our annexing Texas or Cuba to our Union, we should at least keep ourselves free to act as emergencies may arise, and not tie ourselves down to any principle which might immediately afterwards be brought to bear against ourselves.

Mr. Southard inclined much to the same opinion.

The President was averse to any course which should have the appearance of taking a position subordinate to that of Great Britain. . . .

I remarked that the communications recently received from the Russian Minister, Baron Tuyl, afforded, as I thought, a very suitable and convenient opportunity for us to take our stand against the Holy Alliance, and at the same time to decline the overture of Great Britain. It would be more candid, as well as more dignified, to avow our principles explicitly to Russia and France, than to come in as a cock-boat in the wake of the British man-of-war.

This idea was acquiesced in on all sides, and my draft for an answer to Baron Tuyl's note announcing the Emperor's determination to refuse receiving any Minister from the South American Governments was read. . . .

2. *The Message—a Unilateral United States Policy*

It was Monroe's decision to embody a warning to Europe in his message to Congress, rather than to express it in a formal diplomatic circular. After the Message, which temporarily aroused some appreciation in Latin America, the governments of Colombia, Brazil, and Mexico on separate occasions suggested that it be implemented by conclusion of bilateral defensive military pacts. The negative American responses made it clear that the Doctrine was a unilateral policy declaration, to be enforced only at the times and places viewed as necessary by the United States.

Monroe Cautions the Holy Alliance: Annual Message to Congress, December 2, 1823

. . . At the proposal of the Russian Imperial Government, made through the minister of the Emperor residing here, a full power and instructions have been transmitted to the minister of the United States at St. Petersburg to arrange by amicable negotiation the respective rights and interests of the two nations on the northwest coast of this continent. . . . In the discussions to which this interest has given rise and in the arrangements by which they may terminate the occasion has been judged proper for asserting, as a principle in which the rights and interests of the United

States are involved that the American continents, by the free and independent condition which they have assumed and maintain, are henceforth not to be considered as subjects for future colonization by any European powers. . . .

It was stated at the commencement of the last session that a great effort was then making in Spain and Portugal to improve the condition of the people of those countries, and that it appeared to be conducted with extraordinary moderation. It need scarcely be remarked that the result has been so far very different from what was then anticipated. Of events in that quarter of the globe, with which we have so much intercourse and from which we derive our origin, we have always been anxious and interested spectators. The citizens of the United States cherish sentiments the most friendly in favor of the liberty and happiness of their fellow-men on that side of the Atlantic. In the wars of the European powers in matters relating to themselves we have never taken any part, nor does it comport with our policy so to do. It is only when our rights are invaded or seriously menaced that we resent injuries or make preparation for our defense. With the movements in this hemisphere we are of necessity more immediately connected, and by causes which must be obvious to all enlightened and impartial observers. The political system of the allied powers is essentially different in this respect from that of America. This difference proceeds from that which exists in their respective Governments; and to the defense of our own, which has been achieved by the loss of so much blood and treasure, and matured by the wisdom of their most enlightened citizens, and under which we have enjoyed unexampled felicity, this whole nation is devoted. We owe it, therefore, to candor and to the amicable relations existing between the United States and those powers to declare that we should consider any attempt on their part to extend their system to any portion of this hemisphere as dangerous to our peace and safety. With the existing colonies or dependencies of any European power we have not interfered and shall not interfere. But with the Governments who have declared their independence and maintained it, and whose independence we have, on great consideration and on just principles, acknowledged, we could not view any interposition for the purpose of oppressing them, or controlling in any other manner their destiny, by any European power in any other light than as the manifestation of an unfriendly disposition toward the United States. In the war between those new Governments and Spain we declared our neutrality at the time of their recognition, and to this we have adhered, and shall continue to adhere, provided no change shall occur which, in the judgment of the competent authorities of this Government, shall make a corresponding change on the part of the United States indispensable to their security.

The late events in Spain and Portugal shew that Europe is still unsettled. Of this important fact no stronger proof can be adduced than that the allied powers should have thought it proper, on any principle satisfactory to themselves, to have interposed by force in the internal concerns of Spain. To what extent such interposition may be carried, on the same principle, is a question in which all independent powers whose governments differ from theirs are interested, even those most remote, and surely none more so than the United States. Our policy in regard to Europe, which was adopted at an early stage of the wars which have so long agitated that quarter of the globe, nevertheless remains the same, which is, not to interfere in the internal concerns of any of its powers; to consider the government *de facto* as the legitimate government for us; to cultivate friendly relations with it, and to preserve those relations by a frank, firm, and manly policy, meeting in all instances the just claims of every power, submitting to injuries from none. But in regard to those continents circumstances are eminently and conspicuously different. It is impossible that the allied powers should extend their political system to any portion of either continent without endangering our peace and happiness; nor can anyone believe that our southern brethren, if left to themselves, would adopt it of their own accord. It is equally impossible, therefore, that we should behold such interposition in any form with indifference. . . .

John Quincy Adams, Secretary of State, to José Maria Salazar, Colombian Minister to the United States

Washington, *August 6, 1824*—Sir: I have laid before the President of the United States, your confidential Note of the 2d. ultimo, and it has received his deliberate & full consideration. . . .

With respect to the question "in what manner the Government of the United States intends to resist on its part any interference of the Holy alliance for the purpose of subjugating the new Republics or interfering in their political forms" you understand that by the constitution of the United States, the ultimate decision of this question belongs to the Legislative Department of the Government. The probability of such interference of the Holy alliance, having in a great measure disappeared, the occasion for recurring to the dispositions of the Legislature did not occur during the late Session of Congress.

The Sentiments of the President remain as they were expressed in his last annual message to Congress—Should the crisis which appeared then to be approaching, and which gave rise to the remarks then made, hereafter recur, he will be ready to give them effect by recommending to the Legislature the adoption of the measures exclusively of their resort, and by which the principles asserted by him, would with the concurrence if given, be on the part of the United States, efficaciously maintained.

As however the occasion for this resort could arise only by a deliberate and concerted system of the allied Powers to exercise force against the freedom and Independence of your Republic; so it is obvious that the United States could not undertake resistance to them by force of Arms, without a previous understanding with those European Powers, whose Interests and whose principles would secure from them an active and efficient co-operation in the cause—This there is no reason to doubt could be obtained, but it could only be effected by a negotiation preliminary to that of any alliance between the United States and the Colombian Republic, or in any event coeval with it.

The employment of Spanish force in America, while Spain is occupied by a French army and its Government under the influence of France and her allies, does not constitute a case upon which the United States would feel themselves justified in departing from the neutrality which they have hitherto observed—The force itself being necessarily small; and in no wise changing the nature of the contest in the American Hemisphere.

I pray you, Sir, to accept [etc.].

READINGS

1. Idealism and Security

Dexter Perkins has traced the origins and evolution of the Monroe Doctrine in a series of scholarly volumes. In this selection, he acknowledges that commercial motives were involved in the Adams-drafted noncolonization clause of the Monroe Doctrine, but denies that such reasons lay behind the main body of the warning to Europe. Monroe's condemnation of armed European intervention reflected primarily his republican sympathies with Latin America and his concern for the political security of the United States and the Americas.

The Monroe Doctrine

DEXTER PERKINS

The Northwest Boundary Controversy and the Non-colonization Principle. 1823–1824

The famous declaration of December 2, 1823, which has come to be known as the Monroe Doctrine, had a dual origin and a dual purpose. On the one hand, it was the result of the advance of Russia on the northwest coast of America, and was designed to serve as a protest against this advance and to establish a general principle against Russian expansion. Referring to this question of the northwest, President Monroe laid down the principle in his message to Congress that "the American continents, by the free and independent condition which they have assumed and maintain, are henceforth not to be considered as subjects for future colonization by any European powers." On the other hand, the message was provoked by the fear of European intervention in South America to restore to Spain her revolted colonies, and was intended to give warning of the hostility of the United States to any such intervention. "With the governments [that is, of the Spanish-American republics] who have de-

Reprinted by permission of the publishers from Dexter Perkins, *The Monroe Doctrine, 1823–1826.* Cambridge, Mass.: Harvard University Press, Copyright, 1927, 1948 by the President and Fellows of Harvard College. 1955 by Dexter Perkins. pp. 3–5, 7–9, 11–14, 16–19, 40–43, 70–75, 80–81, 85.

clared their independence, and maintained it," wrote the President, "and whose independence we have, on great consideration and just principles, acknowledged, we could not view any interposition for the purpose of oppressing them, or controlling in any other manner their destiny, by any European power, in any other light than as the manifestation of an unfriendly disposition toward the United States."

Of these two aspects of the message, it is no doubt the second which involves the more interesting and important questions. How far did the manifesto of December 2, 1823, actually check European designs on the New World? How great was its immediate influence? Did it lower or raise American prestige? Did it arouse resentment or command respect? These are only some of the more significant questions that suggest themselves in connection with the message in its South American aspects. An examination of the Monroe Doctrine in the days of its origin must inevitably concern itself preponderantly with just these questions.

But, on the other hand, the non-colonization principle must not be neglected. It has a high importance in and of itself. It is indeed the most important *principle* connected with the declaration of 1823. The pregnant sentence directed against Russia was to have a wide influence as time went on. It was to play a rôle of ever-increasing importance. From it were to be deduced many of the corollaries of the Monroe Doctrine, and on it has been based more than one state paper of large significance. It is a matter of great interest, therefore, to study its origins, to understand its logic, and to analyze the effect which it produced at the time of its enunciation.

The introduction to such a study lies in an examination of the northwest controversy with Russia, in the course of which the non-colonization principle was to be laid down. Russian interest in the northwest coast of America goes back to the second quarter of the eighteenth century, to the days of the renowned navigator Vitus Behring, who discovered in 1727 the Straits that now bear his name, and fourteen years later the Alaskan coast in the neighborhood of latitude 58. Behring's explorations were followed by the voyages of fur traders and by the establishment of trading posts on the islands off the American mainland. After years of demoralizing competition on the part of private individuals, the Tsar determined to create a commercial monopoly for the exploitation of the rich fisheries to be found in that part of the world. By the ukase of July 8, 1799, the Russian-American Company was constituted, and to this company were granted exclusive trading rights and jurisdiction along the coast as far south as latitude 55, and the right to make settlements on either side of that line in territory not occupied by other powers.

From an early date the operations of this Russian corporation were impeded by interlopers, very largely American. American vessels sold arms and ammunition to the natives, and secured a considerable part of the fur trade. As early as 1808 and 1810 complaints on the part of the Russian government began to be made to the government at Washington. There was, obviously enough, a situation that might lead to serious friction. . . .

. . . On September 4/16, 1821, the Tsar Alexander I, acting at the instigation of the Russian monopoly, promulgated an imperial decree which renewed its privileges and confirmed its exclusive trading rights. This time the southern limit of these rights on the American coast was set, not at 55, but at 51 degrees. And in addition, all foreign vessels were forbidden, between Behring Straits and 51 degrees, to come within 100 Italian miles of the shore, on pain of confiscation. A Russian warship was dispatched to the northwest coast to enforce this remarkable decree, and every intention was manifested of barring all other nations from any participation whatever in the trade or fisheries of the region. Such a course of action very naturally provoked a protest, not only on the part of the United States, but also on the part of Great Britain. At this time the two Anglo-Saxon powers had joint ownership, under the convention of 1818, of the territory north from 42 degrees to a line yet to be determined, and the Russian claims of exclusive jurisdiction as far south as 51 degrees could hardly fail to be disquieting. Both from London and from Washington, therefore, came strong diplomatic remonstrance, and thus began a controversy which was to have the closest relationship to the famous pronouncement of 1823.

It is neither necessary nor desirable, in connection with this narrative, to trace the negotiations on the northwest question in all their details. What is of special interest here is the evolution of the non-colonization principle in the course of the discussions, the reception which it met at the hands of the interested powers, and the effect which it produced upon the diplomatic interchanges themselves.

It may be said at the outset that the development of the principle was due almost exclusively to the American Secretary of State, John Quincy Adams. With regard to that part of Monroe's pronouncement which refers to South America, there has been a tendency, since the appearance of Mr. W. C. Ford's significant articles, to overestimate the rôle played by the Massachusetts statesman. In this phase of the matter, it is well that fuller credit should be given the President. But, on the northwest question, there can be little doubt that the Secretary of State was responsible for the position assumed, and that his chief did little more than ratify the principle formulated by his chief adviser in matters of foreign policy. Monroe himself was apparently not much concerned about the Russian problem. It was certainly not the most important diplomatic question before the administration either in 1822 or in 1823. The Spanish-American question was of foremost importance. Neither in the President's correspondence, in the diary of Adams, nor in the later recollections of Calhoun, is there the slightest evidence that Monroe held very positive or definite views on the controversy with the Tsar. In all probability he gave Adams a very free hand in the matter. . . .

These discussions, begun in 1822, assumed little importance till the late spring of 1823. By that time it had been agreed that the question should be threshed out at St. Petersburg. In June the cabinet discussed the instructions which were to be sent to Mr. Middleton, American minister at the court of the Tsar. The Secretary of State declared it to be his conviction that the United States ought to contest the right of the Russian government to any territorial establishment on the American continents. Apparently this point of view did not pass unchallenged. It was pointed out that Russia would have little reason to accept such drastic doctrine. The United States, in maintaining it, would be asking everything, and conceding virtually nothing. A compromise was suggested and agreed upon by which this country would recognize the territorial claims of the Tsar north of 55 degrees. On this basis, the negotiations were actually to be conducted.

But Adams, with a curious inconsistency, did not on this account surrender the principle which was taking shape in his mind. At the very moment when he was perfecting the instructions to Middleton along the lines agreed upon in the cabinet, he declared himself to Tuyll, the Russian minister at Washington, in language very much more sweeping.

> I told him specially [he writes in his diary, alluding to an interview of July 17, 1823], that we should contest the right of Russia to *any* territorial establishment on this continent, and that we should assume distinctly the principle that the American continents are no longer subjects for *any* new European colonial establishments.

In this statement, almost five months before the appearance of the President's message, we have the non-colonization principle full-fledged, no longer merely a subject of cabinet debate, but explicitly put forward to the minister of another power, to the minister of the power perhaps most concerned in denying it. One might expect that such a declaration would have been most distasteful to Tuyll. But such evidence as we have leads to a contrary conclusion. There are no indications that the Russian minister challenged or controverted Adams. In his dispatch to St. Petersburg reporting the conversation of July 17, he contented himself with the following allusion to the matter: "The American government will avail itself of the present occasion to ask the acceptance of a general principle by which foreign powers will definitely and finally renounce the right of establishing new colonies in either of the Americas." This is underlined in the text itself, but the Russian minister goes on to say that he sees no great difficulty in the way of a settlement of the northwest question. He clearly did not regard the language of Adams as a serious obstacle to understanding. There was nothing in his attitude which might lead the Secretary of State to modify his position.

We have another statement of the non-colonization dogma almost contemporaneous with the interview with Tuyll. This is found in the instructions to Richard Rush, American minister at the Court of Saint James's. As England had an interest in the northwest controversy, it was obviously desirable that the diplomatic representative of the United States at London should be informed of the views of his government on the subject. Accordingly, on July 22, Adams sent forward a long and careful dispatch, in which he set forth his new theory in greater detail than at any other time. That dispatch will claim our special attention later.

Curiously enough, the instructions to Middleton, of the same date, contain no such clear reference to the non-colonization principle. They do, of course, contest the Russian claims to territorial sovereignty on the northwest coast. They even go so far as to declare that "there can, perhaps, be no better time for saying, frankly and explicitly, to the Russian government that the future peace of the world, and the interest of Russia herself, cannot be promoted by Russian settlements upon any part of the American Continent." This is strong and definite language. But there is, it may fairly be asserted, at least a shade of difference between such language and the enunciation of a general proposition of universal application.

It must, therefore, be a little doubtful just how far Adams intended to push his new theory at this time. Certainly he did not intend to make it the central point in the pending negotiations. He did not specifically direct either Rush or Middleton to press for its positive recognition. He did not develop it at all, as a general diplomatic maxim, in his correspondence with the latter. As a dogma of general purport, Middleton was first to learn of it through the publication of the President's message in the European newspapers.

The process by which it got into that important document was a very simple one.

Adams secured Monroe's assent to his new principle in July, at the time of sending the dispatches just alluded to. Whether that assent was cordial and positive, or whether it was given as a mere matter of routine, we have no way of knowing. The President may have warmly approved the non-colonization doctrine; he may, on the other hand, have been little aware of its significance or its implications. On this point his writings provide us with no illumination. But at any rate, he *did* accept it. When, therefore, the Secretary of State drew up in November, the customary sketch of the topics of foreign policy which might interest the President in connection with the preparation of the forthcoming message, he naturally included in the paragraph on the Russian negotiations a reference to the new dogma. That paragraph was taken over almost without verbal change by Monroe, and thus it appeared in his communication to the Congress. These facts are clear, for we have the actual manuscript of Adams's outline of the diplomatic matters which he wished to draw to the attention of the President, and the language of that outline, so far as the non-colonization principle is concerned, corresponds almost exactly with the language of the message itself.

There was, apparently, no consideration of the principle in the cabinet discussion preceding the publication of the President's declaration. On this point Calhoun, then Secretary of War, was to testify many years later, and the silence of Adams's diary at the time confirms this testimony. There is, after all, nothing strange in such a circumstance. For the question of the hour, in November, 1823, was not the dispute with Russia, but the menace offered by the Holy Alliance to the independence of the States of South America. It was on these problems that all the debates turned; so, very naturally, the other problem was crowded out. . . .

Having thus examined the origins of the non-colonization clause in the message of 1823, we must now turn back to discuss the viewpoint and the reasoning which lay behind it. What was the motive in promulgating such a sweeping theory? What was the logic by which it might be supported?

In later interpretations of this part of the President's declaration, the emphasis has frequently been laid on the dangers involved in bringing the intrigues and conflicting territorial ambitions of Europe across the seas and into the New World. The United States, the argument has run, would thus be swept into the vortex of European politics, and exposed to the wicked influences for which those politics are notorious. Or it has been maintained that the new European territorial establishments would endanger American security, and ought to be opposed on these grounds.

These were not the bases, however, on which John Quincy Adams, in 1823, rested his opposition to colonization. The territorial aspects of colonization were not uppermost in his mind. He was thinking (and the point has been all too little emphasized) primarily of the commercial interests of the United States. In the history of American diplomacy, the principle of non-colonization has a certain affinity with the principle of the open door, asserted three quarters of a century later. It was based on immediate economic factors, not on vague fears of the future. It was because the colonial system meant commercial exclusion that the Secretary of State proclaimed its banishment from the American continents.

A close examination of Adams's point of view makes this clear. The principle of equality of commercial opportunity was one for which he contended with the utmost vigor, not only in the northwest controversy, but in other fields. He fought vigorously against the narrow policy of Great Britain in the British West Indies. He instructed the ministers to the South American states, when they set out in 1823, to contend for the principle that the new republics should treat all nations on the same footing, and that they should give no preferences, not even to their former mother country. The right to which he held most tenaciously in the dispute with Russia was not the right to full possession of the territory on the northwest (on this, as we have seen, it had been agreed to compromise on the line of 55 degrees); the right which he deemed of most importance was the right to trade, and this Middleton was instructed stoutly to maintain. In Adams's opinion the notion of European colonization was flatly opposed to the maintenance of these economic interests. The colonizing methods of the Old World, he told Stratford Canning in November, 1822, had always involved a more or less complete commercial monopoly. "Spain had set the example. She had forbidden foreigners from setting a foot in her Colonies, upon pain of death, and the other colonizing states of Europe had imitated the exclusion, though not the rigor of the penalty." From the very beginning, therefore, the Adams doctrine was knit up with the commercial interests of the United States. And so it remained throughout this early period of its development. Nothing shows this more clearly than the important dispatch of July 22,

1823, to Richard Rush, in which the whole theory of the doctrine found most careful expression. After declaring that the American continents will henceforth no longer be subjects for colonization, the American Secretary of State goes on to say:

> Occupied by civilized independent nations, they will be accessible to Europeans and to each other on that footing alone, and the Pacific Ocean in every part of it will remain open to the navigation of all nations, in like manner with the Atlantic. . . . The application of colonial principles of exclusion, therefore, cannot be admitted by the United States as lawful upon any part of the northwest coast of America, or as belonging to any European nation.

In these clear-cut and precise phrases, the innermost connection of the new dogma with American trading rights stands revealed.

It need not be contended, of course, that there was no more to it than this. It would be a clear exaggeration to say that Adams was contending for trading rights alone. He was thinking also of territorial settlement, as the very dispatch just quoted helps to make clear.

> It is not imaginable [he declared] that, in the present condition of the world, *any* European nation should entertain the project of settling a *colony* on the northwest coast of America. That the United States should form establishments there, with views of absolute territorial right and inland communication, is not only to be expected, but is pointed out by the finger of nature.

But these comments were made with an eye to the future. What was interesting in the immediate sense, "the only useful purpose to which the northwest coast of America" had been or could be made "subservient to the settlement of civilized men," was that of trade and of the fishery. The rights of the United States in this regard it was vital to maintain. On the territorial question there might be compromise; this we have already seen. But on the commercial question there ought to be none. "The right of carrying on trade with the natives throughout the northwest coast they [the United States] cannot renounce." Clearly, it was antagonism to commercial restriction that lay at the basis of the Secretary of State's famous dictum. . . .

The Spanish-American Phase of the Message—The Prelude

The revolt of the Spanish-American colonies followed hard upon the Napoleonic conquest of Spain. From the very beginning, the sympathies of the United States appear to have been engaged upon the side of the revolutionists. American sentiment was distinctly favorable to a movement for independence which had at least a superficial resemblance to that of 1776, and which could easily be regarded as an effort to throw off an odious tyranny and establish throughout the greater part of the New World the blessings of republican government. Fellow feeling in a struggle for liberty and independence was an essential element in forming the policy of the United States with regard to South America.

It was indeed, to all appearances, a far more important element than any hope of material gain. In the formative period of this country's relations with the new states of South America, certainly down to 1822, there is little evidence of the working of economic interest. In the absence of exact statistics for much of the period, and in view of the paucity of references to trade with the Spanish colonies, it is difficult to speak with precision. But certain general observations may safely be made. In the first place, the trade with Cuba and with Spain itself was far more important than the trade with the new republics of the South. A diplomatic policy favorable to the South-American states might jeopardize or even sacrifice commercial interests superior to those which it would promote. If economic reasons were to be regarded as shaping political developments, there were more reasons for a cautious than for an active line of policy. In the second place, there was not, as in the case of Great Britain, any powerful pressure from the commercial classes in favor of colonial independence. The evidence on this point is partly negative, it is true, but it is negative evidence of the strongest kind. One can hardly imagine that the existence of such pressure would pass unnoticed in the debates in Congress, and in such contemporary records as the diary and writings of Adams, and the correspondence of Monroe. But it is not necessary to depend upon this fact alone. Statistics indicate that as late as 1821 only 2.3 per cent of American exports and 1.6 per cent of American imports were South American in destination or origin. In March of the same year Adams could tell Henry Clay that he had little expectation of any commercial advantages from the recognition of the new states. And even later, in 1823, the Secretary of State speaks of commercial development as a matter of hope for the future rather than a present accomplishment. That hope may, of course, have counted for something from the beginning. But, all things considered, it seems highly probable that political sympathy, not economic self-interest, lay at the root of American policy so far as it revealed itself as favorable to the new states of South America.

From the very beginnings of the South American struggle this sympathy asserts itself. As early as 1810, the American government, then headed by Madison, sent agents to South America—Joel R. Poinsett to La Plata and Chile, and Robert Lowry to Venezuela. At the end of 1811, James Monroe, then Secretary of State, thought seriously of raising the question of the recognition of the new states, and of exerting American influence in Europe to secure like action from the principal European powers. He also entered into informal relations with agents from at least one of the revolted provinces. And in Congress, at the same time, in response to the sympathetic language of the President's message, a resolution was passed, expressing a friendly solicitude in the welfare of these communities, and a readiness, when they should become nations by a just exercise of their rights, to unite with the Executive in establishing such relations with them as might be necessary. Thus, very early in the course of the colonial struggle, the general bent of American policy was made plain.

But it was some time before the South-American question became a matter of really first-rate importance. In the years 1810 to 1815, the prime concern of the administration at Washington lay in the preservation of American neutral rights, and, from 1812 to 1814, in the prosecution of the war with Great Britain. Moreover, the course of events in the overseas dominions of Spain was for some time hardly favorable to the revolutionists. In 1814 and 1815, indeed, it seemed entirely possible that the revolutionary movements might be snuffed out. In the north, in Venezuela and Colombia, the army of the Spanish general, Morillo, won victory on victory, and drove the leader of the revolutionists, Bolívar, into exile. In the south, in Chile, Osorio reëstablished the power of the mother country, and in Buenos Aires the struggles of contending factions weakened the new government that had been set up. Under such circumstances, prudence would have dictated a policy of reserve on the part of the United States, even if its government had not been preoccupied with other and more pressing matters.

With the year 1817, however, a change takes place in the status of the colonial question. In the case of one, at any rate, of the new states, the struggle was virtually over. The republic of La Plata had declared its independence and successfully maintained it, so that not a Spanish soldier remained upon its territory; even more, it had dispatched its great general, San Martín, across the Andes, and, with the victory of Chacabuca, taken a great step toward the final liberation of Chile. Perhaps as a result of these developments, interest in favor of the recognition of the new state began to develop in the United States; there were numerous newspaper articles in the summer of 1817, notably the discussions of Lautaro in the Richmond *Enquirer;* and the affairs of South America became a matter of debate both in the councils of the administration and in the halls of Congress.

It is interesting, in the light of later events, to examine these developments. So far as the administration was concerned, the point especially to be emphasized is the warm sympathy of the President himself with the South American cause. There has been a tendency in some quarters, in connection with the evolution of the Monroe Doctrine, to ascribe a very slight importance to the views of the very man who promulgated it. Mr. Monroe has been pictured as "slow-moving and lethargic," as prodded forward only by the more vigorous mind and more determined will of John Quincy Adams, his Secretary of State. But as a matter of fact, Monroe was at all times quite as much interested in the colonial cause, and in as full sympathy with it, as Adams. From the very beginning of his presidency, he showed his concern with regard to it. As early as May, 1817, some months before Adams took office, the President had determined upon a mission of inquiry to the provinces of La Plata, and as early as October he questioned his cabinet on the expediency of recognizing the government of that region. He raised the problem again in the succeeding May, even suggesting the possibility of sending an armed force to the coast of South America, to protect American commerce, "and to countenance the patriots." His views, it is true, were to be overruled or modified by his advisers. But his interest in positive action was very real, and is quite consistent with the character of the man whose flaming sympathy with French republicanism had been so obvious in his earlier career. . . .

The Warning to Europe

The arrival at Washington of the news of Canning's first interviews with Rush was speedily followed by other events of high importance. On October 16, Baron Tuyll called on the Secretary of State and informed him that the Tsar Alexander would not receive any minister or agent from any one of the states just formed in the New World. He also expressed the satisfaction of the Russian government at the attitude of neutrality that had been observed by the United States in the colonial conflict, and at its declared intention to continue to maintain that neutrality. . . . This declaration of policy on the part of Alexander had been entirely unsolicited by the United States. It came at a time when its exact purpose was extremely difficult to fathom. It was like lightning from a clear sky. True, there was nothing necessarily sinister about it. On its face it was no more than a declaration of the Russian viewpoint on South America, and a commendation of the neutral attitude of the United States. But did it indicate a reviving interest on the part of the Tsar in the colonial question? Why compliment the United States on its neutrality? What political principles were those to which the note alluded? Was there here a veiled reference to the right of intervention in behalf of legitimacy? So the President, at any rate, may have feared, for he directed Adams to seek an explanation of the phrase from Tuyll.

A month later came a communication even more disturbing. It was a note written by Nesselrode, dated August 30, 1823, and dealing with the recent intervention in Spain. It was framed, Adams sets down in his diary, in "a tone of passionate exultation," and was

> an "*Io Triumphe*" over the fallen cause of revolution, with sturdy promises of determination to keep it down; disclaimers of all intention of making conquests; bitter complaints of being calumniated, and one paragraph of compunctions, acknowledging that an apology is yet due to mankind for the invasion of Spain, which it is in the power only of Ferdinand to furnish, by making his people happy.

There was nothing in this state paper which directly menaced the liberties of the New World, as a careful reading of its full text will serve to show. The Tsar Alexander, indeed, may well have regarded it as a reassuring explanation of the benevolent intentions of the allied powers. In the main, it was a homily on purely Continental affairs, and contained hardly a reference to the New World. The only phrase which could even by the closest construction be taken to hint at a purpose to intervene in the Spanish colonies is that in which the Tsar speaks of a policy, "whose only object is to guarantee the tranquillity of all the states of which the civilized world is composed." But to anyone aware of Alexander's penchant for sonorous phrase, and sweeping generalization, such a sentence was hardly to be taken too seriously. And yet the principles which the note professed, and the tone in which they were set forth, could hardly fail to be disturbing to the government at Washington, and to furnish an additional reason for setting forth, without delay and in the most explicit terms, the opposition of the United States to the doctrine of intervention, and to interference by the European powers with the affairs of the New World.

Before Tuyll had presented this dispatch to Adams, however, Monroe and his advisers had already discussed the dangers in which the Spanish colonies stood. From the beginning of the cabinet discussions of November, 1823, the President and John C. Calhoun, the Secretary of War, were wholly convinced that the Holy Alliance would soon act to restore the colonies to Spain. The President, wrote Adams, "is alarmed far beyond anything that I could have conceived possible," and "the news that Cadiz has surrendered to the French has so affected him that he appeared entirely to despair of the cause of South America." Calhoun, in Adams's phrase, was "perfectly moonstruck" at the danger.

The Secretary of State himself refused to be thus terrified. It is, indeed, not the least striking evidence of his ability as a diplomat that he viewed the situation without panic, and with superb sense of proportion. Five years before, at the time of the deliberations at Aix-La-Chapelle, he had pointed out that the allies had no interest whatsoever in the reconquest of the colonies. This was still his viewpoint in 1823. He believed that the Holy Alliance "would not ultimately invade South America." If they should actually do so, "they might make a temporary impression for three, four, or five years," said Adams in the cabinet meeting of November 15, but "I no more believe that the Holy Allies will restore the Spanish dominion upon the American continent than that the Chimborazo will sink beneath the ocean." They would have no conceivable reason to restore the old exclusive system of the past. Spain could never maintain herself in the New World alone, and "was it in human absurdity to imagine that they [the allied powers] should waste their blood and treasure to prohibit their own subjects upon pain of death to set foot upon those territories?" If they took action at all, the ultimate result would be to partition the colonies among themselves. But was it reasonable to suppose that they could agree upon any principle of partition? And even if they were able to do so, what inducement could they offer to Great Britain to acquiesce in any such scheme? "The only possible bait they could offer . . . was Cuba, which neither they nor Spain would consent to give her."

But though Adams was very far indeed from the panic fear that the Holy Alliance would reconquer South America, and was strongly inclined to the opinion that no intervention would even be attempted, he was by no means inclined to let the situation pass without an expression of the views of the United States. He believed that the situation required a very definite assertion of American policy. And so, for the matter of that, did all the other members of the cabinet and the President himself. There was not even a disposition to delay action until Canning's overtures could be accepted, and a concert of action established with Great Britain. When Adams, in one of the first of the cabinet meetings, that of November 7, declared that "it would be more candid as well as more dignified, to avow our principles explicitly to Russia and France, than to come in as a cock-boat in the wake of the British man-of-war," his idea "was aquiesced in on all sides." President Monroe himself, who leaned toward the acceptance of the British proposals, was heartily averse to taking any attitude that might be regarded as "subordinate," and was ready to make the position of the United States entirely clear. There was to be no dependence on Great Britain.

The question was not whether action should be taken, but in what form. What answer should be given to Rush? What answer should be given to Tuyll? And, finally, how should the colonial question be treated in the forthcoming communication to Congress? All these matters taken together engaged the attention of the cabinet during the momentous sessions of November, 1823. All of them have a direct relation to the enunciation of the Monroe Doctrine. But it will be best to begin with a discussion of the evolution of the actual message itself.

From the moment when the President set about the preparation of that document he seems to have intended that some reference to the colonial question should be made. The idea—and this fact is of the first importance—was almost certainly his own. There are several reasons for so believing. In the first place, in the sketch prepared by Mr. Adams for his chief, summarizing the matters of foreign policy which might be treated in the message, there is no mention of South American affairs at all. Nowhere in his diary does the Secretary so much as intimate that he wished to see a public declaration of the kind which the President actually penned. He was occupied, as we shall see, with the answer to Rush, and the reply to Tuyll, the latter of which documents, as he himself records, was modelled on the language of Monroe. There is no positive evidence whatsoever to show that he suggested that the colonial problem should be treated in the message, and the negative evidence tends strongly in the other direction. Furthermore, the place of the paragraphs on South America in the President's communication to Congress strongly suggests a separate origin from the other sections dealing with foreign affairs. These latter come near the beginning, and closely follow Adams's sketch. The Monroe Doctrine comes near the end, entirely apart from all other diplomatic matters. Standing by itself, it was, to all appearances, a pronouncement independent of all others, and the special pronouncement of the President himself. . . .

In looking back at these debates, so full of interest to the student of American diplomatic history, one fact seems particularly worth noting. It is the fact of their preponderantly political character. In the discussions upon the northwest controversy, as has been seen, trading influences contributed very materially to the stand which was taken by the administration. But it would be difficult to prove anything of the kind with regard to the warning given to Europe against intervention in South America.

This is not to say that such influences necessarily played no rôle at all. John Quincy Adams, of course, came from the great shipping section of the Union. In his instructions to the American ministers sent out to Colombia and La Plata in the spring of 1823, he had laid a very considerable emphasis upon freedom of commercial opportunity, though he was by no means exuberantly optimistic as to the possibilities of the South American trade. In the cabinet discussions of November, he had, on one occasion, brought forward as a reason for action the fact that if the United States stood aside and Great Britain alone vetoed the designs of the Continental powers, the latter country would gain great commercial advantages. It is worth noting, too, that our commerce with the Spanish-American states was considerably more important in 1823 than it had been two or three years before. But these facts would be a slender foundation on which to base an "economic interpretation" of the Monroe Doctrine. And they are offset by many others. Whoever reads the pages of Adams's diary will find it hard to believe that trading considerations played a very considerable rôle in his mind. The distaste produced by the homilies of the Tsar, a genuine and robust disapproval of the trend of European politics, a desire to set forth the political doctrines of the United States in opposition to those of the Alliance, these are the factors that bulked largest in his thought. Economic considerations there may have been in the background. But it was a profound political antagonism that gave force to the action which he advocated in the councils of President Monroe.

With the President himself, this antagonism was even more keenly felt. The letter to Jefferson, written early in June, seems to express his point of view pretty accurately. He was anxious to strike a blow for liberty, and the situation in the fall of 1823 offered him an excellent opportunity. To this must be added the fact that Monroe, like Calhoun, feared that an assault upon the liberties of the Spanish Americans would be dangerous to the safety of the United States itself. It was these considerations, beyond a doubt, that sharpened his pen as he wrote the declaration of December 2. . . .

. . . Monroe's belief in the superiority of American institutions, his conviction that the extension of European dominion would be dangerous to our peace and safety—these are propositions that are hardly capable of rigorous demonstration. Perhaps their strength lies in just that fact. Yet there is, I think, one thing more to be said for them. In resting his opposition to European intermeddling in Spanish America on the "peace and safety" of the United States, the President was taking up a strong position from the legal and moral point of view. For he was basing American policy on the right of self-preservation, a right that is and always has been recognized as fundamental in international law. If in very truth the interposition of the Holy Alliance in South America imperilled the peace and safety of the United States, then the President's right to protest against it was obvious. Nor was it to be expected that as to the reality of the peril he would accept the conclusions of European statesmen. He stood secure in his own conviction and on his own ground. . . .

2. *A Proclamation of a Mercantilist Empire*

The following selection by William A. Williams strongly suggests that the Monroe Doctrine was a declaration of a new American System for the Western Hemisphere, which would be dominated by the United States and would offer opportunities for political, economic, and territorial expansion. A stimulating writer, whose previous publications have ranged from Russo-American relations to the Turner thesis and foreign policy, Professor Williams thus takes exception to the usual version of the Monroe Doctrine as primarily a defensive political measure.

The Age of Mercantilism: An Interpretation of the American Political Economy, 1763 to 1828

WILLIAM APPLEMAN WILLIAMS

Based upon the suggestion by Curtis P. Nettels that one of the consequences of British mercantilism was the creation "of a new mercantilist state on this side of the Atlantic," and upon recent re-evaluations of mercantilism by William D. Grampp, Gunnar Myrdal, Jacob Viner, Charles Wilson, and others, this essay advances the hypothesis that the central characteristic of American history from 1763 to 1828 was in fact the development and maturation of an American mercantilism. Let it be emphasized that the interpretation is offered as a hypothesis and no more—as an idea to be examined and tested, then accepted, modified, or rejected on the basis of its relevance and validity. There is no intention, furthermore, even to imply that the approach as here stated offers final answers to all the vexing problems connected with understanding early American society. It is merely proposed that a re-examination of the era from this angle may lead to new insights, and hence contribute to a broader interpretation of the period.

At the outset, for example, the use of the concept of mercantilism restores to its properly central place the fact that Americans thought of themselves as an empire at the very beginning of their national existence —as part of their assertive self-consciousness which culminated in the American Revolution. Though it may seem surprising, especially when contrasted with the image of isolationism which has been accepted so long, in reality this early predominance of a pattern of empire thought is neither very strange nor very difficult to explain. Having matured in an age of empires as part of an empire, the colonists naturally saw themselves in the same light once they joined issue with the mother country.

Revolutionary leaders were confident of their ability "not only to take territory by the sword, but to hold and govern it under a colonial status." Long before the break with England, for example, Benjamin Franklin was a leader of those who entertained a "burning interest in westward expansion." At the threshold of the revolution he visualized an American Em-

William Appleman Williams, "The Age of Mercantilism: An Interpretation of the American Political Economy, 1763 to 1828," *The William and Mary Quarterly,* XV (1958), 419–437. Reprinted with the permission of The Institute of Early American History and Culture, Williamsburg, Virginia and *The William and Mary Quarterly.*

pire including Canada, the Spanish Floridas, the West Indies, and perhaps even Ireland. George Washington, John Adams, John Livingston, and Thomas Lee were among those who shared such conceptions of an American Empire. By the end of the war, such men as Silas Deane looked forward to the time when "Great Britain, America and Russia united will command not barely Europe, but the whole world united." And in 1789, after remarking that "it is well known that empire has been travelling from east to west," Congregational minister and geographer Jedidiah Morse concluded that "probably her last and broadest seat will be America . . . the largest empire that ever existed."

While the vigor, even cockiness, of such statements may be explained by the consciousness of having whipped the champion, the underlying emphasis on expansion and empire was an integral part of the general outlook of mercantilism, a conception of the world shared by most of the revolutionary generation. Though they revolted against British mercantilism, there is considerable evidence to suggest that early American leaders did not, as so often is assumed, rebel against the idea and practice of mercantilism itself. In stressing the role of natural-rights philosophy in the thinking of the leaders of the revolution, the traditional view of the American Revolution has slighted this key point.

An acceptance of natural law is not incompatible with mercantilism, as is indicated by John Locke's vigorous espousal of both systems. Much of the talk in America about natural rights, moreover, concerned what Thomas Paine called the "natural right" to one's own empire. And though they were willing to use Adam Smith's polemic in behalf of laissez faire as a weapon against British mercantilism (and against their domestic opponents), most Americans adhered firmly in their own practice to the principle that the state had to intervene in economic affairs. America's romance with Smith's laissez faire came later and was of relatively short duration. Hence it would appear that a better understanding of early American history depends in considerable measure upon a grasp of the nature and practice of American mercantilism as it developed between 1763 and 1825.

Traditionally thought of as little more than a narrow and selfish point of view held by the trading interest, mercantilism was in fact a broad definition and explanation of the world shared by most of Western Europe in the seventeenth and eighteenth centuries. In this sense it was the basic outlook of those who labored to build a dynamic balanced economy of agriculture and business organized on a capitalistic basis within a nationalistic framework. Depending upon their specific function and power at any given stage in the process, mercantilists argued among themselves over the best means to achieve and maintain such a system—and differed in their estimates of whether or not it had been established—but they agreed on the objective and upon the need to use the state as a tool.

Whether agrarian or urban, therefore, mercantilists were essentially nationalists who strove for self-sufficiency through increased domestic production and a favorable balance (and terms) of trade. Their emphasis on production and the control of export markets and sources of raw materials, rather than on consumption and economic interdependence, led them to fear surpluses as a sign of crisis and failure. Thus they dropped the old feudal restrictions on exports and replaced them with taxes on imports. Their greatest fear was a surplus of goods. In this respect, furthermore, mercantilism was reinforced—albeit in a backhanded and even unintentional way—by the broad ethical outlook of Puritanism (which frowned on luxury), even though mercantilism itself was a secular and almost amoral system. Likewise, the concept of a chosen people, so strong in Puritanism, also strengthened the secular and economic nationalism of mercantilism. Thus mercantilists constantly labored to build a tightly organized and protected national market and to increase their share of the world market. The key points in their program were integration at home and expansion abroad.

In the exuberant confidence of their victory over Britain, Americans tended to assume that each new state could survive and thrive as a mercantile empire unto itself. That attitude was not too surprising, for each of the new states appeared to enjoy the raw materials, labor supply, and trading facilities for a balanced economy. That estimate of the situation was supported and reinforced by the conviction, itself part of traditional theory, that a state could remain democratic in political and social life only if it were small and integrated, and by the experiences of the colonies in dealing with Great Britain's imperial policy after 1763. Yet the political outlook and faith contradicted certain basic tenets of mercantilism, which Americans also entertained, or assumed.

The first attempt to reconcile the conflict produced the Articles of Confederation. That instrument of government stressed the independence of the states as self-contained units of mercantilism and democratic republicanism, yet also established a central government for the purposes of war and, as in the case of Canada, future expansion. But specific postwar developments, such as the serious recession, the expansionist conflicts between the states, and the difficulties in dealing with other countries in economic affairs, combined to disillusion many Americans with their experiment in particularistic mercantilism.

Broadly speaking, the resulting movement toward a stronger central government grew out of internal and international economic difficulties analyzed and explained with the ideas of mercantilism. By 1785, for example, most of the states, including the agrarian ones, were switching from tariffs for revenue to tariffs for international retaliation and protection. Merchants demanded American navigation acts, artisans agitated for protection of their labor, and agricultural interests wanted help in balancing their political economy. Various groups of Americans who concerned themselves directly with the problem of strengthening the central government—and there were many who were preoccupied with local and immediate difficulties or opportunities—offered several proposals for handling the problem. Centered in New England, the smallest group favored establishing an aristocratic society at home and rejoining the British Empire as a contractual junior partner. Such men were not willing to return to colonial status, but they did favor economic and social reintegration.

Most Americans opposed that solution, favoring instead either the delegation of more power to the central government under the Articles of Confederation or the substitution of an entirely new instrument of government.

A letter from James Madison to Thomas Jefferson in the spring of 1786 not only indicates that the agrarian as well as the urban interests favored one or the other of those last two approaches, but dramatizes the fundamental mercantilism of the entire movement. "A continuance of the present anarchy of our commerce," Madison explained, "will be a continuance of the unfavorable balance on it, which by draining us of our metals . . . [will bring our ruin]. In fact, most of our political evils may be traced up to our commercial ones, and most of our moral may to our political."

Against this background, the Constitution appears as an instrument of centralized national government framed in the classic manner by men thinking within the framework of mercantilism and blessed with the physical and human resources for a balanced economy. It provided the foundation for a national system of economics and politics and organized American strength for the struggle with other mercantile empires and for the conquest of less powerful peoples. The latter considerations were essential, for the Founding Fathers resolved the contradiction between the stress on expansion in mercantilism and the emphasis on a small state in existing democratic political theory by developing a theory of their own which held that democratic republicanism could be sustained by just such expansion. James Madison, often called the Father of the Constitution provided the most striking formulation of this proposition, but Thomas Jefferson, John Adams, and other early leaders either shared or adopted it in one form or another within a reasonably short time.

Taking his cue from David Hume, the Englishman who attacked Montesquieu's argument that democracy was a system that could work only in small states, Madison asserted that a large state offered a much better foundation for republicanism. Institutional checks and balances could help, and were therefore necessary, but they were not enough in and of themselves. "Extend the sphere," he argued, "and you take in a greater variety of parties and interests; you make it less probable that a majority of the whole will have a common motive to invade the rights of other citizens; or if such a common motive exists, it will be more difficult for all who feel it to discover their own strength, and to act in unison with each other. . . ."

While it is possible to conclude from Madison's remarks that he had in mind a static conception of such a large state, three considerations would appear to weaken that reading of his thesis. First, Madison used the verb "extend" in its active, unlimited sense. Second, he was stating a general theory, not making an argument in behalf of a given territorial settlement. And third, he advocated and vigorously supported the continued expansion of the United States. It seems more probable, therefore, that Madison was proposing, *as a guide to policy and action in his own time,* the same kind of an argument that Frederick Jackson Turner formulated a century later, when he advanced his frontier thesis which explained America's democracy and prosperity as the result of such expansion.

Madison's theory became the key to an American mercantilism. Merchants and manufacturers who wanted their own empire found it convincing and convenient. And Jefferson's thesis that democracy and prosperity depended upon a society of landholding freemen was a drastically simplified version of the same idea. Edward Everett of Massachusetts captured the essence of the interpretation in his judgment that expansion was the "*principle* of our institutions." Additional support for this interpretation is offered by Madison's later prophecy (in 1828–29) that a major crisis would occur in about a century, when the continent was filled up and an industrial system had deprived most people of any truly productive property. In the event, Madison's fears proved true sooner than he anticipated. For in the crisis of the 1890's, when Americans *thought* that the frontier was gone, they advanced and accepted the argument that new expansion was the best—if not the only—way to sustain their freedom and prosperity.

Madison's original statement of the expansionist thesis was important for two reasons. First, it provided the theoretical basis for an American mercantilism combining commercial and territorial expansion with political democracy. Second, by thus re-emphasizing the idea of empire, and proposing expansion as the key to national welfare, Madison opened the way for a discussion of the basic questions facing American mercantilism. Those issues concerned domestic economic affairs, the kind of expansion that was necessary and desirable, and the means to accomplish such gains while the nation was young and weak.

Washington's Farewell Address formulated a bipartisan answer to the problem of basic strategy. The solution was to build a commercial empire (which included markets for agricultural surpluses) by avoiding political involvement in the European system, meanwhile retaining complete freedom of action to secure and develop a continental empire in the Western Hemisphere. Washington's proposition was classically simple: play from the strength provided by America's basic economic wealth and geographic location in order to survive immediate weakness and emerge as *the* world power. "If we remain one people, under an efficient government," he promised, "the period is not far off when we may defy material injury from external annoyance . . . when we may choose peace or war, as our interest, guided by justice, shall counsel." Sharing that objective, and quite in agreement with the strategy, Thomas Jefferson summed it all up a bit later in one famous axiom: "entangling alliances with none." And with the enunciation of the Monroe Doctrine, freedom of action became the avowed and central bipartisan theme of American foreign policy.

As a condition of that persuasive agreement, however, several serious conflicts had to be resolved. Perhaps they can be discussed most clearly by defining and considering them within the framework of the gradual defeat and amalgamation of the pro-British and pro-French minorities by a growing consensus in favor of an American mercantilism. Such an approach has the additional value of making it possible to organize the analysis around familiar personalities as symbols of certain ideas, functional groups, and special interests. Let it be posited, therefore, that the following men are key figures in the evolution of an American mercantilism: Timothy Pickering, John Adams, and John Quincy Adams of Massachusetts; Alexander Hamilton of New York; and James Madison, Thomas Jefferson, and John Taylor of Virginia.

In many respects, at any rate, Pickering and Taylor represented the nether fringes of American mercantilism. Pickering trod the trail from reluctant revolutionary to threatening secessionist in the name of a domestic merchant aristocracy functioning as a quasi-independent contractual member of the British Empire. His ideal was a central government charged with the responsibility (and armed with the power and authority) to establish and sustain a politically and socially stratified society and to provide the economic assistance (especially funded credit) that was necessary for the rationalized operations of overseas correspondents of British mercantilism and for domestic speculative ventures. Though Pickering and his supporters fit the traditional stereotype of mercantilists, they were in fact and function no more than the agents of British mercantilism. They were very successful agents, to be sure, but they did not view or define America in terms of its own mercantilism. Rather did they visualize it as a self-governing commonwealth of the British Empire. Hence it was only very late and with great reluctance, if at all, that they supported the measures necessary for a mercantilist state in America.

At the other extreme, John Taylor developed his program as a variation on a theme first stated by the French physiocrats. He emphasized the primacy of agriculture as narrowly as Pickering stressed the virtue and necessity of the merchant-trader-speculator. Taylor's tirades against funded debts and bank stock, and his soliloquies in praise of the noble farmer, seem alike in their total opposition to the principles of mercantilism. But in other respects his ideas were not so untainted by mercantilism as his rhetoric indicated. As with most other planters, for example, his theory of labor coincided at all essential points with the view held by British mercantilists. So, too, did his conception of the role of western lands in the economy of the seaboard "mother country."

With respect to foreign trade, moreover, Taylor was trapped by the weakness of the physiocrats in that area of economics. Ostensibly free traders, the physiocrats did not favor the navy essential to such a program. Taylor and other American imbibers of the physiocratic elixir awoke to discover that their vision did not correspond to reality. Taylor himself was not very adaptive, and ended his career in attacks on Jefferson and other agrarians who did develop an American mercantilism. But Taylor's position does dramatize the dilemma faced by the agrarians. The contradiction between theory and actuality confronted them with a rather apparent choice: either they could content themselves with slow economic stagnation or they could build an American maritime system, accept dependence upon a foreign naval power, or support an American industry. In that choice lies a key aspect of the rise of a mature American mercantilism; for it developed most consciously and was ultimately practiced most rigorously by the southern agrarians who are often assumed to have been most rabidly antimercantilist. If nothing else, the weakness of their ideal program drove them into mercantilism.

It is particularly important to keep that fact in mind when considering Hamilton, about whom the discussion of American mercantilism has billowed for so long. Joseph Charles was essentially correct in his view that "the standard works on Hamilton evade the main issues which his career raises," and his judgment remains relevant despite the plethora of centennial essays and biographies. The entire question of Hamilton's mercantilism has to be decided with reference to three points: the meaning and significance of the *Report on Manufactures,* his role in the Jay Treaty episode, and his plans to join in the further expansion of the British Empire in the Western Hemisphere. However difficult it may be to pin him down with an alternate characterization, Hamilton simply cannot be considered the fountainhead of American mercantilism unless those aspects of his career can be interpreted within the framework of mercantilist thought and action.

Since the *Report on Manufactures* is often accepted as proof, as well as evidence, of Hamilton's mercantilism, it is convenient to give first consideration to that document. In doing so, it seems wise to recall the chronology of his three state papers on economic affairs. Hamilton was commissioned as Secretary of the Treasury on September 11, 1789; and there followed the manifesto on public credit in January 1790, the report on a central bank in December 1790, and the paper on manufacturing in December 1791. Even the most cursory review of those dates catches the two-year delay between the reports on credit and manufacturers. That interval becomes even more striking when viewed in the context of other events.

It was Madison rather than Hamilton, for example, who gave more attention to protective duties on manufactures during the Constitutional Convention. That is still more illuminating since associations for the promotion of American manufactures had appeared in New York, Boston, Providence, and Baltimore as early as 1785; and resolutions for domestic goods had followed the next year from such additional and widely separated localities as Hartford, Germantown, Richmond, and Halifax (South Carolina). By 1789, furthermore, not only had the anti-Federalists picked up political support from such groups in New England, New York, and Pennsylvania, but the special session of Congress received numerous requests and petitions from various manufacturing societies.

Having passed an emergency revenue bill in the form of tariff legislation, the Congress then *ordered* Hamilton, on January 15, 1790, to prepare a specific report on manufactures. That makes his delay even more noticeable, whatever allowances may be granted for his other duties and the thoroughness of his research. As late as October 1791, moreover, the administration saw no need to increase the tariff of 1789. In matters of chronology, urgency, and emphasis, therefore, it seems clear that Hamilton gave priority to funding the debt and establishing the bank. Those operations represented precisely the needs and objectives of the merchants who were semiautonomous correspondents of British mercantilism, and who were fundamentally opposed to a strong American industry. Their economic, political, and social position would be threatened by a vigorous program of industrialization; for at the very least they would have to make drastic changes in their outlook and actions. Since Hamilton's personal and political position was based on his rapport with that group, it seems relevant to consider whether Hamilton's mercantilism was as thoroughgoing as historians have assumed it was.

In Hamilton's behalf, it can be argued with considerable validity that domestic industry had to have a sound credit system as a cornerstone. But that approach only raises the question of why Hamilton did not present his funding and bank programs as the means to achieve an independent balanced economy. Since he did not, the most relevant explanation would seem to be that Hamilton was in fact a mercantilist who was hamstrung by his political dependence upon the Federalists around Pickering. His association with Tench Coxe would serve to strengthen that analysis. The same argument could then be used to explain why Hamilton delayed his paper on manufactures for almost two years after the Congress had asked for it in January 1790.

The weakest point in that interpretation concerns Hamilton's response to Madison's resolution of January 3, 1794, that "the interests of the United States would be promoted by further restrictions and higher duties in certain cases on the manufactures and navigation of foreign nations employed in the commerce of the United States." Working through William Smith of South Carolina, Hamilton killed Madison's entire program which was designed to promote commercial and industrial independence. Instead, Hamilton's committee in the House reported in favor of more borrowing and further domestic taxes. For that matter, neither Hamilton nor the Federalist party acted to increase protection after 1792.

The explanation of Hamilton's action which does the most to sustain his reputation as an American mercantilist is not as generous to his standing as a reformed monarchist. For given the broad and vigorous agitation from manufacturing societies for greater protection, Madison's resolutions offered Hamilton a striking opportunity to widen the base of the Federalist party. That would have strengthened his hand against the pro-British group within the party and have enabled him to give substance to the *Report on Manufactures*. If it be said that Hamilton favored domestic excise taxes in preference to domestic manufacturing, then his mercantilism appears even more questionable. A stronger argument could be made by reference to Hamilton's known reservations about democracy, which would account for his refusal to court the manufacturers as a counterweight to the merchants around Pickering.

It may be, however, that Hamilton's vigorous opposition to Madison's resolutions of 1794 derived in considerable part from the fact that Madison's program was aimed at Great Britain. Not only was that true in the immediate, particular sense, but it also was the case in that Madison's proposals pointed toward general economic independence. That approach to the question of Hamilton's mercantilism has the virtue of having considerable relevance to his role in Jay's Treaty. An American mercantilist could explain and defend Hamilton's basic attitude and maneuvers behind Jay's back by one or both of two arguments. First, England had to be courted while the United States built a navy. Second, Hamilton stressed the political side of mercantilism.

Neither of those explanations is very convincing: Hamilton always favored the Army over the Navy, and political mercantilism is such a contradiction in terms that it begs the entire issue. That interpretation becomes even less convincing when asked to account for the fact that at the end of his career Hamilton turned not toward manufacturing but in the direction of becoming a partner in Britain's imperial adventures in Latin America. Indeed, Hamilton's foreign policy does less to settle the question of his mercantilism than to recall the report of 1793 that "the English considered Hamilton, [Rufus] King, and [William] Smith, of South Carolina, as main supports of British interest in America. Hamilton, not Hammond, was their effective minister." Perhaps the most to be said of Hamilton's mercantilism is that it was latent and limited, for his actions belied his rhetoric.

As in many other contexts, it is Madison who emerges as the central figure in the development of an American mercantilism. While there are many illustrations, perhaps his resolutions of January 1794 provide the most illuminating evidence. Once again Charles points the way: "The program with which Madison began the first strategic moves against the Federalists was not one which could be called anti-Federalist, particularist, or States' rights." His plan was to combine landed expansion to the west with support for domestic manufacturing and an independent American commercial policy. Considered at the practical political level, it represented a bid to the growing numbers of dissident Federalists who opposed a one-way relationship with Britain. Some of those men eyed a bull market for domestic manufactures. Others thought of an expansionist foreign policy with the established states cast in the role of "mother country." Madison saw such groups as allies for the anti-Federalists, as well as the building blocks of an American mercantilism.

Madison's conception of an American mercantilism was possibly too comprehensive as well as too premature politically to be adopted by Congress in 1794, though it was extensively debated before being sidetracked by Hamilton and Smith. But it did serve as a keen analysis and program for the growing consensus among anti-Federalists. That drive toward economic independence manifested itself in the Non-Intercourse Bill introduced in the summer of 1794, a move which was defeated only by the vote of Vice-President John Adams. Equally significant is the fact that it was backed by congressmen from Pennsylvania and Delaware as well as by those from southern states. Madison's mercantilism picked up new allies very rapidly, and two subsequent events served as catalysts in the process. Considered in the order of their importance, they were Jay's Treaty and the last stage in the defection of John Adams from High Federalism.

Following so closely upon the narrow defeat of the Non-Intercourse Bill, Jay's Treaty added injury to frustration. The great majority of Americans reacted bitterly and vigorously. Already weakened by deep fissures, the Federalist party cracked open under the ensuing attack. It cost them key leaders in such states as New Hampshire and Pennsylvania and alienated unknown numbers of voters south of the Potomac. As one who had cast the deciding vote against the Non-Intercourse Bill only with great reluctance, John Adams provided temporary leadership for such Federalist dissidents.

Adams strengthened his position even more by refusing to go quietly along to war with France at the bidding of the High Federalists. The differences between Hamilton and Adams were numerous, but perhaps none is so important to an appreciation of the maturing American mercantilism as the contrast between Hamilton's passion for a large army and Adams' emphasis on an American navy. Hamilton's military policy was that of the British nabob in North America, while that of Adams represented American mercantilism. Against that background, and in the context of his deciding vote on the Non-Intercourse Bill of 1794, it is possible to appreciate the full impact of Jay's Treaty on Adams. He made peace with France and forced Pickering out of the cabinet.

Little wonder, then, that Jefferson was willing to give way in favor of Adams. But thanks to Madison, who had been organizing a party as well as projecting a theory and a program, Jefferson became President. Once in power, Jefferson and his supporters were prodded by necessity and spurred by their own visions of empire toward the full development of an American mercantilism. There are several explanations for this phenomenon. Among the most important, one might list the following: the foreign-trade dilemma inherent in physiocratic theory (which was intensified by the wars stemming from the French Revolution); the creative leadership provided by such men as Madison and Albert Gallatin (who made his own *Report on Manufactures* in 1810); the political necessities and expediences of unifying and sustaining a national party; and the maturing thought of Jefferson himself. But wherever one chooses to place the emphasis, the fact remains that the Jeffersonians in action were far more mercantilistic than the Federalists had been—even in theory and rhetoric.

As early as 1791, for that matter, Jefferson began to shift away from the physiocratic dogma of free trade. And by 1793 he concluded his *Report on Commercial Policy* with a series of retaliatory proposals that were as mercantilistic as any he criticized. Perhaps even more significant was his early ambivalence toward manufacturing, which he never condemned outright once and for all. Jefferson disliked cities and the factory system for what he judged their negative impact on politics and morals, and for the conditions and style of life they imposed upon human beings, but he never discounted the importance of home manufacturing and commerce. He could not afford to, either as the leader of agrarians beginning to produce surpluses for sale, or as one who sought and accepted support from the increasing number of urban groups of all classes who preferred an empire of their own to rejoining the British system. Even if Jefferson had not caught the intellectual flaw in physiocratic trade theory, its practical consequences were something he could not avoid. In substance, therefore, the Jeffersonians based their strength and their policies on the mercantilistic program of a balanced economy at home and a foreign policy of expansion.

Their strategy was to exploit the policy of neutrality initiated by Washington and continued by John Adams. To do so, Jefferson ultimately resorted to the intensely mercantilistic policies of the embargo and nonimportation against Britain and France. It was with obvious pride that he remarked, in 1809, that those policies "hastened the day when an equilibrium between the occupations of agriculture, manufactures, and commerce, shall simplify our foreign concerns to the exchange only of that surplus which we cannot consume [in return] for those articles of reasonable comfort or convenience which we cannot produce." Not even Madison ever provided a more classic statement of American mercantilism.

Quite in line with Jefferson's recommendations of the 1790's, and his actions between 1800 and 1809, his successors acted vigorously against such weaker opponents as the Barbary Pirates who threatened American trade. On a more general level, Jefferson's argument that American democracy depended upon a surplus of land was but another, even more overtly formulated, version of Madison's theory that extending the sphere was the key to controlling factions. Hence he and his followers initiated and encouraged such expansion wherever they could, as in Florida and to the West; and it was precisely Jefferson's general expansionist outlook which overrode his concern that the Louisiana Purchase was unconstitutional.

The Louisiana Purchase opened the way to apply the tenets of American mercantilism to the entire hemisphere. It also encouraged an explicit American formulation of the expansionist philosophy of history that was implicit in mercantilism. Americans began to call openly and militantly for further expansion whenever and wherever they encountered domestic or foreign difficulties. Indians and Spaniards had to be pushed out of the way or destroyed. Interference with exports had to be stopped, by war if necessary. Canada offered the solution to other domestic economic problems, and should be taken forthwith.

After 1807, when economic troubles appeared at home, that expansionist outlook and program focused on Great Britain as the chief offender against the American Empire. Growing out of an alliance of business and agrarian interests which favored war to relieve immediate difficulties and forestall future crises, the War of 1812 was a classic mercantilist conflict for trade and colonies. The Jeffersonians' earlier economic and maritime warfare, which almost secured the immediate objectives, and which had appeared capable of clearing the way for a general advance, was just as mercantilistic in nature. Though in many ways it failed to attain its avowed objectives, the War of 1812 was in no sense a strategic defeat for American mercantilism. If only in turning Americans to the west and the south, it focused the general spirit of expansion in a new and powerful manner. Perhaps even more significant, the stalemate strengthened the idea of an American System as opposed to the rest of the world. It was in the wake of the War of 1812, after all, that the vapors of Manifest Destiny gathered themselves for an explosion westward to the Pacific.

John Quincy Adams formulated his own concept of Manifest Destiny as early as 1796, when he assured President Washington that the American System would "infallibly triumph over the European system. . . ." Fifteen years later he defined America as "a nation, coextensive with the North American Continent, destined by God and nature to be the most populous and most powerful people ever combined under one social compact." He pushed overseas economic expansion just as vigorously. Even his harshest critics, the High Federalists of New England who wanted to re-enter the British Empire in some form or another, recognized his mercantilism. They called him one of the species of "amphibious politicians, who live on both land and water. . . ."

Both before and after he served as Secretary of State under President James Monroe, Adams devoted his energies to building such an American Empire. His rational program for a dynamic balanced economy at home was too demanding for his countrymen. They grew ever more enamored of a philosophy that assured them that expansion was the way to ease their dilemmas and realize their dreams. Hence they paid little heed to his proposals for domestic development or to his warning that America should go "not abroad in search of monsters to destroy." But to the extent that Adams wanted an empire big enough to sustain such a balanced economy, and to the degree that he partook of the expansionist elixir, he won support and influence. And, indeed, his very presence in the cabinet of Monroe was a symbol of the maturity of American mercantilism. Having broken with the old pro-British party to vote for the Louisiana Purchase and the measures of economic warfare against Europe, Adams became the leader of those business interests which supported territorial as well as commercial expansion.

In timing, authorship, and content, the Monroe Doctrine was the classic statement of mature American mercantilism. Seizing the opportunity presented by the decay of the Spanish Empire, Monroe and Adams moved quickly, decisively, and independently to give substance to Henry Clay's fervent exhortation to "become real and true Americans and place ourselves at the head of the American System." Adams caught the tone and meaning of the doctrine in his famous remark that it was time for America to stop bobbing along as a cock-boat in the wake of the British Empire. Acting in that spirit, he spurned Secretary George Canning's not-so-subtle suggestion that America join England in a joint guarantee of Latin American independence and a pledge against their own expansion in the region. Canning claimed high honors for having brought in the New World to redress the balance of the Old, but one would like to think that Adams enjoyed a hearty chuckle over such ability to put a rhetorical gloss on a policy defeat. For what Canning had done was to block the old empires only to be confronted by the challenge of a mature American mercantilism.

In the negative sense, the Monroe Doctrine was designed to check further European colonization in the Western Hemisphere. But Americans were quite aware of the positive implications of the strategy: it left the United States as the most powerful nation on the scene. America's ultimate territorial and commercial expansion in the New World would be limited only by its energies and its preferences—just as Washington had argued. The negative side of the Monroe Doctrine is the least significant feature about it: the crucial point is that it was, in the minds of its authors, in its language, and in its reception by Americans, the manifesto of an American Empire.

The Monroe Doctrine was the capstone of a system destined to succumb to its own success. For in broad historical perspective, the classic function of mercantilism was to build a system strong enough to survive the application of the principles of Adam Smith. Without an American mercantilism there could have been no Age of Jacksonian Laissez Moi Faire. Perhaps, indeed, the greatest tribute to the leaders of American mercantilism lies in the fact that their handiwork withstood the trauma of a civil war and the sustained shock of unrestrained and irrational exploitation for some seventy years—until it became necessary in the Crisis of the 1890's to undertake the building of a new corporate system.

Additional Reading

S. F. Bemis, *John Quincy Adams and the Foundations of American Foreign Policy* (1949).

———, *The Latin American Policy of the United States* (1943).

George Dangerfield, *The Era of Good Feelings* (1952).

G. W. McGee, "The Monroe Doctrine—A Stopgap Measure," *Mississippi Valley Historical Review*, XXXVIII (1951), 233–250.

Dexter Perkins, *A History of the Monroe Doctrine* (1955).

J. Fred Rippy, *Rivalry of the United States and Great Britain over Latin America, 1808–1830* (1929).

E. H. Tatum, Jr., *The United States and Europe, 1815–1823* (1936).

A. P. Whitaker, *The United States and the Independence of Latin America, 1800–1830* (1941).

7 *THE OREGON TREATY: Pioneer Pressures or Commercial Motives?*

The 1830's and 1840's were marked by an increase of Anglophobia, or hatred of England, in the United States. Much of the bitterness dated back to the late colonial clashes with the mother country and to the problems the young republic faced after 1783 in getting Britain to recognize fully the political and economic independence of the United States. Controversies over neutral commerce led to war in 1812 and after 1815 further irritants were created by the abortive revolution in Canada and quarrels over the northeastern boundary. British travelers to America, and they came in considerable number in this period, were usually high Tory in outlook and most critical of American democratic society. In addition, many Britishers were annoyed at the widespread debt-defaulting of American states and local governments after the Panic of 1837 and English literary circles bitterly resented the lack of an international copyright protection in America. The result was the publication of a series of critical travel books in England on all phases of American life and a "literary war" of attack and counterattack by periodicals on both sides of the Atlantic. Yet despite the poisoned atmosphere, the two governments were aware of mutual economic ties and had a will to peace. As a result, the Webster-Ashburton Treaty of 1842 settled the tangled northeastern boundary dispute and in 1846 a treaty was completed which divided satisfactorily the Oregon territory.

The Oregon settlement has raised several questions of interest to students of history: why did Great Britain make such great concessions in an area where its claims were stronger? and was the American interest in Oregon the result of Manifest Destiny drives and the pioneer desire for land, or commercial interests in good ports suitable for expanding trade in the Pacific?

DOCUMENT

A British Surrender

If the Webster-Ashburton Treaty was an American retreat in an area where its claims were strongest, as many historians believe, the Oregon Treaty was clearly an American victory. The boundaries of the jointly-claimed area had been delineated by treaties with Spain in 1819 and Russia in 1824–1825 as north of the 42nd parallel, south of the line 54°40′ and west of the Rocky Mountains. Within this area, the Hudson's Bay Company carried on trapping and trading activities as far south as the Columbia River, and established an agricultural colony at Puget Sound. American missionaries and settlers came in later and located south of the Columbia. Even after the "Oregon fever" of

the 1840's substantially increased the American population, the settlers with a few exceptions were still south of the river and the British were in occupancy to the north. Yet by the 1846 treaty, that area up to the 49th parallel was granted to the United States.

The Oregon Treaty of June 15, 1846

Article I. From the point on the forty-ninth parallel of north latitude where the boundary laid down in existing treaties and conventions between the United States and Great Britain terminates, the line of boundary between the territories of the United States and those of Her Britannic Majesty shall be continued westward along the said forty-ninth parallel of north latitude to the middle of the channel which separates the continent from Vancouver's Island; and thence southerly through the middle of the said channel, and of Fuca's Straits to the Pacific Ocean; provided, however, that the navigation of the whole of the said channel and Straits south of the forty-ninth parallel of north latitude remain free and open to both Parties.

Article II. From the point at which the forty-ninth parallel of north latitude shall be found to intersect the great northern branch of the Columbia River, the navigation of the said branch shall be free and open to the Hudson's Bay Company and to all British subjects trading with the same, to the point where the said branch meets the main stream of the Columbia, and thence down the said main stream to the Ocean, with free access into and through the said River or Rivers, it being understood that all the usual portages along the line thus described shall in like manner be free and open. In navigating the said River or Rivers, British subjects with their goods and produce, shall be treated on the same footing as citizens of the United States; it being however always understood that nothing in this article shall be construed as preventing, or intended to prevent, the Government of the United States from making any regulations respecting the navigation of the said river or rivers, not inconsistent with the present treaty.

Article III. In the future appropriation of the territory, south of the forty-ninth parallel of north latitude, as provided in the first article of this Treaty, the possessory rights of the Hudson's Bay Company and of all British subjects who may be already in the occupation of land or other property, lawfully acquired within the said Territory, shall be respected.

Article IV. The farms, lands, and other property of every description belonging to the Puget's Sound Agricultural Company on the north side of the Columbia River, shall be confirmed to the said Company. In case however the situation of those farms and lands should be considered by the United States to be of public and political importance, and the United States' Government should signify a desire to obtain possession of the whole, or of any part thereof, the property so required shall be tranferred

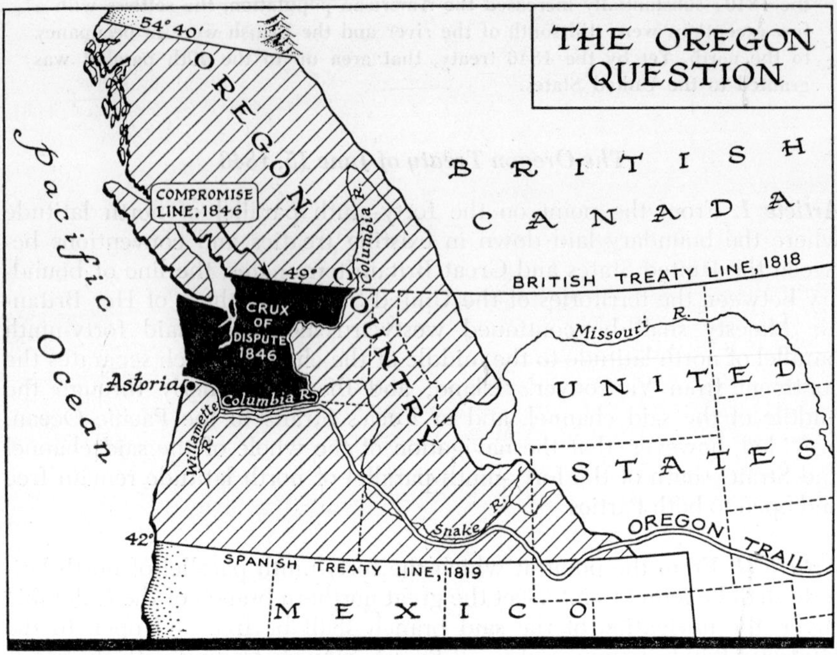

to the said Government, at a proper valuation, to be agreed upon between the Parties.

Article V. The present Treaty shall be ratified by the President of the United States, by and with the advice and consent of the Senate thereof, and by Her Britannic Majesty; and the ratifications shall be exchanged at London, at the expiration of six months from the date hereof, or sooner if possible.

In witness whereof, the respective Plenipotentiaries have signed the same, and have affixed thereto the seals of their arms.

Done at Washington the fifteenth day of June, in the year of our Lord one thousand eight hundred and forty-six.

[Seal] JAMES BUCHANAN
[Seal] RICHARD PAKENHAM

READINGS

1. Pioneers and Manifest Destiny

The question of why Great Britain conceded the 49th parallel in 1846, after refusing to do so on several previous occasions, is attributed by Melvin C. Jacobs, a student of Pacific Northwest history, primarily to the pressure of American pioneer settlers. The growing density of American agricultural settlements, the consequent decline in fur-bearing animals, and the possibilities of

armed clashes with the unruly pioneers led the Hudson's Bay Company to move its center of operations to the north. The company comprised the chief British interest in the area between the Columbia River and Puget Sound, and its withdrawal opened the way to acceptance by Britain of a boundary at the 49th parallel. The cutting edge of American westward expansion into Oregon and California thus had been the restless pioneer, driven by Manifest Destiny sentiments and the desire for new agricultural lands.

Winning Oregon Territory for the United States

MELVIN C. JACOBS

According to evidence cited in the foregoing, the pioneer migrated to Oregon in the spirit of restlessness and adventure, seeking free lands and a salubrious climate. Some also thought they were helping to win the territory for the United States. Representatives in Congress were agitating the Oregon Question and were attempting to legalize land grants as an inducement for people to emigrate to that country. A Government which had been turning a deaf ear to agitation for free lands was now proposing to give a square mile of land to any family appearing on the scene and staking a claim. As the pioneer listened to the proposal and followed arguments favoring it, he had arrived at the conclusion that land was to be granted as a compensation for perfecting the title of his country to this territory.

The idea that the missionaries, Jason Lee, Marcus Whitman, or any other individual "saved Oregon" has been demonstrated by various students of the subject to be untenable. *No single individual saved Oregon.* The task was difficult and complex. Parts in the task were played by explorers, hunters, traders, missionaries, diplomats, congressmen, Presidents, and settlers. What part did the pioneers—the settlers of Oregon—play in drawing the boundary *when* it was delimited, and the place *where* it was drawn? American diplomats had repeatedly attempted to establish the boundary along the forty-ninth parallel and were unsuccessful because England refused to agree on a boundary located that far north. In 1818, when the Joint Occupation Treaty was being formulated, the forty-ninth parallel was offered as a boundary, and rejected by England. This proposal was repeated in 1826, when joint occupation was renewed. Again, in 1845, this boundary was tendered, with modifications, only to be summarily rejected.

What difference in the boundary situation was brought about by the presence of American settlers in Oregon? When the settlers under the leadership of Elijah White arrived in the Willamette Valley in 1842, they, together with earlier settlers, set up a provisional government July 5, 1843. With the arrival of an increasing number of Americans in the valley, even the Hudson's Bay Company employees at Fort Vancouver joined this provisional government for their own protection.

In the autumn of 1843 the celebrated expedition of what is known as the "thousand" emigrants appeared in the Willamette Valley and turned

Melvin Clay Jacobs, *Winning Oregon: A Study of an Expansionist Movement* (Caldwell, Idaho: The Caxton Printers, Ltd., 1938), 209–212, 217–223, 226–227, 229, 234–242. Reprinted with permission.

the small American majority into an overwhelming majority. It was influential beyond its numbers. It was the direct result of the "Oregon fever" on the frontier. This fever was fostered through agitation, education, and organization for Oregon. Its influence produced results in Oregon, in England, on the frontier, at Washington, and throughout the country. The successive contingents of settlers which appeared in the years immediately following that of 1843 made American the settlement south of the Columbia River.

However, that part of Oregon territory lying south of the Columbia River could have been accepted by the Federal Government at any time during the joint occupation, without a solitary settler within its bounds. When the settlers did appear they located south of the Columbia, in that part of the territory over which there was no dispute. The American Government could not claim the section north of the river on the basis of possession or actual settlement. The land lying north of the Columbia was actually occupied by the British when the boundary was settled. This being true, what part did the pioneer play in winning that section of Oregon which he neither occupied nor settled? The answer to this question involves a consideration of his influence upon the Western part of the United States, upon the Hudson's Bay Company, and upon the English Government, as well as upon the Federal Government. A cursory glance at the situation may cause one to think that the boundary was drawn by the Federal Government through channels of diplomacy and that the pioneers had nothing to do with its settlement. The pioneer influence upon the situation must be carefully investigated if one desires to evaluate properly the relative contributions to the "saving" of that part of Oregon which was in dispute and which finally became part of the United States.

In considering the significance of the settler in the determination of the boundary, let us turn to the settler himself. *The Oregon pioneer thought he was perfecting the title to Oregon.* Mr. J. Quinn Thornton, emigrant in 1846, an Oregon judge, and later Governor of California, stated that "imperfect legislation, letters from the Secretary of State and from Hon. T. H. Benton and other distinguished gentlemen whom we regarded as our friends and protectors, and to whom we looked with respect and even reverence, invited us to come to this beautiful land, and to make farms and build houses and towns. By doing this we laid a broad and deep foundation upon which to build up a title to the country which nothing could shake down." . . .

. . . If the pioneers went to Oregon with the object of aiding the movement to win the country, why did they not locate north of the Columbia, in the strip of land which was in dispute? There are several reasons why they located south of the Columbia. The inaccessibility of the land to the north to overland travel was a deterrent to its settlement. The Willamette Valley was more accessible. The Willamette and Columbia Rivers served as natural highways to Fort Vancouver, the trading mart of the country. The land about Puget Sound was covered with timber. Clearings were necessary before houses could be built and land devoted to cultivation.

The country south of the Columbia contained only patches of timber in the midst of rich grazing land. As the number of settlers increased in the Valley the price of real estate rose. Settlers located there to reap these gains. Moreover, the Hudson's Bay Company had spread over the country to the north and discouraged American settlement there. Members of the company reported that the land north of the Columbia was not suitable for agriculture.

When discussions on drawing the boundary of Oregon were carried on in Congress, members of Congress stated on the floor that no American settlers were located north of the Columbia. No Congressman contradicted the statement. It is obvious that the staunchest advocates for annexation of the whole of Oregon were not cognizant of the fact that any citizens had settled there. Mr. George H. Himes, resident of Olympia during the period of 1853–64, conducted a careful investigation on the number of American settlers residing north of the Columbia on June 15, 1846. He listed five families and two men, a total number of thirty-one persons. On a liberal estimation, one can say that there were less than forty American citizens, including children, north of the Columbia River when the treaty was ratified, and that those who negotiated the treaty were unaware that any American people were located there.

An estimation of the effect of the settler in Oregon, upon the boundary situation, must take into consideration that the Hudson's Bay Company was organized for gathering pelts and disposing of them in the markets of the world. It had been their policy to foster wilderness rather than settlement. With the appearance of the settler, wild animals disappeared. The resulting dearth of fur defeated the objects of the company. *The American settler rendered the position of the company increasingly unprofitable and untenable in the inland districts, where their chief operations had been carried on.* The pressure placed upon the English Government by the Hudson's Bay Company to retain the country north of the Columbia, and the company's insistence on the right of free navigation of the river, was to be found in the desire to operate the trading posts established in the interior. The gradual weakening of the fur trade in the interior brought on a gradual weakening of the English grip upon Oregon territory in general.

The incoming settlers brought a close proximity of Americans and English in a territory under joint occupation, a territory which was daily becoming a disputed land. The frontiersman brought with him his hereditary antipathy for the English. He regarded them as rivals and interlopers. Many pioneers were led to believe that the whole of Oregon belonged to the United States. *A forceful argument in Congress for the immediate settlement of the boundary was found in the fact that there was an impending danger of a clash between the settlers and the employees of the Hudson's Bay Company.* Had not the "Aristook War" broken out between the Canadians and the people of Maine? Knowing the pugnacious spirit of the backwoodsmen, Congressmen regarded any measure which meant delay as likely to lead to greater difficulties.

Englishmen also recognized this danger. Lord Ashburton wrote to

Daniel Webster from London, January, 1846: "The Oregon dispute was mainly invented," he said, "before we settled the Maine boundary, and when it is closed some new grievance will soon be opened. As long as we are neighbors on the great Continent which you begin to think should wholly belong to you we shall never really be friends, and I long wished we could find a decent excuse to let the work of Annexation be completed."

The Secretary of State, Buchanan, wrote the American Minister to England, February 26, 1846: "Meanwhile the tide of emigration from the United States to Oregon would be constantly swelling, and the danger of collisions between the British subjects and American citizens in that territory would be constantly increasing. In my opinion, in order to secure a peaceful, there must be a prompt settlement of the controversy. There never was a question in which delay will prove more dangerous."

The Hudson's Bay Company also feared that a clash might take place between their employees and the Americans. At the request of McLoughlin a war vessel was stationed at Fort Vancouver. Cannon were mounted, and an additional guard was formed for the protection of the fort. Some of the most rabid, unruly, and lawless elements of the Americans threatened to burn the fort, which was constructed of pine logs and would have burned like tinder. Representatives of the company reported their fears to headquarters in London. When the company moved to Vancouver Island they were influenced by the desire to withdraw from the vicinity of the American settlements.

Through the influx of settlers the harvest of pelts in the interior diminished in number. The company was not able to protect the game as it did in the north where it exercised full supervision. With the diminishing number of fur-bearing animals in the interior, the retention of the Columbia as an outlet from the hinterland no longer appeared indispensable. England was able to surrender her claims to it without violent opposition from any group at home. The way of diplomacy was made smooth for negotiation, with the forty-ninth parallel as a boundary, when the Hudson's Bay Company decided to move its Western headquarters to Vancouver Island. At least three factors in the situation appear to have induced them to change their chief fort, namely, (1) to withdraw from close proximity to American settlers, (2) the decline in pelts in the interior, (3) an increasing development, and consequent interest in the coastwise trade. In storing the goods designed for coastwise trade at Vancouver Island rather than at Fort Vancouver, they avoided the hazardous passage at the mouth of the Columbia. . . .

Someone may remark that it is not according to facts to say that the United States would necessarily have lost all the land north of the Columbia if settlers had not appeared upon the scene. When Albert Gallatin was negotiating with England on the Oregon problem in 1826, Americans were insisting that they be given an outlet to the sea. Placing the boundary along the middle of the channel of the Columbia would have given America the dangerous, and at times impassable, channel of the Columbia as the only means of access by water to the country bordering on the Pacific, or as a haven for numerous American vessels engaged in whale fishing, coastwise trade, or trade with the Sandwich Islands and the Orient. To meet this objection, George Canning offered, in addition to the boundary of the Columbia, the harbor at Port Discovery on the Strait of De Fuca, with a five-mile radius about it. If this was not satisfactory, they would give up a triangle north of the Columbia on the Pacific Coast, bordered by Juan de Fuca Strait on the north, and Hood Canal, with a line drawn from its southern extremity to a point ten miles south of Grays Harbor as the other boundary. The American Government refused to consider this proposition because the harbor tendered would have been surrounded by English territory and entirely cut off from American communications overland. In later interviews England did not submit proposals of this sort. The Hudson's Bay Company was occupying that domain and claiming it by right of possession.

We have observed that it has been asserted that the diplomatic agents of the Federal Government carried on the negotiations which led to the agreement upon the Northwest boundary, that the pioneer had no voice in the negotiation. Diplomats are but agents of governments. Previous to the time when the boundary was finally drawn, diplomats and Government officials were unwilling to press the issue to a conclusion. Settlers in Oregon, agitation of the Oregon Question in the Western part of the country, Western influence in politics, and Western pressure in Congress furnished the "logic of events" which made it difficult for diplomacy to dodge the question any longer. . . .

Conclusion

Oregon territory, like Florida, Louisiana, Texas, and California, was won as a part of the Union in the process of growth and expansion in population. This expansion continued until the thirteen original states appeared as but a narrow fringe along the eastern border of an extensive federation of states. Pressure of population was a determining factor in the process. The method of winning Oregon was no exception to the rule. We have noted the change in the Oregon situation through the influx of settlers. With the advent of the settler, the inevitable depletion of the fur trade took place. Disputed claims over the right to free navigation of the Columbia River became, with the decline of the fur supply in the interior, of little interest or value to the British. The Hudson's Bay Company held the interior by means of trading posts and forts. These having lost the object of their existence, England was able to retreat without opposition from the company, and without loss of dignity. . . .

Additional evidence that the movement for winning Oregon was a frontier movement, distinct from New England missionary activity, is found in the fact that the movement for winning Oregon and for winning California was simultaneous and identical. Oregon and California settlers left the frontier in a unit, usually separating at Fort Hall, in what is now the state of Idaho. As early as 1841, in a contingent of about fifty persons departing for the Far West, the greater part were on their way to California. As the number of emigrants to Oregon increased, a larger number were also attracted to California. By 1845, frontiersmen were talking more of California than of Oregon.

It is interesting to observe the almost identical impressions made upon, and the almost identical conclusions drawn by, Commodore Wilkes, of the United States Navy, and Governor General George Simpson, of the Hudson's Bay Company, when they visited California on their itineraries of investigation. Wilkes reported that "the situation of Upper California will cause its separation from Mexico before many years. . . . It is very probable that this country will become united with Oregon, with which it will perhaps form a state that is destined to control the destinies of the Pacific. This future state is admirably situated to become a powerful maritime nation, with two of the finest ports in the world,—that within the straits of Juan de Fuca, and San Francisco." He added: "Possessed as it must be by the Anglo-Norman race, and having none to enter into rivalry with it but the indolent inhabitants of warm climates, is evidently destined to fill a large space in the world's future history."

Governor Simpson arrived in California shortly after the departure of Wilkes. He, too, was spying out the land and meditating on its prospects for the future. "If Sutter really has the talent and the courage," he remarked, "to make the most of his position, he is not unlikely to render California a second Texas. Even now, the Americans only want a rallying point for carrying into effect their theory, that the English race is destined by 'rights divine' to expel the Spaniards from their ancient seats—a theory which has begun to develop itself in more ways than one." He concluded that "San Francisco will, to a moral certainty, sooner or later fall into possession of Americans; the only possible mode of preventing such a result, being the previous occupation of the port on the part of Great Britain."

It is not pertinent to the object of this study to follow in detail the early migrations of the frontiersmen to California. It is, however, pertinent to observe that these early migrations to Oregon and California were part of the same movement. Both migrations were part of America's manifest destiny.

Western people have frequently charged Congress with ignorance and indifference concerning Oregon. Both charges are contrary to the facts. When representatives in Congress declared that Oregon was a barren, worthless desert, or rendered unsuitable for habitation on account of continuous rain, or that it was worthless commercially, they were seizing upon descriptions applicable to certain sections or conditions in order that they might justify their opposition to westward expansion, or justify their opposition to expansion into territories which were likely to be closed to slavery. Congressmen had numerous and various sources at their disposal for gaining a knowledge of the country. Even those who refused to read would have been compelled to refuse to hear had they determined to remain ignorant on the subject. Western advocates for Oregon poured information on the subject into their speeches until the most indifferent or ill-informed could scarcely plead ignorance.

Congress was struggling under the weakness of sectionalism; the executive, together with the entire treaty-making powers of the Government in general, were handicapped by the peculiar situation of the Joint Occupation Treaty; the entire Government was embroiled in the lack of a clear title. Part of that country which the United States refused to surrender was occupied by the rival claimant. These peculiar combinations of circumstances prevented the Government from taking prompt and aggressive action on the subject. The weakness of sectionalism was partially overcome when the Oregon Question became national and political; the weakness in the lack of a clear title was changed into preponderating advantage when the settlers arrived in the country and staked their claims; the joint occupation agreement for trapping and trading was recognized by both parties to be no longer tenable. The frontier movement effected the change. A flank movement in Congress, while a front movement was enacted on the frontier, eventuated in a settlement which was advantageous and fortunate for the United States. The loss of interest in the navigation of the Columbia through the decline of the fur trade, the desire to withdraw from close proximity to American settlers, together with British intense interest in domestic problems at that time, presents a combination of conditions favorable to the United States in 1846 seldom found at a single interval.

A study of the Oregon agitation in Congress reveals that the majority in neither house were at any time ready to vote for any bill that would force the issue of American contention for the whole of Oregon. Neither were there indications that at any time were the majority of either house ready to vote for a settlement that would limit the northern boundary to the middle channel of the Columbia River. During the administration of Tyler, while Pakenham was discussing the Oregon Question with the Secretary of State, Calhoun, the Secretary informed him that if he could bring himself to accept a less advantageous boundary than that of the forty-ninth parallel, "it would be idle to propose such an arrangement to the Senate for that it most *certainly would not be ratified.*"

England had repeatedly offered the channel of the Columbia River as a boundary, and had met with an emphatic refusal. America had repeatedly offered the forty-ninth parallel, and had met refusals from England. This confined the bone of contention, in a large measure, to the land lying between the Columbia and the forty-ninth parallel. England, although actually occupying this land in dispute, surrendered it to the Americans. The United States gained practically all, except the southern point of Vancouver Island; and this had been in possession of the British.

We have observed that the Hudson's Bay Company had mapped out plans for expansion in the Columbia Valley, as conditions became favorable for carrying out their purposes. In the period of joint occupation, during the ten-year agreement of 1818–28, both the company and the British Government made plans and adjustments for holding the country north of the Columbia, at the expiration of that treaty. When an agreement upon a boundary seemed remote, and it was decided to extend the period of joint occupation indefinitely, the Hudson's Bay Company immediately began to exploit the country south of the Columbia, to prevent it from being occupied by American traders and trappers.

In this move they were successful, their organized and rich monopoly becoming a formidable and triumphant rival. Not content with this attainment, they began to map out a course for the exclusion of "American adventurers" from coastwise trade. By capturing contracts for furnishing the Russians their food supplies, and by underselling Americans, they were able to report to headquarters in London that they had driven the Americans from the coast. The undertaking to furnish food for the Russians necessitated a farming enterprise. To meet this need, the Puget's Sound Agricultural Company was organized for farming on a large scale. The conveyance of settlers from the Red River Valley served the dual purpose of furnishing farmers to grow products for the Russian trade and of interposing settlers on the north side of the Columbia as a counter-movement to the incoming American settlers on the south side.

For emphasis, let us sum up the nature of occupation on the part of England, which extended across the land north of the Columbia. Americans in and out of Congress reported that the Hudson's Bay Company had seized the valuable land sites and occupied the strategic points. They charged that the English were discouraging and impeding the Americans from locating north of the Columbia. At Fort Vancouver, twelve or more sections of land were in use for farming and pasture. Twelve hundred acres of this were under cultivation; the remainder was used for pasturing 700 brood mares, 1600 hogs, 3400 cattle and sheep. From 150 to 200 men were employed in the fields, dairies, mills, shops, and stores of the establishment. As early as 1837, William A. Slacum estimated that they, their half-breed children, and Indian wives, comprised a settlement of from 750 to 800 persons.

The Cowlitz Plains were the center of operations of the Puget's Sound Agricultural Company. The farm was composed of 3000 acres at this place, 1200 of which were under the Roman Catholic Mission and about a half-dozen retired settlers. Here, the attempt at colonization was made by means of the emigrants from the Red River. One hundred and sixteen persons had arrived in 1841, with the expectation that more would follow. Fourteen of these represented heads of families, with a total of seventy-seven persons in the families. A total of eighty-five to ninety men were employed here.

Fort Nisqually, on Puget Sound, was another enterprise of the Puget's Sound Agricultural Company. The herding activities were located there. On a tract of 167,000 acres, 5800 sheep, 200 horses, and 1850 cattle were pastured. Besides these farming enterprises and possessions, the Hudson's Bay Company had a network of trading posts spun along the Columbia River and its branches. These facts were placed before the British Government in reports which exaggerated the importance and significance of occupation of this nature.

When England agreed to draw the boundary along the forty-ninth parallel, the Hudson's Bay Company, their employees, the British press, the British Government, all thought they were making concessions to America in the interest of peace. When Lord Aberdeen submitted the Oregon Treaty to Washington, in his private letters to Pakenham, he spoke of the sacrifices that the English must undergo. The concession of the forty-ninth parallel will "interfere with the possessions of British colonists resident in a district in which it is believed that scarcely an American citizen as a settler, has ever set foot," he lamented.

The *Weekly Tribune*, New York, November 29, 1845, discussed England's rights to Oregon territory. It advanced the following arguments in behalf of England: (1) Contiguity. Oregon is contiguous to English territory as well as to American. (2) The oldest settlements there are British. Nine tenths of all the settlements there are British. English settlements were there thirty years ago; American settlements are but of a decade. (3) We commenced negotiating with Great Britain for part of the territory; now we demand all. In another issue it called attention to the fact that David Thompson, in the employ of the North West Company, was on the north branch of the Columbia River five years before Lewis and Clark appeared in Oregon. Twelve years before the explorations of Lewis and Clark, Mackenzie had traversed the northern part of the territory.

Taking into consideration the indefiniteness and weakness of claims to new territory on the basis of discovery and exploration, in contrast to occupation and settlement, instead of raising the question as to the reasons why America did not secure the whole of Oregon to fifty-four degrees and forty minutes, it appears to be more appropriate to raise the question as to why England lost the territory between the Columbia River and the forty-ninth parallel after she had both occupied and, apparently, possessed it.

2. *Commerce and Good Harbors on the Pacific*

Norman A. Graebner, a productive scholar who has also written extensively on recent American diplomacy, contends that the shape of American policy toward the Pacific coast areas was determined by commercial interests, not vague Manifest Destiny urges or by pioneer farmers. The Pacific was the highway to a rich Far Eastern trade and initial American contacts with the Pacific Coast had resulted from commercial ventures—China traders, sea otter hunters, whalers, and hide and tallow purchasers. The west coast of North America is lacking in good ports. It was soon realized that the best harbors were San Francisco Bay and Puget Sound. Consequently American policy, reflecting commercial desires, sought acquisition of these two ports long before any considerable pioneer settlements had been established in either California or Oregon.

Empire on the Pacific

NORMAN A. GRAEBNER

North from the Columbia

I

When James K. Polk entered the White House in March, 1845, the United States had no clear title, guaranteed by treaty, to frontage on the Pacific Ocean. Even its uncontested claims were limited to a wild

From *Empire on the Pacific—A Study in American Continental Expansion*, by Norman A. Graebner. Copyright, 1955, the Ronald Press Company, pp. 22–34, 137–142, 147–149, 226–228.

fringe of land stretching southward three hundred miles from the Columbia River to the California border. Despite the rugged beauty of this coast, it was hardly inspiring to American commercial interests. It comprised a variety of rocky beaches strewn with half-hidden boulders hulking out of the surf, impermeable sand dunes, and trees twisted and deformed by the winds of centuries. Forested headlands, rising in the coastal range to the east, terminated frequently in forbidding cliffs which jutted precipitously from the sea. Nowhere along this shore was there a port accessible to even the smallest sea-going vessels. Few coves furnished anchorage even under the most favorable conditions of weather and season. The mouth of the Umpqua, its entrance hemmed by encroaching sand, was rendered useless by hidden dangers and a relentless surf. After decades of maritime activity in Oregon, this coastal strip was almost as untouched as the day Lewis and Clark first sighted the Pacific.

This frontage alone had been conceded to the United States in 1845, and that by unwritten agreement. Jefferson's purchase of Louisiana had bridged the immense gap between the Mississippi and the Pacific shores, but it left United States claims to a corridor west of the Rockies uncertain and inconclusive. By the Spanish treaty of 1819, which defined the Louisiana boundary, that nation conceded to the United States all claims above the forty-second parallel west of the Rockies. In 1818 the United States and Great Britain had negotiated the northern boundary of Louisiana along the forty-ninth parallel westward from the Lake of the Woods to the "Stony Mountains." Beyond the Rockies, however, the United States found itself in conflict with the expanding British Empire then pushing southward from western Canada with the Hudson's Bay Company in the vanguard. In the convention of 1818 the two contending powers agreed to leave the region equally and freely accessible for a period of ten years to the vessels and citizens of either nation without prejudice to their respective claims. In lieu of a territorial settlement, the negotiations of 1826–27 extended the principal of joint occupancy indefinitely, each nation obtaining the privilege of terminating the arrangement upon a twelve-month notice of such intention. As late as the forties Oregon was still held in this state of equilibrium by two empires struggling for mastery of the Northwest coast.

Early in the contest for Oregon both the United States and Great Britain put forth their claims to the region in vigorous terms, confident in the strength of their contentions. Through two decades of negotiation these respective claims changed imperceptibly. American diplomats assumed the position that Captain Robert Gray's discovery of the Columbia, the Northwest fur trade, the Lewis and Clark expedition, and the American Fur Company post at Astoria gave the United States prerogatives not only to the entire valley of the Columbia but also to the regions northward at least to the traditional boundary line of the forty-ninth parallel. Even the famed British explorer George Vancouver, they noted, readily admitted that Gray had discovered the mouth of the Columbia. Its course, without question, had been explored first by Lewis and Clark. The waters of Juan de Fuca Strait and Puget Sound, conceded the Americans, had been explored gradually by Spanish, British, and United States navigators, but even in this region American diplomats claimed the Spanish rights and the prerogatives accruing from the fur trade. Astoria at the mouth of the Columbia merely added the right of prior settlement. Lastly, American negotiators insisted that the territory between the forty-second and forty-ninth parallels west of the mountains was a natural extension of United States possessions to the Pacific Ocean.

The British were far less sanguine, but hoped that by neutralizing the American claims of prior discovery, exploration, and settlement they could reduce the contest to a matter of actual occupation. The British, therefore, emphasized the early British explorations of the Columbia and the Strait of Fuca. They insisted, further, that the Spaniards had terminated their claims to the Oregon country in the Nootka settlement of 1790—that for the United States the Spanish rights were no rights at all. It was the British thesis that pretensions based on discovery and exploration were at best confused and controversial and that Oregon should be divided on the basis of possession.

For twenty years and as late as 1845 this remained a strong British position, for the entire region north of the Columbia had been continuously in the possession of the Hudson's Bay Company. Except for a few American trappers who ventured into the region during the 1820's, the British company, partner of the crown in the building of a North American empire, was the sole occupant of the entire area held in contention. Travelers in the forties estimated the number of Hudson's Bay employees at three thousand and described their situation as far stronger commercially and agriculturally than that of the American pioneers then in Oregon. Hudson's Bay controlled a series of posts extending from Fort Hall and Fort Boise on the Snake River in eastern Oregon to Fort Walla Walla on the south bank of the Columbia, and along that river to Fort George near its mouth. Fort Vancouver, located on the north bank of the Columbia opposite the mouth of the Willamette, was the chief Hudson's Bay post in Oregon. It had been established in 1825 by Dr. John McLoughlin as part of the process of overhauling the Columbia Department and strengthening the hold of the British on the entire Columbia Valley. Northward into Canada, Hudson's Bay was unchallenged. To Sir George Simpson, long-time company official and after 1839 Governor-in-Chief of American Operations, continued possession of the Columbia was essential for the maintenance of the British fur trade in Oregon. And the demands of the fur trade determined the objectives of British diplomacy.

While adamant on the Columbia line, the British gave up all pretensions south of that line even though the Hudson's Bay Company continued to maintain scattered posts in that region. George Canning, British Foreign Minister during the twenties, and other British officials pursued the principle that the concession of territory south of the Columbia would strengthen British claims to territory north of that river. Thus it was that United States claims to Oregon were unchallenged in that broad strip of land between the Columbia and the forty-second parallel. The American title to this region was not official for the sole reason that no American official would affix his signature to such an agreement. For the United States, such a division of the Oregon country was unacceptable because a settlement along the Columbia would not achieve the essential American objectives in the Pacific Northwest.

II

Diplomacy could dispose of rival claims to Oregon only after it had resolved the deeper struggle for commercial position on the Pacific Coast. Behind the façade of diplomatic maneuvering on the basis of the prior rights of discovery, exploration, and settlement was the crucial drive for ocean frontage—for a window on the sea as a "point of departure" for an Asiatic mercantile empire. It was the struggle for commercial supremacy in the Pacific that rendered the British proposal of the Columbia unacceptable. Of those factors in American expansion which sought solution in the Oregon negotiations, none appeared of greater concern to the people of the United States than the disposition of Asiatic trade. From the beginning of the Northwest fur trade and commercial relations with the Far East, American goals in Oregon had been fashioned by the sea.

Since the days of Jefferson the common ambition of American politicians and merchants in the Far Northwest had been to find outlets for the exploitation of the rich commerce of the Pacific. Jefferson's initial task was that of opening a commercial route across the continent. What he asked of André Michaux in conducting his western explorations was that he "seek for and pursue that route which shall form the shortest and most convenient communication between the high parts of the Missouri and the Pacific Ocean." Again his instructions to Meriwether Lewis in 1803 revealed his commercial purposes in unmistakable terms. "The object of your mission," he charged the young frontiersman, "is to explore the Missouri River, and such principal streams of it, as by its course and communication with the waters of the Pacific Ocean, may offer the most direct and practicable water communication across the continent for the purposes of commerce." For Jefferson, as for those who followed him, the great objective in continental expansion was the acquisition of a passage through Oregon to the potential wealth of the Orient. With the United States in possession of good ports on the Pacific, predicted Francis Baylies in 1823, "the commercial wealth of the world is ours, and imagination can hardly conceive the greatness, the grandeur, and the power that await us."

To later travelers Oregon was likewise a key to the Pacific. "Commercially," wrote John C. Fremont in 1844, "the value of the Oregon country must be great, washed as it is by the north Pacific ocean—fronting Asia—producing many of the elements of commerce—mild and healthy in its climate—and becoming, as it naturally will, a thoroughfare for the East India and China trade." John C. Calhoun, who accepted this conclusion uncritically, scarcely dared to estimate the magnitude of Oregon's future commerce. Opportunities in China, he prophesied, will "be followed in Japan, and all the eastern portions of the continent. These ports, like the Chinese, will be opened; and the whole of that portion of Asia, containing nearly half the population and wealth of the globe, will be thrown open to the commerce of the world and be placed within the pales of European and American intercourse and civilization." Oregon, in short, offered strategic position on the shores of the Pacific.

But commercial expansionism did more than merely define American interests in Oregon. Its focus on ports guided American territorial objectives relentlessly northward from the Columbia. With increasing insistence, the writings of such leading authorities on the Pacific Northwest as Robert Greenhow, Thomas J. Farnham, Charles Wilkes, and Eugène Duflot de Mofras had convinced the representatives of commerce that the Columbia, although traditionally associated with the Northwest trade, was of questionable value as an ocean port. Their writings made axiomatic the dangers of the sand bar between Cape Disappointment and Point Adams, created by the vast quantities of sand carried down the Columbia and hurled back by the surf. "Mere description," wrote Wilkes, "can give little idea of the terrors of the bar of the Columbia: all who have seen it have spoken of the wildness of the scene, and the incessant roar of the waters, representing it as one of the most fearful sights that can possibly meet the eye of the sailor." Mofras, the noted French traveler, recalled the "hideous spectacle" of the bar, "with the foam cloaking the horizon far out at sea as if to form an insurmountable barrier to ships entering or leaving the river."

During the winter months violent storms rendered the entrance all but impassable. These travelers reported that vessels often stood off the coast or inside the entrance for as long as two months awaiting a favorable opportunity for running the bar. Mofras's ship, for example, lay off the Cape for nineteen days secured by three anchors, unable either to ascend the river or beat out to sea because of the violence of the wind and current. Among the harbor's victims were several Hudson's Bay ships and cargoes and the United States warship *Peacock*. This record of destruction led critics of the Columbia to conclude that a greater proportion of men and ships had been lost entering this port than any other in the world.

In sharp contrast was their description of the Fuca Strait and the sea arms to the east of it. "No part of the world," wrote Farnham, "affords finer inland sounds or a greater number of harbours than can be found here. . . ." Wilkes's description was equally glowing: "Nothing can exceed the beauty of these waters, and their safety: not a shoal exists within the Straits of Juan de Fuca, Admiralty Inlet, Puget Sound, or Hood's Canal, that can in any way interrupt their navigation by a seventy-four gun ship. I venture nothing in saying, there is no country in the world that possesses waters equal to these." Here were the only harbors in Oregon that could be entered or left under any wind during any season of the year. This was the only region on the entire Northwest Coast that could control the waters of the north Pacific. Herein lay the primary objectives in Oregon of commercial America.

What was obvious to American expansionists in the forties had been accepted in principle by President John Quincy Adams as early as his Oregon negotiations of 1826. Adams, in search of a good naval base on the Pacific, had been convinced, perhaps by the letters of "Bill" Sturgis to the Boston *Daily Advertiser,* that Port Discovery was preferable to the Columbia for a United States naval base. That Adams clung to the forty-ninth parallel despite the pressure of Albert Gallatin, his negotiator, to concede to the British the drainage basin of the Strait is evidence of the value he placed on those waters. Yankee that he was, he viewed the controversy in the Pacific Northwest as primarily a struggle for ocean frontage. He vastly preferred to prolong the diplomatic stalemate rather than to allow Britain to endanger permanently American maritime interests in the Pacific. In his policy of containment toward England, Adams formulated the chief diplomatic tradition of the United States toward Oregon. As late as the mid-forties the demands of commercial America coincided with this historic position of United States diplomacy.

For the British two important streams of trade met in Oregon waters —commerce with the Orient and the fur trade of the Hudson's Bay Company. To British officials and traders, therefore, the Columbia River presented a watercourse of peculiar significance, furnishing both an ocean port and an access to the interior fur-bearing regions. Pressure from the Hudson's Bay Company held British officials to the Columbia boundary during the early Oregon negotiations, but increasingly British interests were shifting from the fur trade to the commerce of the Pacific.

Canning as early as 1826 was restive at the expansion of United States trade in the Far East, for British enterprise in that area was limited until the mid-thirties by the British East India Company monopoly. The British Minister anticipated keenly the day when Britain would compete on equal terms for the commerce of Asia. "Its fabled wealth," he wrote, "its teeming millions, its stores of teas, silks, and spices—all the elements that had once fired the mind of Marco Polo—were an invitation still held out to the West. The East was a golden market to which Britain would send, once the fetters of the East India Company had been broken, her surplus for exchange." The real value of Oregon would become apparent, he predicted, when the China trade would be opened to British as well as to American commerce.

Giving evidence of this commercial motivation during the 1826 negotiations, Canning wrote that he would not care to have his "name affixed to an instrument by which England would have foregone the advantage of our immense direct intercourse between China and what may be, if we resolve not to yield them up, her boundless establishments on the N. W. Coast of America." Keenly aware of the underlying competition for ports between the two powers in Oregon, he attempted unsuccessfully to quiet the American demand for 49° by offering a frontage of isolated territory on the Strait. Canning and Adams had defined the real issue in Oregon —the quest for ocean frontage.

Alphonse Pageot, French minister in Washington, also recognized clearly the maritime factor in the conflict. His writings reflect the concern of a neutral commercial power which viewed as momentous the struggle between England and the United States for control of the Oregon coast. "The commerce of the whole world in the Pacific Ocean," he wrote in November, 1843, "is going to acquire a development that will give to all places on its shores, susceptible of being used for ports of repair or of commerce, a considerable importance."

With the gradual shift of British interests from the fur trade to Asiatic commerce, a new British policy toward the Northwest Coast was dawning. The Columbia as key to the fur trade was losing its importance, and its inadequacies as an ocean port were driving British maritime interests northward as it had those of the United States. Simpson complained in 1841 that the uncertainty in crossing the bar was "deranging the best laid plans, burdening the different branches of the business with very heavy shipping charges, and depriving us of the means of embarking in other branches of commerce, which might be carried on with great advantage, had we a depot eligibly situated on the coast." Fort Vancouver, he warned, was no longer a satisfactory station for the West Coast trade. He recommended that it be replaced with an advantageous site on the southern tip of Vancouver Island.

Simpson's conversion of the requirement of a more northerly post was the one crucial alteration in British thought toward Oregon prior to 1845. Only a British surrender of the Columbia would make a peaceful settlement possible. And Wilkes's close examination of the Strait, Puget Sound, Hood's Canal, and the Gulf of Georgia in 1841 had convinced Simpson that the United States would never consent to any settlement which would bar the United States from these harbors. At that moment the British position still appeared secure, for Hudson's Bay dominated the area in dispute. Until the United States could counterbalance British occupation, it lacked the force required to challenge the demands of Britain for the Columbia River boundary.

III

Albert Gallatin anticipated the time when American pioneers would resolve the Oregon question. With remarkable foresight he had favored the postponement of a settlement in 1827 "until the citizens of the United States shall have acquired a respectable footing in the country." Throughout the thirties interest in Oregon dragged, however, and as late as 1842 American settlers in no way challenged Hudson's Bay for possession of the Northwest country. Yet Oregon never completely escaped the consciousness of the American people. During a dozen lean years the ground had been well prepared for the great migrations of 1843 and 1844 and a new burst of interest and enthusiasm.

Many factors after 1842 pointed the attention of a restless, energetic, pioneering people, recovering from years of depression, toward this distant land of promise. The early efforts of such Oregon promoters as Hall Jackson Kelley and Nathaniel Wyeth of New England, the often heroic response of such missionaries as Jason and Daniel Lee, Samuel Parker, Marcus Whitman, and Father Pierre de Smet to the call of the Northwest—these endeavors had brought only a few settlers to Oregon. As late as 1840, settlement in the Willamette Valley comprised just sixty families of missionaries, trappers, and Canadians who had been employed by the Hudson's Bay Company. If the letters, editorials, addresses, and pamphlets of these enthusiasts had secured few settlers for Oregon, they had advertised the region fully.

Several other sources of information after the middle thirties fed knowledge of Oregon to the American people. Between 1837 and 1839 Congress received and published a series of reports on the region by William A. Slacum, a purser in the Navy, Caleb Cushing, and Dr. Lewis F. Linn of Missouri. Secondly, a number of travelers' accounts published after 1835 helped to supply the growing demand for facts regarding the Pacific Northwest. Washington Irving's *Astoria* and his *Rocky Mountains* were followed in rapid succession by Zenas Leonard's *Narratives* (1838), C. A. Murray's *Travels in North America* (1838), Farnham's *Travels* (1839), and Greenhow's *Memoir . . . on the Northwest Coast of North America* (1840).

These accounts pointed to the general agricultural attractiveness of certain portions of Oregon, especially that of the Willamette Valley, which opened southward from Fort Vancouver on the Columbia. This valley, travelers agreed, was the most desirable portion of Oregon. It possessed the soil, climate, and the happy combination of timber and prairie to invite agricultural enterprise with the promise of easy and ample returns. In the Willamette, moreover, were rich markets, made accessible by the nearby Pacific. For many years, prophesied these writers, the home market created by persistent immigration would consume the staples of grain, pork and beef, hides and tallow, fish, wool, and lumber produced there in surplus. Thereafter China and the islands of the Pacific would afford permanent marts for all commodities of export. Already Oregonians boasted prices in excess of those in the Mississippi Valley. In the Willamette, furthermore, settlement could be made peacefully and under the aegis of the United States, for it lay in territory not claimed by the Hudson's Bay Company.

After 1843 the tendency of the Midwest to swarm periodically had its repercussions on the Pacific. Farmers of the settled regions of Ohio, Indiana, and Illinois were swelling the tide into the newer lands of Michigan, Wisconsin, and Iowa. Between the Lakes and the Ohio were now three million cultivators of the soil where a half century earlier existed only a few scattered French settlements. In the half-formed villages of the Mississippi Valley were restless, adventurous souls to whom locomotion was still the ruling principle—men and women who were ready to undertake any movement that would perpetuate the pioneering exploits of previous generations of Americans. Now the attractiveness of Oregon, as revealed by the reports of a decade, propelled a thousand emigrants from the Midwest into Oregon in 1843 and a like number in 1844.

This migration sealed the fate of Oregon. It revealed for the first time the practicability of hauling wagons to Oregon over the Oregon Trail and thereby laid the foundation for almost limitless migration in future years. Yet this new threat to Hudson's Bay dominion was still limited as late as 1845 almost entirely to regions south of the Columbia. . . .

. . . American historians have analyzed thoroughly the factors which compelled Great Britain to settle the Oregon question at the forty-ninth parallel in 1846. In fact, in British rather than in American policy is to be found the key to the several well-known interpretations of the Oregon compromise. England had long since quit her claim to the regions south of the Columbia, while the United States had traditionally offered to yield all territory north of 49°. As late as July, 1845, Polk had offered to treat on that line. Viewed from diplomatic history, therefore, a compromise at 49° was a British surrender. . . .

Students of the Oregon question have attributed the British inclination to retreat from the Columbia to a variety of factors. First, such historians as Thomas P. Martin and St. George Sioussat have concluded that the harvest shortage of 1845 and the corresponding need of American grain contributed to British pacifism. Frederick Merk, however, has questioned this interpretation by citing evidence that the scarcity of food in the British Isles was not sufficient to alter either prices or trade considerably.

Secondly, historians have found the key to the Oregon settlement in the improved commercial relations between the United States and Great Britain during the spring of 1846. This popular interpretation—the free-trade analysis—rests primarily on evidence that, to several important British and American officials, commercial intercourse between the two nations was of greater interest and concern than the Oregon question. This thesis takes strength from a variety of British statements, such as one of Sir Robert Peel: "The admission of Maize will I believe go far to promote the settlement of Oregon." Lord Aberdeen, the Foreign Secretary, also wrote in December, 1845: "The access of Indian corn to our markets would go far to pacify the warriors of the Western States." Apparently these British spokesmen believed that the opening of the British grain market would provide an outlet for the surplus wheat of the Old Northwest and reduce, in direct proportion, the persistent Anglophobia of the region.

There is evidence, furthermore, that low tariff advocates in the United States, such as Calhoun, wanted to compromise the Oregon issue not only to avoid war but also to facilitate the acceptance of low tariff policies on both sides of the Atlantic. The Charleston *Mercury* gave evidence of the Southern preference for free trade to the acquisition of the whole of Oregon when it declared that Southern statesmen would not maintain a clear and unquestioned title at 54° 40′ at the price of two million bales of cotton per year. Thomas P. Martin has shown that American free traders urged British officials to drop their antislavery policy and repeal the Corn Laws to conciliate the powerful Democratic elements of both the South and West behind a low tariff policy in the United States. Even President Polk agreed that markets for manufactured goods were of infinitely more value to Britain than any portion of Oregon, and he predicted optimistically that a reduction of American tariffs might tempt the British to surrender all of Oregon. Whigs in Congress feared that the Democratic administration would pursue the course of soothing the British with tariff reductions so enthusiastically that it would destroy the budding manufacturing interests of the United States.

Perhaps more agrarian tempers were vexed than soothed by the repeal of the British Corn Laws, however; for it removed the advantage of easy entry into the British Empire trade through Canada. Many Westerners, moreover, refused to admit any relationship between the tariff and the Oregon question. The free-trade editor of the *Ohio Statesman* wrote: "Withered be the hand that dismembers Oregon, and palsied the tongue that consents to an act so treasonable, foul and unnatural." Hannegan spoke for the "ultras" in the Senate: "Free trade I love dearly, but it will never be bought by me by the territory of my country." Orlando Ficklin of Illinois warned against placing reliance in the British repeal bill. "Great Britain has a sliding scale not only in regard to her corn laws," he cried, "but she has one also in regard to the faith which she keeps with other nations." The hope that the British action would facilitate a settlement of the Oregon question proved false. The South and East were highly pleased, but the West, for whom the sedative was intended, continued to fume with customary vehemence.

A third interpretation of the settlement of the Oregon question attributes British conciliation to the pressure of American pioneers. There were few Americans north of the Columbia in 1846, but it is unquestionably true that the British viewed the growing numbers of pioneers south of the river with dismay, for they endangered the peace and threatened to disrupt the fur trade. When in 1845 the Hudson's Bay Company moved its main depot to Vancouver Island because of the decline of the fur traffic and American immigrant pressure, it admitted that its perennial *sine qua non* in any treaty, the Columbia, was no longer its vital trade route. This surrender of the Columbia, says Merk, was the key to the Oregon settlement.

There was yet a fourth dimension in the British inclination to retreat —the maritime factor. Lord Aberdeen, who as Foreign Secretary led the British government toward compromise, analyzed cogently his own predisposition for compromise in terms of Pacific ports. He wrote to Sir Robert Peel in September, 1844:

> I believe that if the line of the 49th degree were extended only to the waters edge, and should leave us possession of all of Vancouver's Island, with the northern side of the entrance to Puget's Sound; and if all the harbors within the Sound, and to the Columbia, inclusive, were made free to both countries; and further, if the river Columbia from the point at which it became navigable to its mouth, were also made free to both, this would be in reality a most advantageous settlement.

A year later Aberdeen admitted that England could obtain everything worth contending for in Vancouver Island, the navigation of the Columbia, and free access to all ports between the Columbia and 49°.

Aberdeen's purpose in 1845 and 1846 was to propagandize the British people into an acceptance of this view. His specific task was to convince them that British claims to Oregon were imperfect, that Oregon was not worth a dispute with the United States, that the British fur trade was dying, that the Columbia offered little security for heavy commerce, and that the United States had reasonable claims to good harbors on the Pacific.

Several major British journals spread these doctrines for him. In an anonymous article the *Edinburgh Review* of July, 1845, emphasized the unattractiveness of Oregon and the worthlessness of the ports south of the Strait. Similarly the *London Illustrated News* concluded later that year: "The value of the whole territory in fee simple would not be worth the expense of one year's war." The *Quarterly Review* termed a settlement of 49° a "subject of honorable negotiation and compromise." Convinced that the United States would concede no more, the writer accepted that line as "best for our interests and sufficient for our honor." By January, 1846, the London *Times* became the special champion of Aberdeen's foreign policy, and its conversion helped the Foreign Secretary marshal the support of many other leading British newspapers such as the London *Spectator*, the *Manchester Guardian*, the Liverpool *Times*, and the Leeds *Mercury*. Thus the British willingness to compromise in 1846 was in a sense a triumph for Aberdeen's maritime views.

The real significance of the famous British Corn Law crisis in motivating compromise rested in its creation of a realignment of British parties that brought into power in England a coalition that was willing to settle the Oregon issue for an equitable distribution of ports. The essential fact is that by May, 1846, Aberdeen, upon the passage of the resolution by the United States Congress to terminate the Joint Convention of 1827, was permitted by both the British government and British public opinion to proffer to the United States an acceptable treaty.

V

That President Polk without hesitation presented the British proposal to the Senate indicates that he had moved far from his public position of 1845. Historical analyses of this apparent policy shift fall basically into two categories. Julius Pratt has developed the thesis that Polk was convinced by Minister Louis McLane early in 1846 that the British would fight rather than concede more than the forty-ninth parallel, and that thereafter the President was less inclined to look John Bull in the eye. Other historians, such as Albert K. Weinberg, attribute Polk's desire to compromise to the growing threat of war with Mexico.

Since Polk bore the responsibility for the conduct of American diplomacy, he became the focus of all pressures for peace with England. Politicians and the press sought vigorously to assure the administration that the overwhelming majority of the American people would sustain it in the face of the current popular outcry against England. "Six clear heads in Washington," argued one editor in an effort to stiffen the executive, "are much more likely to come to a correct conclusion of the Nation's welfare, than hundreds of popular meetings composed of tens of thousands of excited individuals." Those who urged the President to assume the diplomatic initiative sensed correctly a peaceful intent in the administration.

This tremendous pressure to avoid war was only one factor motivating compromise in the President. It must be remembered that long before he forced the Oregon issue upon Congress and the British ministry in December, 1845, his vision of America's future position in the West had been fashioned by the Pacific. As early as July, 1845, he indicated a willingness to compromise the Oregon question on a fair distribution of the coastal inlets. It was largely his interest in ports that turned his attention to California in 1845 and stimulated his desire to limit British encroachment in North America. He demonstrated this interest again when he attempted to purchase San Francisco from Mexico in the Slidell mission of November, 1845. Yet at no time did the President lose sight of the Strait of Fuca. In his first message to Congress he declared that the United States could never accept a settlement in Oregon that "would leave on the British side two-thirds of the whole Oregon territory, including the free navigation of the Columbia and all valuable harbors on the Pacific." Before the end of December, Polk noted in his diary that he would submit to the Senate for its previous advice any British offer that would grant to the United States the Strait of Fuca and some free ports to the north. . . .

. . . The ratified Oregon Treaty differed in only two minor respects from Polk's proposals of July, 1845. The President had demanded the extension of the forty-ninth parallel to the Pacific, with Britain ceding to the United States the southern tip of Vancouver Island. He omitted all reference to British navigation on the Columbia. Aberdeen countered with the British position: the forty-ninth parallel to the middle of the channel between the mainland and Vancouver Island, and then southward through King George's Sound and the Strait of Fuca to the Pacific. This line would convey all of Vancouver Island to Great Britain. In addition, Aberdeen demanded common use of the Columbia.

McLane in 1846 urged the acceptance of the British position, for he was convinced that the British would not retreat on either demand. Polk conceded the loss of Vancouver Island early, but he believed this concession sufficient to terminate all further conversation over free ports to the south of the Strait. He resisted granting the British perpetual navigation of the Columbia, fearing that some unforeseen conflict might again challenge peace between the two nations. As a compromise on the Columbia River question, McLane recommended that its use be limited to the Hudson's Bay Company. These two modifications of Polk's initial position, agreed to in advance by both governments, comprised the only real diplomatic achievement on the Oregon question.

For neither Polk nor Aberdeen, who had long been in essential agreement over the equitable distribution of Oregon waterways, was the Oregon Treaty a major compromise at all. For large portions of both the British and American people, however, the final settlement was viewed as a sacrifice. The task of leadership in the crisis consisted of bringing public opinion in both nations to an acceptance of the forty-ninth parallel. Since domestic partisanship effectively tied Polk's hands, the movement for compromise in the United States had to come from Congress and the metropolitan press. For Aberdeen the task of securing support was even more difficult, since Britain, unlike the United States, was forced to retreat from its traditional offer.

Both nations as a whole were content with the distribution of lands and ports. During the closing argument on the Oregon Treaty Benton passed final judgment on the forty-ninth parallel: "With that boundary comes all that we want in that quarter, namely, all the waters of Puget's Sound, and the fertile Olympian district which borders upon them." The Oregon settlement brought to the business community on both sides of the Atlantic relief from the evils of suspense and uncertainty. A brief poem of America's leading expansionist press, the New York *Herald*, summed up well the attitude of the English-speaking world:

> Old Buck and Pack
> Are coming back
> And will soon together dine.
> And drink a toast
> Upon their roast
> To number forty-nine.

Historians have tended to exaggerate the natural urge of the American people to expand in the forties. For that reason they have attributed an unrealistic importance to the impact of pioneers, public sentiment, and war on American continental expansion. None of these had any direct bearing on the determination of United States boundaries along the Pacific. American frontiersmen never repeated the role they played in the annexation of Texas. In time they might have secured possession of California, but in 1845 hardly a thousand had reached that province. More numerous in Oregon, American pioneers were still limited to regions south of the Columbia. If they prompted the British to retreat from that line, they hardly explain why the United States insisted on that British retreat.

What mattered far more in the definition of American purpose were the travelers who toured the Pacific coasts and recorded the location and significance of waterways. These men, not pioneers, formulated the objectives of American officials from Adams to Polk. For two decades the official analysis of United States needs on the Pacific changed imperceptibly. Pioneers undoubtedly strengthened the American urge to expand westward, but they had little effect on the extent to which the nation would expand.

Public opinion as reflected in the spirit of manifest destiny played no greater role in the determination of United States ocean frontage than did the pressure of pioneers. Politicians had aroused sufficient interest in Oregon by 1844 to turn it into a popular issue. But to the extent that the Oregon settlement was a mandate, the American people voted for 54° 40′, a boundary which they never acquired.

California was never a campaign issue at all. Its annexation was never the result of popular demand. After the metropolitan press turned its attention to that region in 1845, the Mexican province undoubtedly became a coveted objective for thousands of Americans. Yet for the mass of citizens it remained a remote, unknown region. California persisted probably as an area of vital concern for those relatively few merchants, politicians, travelers, and officials who appreciated its commercial significance. Whig success in attacking Democratic expansionist policy during 1848 reveals an extensive lack of interest in Polk's diplomatic achievement. The Washington *National Intelligencer* interpreted the Whig victory as proof that the American people had rejected the seductive visions of manifest destiny.

American triumphs in Mexico were essential to the success of the expansionist program, but they had no bearing on administration goals. These had been defined by Polk and his cabinet before the war was hardly under way. Manifest destiny revealed itself in the Mexican War only when it clamored for the whole of Mexico, but even that final burst or agrarian nationalism was effectively killed by the Treaty of Guadalupe Hidalgo. Polk's objectives, clear and precise, were ever limited to two ocean ports. Victories along the road to Mexico City were important only in that they eventually brought to the President the opportunity to secure what he had once hoped to achieve by diplomacy alone.

Nor can Nicholas P. Trist be overlooked in the fulfillment of United States territorial growth, for in the final analysis it was he, lonely and unobserved, who secured the southern boundary of California. If the nation achieved all this through the dictates of manifest destiny, that destiny revealed itself through some exceedingly devious patterns.

Particularism had its way in both the Oregon and Mexican treaties. Administration goals, therefore, had to be achieved through private diplomacy, England assuming the leadership in the former negotiations. This was essential, for only thus could the President defy that public opinion and avoid those pressures of American politics that sought to prevent both the peaceful settlement of the Oregon question and the acquisition of California.

Indeed, manifest destiny is an inadequate description of American expansionism in the forties. The mere urge to expand or even the acceptance of a destiny to occupy new areas on the continent does not create specific geographical objectives. Nor do these factors take into account the role of chance or the careful formulation and execution of policy. It was not by accident that the United States spread as a broad belt across the continent in the forties. It was rather through clearly conceived policies relentlessly pursued that the United States achieved its empire on the Pacific.

Additional Reading

Edward McNall Burns, *The American Idea of Mission* (1957).
J. S. Galbraith, *The Hudson's Bay Company as an Imperial Factor, 1821–1869* (1958).
Frederick Merk, "The Genesis of the Oregon Question," *Mississippi Valley Historical Review*, XXXVI (1950), 583–612.
———, "The Oregon Pioneers and the Boundary," *American Historical Review*, XXIX (1924), 681–699.
———, "British Party Politics and the Oregon Treaty," *American Historical Review*, XXXVII (1932), 667–672.
———, "The British Corn Crisis of 1845–46 and the Oregon Treaty," *Agricultural History*, VIII (1934), 95–123.
———, *Albert Gallatin and the Oregon Problem* (1950).
E. A. Miles, " 'Fifty-Four Forty or Fight'—An American Political Legend," *Misissippi Valley Historical Review*, XLIV (1957), 291–309.
A. K. Weinberg, *Manifest Destiny* (1935).

8 *THE MEXICAN WAR: American Imperialism or Mexican Intransigence?*

The Mexican War (1846-1848) was obviously an imperialistic war in terms of results, for the United States not only made good its claim to a Texas boundary at the Rio Grande River but secured title by conquest to New Mexico and California. The question of the cause of the war is, however, a different problem and one about which historians have sharply disagreed.

One group has criticized American governmental policy, and above all President James K. Polk, for forcing war on a weak and turbulent Mexico. While the war was underway, Whig party leaders and Northern critics of slavery began to charge that Polk and his Southern advisers had deliberately provoked hostilities in order to expand the slave system and to advance the political aspirations of the Democratic administration. After the Civil War, some Northern historians spoke of a slave-owners' conspiracy to expand slavery by wars of conquest and ultimately to nationalize the peculiar institution within the United States.

In the early years of the 20th century, after old hatreds and suspicions had abated, it was possible to take a more dispassionate view of the Mexican War and the sectional controversy culminating in the Civil War. Historians soon realized that there was little substantiating evidence for a slave-holders' conspiracy allegedly responsible for Texas annexation and the 1846 war. Still, the question remained whether or not Polk and the American government were responsible for the war. The second reading selection illustrates an attempt to exonerate Polk and the United States from primary responsibility.

DOCUMENTS

War and Peace with Mexico

American settlers entered the Spanish-Mexican province of Texas in the 1820's. Most of the immigrants were from the southern United States, by reason of geographical access, but few were large slave holders. Conflicts with Mexican authorities led to revolution in 1835 and the establishment of an independent republic. Largely because of the domestic political situation in the United States, annexation was not consummated until early 1845. By then Texas had been independent for nine years, and had been accorded diplomatic recognition by Great Britain and France. Two problems confronted the United States: Texan claims to the Rio Grande boundary, instead of the Nueces River, and continued Mexican refusal to recognize the loss of Texas.

In his War Message, Polk emphasized as causes for hostilities Mexican turbulence, refusal to satisfy the legitimate damage claims of American citizens, disruptions of commerce, and the initiation of armed clashes along the Rio Grande border claimed by the United States. His assertion that Mexico had shed American blood on American soil soon came under sharp attack from the opposition in Congress and subsequently by many historians writing in the 19th century. The Treaty of Guadalupe Hidalgo, negotiated by a repudiated executive agent, Nicholas Trist, ended the war in 1848 with vast cessions by Mexico and an American "conscience-money" gift.

Polk's War Message

WASHINGTON, *May 11, 1846.*

To the Senate and House of Representatives:

The existing state of the relations between the United States and Mexico renders it proper that I should bring the subject to the consideration of Congress. . . .

The strong desire to establish peace with Mexico on liberal and honorable terms, and the readiness of this Government to regulate and adjust our boundary and other causes of difference with that power on such fair and equitable principles as would lead to permanent relations of the most friendly nature, induced me in September last to seek the reopening of diplomatic relations between the two countries. . . . An envoy of the United States repaired to Mexico with full powers to adjust every existing difference. But though present on the Mexican soil by agreement between the two Governments, invested with full powers, and bearing evidence of the most friendly dispositions, his mission has been unavailing. The Mexican Government not only refused to receive him or listen to his propositions, but after a long-continued series of menaces have at last invaded our territory and shed the blood of our fellow-citizens on our own soil.

It now becomes my duty to state more in detail the origin, progress, and failure of that mission. In pursuance of the instructions given in September last, an inquiry was made on the 13th of October, 1845, in the most friendly terms, through our consul in Mexico, of the minister for foreign affairs, whether the Mexican Government "would receive an envoy from the United States intrusted with full powers to adjust all the questions in dispute between the two Governments," with the assurance that "should the answer be in the affirmative such an envoy would be immediately dispatched to Mexico." The Mexican minister on the 15th of October gave an affirmative answer to this inquiry. . . . On the 10th of November, 1845, Mr. John Slidell, of Louisiana, was commissioned by me as envoy extraordinary and minister plenipotentiary of the United States to Mexico, and was intrusted with full powers to adjust both the questions of the Texas boundary and of indemnification to our citizens. The redress of the wrongs of our citizens naturally and inseparably blended itself with the question of boundary. The settlement of the one question in any correct view of the subject involves that of the other. I could not for a moment entertain the idea that the claims of our much-injured and long-

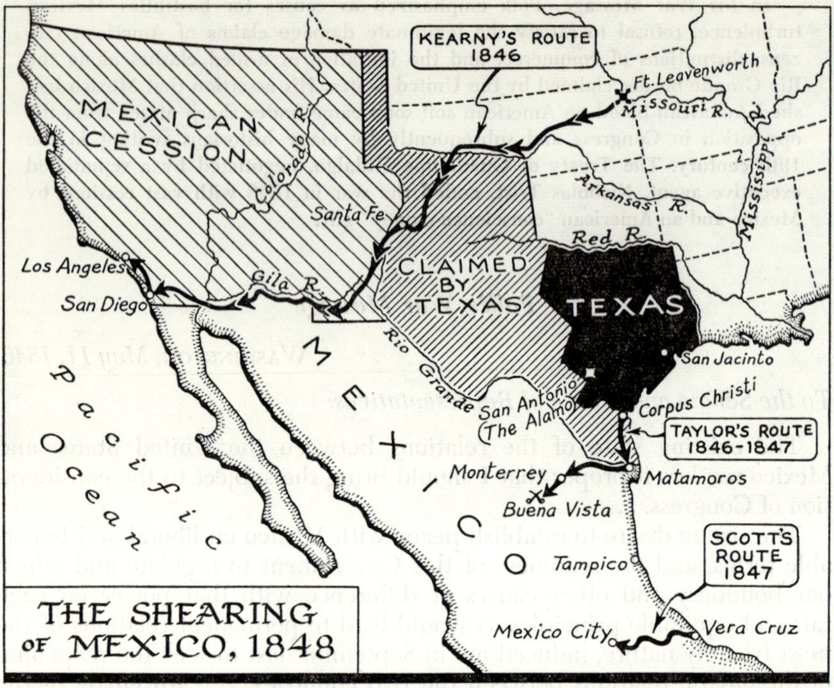

THE SHEARING OF MEXICO, 1848

suffering citizens, many of which had existed for more than twenty years, should be postponed or separated from the settlement of the boundary question.

Mr. Slidell arrived at Vera Cruz on the 30th of November, and was courteously received by the authorities of that city. But the Government of General Herrera was then tottering to its fall. The revolutionary party had seized upon the Texas question to effect or hasten its overthrow. Its determination to restore friendly relations with the United States, and to receive our minister to negotiate for the settlement of this question, was violently assailed, and was made the great theme of denunciation against it. The Government of General Herrera, there is good reason to believe, was sincerely desirous to receive our minister; but it yielded to the storm raised by its enemies, and on the 21st of December refused to accredit Mr. Slidell upon the most frivolous pretexts. These are so fully and ably exposed in the note of Mr. Slidell of the 24th of December last to the Mexican minister of foreign relations, herewith transmitted, that I deem it unnecessary to enter into further detail on this portion of the subject.

Five days after the date of Mr. Slidell's note General Herrera yielded the Government to General Paredes without a struggle, and on the 30th of December resigned the Presidency. This revolution was accomplished solely by the army, the people having taken little part in the contest; and thus the supreme power in Mexico passed into the hands of a military leader.

Determined to leave no effort untried to effect an amicable adjustment with Mexico, I directed Mr. Slidell to present his credentials to the Government of General Paredes and ask to be officially received by him. There would have been less ground for taking this step had General Paredes come into power by a regular constitutional succession. In that event his administration would have been considered but a mere constitutional continuance of the Government of General Herrera, and the refusal of the latter to receive our minister would have been deemed conclusive unless an intimation had been given by General Paredes of his desire to reverse the decision of his predecessor. But the Government of General Paredes owes its existence to a military revolution, by which the subsisting constitutional authorities had been subverted. The form of government was entirely changed, as well as all the high functionaries by whom it was administered.

Under these circumstances, Mr. Slidell, in obedience to my direction, addressed a note to the Mexican minister of foreign relations, under date of the 1st of March last, asking to be received by that Government in the diplomatic character to which he had been appointed. This minister in his reply, under date of the 12th of March, reiterated the arguments of his predecessor, and in terms that may be considered as giving just grounds of offense to the Government and people of the United States denied the application of Mr. Slidell. Nothing therefore remained for our envoy but to demand his passports and return to his own country.

Thus the Government of Mexico, though solemnly pledged by official acts in October last to receive and accredit an American envoy, violated their plighted faith and refused the offer of a peaceful adjustment of our difficulties. Not only was the offer rejected, but the indignity of its rejection was enhanced by the manifest breach of faith in refusing to admit the envoy who came because they had bound themselves to receive him. Nor can it be said that the offer was fruitless from the want of opportunity of discussing it; our envoy was present on their own soil. Nor can it be ascribed to a want of sufficient powers; our envoy had full powers to adjust every question of difference. Nor was there room for complaint that our propositions for settlement were unreasonable; permission was not even given our envoy to make any proposition whatever. Nor can it be objected that we, on our part, would not listen to any reasonable terms of their suggestion; the Mexican Government refused all negotiation, and have made no proposition of any kind.

In my message at the commencement of the present session I informed you that upon the earnest appeal both of the Congress and convention of Texas I had ordered an efficient military force to take a position "between the Nueces and the Del Norte." This had become necessary to meet a threatened invasion of Texas by the Mexican forces, for which extensive military preparations had been made. The invasion was threatened solely because Texas had determined, in accordance with a solemn resolution of the Congress of the United States, to annex herself to our Union, and under these circumstances it was plainly our duty to extend our protection over her citizens and soil.

This force was concentrated at Corpus Christi, and remained there until after I had received such information from Mexico as rendered it probable, if not certain, that the Mexican Government would refuse to receive our envoy.

Meantime Texas, by the final action of our Congress, had become an integral part of our Union. The Congress of Texas, by its act of December 19, 1836, had declared the Rio del Norte to be the boundary of that Republic. Its jurisdiction had been extended and exercised beyond the Nueces. The country between that river and the Del Norte had been represented in the Congress and in the convention of Texas, had thus taken part in the act of annexation itself, and is now included within one of our Congressional districts. Our own Congress had, moreover, with great unanimity, by the act approved December 31, 1845, recognized the country beyond the Nueces as a part of our territory by including it within our own revenue system, and a revenue officer to reside within that district has been appointed by and with the advice and consent of the Senate. It became, therefore, of urgent necessity to provide for the defense of that portion of our country. Accordingly, on the 13th of January last instructions were issued to the general in command of these troops to occupy the left bank of the Del Norte. This river, which is the southwestern boundary of the State of Texas, is an exposed frontier. From this quarter invasion was threatened; upon it and in its immediate vicinity, in the judgment of high military experience, are the proper stations for the protecting forces of the Government. In addition to this important consideration, several others occurred to induce this movement. Among these are the facilities afforded by the ports at Brazos Santiago and the mouth of the Del Norte for the reception of supplies by sea, the stronger and more healthful military positions, the convenience for obtaining a ready and a more abundant supply of provisions, water, fuel, and forage, and the advantages which are afforded by the Del Norte in forwarding supplies to such posts as may be established in the interior and upon the Indian frontier.

The movement of the troops to the Del Norte was made by the commanding general under positive instructions to abstain from all aggressive acts toward Mexico or Mexican citizens and to regard the relations between that Republic and the United States as peaceful unless she should declare war or commit acts of hostility indicative of a state of war. He was specially directed to protect private property and respect personal rights.

The Army moved from Corpus Christi on the 11th of March, and on the 28th of that month arrived on the left bank of the Del Norte opposite to Matamoras, where it encamped on a commanding position, which has since been strengthened by the erection of fieldworks. A depot has also been established at Point Isabel, near the Brazos Santiago, 30 miles in the rear of the encampment. The selection of his position was necessarily confided to the judgment of the general in command.

The Mexican forces at Matamoras assumed a belligerent attitude, and on the 12th of April General Ampudia, then in command, notified General Taylor to break up his camp within twenty-four hours and to retire beyond the Nueces River, and in the event of his failure to comply with these demands announced that arms, and arms alone, must decide the question. But no open act of hostility was committed until the 24th of April. On that day General Arista, who had succeeded to the command of the Mexican forces, communicated to General Taylor that "he considered hostilities commenced and should prosecute them." A party of dragoons of 63 men and officers were on the same day dispatched from the American camp up the Rio del Norte, on its left bank, to ascertain whether the Mexican troops had crossed or were preparing to cross the river, "became engaged with a large body of these troops, and after a short affair, in which some 16 were killed and wounded, appear to have been surrounded and compelled to surrender."

The grievous wrongs perpetrated by Mexico upon our citizens throughout a long period of years remain unredressed, and solemn treaties pledging her public faith for this redress have been disregarded. A government either unable or unwilling to enforce the execution of such treaties fails to perform one of its plainest duties.

Our commerce with Mexico has been almost annihilated. It was formerly highly beneficial to both nations, but our merchants have been deterred from prosecuting it by the system of outrage and extortion which the Mexican authorities have pursued against them, whilst their appeals through their own Government for indemnity have been made in vain. Our forbearance has gone to such an extreme as to be mistaken in its character. Had we acted with vigor in repelling the insults and redressing the injuries inflicted by Mexico at the commencement, we should doubtless have escaped all the difficulties in which we are now involved.

Instead of this, however, we have been exerting our best efforts to propitiate her good will. Upon the pretext that Texas, a nation as independent as herself, thought proper to unite its destinies with our own she has affected to believe that we have severed her rightful territory, and in official proclamations and manifestoes has repeatedly threatened to make war upon us for the purpose of reconquering Texas. In the meantime we have tried every effort at reconciliation. The cup of forbearance had been exhausted even before the recent information from the frontier of the Del Norte. But now, after reiterated menaces, Mexico has passed the boundary of the United States, has invaded our territory and shed American blood upon the American soil. She has proclaimed that hostilities have commenced, and that the two nations are now at war.

As war exists, and, notwithstanding all our efforts to avoid it, exists by the act of Mexico herself, we are called upon by every consideration of duty and patriotism to vindicate with decision the honor, the rights, and the interests of our country.

Anticipating the possibility of a crisis like that which has arrived, instructions were given in August last, "as a precautionary measure" against invasion or threatened invasion, authorizing General Taylor, if the emergency required, to accept volunteers, not from Texas only, but from the States of Louisiana, Alabama, Mississippi, Tennessee, and Kentucky, and corresponding letters were addressed to the respective governors of those States. These instructions were repeated, and in January last, soon after the incorporation of "Texas into our Union of States," General Taylor was further "authorized by the President to make a requisition upon the executive of that State for such of its militia force as may be needed to repel invasion or to secure the country against apprehended invasion." On the 2d day of March he was again reminded, "in the event of the approach of any considerable Mexican force, promptly and efficiently to use the authority with which he was clothed to call to him such auxiliary force as he might need." War actually existing and our territory having been invaded, General Taylor, pursuant to authority vested in him by my direction, has called on the governor of Texas for four regiments of State troops, two to be mounted and two to serve on foot, and on the governor of Louisiana for four regiments of infantry to be sent to him as soon as practicable.

In further vindication of our rights and defense of our territory, I invoke the prompt action of Congress to recognize the existence of the war, and to place at the disposition of the Executive the means of prosecuting the war with vigor, and thus hastening the restoration of peace. To this end I recommend that authority should be given to call into the public service a large body of volunteers to serve for not less than six or twelve months unless sooner discharged. A volunteer force is beyond question more efficient than any other description of citizen soldiers, and it is not to be doubted that a number far beyond that required would readily rush to the field upon the call of their country. I further recommend that a liberal provision be made for sustaining our entire military force and furnishing it with supplies and munitions of war.

The most energetic and prompt measures and the immediate appearance in arms of a large and overpowering force are recommended to Congress as the most certain and efficient means of bringing the existing collision with Mexico to a speedy and successful termination.

In making these recommendations I deem it proper to declare that it is my anxious desire not only to terminate hostilities speedily, but to bring all matters in dispute between this Government and Mexico to an early and amicable adjustment; and in this view I shall be prepared to renew negotiations whenever Mexico shall be ready to receive propositions or to make propositions of her own.

I transmit herewith a copy of the correspondence between our envoy to Mexico and the Mexican minister for foreign affairs, and so much of the correspondence between that envoy and the Secretary of State and between the Secretary of War and the general in command on the Del Norte as is necessary to a full understanding of the subject.

Treaty of Guadalupe Hidalgo, February 2, 1848

Article V. The Boundary line between the two Republics shall commence in the Gulf of Mexico, three leagues from land, opposite the mouth of the Rio Grande, otherwise called Rio Bravo del Norte, or opposite the mouth of it's deepest branch, if it should have more than one branch emptying directly into the sea; from thence, up the middle of that river, following the deepest channel, where it has more than one, to the point where it strikes the southern boundary of New Mexico; thence, westwardly, along the whole southern boundary of New Mexico (which runs north of the town called *Paso*) to it's western termination; thence northward, along the western line of New Mexico, until it intersects the first branch of the river Gila; (or if it should not intersect any branch of that river, then, to the point on the said line nearest to such branch, and thence in a direct line to the same;) thence down the middle of the said branch and of the said river, until it empties into the Rio Colorado; thence, across the Rio Colorado, following the division line between Upper and Lower California, to the Pacific Ocean. . . .

Article XII. In consideration of the extension acquired by the boundaries of the United States, as defined in the fifth Article of the present Treaty, the Government of the United States engages to pay to that of the Mexican Republic the sum of fifteen Millions of Dollars.

Immediately after this treaty shall have been duly ratified by the Government of the Mexican Republic, the sum of three millions of dollars shall be paid to the said Government by that of the United States at the city of Mexico, in the gold or silver coin of Mexico. The remaining twelve millions of dollars shall be paid at the same place and in the same coin, in annual instalments of three millions of dollars each, together with interest on the same at the rate of six per centum per annum. This interest shall begin to run upon the whole sum of twelve millions, from the day of the ratification of the present treaty by the Mexican Government, and the first of the instalments shall be paid at the expiration of one year from the same day. Together with each annual instalment, as it falls due, the whole interest accruing on such instalment from the beginning shall also be paid.

Article XIII. The United States engage moreover, to assume and pay to the claimants all the amounts now due them, and those hereafter to become due, by reason of the claims already liquidated and decided against the Mexican Republic, under the conventions between the two Republics severally concluded on the eleventh day of April eighteen hundred and thirty-nine, and on the thirtieth day of January eighteen hundred and forty-three: so that the Mexican Republic shall be absolutely exempt for the future, from all expense whatever on account of the said claims.

Article XIV. The United States do furthermore discharge the Mexican Republic from all claims of citizens of the United States, not heretofore decided against the Mexican Government, which may have arisen previously to the date of the signature of this treaty: which discharge shall be final and perpetual, whether the said claims be rejected or be allowed by the Board of Commissioners provided for in the following Article, and whatever shall be the total amount of those allowed.

Article XV. The United States, exonerating Mexico from all demands on account of the claims of their citizens mentioned in the preceding Article, and considering them entirely and forever cancelled, whatever their amount may be, undertake to make satisfaction for the same, to an amount not exceeding three and one quarter millions of Dollars. To ascertain the validity and amount of those claims, a Board of Commissioners shall be established by the Government of the United States, whose awards shall be final and conclusive: provided that in deciding upon the validity of each claim, the board shall be guided and governed by the principles and rules of decision prescribed by the first and fifth Articles of the unratified convention, concluded at the City of Mexico on the twentieth day of November, one thousand eight hundred and forty-three; and in no case shall an award be made in favour of any claim not embraced by these principles and rules. . . .

READINGS

1. The War of "Polk the Mendacious"

Hermann Von Holst published a multi-volume history of the United States in the late 19th century which reiterated earlier Whig and Northern criticism of the Mexican War. Von Holst, a German-trained historian who served as the first chairman of the history department at the newly established Univeristy of Chicago, was an ardent nationalist and a moralist who envisioned American history prior to 1865 as a long struggle between the forces of righteousness, for union and against slavery, and the morally wrong Southern advocates of slavery and states' rights. Consequently, he interpreted the Mexican War as deliberately precipitated by a pro-slavery expansionist administration. He was not alone in holding that view: as late as 1902, the well-known historian James Ford Rhodes asserted that "Mexico was actually goaded on to war" (*History of the United States from the Compromise of 1850*, I, 87).

Polk Weaves the Warp of the Mexican War

HERMANN VON HOLST

Three weeks after the passage of the resolutions of annexation, the War Department instructed General Zachary Taylor, then stationed in Louisiana, to hold part of his troops in readiness for an expedition into Texas. May 28, 1845, the Secretary of War informed him, that Texas would in all probability shortly accept the conditions of annexation, and that the President would then consider her a component part of the United States, or sufficiently so to have a claim to protection against invasion by foreign powers and Indian incursions. Taylor was, therefore, to post the troops, then or thereafter, at his command, in such a way as to insure the promptest and most effective protection to Texas. In order to suppress any hostilities on the part of the Indians, it would, however, probably suffice to cross

Hermann Von Holst, *The Constitutional and Political History of the United States* (Chicago, 1881), III, 79–89, 94–97, 102–113.

the Sabine or Red river, with the troops designated in the instructions already mentioned, of March twenty-first. It was thus only in view of a possible invasion, that the President considered it proper to go beyond those instructions, and to take into consideration the strengthening of Taylor's fighting force.

Was there any real reason for anxiety lest Mexico should answer annexation with an invasion? If one confined himself simply to Mexico's emphatic declarations, this could appear by no means doubtful. The Mexican Government had repeatedly, without any sort of qualification, signified to the United States that it would consider the annexation of Texas as a declaration of war. Almonte had at once (March 6), protested against the "joint resolution," and demanded his passports. March 28, Cuevas, the Minister of Foreign Affairs, acquainted the American ambassador, W. Shannon, with the rupture of diplomatic relations between the two countries. When Shannon returned a written answer, he was informed that no further relations of any kind could be held with him. June 4, Herrera issued a proclamation, which asserted that it was evidently Mexico's right to oppose annexation, up to the last moment, with all the strength at her command, and announced the determination of the government to put into the field the whole armed force of the country. July 12, the Minister of War, Garcia Conde, declared in a circular-letter, that the government had decided upon a declaration of war against the United States, and four days later he spoke of the war as a fact already in existence. A later report of Cuevas (July 20), to the Chamber of Deputies spoke, however, only of the resolve of the government to declare war, and proposed that this should be carried out, if the annexation was accomplished, or if United States troops should enter the territory of the Republic.

. . . Indeed, it was generally expected that Mexico would make great ado over annexation, but it was considered utterly improbable that her actions would follow her words, or would, in any way, correspond to them. The conclusion of the preliminary peace involving the eventual recognition of the independence of Texas, had been a confession that she was too weak to again subjugate that country. It must, therefore, have been impossible for her to believe herself sufficiently strong to tear Texas away from the United States, and so it was not to be expected that she would begin an utterly hopeless war for the sake of a mere point of honor, so long as the fact of annexation was the only question at issue. However great Mexican pride might be, it had already bowed under the weight of facts, before Texas alone. It would have been, then, quite wonderful, if, when the weight of facts had become so very much greater, that pride should now, without further provocation, carry Mexico back to the standpoint which she had taken in the years immediately following the day of San Jacinto. The Mexican character was best understood in the Gulf States, which had, on account of climatic conditions and a strong admixture of the Latin races, a population most like her own. In those States, thoughtful people considered it ridiculous to take the Mexican rodomontades in earnest. This judgment was just. The Mexican Congress adjourned, without having come to any conclusion on the proposal of the government to declare war. It authorized, of course, the suggested loan of $15,000,000, but it took no pains to make its negotiation possible. One month after another slipped by, and Mexico did nothing to carry out her threats. Towards the end of the year, Polk had to bear official witness to the fact that she had made "no aggressive movement." He did not assert that his measures for meeting force with force had accomplished this. But if it was not on account of fear that Mexico contented herself with pompous phrases, then his "precautionary measure" had been, in truth, a blameworthy bit of imprudence; provided he really wished, as he said he did, to maintain peace. In his opinion, he was bound to express to the commander of the troops in Texas and the squadron on the Mexican coast, before the whole people, his recognition of the fact that they had prevented any breach of the peace, by their discretion in the execution of his instructions. If Congress had been of the opinion, when it passed the "joint resolution," that the annexation would not result in a war, or if it could and must have been expected that Mexico would not base her conduct exclusively upon her pretended rights, but mainly upon the comparative strength of the two countries, in such a case, the discretion of the President himself appears in a very dubious light, when he gave the commanders of the army and navy instructions which needed such a discreet execution, in order not to lead to a breach of the peace. Polk had either been much too cautious (and this could scarcely be assumed of a man who had flung down the gauntlet before England in such defiant fashion), or he had gone to work with too painful a conscientiousness to fulfill his declared duty of protecting Texas, even before her formal incorporation into the Union, against every possible danger. We must seek in the instructions the answer to the question whether Polk could, in fact, boast such a sensitive conscience.

June 15, Taylor received orders to march immediately to the mouth of the Sabine, or to some other point, which, in his judgment, was best adapted for the embarkation of troops for the western boundary of Texas; the latter was to be his final aim, and there, or upon the Rio Grande del Norte, which would be the western boundary of the United States in case of annexation, he was to encamp at some fit place. Is it not remarkable that the War Department considered it necessary to inform the general where the western boundary of Texas was, that is, where that of the United States was to be? If Taylor had been marching against Canada, he would certainly have been spared such geographical instruction. That the Government considered it necessary to give him this information, was an indirect recognition of the fact, that, upon this point, not only were different views possible, but radically different views prevailed. What his instructions clothed in the form of a statement of fact, was, in truth, only an assertion. As long as a controversy existed, which bore not only an academic character, but was an open political question, saying: "This is the boundary," meant only: "I declare this to be the boundary." Polk, indeed, had never confessed this, but had always asserted that the fact was unquestionable. Yet his own argument is a sufficient answer to this assertion. In his message of May 11, 1846, he says: "The Congress of Texas, by its act of December 19, 1836, had declared the Rio del Norte to be the boundary of that Republic." This was the only basis for his assertion. He planted himself, therefore, neither upon the undeniable, actual condition of things, nor upon a once recognized title, but only upon a declaration of the Texan Congress. But that declaration was a revolutionary act, as was everything which that Congress did. It had, therefore, in itself, no legal force, and could have the force of law, at most, only in so far as Texas succeeded in making the actual condition of affairs correspond to it. The next question is, therefore, how far this had happened.

. . . That territory had never belonged, under the Mexican government, to Texas, but to the State of Tamaulipas. The Nueces was the boundary between Tamaulipas and Texas. In the debates over annexation in the Senate, the president of the constitutional convention of Texas was quoted as a witness to the fact, that Texas had declared the Rio del Norte to be her western boundary only to be able thereafter, in the negotiations with Mexico, to waive her claims to considerable stretches of territory, as a consideration for the recognition of her independence. Moreover, years after the Republic had won her actual independence, the Texan government evidently looked upon the boundary clauses of the act of December 19, 1836, in the same way. In 1839, an attempt was made, under the leadership of General Canales, to create an independent state under the name of the Rio Grande Republic, out of Tamaulipas, Coahuila, and Durango. Canales, who had been elected president by the revolutionists, concluded a secret treaty with the government of Texas. Its main provisions were the following: Canales bound himself to proclaim the independence of the Republic of the Rio Grande; this was to recognize the independence of Texas; Texas was to aid the new Republic in its own struggle for independence. With the aid of Texan troops, Canales occupied Laredo, a town in Tamaulipas, upon the eastern shore of the Del Norte. He was, however, compelled to flee into Texas in April, 1840, when he was attacked by Arista. With his flight the Republic of the Rio Grande ended its short life upon paper. It is rescued from oblivion solely by the fact, that the Texan government, in this secret treaty, made no claim to the Rio del Norte as the boundary of Texas, and was willing to allow all Tamaulipas to form a component part of the new Republic, without considering it necessary to formally renounce any claims of its own to the territory on the east bank of the river. A formal renunciation, or accession, would have been entirely superfluous, in so far as the act of December 19, 1836, was legally but a piece of paper, and Texas had never actually occupied the country. In this regard, the real condition of affairs remained entirely unchanged up to the time of annexation. Texas, indeed, made a few attempts to take possession of the country, but they were pitiable failures.

Polk's assertion that the annexation had made the Rio Grande the western boundary of the Union, rested, therefore, only upon the declaration contained in the law of Dec. 19, 1836. When the annexation was still an open question, even its most ardent advocates had not claimed that this law was certainly and unconditionally decisive. Ch. J. Ingersoll, who, as chairman of the House committee on foreign affairs, spoke on this matter with a certain authority, simply put aside the Rio Grande, and declared that the desert waste which lay between this river and the Nueces formed "the natural boundaries" between the two states. This was, in fact, the natural boundary, if any such existed, for in a land without mountains there can be no more natural and effective boundary marks than deserts.

Polk asserted, indeed, in his message of May 11, 1846, that Texas had actually exercised jurisdiction beyond the Nueces; and this was true. But if the President had wished to represent correctly the actual condition of affairs, he would have been forced to add that this "beyond" was limited to the river. Corpus Christi, at the mouth of the Nueces, and the little town of San Patricio, higher up, and peopled by about twenty families, were the only points beyond the Nueces held by Texas. In like manner it was only a half-truth, and it presented the actual condition of affairs in a false light, when the President asserted, further, that Congress, by the law of December 31, 1845, had "recognized the country beyond the Nueces as a part of our territory by including it within our revenue system." This law said nothing about the boundaries of Texas, but simply made Corpus Christi, with several other Texan towns, a port of delivery, requiring a collector of customs. By another law, however, and at a time when the United States was not the judge of its own cause, Congress had shown in the most certain way that it, at least, did not look upon the whole line of the Rio Grande as either the actual or the rightful boundary of Texas. A law of March 3, 1845, contained provisions for the paying back of duties in "Chihuahua and Santa Fé, in New Mexico." Texas had made no objection to this law, and would have simply made herself ridiculous if she had tried to object; for New Mexico was in the unquestioned possession of Mexico, and showed no inclination whatever to be incorporated with Texas. And not only at Santa Fé, but at Brazos, a town at the mouth of the Rio Grande, American merchants paid the duties imposed by the Mexican tariff at the Mexican custom houses, both before and after the annexation, without complaint.

Polk, of course, knew these facts, and there is no reason for impugning his intellect by supposing that he could not measure their scope. That his silence about them was deliberately designed is made clearer than day by the false coloring by means of which he manages, without exciting distrust by bold misrepresentations, to give to things which supported his assertion a weight which they did not remotely deserve. He knew enough of international law, and of practical politics to know, that the boundary-question could not be determined exclusively and unquestionably by the act of the Texan Congress, of December 19, 1836. . . .

. . . July 30, orders were sent to Taylor to occupy, protect, and defend the territory of Texas, so far as it had been occupied by the Texans. He was, however, to avoid in his occupation of the country, those posts and settlements which were held by Mexican troops, or which had not been, at the time of annexation, in the possession of Texas. Yet he was also commanded to approach the Rio Grande, as nearly as might seem prudent, and to extend his protection as far as that river. These two instructions could be reconciled, only if there were Texan settlements between Corpus Christi and the Rio Grande. But Polk and [Secretary of War] Marcy knew well enough that this was not the case, and they must, therefore, have been also fully aware that the orders of July 30th to Taylor said yes and no at the same time. What was the aim of this? The answer must be sought in the subsequent instructions to Taylor.

The general had, meanwhile, marched towards the west, and was seeking a suitable place for encampment. At the beginning of August, he decided upon Corpus Christi. His announcement that he had reached there in safety with a part of his troops, was crossed by a dispatch from the adjutant-general, dated August 6, which informed him that a regiment of infantry and a detachment of dragoons had received orders to reinforce him, and that he was authorized, in case of necessity, to muster Texan volunteers into the service of the United States. The reason assigned for these steps was that, even in case Mexico did not begin war and did not attempt an invasion, he might be placed in a position to meet any possible emergency. As early as August 23, before Taylor's report, already mentioned, of August 15, had reached Washington, another dispatch was sent him by the Secretary of War, which informed him that the fleet in the Gulf of Mexico had received orders to coöperate with him, and authorized him to muster into the service also volunteers from Louisiana, Alabama, Mississippi, Tennessee and Kentucky. This haste to enable Taylor to bring together in Texas, in a short time, and without further instructions, a considerable army, was the more remarkable, inasmuch as Marcy's letters of August 25 and 28, to the Governors of the States named, in regard to the powers conferred upon Taylor, pointed out the fact that Congress had not foreseen the necessity for such a course, and had, therefore, made no appropriation for the payment of the militia. But since it was not pretended that there was any immediate necessity for raising volunteers, this lack of foresight could still be readily repaired. Why did not the President immediately call a special session of Congress? The affair was surely important enough to justify such a course. A necessity for calling militia into the service of the Union could arise, only if the probability of war bordered upon certainty, and the right of declaring war belonged to Congress alone. It would, therefore, have been only loyal if the President had sought to offer Congress an opportunity to express its wish and will before it found itself confronted by already accomplished facts. But however obvious and well-founded such reasoning might be, the President could not think of summoning Congress to Washington before the regular time, and this, simply because nothing whatever had happened, apart from the things done and left undone by the President himself, which Congress had not foreseen before its last adjournment. There were all sorts of reports, indeed, of great Mexican armies upon the border, but, if the Government could, in good faith, think that these reports were not made out of whole cloth, it nevertheless considered them greatly exaggerated. It never spoke of the possibility that bankrupt Mexico could secretly put a force of troops in the field sufficient seriously to threaten Texas alone, apart from the rest of the Union. However audacious Polk and his Cabinet might be in their assertions, they never ventured to assign the *periculum in mora* as a ground of justification. There must have been, therefore, another reason for their haste.

We have already heard how Donelson, who was far-sighted and prudent in the boundary question, expressed his opinion that, in case of an attack on the line of the Nueces, the right of self-defense would justify driving the Mexicans back over the Rio Grande. But if the Government shared the wish of its agent for an attack, was it not, then, a surer plan to go somewhat further to meet the Mexicans? In any event, Polk wished Taylor to go towards them as far as possible, that is, up to the line of the Rio Grande. . . .

One might think—Polk himself might have believed—that he had done enough to satisfy his sensitive feeling of duty when, despite his earnest wish to maintain peace, he had deduced all these results from the Texan law of December 19, 1836. But the instructions of August 30 went still a step further. Not only if war were declared, but also in case Mexico should have brought on an actual state of war by the hostile acts indicated, Taylor was not to confine himself exclusively to protecting Texas. If he had sufficient force, he was to cross the Rio Grande and seize upon Matamoras and other places. These directions explain why it had been thought necessary to put Taylor in such comparatively excellent fighting trim, although a handful of Texans had won Texan independence at San Jacinto. If the first gun shot was to be the signal for a war of conquest, more troops were certainly needed.

The instructions of August 30 were crossed by a dispatch from Taylor, dated September 6, which announced that, according to trustworthy reports, Mexico was making no military preparations on the Rio Grande, and a declaration of war was not likely, and that, while he would continue to prepare for war, he wished no volunteers sent him without a requisition, for he probably would not need them. A former American consul at Matamoras soon gave Taylor the same information. General Arista had given this gentleman his solemn assurance that only small parties of Mexican troops should be sent across the Rio Grande, and that they would be sent only to hold the Indians and the smugglers in check.

In Washington there was no doubt of the trustworthiness of these tidings. Quite apart from them, the President and his cabinet had, by this time, come to the conclusion that at least for the present, neither declaration of war nor invasion was to be expected. Marcy's dispatch of October 16, to Taylor, expressed this frankly, but yet repeated his orders to approach the Rio Grande as nearly as might be. The "threatened invasion" now shrivels into "any attempted incursions," which were to be prevented. Between the lines there seems to glimmer a wish that the General should consider any transfer of troops to the left bank of the Rio Grande as an "incursion." At least, the despatch says not a word about the protection to which the Texans were entitled but emphasizes, as of prime importance, the fact that the "government of the United States"—since when had the President become the government of the United States?—was determined to maintain its claim to the boundary of the Rio Grande. How far this directed him to go, or made it his duty to go, Taylor was left to decide for himself. The Secretary of War wished exhaustive information as to his plans and views, recommended him to be fully prepared for any emergency, and instructed him not to wait for orders from Washington.

There was no need of this last hint, to acquaint Taylor with what was wished of him, but he was not ready to gratify the administration by pulling hot chestnuts out of the coals. He had already, on October 4, sent a dispatch to the Adjutant-General, in which he advised an immediate advance to the Rio Grande, provided this boundary-line was to be the "ultimatum"; but if this plan were adopted, the war department would have to order the advance, for he did not feel authorized by his earlier instructions to take such a step. This position was entirely correct. Taylor, in his official capacity, had nothing to do with the political and legal phases of the question; it concerned him only from the military standpoint, and from that his advice was unquestionably sound. But he could not allow, and ought not to have allowed, the political responsibility for a step which made war practically certain to be shoved upon him, by his taking that step under vague and general instructions. If the President wished the step to be taken, he would have to assume the whole responsibility for it by an express and entirely unambiguous command.

The War Department, as far as can be gathered from the published records, answered this dispatch by profound and protracted silence. It was evidently useless to write further variations on the theme which had now been handled for seven months in the instructions to Taylor. The energetic pursuit of the wished-for end was not checked for an instant on this account, but before the administration decided to send Taylor the order he required—the last resource, to which resort could be had at any moment—it wished to see whether the game would not yet lend itself to the original scheme, although Taylor declined to play the trump-card thrust upon him. Buchanan had already, on the 17th of September, commissioned one Black, a consul in Mexico, to enquire of the Mexican government whether it would receive an "envoy," in order to consider and to try to adjust, in a peaceful way, "all" the questions at issue. The reason of this suggestion was, according to Buchanan, that Mexico seemed inclined to resume diplomatic intercourse, and the President now, as before, wished to see the most heart-felt and friendly relations prevail between the two sister republics; he had taken measures, as in duty bound, to cope successfully with the threatened invasion, but he wished to maintain peace, although he was prepared for war. It is clear from the latter phrases that the introduction of diplomacy did not mean a change of front, but had been part of the plan of operations from the beginning. Before the right hand of the negotiator offered a treaty, his left was to be able to point to an army, ready for battle, encamped upon the frontier.

Peña y Peña, Minister of Foreign Affairs, answered this suggestion, October 15, saying that Mexico, although seriously wronged by the advance of the United States forces into Texas, was ready to receive a "commissioner" in order "to settle the present dispute in a peaceable, reasonable, and honorable manner"; but as Mexico did not wish to appear to be acting under duress, the United States squadron then lying off Vera Cruz would have first to be removed. This answer reached Washington November 9, and Polk considered it an acceptance of his propositions. On the following day, he named John Slidell, of Louisiana, as envoy extraordinary, and gave him full power to make a final settlement of all contested questions between the two powers, including those in relation to boundaries.

Had Polk by this time come to know that the annexation resolutions did not decisively and irrevocably make the Rio Grande the boundary of the United States, in the event of the incorporation of Texas? By no means. His position was precisely the same as before. He had always wished to "negotiate" the boundary question with Mexico, but his "ultimatum" was now, and had always been intended to be, that Mexico must yield to the United States every foot of land which the United States claimed. If she would not agree to this, then she must herself, in Polk's opinion, be responsible for the consequences; and the latter would not be light. It would not be his fault, at any rate, if she did not have to pay a heavy price for having learned so ill the lesson that might makes right. From the beginning, he had had this possibility in view, had considered it the most probable event, and had prepared everything to make the best use of it.

Nevertheless, the orders to Taylor to reduce "Matamoras and other places," under certain circumstances, are no convincing proof that the President was planning conquests; taking the offensive might be considered the best plan of defense. As early as the 11th of July, Commodore Connor, the commander of the Gulf squadron, had been informed by Bancroft that the President was determined to force Mexico to conclude peace, if she declared war, by the most energetic measures. Did this mean that she was to be forced to conclude peace upon the basis of the Rio Grande boundary? Bancroft's instructions of June 24 to Commodore Sloat, who commanded the fleet on the Pacific, declared still more emphatically that the President wished most earnestly to maintain peace, and warned the commodore to avoid everything which might endanger the fulfillment of this wish. If, however, Sloat received certain intelligence of a declaration of war by Mexico, he was to possess himself at once of San Francisco and other ports. If the only thing desired was to conquer peace, it is certainly surprising that San Francisco was put so prominently in the foreground, since, according to Bancroft's own testimony, there was, practically, no connection between California and Mexico. Mexico's power of armed resistance, would, therefore, be least impaired by a blow in just this spot. But if the immediate injury to Mexico from such a seizure would be slight, the seizure might be of incalculable value to the United States, in case the war was intended to do something more than merely to force Mexico to recognize the Rio Grande as the boundary. If this was the ruling idea of the policy pursued at Washington, the instruction to Sloat is intelligible enough. And in the light of this consideration, one may easily see, too, why Sloat was so strictly commanded, in case of a seizure, to "preserve, if possible, the most friendly relations with the inhabitants," and, where he could do so, "to encourage them to adopt a course of neutrality."

The instructions must be read in the light of preceding and subsequent events. If this is done, no impartial critic can object that this interpretation introduces anything into them which they do not contain. We remember how Wise, of Virginia, declared, in the House of Representatives, in April, 1842, that he would allot California a place where all the power of England could not reach her, and how Commodore Jones in October of the same year raised the stars and stripes at Monterey. Mexico, which had had her wits sharpened by her experience with Texas, knew what this sign of the times meant. All citizens of the United States in California and the neighboring departments were ordered to leave the country. When Waddy Thompson, the American ambassador, was informed of this order in December, 1843, he naturally complained of it, but effected nothing by his representations until, without being authorized to do so by his Government, he demanded his passports. He afterwards confessed that this rough demeanor had cost him some pangs of conscience, for he knew that his protegés had prepared to repeat the drama of Texas. The project was not carried out at the time, but it was not given up. It was merely postponed to a more favorable opportunity. In the United States itself, longing eyes were kept fastened upon the beautiful land. From the spring of 1845, the newspapers, favorable to annexation, openly spoke of the acquisition of California, and on the 15th of December Cass expressed in the Senate his hope that the Administration would bring this to pass.

Was this statement a mere shot in the air, which, wholly by chance, hit the mark? Cass's position in the Senate was too important to permit of his giving expression to such ideas lightly, and he had shown himself at other times too deeply versed in the policy of the President to let it seem improbable that he had, on this occasion, been informed of Polk's plans and wishes. And the acquisition of California was, by this time no longer a mere wish of Polk, but his steadfast plan, which had already reached the first stage of its accomplishment. The instructions to Slidell, which the President refused to communicate officially to the House of Representatives, two years afterwards, had quickly found their way into the public press, and had laid bare Polk's policy to the light. The President thought he had, in the old claims against Mexico, an excellent means of reaching a settlement on the boundary question. Mexico had, he considered, an excellent opportunity thus afforded to her to rid herself finally of this burden and to earn a considerable sum of money besides. Polk's liberal offer was that the United States would itself pay the American claimants and would besides pay Mexico $5,000,000 for New Mexico, or would assume the claims and pay $25,000,000 besides for New Mexico and California.

This construction of the annexation resolutions is, perhaps, the most glittering example the history of the world affords of skill in interpretation. Slidell was to open negotiations upon the question, not as to whether the Nueces or the Rio Grande, but as to whether the Rio Grande or the Pacific Ocean, should be the boundary. If Mexico had been willing to regard the matter from the tradesman's standpoint, she would probably have done well to accept the offer, for she certainly had scant chance of defending these territories permanently from her too powerful neighbor, if the latter were once determined to annex them. But Mexico would have had to have lost the last traces of honor if she had now, after repeatedly declaring that the annexation of Texas would necessarily be equivalent to a declaration of war, voluntarily surrendered an additional and boundless territory to the United States for base gold, even if Polk's offer had been increased a hundred fold. An unmeasured, sensitive pride, was the one thing which this unhappy people had preserved unimpaired through their endless civil wars. It was much, very much, that Mexico, conscious of her weakness, had decided to submit quietly to the annexation of Texas, giving herself only the idle comfort of pompous phrases and high-sounding protests. And that she had wrung this hard resolve from her pride was admitted even by fanatic Southerners. But no Mexican government could yield a single inch further, for even if it had wished to do so, the thing would have become impossible the instant it was attempted. . . .

2. *The Case against Mexico*

Writing shortly after World War I and in the afterglow of the heightened patriotism it aroused, Justin H. Smith of Dartmouth answered the charges previously raised against the Polk administration. He attributed the war, in the final analysis, to Mexican turbulence, pride, and lack of realism in foreign affairs. Polk was not ambitious for personal glory and although eager for California was willing to seek it by means other than war. Historians today are more inclined to accept Smith's interpretation than that of Von Holst and Rhodes, though perhaps he has too completely exonerated the United States of all responsibility.

The War With Mexico

JUSTIN H. SMITH

. . . Turning now to the attitude of the government, we art told at once that Polk deliberately intended to attack Mexico, and are offered various reasons for so believing. One accuser says that he was ambitious for personal glory; another, that he desired to perpetuate the power of his party; a third, that he felt anxious to cover up the humiliating result of the Oregon negotiation; still another, that he wished to be reëlected; and more than one allege that he was determined to obtain California. For this last view there is just evidence enough to create a suspicion. For example, Bancroft [George Bancroft, then Secretary of the Navy] remarked more than forty years after the event that Polk said the acquisition of that province would be one of his aims, and this remark has been cited as if it proved the charge. But there was not the slightest impropriety in his desiring an immensely valuable territory that Webster had endeav-

Justin H. Smith, *The War with Mexico* (New York: The Macmillan Company, 1919, 2 vols.), I, 127–140, 144–145, 149–155, 187–190. Reprinted with the permission of The American Missionary Association.

ored a few years before to acquire, and in 1845 Bancroft himself represented the President's feeling toward Mexico as "most conciliatory." Indeed, after the conflict had begun, Bancroft wrote privately to Samuel Hooper, "We were driven reluctantly to war."

Again, certain facts are cited and aligned: Polk wanted California, a war occurred, and he promptly took advantage of the war to occupy the desired territory. But the existence of several points in line does not prove the existence of a path connecting them, and there is weighty evidence against the suspicion which these facts naturally excite. While directing Slidell to obtain the cession of northern California, if he could, Buchanan intimated, as we have seen, that he should not press this matter, if so doing would prevent the restoration of amicable relations with Mexico. In other words, instead of desiring to precipitate a war for the sake of obtaining California, Polk was ready to let California go—or at least wait—for the sake of maintaining peace. Besides, as we shall find when we come to the operations on the western coast, Polk had a policy for the acquisition of that region, and this policy did not contemplate war. With nothing solid to stand upon, then, and much to stand against, this theory must be given up.

The other explanations of Polk's alleged intention to fight Mexico are evidently mere conjectures, and prove nothing. The idea that contracts and offices could strengthen the administration and build up the party is mainly, or perhaps entirely, fallacious. There were not enough to satisfy more than a small percentage of the hungry patriots, and the rest were likely to take offence. Moreover, if given to Democrats, these favors could make no converts; while if given to Whigs, the Democrats were sure to complain, and few of the recipients could change their party for such a reason. Many of Polk's chief troubles, as his diary shows, came from dissatisfied applicants for commissions, and any person well versed in public affairs could have foreseen that it would be so. And yet, after all, the charge that he purposely brought on the war has been so commonly believed, or at least so frequently repeated, that it can fairly demand a more extended examination.

First of all, then, we must form an estimate of Polk. For this purpose his diary is extremely useful. No doubt, like other documents of the sort, it colors some things and omits others; but so extremely busy a man could not have practised systematic misrepresentation in his daily record without hopelessly enmeshing and entangling himself and incurring the risk of detection at many points, while—occupying, as he did, a position where his every word and act were noted by others—he would have exposed himself often to documentary refutation. Besides, the marks of good faith are without number. The diary should therefore be accepted, and has been accepted, as essentially truthful; and the man it shows us—revealed also by a large amount of other evidence—is a cold, narrow, methodical, dogged, plodding, obstinate partisan, deeply convinced of his importance and responsibility, very wanting in humor, very wanting in ideality, very wanting in soulfulness, inclined to be sly, and quite incapable of seeing great things in a great way. All know the type. It is the leading citizen and schemer of the small town, who marches up the centre aisle on public occasions with creaking shoes and a wooden smile, and takes his seat with a backward, all-embracing glance.

Such a person—lean, stiff, angular, with sharp gray eyes in a sad face, and long, grizzled hair brushed straight back behind his ears—makes no appeal to our sympathies, and for that reason is almost sure to be judged unfairly. For example, Polk has been called the "Mendacious"; but that is unjust. Many things are done in good society which, if thrown upon a screen before two thousand people, would be recognized instantly as mean; and the same is true in the world of affairs. As a lawyer and politician of Nashville, Polk no doubt resorted to devices of this kind, and he was not the man to realize the difference between a provincial town and a nation, and adapt himself to his new position. Compelled to act, he acted as he could; used the tactics with which he was familiar. In this manner he deceived men or permitted men to deceive themselves, and those accustomed to broader and larger and nobler methods thought he lied. In reality he was not Polk the Mendacious, but simply Polk the Mediocre.

Yet he was mediocre only as compared with great standards. He could by no means be called insignificant. George Bancroft, secretary of the navy, has testified that he surpassed every member of his Cabinet in ability—not as high a distinction, perhaps, as might have been wished, but still high. His will-power was ample, and his output of mental energy large. In seriousness, industry and fidelity he left nothing to be desired. Though strongly inclined to be positive, he would listen patiently to others, discuss weighty matters at length, and if convinced would yield. He reflected long, and yet when the time for decision came, he did not shrink from taking a stand. He intended to do his duty as he, Polk, was able to see it, and spent himself liberally in that cause. He certainly was religious, and no doubt—though blind to the beauty of uprightness and unresponsive to the delicacy of honor—he fully believed that he was conscientious.

To regard such a man, uninspired and uninspiring, as capable of playing the brilliant villain's rôle in a grand international tragedy, of dreaming the conqueror's dream and sacrificing his fellow-citizens on the altar of gory but gorgeous ambition, of smelling the battle from afar like the war-horse and crying, "Ha, ha!"—this is out of the question. It was not in him. Neither intellect, conscience nor imagination permitted it. The Cabinet, which he selected with care, hampered by no preëlection agreements, was much like him; and as Benton said, it is "impossible to conceive of an administration less warlike, or more intriguing." "Mr. Polk never dreamed of any other war than a war upon the Whigs," admitted Robert Toombs, then a Whig member of Congress, in February, 1846.

A number of circumstances almost committed him to a peaceable course toward Mexico. During the discussions of the annexation project one of the strongest objections had been that it would involve the country in war, and its advocates had strenuously denied this allegation. The President belonged to that group, and Webster said: "That Mr. Polk and his Cabinet will desire to keep the peace, there is no doubt. The responsibility of having provoked war by their scheme of annexation is what they would greatly dread." Though many plain citizens desired a fight, an influential body of merchants, financiers and conservatives did not; and in the view of a still greater number a vital discrepancy between the predictions of the annexationists and their later conduct would surely have been damaging. The Oregon question threatened to prove serious; and it is hardly credible that Polk, even if quite willing to meet an attack from Mexico, would have desired to attack her before settling this controversy with England. The secretaries of state, war and the navy did not hail from fire-eating communities. The head of the army, General Scott, was a Whig and a recognized candidate for the Presidency; and the chiefs of the Democratic party had fully sense enough to understand that a war might enable him to succeed Polk. In fact the President's diary exhibits painful writhings due to such a possibility. Finally war, no matter how successful, would mean taxes, and even those who demanded a fight might not be willing to pay for it. Certainly Polk was not self-sacrificing enough to desire the odium of laying war taxes for the sake of bringing Scott into the White House. Besides, it looked as if war expenses could not fail to strengthen the tariff system, and that was obnoxious to a great number of the Democrats.

Polk's professions were every way most pacific. The assurances conveyed to Almonte after he made his protest have already been mentioned. In August, 1845, Polk wrote confidentially to a Senator, "We will not be the aggressors upon Mexico." A month later Buchanan declared in a "Private and Personal" letter to our minister at London: "The President does not intend to proceed beyond a just and righteous self-defence, and he is ready to present the olive branch to Mexico the moment he knows it will be accepted." It is hardly supposable that our secretary of state intended to deceive our most important representative abroad, or that he was deceived himself by Polk in so vital a matter.

The confidential orders of the government were emphatically unwarlike in tone. To Conner, commanding in the Gulf, the secretary of the navy wrote in March, 1845, "The disposition of the President is to maintain the most friendly relations with the Mexican Republic," and in substance this declaration was repeated in the following July and August. "Take special care," the department said to Stockton, who had a few vessels on the Texas coast, "to avoid every act that can admit of being construed as inconsistent with our friendly relations" with Mexico. Commodore Sloat, in the Pacific, was told in "Secret and Confidential" instructions dated June 24, 1845, "The President hopes, most earnestly, that the peace of the two countries may not be disturbed . . . do everything consistent with the national honor" to avoid a rupture; and these instructions to Sloat were most noteworthy, for the commander on the Pacific station was liable to be out of touch with the government for a year at a time, and he needed to be sure as to its general policy.

For the guidance of our chargé in Texas, where many feared a Mexican invasion and called for American troops, a clear statement of our intentions was equally necessary, and Buchanan wrote to Donelson at about the same time, "The Government will studiously refrain from all acts of hostility towards that republic [Mexico], unless these should become absolutely necessary in self-defence." Quite in line with all this was the order cancelling Frémont's second exploring trip to the far west, because he had equipped his party in a military style—an order that was decidedly over-strict, since precautions against the Indians could not be neglected. In his Message to the Senate, March 24, 1846, the President declared it his "settled purpose" to maintain peace with Mexico, and it is believed that no expression of his indicating a desire to provoke a conflict can be found.

The measures of the administration corresponded with its professions. In the first place this was true negatively. It would not be easy to deny that Mexico's refusal to pay the instalments of our awards could have been handled by our government in a way to enrage this nation, already so eager for the fray, and probably her severance of diplomatic relations might have been used to precipitate an issue; but no advantage was taken of either opportunity. Another instance is even more signal. One can hardly doubt that Polk might have brought on a war in the summer of 1845, had he so desired. Not only had Mexico grossly insulted us, refused to pay those awards, and severed relations with us both at her capital and at our own, but she had solemnly announced that our annexing Texas would be regarded as equivalent to a declaration of war, notified her agents privately and the world at large publicly that she was going to fight, and begun preparations for immediate hostilities. Had Polk summoned Congress and laid all the facts before it, a declaration of war, or at least an ultimatum that Mexico would in all probability have rejected, must certainly, or almost certainly, have been the response; and if one may judge from the state of mind existing in the United States at the time, our people would in the main have supported such a course. "The current of public opinion," said the St. Louis *Republican*, "seems now strongly inclined in favor of a war with Mexico." "All the better portions of the press of the country," was the summary of the New Orleans *Picayune*, "are urgent for the adoption of the most energetic measures" against that country. Almost every Democratic journal and a vast majority of the Whig journals, declared the Washington *Globe*, were for crushing Mexico at once. "The people will approve" of vigorous action, admitted even the Charleston *Courier*.

But Polk did not adopt a course of that sort. He took no such steps to settle matters with England as a President of ordinary common sense would have taken, if anxious to fight Mexico; and no serious measures were adopted to increase our nominal army or our insufficient fleet. In September, he requested the members of the Cabinet to make their estimates for the coming year on "the most economical scale," and in fact only twenty-six hundred additional men were asked for the army —none for the navy. A note from the secretary of the navy to Captain Perry—"We are jogging on quietly this winter, not anticipating war"— well represents our military and naval programme; and a letter to Conner explains it: "We all hope Mexico will agree to a peace." Knowing, as Polk must have known, the deep and widespread fear of Mexican privateers, he would have been prevented by a merely selfish regard for the good opinion of the public from planning war without making some dispositions to protect, or at least warn, our millions of floating property. And apparently even the ardor of our young men for combat did not seriously move him.

In the second place, Polk's action pointed the same way as his non-action. No one could think of any rational method to conciliate Mexico that he did not put into operation. The chief object of Parrott's mission, which was private and therefore could not have been intended for effect upon the world, was understood by Parrott himself to be, "preventing a declaration of war, by Mexico, against the United States." In appointing Slidell, as even the *American Review* admitted, the President was evidently sincere. At the end of March, 1846, Polk received advices from Slidell which made it seem quite possible that he would finally be given a hearing, and immediately he set on foot a plan to furnish Paredes with funds, enable him to keep the army faithful, and thus encourage him to settle matters amicably. Indeed, all that is known of this mission from beginning to end, including Slidell's private letters to Buchanan and numerous details that it would be wearisome to hear specified, show that Polk strongly desired—as the Mexicans accused him of desiring—a restoration of friendly intercourse; and when the purpose had evidently failed, Slidell gave final evidence of that disposition by writing: "I am greatly mortified at the total failure of a mission commenced under auspices apparently the most flattering, but that mortification is much mitigated by the consciousness, that no fault of omission or commission, can justly be attributed either to the Government or to the Legation."

In short, then, we find that Polk had the gravest reasons for desiring friendly intercourse with Mexico, and probably felt none for plotting war; that a variety of personal and political circumstances naturally inclined him toward peace; that his declarations, both public and private, pointed consistently in that direction as long as any hope of an amicable settlement remained; and that what he did in repeated and most significant ways, as well as what he refrained from doing, had the same meaning. We must therefore give up the idea that he desired, and from the first intended, to have a war with Mexico.

All prospects of negotiation came to an end, however, and the administration found itself confronted by a crisis. The dignity of the United States had certainly been outraged in a defiant and contemptuous manner. By the acts of Mexico, diplomatic relations had been completely severed, and she would not renew them on any terms which the United States could think of accepting. Commercial intercourse was practically at an end, and the interests of our citizens were so greatly prejudiced, that from this point of view even a London paper, the *Examiner*, admitted reluctantly that the situation was becoming "intolerable to the United States." Our claims and our awards were still facts. "The honor of this government is pledged to our own people for the diligent and proper prosecution of these claims," our secretary of state had said in 1843, and it was perfectly true. To let them go unpaid, in addition to being internationally immoral, would have wronged our aggrieved citizens; and to pay them from our own revenues, besides being immoral, pusillanimous and ridiculous, would have been unfair to all of our tax-payers. We had observed no more willingness, although the Mexican government had nearly always been sufficiently strong, to do us justice before annexation became an issue than afterwards; and in fact Ashburnham, a British representative at Mexico, did not exaggerate when he wrote, "They *will* not pay but on compulsion." There was therefore no way to collect our due except by force.

If our long forbearance appeared to American editors a mistake, much more reason had the administration to entertain that opinion, for our ministers and consuls in Mexico had repeatedly urged it, and Slidell had summed up his experience there in the following words, amply justified by the sequel: "We shall never be able to treat with her on fair terms until she has been taught to respect us . . . here all amicable advances are considered as indicative either of weakness or treachery." "Be assured," he added privately to Buchanan, "that nothing is to be done with these people, until they shall have been chastised." The solemn declarations of a succession of trusted agents that our forbearance was a tactical error were facts that our government was bound to consider; and by way of confirmation it had not only our complete failure to get on with Mexico, but the success of a power which seemed to have pursued a very different course, for in October, 1845, our consul at Vera Cruz had given the state department a specimen of England's tone. Mexico, said she to the minister of relations, must fulfil to the letter every contract with a British subject.

Furthermore our government felt seriously concerned about the European monarchical schemes. Early in January, 1846, the London *Times* printed a letter from its correspondent at Mexico in which the opinion was expressed that a foreign prince, if "seconded by any leading European power," could gain a Mexican throne. A week later the same journal, recommending a Spanish king as the only possible cure for the ills of Mexico, had remarked that the United States could not oppose the "united policy of the European Powers"; and at about the same time the *Picayune* had announced, that it was proposed to give Cuba to England for her coöperation in the monarchical plan. Our government had, and could have, no intention of submitting to such European manoeuvres. Any attempt of England and France to place a king on the throne of Mexico, wrote Buchanan, "would be resisted by all the power of the United States"; and the best way to oppose it was to effect a definitive settlement of our difficulties with Mexico at once—first, because this of itself would very likely make the development of the rather complicated scheme appear, in view of the "Monroe Doctrine," impracticable, and, secondly, because no European power could, with any show of decency, interfere in the domestic affairs of that country, while she was actually at war.

Chivalry does not govern international relations even at the present day, and in 1845 sentiment was perhaps less tender on the subject than it now is. Vattel, the recognized authority on the law of nations, wrote thus: "Every nation . . . has, therefore, a right . . . to preserve herself from all injuries. . . . When the evil is done, the same right to security authorizes the offended party to endeavour to obtain a complete reparation, and to employ force for that purpose, if necessary."

Moreover, the United States could appeal, not only to strict law, but still more forcibly to broad equity. To sum up the case in one sentence, Mexico, our next neighbor, on no grounds that could be recognized by the United States, repudiated her treaties with us, ended official relations, aimed to prevent commercial intercourse, planned to deprive us of all influence on certain issues vitally connected with our declared foreign policy, seemed likely to sell California to some European rival of ours, made it impossible for us to urge long-standing claims or watch over citizens dwelling within her borders, refused to pay even her admitted debts to us, claimed the privilege of applying to our government publicly the most opprobrious epithets in the vocabulary of nations, designed to keep our people in a constant state of uncertainty and alarm, intended to cause us the expense of maintaining for defensive purposes a large army and a large navy, planned to destroy our commerce by commissioning privateers, claimed the right to harry Texas, a part of the Union, at will, threatened and prepared for war, and proposed to assume such an attitude that, whenever encouraged by foreign support or any other circumstances she could open fire upon us without even giving notice. She had informed the world that it was her privilege to keep on harrying Texas from generation to generation; and on a broader scale, but in a manner precisely analogous, it was now proposed to hang upon the flank of the United States. Foreign mediation could not be invoked, for all the American states were naturally supposed to be prejudiced, and it was contrary to our interest and avowed policy to allow European intervention in the affairs of this continent; and no end of what had become truly an intolerable state of affairs could be seen, for Mexico declared she would never give up her pretensions until she had recovered Texas, which it was now beyond her power to do.

It rested with our government, therefore, as the agent of national defence and the representative of national dignity and interests, to apply a remedy. Of course, too, all the pressure of warlike sentiment among our people, especially in the President's party, and even the pressure of motives distinctly selfish, had to be recognized more or less, for such is the nature of popular government. Very likely Polk's abandoning a part of our Oregon claim rendered it the more necessary to avoid flinching in the Mexican affair; and accordingly on April 21, 1846, after long consideration of the matter, he informed the Cabinet that our relations with Mexico "could not be permitted to remain" as they were, and that he thought he should recommend to Congress the adoption of energetic measures for the redress of our grievances, which meant also of course a full settlement of our differences with that power. In truth no other course would have been patriotic or even rational.

Strangely enough, although our diplomatic troubles with Mexico would almost certainly have led to hostilities, the war actually came about in a totally different way.

During the spring and early summer of 1845, in view of Mexican threats and of reports from trustworthy sources that an invasion of Texas might be expected, it was decided by our government that when her people should have accepted our annexation proposal, as they were almost sure to do, it would become the duty of the United States to defend her; and this decision made the question where her southern boundary lay a practical matter. It was a thorny subject. In 1834 Mexico herself did not feel sure about the line; and according to the chief technical officer in our state department, sole commissioner to negotiate the treaty of peace with Mexico, if an official demarcation had existed, the war between Texas and the mother-country had rubbed it out. The former now claimed the territory as far as the Rio Grande, but she did not establish her title by occupying completely and effectively the region south of the Nueces. Only by an agreement with Mexico, indeed, could limits have been fixed. So far as it concerned the republic of Texas, this was in effect the situation.

For the United States, however, this was not the whole story. Down to 1819 our government had insisted that Louisiana extended to the Rio Grande. In other language, since the southern part of Louisiana was called Texas, the official view was that Texas bordered on that stream. Such, then, was in effect the contention of Jefferson, Madison, Monroe, John Quincy Adams, Pinckney, Livingston and Clay, who represented three administrations in upholding the claim. By the treaty of 1819 we did not withdraw from our position, but merely arranged to "cede" whatever possessions we had west of the Sabine for certain valuable considerations. From 1819 to 1845, Texas, considered under its geographical and historical aspects as a district of old Louisiana, appeared to border on the Rio Grande not less truly than before, for no other line became established. Hence it seemed evident from this point of view, that by annexing Texas we revived our old claim, our old official view, and the testimony of all those eminent statesmen. Our government so held. November 10, 1845, in explaining to Slidell the extent of Texas, Buchanan went back to Jefferson, Madison, Monroe, Pinckney and the discussion of the Louisiana boundary. Polk, as the head of our government, could not well repudiate, simply on his own authority, the solemn declarations of Presidents and other high officials, in which through a term of years the nation had acquiesced. The fact that for a considerable time the Texans, asserting the Rio Grande line, had maintained themselves against Mexico perhaps had some confirmatory value; and Polk was further bound, not only by his apparently sincere belief in our old claim, but by the pledge he had given to Texas and the pledge our official representative had given her, expressly to promote the cause of annexation, that he would maintain the claim as President. These were grips of steel. . . .

Toward the end of August Marcy wrote: "Should Mexico assemble a large body of troops on the Rio Grande and cross it with a considerable force, such a movement must be regarded as an invasion of the United States and the commencement of hostilities." This declaration called forth protests, but was quite fair. By stationing troops peaceably in the "intermediate region" between the Nueces and the Rio Grande we only placed ourselves on an equality with Mexico; and, as we ordered [General Zackary] Taylor to leave her posts undisturbed, we showed a friendly recognition of the principle of pacific joint-occupation during negotiations. Our forces, to be sure, outnumbered hers, but her attitude made it unsafe to despatch a smaller representation. Unlike us, Mexico had no occasion to send an army into that region for defensive purposes. The United States had shown every sign of desiring peace and none of desiring war, and at this time was endeavoring to bring about a friendly settlement. Such an army could not have prevented us from entering the intermediate region, for at Corpus Christi Taylor was already there; and it could not have saved the Mexican posts and citizens, for they were not menaced. Mexico, on the other hand, had threatened us and made open preparations to strike; it was now understood at Washington that no declaration of war should be expected to precede a blow; her generals had proclaimed that hostilities were on the point of beginning; and it was only common sense to assume that, should a Mexican army cross the Rio Grande, it would come to execute the announced intention of those who sent it.

During the evening of January 12, 1846, despatches from Slidell and Black arrived at Washington, and made the rejection of our pacific overture look almost certain. This unexpected turn of affairs gave new seriousness and fresh urgency to the Mexican issue; and the next day Taylor was ordered to encamp on the Rio Grande at whatever point he should consider most advantageous. He was cautioned, however, against regarding Mexico as a enemy, unless war should be declared or hostilities be undertaken by her, and against provoking a conflict by insistence upon the joint navigation of the river, which our claim implied. . . .

Ampudia's orders and intention had been to attack the Americans as soon as possible, but his glorious prospects darkened immediately. Though given the place of Major General Arista, long at the head of military affairs in this quarter, because he supported the revolution of Paredes while Arista not only frowned upon it, but seemed to aim at making northeastern Mexico independent, Ampudia was detested and thought incompetent—an opinion he did not share—by not a few in the northern army, whereas Arista stood high in his caste, and, as a person of wealth and position, had strong friends well able to make trouble for the central government. Consequently an order dated April 4 made Arista commander-in-chief with Ampudia as lieutenant. The latter was immediately forbidden to shine on the field of glory, and, finding his officers would not support him in disobedience, he submitted.

Arista, however, bearing instructions dated April 4 to attack the Americans, reached the scene on the 24th, and ordered his cavalry general, Torrejón, to cross above Matamoros with about 1600 men. Hearing a rumor of this movement, Taylor sent Captain Thornton and about sixty dragoons late that afternoon to reconnoitre; and the next morning, some twenty-eight miles from camp, finding himself completely shut in by overwhelming forces, the Captain tried to break through, lost several men killed and wounded, and then with all the rest surrendered. This was war. "Hostilities have begun," announced Arista on the day of his arrival. "Hostilities may now be considered as commenced," reported Taylor on the 26th; and—besides advising Polk to organize twelve-months volunteers—he at once called upon Texas and Louisiana for about 5000 men.

It was a tragic and most regrettable dénouement; yet, on a close review of all the data now accessible, one does not find it easy to censure Polk. If he had wished and meditated war from the first, why did he work for an amicable settlement through Parrott, Black and Slidell? For the sake of appearances, many said. But in the first place we have found that Polk was honest in those negotiations; and, in the second, had war been his aim and appearances his care, he would not have permitted the order of January 13 to be issued that day. On January 12 it looked at Washington as if the question of receiving Slidell would soon be decided. The President could afford to wait a little, and he would have done this, for it was clear that an unnecessary military step, taken while he was extending the olive branch, would needlessly make him appear either treacherous or ridiculous. Moreover if he sought a war, he knew on January 12 that matters were shaping themselves to his taste; that Mexico was almost sure to close the door of negotiation soon; and consequently that he would soon be able to demand of Congress the forcible redress of our grievances.

Here lay a *casus belli* amply endorsed by international law, the practice of civilized powers, and the general opinion of the world. It was a ground, too, that Polk himself, as we have seen, felt entirely satisfied to stand upon, and one that our people, feeling as they did, would almost certainly have accepted. Having, then, apparently within his reach a pretext for war that almost everybody thought good, he would not have exerted himself to obtain one that almost everybody thought bad; and in fact—evidently expecting no event of decisive importance to occur near the Rio Grande—he went on day after day with his plan to lay our grievances before Congress, until news of the attack on Thornton burst upon Washington like a rocket. On the hypothesis that he had wished and meditated war from the first and merely stuck at appearances, his conduct was therefore irrational; and, besides, we have seen adequate reasons for believing that he desired peace.

Discarding that hypothesis, however, leaves us the important question, How did the idea of sending Taylor forward present itself to Polk? First, then, from his point of view it seemed entirely permissible. A proprietor is not debarred from going where a squatter has built a cabin; and in the light of our official claim and arguments Mexican occupation above the Rio Grande was merely by sufferance. The so-called "provocative act" of pointing guns at Matamoros could not be charged against the government, for Marcy had suggested other points also for Taylor's camp, leaving the choice to him. It was a defensive measure adopted by the General for military reasons in conjunction with pacific assurances and proposals; and we learn from Arista and others that it had a sedative effect on the property owners of that flimsily built city and on the army authorities.

No encroachment upon the powers of Congress appeared to be involved. Had Polk's aim been, as Calhoun alleged, to establish a boundary, he could not have tolerated Mexican posts, for the troops of foreign states cannot be permitted to sojourn within our officially defined limits. Besides, Polk had sent Slidell to treat on this very question, and Slidell had not given up the task. Though it rested with Congress to declare war, a President could legally, in the exercise of his discretion, take steps liable to bring about hostilities. Moreover Congress appeared to have authorized Taylor's movement. Corpus Christi, claimed by Tamaulipas, had been made an American port of delivery. A collection district had been established in the intermediate region. The declaration of Polk's Message, December, 1845, that our jurisdiction had been extended to the Rio Grande, and Marcy's appended report, which announced that Taylor's instructions were to regard that stream as our boundary, had raised no storm. For six months, admitted the chief Whig organ, our doings in this field not only had appeared to be endorsed by the people, but had gone on openly without calling forth "a single question from any public authority." Officially notified of the military occupation of Corpus Christi, Congress, instead of protesting, had voted supplies for the troops. Finally, Congress had instructed the Executive, in the resolutions for annexing Texas, to reach an agreement with Mexico regarding the boundary; it was his duty to persevere in the attempt until convinced he could not succeed; and Taylor's advance, as will presently be seen, appeared to him a proper step in the discharge of this obligation.

Familiar precedents and principles were believed to sanction the movement of our troops. In 1794 Washington had ordered Wayne to conduct hostilities in disputed territory, and had threatened to destroy a British fort there. In accordance with a resolution of Congress, Madison had seized the "Florida parishes" claimed by Spain. Just before Taylor was ordered to move, Hilliard informed the House of Representatives that England had magistrates in the southern part of Oregon; and John Quincy Adams proposed to take military possession of that disputed territory before concluding negotiations. If such a method could be employed in dealing with countries willing to treat, very naturally—in the case of one that had pronounced for war—pacific occupation, leaving the competing jurisdiction undisturbed, seemed fully justifiable.

Taylor's advance appeared also to be highly expedient. For one thing, our claim upon the intermediate region would have been weakened, had we refrained from sharing with Mexico in the occupation of it. For another, it seemed wise to place ourselves in a strategic position that would be of great value, should Mexico's threat of war be carried into effect. And for a third it was believed that a bold military attitude, indicating that at last the United States had made up its mind, would count with

Mexico as a strong argument for negotiation. Such was the opinion of Parrott, Slidell, Worth, Taylor, Scott, Archer, now chairman of the Senate committee on foreign relations, Brantz Mayer, formerly secretary of legation at Mexico, Polk himself, the administration circle in general, and well-informed persons outside it. January 17 Conner was ordered to assemble all his vessels and exhibit them off Vera Cruz—evidently in pursuance of this design. The government organ stated, and opposition writers conceded, that such a purpose was in view.

But essentially, as already has been suggested, Taylor's advance rested on the necessity of military defence; and indeed there is reason to consider Scott the prime factor in the business, for the order of January 13 was based upon, and in part verbally reproduced, a "projet'" submitted by him, whereas Polk's diary for January 12 and 13 does not even allude to the subject. Now not only were defensive measures called for on general principles, as we have just been informed by the London *Times,* but the Texans actually and urgently needed a sheltering arm. During the latter part of 1845 the chief Mexican engineers drew detailed plans for crossing, not only the Rio Grande, but the Sabine. Merely the refusal of Paredes, growing out of his revolutionary designs, to reinforce the troops on the frontier with 2400 men prevented an attack at this time. Almonte, who had particularly recommended incursions into Texas, held the post of war minister in January, 1846. The Mexican troops were extremely mobile. Ampudia's main force, at the end of a long march, did 180 miles in four days. Screened by rancheros and living on a little corn and jerked beef carried in their pouches, a body of light cavalry could have reached San Antonio by way of Laredo, ruined the town, and been well on their way toward home before their movement would have been suspected at Corpus Christi. The government received warnings of this danger from Dimond and from Parrott in 1845; Marcy and Polk feared it; and the probable rejection of Slidell—which meant a triumph of the war party—seemed likely to accentuate the peril. In fact Mejía ordered irregulars into Texas on February 16 and March 17, though, as their commander aspired to execute a revolution with American aid, he did us no harm.

Nor were only such formal incursions to be guarded against. The war of 1836 in Texas had shown what outrages Mexicans were capable of committing, and similar affairs had now begun to occur. In one instance a party of fifteen, including women, after having been induced to surrender, were all butchered except a single person, who survived though seriously wounded. In April, 1846, the Mexicans opposite Matamoros confessed that bloodthirsty guerillas were abroad. Ampudia, whose murderous record had been his chief distinction, commanded there. May 13 the British consul in that city reported that licensed bands of assassins, "caressed, rewarded, and encouraged" by the authorities, were committing atrocities near the Rio Grande; and, had the way been open, such gangs might have robbed and murdered in the settlements of Texas. . . .

But the challenge was triumphantly thrown out: Can it be denied that our taking a position on the river did in fact cause the war? In view of the data it can and should be denied. First, joint occupation of the disputed region might have gone on peaceably, as occupation of that character has continued elsewhere, but for a distinctly aggressive step on the part of Mexico; and, secondly, for her the Rio Grande had no particular significance. She claimed all of Texas, and intended to drive us from it, if she could. Furthermore, the crass vanity and ambition of Mexican generals and the exigencies of domestic politics would probably have led to an attack upon us, had Taylor remained at Corpus Christi, or even pitched his camp at San Antonio. In spite of express orders, Mejía actually attempted an offensive in the intermediate region. When the Mexican government gave formal notice to England and France in the summer of 1845 that war had become inevitable, our army lay far from the Rio Grande. Taylor's advance to the Bold River no more produced the war than Pitcairn's march to Lexington produced the American revolution. It was an effect and an occasion, but not a cause.

Finally, as a matter of fact, the hostilities were deliberately precipitated by the will and act of Mexico. The circumstances proved this and testimony illuminates them. In October, 1847, a pamphlet written by Mariano Otero, editor of *El Siglo XIX* and Senator from the state of Jalisco, appeared. His object was by no means to defend the United States, but he said: "The American forces did not advance to the Rio Grande until after the war became inevitable, and then only as an army of observation. . . . The military rebellion of San Luis [Potosí] gave rise to a government [that of Paredes] pledged to resist all accommodation [with the United States] . . . which government . . . began hostilities." Arista declared in December, 1847, "I had the pleasure of being the first to begin the war." In short, Polk told only the truth when he said the conflict was forced upon us. Mexico wanted it; Mexico threatened it; Mexico issued orders to wage it; and on April 18 her President, no doubt in view of his political difficulties, insisted upon those orders. "It is indispensable," he wrote urgently to Arista, "that hostilities begin, yourself taking the initiative."

We were, then, under arms; but, after all, why? What was the cause of the war? It was not—as will plainly appear in another chapter, it is believed—an unholy determination to obtain California at the cost, if necessary, of fifty thousand lives. It cannot have been a difficulty as to the boundary of Texas, for two nations do not fight over an issue that exists for only one of them—and that one not the aggressor; and for Mexico the question between the Nueces and the Rio Grande had no international significance except when it could be used, as an *argumentum ad hominem,* to embarrass Americans.

Nor was it a scheme to extend the field of negro servitude. Even a cormorant requires time for digestion, and in 1845 the acquisition of Texas appeared so powerful a bulwark for the peculiar institution, that no strong and widespread craving for additional areas can be supposed to have existed at the beginning of 1846. Besides, as pro-slavery Taylor, Calhoun and Polk, anti-slavery Webster and time-serving Buchanan agreed, free labor was practically sure to dominate California; and hence, in view of the slight probability that much cultivable territory could be obtained in the south against the stubborn opposition of the free states, the war seemed more likely to diminish than to increase the relative strength of slavery. Moreover, the soil south and west of the Rio Grande was unsuitable for cotton, sugar, rice or tobacco. Rich proprietors already owned the land, and had no thought of parting with it. The system of peonage was extremely economical, and it held the ground so firmly that negro slavery, though tried, had been unable to make headway against it. The free laborers of northeastern Mexico would have been, admitted the *North American*, particularly hostile to our southerners and their methods; and the colored population, it was pointed out, could have escaped gradually from its bonds by amalgamating with the natives. Now the leaders of the "slavocracy" doubtless inquired into the conditions; and, as most of our ministers and probably most of our consuls in Mexico were from their section, they could easily obtain information. Waddy Thompson and A. J. Donelson, for example, believed and said, that slavery would not thrive in northern Mexico.

Polk's diary and papers reveal no evidence that he seriously considered the interest of the peculiar institution in connection with our Mexican problem. The debates of Congress are equally barren. Soon after the war opened, as we shall discover, northeastern Mexico seemed ready to join the United States or accept our protection, and there is no sign that the slavocracy attempted to improve the opportunity. The politicians most eager to acquire Mexican territory were Dickinson of New York, Hannegan of Indiana and Walker, an anti-slavery man. A northern correspondent of Calhoun wrote that many in New York insisted on extending that way "to augment the strength of the non-slaveholding states," while a Mobile correspondent said, "I would let the war continue forever before I would take 697,000 [square miles] of territory, which must be free territory." A meeting in Ohio declared for taking all of that country, and this does not seem to have been paralleled in the South. South Carolina was preëminently the champion of slavery, yet Governor Aiken publicly opposed making acquisitions in that quarter. Calhoun, the leader of the southern ultras there and elsewhere, did the same. So did Waddy Thompson, Botts, Toombs, Lumpkin, Campbell and many other southerners. W. R. King said that while the South would insist—as a point of pride and right—upon sharing the benefit of any territory gained from Mexico, it was a gross libel to represent her as desiring to increase in that way the strength of slavery.

King deplored the war. One of the South Carolina Senators wrote that it was detested nowhere more than in his state. In Georgia, too, the conflict was bitterly opposed. The people did not desire the war, said Toombs. Half of the slaveholders oppose it, admitted Ritchie, a Virginian, editor of the administration organ. Besides all other objections, it was pointed out that the southern policy of conservatism and her stand for a strict construction of the Constitution would be endangered by absorbing a large area mainly populated by extremely inferior aliens. To combat all this evidence, we find hardly anything except the characteristic hints, imaginings and assertions of certain abolitionists.

On the other hand, the evidence that the annexation of Texas was essentially the cause of the war is impressive both in quantity and in quality. Benton, Clay, Robert C. Winthrop, Stephen A. Douglas, Andrew Johnson and many other public men agreed on this point. As Van Buren and substantially all the Whig organs had predicted that immediate annexation would entail war with Mexico, they must be counted in the same class. Charles Sumner drew up a resolution declaring that such was the primary cause, and it passed the legislature of Massachusetts, where the subject was rather closely studied, by overwhelming majorities. The House committee on foreign affairs took that ground in its report of February 24, 1847. All agree upon this, was Winthrop's declaration. Paredes expressed the same view in the most formal manner. The Mexican minister of war under the government that overthrew Paredes publicly endorsed it; and at least two well-qualified foreign observers, Duflet de Mofras and the biographer of Lord Aberdeen, took the same view. Indeed, the proposition seems demonstrated by the plain course of events.

The mere annexation of Texas cannot, however, be regarded as the sole cause of the war. But for the loudly expressed wrath of the Americans, due mainly to Mexican barbarities in Texas and outrages upon the persons and property of American citizens, Mexico would have been far less irritable, and the annexation difficulty, which came so near to being patched up, might have been adjusted; while, as Polk maintained, if the policy of the United States regarding our claims had been firm, consistent and strong from the first, Mexico would not have dared to risk so much in dealing with us later.

The general cause of hostilities was, therefore, the series of unpleasant incidents occurring in the mutual relations of the two countries from the scandalous treatment of Poinsett down to the scandalous treatment of Slidell, from the first mutterings of discontent in Texas down to the setting of her one fair star in the broad sea of the American Union; and in this long series the annexation of Texas was the chief event.

But one can speak much more definitely. For a term of years, mainly in consequence of the use made of these affairs by self-seeking politicians, the people of Mexico had fed on the ideas of despising, fearing, hating and fighting the United States; Paredes had gained supreme authority on this basis; public sentiment demanded that he should pursue the route marked out by his professions; to beat the small and apparently demoralized American army, led by a backwoods general, seemed quite feasible; it appeared likely that a victory would confirm the dictator's power, while a failure to strike would ensure his doom; and hence an attack upon our army was ordered. This was the precise cause of the war. . . .

Additional Reading

S. F. Bemis, *The Latin American Policy of the United States* (1943).
William C. Binkley, *The Texas Revolution* (1952).
James M. Callahan, *American Foreign Policy in Mexican Relations* (1932).

John D. P. Fuller, *The Movement for the Acquisition of All Mexico, 1846–1848* (1936).
Norman A. Graebner, *Empire on the Pacific* (1955).
E. I. McCormac, *James K. Polk: A Political Biography* (1922).
Allan Nevins, *Fremont: Pathmarker of the West* (1939).
J. Fred Rippy, *The United States and Mexico* (1931 ed., 2nd).
Joseph W. Schmitz, *Texan Statecraft, 1836–1845* (1941).
Otis A. Singletary, *The Mexican War* (1960).

9 *POST CIVIL WAR EXPANSIONISM*

Manifest Destiny had been halted by the sectional struggle of the 1850's but after The Civil War an effort was made to revive the expansionist drive. Problems experienced during the recent struggle in blockading the Confederacy and destroying Southern commerce raiders indicated the need for naval bases and coaling stations in the Caribbean Sea and in the Pacific. Secretary of State William H. Seward threw his full energies behind expansionist plans to acquire the Danish West Indies, ports in Santo Domingo, and Pacific bases.

The popular mood, however, was generally opposed or indifferent to further territorial acquisitions. Domestic problems of reconstruction, industrialization, and agricultural growth absorbed the national energies, and the bloodletting of the Civil War had satiated the lust for martial adventure. Furthermore, past territorial expansion had been on the mainland of North America, contiguous to the United States, and had involved areas suitable for eventual statehood. Projected acquisitions after 1865 involved noncontiguous areas with alien populations and race problems, and if secured would presumably be administered as colonies. Many thoughtful Americans believed that such additions would weaken the democratic processes and corrupt the soul of a republic founded on the premise of government by consent. For these reasons, the schemes of Seward and later of President Ulysses S. Grant for Caribbean expansion failed; the only acquisitions were the purchase of Alaska in 1867 and the occupation of uninhabited Midway Island in the Pacific in the same year.

DOCUMENT

"Seward's Icebox"

Note the provisions for extension of citizenship to the inhabitants of Russian America. The historian Julius W. Pratt has called the treaty a half-way house on the road to colonialism, for in contrast to previous acquisitions nothing was said about eventual statehood; later treaties transferring areas to the United States were silent even on citizenship.

The Alaska Treaty With Russia

Article I. His Majesty the Emperor of all the Russias agrees to cede to the United States, by this convention, immediately upon the exchange of the ratifications thereof, all the territory and dominion now possessed by his said Majesty on the continent of America and in the adjacent islands, the same being contained within the geographical limits herein set forth, to wit: The eastern limit is the line of demarcation between the

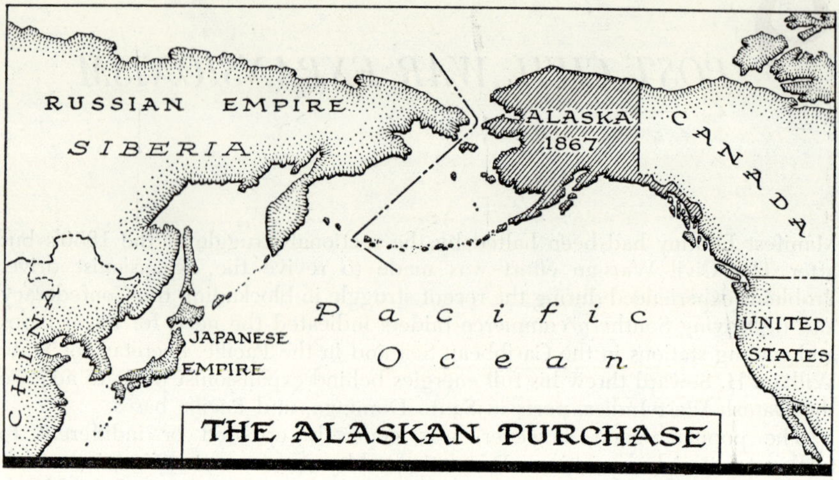

Russian and the British possessions in North America, as established by the convention between Russia and Great Britain, of February 28–16, 1825, and described in Articles III and IV of said convention. . . .

Article III. The inhabitants of the ceded territory, according to their choice, reserving their natural allegiance, may return to Russia within three years; but if they should prefer to remain in the ceded territory, they, with the exception of uncivilized native tribes, shall be admitted to the enjoyment of all the rights, advantages, and immunities of citizens of the United States, and shall be maintained and protected in the free enjoyment of their liberty, property, and religion. The uncivilized tribes will be subject to such laws and regulations as the United States may, from time to time, adopt in regard to aboriginal tribes of that country.

Article VI. In consideration of the cession aforesaid, the United States agree to pay at the treasury in Washington, within ten months after the exchange of the ratifications of this convention, to the diplomatic representative or other agent of his Majesty the Emperor of all the Russias, duly authorized to receive the same, seven million two hundred thousand dollars in gold. The cession of territory and dominion herein made is hereby declared to be free and unencumbered by any reservations, privileges, franchises, grants, or possessions, by any associated companies, whether corporate or incorporate, Russian or any other, or by any parties, except merely private individual property holders; and the cession hereby made, conveys all the rights, franchises, and privileges now belonging to Russia in the said territory or dominion, and appurtenances thereto.

READINGS

1. Alaska and Russo-American Friendship

That Russian-America, renamed Alaska, was the only sizable territorial acquisition in the post Civil War period has long been explained by historians on the grounds of America's friendship for Russia. F. R. Dulles of Ohio State University, the contributor of several studies on American diplomatic and social history, shares that view. Engineered by the expansionist Secretary of State Seward, the purchase of Alaska was accepted by a reluctant American people and Congress largely because Russia during the recent Civil War had seemed to be the only European friend of the Union cause. To reject the offer of sale would be to return injury where gratitude was due and might wreck the traditional cordiality between the two countries.

Seward's Folly

F. R. DULLES

Four years after the Civil War visit of the Russian fleets to American waters, a momentous deal was concluded between the governments at Washington and St. Petersburg. Russian America was purchased by the United States for $7,200,000. That cold, forbidding country, where Baranov had once ruled with an iron hand and offered at his "Castle" at Sitka such a roistering welcome to American visitors, became the territory of Alaska. And had it not been for the close bonds that were forged as Russia proved herself "our friend when the world was our foe," it is highly improbable that the American people would have approved this transfer of territory.

For the United States did not really want to buy Alaska. It was Russia that wanted to sell. Among American statesmen and political leaders, only Secretary of State Seward showed any enthusiasm over the transaction. He engineered it singlehanded. It was his ambitious imperialism, his soaring vision of the future importance of the Pacific, that was primarily responsible for this new addition to American territory. Few of his countrymen recognized either Alaska's economic potentialities or its highly strategic geographic location. Before the congressional and public debate upon the treaty he negotiated with Russia was concluded, Seward had been able to convince the country that Alaska was possibly worth the $7,200,000 we had agreed to pay for it, but this alone could not clinch the bargain in view of the public apathy at this time toward expansion. Popular friendship for Russia played a decisive part in securing both ratification of the treaty and the appropriation of the necessary money. We were repaying a debt of gratitude.

If today it appears surprising that there should have been any hesitation over taking Alaska off Russia's hands on such relatively easy terms, it must be remembered that in the 1860's little was known of its material

Reprinted from *The Road to Teheran: The Story of Russia and America,* 1781–1943 by Foster Rhea Dulles by permission of Princeton University Press. Copyright, 1944, by Princeton University Press. Pp. 63–77.

wealth. Prevalent ideas of its climate had convinced the few Americans who had ever heard of Alaska that such a frigid, barren country could hardly have any real value for the United States. It was also believed to lie too far north to have any commercial or strategic importance. After all it is only the airplane that has given validity to Seward's conception of Alaska as a drawbridge linking America and Asia, and in 1867 our modern conquest of the air was not even a gleam in the eye of statesmanship. Not until well into the twentieth century, perhaps not until the 1940's, could the American people appreciate the tremendous significance of what at that time they derisively called "Seward's Folly."

After the death of Baranov in 1819 there had been a steady decline in the fortunes of the Russian American Company. Alexander I had not responded to the occasional urgings of those who tried to revive the dream of imperial expansion on the American continent, and the Russo-American treaty of 1824 had marked the abandonment of all idea of acquiring new territory. Russians remained in control of the settlement at Fort Ross for some time, not withdrawing from this outpost until the eve of our own acquisition of California, but this colony dwindled in importance even more than that at Sitka. The gradual extermination of the sea otter was in large part responsible for the hard times that fell upon the Russian American Company. As the century advanced it was no longer possible for it to send home an annual fleet laden with a cargo of priceless skins, and other ventures undertaken to compensate for these losses did not greatly prosper. Alaska was becoming a liability rather than an asset. The Czarist government lost what slight interest it had ever had in the territory, and the officials at St. Petersburg began to feel that the difficulties in holding it and providing for its protection outweighed its possible value.

Suggestions for the transfer of Alaska to the United States were in the air around the middle of the century. Cassius M. Clay, our minister to St. Petersburg in the 1860's, was the doubtful authority for a report that Russia would have been willing to cede the territory without compensation at the time when the United States and Great Britain were involved in controversy over the division of Oregon. During the Crimean War there were rumors that Russia was anxious to sell. These reports were denied by Minister Stoeckl but they had at least some slight foundation. A fictitious sale to a San Francisco company had been proposed with the idea of averting possible attack by Great Britain. This plan was soon dropped and Alaska's neutrality during the Anglo-Russian hostilities had then been assured through an agreement with the Hudson's Bay Company, to which the Russian American Company had leased certain of its property.

The Crimean War, however, brought home to St. Petersburg the exposed situation of Alaska, and the idea of selling it was given serious consideration in 1857. The Grand Duke Constantine now took the lead in urging cession of territory which Russia could not hope to hold in the event of another war. He was strongly supported in these views by Stoeckl. The Russian minister agreed that Alaska was virtually defenseless, and he also pointed out that it represented a possible source of needless friction with the United States which might well jeopardize Russian-American friendship. There had been continuing controversies over American fishing rights in Alaskan waters since the expiration of the clause in the treaty of 1824 granting us such privileges, but—far more important—Stoeckl was convinced that some day the United States would seek to absorb Alaska as it had already absorbed Oregon and California. He reported to his government in some alarm that there were rumors that the Mormons under Brigham Young planned a northern emigration. Alexander wrote on the top of his minister's dispatch that this fresh complication provided additional support for the views of those who were urging that Alaska be sold.

As a result of these developments Stoeckl was instructed to be ready to take advantage of any suggestion that the United States might be interested in acquiring the territory. Early in 1860 he reported that the idea had been broached in conversations with Senator Gwin of California and Assistant Secretary of State Appleton. He was informed that President Buchanan favored purchase and a price of $5,000,000 was mentioned. Neither government, however, was prepared to commit itself definitely on the proposition. Secretary of State Cass was apparently not even informed of what was going on, and Foreign Minister Gorchakov advised Stoeckl to proceed with extreme caution. Meanwhile the shadow of impending Civil War crept over the horizon and the negotiations lapsed under the stress of far more important problems.

Six years later the issue came up again at St. Petersburg. Affairs had been going from bad to worse in Alaska. The charter of the Russian American Company had expired and its tangled finances left it on the verge of bankruptcy. If Alaska were to be maintained as a Russian colony, the government had either to subsidize the company heavily or itself take over administration of the territory. All the arguments advanced a decade earlier in favor of its possible transfer to the United States appeared now to be more valid than ever. Stoeckl, home on leave, was still certain that the time would come when Americans would overrun the territory and he strongly felt that it would not be to Russia's interest to become involved in a hopeless struggle to retain something she did not really want. It was now known in Russian official circles that there was gold in Alaska. But ironically enough this served only to make Stoeckl more anxious to sell the territory because he feared that once the fact became known there would be no resisting the American onrush whatever Russia sought to do. His position was that Russia was bound to lose Alaska sooner or later, either to Great Britain or to the United States, and that it should be sold before it was too late.

The whole matter was threshed over at a council of ministers at St. Petersburg in December 1866 and, in the face of some opposition from those who felt that Russia should preserve "every clod of earth along the coast of an ocean which has world-wide importance," the proponents of sale won the day. The United States was of course the logical customer, for Russia as always sought to strengthen this country at the expense

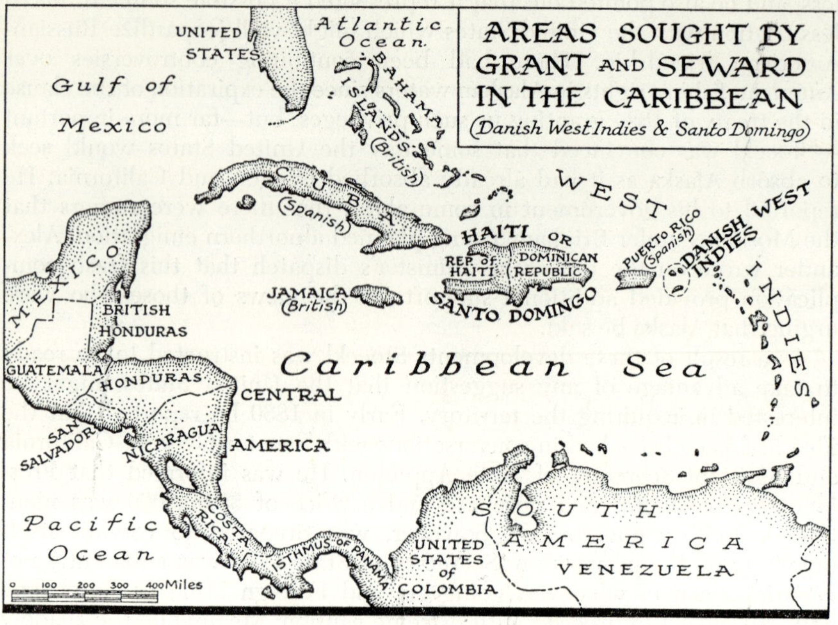

AREAS SOUGHT BY GRANT AND SEWARD IN THE CARIBBEAN (Danish West Indies & Santo Domingo)

of Great Britain, and the decision was now definitely reached that the transfer should be urged upon the American government at the earliest opportunity. Stoeckl was commissioned to return to Washington and to carry out the agreed-upon policy to the best of his ability. The minimum price he was authorized to accept was $5,000,000.

The moment of his return was unexpectedly propitious. Secretary Seward was looking about for new territories the United States might acquire, ready to give free rein to his expansionist ambitions. He wanted to annex Santo Domingo and to purchase the Danish West Indies; he hoped to negotiate a treaty of either annexation or reciprocity with the Hawaiian Islands, and he had quietly appropriated Midway Island. With his main interest centered upon the Pacific, which he so confidently believed to be "the chief theatre of events in the world's great hereafter," nothing could have fitted more neatly into his plans than the purchase of Alaska.

There were not many other Americans who felt as did Seward. The public was far too much absorbed in domestic questions arising out of the Civil War, as the Secretary of State himself wrote somewhat despairingly, to entertain "the higher, but more remote, questions of national extension." As for Alaska itself, it was so far away that the American people not only had no direct contacts with it whatsoever but hardly knew of its existence. There were only two slender threads which might be considered as linking the United States with the Russian colony now on the market. One involved the project of a telegraph line to Europe by way of Alaska and Siberia, and the other was the question of fishing privileges on the Alaskan coast. Here were the sum and total of American interests in Alaska outside the fertile and imaginative mind of Secretary Seward.

In connection with the proposed telegraph line the Western Union Company had obtained from the Russian government, with the enthusiastic cooperation of Cassius Clay, the necessary charter and privileges. It had conducted extensive surveys throughout Alaska. The whole project nevertheless fell through in 1866 when an Atlantic cable was at last successfully laid and a telegraph line across Alaska consequently no longer justified the great expense of its construction. The old issue of fishing privileges, however, had been revived with the presentation to President Johnson of a memorial from the legislature of Washington Territory urging conclusion of a new treaty with Russia to obtain for American vessels the right to fish off the Alaskan coast and visit Alaskan ports. The memorial did not reflect any wide popular demand, even on the West coast. It was largely the work of one Joseph Lane MacDonald who had organized the Puget Sound Steam Navigation Company and hoped to extend its operations to the north.

Secretary Seward knew of these developments and the memorial concerning fishing privileges, presented early in 1866, appeared to him to afford an opportunity for which he had long been looking. Why not use it as an opening wedge to persuade the Russian government to sell Alaska to the United States? Without any knowledge of the instructions which Stoeckl was actually bringing back with him from St. Petersburg, the ambitious Secretary of State decided on just this step. He made the memorial so conveniently adopted by the Washington legislature the occasion for communicating to Stoeckl, in his own words, "the importance of some early and comprehensive arrangement between the two countries, to prevent the growth of difficulties arising out of the fisheries in the Russian possessions."

One may easily imagine the surprise and gratification with which the shrewd and skillful Russian diplomat, upon reaching Washington in March 1867, listened to the impulsive Seward's suggestion. Nothing could have more directly played into his hands. Negotiations for the transfer of Alaska were consequently taken up at once between two such willing partners and carried forward with both haste and complete secrecy.

Seward offered $5,000,000 as a purchase price; Stoeckl asked $7,000,000. A compromise between these two figures appeared logical and the Russian minister actually reported to his government that he was ready to accept anything from $6,000,000 to $6,500,000. But he soon realized there was no need to reduce the price for so eager a purchaser. He stood by his original demand. After some half-hearted haggling on Seward's part, the final price of $7,000,000 was agreed upon. Moreover, when the question arose of various franchises and concessions leased by the Russian American Company, the Secretary of State went even further in declaring that he would add $200,000 to the price if Alaska came to the United States free of all encumbrances. The bargain was quickly sealed under these happy circumstances. Seward obtained the somewhat sceptical approval of President Johnson and Stoeckl telegraphed his government by means of the new Atlantic cable for final authorization to sign a treaty.

"On Friday evening, March 29," as the next step in this remarkable transaction has been recorded by the Secretary of State's son, "Seward was playing whist in his parlor with some of his family, when the Russian minister was announced.

"'I have a dispatch, Mr. Seward, from my Government by cable. The Emperor gives his consent to the cession. Tomorrow if you like, I will come to the department, and we can enter upon the treaty.'

"Seward, with a smile of satisfaction at the news, pushed away the whist table, saying:

"'Why wait till tomorrow, Mr. Stoeckl? Let us make the treaty to-night.'"

Startled secretaries were at once routed out; Charles Sumner, chairman of the Senate Foreign Relations Committee, hastily summoned, and the two men repaired to the State Department. By four o'clock the next morning the treaty had been drawn up and signed. Passers-by, wondering why the Secretary of State's office should be so brilliantly lighted at such an unlikely hour in the morning, little suspected that it signified their country's acquisition of new territory totaling some 591,000 square miles, an area more than twice the size of Texas and equal to nearly one-fifth of continental United States. Nor could any legislative body have been more surprised than was the Senate when later that same day it received a special message from President Johnson, laconically submitting for its approval "a treaty for the cession of Russian America."

So secretly had the brief negotiations been conducted that outside of a handful of people in Washington, no one had even suspected that the United States was seriously considering the purchase of Alaska. The announcement of Seward's dramatic coup was at first greeted with stunned surprise. Newspaper editors throughout the country hurried to their atlases and encyclopedias to discover what they could of Russian America, and in some cases launched into descriptions of the territory even without the benefit of such hastily acquired information. An even more ignorant public was treated to some amazing descriptive material. It was confidently stated that the ground in Alaska was frozen throughout the year to a depth of some six feet, that the streams were all glaciers, and that the territory's only products were icebergs and polar bears. While "Seward's Folly" became the most popular name for our prospective new possession, it was also joyously termed "Walrussia," "Johnson's Polar Bear Garden," and "Seward's Icebox." Although it would later support the cession, the *New York Herald* took its fling at the Secretary of State by advising him to purchase Patagonia "to make both ends meet," publishing a fictitious advertisement:

> CASH! CASH! CASH!—Cash paid for cast-off territory. Best price given for old colonies, North or South. Any impoverished monarchs retiring from the colonization business may find a good purchaser by addressing W. H. S., Post Office, Washington, D.C.

The anti-administration papers, bitter against President Johnson on the eve of the impeachment proceedings resulting from his conflict with Congress over reconstruction in the South, automatically condemned anything for which he could directly or indirectly be held responsible. His Secretary of State was consequently denounced for his "bad bargain" and the "egregious folly" of the whole affair. It was a "dark deed done in the night."

Although this outburst was somewhat dismaying, and Senator Sumner actually advised Stoeckl to withdraw the treaty rather than risk its rejection by the Senate, Seward believed he could win sufficient popular support to ensure favorable action. He launched a nationwide propaganda campaign to convince the country that Alaska was well worth the $7,200,000 being paid for it. Friendly newspapers were furnished with abundant copy emphasizing the reasons why we should acquire the territory. The argument was put forward that opposition to this purchase was based upon the same shortsightedness and provincialism that had sought to block that of Louisiana. The known resources of Alaska in fish, furs and lumber, and its commercial and strategic importance in the Pacific area, were carefully elaborated upon as wholly justifying the cession. The final and supposedly conclusive reason advanced for ratifying the treaty, however, was that since the Czar desired to sell, and an agreement had actually been reached, our debt to Russia for support during the Civil War did not permit us to rebuff her overtures.

The backing of Senator Sumner proved to be Seward's most powerful asset in securing approval by the Senate. The treaty could hardly have been ratified without it. The Massachusetts statesman did not share Seward's glowing dream of Pacific expansion. He had doubts upon the advisability of the purchase. But he was won over to its support, despite his opposition to the Johnson administration on so many other counts, because of his desire to have the United States retain the friendship of Russia. "The Russian treaty tried me severely," Sumner later wrote; "abstractly I am against further acquisitions of territory, unless by the free choice of their inhabitants. But this question was perplexed by considerations of politics and comity and the engagements already entered into by the Government. I hesitated to take the responsibility of defeating it." Having once made up his mind, however, the influential senator from Massachusetts threw himself wholeheartedly into the fight to secure prompt ratification.

In a memorable speech before the Senate which is still a mine of information about Alaska, Sumner declared that possession of the Russian territory would immensely strengthen our naval and commercial position in the Pacific. It was essential, he said, that we should take advantage of this opportunity to acquire it. Otherwise it might well fall some day into the hands of Great Britain and afford her control over an ocean which should be kept free for American trade and commerce. Describing the Aleutian Islands as "extending a friendly hand to Asia," he further emphasized Alaska's role as a link with the people of China and Japan. But the argument upon which he laid the greatest stress and to which he repeatedly returned, as had the newspaper articles inspired by Seward, was our international obligation. "It is difficult to see," he stated emphatically, "how we can refuse to complete the purchase without putting to hazard the friendly relations which happily subsist between the United States and Russia."

So decisive was Sumner's attitude that he persuaded his fellow senators to accept the agreement, whatever their feelings as to its wisdom, rather than affront Russia by rejecting it. The treaty was ratified on April 9, 1867, by a majority of 27 to 12. A motion was then introduced to make the vote unanimous as a gesture of cordiality toward Russia, "the old and faithful friend of the United States," but two ballots were still cast in the negative.

It was now necessary to secure House approval for the appropriation of the $7,200,000 purchase price. Consideration of the necessary bill was long delayed by the absorption of Congress in the impeachment proceedings against President Johnson, and for a time it appeared highly doubtful if favorable action would ever be taken. The political situation stacked all cards against the administration. Stoeckl grew so despairing that he even suggested to his government that it offer to forego all payment for Alaska in the hope of shaming Congress into making the funds available. Foreign Minister Gorchakov vetoed this idea. Possibly he feared the Congress would take advantage of it.

Justification for such cynicism existed in the fact that certain private claims had been brought against the Russian government and there was at least some congressional support for demanding their settlement as a condition of paying for Alaska. These claims were shown to be fraudulent and the proposition rejected. Nevertheless even their discussion introduced an unsavory element into the transaction foreshadowing the scandals which would soon become so notorious in Washington during the Grant administration. Rumors were also spread about somewhat later which hinted at bribery and corruption as a means of winning support for the treaty. There was no question that Seward and Stoeckl spent large sums for propaganda, but how much further their agents may have gone cannot be definitely answered. A memorandum subsequently discovered among the papers of President Johnson quoted Seward as having told the President that the Russian envoy had actually paid considerable sums to certain important Washington figures to win their support. Thaddeus Stevens was said to have received $10,000, N. P. Banks, chairman of the House Foreign Relations Committee, $8,000, John W. Forney $30,000, and R. J. Walker and F. P. Stanton $20,000 apiece.

This hearsay evidence is not in itself proof of corruption, but the testimony given at the time by the principals in the transaction is not altogether reassuring. While Seward stated before a congressional committee investigating the "Alaska Swindle" that "no engagement was ever made with anybody for any part of the purchase-money, or any fund," he was not altogether candid in certain of his other statements. For his part Stoeckl reported to the Russian government that the greater part of the $200,000 added to the purchase price had been used for "secret expenses," and he finally asked that he be transferred to some other post where he could "breathe an atmosphere purer than that of Washington."

The debate in the House upon the appropriation bill, apart from these aspects of the question, reflected the public attitude toward Alaska's purchase. Partisan opposition to the Johnson administration, the constitutional issue involved in the right of the Senate to ratify a treaty dependent upon a congressional appropriation, the value of Alaska to the United States and our obligations to Russia all played their part in the discussion. There were those who followed Seward's lead in declaring that acquisition of the territory would give us control of the Pacific, and bitter opponents of the transfer who saw in Alaska nothing at all but a useless and expensive burden. The argument stressing our debt to Russia was brought up repeatedly, to be answered in one instance with the statement that if it involved the payment of $7,200,000, we should meet it promptly but not accept Alaska even as a free gift.

"Alaska, with the Aleutian Islands," Ferris of New York caustically remarked, "is an inhospitable, wretched, and Godforsaken region, worth nothing, but a positive injury and incumbrance as a colony of the United States." Washburn of Wisconsin blandly suggested that if we were determined upon acquiring a white elephant, we could get a much superior one "in Siam or Bombay for one-hundredth part of the money, with not one ten-thousandth part of the expense in keeping the animal in proper condition." Let Russia keep Alaska was the burden of these critics' song. "Have the people desired it?" Williams of Pennsylvania demanded. "Not a sensible man among them ever suggested it. The whole country exclaimed at once, when it was made known to them, against the ineffable folly, if not the wanton profligacy, of the whole transaction."

Proponents of the purchase stood their ground against all such attacks. There was strong support for purchasing the territory from the West coast, where the value of the Alaskan fisheries was better known, and a number of representatives dwelt upon the importance of our trade in the Pacific. Maynard of Tennessee echoed Seward's views in stating that possession of Alaska would give the United States "commercial and naval supremacy on the Pacific as complete as Great Britain has for two centuries enjoyed on the Atlantic Ocean." N. P. Banks shared—or perhaps borrowed—the Secretary of State's prophetic visions of the Pacific. "That ocean will be the theatre of the triumphs of civilization in the future," he grandiloquently proclaimed. "It is on that line that are to be fought the great battles of the hereafter. It is there that the institutions of the world will be fashioned and its destinies decided. If this transfer is successful, it will no longer be an European civilization or an European destiny that controls us. It will be a higher civilization and a nobler destiny. It may be an American civilization, an American destiny of six hundred million souls."

Long before these floods of impassioned oratory inundated the halls of Congress, Seward had gone ahead with the formal process of taking possession of Alaska, and the American flag had been impressively raised at Sitka on October 18, 1867. By the time the House got around to taking final action, in the summer of 1868, it was actually confronted with a *fait accompli.* Refusal of the necessary appropriation had become more than ever difficult. "Shall that flag which waves so proudly there now be taken down?" cried Representative Orth of Indiana. "Palsied be the hand that would dare to remove it. Our flag is there, and there it will remain." This was a decisive argument. And four days later, on July 23, the House at last acted. The appropriation was approved by a vote of 113 to 43.

It is clearly evident both in this vote and in the newspaper comment of the period that there was no overwhelming popular demand for Alaska. Seward had fought an uphill battle in winning public support for his treaty. It would also appear that despite such converts as he may have made to his own expansionist doctrines, there might have been no purchase of Alaska if it had been owned by any other nation than Russia. The Secretary of State did not succeed in any of his other attempts to acquire new possessions. "I doubt that there was any member of either house of Congress," John Bigelow, a friend of Seward, later wrote on the basis of contemporary conversations, "who supposed the Government then had any other motive in the purchase of Alaska than to recognize the obligations to the Czar. . . ." While this was most certainly not true of Seward himself, it was an attitude widely held and probably decisive in the final acceptance of the transfer.

Not many years were to pass before the value of Alaska would be proved far beyond the most optimistic predictions of Seward and his supporters. Taxes upon Alaskan industries poured back into the Treasury within a few decades a sum greater than the territory's total purchase price. Even before the Klondike Rush in 1896, gold production had far surpassed this figure of $7,200,000, while the mounting profits of the fisheries and fur seal industry completely dwarfed a sum which had loomed so large in the minds of timid congressmen. The "ineffable folly, if not wanton profligacy" of our deal with Russia turned out to be one of the shrewdest bargains the country ever concluded.

While the fisheries, fur sealing industry and gold mining early revealed Alaska's economic significance, its role as a base for air transport has more recently demonstrated many times over its tremendous strategic value to the United States. "Alaska is the most central place in the world for aircraft," Brigadier General William Mitchell even went so far as to write in 1935. "And that is true either of Europe, Asia or North America, for in the future I think whoever holds Alaska will hold the world, and I think it is the most important strategic place in the world."

With the outbreak of the Pacific war in 1941, this aspect of the territory was doubly emphasized. Whatever might have been the role of Alaska in the hands of a foreign power, its possession by the United States provided a northern anchor for a vital defensive line which stretched from the Aleutian Islands through Hawaii to the Panama Canal. Perhaps even more important, the rocky and fog-girt Aleutians had fulfilled Seward's nineteenth century prophecy. They were at last becoming "this drawbridge between America and Asia, these stepping stones across the Pacific Ocean."

2. *The Alaska Purchase—a National Decision*

A view contrary to the previous selection is advanced in the following account by R. E. Welch, a young diplomatic historian. Although at first little aware of the attractions of Alaska, public opinion as reflected in the press soon acquired knowledge and came to support the acquisition of Alaska on national grounds: its economic offerings and good harbors, and the advancement of Manifest Destiny. Friendship for Russia was of secondary importance.

American Public Opinion and the Purchase of Russian America

RICHARD E. WELCH, JR.

The American purchase of Alaska from Russia in 1867 is often cited today as an example of providential intervention in behalf of America's national security. Commentators shudder at the thought of Soviet air bases in what was once Russian America and praise the near miraculous foresight of Secretary of State William Seward.

Comprising as it does the only real estate transaction ever completed by Russia and America, Seward's annexation of Alaska properly holds a rather unique place in the diplomatic annals of both countries. The tendency of textbook writers to over-dramatize the role of Providence and to imply that Seward alone saw the value of Russian America is, however, both mistaken and unfortunate. It tends to make the Alaskan Treaty of 1867 the mysterious property of a single individual, a thing foisted on the American people and accepted by them, reluctantly, only from a sense of obligation to Russia for her supposed aid to the Union government during the Civil War. It is possibly congenial to our current self-esteem to believe that only in our generation have Americans appreciated the value of American ownership of Alaska. Such a view, if gratifying, is incorrect. Contemporary public opinion—as reflected in the newspapers of the day—was far from universally opposed to our purchase of Alaska.

The initial response of certain newspapers, upon hearing of the unexpected transaction, was one of some bewilderment. But the editorial mind of many was soon affected by the March 30th dispatch of the Associated Press, by the quantities of information eagerly supplied by the State Department, or by a reasoned weighing of the increasingly available evidence. Each of these influences requires perhaps a brief explanation.

The March 30th dispatch of the Associated Press was a lengthy account, relating the existence of the treaty, its chief provisions, and its supposed origin. It was not dictated by Secretary Seward, but he was certainly its anonymous, responsible source. The dispatch implied that the Johnson Administration, inspired by a concern for the economic welfare of our citizens in the Washington Territory, was solely responsible for initiating the treaty. The implication was clear. If this treaty was rejected,

Richard E. Welch, Jr., "American Public Opinion and the Purchase of Russian America," *The American Slavic and East European Review,* XVII (1958), 481–494. Reprinted with permission.

the innocent and obliging Russian Emperor would consider himself insulted and betrayed, and let all remember that Alexander II was the one European monarch who had "befriended" the United States during the Civil War.

The influence of the State Department on the American Press, in general, though apparent, was not conclusive. Surely Secretary Seward "planted" some information, and made available to the press certain letters he had received, various official scientific reports, and copies of Charles Sumner's eloquent speech in the Senate; surely all the information so distributed was favorable to the purchase. This need neither surprise the historian, however, nor give rise to the assumption that the press was bribed or controlled by Secretary Seward. Charges current at the time, and later, that vast sums of government money were expended by Seward to subsidize large portions of the press, seem definitely unfounded. What Seward termed his "education campaign" was neither extravagant nor illegal; indeed, it has perhaps been rather over-emphasized by certain writers. Indirectly, this educational campaign influenced both congressional approval and the acquiescence of a large part of the articulate public. It did not alone create this approval and acquiescence. Any belief in Seward's omnipotence is perhaps disproved by the fate of the Secretary's West Indian project.

For the purpose of this paper the *extent* of Seward's influence on the press is somewhat irrelevant. It is with the opinions and given reasons of American journalists that we are concerned; whether they obtained these opinions and reasons from prepared releases or original research is relatively unimportant.

The press was not dependent for information on Alaska solely from Secretary Seward, in any case. It is quite erroneous to believe that Alaska was *terra incognita* for all Americans in March, 1867. Not only had New England whalers brought back news of seal furs and walrus ivory, as well as sperm oil and ambergris, but the mishaps of the Percy Collins-Western Union Telegraph project, and the exploits of the "Rebel pirate," *Shenandoah* had acquainted various Americans with Alaska's existence. Moreover, after March, 1867, information on Alaska increased considerably, thanks to the reports of the combined coast survey-scientific expedition sent out by the Government in 1867; the research efforts of Professors Baird, Bannister, and Henry of the Smithsonian Institute; the literary labors of Frederick Whymper, artist of the ill-fated "Telegraph Expedition"; and the "Alaskan lectures" of the indefatigable William H. Dall.

Editors would also, of course, consult local leaders whose views would reflect local economic interests. New England papers, for example, mentioned the whalers of New Bedford; West Coast papers, the needs and desires of Louis Gladstone and the California fur traders.

As the initial bewilderment of many papers was overcome by second thoughts and growing information, one must not accept the first editorial comment as the considered judgment of a paper; neither must one confuse a touch of good-natured raillery with confirmed antagonism. The walrus and the polar bear lent themselves to jest and remarks of supposed wit, and even many pro-Alaska editors could not resist a facetious comment or two. James Gordon Bennett of the New York *Herald* favored the treaty, but could not forbear to print certain editor-manufactured advertisements to the effect that any impoverished European monarch who wanted to sell worthless territory "should apply to W. H. Seward, State Department, Washington, D.C."

The forty-eight newspapers consulted (for the months of April, 1867, and July, 1868) constitute, it is believed, a reasonably representative sample, geographically and politically. Most of the quotations will be found to carry an April, 1867, dateline. Very few editors seem to have taken the trouble to express any real interest in the House proceedings of July, 1868, when the appropriation bill was debated. This can perhaps be accounted for on the grounds that the physical transfer of the territory was then an accomplished fact, and the presidential campaign of 1868 well under way.

The papers consulted will be divided geographically. Chief concentration will be placed on the Eastern newspaper capitals of Boston, New York, and Philadelphia, and for all sections only those papers will be mentioned which offered opinionated editorial comment concerning the Alaskan Purchase.

The Boston press was almost uniformly favorable to the purchase, evincing no trace of fear that the Alaskan fishing grounds would affect adversely New England interests in the North Atlantic fisheries.

The Boston *Herald* (moderate Republican) of April 11, 1867, declared, regarding Alaska, that:

> . . . those who know most about it, estimate it most highly. The climate on the Pacific side [at that latitude] is not to be compared to that on the Atlantic side of the continent. . . . The country is reported to abound in furs, forest, and minerals, while its rivers and bays on its coast swarm with as fine fish as ever were caught. [Alaskan timber] will be particularly valuable in the development of our domain on the Pacific coast and the commerce of the Pacific which has just been entered upon. As to the price, there can be but one opinion—it is dog cheap.

The Boston *Daily Evening Transcript* (April 3, 1867) emphasized "the great value and growing importance of our fisheries, both for whale and cod, in the waters of the North Pacific. . . ." Though by no means ardent in its favor of the purchase, the *Transcript* seemed to think Alaska a reasonably good buy at $7,200,000 dollars. It had not changed its mind fifteen months later, though it expressed shock at the rumors that only four of the seven millions would reach Russian soil.

The Boston *Advertiser* (Democratic) warned that the "treaty is not a matter to be dismissed lightly in ignorance." There was involved "the great whale fishery of the Northern Pacific and of Behring Straits, in which Massachusetts is so deeply interested." The western tip of Alaska, moreover, would provide a commanding naval station. (April 6).

A letter to the editor (April 9) declared that the Aleutian Islands would make fine coaling stations between our country and China, and that the products of India would soon be flowing across the Pacific to America, in ever-mounting quantities.

The Republican *Daily Evening Traveller* gloated over the supposed excitement the purchase had caused among the British, and editorialized to the effect that Alaska's "chief value is now its fur trade and its fisheries; but . . . of vastly more importance than all other things, will be the command it will give us of the western and the northwestern territory of this continent."

This paper could not resist mocking (April 12) the "great change [that] has come over the American mind with respect to Russian America. Everybody is looking at Russian America, and it is discovered that that country, which *once* was scarcely supposed fit for the presence of civilized men, is one of the finest parts of the globe." The *Traveller*, however, by no means condemned the turn the public mind had taken. "It deserves praise rather than censure." Whether the bargain would be a good or bad one would depend in the final analysis on the use that should be made by America of the acquisition. ". . . the change in Russian America, there is reason to hope and expect, will prove as great as that which within living memory has taken place in the country purchased from Napoleon. . . ."

The Boston *Journal* (Republican) made little editorial comment on the purchase, but its Washington correspondent proclaimed that Sitka would follow the example of San Francisco, and in ten years would be a city of 50,000 persons.

The leading northern New England papers of the period were the Bangor (Maine) *Daily Times* and the Manchester (New Hampshire) *Daily Union*. Though for a time rather neutral, both finally concluded that the purchase was a good thing. In the opinion of the editor of the *Daily Union* (Democratic), it was well worth seven millions "to get good boundaries like the Pacific and Arctic Oceans." (April 10).

Of the seven New England papers consulted not one may be classified as an opponent of Alaskan annexation.

Among New York papers was the great journalistic opponent of the treaty, Horace Greeley's New York *Tribune* (then radical Republican). It opened fire on April 1 with a charge that the Administration was trying to divert attention from its domestic difficulties by plunging the country into foreign complications. We had no use for this territory and were putting "ourselves in the attitude of seeking ostentatiously the friendship of a power not friendly to England, and of contracting what is tantamount to an alliance for the sake of an affront."

By April 8 the *Tribune* was complaining that "national good will does not usually extend so far that one nation will sacrifice its interest merely to oblige another," and warning that Alaska was "territory on which Great Britain holds a virtual mortgage, and in which her fishermen and hunters will have equal rights with ours." On the following day the *Tribune* printed a story to the effect that Admiral Fox had once been told by Prince Gortchakoff that Russia would gladly *give* Alaska to the United States, just to be rid of it. The lobbying activities of Seward and his "Esquimaux ring" were steadily criticized by Greeley, and the Senate, when it ratified the treaty, was accused of land mania—"if it is at the North Pole, no matter." (April 10).

The *Tribune* initially expressed the hope that the House would refuse to appropriate the money to effect this hideously expensive and tax-burdensome folly, this acquisition of impossible "deserts of snow" (April 11); but by July 16, 1868, was grandly conceding: "We have not felt justified in urging the House to refuse the acquisition appropriation. We believe it was advisable to pay the money. Having received it, we wish Russia would consent to receive back the territory as a free gift from this Republic."

Of the other New York papers only the *Independent* (April 18, 1867) and the *Sun* (July 1, 20, 1868) joined the *Tribune* in real opposition to the acquisition of Alaska. The *World, Commercial Advertiser, Times,* and *Herald* were all on the other side of the fence.

The New York *World* (Democratic) was increasingly favorable to the acquisition as the first week of April, 1867, wore on. In its first editorial (April 1), it asked: "But have we done wisely in buying it? If estimated by what it is now, certainly no; if by what the purchase may hereafter lead to, perhaps yes." As an advocate of expansion the *World* was inclined to favor the treaty because, "It is an advancing step in that manifest destiny which is yet to give us British North America."

Twenty-four hours were sufficient to evoke other arguments in the treaty's favor. "The whaling merchants of New England and settlers in Oregon and California will no doubt find some way of profiting by the annexation. . . . Our commerce . . . ought pretty certainly to be benefited by the opening of ports along this extreme verge of the continent, and by the attendant expansion of the fur trade and the fisheries."

The New York *Commercial Advertiser* (Democratic) was both pro-Seward and pro-treaty, and in the New York *Times* the purchase had one of its most influential advocates.

> While narrow minded political bigots have been exhausting all their resources in branding him [Seward] as a traitor to his party, he has been quietly pursuing great objects of permanent and paramount interest for his country. The main importance of this acquisition grows out of its bearing upon our future trade with Japan, China, and the other countries of Eastern Asia. . . . Reluctant as that body [the Senate] may be to accept even so great a boon as this from the hands of the President and Mr. Seward, its sense of public duty will constrain its ratification. (*Times,* April 1).

With its next issue the *Times* was ready boldly to declare that the purchase was "a natural though perhaps unexpected consummation of negotiations dating back to the time of Monroe, and its tendency is to lessen the likelihood of 'further entanglements' by removing Russia from the diplomatic area so far as the future policy of this continent is concerned."

In later editorials it mentioned the undeveloped coal seams of the new territory, spoke of the possibilities of the Aleutian Islands as a naval station, and declared that seven millions "was a mere bagatelle compared with the magnitude and importance of the acquisition." (April 8, 10).

The New York *Herald* (Republican) favored the treaty mainly on grounds of international policy:

> Politically considered, however, this cession of Russian Alaska becomes a matter of great importance. It indicates the extent to which Russia is ready to carry out her "entente cordiale" with the United States. . . . it places British possessions on the Pacific coast in the uncomfortable position of a hostile cockney with a watchful Yankee on each side of him. . . . [It is a] flank movement for this greater object (Canada). . . . we are satisfied that the proposed purchase from its political bearings will be at once approved by the public sentiment of the country and will, perhaps, be considered a bargain at seven millions, simply as a speculation in fish oil and the fur business. (April 1).

The *Herald* was a sharp critic of the "pushing" tactics of Mr. Seward, however, and with reference to Seward's "promotional" dinner parties declared: "But with his Pennsylvania roast beef, his Virginia oysters, his smoked walrus from Behring Strait, his Esquimaux stews and ice, his California wines and Kentucky Bourbon, his seven millions and the lobby, the undaunted Seward, perhaps, will best them yet" (April 9).

Despite such exercises in literary irony, the *Herald* was a treaty advocate. The leading paper in extracting names and quotes from the executive sessions of the Senate, and the first paper to publish the treaty text, the *Herald* was sure that this new empire, "in area more than twice the size of France" would prove valuable as a factor in the international scene and valuable, too, for its fisheries, whales, fur trade, and coal. (April 12).

The New York Evening *Post* demonstrated an inexplicable example of editorial indecision. In its first edition of April 1, it declared that the territory was a "frozen, sterile, desert region . . . of no value present or prospective . . ." In its second edition of the same date, it asserted: "The purchase of the Russian Territory is a step towards the retrieval of this blunder [the Oregon 'Compromise' of 1846] not only by giving us the undisputed prominence on the American coast of the Pacific, but by pushing it out of the power of England to extend her territory in that quarter." The forests there were immensely valuable, its agricultural capabilities had never been developed, and, as for its fisheries, "the advantage of our whaling and fishing interest in these northern seas, in having always ports of their own country to run into, will develop its value with the advance of our population in the Pacific."

On April 8, however, the *Post* declared, "We hope the Senate will reject the proposed purchase." The next day it spoke in resigned tones of the acquisition, and on April 19, went so far as to make plans for the future of the various areas of Alaska when "the increase of population and of trade requires a division of the territory."

The only thing that seems certain about the attitude of the *Post* is that it was neither decisively for or against the treaty. Of the seven New York papers which took a definite stand, four were, on balance, favorable to Alaskan annexation.

In Philadelphia the editor of the *Inquirer* (Republican) was a most ardent advocate of the purchase:

> [Alaska] might become very useful to any power having naval interests in the Pacific. . . . A time may come, when the possession of this territory will give us the command over the Pacific, which our extensive possessions there require. (April 1).
>
> . . . If there is any value in the timber, furs, and fisheries of that region, and it must be great, the consideration of the cost of the territorial government is not worthy of a moment's thought. (April 8).

The *Inquirer's* Washington correspondent was equally enthusiastic over the territory's possibilities and spoke of the Pacific Coast's desire for Alaska, and of the treaty's value in preserving the Union Party in the Far West. Numerous letters to the editor were published, all of them favorable to the purchase.

The Philadelphia *Ledger* (Democratic) was less decided in its support of the treaty, but despite some merriment over the possibilities of political elections among the polar bears (April 11), offered no real objection to the treaty. The expansionist-minded *North American Gazette* (Republican) also favored the results of Seward's latest project. Philadelphia, indeed, produced little or no journalistic opposition to Seward's treaty.

Moving South, the press of Washington, D.C. was generally favorable. The Washington *Evening Star* scouted the opposition to the treaty, jibing that it paralleled the foolish reluctance of some in 1803 to accept the Louisiana Purchase. It viewed the treaty as a proper piece of expansionism and dogmatically pronounced: "There are few full-blooded Americans who do not devoutly believe in the doctrine that this country is to absorb not only Russian America, but all the British possessions in North America." (December 21).

The *National Intelligencer* was equally convinced:

> The Russian possessions will secure us furs, fish and lumber in the greatest abundance to say nothing of the undisputed route of an overland telegraph. The fisheries, in the hands of our hardy seamen, would be of priceless value, and, as we are soon to have the Pacific railway, which will give an extraordinary impetus, we wonder that American statesmen should hesitate. (April 5).

The *National Republican* voiced its support in turn. In an editorial entitled, "Now is the Day and Hour for the Confirmation of the Treaty with Russia" (April 6), it lectured to the following effect: "American civilization has pushed itself through to the Pacific sea, where a commerce is growing up . . . which demands that the United States have absolute sovereignty over the entire coast from California to Bhering [*sic*] Straits." In listing various reasons for desiring the territory, the *National Republican* mentioned the protection it would afford our fisheries and fishermen there, the splendid nature of the rivers and harbors of Russian America, the territory's use as a broad base of trade with Japan and China, and the chance it gave us to fill out and protect our Continental Republic. The friendship of Russia was noted by way of further justification, and the warning given that "if we shall ever need the aid of any foreign power . . . it will be the immense and almost immaculate power of Russia." (April 8).

Whatever might have been the case when the purchase was before the House, it is most likely that John Forney's *Daily Morning Chronicle* was a free and unbribed agent in April, 1867, quite uninfluenced by the labors of former Senator Robert Walker or the purse of Minister Stoeckl. In this early and "amateur" phase, the *Chronicle* heartily applauded the treaty, if not with the violence it was to exhibit later: "Our people have faith in the manifest destiny of the nation. They look to the eventual absorption of the whole North American continent, and the Senate has undoubtedly gratified a national instinct in ratifying the treaty. . . ." (April 11).

The favor with which the *Chronicle* received this treaty is indicated by its quoting in full—and with marked approval—an editorial in the Rochester (New York) *Democrat*, which virtually eulogized the possibilities of the Alaskan territory.

The Wilmington (Delaware) *Daily Commercial* favored the acquisition of the territory, but opposed its purchase: "It seems to us the worst of policies, for it . . . is certainly to become ultimately the property of our Yankee nation, and we consider it fair to presume at a price next to nothing at all. If this were our last chance, and the lowest offer likely to be made, we might urge its acceptance. . . ." (April 4).

The Baltimore *Sun* (Democratic) and *American and Commercial Advertiser* (Republican) were not so economy-minded. The latter printed the highly favorable and nationally quoted Associated Press dispatch of March 31 as its first news of the treaty, and followed this up with a pair of editorials in which the value of the area's fisheries and fur trade was discussed at great length.

The *Daily Journal* of Wilmington, North Carolina approved the purchase only "in view of ulterior events." The expansion of the fur trade and whale fisheries on the Pacific Coast and the increased likelihood of garnering the British possessions in North America furnished such "events." (April 4).

The Louisville (Kentucky) *Daily Journal* favored the treaty, observing: "The great commercial advantages secured by it are universally admitted." (April 3).

The Memphis *Daily Post* (moderate Republican) urged the purchase in these terms:

> In view of our growing commerce in the Pacific, the establishment of lines of steamers to run regularly between China, Japan, and Australia, the increase of the coastwise trade, the completion of the Pacific Railroad and the Russo-American telegraph . . . the acquisition of this vast possession is desirable, and seven millions of dollars is a small consideration to pay for it. (April 5).

The Memphis paper, however, reviled the manner in which Seward had "unscrupulously urged" the treaty, and insisted that the actions of the

Secretary and the President in this connection would further damn them in the eyes of the public. (April 15).

The Washington dispatches of both the Savannah *Daily Republican* and the Augusta *Daily Press* included press releases, telegrams and Seward-inspired "reports from Washington" highly favorable to the purchase.

Of the New Orleans papers the *Commercial Bulletin* seems to have been the most enthusiastic, virtually urging an alliance between the now-enlarged Northwest and the South:

> The demands for cotton goods in the new region of the Northwest will be enormous, and there is no reason why these goods should not be manufactured in the South, thereby employing our poor and industrious population, and adding greatly to our resources. . . . it will be seen that the South will be greatly advanced by the acquisition and settlement of the Russian American possessions. (April 15).

The New Orleans *Times* and the newborn New Orleans *Republican* contained a large number of dispatches and letters favorable to the purchase, but *La Tribune de la Nouvelle-Orleans* had mild doubts about the value of the territory. It suspected that if the Russians were willing to shed the territory it must be of little value. (". . . évidemment inutile aux Russes, elle ne peut pas être d'un bien grand profit pour les Americains.") (April 3).

The Galveston *Republican,* though making no editorial comment, printed at considerable length the panegyric on Alaska delivered by Representative Banks during the debate in the House. (July 13).

Of the sixteen Southern newspapers consulted, only two may be labelled outright opponents of the Alaskan Purchase.

In the Middle West, the city of Chicago saw its two leading papers somewhat divided on the desirability of Alaska. The *Evening Journal* cheered the purchase without qualification of any kind, but the reaction of the *Republican* was less clear. The Washington correspondent of that paper was vehemently anti-treaty; its editor, tepidly favorable. The same issue of the *Republican* that found the correspondent calling the treaty a "huge farce," found the editor pontificating that it was "very natural that Russia and the United States should form an alliance. . . . Russia has demonstrated her good faith in this matter by ceding to our Government all her possessions on the American continent." (April 1). Even though the editor jocosely declared some four days later that the real reason for the purchase was to give the Fenians a base of operations, and even later (April 13) spoke of the danger of soon seeing in the House a representative from Sitka "dressed in a grizzly bear-skin overcoat and seal-skin unmentionables," the attitude of the paper seems to have been, on the whole, one of hesitant favor. "As evidence of the good will of the Russian Government toward the United States, this treaty has its chief significance. Future explorations may prove it to be rich in mines, while it will undoubtedly prove of increasing value to the Pacific states for its fisheries." (April 10).

The Cincinnati *Daily Gazette* rather opposed the purchase, but its sister paper, the *Commercial,* favored it. Other affirmative voices were those of the Detroit Free *Press* and the St. Louis *Times* and *Daily Missouri Democrat.* The latter stressed the wonderful effect of the Japanese current on the climate of Alaska, and asserted that the acquisition "affords another perspective of Uncle Samuel's 'manifest destiny' to absorb the continent." (April 11).

The Alaskan Treaty does not seem to have interested Mid-Western editors to the extent it did those on the East and West coasts, but even the few examples given show that the press of this section was in no sense solidly opposed to the purchase.

What then can be said of the reaction of the press as a whole? First, that all statements to the effect that the newspapers were uniformly unfavorable to the treaty are erroneous. Secondly, that though the sample of newspapers consulted is perhaps too small to support any sweeping generalizations, it can be suggested that a majority of the American press seems either to have favored the treaty or at least not to have been opposed to it. Thirdly, that neither the political allegiance nor the geographic location of a newspaper was usually decisive in determining its stand. Finally, that the main arguments advanced by the press in support of the purchase, listed perhaps in order of increasing importance, were: the propriety of maintaining the friendship of Russia; the possibility that the purchase would facilitate the acquisition of British Columbia and generally promote our predestined expansion and power; and the probability that we should derive great economic benefits from the purchase.

"Russian friendship" and the "assistance" Russia gave the Federal Government during the Civil War was often mentioned by the American press, though usually as an auxiliary argument.

Contemporary press opinion indicates that there was a good deal of latent expansionism in the United States in 1867. The Civil War had caused certain Americans to think for the first time of the desirability of such objects as naval and commercial bases, and that quasi-mystical doctrine, "Manifest Destiny," had still its supporters. Belief in the inevitable and benevolent assimilation of North America by the politically and morally superior United States was nurtured in many an editorial heart and column. In so far as Manifest Destiny was basically an agrarian movement, the desire of certain Americans for Alaska was not an offshoot of Manifest Destiny. But Manifest Destiny also had its "commercial" side, and in this sense, the Purchase was the vestigial remain of that nation-shaping doctrine. Certain papers emphasized the importance of Alaska's harbors for our Oriental trade, and more spoke of the necessity of checking British expansion and securing a favorable balance of power for the United States in the Pacific West. Various editors on the Pacific Coast went so far as to express hope that the purchase of Alaska, by putting British Columbia in "an American vice," would mean the ultimate acquisition of that choice and strategic area by the United States.

The chief argument of those members of the press who supported the purchase, however, was that, in economic terms, Alaska was worth the purchase price. Because of its supposed resources in fish, whales, furs, timber, and minerals, because of its very real commercial value, Alaska was thought a good bargain.

These were arguments and motives that could have clear appeal for the average educated American. Surely they were such as to deter press or public from howling in united chorus, "Seward's Folly!"

Additional Reading

T. A. Bailey, *America Faces Russia* (1950).

D. M. Dozer, "Anti-Expansionism during the Johnson Administration," *Pacific Historical Review*, XII (1943), 253–275.

V. J. Farrar, *The Annexation of Russian America to the United States* (1937).

B. P. Thomas, *Russo-American Relations, 1815–1867* (1930).

William A. Williams, *American-Russian Relations, 1781–1941* (1952).

PART II

Emergence of the United States as a Great World Power

1890-1963

INTRODUCTION

The major themes in American diplomatic history after 1889 are the emergence of the United States as a major world power and the reflection in its foreign policies of the domestic conflict between the "isolationists" and the "internationalists."

From birth, the United States was a world power, as historian T. A. Bailey has pointed out, seriously considered by European states in matters affecting the Western Hemisphere. In the watershed or transitional decade of the 1890's, America clearly became a major or great world power whose wealth, population, and potential military strength made it important in the scales of the global balance of power. The United States began to build a modern navy and to become greatly interested in overseas markets and bases, and in 1898 had a spectacular "coming-out" party in the brief but eminently satisfying Spanish-American War. By 1900 these developments, including acquisition of overseas empire, had inextricably involved America in international politics.

Yet the American people retained a psychological isolationism. In the 19th century, as historian C. Vann Woodward has aptly described it, the United States had enjoyed a long period of "free security," of relative immunity from external threats. This had resulted less from American power and efforts, and more from the existence of a favorable power structure in Europe capped by the generally benevolent sea power of Great Britain. Although this condition ended by 1914, most Americans failed to appreciate the change and remained committed to the older isolationist policies and sentiments. By the turn of the 20th century, the balance of power in Europe and the Far East was shifting and a cycle of incredibly destructive wars was in the offing. The United States henceforth would have to pay a much higher price for security.

By the 1960's, two world wars and a "police action" later, Americans at last were accepting the fact of inescapable involvement and responsibilities in world affairs. Even so, it was for many a most reluctant acceptance—hence the often bitter post-1945 debates over foreign aid and levels of military strength. Isolationism perhaps was dead as a viable policy, but its emotional attitudes have lingered and maturity in foreign affairs is by no means yet achieved.

10 *THE SPANISH-AMERICAN WAR: A Popular Crusade?*

The United States had attained a high level of agricultural and industrial production by the 1890's and was in the flush of a newly aroused interest in world affairs. Reconstruction was over, the frontier process largely completed, population neared seventy millions, and economic production had achieved such miracles of abundance as apparently to require a more vigorous drive for external markets and raw material sources of supply. Psychologically, the generation of the 1890's was in an expansionist and adventurous mood. Civil War bloodshed and suffering had been dimmed by the passage of time, and nationalism had welled to a new peak of intensity. The result was what historians describe as a revival of Manifest Destiny, a revival of a conviction that America was destined to play a more active role in the world and a renewed interest in overseas colonies and coaling stations. The quickened national tempo was expressed in a number of ways: the launching of the modern Pan American movement in 1889, rivalry with Germany and Great Britain in Samoa, annexation schemes for Hawaii, and clashes with Chile and Great Britain in the Western Hemisphere. The new spirit culminated in the 1898 Spanish-American War over Cuba.

The war in 1898 raises several important questions for students of history. Why did the United States intervene in the Cuban strife, after an earlier abstention during the equally bloody Ten Years' War (1868–1878)? What role did endangered American economic interests in Cuba have in the decision for war? What was the attitude of the big business community within the United States? Was the sensationalist press primarily responsible for the popular demand for intervention? And, finally, why did a war to free Cuba transform the United States into an imperial power?

DOCUMENTS

1. McKinley Decides for War

On March 25 and 27, 1898, Assistant Secretary of State William R. Day instructed the American Minister Stewart L. Woodford to request of the Spanish government the proclamation of an armistice in Cuba until October, the revocation of the reconcentration policy affecting the Cuban population in rebellious areas, and acceptance of American mediation. Although Woodford's reports, on April 9 and 10, indicated that the Madrid regime was beginning to comply, President McKinley in effect asked Congress on April 11 to declare war. Subsequently, historians have roundly condemned him for thus rejecting a peaceful solution and capitulating to popular jingoistic pressures. Yet it should be noted,

as his message made clear, the costly patience of the American government in the preceding three years of the civil war. It was by no means probable that the Cuban rebels would accept the armistice and the Spanish authorities were not prepared to consent to an American mediation culminating in Cuban independence.

Congress authorized the use of force on April 19 and war was declared subsequently as of April 21.

McKinley's Address to Congress, April 11, 1898

EXECUTIVE MANSION, April 11, 1898

To the Congress of the United States:

Obedient to that precept of the Constitution which commands the President to give from time to time to the Congress information of the state of the Union and to recommend to their consideration such measures as he shall judge necessary and expedient, it becomes my duty to now address your body with regard to the grave crisis that has arisen in the relations of the United States to Spain by reason of the warfare that for more than three years has raged in the neighboring island of Cuba.

I do so because of the intimate connection of the Cuban question with the state of our own Union and the grave relation the course which it is now incumbent upon the nation to adopt must needs bear to the traditional policy of our Government if it is to accord with the precepts laid down by the founders of the Republic and religiously observed by succeeding Administrations to the present day.

The present revolution is but the successor of other similar insurrections which have occurred in Cuba against the dominion of Spain, extending over a period of nearly half a century, each of which during its progress has subjected the United States to great effort and expense in enforcing its neutrality laws, caused enormous losses to American trade and commerce, caused irritation, annoyance, and disturbance among our citizens, and, by the exercise of cruel, barbarous, and uncivilized practices of warfare, shocked the sensibilities and offended the humane sympathies of our people. . . .

Our people have beheld a once prosperous community reduced to comparative want, its lucrative commerce virtually paralyzed, its exceptional productiveness diminished, its fields laid waste, its mills in ruins, and its people perishing by tens of thousands from hunger and destitution. We have found ourselves constrained, in the observance of that strict neutrality which our laws enjoin and which the law of nations commands, to police our own waters and watch our own seaports in prevention of any unlawful act in aid of the Cubans.

Our trade has suffered, the capital invested by our citizens in Cuba has been largely lost, and the temper and forbearance of our people have been so sorely tried as to beget a perilous unrest among our own citizens, which has inevitably found its expression from time to time in the National Legislature, so that issues wholly external to our own body politic engross attention and stand in the way of that close devotion to domestic advancement that becomes a self-contained commonwealth whose primal maxim has been the avoidance of all foreign entanglements. All this must needs awaken, and has, indeed, aroused, the utmost concern on the part of this Government, as well during my predecessor's term as in my own. . . .

The war in Cuba is of such a nature that, short of subjugation or extermination, a final military victory for either side seems impracticable. The alternative lies in the physical exhaustion of the one or the other party, or perhaps of both—a condition which in effect ended the ten years' war by the truce of Zanjon. The prospect of such a protraction and conclusion of the present strife is a contingency hardly to be contemplated with equanimity by the civilized world, and least of all by the United States, affected and injured as we are, deeply and intimately, by its very existence.

Realizing this, it appeared to be my duty, in a spirit of true friendliness, no less to Spain than to the Cubans, who have so much to lose by the prolongation of the struggle, to seek to bring about an immediate termination of the war. To this end I submitted on the 27th ultimo, as a result of much representation and correspondence, through the United States minister at Madrid, propositions to the Spanish Government looking to an armistice until October 1 for the negotiation of peace with the good offices of the President.

In addition I asked the immediate revocation of the order of reconcentration, so as to permit the people to return to their farms and the needy to be relieved with provisions and supplies from the United States, cooperating with the Spanish authorities, so as to afford full relief.

The reply of the Spanish cabinet was received on the night of the 31st ultimo. It offered, as the means to bring about peace in Cuba, to confide the preparation thereof to the insular parliament, inasmuch as the concurrence of that body would be necessary to reach a final result, it being, however, understood that the powers reserved by the constitution to the central Government are not lessened or diminished. As the Cuban parliament does not meet until the 4th of May next, the Spanish Government would not object for its part to accept at once a suspension of hostilities if asked for by the insurgents from the general in chief, to whom it would pertain in such case to determine the duration and conditions of the armistice. . . .

With this last overture in the direction of immediate peace, and its disappointing reception by Spain, the Executive is brought to the end of his effort. . . .

The grounds for . . . intervention may be briefly summarized as follows:

First. In the cause of humanity and to put an end to the barbarities, bloodshed, starvation, and horrible miseries now existing there, and which the parties to the conflict are either unable or unwilling to stop or mitigate. It is no answer to say this is all in another country, belonging to another nation, and is therefore none of our business. It is specially our duty, for it is right at our door.

Second. We owe it to our citizens in Cuba to afford them that protection and indemnity for life and property which no government there can or will afford, and to that end to terminate the conditions that deprive them of legal protection.

Third. The right to intervene may be justified by the very serious injury to the commerce, trade, and business of our people and by the wanton destruction of property and devastation of the island.

Fourth, and which is of the utmost importance. The present condition of affairs in Cuba is a constant menace to our peace and entails upon this Government an enormous expense. With such a conflict waged for years in an island so near us and with which our people have such trade and business relations; when the lives and liberty of our citizens are in constant danger and their property destroyed and themselves ruined; where our trading vessels are liable to seizure and are seized at our very door by war ships of a foreign nation; the expeditions of filibustering that we are powerless to prevent altogether, and the irritating questions and entanglements thus arising—all these and others that I need not mention, with the resulting strained relations, are a constant menace to our peace and compel us to keep on a semi war footing with a nation with which we are at peace. . . .

In view of these facts and of these considerations I ask the Congress to authorize and empower the President to take measures to secure a full and final termination of hostilities between the Government of Spain and the people of Cuba, and to secure in the island the establishment of a stable government, capable of maintaining order and observing its international obligations, insuring peace and tranquillity and the security of its citizens as well as our own, and to use the military and naval forces of the United States as may be necessary for these purposes.

And in the interest of humanity and to aid in preserving the lives of the starving people of the island I recommend that the distribution of food and supplies be continued and that an appropriation be made out of the public Treasury to supplement the charity of our citizens.

The issue is now with the Congress. It is a solemn responsibility. I have exhausted every effort to relieve the intolerable condition of affairs which is at our doors. Prepared to execute every obligation imposed upon me by the Constitution and the law, I await your action.

Yesterday, and since the preparation of the foregoing message, official information was received by me that the latest decree of the Queen Regent of Spain directs General Blanco, in order to prepare and facilitate peace, to proclaim a suspension of hostilities, the duration and details of which have not yet been communicated to me.

This fact, with every other pertinent consideration, will, I am sure, have your just and careful attention in the solemn deliberations upon which you are about to enter. If this measure attains a successful result, then our aspirations as a Christian, peace-loving people will be realized. If it fails, it will be only another justification for our contemplated action.

2. *The March of the Flag*

Entering the war to free Cuba, the United States ended it by annexing Puerto Rico, Guam, and the Philippine Islands. Spain was compensated in the peace treaty, signed December 10, 1898, by the sum of 20 million dollars. President McKinley explained to a group of visiting Methodists the mixture of motives—economic, patriotic and missionary—for the decision to acquire the Philippines. Albert J. Beveridge, Republican Senator from Indiana and an ardent expansionist, expressed the same arguments more fully in a flamboyant address known as the "March of the Flag."

McKinley Explains Acquisition of the Philippines

. . . The truth is I didn't want the Philippines, and when they came to us, as a gift from the gods, I did not know what to do with them. When the Spanish War broke out, Dewey was at Hongkong, and I ordered him to go to Manila and to capture or destroy the Spanish fleet, and he had to; because, if defeated, he had no place to refit on that side of the globe, and if the Dons were victorious, they would likely cross the Pacific and ravage our Oregon and California coasts. And so he had to destroy the Spanish fleet, and did it! But that was as far as I thought then.

When next I realized that the Philippines had dropped into our laps I confess I did not know what to do with them. I sought counsel from all sides—Democrats as well as Republicans—but got little help. I thought first we would take only Manila; then Luzon; then other islands, perhaps, also. I walked the floor of the White House night after night until midnight; and I am not ashamed to tell you, gentlemen, that I went down on my knees and prayed Almighty God for light and guidance more than one night. And one night late it came to me this way—I don't know how it was, but it came: (1) That we could not give them back to Spain—that would be cowardly and dishonorable; (2) that we could not turn them over to France or Germany—our commercial rivals in the Orient—that would be bad business and discreditable; (3) that we could not leave them to themselves—they were unfit for self-government—and they would soon have anarchy and misrule over there worse than Spain's was; and (4) that there was nothing left for us to do but to take them all, and to educate the Filipinos, and uplift and civilize and Christianize them, and by God's grace do the very best we could by them, as our fellow-men for whom Christ also died. And then I went to bed, and went to sleep, and slept soundly, and the next morning I sent for the chief engineer of the War Department (our map-maker), and I told him to put the Philippines on the map of the United States [pointing to a large map on the wall of his office], and there they are, and there they will stay while I am President!

Albert J. Beveridge's "March of the Flag" Speech

Fellow citizens, It is a noble land that God has given us; a land that can feed and clothe the world; a land whose coast lines would enclose half the countries of Europe; a land set like a sentinel between the two imperial oceans of the globe, a greater England with a nobler destiny. It is a mighty people that he has planted on this soil; a people sprung from the most masterful blood of history; a people perpetually revitalized by the virile, man-producing workingfolk of all the earth; a people imperial by virtue of their power, by right of their institutions, by authority of their heaven-directed purposes—the propagandists and not the misers of liberty. It is a glorious history our God has bestowed upon his chosen people; a history whose keynote was struck by Liberty Bell; a history heroic with faith in our mission and our future; a history of statesmen who flung the boundaries of the Republic out into unexplored lands and savage wildernesses; a history of soldiers who carried the flag across the blazing deserts and through the ranks of hostile mountains, even to the gates of sunset; a history of a multiplying people who overran a continent in half a century; a history of prophets who saw the consequences of evils inherited from the past and of martyrs who died to save us from them; a history divinely logical, in the process of whose tremendous reasoning we find ourselves today.

. . . Shall the American people continue their resistless march toward the commercial supremacy of the world? Shall free institutions broaden their blessed reign as the children of liberty wax in strength, until the empire of our principles is established over the hearts of all mankind?

Have we no mission to perform, no duty to discharge to our fellowman? Has the Almighty Father endowed us with gifts beyond our deserts and marked us as the people of his peculiar favor, merely to rot in our own selfishness, as men and nations must, who take cowardice for their companion and self for their Deity—as China has, as India has, as Egypt has?

Shall we be as the man who had one talent and hid it, or as he who had ten talents and used them until they grew to riches? And shall we reap the reward that waits on our discharge of our high duty as the sovereign power of earth; shall we occupy new markets for what our farmers raise, new markets for what our factories make, new markets for what our merchants sell—aye, and, please God, new markets for what our ships shall carry?

Shall we avail ourselves of new sources of supply of what we do not raise or make, so that what are luxuries to-day will be necessities to-morrow? Shall our commerce be encouraged until, with Oceanica, the Orient, and the world, American trade shall be the imperial trade of the entire globe? . . .

. . . For William McKinley is continuing the policy that Jefferson began, Monroe continued, Seward advanced, Grant promoted, Harrison championed, and the growth of the republic has demanded. Hawaii is ours; Porto Rico is to be ours; at the prayer of the people Cuba will finally be ours; in the islands of the East, even to the gates of Asia, coaling-stations are to be ours; at the very least the flag of a liberal government is to float over the Philippines, and I pray God it may be the banner that

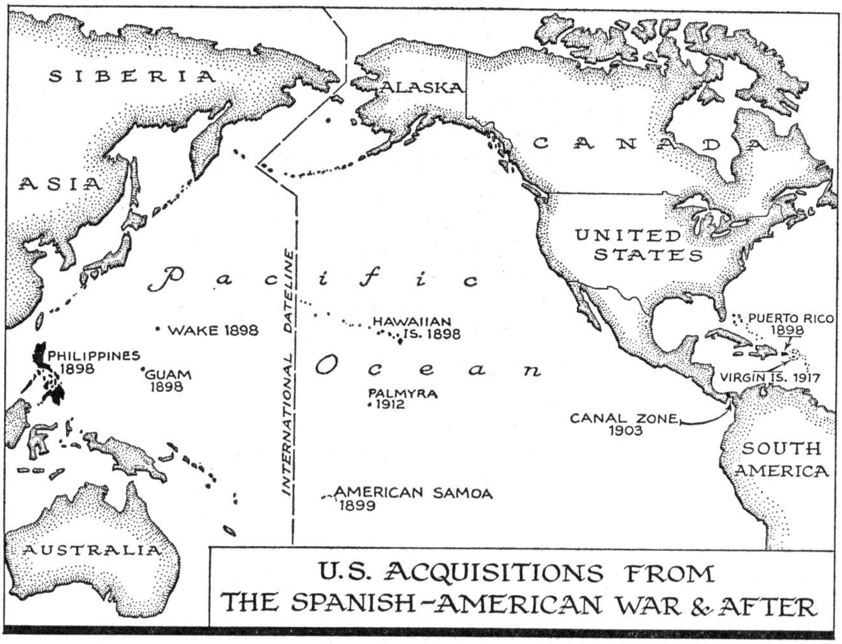

U.S. ACQUISITIONS FROM THE SPANISH-AMERICAN WAR & AFTER

Taylor unfurled in Texas and Fremont carried to the coast—the Stars and Stripes of glory. . . .

The Opposition tells us that we ought not to govern a people without their consent. I answer, The rule of liberty that all just government derives its authority from the consent of the governed, applies only to those who are capable of self-government. I answer, We govern the Indians without their consent, we govern our territories without their consent, we govern our children without their consent. I answer, How do you assume that our government would be without their consent? Would not the people of the Philippines prefer the just, humane, civilizing government of this republic to the savage, bloody rule of pillage and extortion from which we have rescued them?

. . . And, now, obeying the same voice that Jefferson heard and obeyed, that Jackson heard and obeyed, that Monroe heard and obeyed, that Seward heard and obeyed, that Ulysses S. Grant heard and obeyed, that Benjamin Harrison heard and obeyed, William McKinley plants the flag over the islands of the seas, outposts of commerce, citadels of national security, and the march of the flag goes on! . . .

Distance and oceans are no arguments. . . .

Steam joins us; electricity joins us—the very elements are in league with our destiny. Cuba not contiguous! Porto Rico not contiguous! Hawaii and the Philippines not contiguous! Our navy will make them contiguous. Dewey and Sampson and Schley have made them contiguous, and American speed, American guns, American heart and brain and nerve will keep them contiguous forever. . . .

. . . to-day, we are raising more than we can consume. To-day, we are making more than we can use. To-day, our industrial society is congested; there are more workers than there is work; there is more capital than there is investment. We do not need more money—we need more circulation, more employment. Therefore we must find new markets for our produce, new occupation for our capital, new work for our labor. And so, while we did not need the territory taken during the past century at the time it was acquired, we do need what we have taken in 1898, and we need it now.

Think of the thousands of Americans who will pour into Hawaii and Porto Rico when the republic's laws cover those islands with justice and safety! Think of the tens of thousands of Americans who will invade mine and field and forest in the Philippines when a liberal government, protected and controlled by this republic, if not the government of the republic itself, shall establish order and equity there! Think of the hundreds of thousands of Americans who will build a soap-and-water, common-school civilization of energy and industry in Cuba, when a government of law replaces the double reign of anarchy and tyranny!—think of the prosperous millions that Empress of Islands will support when, obedient to the law of political gravitation, her people ask for the highest honor liberty can bestow, the sacred Order of the Stars and Stripes, the citizenship of the Great Republic!

What does all this mean for every one of us? It means opportunity for all the glorious young manhood of the republic—the most virile, ambitious, impatient, militant manhood the world has ever seen. It means that the resources and the commerce of these immensely rich dominions will be increased as much as American energy is greater than Spanish sloth; for Americans henceforth will monopolize those resources and that commerce. . . .

Fellow Americans, we are God's chosen people. Yonder at Bunker Hill and Yorktown his providence was above us. At New Orleans and on ensanguined seas his hand sustained us. Abraham Lincoln was his minister and his was the Altar of Freedom, the boys in blue set on a hundred battlefields. His power directed Dewey in the East and delivered the Spanish fleet into our hands on the eve of Liberty's natal day, as he delivered the elder Armada into the hands of our English sires two centuries ago. His great purposes are revealed in the progress of the flag, which surpasses the intentions of Congresses and Cabinets, and leads us like a holier pillar of cloud by day and pillar of fire by night into situations unforeseen by finite wisdom, and duties unexpected by the unprophetic heart of selfishness. The American people cannot use a dishonest medium of exchange; it is ours to set the world its example of right and honor. We cannot fly from our world duties; it is ours to execute the purpose of a fate that has driven us to be greater than our small intentions. We cannot retreat from any soil where Providence has unfurled our banner; it is ours to save that soil for Liberty and Civilization. For Liberty and Civilization and God's promise fulfilled, the flag must henceforth be the symbol and the sign to all mankind—the flag!—

Flag of the free heart's hope and home,
By angel hands to valor given,
Thy stars have lit the welkin dome,
And all their hues were born in heaven!
Forever wave that standard sheet,
Where breathes the foe but falls before us,
With freedom's soil beneath our feet
And freedom's banner streaming o'er us.

READINGS

1. Economics and the Spanish War

Several historians, including Charles A. Beard, have explained American imperialism and the Spanish war on economic grounds: the desire for markets, and the 150 million American dollars invested in Cuban sugar and trade. Challenging that interpretation, Julius W. Pratt, in the following selection, examines the attitude of business groups toward intervention in Cuba and demonstrates conclusively that powerful economic groups were opposed to war in 1897 and early 1898. Yet there can be little doubt that economic interests were to some degree involved in the revival of Manifest Destiny in the 1890's, and played an even more significant role in the decision to retain the Philippines.

Expansionists of 1898

JULIUS W. PRATT

. . . So reliable a scholar as Professor H. U. Faulkner has asserted that "the great cause for the war" with Spain is to be found in the fact that by 1898 the United States was "sufficiently advanced for financial imperialism," implying that the war was fought for markets and fields for investment. This interpretation was directly contradicted by the late James Ford Rhodes, who declared quite as categorically that "the financial and business interests of the country were opposed to the war." We may well enquire, therefore, what was, in reality, the attitude of American business both to the war (or to the intervention in Cuba, which brought on the war) and to the question of territorial expansion.

We may begin with a generalization, the evidence for which will be presented as the chapter proceeds. American business, in general, had strongly opposed action that would lead to war with Spain. American business had been either opposed or indifferent to the expansionist philosophy which had arisen since 1890. But almost at the moment when the war began, a large section of American business had, for reasons that will become apparent, been converted to the belief that a program of territorial expansion would serve its purposes. Hence business, in the end, welcomed the "large policy" and exerted its share of pressure

Julius W. Pratt, *Expansionists of 1898* (Baltimore: The Johns Hopkins Press, 1936), 232–237, 239–242, 246, 248–252, 266–267, 273–274, 278. Reprinted with permission.

for the retention of the Spanish islands and such related policies as the annexation of Hawaii and the construction of an isthmian canal.

One public man to whom the welfare of American business was of so much concern that he may almost be considered its spokesman in the Senate, was McKinley's friend, Mark Hanna. No one was more unwilling than he to see the United States drift into war with Spain. To Hanna, in the words of his biographer, "the outbreak of war seemed to imperil the whole policy of domestic economic amelioration which he placed before every other object of political action." Hanna's attitude appears to have been identical with that of leading business men. This conclusion is based not only upon the few published biographies of such men, but also upon the study of a large number of financial and trade periodicals, of the proceedings of chambers of commerce and boards of trade, and of material in the *Miscellaneous Files* of the Department of State, containing numerous letters and petitions from business men and organizations.

That business sentiment, especially in the East, was strongly anti-war at the close of 1897 and in the opening months of 1898, is hardly open to doubt. Wall Street stocks turned downward whenever the day's news seemed to presage war and climbed again with information favorable to peace. Bulls and bears on the market were those who anticipated, respectively, a peaceable and a warlike solution of the Cuban question. The "jingo," in Congress or the press, was an object of intense dislike to the editors of business and financial journals, who sought to counteract his influence by anti-war editorials in their columns. Boards of trade and chambers of commerce added their pleas for the maintenance of peace to those of the business newspapers and magazines. So marked, indeed, was the anti-war solidarity of the financial interests and their spokesmen that the jingoes fell to charging Wall Street with want of patriotism. Wall Street, declared the Sacramento *Evening Bee* (March 11, 1898), was "the colossal and aggregate Benedict Arnold of the Union, and the syndicated Judas Iscariot of humanity." Senator Thurston, of Nebraska, charged that opposition to war was found only among the "money-changers," bringing from the editor of *The American Banker* the reply that "there is not an intelligent, self-respecting and civilized American citizen anywhere who would not prefer to have the existing crisis culminate in peaceful negotiations."

This anti-war attitude on the part of several leading financial journals continued up to the very beginning of hostilities. The New York *Journal of Commerce and Commercial Bulletin* declared on February 28 that the only possible excuses for war would be (1) a finding by the naval board investigating the "Maine" disaster that the ship had been destroyed by an official act of the Spanish Government; or (2) a refusal by Spain to make reparation if the board should hold that she had failed to exercise due diligence in safeguarding the vessel. Either of these events it held to be almost inconceivable. The *Commercial and Financial Chronicle* expressed the belief on March 12 that the opposition of the financial interests would yet prevent war; and on April 2 the same journal branded as "monstrous" the proposition to settle the Cuban and "Maine" questions by war while the slightest chance remained for a peaceful solution. On April 16, after the House of Representatives had passed the Cuban resolutions, the Boston *Journal of Commerce* declared: "Sober second thought had but little to do with the deliberations. . . . The members were carried off their feet by the war fever that had been so persistently worked up since the Maine explosion. . . ."

The reasons for this attitude on the part of business are not far to seek. Since the panic of 1893 American business had been in the doldrums. Tendencies toward industrial revival had been checked, first by the Venezuela war scare in December, 1895, and again by the free silver menace in 1896. But in 1897 began a real revival, and before the end of the year signs of prosperity appeared on all sides. The New York *Commercial* conducted a survey of business conditions in a wide variety of trades and industries, from which it concluded that, "after three years of waiting and of false starts, the groundswell of demand has at last begun to rise with a steadiness which leaves little doubt that an era of prosperity has appeared.". . .

To this fair prospect of a great business revival the threat of war was like a spectre at the feast. A foreign complication, thought the *Commercial and Financial Chronicle* in October, 1897, would quickly mar "the trade prosperity which all are enjoying." Six months later (April 2, 1898), after a discussion of the effect of war rumors on the stock exchange, it declared: ". . . Every influence has been, and even now is, tending strongly towards a term of decided prosperity, and that the Cuban disturbance, and it alone, has arrested the movement and checked enterprise." The *Banker and Tradesman* saw in the Cuban complication the threat of a "material setback to the prosperous conditions which had just set in after five years of panic and depression." The same journal summarized a calculation made by the Boston *Transcript* showing that in February, 1898, the wave of prosperity had carried the average price of twenty-five leading stocks within 5½ points of the high for the preceding ten years and 30 points above the low of 1896, and that the Cuban trouble had, in a little over two months, caused a loss of over ten points, or more than one-third of the recent gain. "War would impede the march of prosperity and put the country back many years," said the *New Jersey Trade Review*. The *Railway Age* was of the opinion that the country was coming out of a depression and needed peace to complete its recovery. "From a commercial and mercenary standpoint," it remarked, "it seems peculiarly bitter that this war should have come when the country had already suffered so much and so needed rest and peace.

The idea that war could bring any substantial benefits to business was generally scouted. It would endanger our currency stability, interrupt our trade, and threaten our coasts and our commerce, thought the *Commercial and Financial Chronicle*. It would "incalculably increase the loss to business interests," said the *Banker's Magazine;* while the *United States Investor* held that war was "never beneficial from a material standpoint, that is, in the long run." The *Railroad Gazette* predicted that war would result in "interruption of business enterprise of every kind, stopping new projects and diminution of the output of existing businesses and contraction of trade everywhere." Railroads would lose more than they would gain. Even arms manufacturers were not all agreed that war would be desirable. Journals speaking for the iron and steel industry also argued that war would injure business. It "would injure the iron and steel makers ten times as much as they would be benefited by the prevailing spurt in the manufacture of small arms, projectiles and steel plates for war ships," in the opinion of one of these. The *American Wool and Cotton Reporter* of New York and the *Northwestern Miller* of Minneapolis agreed that war was never materially beneficial in the long run, while trade journals in Atlanta, Chattanooga, and Portland, Oregon, saw as fruits of the approaching conflict only destruction, debt, and depressed industry.

Many conservative interests feared war for the specific reason that it might derange the currency and even revive the free-silver agitation, which had seemed happily dead. The subsistence of that agitation and the prospect of currency reform were among the hopeful factors at the close of 1897. It was not uncommonly charged that the jingoes were animated in part by the expectation that war would lead to inflation in paper or silver. . . .

. . . It remains to examine the attitude of certain American business men and corporations having an immediate stake in Cuba, or otherwise liable to be directly affected by American intervention. Much American capital, as is well known, was invested in the Cuban sugar industry. Upon this industry the civil war fell with peculiarly devastating effect, not only cutting off profits on capital so invested, but also crippling a valuable carrying trade between Cuba and the United States. Naturally enough, some firms suffering under these conditions desired to see the United States intervene to end the war, though such intervention might lead to war between the United States and Spain. In May, 1897, a memorial on the subject bearing over three hundred signatures was presented to John Sherman, Secretary of State. The signers described themselves as "citizens of the United States, doing business as bankers, merchants, manufacturers, steamship owners and agents in the cities of Boston, New York, Philadelphia, Baltimore, Savannah, Charleston, Jacksonville, New Orleans, and other places, and also other citizens of the United States, who have been for many years engaged in the export and import trade with the Island of Cuba." They called attention to the serious losses to which their businesses had been subjected by the hostilities in Cuba and expressed the hope that, in order to prevent further loss, to reestablish American commerce, and also to secure "the blessings of peace for one and a half millions of residents of the Island of Cuba now enduring unspeakable distress and suffering," the United States Government might take steps to bring about an honorable reconciliation between the parties to the conflict.

Another memorial, signed by many of the same subscribers, was presented to President McKinley on February 9, 1898, by a committee of New York business men. It asserted that the Cuban war, which had now continued for three entire years, had caused an average loss of $100,000,000 a year, or a total loss of $300,000,000 in the import and export trade between Cuba and the United States, to which were to be added "heavy sums irretrievably lost by the destruction of American properties, or properties supported by American capital in the Island itself, such as sugar factories, railways, tobacco plantations, mines and other industrial enterprises; the loss of the United States in trade and capital by means of this war being probably far greater and more serious than that of all the other parties concerned, not excepting Spain herself."...

How much weight such pressure from special interests had with the administration there is no way of knowing. But it is to be noted that the pressure from parties directly interested was not all on one side. Mr. E. F. Atkins, an American citizen who divided his time between Boston and his sugar plantation of Soledad near Cienfuegos, Cuba, which he had developed at a cost of $1,400,000 had been able, through protection received from the Spanish Government and through a corps of guards organized and paid by himself, to continue operations throughout the period of the insurrection. He was frequently in Washington, where he had influential friends, during both the Cleveland and McKinley administrations and worked consistently against the adoption of any measures likely to provoke war.

Unlike some of the sugar plantations, American-owned iron mines in Cuba continued to do active business despite the insurrection. Three American iron and manganese enterprises in the single province of Santiago claimed to have an investment of some $6,000,000 of purely American capital, a large proportion of which was in property which could easily be destroyed. "We are fully advised as to our status in case of war," wrote the representative of one company to the Assistant Secretary of State, "and that this property might be subject to confiscation or destruction by the Spanish Government." War between Spain and the United States, wrote the president of another company, "will very likely mean the destruction of our valuable plant and in any event untold loss to our Company and its American stockholders." An American cork company with large interests in Spain; a New York merchant with trade in the Mediterranean and Black Sea; a Mobile firm which had chartered a Spanish ship to carry a cargo of timber—these are samples of American business interests which saw in war the threat of direct damage to themselves....

It seems safe to conclude, from the evidence available, that the only important business interests (other than the business of sensational journalism) which clamored for intervention in Cuba were those directly or indirectly concerned in the Cuban sugar industry; that opposed to intervention were the influence of other parties (including at least one prominent sugar planter) whose business would suffer direct injury from war and also the overwhelming preponderance of general business opinion. After the middle of March, 1898, some conservative editors came to think intervention inevitable on humanitarian grounds, but many of the most influential business journals opposed it to the end....

In the light of . . . widespread and intense interest in the preservation of the Chinese market, we can perhaps understand why American business, which had been, to all appearances, anti-war and anti-imperialist, was filled with sudden enthusiasm at the news of Dewey's victory at Manila Bay. Not only did the news dissipate all fears of a long and costly war and send stock prices rapidly upward; still more important, it seemed to place in American hands, all unexpectedly, the key to the trade of the Orient. The attack on the Spanish fleet at Manila had been anticipated for months and well advertised by the American press. Some papers had speculated upon the value of the islands as an American colony and had foreseen that a victory there might greatly alter our relation to the imbroglio in China. But for most, this thought did not occur until arrival of the news that the Spanish fleet was destroyed and Dewey safely in possession of Manila Bay. Then, at last, business men joined the jingoes in their acclaim of imperial conquests. Senator Lodge's exclamation—"We hold the other side of the Pacific, and the value to this country is almost beyond recognition"—was matched by many a formerly conservative business journal. It was not the intrinsic value of the Philippines or their trade that most impressed American writers, though this angle of the subject was not overlooked. Rather, their importance appeared to lie in their position as a gateway to the markets of Eastern Asia. . . .

There is no way of measuring accurately the strength of business opinion for and against the retention of the Philippines. Judging opinion as best we can from the available expressions of it, it seems safe to conclude that after the battle of Manila Bay American business became definitely imperialistic—that is, if a wish to retain the Philippines is an evidence of an imperialistic attitude. It seems certain, too, from the prominence given to the Chinese situation in nearly every discussion of the value of the islands, that the conversion of business opinion was accomplished by the combination of a European threat against the freedom of the American market in China, present and prospective, with the dramatic coup of the American fleet in a fine harbor so near the Chinese coast. In one paper, the New York *Journal of Commerce,* there appears with beautiful clarity the shift of position induced by the action of the European Powers in China. In November, 1897, against all schemes of colonial or naval expansion; in December, for a canal, Hawaii annexation, and a big navy; in May and thereafter, for retention of the entire Philippine archipelago and aggressive assertion of American rights in China—the *Journal* reveals a process of thought which perhaps occurred less clearly and consciously in the minds of many business men.

Having concluded that the Philippines were wholesome and digestible, business was disposed to treat itself to more of the same diet. The venture in the Philippines strengthened immeasurably the demand for the annexation of Hawaii. "The battle of Manila Bay," said the *Journal of Commerce,* May 31, "makes it imperative that we should establish permanent arrangements which will make the [Hawaiian] islands a half-way house on the road to the Philippines." But there were other Pacific islands that beckoned. "Bridge the Pacific!" cried the Philadelphia *Press.* "With the Philippines go the Carolines, a Spanish possession, Samoa and the Hawaiian Islands complete the chain." The war in the Pacific, the prospect of new possessions there, and the voyage of the "Oregon" also gave new force to the demand for an isthmian canal. . . .

American business had yielded reluctantly to the necessity of a war with Spain, forced upon the United States by popular reaction to the distressing situation in Cuba. It had not foreseen, or if it foresaw had feared, the colonial responsibilities to which such a war might lead. But when Dewey's dramatic victory on the first of May offered a Far Eastern base from which the threatened markets in China might be defended, it had gladly accepted the result, and long before the conclusion of peace with Spain, it was building high hopes upon the supposed opportunities for trade and exploitation in a string of dependencies stretching from the Philippines to Puerto Rico.

2. *The Yellow Press and the Coming of the War*

Joseph E. Wisan, an American diplomatic and intellectual historian, agrees with the Pratt view that business groups generally were opposed to involvement in the Cuban imbroglio. He believes the war to have been a people's war, forced on the reluctant McKinley administration by popular emotions and demands. The key to the aroused public feeling was the development of sensation-seeking journalism and above all the circulation war between the New York City press giants, Hearst and Pulitzer.

The Cuban Crisis

JOSEPH E. WISAN

The Press in 1895

The decade of the 1890's which witnessed the final crisis of the long continued friction between Spain and her Cuban colony marked also the appearance of a new type of journalism in New York City. While a number of veteran newspaper men were grimly attempting to maintain conservative standards, a new school in newspaper making with its reckless headlines, "popular" features, and sensational appeals to the masses reached many readers previously impervious to the comparatively staid sheets of the old order. . . .

In 1895 the important metropolitan morning newspapers were the *World*, the *Journal*, the *Sun*, the *Herald*, the *Tribune* and the *Times;* the leading evening sheets were the *Evening Post*, the *Commercial Advertiser*, and the *Mail and Express*. The *Journal of Commerce* represented the financial and commercial elements.

The *World* was owned by Joseph Pulitzer, whose career in the field of journalism had been most unusual. An ambitious immigrant in 1864, Pulitzer had served in many humble occupations. His newspaper ex-

Joseph E. Wisan, *The Cuban Crisis as Reflected in the New York Press, 1895–1898* (New York: Columbia University Press, 1934), 21–26, 187–191, 200–205, 324–332, 389–393, 455–458. Reprinted with permission.

perience began in Carl Schurz's *Westliche Post* in which he later bought an interest. He was employed by the New York *Sun,* purchased the St. Louis *Evening Post* which he transformed into the *Post-Dispatch,* and, in 1883 bought the *World* from Jay Gould. The newspaper was in poor shape when the change in ownership occurred. Pulitzer made a remarkable success of the enterprise. He created a new type of journal, "a journal that is not only cheap but bright, not only bright but large, not only large but truly democratic—dedicated to the cause of the people rather than of purse-potentates—devoted more to the New than the Old World—that will expose all fraud and sham, fight all public evils and abuses—that will serve and battle for the people with earnest sincerity." A week later his platform appeared—taxation of luxuries, of inheritances, of large incomes, of monopolies and privileged corporations, a tariff for revenue, civil service reform, punishment for corruption in office, vote buying and political coercion. Pulitzer employed every device to interest new readers. Screaming headlines, lurid style, profuse illustrations disgusted conservative readers but swelled circulation. Pulitzer outdid the earlier efforts of the Bennetts and the appearance of Hearst as an arch rival for the patronage of the lower classes compelled a reluctant adoption of even more spectacular methods. . . .

A Democrat since 1876, Pulitzer had supported Cleveland in 1884, 1888, and 1892, yet he took sharp issue with the President in several important instances. The *World* believed Cleveland too close to Wall Street; it denounced the sale of bonds to the Morgan-Rothschild syndicate early in 1895 and the failure to prosecute the trusts. It criticized Cleveland's Venezuela message as jingoistic and advocated peace. Olney it detested. . . .

Pulitzer's success with the *World* may be gauged by its increase in circulation. In 1883 the eight-page paper sold about 15,000 copies daily. In 1895 the sixteen page *World,* selling for the same price of two cents, boasted a circulation of 555,570 daily. For the year 1896, the *World* claimed an average week-day circulation of 743,024 and an average Sunday circulation of 562,903. According to its own statement there had been an average increase of 182,934 in the week-day issues and of 176,287 in the Sunday paper. By 1898 the circulation reached over five million copies per week, "the largest of any newspaper printed in any language in any country."

William Randolph Hearst, Pulitzer's chief rival, began his career in New York journalism on September 25, 1895, when, at the age of thirty, he purchased the New York *Morning Journal* from John R. McLean. Hearst's wealthy father had given him control in 1887 of the San Francisco *Examiner,* a newspaper the elder Hearst had taken over for a bad debt some years before. Hearst succeeded in making a financial success of the sheet, raising its circulation from almost nothing to 80,000 in a city of 300,000. This success he achieved by adopting sensational methods copied, generally, from Pulitzer. It was Hearst's ambition to surpass Pulitzer in sensationalism, circulation, and power, and his entrance into New York journalism began an intense rivalry between the two papers.

Hearst reduced the price of the *Journal* to one cent and improved its staff by transfers from his San Francisco *Examiner* and by acquisitions from his New York rivals. Associated with him at various times were Creelman, Grover Flint, Cuban correspondent with Gómez's army for four months, Alfred Henry Lewis, Washington correspondent, Julian Hawthorne, Richard Harding Davis, Karl Decker, Frederic Remington, and George Eugene Bryson. Melodrama, crime, vice, advice to the lovelorn, bizarre treatment of alleged scientific discoveries, became "news"; or as the *Journal* described it, "true stories of the new romances, mystery, pathos and humor caught from the whirl of everyday life." The *Journal* ran theatrical benefits for the city's poor; it offered rewards for the capture of notorious criminals; it interviewed kings; it hired prominent men for special assignments. A favorite trick was to wire statesmen for their views on important questions and to broadcast their replies conspicuously. A special Hoe color press, making possible an eight page comic section for the Sunday *Journal,* was installed. Streamer headlines, introduced in the Sunday *Journal,* were later adopted by the daily.

In international affairs Hearst invariably adopted an anti-foreign attitude. Spain, England, France, Japan, China, were all attacked for purposes of circulation.

In 1897 the *Journal* was increased in size, the regular edition being supplemented by a "magazine" devoted to "science in popular form, news of the week, and human interest," and a 24 page woman's supplement. The Eastern Sunday edition in 1897 reached 116 pages; a special Christmas edition, 112. This was rendered possible by an amazing growth in circulation. Hearst claimed an average daily increase of 1500 new readers during the first year of his proprietorship. The paper advertised an increase from 77,239 to 430,410 for the daily and 54,308 to 408,779 for the Sunday edition. On the day following McKinley's election the *Morning Journal* printed 956,921 copies. This, Hearst declared, was "an achievement not only unparalleled in the history of the world but hitherto undreamed-of in the realm of modern journalism." During each of the three days following the destruction of the *Maine,* the *Journal* printed over a million copies. After Dewey's victory at Manila its circulation exceeded 1,600,000 and it remained well over 1,250,000 during the war. . . .

Weyler and the New Press

The sensational press treatment of the multifarious phases of the Cuban crisis was due only in part to the nature of the events themselves. Much of it resulted from the development of the "new journalism," the roots of which lay in the past, but which reached full development during the years 1897–1898.

The typical new journal was jealous of its power; it was proud of itself and of its circulation, of which it blatantly boasted. It spent money lavishly. It hired special correspondents for important assignments. It "did things" as well as wrote about them. It was contemptuous of its rivals.

The *Journal* offered the most conspicuous example of this attitude and policy. Anxious to wrest circulation leadership from Pulitzer's *World,* it spared no expense to furnish exciting news. To its already costly staff covering the Cuban situation, it added Richard Harding Davis and Frederic Remington for special service. . . .

The *Journal* was the first newspaper to send to Cuba its own dispatch boat, the *Vamoose.* This was done in order to counteract the effects of Weyler's [Spanish commander in Cuba] rigid censorship. It boasted that the *Vamoose* was "the fastest boat in American waters," and that, despite De Lome's [Spanish ambassador in Washington] efforts to delay the progress of her mission to Cuba, she would get the news.

The *Journal* ridiculed the attempts of the other newspapers to keep up with it. It scoffed at "the sneers and snarls of the tired representatives of the old journalism attempting to discredit the *Journal's* exclusive news." The close relationship between the development of the new journalism and the Cuban crisis is well illustrated in an editorial boasting of its priority in reporting the contemplated grant of autonomy. No matter of international discussion interests the people of the United States more than the struggle of the Cubans for liberty. . . . Recognizing the existence of this universal interest, the *Journal* has spared no pains and no expense in its effort to gather and publish every piece of trustworthy information on the subject. It has sent to Cuba from time to time correspondents who represent the highest journalistic, military, political, literary or artistic attainments. It dispatched to Madrid Mr. James Creelman who antedated by sixteen days the *Herald's* instructive 'news' of yesterday. To those eminent exponents of the old journalism, the *Herald,* which copies after sixteen days the news the *Journal* obtained from headquarters at Madrid, and the *World,* which positively contradicted statements of fact which the *Herald* now affirms, the *Journal* presents its compliments and promises to leave them to the uninterrupted practice of their style of newspaper making. The new journalism prints what is new and prints it first."

The *World,* in an attempt to counteract the *Journal's* methods, claimed a series of scoops. In this Scovel was its greatest asset, although Dr. Bowen continued to send extremely good reports from the field. Pulitzer claimed an exclusive Gómez interview obtained at Gómez's camp near Salado, Santa Clara, in which the Cuban general denied his willingness to accept autonomy for the island. Its cruelty-affidavit scoops of early December it considered a real achievement. It prided itself upon an exclusive Weyler statement denying the charge that Maceo had been assassinated. It claimed to have presented "the first authentic news of the movements of the Cuban patriot armies that has reached New York in many weeks." . . .

When subjected to criticism the Pulitzer and Hearst newspapers seemed pleased. A Havana newspaper having published a three-column attack on the American press, charging it with a systematic attempt to deceive, the *World* expressed pleasure that it had been singled out for particular criticism. When Weyler blamed the "pernicious activity" of the newspapers of the United States for his failure to subdue the insurgents earlier, the *Journal* applauded his "tribute to the press," and declared, "it is a grateful compliment. . . . It is true that the press of this country has done what it could to create public sentiment against the infamous cruelty of the Spanish pirate in Cuba and in favor of intervention by this government." The *Evening Post* reported that Spanish officials in Puerto Rico destroyed American newspapers whenever they could find them. . . .

. . . During this period tales of Spanish atrocities increased in frequency. The *World* and *Journal* led, followed by the *Sun* and the *Mail and Express*, while the *Herald*, *Commercial Advertiser*, and *Times* printed reports occasionally. The stories were similar to those ordinarily believed by a nation at war. One favorite was the tale of political prisoners shot without trial. The *Journal* reported that Spanish officials kept their jails crowded so that they might profit by providing inferior food to the prisoners. The horrors of imprisonment in Spain's African penal settlement were described at great length by the *Mail and Express*. "The butcheries in Cuba would . . . seem almost merciful in comparison. . . . The patriots are . . . buried in a living grave. . . . The true story of the refinement of Spain's bloody cruelty lies hidden in far away Africa, rivaling the Inquisition in horror and surpassing the fastnesses of Siberia in secrecy." Some were reported drowned at night by Havana police; the *Journal's* headline on this was "Feeding Prisoners to Sharks." The *Mail and Express* reported that this practice had continued since September 1, and that sixty-three prisoners had disappeared in this way, officers in Morro Castle complaining because the cries of those doomed disturbed their sleep. Many crimes against non-combatants were reported. Madrid was said to have ordered Weyler to "shoot or bury all those opposed to Spain." Tejeda, "the Dominican Butcher," was reported to be killing peaceful men, women and children in eastern Cuba. The *Sun* asked whether Minister Taylor had received instructions "to invite the attention of the Spanish government to the barbarous manner in which prisoners and non-combatants were being put to death." A drunken Spanish major was reported to have killed fifty Cuban citizens; others, "old men and little boys, were cut down and their bodies fed to the dogs." One Spanish regiment was said to have proudly claimed 140 non-combatant victims. In the opinion of the *Sun*, Spain was "bent on wiping out the whole Cuban population," and officers who killed the most peasants "were decorated and promoted." Eight hundred peaceful inhabitants of the Rubi Hills were reported murdered during Weyler's brief November campaign in that area. Merciless attacks upon hospitals were alleged to be perpetrated by the Spaniards. One such report, describing raids on rebel hospitals at Isabel and Magdalena, declared: "The helpless and wounded were assassinated in their cots and the buildings then burned over their heads to cover up the crime." Another described the butchering of forty wounded prisoners. The poisoning of provisions furnished another type of atrocity story; and the maltreatment of women and the punishment of men attempting to defend women was another usual story.

During June the *World* printed an unusually large number of atrocity stories and also devoted frequent editorials to the subject. It pretended to believe the Spaniards capable of any crime. "Under the impulse of barbaric patriotism the average Spaniard is easily convinced that anyone who, on any account, dares to oppose Spain, is worthy of death in its worst form. Cruelty thus becomes almost a religion with the Spanish soldier." It referred to "the old Spanish habit of fusillading unarmed prisoners." "Genghis Khan and Timour, who made trophies of the skulls of their slaughtered enemies, were no more barbaric than is the Captain-General of Cuba, whose policies are outlined by the corpses of bound prisoners left lying along the march of his troops." Creelman was especially active in writing atrocity stories, and the following quotation is from his pen: "The horrors of the barbarous struggle for the extermination of the native population are witnessed in all parts of the country. Blood on the roadsides, blood in the fields, blood on the doorsteps, blood, blood, blood! The old, the young, the weak, the crippled, all are butchered without mercy. There is scarcely a hamlet that has not witnessed the dreadful work." In a featured article, the *World* presented a fearful record of Spanish atrocities claimed to have been committed in the province of Pinar del Rio under Weyler's command, some 200 victims being catalogued with names and places of residence. The editor claimed to have in his possession a score of affidavits of eye-witnesses sustaining the statements of its correspondent.

Weyler was regarded as the very incarnation of Spanish cruelty. The *Journal* devoted a special Sunday feature "to the prince of all the cruel generals this century has seen." "Spain . . . has at last played her trump card and sent on the field of battle . . . her most ferocious and bloody soldier . . . the fiendish despot whose hand Cuba well knows. . . . A panic has spread over Cuba. . . . Hundreds of Cuban women, maids and matrons, shudder. . . . It is not only Weyler the soldier . . . but Weyler the brute, the devastator of haciendas, the destroyer of families, and the outrager of women. . . . Pitiless, cold, an exterminator of men. . . . There is nothing to prevent his carnal, animal brain from running riot with itself in inventing tortures and infamies of bloody debauchery." The *Sun* said, "He has the ways of a coward"; the *Mail and Express* referred to him as "a menace to Spain"; and the *World* declared him "a barbarian, bred in an atmosphere of medievalism."...

. . . Evangelina Cisneros was the daughter of a Cuban insurgent who had been arrested in June, 1895 and imprisoned in Cienfuegos. She had succeeded through an accidental meeting with Martínex Campos's son in securing a commutation of her father's death sentence to one of life imprisonment at Ceuta. Through a personal appeal to Weyler she succeeded in having her father transferred to the penal settlement on the Isle of Pines, to which Miss Cisneros and her sister accompanied him. A moderately pleasant existence on the island was interrupted by the advent of the new military commander, Col. Berriz, nephew of Azcárraga and close friend of Weyler. According to the girl's story, Berriz attempted a brutal assault upon her but received a beating at the hands of a group of fellow-exiles summoned by her cries for help, only the intervention of Spanish soldiers saving him from more severe punishment.

Miss Cisneros was charged with rebellion, removed to Havana and incarcerated in the "Recojidas" prison. None of these events had received newspaper attention when they occurred. On August 17, 1897, some nine months after the transfer of the girl to Havana, the *Journal* told the dramatic story of the case, accepting her version in every detail; it reported that Miss Cisneros had been convicted of sedition and warned that she might be sentenced to twenty years' imprisonment in the African penal settlement. During the next fortnight, in both the news and editorial columns, it championed the girl's cause so vociferously that the case assumed international prominence. In its opinion, Spanish viciousness and cruelty were exemplified in this case. "This tenderly nurtured girl was imprisoned at eighteen among the most depraved negresses of Havana, and now she is to be sent in mockery to spend twenty years in a servitude that will kill her in a year." "The unspeakable fate to which Weyler has doomed an innocent girl whose only crime is that she has defended her honor against a beast in uniform has sent a shudder of horror through the American people." "Miss Cisneros is, according to all who have seen her, the most beautiful girl in the island of Cuba. . . . She was reared in seclusion and, almost a child in years, is as ignorant of the world as a cloistered nun." "This girl, delicate, refined, sensitive, unused to hardship, absolutely ignorant of vice, unconscious of the existence of such beings as crowd the cells of the Casa de Recojidas, is seized, thrust into the prison maintained for the vilest class of abandoned women of Havana, compelled to scrub floors and to sleep on bare boards with outcast negresses, and shattered in health until she is threatened with an early death." Berriz was a "lecherous and foiled scoundrel." The *Journal* sent a telegram to Weyler asking for mercy for the girl. It sent telegrams to prominent women of the United States, urging them to petition the Pope and the Queen-Regent of Spain in her behalf. Among those who responded were Julia Ward Howe, Mrs. Jefferson Davis, Mrs. Mark Hanna, the mother of President McKinley, Mrs. Julia Dent Grant, widow of ex-President Grant, Mrs. Sherman, wife of the Secretary of State, Mrs. Letitia Tyler Semple, daughter of ex-President Tyler, Miss Eugenia Washington, grandniece of George Washington, Mrs. John G. Carlisle, wife of ex-Secretary of the Treasury Carlisle, Clara Barton, and Mrs. W. C. Whitney. Among many prominent men who publicly congratulated the *Journal* on its enterprise were Secretary Sherman, Senators Money, Jones, Turner, Governor Mount of Indiana, and ex-Governor Crittenden of Missouri.

Meanwhile, the *World*, jealous of its rival's exploit, attempted to minimize its importance by publishing a telegram from Weyler denying the truth of the *Journal's* story. According to Weyler's version, the girl had "deceitfully lured to her house the military commander of the Isle of Pines, had men posted secretly who tied him and attempted to assassinate him." He also denied that the case had been decided and that sentence had been yet passed. An accompanying *World* editorial bewailed the *Journal's* sensationalism. . . .

During the first week in September the case continued to furnish front-page material. The Queen-Regent's order to Weyler to remove the girl to a convent pending the completion of the case, the Governor-General's angry refusal to obey the order, the testimony of witnesses to the innocence of the girl and to the shameful jail conditions, the progress of a petition organized by Lady Rothschild and Mrs. Ormiston Chant and widely circulated among the women of England, the reported attempt of Berriz to obtain the girl's freedom in exchange for letters incriminating himself, the Pope's intercession for clemency for the girl, all were fully reported. The *World* continued its sniping tactics. It refuted the *Journal's* claim that the girl was related to the Marquis of Santa Lucía, Cuban President, and was rewarded by a *Journal* editorial directed against the snobbery of "the aristocratic Mr. Pulitzer's *New York World.*" It declared that only the Hearst publicity had prevented Weyler from carrying out his original intention to free the girl on Lee's request. It obtained an interview with the girl and described prison conditions as much more satisfactory than those depicted by its rival. It reported fully Lee's criticism of the sensational journalistic misrepresentation of the case.

After a month's absence from the front page, the case entered its second sensational phase with the news that the girl had escaped from jail. The following day some newspapers reported that she had had outside help in effecting her escape. Not until October 10th (Sunday), did the *Journal* make the amazing announcement that it had rescued the prisoner. The first three pages of the issue were devoted to the story. Karl Decker (Charles Duval), a *Journal* reporter replacing the expelled Bryson, had reached Cuba August 28th. Failing in his attempts to bribe the guards, he had, with the help of the prisoner, worked out a plan to free the girl. With two aides, Hernandon and Mallory, he had rented a house next to the prison and, using a ladder to get to the roof, sawed through the cell bars to effect the escape. The other inmates had been drugged. With the girl disguised as a boy, and Decker using a forged visa on his passport, they made their escape on the Ward liner *Seneca.*

For many days the *Journal* reaped a full return of glory for its exploit, which, in its own opinion, was paralleled only by the rescue of Mary Queen of Scots. Congratulatory comments from prominent people were published—Mrs. Grant, Mrs. Sherman, Mrs. Carlisle, Mrs. Governor Bradley, Mrs. Senator Mason, Clara Barton, Senators Money, Jones, Turner, Elkins, Thurston, Governor Mount of Indiana, and many more, including even Secretary Sherman. The Bishop of London congratulated Hearst on his "magnificent journalism." Governor Sadler of Missouri suggested that the *Journal* send five hundred of its reporters to free the island.

There were many columns quoting the congratulatory statements of other newspapers—all from other cities in the United States and in Europe.

A novelized version of the entire case ran as a special Sunday *Journal* feature for three months. In conjunction with the Junta, the newspaper arranged an elaborate dinner at Delmonico's and a monster reception for the girl in Madison Square Garden, at which Henry George spoke. Miss Cisneros's visits to historic New York places were duly chronicled, as was her announced intention to become an American citizen. An interview with President McKinley was arranged, Mrs. Logan presenting the girl and Decker to the President. . . .

. . . The loss of the ship [*Maine*], important in itself, assumed far greater significance in view of the circumstances which surrounded it. It occurred in the harbor of Havana, where loyalist nerves had been frayed by the events of the preceding months and where the *Maine's* presence had been deeply and openly resented. Following closely the January riot and the De Lome letter, it came at a time when Spanish-American relations were highly strained. Suspicion of foul play was inevitable especially among those who for three years had been trained by the pro-Cuban journals to despise the Spanish monarchy and its policies.

An official investigation was inaugurated on February 17th by [Navy] Secretary Long's order that Admiral Sicard select officers from the ships of the North Atlantic Squadron to compose a Court of Inquiry. The Court left for Havana on February 20th. After an investigation of twenty-three days, every effort being made to achieve complete secrecy during its progress, the report of the Court of Inquiry was sent to Congress March 28th.

Those in positions of responsibility acted to prevent the engulfment of the nation in a tide of hysteria. Captain Sigsbee in his first telegraphic report, sent from the *City of Washington,* advised that "public opinion should be suspended until further report." Lee telegraphed a similar request: "Hope our people will repress excitement and calmly await decision." Secretary Long publicly announced his opinion that an explosion in the *Maine's* magazine had caused the accident. President McKinley also expressed his opinion that the catastrophe had resulted from an internal explosion.

However, the sensational newspapers were fully alive to the public's excited interest in the event and to the opportunity offered to themselves and made frantic efforts to get—or manufacture—the news, and to present it in the most lurid fashion. During the week beginning February 17th, the *Journal* devoted a daily average space of 8½ pages to the *Maine* —news, editorials, and pictures. It sent the yachts *Buccaneer* and *Anita* and the tug *Echo* to Havana, and massed at the Cuban capital its group of special correspondents—Hawthorne, Decker, Creelman, Lewis, Bryson, and artists Remington and Bengough. It offered a reward of fifty thousand dollars "for the conviction of the criminals who sent 258 American sailors to their death." Declaring that "the government has set an investigation on foot, and the *Journal* has independently undertaken another," it boasted, "between them the truth will soon be known." It inaugurated a fund to build a monument in memory of the *Maine* victims, associating with itself in this endeavor many names prominent in civil and military life, including Levi P. Morton, General Miles, Rear Admiral Selfridge, O. H. P. Belmont, George Gould, Depew, and General O. O. Howard. The *World* chartered a special tug and engaged divers to investigate the wreck, and was disappointed when refused permission to do so. According to its own figures the *Journal's* circulation for the week of January 9th had averaged 416,885; on February 17th it reached 1,025,624; on February 18th, 1,036,140. For the week beginning February 27th the average figure was 632,217.

The news columns of Hearst's paper seemed deliberately intended to inflame the public. "The warship *Maine* was split in two by an enemy's secret infernal machine"; "Captain Sigsbee practically declares that his ship was blown up by a mine or a torpedo"; "Strong evidence of crime"; "There are many among the Spanish officers and privates who hate Americans to the point of frenzy"; "If this can be proven, the brutal nature of the Spaniards will be shown in that they waited to spring the mine until after all men had retired for the night. The Maltese Cross [referring to an accompanying illustration] shows where the mine may have been fired." One leading headline read, "THE WHOLE COUNTRY THRILLS WITH WAR FEVER." The governors of many states reported the readiness and anxiety of the militia for service. One picture was captioned, "Divers searching for the dead and the evidence that they were murdered under the murky waters of Havana Bay." On February 20th (the day the Court of Inquiry left for Havana to begin its investigation) the *Journal* presented "proof of a submarine mine." Under a headline, "HAVANA POPULACE INSULTS THE MEMORY OF THE MAINE VICTIMS," appeared the statement that Spanish officers had boasted that any other American ship visiting Havana would "follow the *Maine*." "THE MAINE WAS DESTROYED BY TREACHERY" was another headline. A few days later Karl Decker claimed to have "the secret testimony on which the Court of Inquiry will base its portentous report." The *Journal* quoted authorities (far removed from Havana) to prove its contention that the explosion was external and deliberate—Assistant-Secretary Roosevelt, Chief Constructor Philip Hichborn, Rear Admiral George E. Belknap (retired), and Naval Constructor Bolles. Captain Zalinski (a retired naval officer and "dynamite expert") judged from the *Journal's* photographs that a mine blew up the *Maine*. The Italian ex-Premier Crispi's opinion that the *Maine's* destruction was not accidental was made the subject of a leading editorial.

Though the *World* did not quite match its rival's sensationalism, it adopted similar tactics. Turning from its earlier headline guesses that "The *Maine* explosion was caused by a bomb" and that there was "Suspicion of a torpedo," and emphasizing the work of its own special investigators, it announced on February 20th that the "*World's* discoveries prove the mine theory." Another headline read, "War spirit rising from *World's* evidence." And still another, "Government accepts mine theory of *World*." It featured a report that Sigsbee had attributed the explosion to external forces. It warned of the damage possible from the guns of the *Vizcaya*, expected to arrive that day. "While lying off the Battery, her shells will explode on the Harlem River and in the suburbs of Brooklyn." A full page streamer announced that the President and Congress were "ready for action." It described the elaborate preparations of the Government to improve the Atlantic Coast defense and insisted that we were fully prepared for war. A large picture representing American cannon pointed at the *Vizcaya* accompanied this article. . . .

Conclusion

The Spanish-American War, so momentous in its consequences, was a popular crusade. Neither the business interests of the nation nor the Government executives desired it. The public, aroused by the press, demanded it.

The leading commercial and financial interests of the nation favored an early restoration of stability in Cuba. They sought not only to avoid war, but to minimize its possibility. Investors in Cuban enterprises, anxious above all else to restore the security of their properties, attributed their losses to the tactics of the insurgents, and opposed all direct or indirect aid to them. Edwin F. Atkins, one of the leading American investors in Cuba, and influential with high officials of both the Cleveland and McKinley Administrations, sought constantly to prevent such aid. Indeed, he was accused of poisoning Olney's mind against the insurgents. General industrial and banking interests, emerging from the serious depression of 1893, and anxious to permit the unhampered operation of McKinley's policies, feared the possible effects of war. Furthermore, the 1896 campaign had not ended the menace of free silver; a war, possibly prolonged and certain to be costly, would strengthen the position of the silverites. It was no mere accident that most of the leading proponents of intervention in Congress represented southern and western states where populism and silver were strongest.

Wall Street served as a sensitive index of the fears of the financial interests. Rumors of increased tension in Spanish-American relations were almost invariably accompanied by a decline in stock prices and by editorial demands for peace from financial organs. Examples of this tendency may be seen in the falling prices which resulted from the Senate's adoption of the belligerency resolutions (Feb. 29, 1896), the conviction of the *Competitor* prisoners (May 12, 1896), a report that the St. Louis convention would demand armed intervention in Cuba (June 18, 1896), the Maceo assassination story (December 15, 1896); the Senate Committee on Foreign Relations' adoption of the Cameron resolution (December 19, 1896), the publicity given to the views of Hannis Taylor (November 5, 1897), the destruction of the *Maine* (February 16, 1898), and the passage of the $50,000,000 defense bill (March 7, 1898). On the other hand, reports of incidents making for peace between the two nations rallied prices. For example, gains were recorded when Cleveland indicated a strong desire to adjust our difficulties amicably (March 10, 1896, April 14, 1896), when Madrid ordered a postponement of the execution of the *Competitor* prisoners (May 13, 1896), and when Olney announced that Cleveland would not be bound by the Congressional Resolution of December, 1896 (December 20, 1896; December 22, 1896). Mark Hanna's determined opposition to the war is typical of the attitude of the nation's leading business men. The *Journal of Commerce* consistently opposed American intervention.

Spain's inability to protect American property in Cuba was annoying, as were the hindrances she imposed upon American commerce during the early part of the insurrection. However, during the later stages of the revolt she did everything possible to offer protection and she removed the curbs on American business in Cuba. American claims for damages could have been settled easily with a nation striving to maintain peace. Spanish historians, such as Maura and Ortega, attach little significance to this aspect of the controversy between the two nations, condemning American Jingoes, not American business men, as the provokers of an unjustifiable war. Indeed, the most bitter complaints of Spain's interferences with American business came from the ranks of the Jingoes thirsting for war, not from among the business men whose financial interests were immediately involved.

Responsible officials of both the Cleveland and McKinley Administrations strove to avoid an open break. Energetic and generally effective steps were taken to prevent filibustering. Cleveland's proclamations of neutrality, his repeated criticism of overzealous Cuban sympathizers in America, his offer of American mediation towards a permanent solution in which Spanish sovereignty would be safeguarded, his anxiety to obtain from the Supreme Court a decision setting clearly defined legal limits to filibustering operations, all bespeak his efforts on behalf of peace. Despite an increasing irritation at Spain's inability to restore peace, he and Olney were a constant bulwark against the Jingoes. McKinley, more responsive to popular and party demands, and willing to add to the prestige of his Administration by minor diplomatic victories, was equally anxious to avoid war, as was his entire cabinet, with the exception of Alger. Despite the presence of bellicose individuals such as Lodge and Roosevelt, the force of Republican leadership was exerted for peace. Woodford's sincere efforts to maintain peace during March and April, 1898, were undertaken to please and help his superiors, not to make their position more awkward. McKinley's problem was made easier by Spain's mounting domestic difficulties and her increasing willingness to accede to American demands, particularly after the accession of the Sagasta Ministry and the removal of Weyler. It was made more difficult by the public's increasing sympathy for Cuba and its growing hatred of Spain. It was made impossible by the high emotional pitch to which the public was raised following the destruction of the *Maine*. Responsibility for this state of mind rests primarily with the press.

In the opinion of the writer, the Spanish-American War would not have occurred had not the appearance of Hearst in New York journalism precipitated a bitter battle for newspaper circulation. The Cuban insurrection and its attendant horrors furnished a unique opportunity to the proprietors of the sensational press to prove their enterprise and provide the type of news that sold papers. Even the conservative journals, irritated by the emphasis the "new journalists" placed upon Cuba, were compelled by that very emphasis to devote considerably more space to Cuban affairs than they otherwise would have done. . . .

3. The Psychic Crisis of the 1890's

Utilizing psychological insights, Richard Hofstadter, the historian of American reform movements and political leaders, suggests that the popular demand for war was not created by the Yellow Press but was the result of a mass sense of frustration and fear, and the seeking of relief through a foreign crusade in Cuba. Acquisition of the Philippines is a separate problem, however, and was the achievement of the plans and actions of a small group of avowed imperialists.

Manifest Destiny and the Philippines

RICHARD HOFSTADTER

The taking of the Philippine Islands from Spain in 1899 marked a major historical departure for the American people. It was a breach in their traditions and a shock to their established values. To be sure, from their national beginnings they had constantly engaged in expansion, but almost entirely into contiguous territory. Now they were extending themselves to distant extra-hemispheric colonies; they were abandoning a strategy of defense hitherto limited to the continent and its appurtenances, in favor of a major strategic commitment in the Far East; and they were now supplementing the spread of a relatively homogeneous population into territories destined from the beginning for self-government with a far different procedure in which control was imposed by force on millions of ethnic aliens. The acquisition of the islands, therefore, was understood by contemporaries on both sides of the debate, as it is readily understood today, to be a turning-point in our history.

To discuss the debate in isolation from other events, however, would be to deprive it of its full significance. American entrance into the Philippine Islands was a by-product of the Spanish-American War. The Philippine crisis is inseparable from the war crisis and the war crisis itself is inseparable from a larger constellation that might be called "the psychic crisis of the 1890's."

Central in the background of the psychic crisis was the great depression that broke in 1893 and was still very acute when the agitation over the war in Cuba began. Severe depression, by itself, does not always generate an emotional crisis as intense as that of the nineties. In the 1870's the country had been swept by a depression of comparable acuteness and duration which, however, did not give rise to all the phenomena that appeared in the 1890's or to very many of them with comparable intensity and impact. It is often said that the 1890's, unlike the 1870's, form some kind of a "watershed" in American history. The difference between the emotional and intellectual impact of these two depressions can be measured, I believe, not by any difference in severity, but rather by reference to a number of singular events that in the 1890's converged with the depression to heighten its impact upon the public mind.

Reprinted from "Manifest Destiny and the Philippines," by Richard Hofstadter, in *America in Crisis* edited by Daniel Aaron, pp. 173–176, 180–187, 189–191, by permission of Alfred A. Knopf, Inc.

First in importance was the Populist movement, the free-silver agitation, the heated campaign of 1896. For the first time in our history a depression had created an allegedly "radical" movement strong enough to capture a major party and raise the specter, however unreal, of drastic social convulsion. Second was the maturation and bureaucratization of American business, the completion of its essential industrial plant, and the development of trusts on a scale sufficient to stir the anxiety that the old order of competitive opportunities was approaching an eclipse. Third, and of immense symbolic importance, was the apparent filling up of the continent and disappearance of the frontier line. We now know how much land had not yet been taken up and how great were the remaining possibilities of internal expansion both in business and on the land; but to the mind of the 1890's it seemed that the resource that had engaged the energies of the people for three centuries had been used up; the frightening possibility suggested itself that a serious juncture in the nation's history had come. As Frederick Jackson Turner expressed it in his famous paper of 1893: "Now, four centuries from the discovery of America, at the end of one hundred years of life under the Constitution, the frontier has gone, and with its going has closed the first period of American history."

To middle-class citizens who had been brought up to think in terms of the nineteenth-century order, things looked bad. Farmers in the staple-growing region seemed to have gone mad over silver and Bryan; workers were stirring in bloody struggles like the Homestead and Pullman strikes; the supply of new land seemed at an end; the trust threatened the spirit of business enterprise; civic corruption was at a high point in the large cities; great waves of seemingly unassimilable immigrants arrived yearly and settled in hideous slums. To many historically conscious writers, the nation seemed overripe, like an empire ready for collapse through a stroke from outside or through internal upheaval. Acute as the situation was for all those who lived by the symbols of national power—for the governing and thinking classes—it was especially poignant for young people, who would have to make their careers in the dark world that seemed to be emerging.

The symptomatology of the crisis might record several tendencies in popular thought and behavior that had not been observable before or had existed only in pale and tenuous form. These symptoms fall into two basic moods. The key to one of them is an intensification of protest and humanitarian reform. Populism, Utopianism, the rise of the Christian Social gospel, the growing intellectual interest in Socialism, the social settlement movement that appealed so strongly to the college generation of the nineties, the quickening of protest in the realistic novel—all these are expressions of this mood. The other is one of national self-assertion, aggression, expansion. The tone of the first was sympathy, of the second, power. During the 1890's far more patriotic groups were founded than in any other decade of our history; the naval theories of Captain Mahan were gaining in influence; naval construction was booming; there was an immense quickening of the American cult of Napoleon and a vogue of the virile and martial writings of Rudyard Kipling; young Theodore Roosevelt became the exemplar of the vigorous, masterful, out-of-doors man; the revival of European imperialism stirred speculation over what America's place would be in the world of renewed colonial rivalries. But most significant was the rising tide of jingoism, a matter of constant comment among observers of American life during the decade.

Jingoism, of course, was not new in American history. But during the 1870's and '80's the American public had been notably quiescent about foreign relations. There had been expansionist statesmen, but they had been blocked by popular apathy and statecraft had been restrained. Grant had failed dismally in his attempt to acquire Santo Domingo; our policy toward troubled Hawaii had been cautious; in 1877 an offer of two Haitian naval harbors had been spurned. In responding to Haiti, Secretary of State Frelinghuysen had remarked that "the policy of this Government . . . has tended toward avoidance of possessions disconnected from the main continent." Henry Cabot Lodge, in his life of George Washington published in 1889, observed that foreign relations then filled "but a slight place in American politics, and excite generally only a languid interest." Within a few years this comment would have seemed absurd; the history of the 1890's is the history of public agitation over expansionist issues and of quarrels with other nations.

Historians say that the war was brought on by sensational newspapers. The press, spurred by the rivalry between Pulitzer and Hearst, aroused sympathy with the Cubans and hatred of Spain and catered to the bellicosity of the public. No one seems to have asked: *Why was the public so fatally receptive to war propaganda?* I believe the answer must be sought in the causes of the jingoism that had raged for seven years before the war actually broke out. The events of the nineties had brought frustration and anxiety to civically conscious Americans. On one hand, as Mark Sullivan has commented, the American during this period was disposed "to see himself as an underdog in economic situations and controversies in his own country"; but the civic frustrations of the era created also a restless aggressiveness, a desire to be assured that the power and vitality of the nation were not waning. The capacity for sympathy and the need for power existed side by side. That highly typical and symptomatic American, William Allen White, recalls in his *Autobiography* how during the nineties he was "bound to my idols—Whitman, the great democrat, and Kipling, the imperialist." In varying stages of solution the democrat and imperialist existed in the hearts of White's countrymen—the democrat disposed to free Cuba, the imperialist to vent his civic spleen on Spain.

I suspect that the readiness of the public to over-react to the Cuban situation can be understood in part through the displacement of feelings of sympathy or social protest generated in domestic affairs; these impulses found a safe and satisfactory discharge in foreign conflict. Spain was portrayed in the press as waging a heartless and inhuman war; the Cubans were portrayed as noble victims of Spanish tyranny, their situation as analogous to that of Americans in 1776. When one examines the sectional and political elements that were most enthusiastic about the war, one finds them not primarily among the wealthy Eastern big-business Republicans who supported McKinley and read the conservative dignified newspapers, but in the Bryan sections of the country, in the Democratic party, and among the patrons of the yellow journals. During the controversy significant charges were hurled back and forth; conservative peace-advocates claimed that many jingoists were hoping for a costly war over Cuba that could be made the occasion of a return to free silver; in return, the inflammatory press often fell into the pattern of Populist rhetoric, declaiming, for example, about "the eminently respectable porcine citizens who—for dollars in the money-grubbing sty, support 'conservative' newspapers and consider the starvation of . . . inoffensive men, women and children, and the murder of 250 American sailors . . . of less importance than a fall of two points in a price of stocks." Although imputations of base economic motives were made by both sides, it is also significant that the current of sympathy and agitation ran strong where a discontented constituency, politically frustrated by Bryan's defeat, was most numerous. An opportunity to discharge aggressions against "Wall Street interests" coolly indifferent to the fate of both Cuban *insurrectos* and staple farmers may have been more important than the more rationalized and abstract linkage between a war and free silver. The primary significance of the war for the psychic economy of the nineties was that it served as an outlet for aggressive impulses while presenting itself, quite truthfully, as an idealistic and humanitarian crusade. The American public was not interested in the material gains of an intervention in Cuba. It never dreamed that the war would lead to the taking of the Philippines. Starting a war for a high-minded and altruistic purpose and then transmuting it into a war for annexation was unthinkable; it would be, as McKinley put it in a phrase that later came back to haunt him, "criminal aggression."

There is one odd paradox in the evolution of sentiment from a war over freeing Cuba to a peace treaty acquiring the Philippines by conquest. The big-business-conservative-Republican-McKinley element, overwhelmingly hostile to this romantic and sentimental war, quickly became interested in the imperialism that grew out of it. The popular Populist-Democratic-Bryanite element, which had been so keen for the war, became the stronghold—although by no means resolute or unbroken—of opposition to the fruits of war. This much, however, must be said of both the populace and the business community: if the matter had been left either to public clamor or to business interests, there would have been no American entrance into the Philippines in 1898.

The dynamic element in the movement for imperialism was a small group of politicians, intellectuals, and publicists, including Senator Henry Cabot Lodge, Theodore Roosevelt, John Hay, Senator Albert J. Beveridge, Whitelaw Reid, editor of *The New York Tribune,* Albert Shaw, editor of the *Review of Reviews,* Walter Hines Page, editor of the *Atlantic Monthly,* and Henry and Brooks Adams.

Most of these men came from what are known as good families. They were well educated, cultivated, patrician in outlook, Anglo-Saxon in background, noncommercial in personal goals and standards, and conservative reformers in politics. Although living in a commercial world, they could not accept business standards for their own careers nor absorb themselves into the business community. Although they lived in a vulgar democracy, they were not democratic by instinct. They could not and did not care to succeed in politics of the corrupt sort that had become so common in America. They had tried their hands at civic reform, had found it futile, and had become bored with it. When they did not, like Henry Adams, turn away from American life in bitterness, they became interested in some large and statesmanlike theater of action, broader than American domestic policy. Although there were men of this sort in the Democratic ranks, like Walter Hines Page, they were most influential within the Republican Party, which during the mid-nineties had become committed to a policy of expansion.

In general, this group of imperialists was inspired by the navalist theories of Mahan and by the practical example of what they sometimes referred to as Mother England. They saw that a new phase of imperialism had opened in the Western world at large, and they were fearful that if the United States did not adopt a policy of expansion and preparation for military and naval struggle, it would be left behind in what they referred to as the struggle for life or, at other times, as the march of the nations. They were much concerned that the United States expand its army and particularly its navy; that it dig an isthmian canal; that it acquire the naval bases and colonies in the Caribbean and the Pacific necessary to protect such a canal; that it annex Hawaii and Samoa. At their most aggressive, they also called for the annexation of Canada, and the expulsion of European powers from the Western hemisphere. They were much interested in the Far East as a new theater of political conflict and investment possibilities. They were, indeed, more interested than business itself in the Pacific area, particularly in China, as a potential market. As Professor Pratt has observed: "The need of American business for colonial markets and fields for investment was discovered not by businessmen but by historians and other intellectuals, by journalists and politicians."

The central figure in this group was Theodore Roosevelt, who more than any other single man was responsible for our entry into the Philippines. Throughout the 1890's Roosevelt had been eager for a war, whether it be with Chile, Spain, or England. A war with Spain, he felt, would get us "a proper navy and a good system of coast defenses," would free Cuba from Spain, and would help to free America from European domination, would give "our people . . . something to think of that isn't material gain," and would try "both the army and navy in actual practice." Roosevelt feared that the United States would grow heedless of its defense, take insufficient care to develop its power, and become "an easy prey for any people which still retained those most valuable of all qualities, the soldierly virtues." "All the great masterful races have been fighting races," he argued. There were higher virtues than those of peace and material comfort. "No triumph of peace is quite so great as the supreme triumphs of war." Such was the philosophy of the man who secured Commodore Dewey's appointment to the Far Eastern Squadron and alerted him before the actual outbreak of hostilities to be prepared to engage the Spanish fleet at Manila.

Our first step into the Philippines presented itself to us as a "defensive" measure. Dewey's attack on the Spanish fleet in Manila Bay was made on the assumption that the Spanish fleet, if unmolested, might cross the Pacific and bombard the west coast cities of the United States. I do not know whether American officialdom was aware that this fleet was so decrepit that it could hardly have gasped its way across the ocean. Next, Dewey's fleet seemed in danger unless its security were underwritten by the dispatch of American troops to Manila. To be sure, having accomplished his mission, Dewey could have removed his "danger" simply by leaving Manila Bay. However, in war one is always tempted to hold whatever gains have been made, and at Dewey's request American troops were dispatched very promptly after the victory and arrived at Manila in July 1898. Thus our second step into the Philippines was again a "defensive" measure. The third step was the so-called "capture" of Manila, which was actually carried out in co-operation with the Spaniards, who were allowed to make a token resistance, and in exclusion of the Filipino patriots under Aguinaldo. The fourth step was an agreement, incorporated in the protocol suspending hostilities between the United States and Spain, that the United States would occupy the city, bay, and harbor of Manila pending a final settlement in the peace treaty. The fifth step came much later, on December 21, 1898, when McKinley instructed the War Department to extend the military government already in force at Manila to the entire archipelago. This began a fierce revolt by the Filipino patriots, who felt that they had been led to expect a much different policy from the American government. Two days before the vote was taken in the Senate on the ratification of the peace treaty, the patriots and the American forces fought their first battle and American soldiers were killed, a fact that seems to have had an important influence on public discussion. Once again, administrative action had given a sharp bias to the whole process of political decision. Tyler Dennett goes so far as to say that by authorizing a campaign of conquest while the Senate was still dicussing the situation, McKinley "created a situation . . . which had the effect of coercing the Senate." This is a doubtful conclusion, but there is some reason to believe that the hand of expansionists was strengthened by the feeling that opposition to the administration's policy would be unpatriotic.

This much can certainly be said: by the time our policy could be affected by public discussion a great deal had already been accomplished by the annexationists. The tone of the argument was already weighted towards staying in simply because we were there. As McKinley put it: "It is not a question of keeping the islands of the East, but of leaving them." It is not an easy thing to persuade a people or a government during the pitch of war enthusiasm to abandon a potential gain already in hand. Moreover, a great social interest hitherto indifferent to the Philippines, the business community, quickly swung around to an expansionist position. The Protestant clergy, seeing a potential enlargement of missionary enterprise, also threw in its weight. For the first time the group of imperialists and navalists had powerful allies. Business began to talk about the Philippines as a possible gateway to the markets of eastern Asia, the potentialities of which were thought to be very large. The little imperialist group itself was much heartened and, with the help of Navy officers, put increasing pressure upon a rather hesitant administration to follow through. . . .

Who was for and who against annexation? In large measure it was a party issue. The *New York Herald* poll showed that of 241 Republican papers 84.2 per cent were *for* expansion, and of 174 Democratic papers 71.3 per cent were *against* expansion. In some degree it was also a young man's movement. Geographically it extended throughout all sections of the country, and seems to have been favored everywhere but in the South, although even there it was strong. We do not have a clear index of public opinion for the period, but the practical politicians, whose business it was to gauge public sentiment in the best way they knew, concluded that the preponderant feeling was overwhelmingly for annexation.

The debate over the acquisition of the Philippines was perhaps no more than a ceremonial assertion of the values of both sides. The real decisions were made in the office of Theodore Roosevelt, in the Senate cloakroom, in the sanctums of those naval officers from whom the McKinley administration got its primary information about the Philippines during its period of doubt over annexation, and, by McKinley's own testimony, in the privacy of his chambers late at night. The public was, by and large, faced with a *fait accompli* that, although theoretically reversible, had the initial impetus of its very existence to carry it along. The intensity of the public discussion, at any rate, showed that the American conscience had really been shocked. No type of argument was neglected on either side. Those who wanted to take the Philippines pointed to the potential markets of the East, the White Man's Burden, the struggle for existence, "racial" destiny, American traditions of expansion, the dangers of a general war if the Philippines were left open to a European scramble, the almost parental duty of assuming responsibility for the allegedly childlike Filipinos, the incapacity of the Filipinos for self-government, and so on. The anti-imperialists based their essential appeal on political principle. They pointed out that the United States had come into existence pledged to the idea that man should not be governed without his consent. They suggested that the violation of these political traditions (under which the nation had prospered) was not only a gross injustice to others, of which we should feel deeply ashamed, but also a way of tempting Providence and risking degeneration and disintegration as a sort of punishment for the atrophy of one's own principles. They pointed also to the expense of overseas dominions, standing armies, and navalism, and the danger of being embroiled in imperialist wars.

Many leading anti-imperialists were men of great distinction; their ranks included by far the greater part of the eminent figures of the literary and intellectual world. Most of them were, however, in the unfortunate position of opposing the fruits of a war that they had either favored or failed to oppose. Unlike the expansionists, they did not have complete control of a major party (there were more expansionists among the Democrats than there were anti-expansionists among the Republicans). They were hopelessly heterogeneous: Gold Democrats, Bryan Democrats, New-England-conscience Republicans, and a scattering of reformers and intellectuals.

They organized late—the Anti-Imperialist League grew up in the months after November 1898—and their political leadership, however ardent in sentiment, pursued a hesitant and uncertain course. Their most eminent political leaders were chiefly old men, and the strongest appeal of the anti-imperialist movement seems to have been to the old, high-principled elements in the country, while the imagination of the young was fired far more by the rhetoric of expansionism. It seems clear that the main chance of this minority was to use its position in the Senate to deny the necessary two-thirds approval to the peace treaty acquiring the islands from Spain. Here the opponents of annexation might have delayed it long enough to give themselves a chance to reach the public. But William Jennings Bryan, for reasons that are not altogether clear, persuaded enough members of his party to vote for the treaty to lose the case. Bryan hoped to continue the fight, of course, and grant independence later, but over his conduct and his explanations there hangs a heavy sense of inevitable defeat, stemming from his recognition that the voice of the majority demanded the bold and aggressive policy. . . .

Additional Reading

G. W. Auxier, "Middle Western Newspapers and the Spanish-American War, 1895–1898," *Mississippi Valley Historical Review*, XXVI (1940), 523–534.

E. J. Benton, *International Law and Diplomacy of the Spanish-American War* (1908).

F. E. Chadwick, *The Relations of the United States and Spain: Diplomacy* (1909).

Foster Rhea Dulles, *The Imperial Years* (1956).

Margaret Leech, *In the Days of McKinley* (1959).

Ernest R. May, *Imperial Democracy: Emergence of America as a Great Power* (1961).

Walter Millis, *The Martial Spirit* (1931).

M. M. Wilkerson, *Public Opinion and the Spanish-American War* (1932).

II THE "OPEN-DOOR" POLICY: *Markets and Morality*

The traditional trading policy of the United States in China was an insistence on commercial equality with other powers, expressed in treaty form as "the most favored nation" principle. When Great Britain, at the conclusion of the Opium War, compelled the Chinese imperial government to open five ports to British trade, the United States secured similar privileges in the 1844 Treaty of Wanghia. Other nations interested in the China trade obtained the same rights. The principle of commercial equality in China was thus the first phase of the "Open-Door" policy: equal privileges, uniform tariff rates, port charges, and transportation fees.

In the last years of the 19th century, the economic situation began to change. Western interests in the Celestial Empire had heretofore been commercial; now, the emphasis began to be placed on mining concessions, railroad construction, and financial investments. The major powers scrambled for leased ports and spheres of influence in China, within which discrimination was usually practiced against all other foreign competitors. The weak Chinese government was unable to resist successfully these demands and China appeared to be on the verge of dismemberment and partition. Russia was driving southward from maritime Siberia into Manchuria and northern Korea; Germany acquired leaseholds in 1897 in Shantung province; France pushed northward from Indo-China; and Japan made substantial gains after victory in the 1894–95 Sino-Japanese War.

British trading interests had been predominant in China in the past and were obviously endangered by these threats to the principle of commercial equality. Alarmed at the danger and seeking closer Anglo-American relations, the British government in 1898 and early 1899 proposed to the United States joint action in behalf of the preservation of commercial equality in China. The McKinley administration, aware of the small American interest in China and because of traditional isolationist policies, declined. A reversal, however, took place after the Spanish-American War. Secretary of State John Hay enunciated in two notes to the major powers what came to be known as the "Open-Door" policy. Though the two statements were unilateral declarations, scholars have asked if they were not undertaken at the British initiative and in the British behalf, and in an area of little real concern to the United States. Or, if the notes represented concrete American interests in China, what were those interests and to what extent were they exaggerated as the basis for action?

DOCUMENTS

1. Commercial Equality of Opportunity

The first "open-door" note has often been misunderstood. Secretary of State John Hay did not object to spheres of influence but merely requested that within leased ports and spheres discrimination should not be practiced against other foreign commerce. The September 6 note here reprinted was sent to Germany, Britain, Russia, France, Japan and other powers. The replies generally were evasive, contingent upon acceptance by other governments and exempting certain areas from observance of the commercial open door. The Russian response, of December 18–30, was the most evasive and reluctant of all. Yet Secretary Hay blandly announced that the replies had been satisfactory. His statement of March 20, 1900, has been praised by some as a masterpiece of diplomatic maneuver, and by others as an unfortunate bluff falsely giving the American people the impression that moral platitudes and pronouncements suffice in a power-system world.

Secretary of State John Hay's "Open-Door" Note

DEPARTMENT OF STATE,
Washington, September 6, 1899.

At the time when the Government of the United States was informed by that of Germany that it had leased from His Majesty the Emperor of China the port of Kiao-chao and the adjacent territory in the province of Shantung, assurances were given to the ambassador of the United States at Berlin by the Imperial German minister for foreign affairs that the rights and privileges insured by treaties with China to citizens of the United States would not thereby suffer or be in anywise impaired within the area over which Germany had thus obtained control.

More recently, however, the British Government recognized by a formal agreement with Germany the exclusive right of the latter country to enjoy in said leased area and the contiguous "sphere of influence or interest" certain privileges, more especially those relating to railroads and mining enterprises; but as the exact nature and extent of the rights thus recognized have not been clearly defined, it is possible that serious conflicts of interest may at any time arise not only between British and German subjects within said area, but that the interests of our citizens may also be jeopardized thereby.

Earnestly desirous to remove any cause of irritation and to insure at the same time to the commerce of all nations in China the undoubted benefits which should accrue from a formal recognition by the various powers claiming "spheres of interest" that they shall enjoy perfect equality of treatment for their commerce and navigation within such "spheres," the Government of the United States would be pleased to see His German Majesty's Government give formal assurances, and lend its cooperation in securing like assurances from the other interested powers, that each, within its respective sphere of whatever influence—

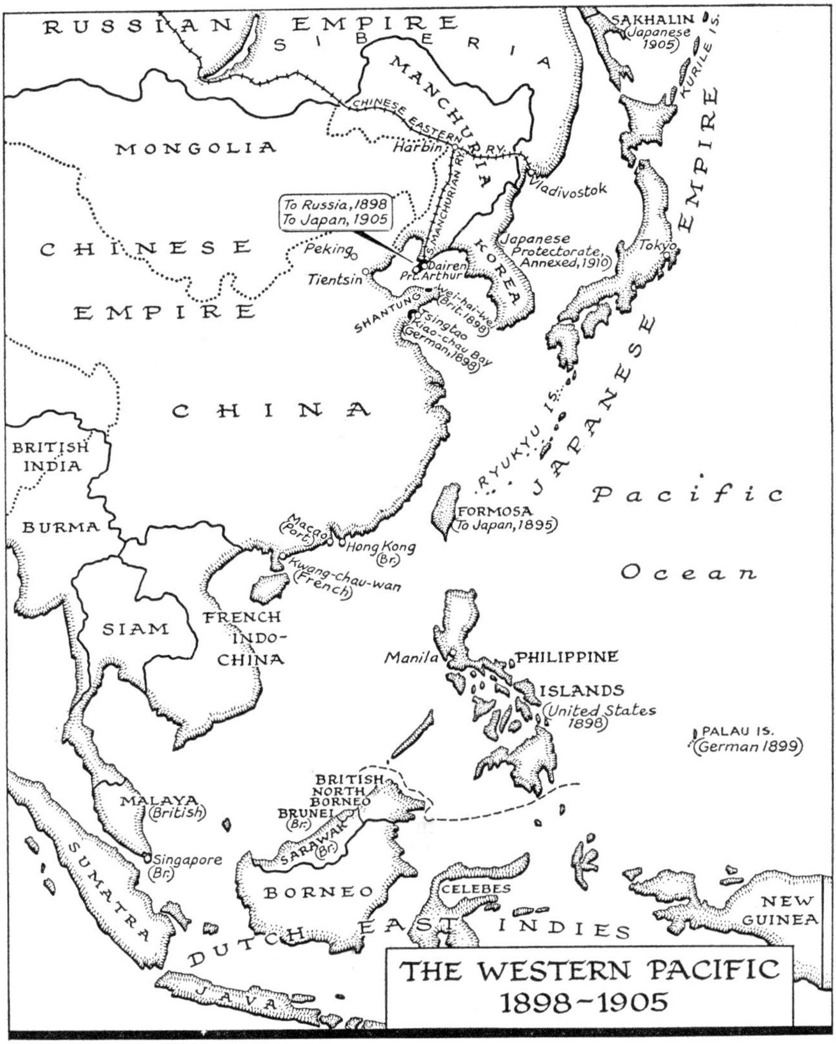

THE WESTERN PACIFIC 1898–1905

First. Will in no way interfere with any treaty port or any vested interest within any so-called "sphere of interest" or leased territory it may have in China.

Second. That the Chinese treaty tariff of the time being shall apply to all merchandise landed or shipped to all such ports as are within said "sphere of interest" (unless they be "free ports"), no matter to what nationality it may belong, and that duties so leviable shall be collected by the Chinese Government.

Third. That it will levy no higher harbor dues on vessels of another nationality frequenting any port in such "sphere" than shall be levied on vessels of its own nationality, and no higher railroad charges over lines built, controlled, or operated within its "sphere" on merchandise belonging to citizens or subjects of other nationalities transported through such "sphere" than shall be levied on similar merchandise belonging to its own nationals transported over equal distances.

The liberal policy pursued by His Imperial German Majesty in declaring Kiao-chao a free port and in aiding the Chinese Government in the establishment there of a custom-house are so clearly in line with the proposition which this Government is anxious to see recognized that it entertains the strongest hope that Germany will give its acceptance and hearty support.

The recent ukase of His Majesty the Emperor of Russia declaring the port of Ta-lien-wan open during the whole of the lease under which it is held from China to the merchant ships of all nations, coupled with the categorical assurances made to this Government by His Imperial Majesty's representative at this capital at the time and since repeated to me by the present Russian ambassador, seem to insure the support of the Emperor to the proposed measure. Our ambassador at the Court of St. Petersburg has in consequence been instructed to submit it to the Russian Government and to request their early consideration of it. A copy of my instruction on the subject to Mr. Tower is herewith inclosed for your confidential information.

The commercial interests of Great Britain and Japan will be so clearly served by the desired declaration of intentions, and the views of the Governments of these countries as to the desirability of the adoption of measures insuring the benefits of equality of treatment of all foreign trade throughout China are so similar to those entertained by the United States, that their acceptance of the propositions herein outlined and their cooperation in advocating their adoption by the other powers can be confidently expected. I inclose herewith copy of the instruction which I have sent to Mr. Choate on the subject.

In view of the present favorable conditions, you are instructed to submit the above considerations to His Imperial German Majesty's Minister for Foreign Affairs, and to request his early consideration of the subject.

Copy of this instruction is sent to our ambassadors at London and at St. Petersburg for their information.

The Russian Reply to the American Ambassador

MINISTRY OF FOREIGN AFFAIRS,
December 18–30, 1899.

Mr. Ambassador: I had the honor to receive your excellency's note dated the 8th–20th of September last, relating to the principles which the Government of the United States would like to see adopted in commercial matters by the powers which have interests in China.

In so far as the territory leased by China to Russia is concerned, the Imperial Government has already demonstrated its firm intention to follow the policy of "the open door" by creating Dalny (Ta-lien-wan) a free port; and if at some future time that port, although remaining free itself, should be separated by a customs limit from other portions of the territory in question, the customs duties would be levied, in the zone subject to the tariff, upon all foreign merchandise without distinction as to nationality.

As to the ports now opened or hereafter to be opened to foreign commerce by the Chinese Government, and which lie beyond the territory leased to Russia, the settlement of the question of the customs duties belongs to China herself, and the Imperial Government has no intention whatever of claiming any privileges for its own subjects to the exclusion of other foreigners. It is to be understood, however, that this assurance of the Imperial Government is given upon condition that a similar declaration shall be made by other powers having interests in China.

With the conviction that this reply is such as to satisfy the inquiry made in the aforementioned note, the Imperial Government is happy to have complied with the wishes of the American Government, especially as it attaches the highest value to anything that may strengthen and consolidate the traditional relations of friendship existing between the two countries.

Hay's Instructions to the United States Ambassadors at London, Paris, Berlin, St. Petersburg, and Rome, and to the United States Minister at Tokyo

DEPARTMENT OF STATE,
Washington, March 20, 1900.

The ——— Government having accepted the declaration suggested by the United States concerning foreign trade in China, the terms of which I transmitted to you in my instruction No. ——— of ———, and like action having been taken by all the various powers having leased territory or so-called "spheres of interest" in the Chinese Empire, as shown by the notes which I herewith transmit to you, you will please inform the Government to which you are accredited that the condition originally attached to its acceptance—that all other powers concerned should likewise accept the proposals of the United States—having been complied with, this Government will therefore consider the assent given to it by ——— as final and definitive.

You will also transmit to the minister for foreign affairs copies of the present inclosures, and by the same occasion convey to him the expression of the sincere gratification which the President feels at the successful termination of these negotiations, in which he sees proof of the friendly spirit which animates the various powers interested in the untrammeled development of commerce and industry in the Chinese Empire, and a source of vast benefit to the whole commercial world.

2. *Chinese Territorial Integrity*

The July 3, 1900, circular from Hay to the great powers was occasioned by the Boxer Rebellion in China and the resultant threat of an imminent partition of the empire. It did not request formal replies and was intended to avert the danger without unduly affecting the presidential campaign under way in the United States. Probably Hay did not intend to inaugurate a new policy, binding on subsequent administrations, yet such was to result from his vague commitment of the United States to the preservation of Chinese independence and integrity. American policy in the past had been to observe that principle itself, but Hay now seemed to imply that the United States would try to protect China against all other powers.

Hay's Note of 1900 to the Great Powers

DEPARTMENT OF STATE,
Washington, July 3, 1900.

In this critical posture of affairs in China it is deemed appropriate to define the attitude of the United States as far as present circumstances permit this to be done. We adhere to the policy initiated by us in 1857, of peace with the Chinese nation, of furtherance of lawful commerce, and of protection of lives and property of our citizens by all means guaranteed under extraterritorial treaty rights and by the law of nations. If wrong be done to our citizens we propose to hold the responsible authors to the uttermost accountability. We regard the condition at Pekin as one of virtual anarchy, whereby power and responsibility are practically devolved upon the local provincial authorities. So long as they are not in overt collusion with rebellion and use their power to protect foreign life and property we regard them as representing the Chinese people, with whom we seek to remain in peace and friendship. The purpose of the President is, as it has been heretofore, to act concurrently with the other powers, first, in opening up communication with Pekin and rescuing the American officials, missionaries, and other Americans who are in danger; secondly, in affording all possible protection everywhere in China to American life and property; thirdly, in guarding and protecting all legitimate American interests; and fourthly, in aiding to prevent a spread of the disorders to the other provinces of the Empire and a recurrence of such disasters. It is, of course, too early to forecast the means of attaining this last result; but the policy of the Government of the United States is to seek a solution which may bring about permanent safety and peace to China, preserve Chinese territorial and administrative entity, protect all rights guaranteed to friendly powers by treaty and international law, and safeguard for the world the principle of equal and impartial trade with all parts of the Chinese Empire.

You will communicate the purport of this instruction to the minister for foreign affairs.

READINGS

1. The Open Door: an Altruistic Policy

The journalist Mark Sullivan expresses in the following excerpt the popular view held by most Americans of the Hay "Open-Door" notes. Detecting the selfish plans of the other great powers, the American government on its own initiative acted to uphold commercial equality in China and to prevent the dismemberment of the empire. Far-visioned statesmanship and vigorous, imaginative, diplomacy averted the peril.

Our Times

MARK SULLIVAN

On January 2, 1900, Hay announced to the Cabinet that he had completed negotiations for the "open door" in China. The negotiations consisted of securing assurances from the various Powers, Great Britain, France, Germany, Russia, Japan, and Italy, who then had or looked to acquiring interests in China, that in whatever influence they might exercise over China or any part of it, the treaty rights of the United States, and of all other nations, with China, would be respected; that neither our citizens and commerce, nor those of any other nation, would be placed at a disadvantage by any discriminating tariff laws or other conditions.

The "open door" policy in China was an American idea. It was set up in contrast to the "spheres-of-influence" policy practised by other nations. "Spheres of influence" was really a euphemism for the "partition of China," which in 1900 was looked upon as well under way. Since her defeat by Japan in 1894, it had been realized that China was not a fighting nation, and could not defend herself against modern armies and navies. She lay like a stranded whale.

While Hay put his negotiations on the ground of maintaining the existing status of the interests of the United States in territory grabbed by other Powers (which was the only aspect he had a clear right to discuss), its effect was to take away some of the motive of the Powers for aggrandizement, and ultimately to save the territorial and national integrity of China.

The "open door" is one of the most creditable episodes in American diplomacy, an example of benevolent impulse accompanied by energy and shrewd skill in negotiation. Not one of the statesmen and nations that agreed to Hay's policy wanted to. It was like asking every man who believes in truth to stand up—the liars are obliged to be the first to rise. Hay saw through them perfectly; his insight into human nature was one of his strongest qualities. Doubtless he had his own moments of indignation, but he had learned something of patience and long-suffering self-restraint from Lincoln, although even in his mellow maturity he never quite ceased to be what his college mates described: "A fellow who would never do a mean act, nor tolerate one."

Every aspect of Hay's achievement excites enthusiasm. His vision and idealism were the more remarkable, since he was going against the current of the age, as only a scholar, a man who knew the world and history, would. The atmosphere of the time took the dismemberment of China for granted. The air was full of a hypocritical cant which put greed in words of benevolence—everybody not a White Man was regarded as a White Man's Burden. It was Europe, mainly, that was grabbing, but we were in it too, and there were plenty who would have counselled that our policy should be to join the scramble, take our share and take it in time. There was much talk about using the Philippines as a foothold for further expansion in the Orient. Hay took his course without any appearance of doing a daring thing; even in his own mind he did not seem to set it up as anything dramatic—it was just the natural expression of honesty and wisdom, the ordinary day's work of a gentleman in high office.

The "open-door" policy survived, and despite some setbacks, grew so that in 1925 the integrity of China was far more secure than had seemed likely in 1900.

Less than a month after the announcement of success in the "open-door" negotiations, Hay's altruistic course was made more difficult by the necessity of uniting with Great Britain, France, and Germany, in a joint note to the Chinese Government demanding protection for missionaries who, with other foreigners, were being subjected more and more to threats by the natives. The anti-foreign movement came to a head in June, 1900, when the foreign legations in Pekin were attacked. . . .

Troops of all the Great Powers were sent to relieve their legations, and to put down the uprising, for the Chinese Government was not only too feeble to resist foreign aggression, but even to put down internal conflict. The conditions seemed not only to tempt but almost to justify seizure of Chinese territory. The German Von Waldersee, as the highest in rank among the foreign commanders, was made commander-in-chief. Leaving Berlin, he wore the uniform presented to him by Emperor William, which the latter had worn on his voyage to Jerusalem. The German troops before leaving for China were harangued by the War Lord, who instructed them to so comport themselves in China that "no Chinese shall ever again dare even to look at a German askance." As it turned out, the Germans were no more ruthless than the troops of some other nations.

While the American Government participated energetically with troops and otherwise in rescuing foreigners and suppressing the outbreak, President McKinley and Secretary Hay maintained an attitude of sympathetic understanding of the cause, and controlled the situation in such a way as to avoid its being used as an occasion for the disruption of China's national and territorial entity. Hay persuaded the Powers to agree to joint occupation until the issues were settled, shrewdly assuming that in a joint occupation mutual jealousies would prevent any one Power from seizing any portion of the empire. He then persuaded England and

Germany not to demand territory, and to oppose such a demand from the others. Thereafter it was agreed that the reparations should be in the form of money.

2. The British Influence

A. Whitney Griswold, a respected authority on American policies in the Orient, emphasized the role of Great Britain in triggering the "Open-Door" notes. Hay's two declarations were not mere reiterations of traditional American policies in the Far East, but instead were major forays into world politics. China was saved from further partition, he concludes, not by the American actions—for these were not backed by force—but by the precarious balance of power prevailing in Europe and the Far East. Yet Hay had helped frame policies which were subsequently viewed as permanent American commitments and which eventually were to result in conflict with Japan.

Writing the Open-Door Notes

A. WHITNEY GRISWOLD

. . . Business and diplomacy were not the only forces impelling Hay toward his fateful decision. American missionaries in the Far East had also been thrilled by the conquest of the Philippines. In 1899 there were between one thousand and fifteen hundred of them in China where they, and their predecessors, had early assumed a political importance out of all proportion to their numbers. Now their situation was very comparable to that of American businessmen in China. Just as they were rejoicing in the annexation of the Philippines for the aid and comfort they thought it would give their cause, they found themselves confronted by an anti-foreign movement stirred up partly by the concessions-scramble, partly by their own proselytizing, that was to culminate in the Boxer Rebellion. In 1899 they, too, wished the United States to show a strong hand in China.

So far the McKinley Administration had adhered strictly to precedent in the Far East. It had kept free of alliances or understandings with foreign powers. It had called the attention of Europe to the long-established interest of the United States in the open door and the preservation of existing treaty rights. From the two particular nations that caused it most alarm it had obtained assurances. The President had declared himself satisfied with these, and proved it by rejecting Pauncefote for the second time within a year. In spite of the concessions-scramble, American trade with China, small though it was, was actually increasing. If it appeared likely to certain business groups that Russia would some day close them out of Northern China, others comtemplated great profit in the sale of products essential to Russia in the development of that region. As yet Germany had been no less hospitable to American trade and

From *The Far Eastern Policy of the United States* by A. Whitney Griswold, copyright, 1938, by Harcourt, Brace & World, Inc., and reprinted with their permission. Pp. 61–65, 67–69, 74–76. 77–86.

capital in Shantung than England had been in the Yangtse Valley. American fears of exclusion, like American hopes of gain, were all in the future. Up to the summer of 1899 neither had been strong enough to cause a departure from the diplomatic traditions and precedents of the past hundred years.

Then, in July and August, through informal, personal channels, the British influence was once more turned on Hay, this time with success.

Like most Secretaries of State, John Hay had only a superficial knowledge of conditions in the Far East. To advise him on this complicated subject he had chosen a friend and, as it happened, one of the best-informed authorities on China of his generation, William W. Rockhill. Born in Philadelphia in 1854, Rockhill's early youth was spent in France, where he completed his education at the military school at Saint Cyr, and where he acquired an interest in the Chinese language and literature. After three years of service as lieutenant in the French Foreign Legion in Algeria, he returned to the United States, and in 1884 procured an appointment as Second Secretary of the Peking Legation. The next year he was promoted to First Secretary. During the winter of 1886–1887 he served as Chargé d'Affaires at Seoul, Korea. He had entered the diplomatic service as a means of pursuing his Chinese studies. He resigned because of personal incompatibility with Denby. After two famous journeys of exploration through Mongolia and Tibet (1888–1889 and 1891–1892) he returned to the diplomatic service as Chief Clerk of the State Department in 1893. From February 14, 1896, to May 10, 1897, he served as Assistant Secretary of State under Olney, during part of which period (March 4 to May 10, 1897) he filled the gap between Olney and Sherman as Acting Secretary.

By this time Rockhill's scholarly writings and explorations had brought him membership in learned Oriental societies and scientific institutes all over the world. His wide experience in the Far East and in the Department of State had established his reputation as an expert on China and earned him the friendship and admiration of influential Republicans including Roosevelt, Lodge and Hay. When it became evident that Denby was to be replaced, Rockhill's friends urged McKinley to appoint him Minister to China, a post his training pre-eminently qualified him to fill. They were disappointed. Rockhill was sent to Athens as Minister to Greece, Roumania and Servia. It was from this post that Adee and Hay rescued him in April, 1899, by helping to secure his appointment as Director of the Bureau of American Republics in Washington, presumably in order to have the benefit of his counsel on affairs in Eastern Asia. In any event, Rockhill had no sooner assumed his new office (May 22) than the Secretary of State began to solicit his advice.

Rockhill, too, had his confidential adviser in Alfred E. Hippisley, a British subject and a member of the Chinese Imperial Maritime Customs Service. Hippisley was an old China hand. It should be recalled that the Chinese customs service was administered by the British, a privilege ultimately sanctioned by treaty in 1898 for as long as England's share of China's foreign trade should exceed that of any other nation. A member of this service since 1867, Hippisley had long followed political affairs in China with a sharp, intelligent eye. His acquaintance with Rockhill dated from the autumn of 1884 when the latter first joined the staff of the American legation in Peking. "In a small community such as that of Peking," wrote Hippisley many years later, "acquaintance quickly ripens into intimacy between persons who have similar tastes, and both Rockhill and I were deeply interested in China and Chinese politics, and in my case the intimacy was made the closer by my marriage in the following year with Miss Howard, a friend of long standing of Mrs. Rockhill's, who had accompanied the latter and her husband from Baltimore." What Rockhill was to Hay, Hippisley was to Rockhill: an old friend and trusted adviser on the Far East.

Mutual friendship—and fate—drew the three men together in the early summer of 1899. Simultaneously with Rockhill's inauguration as Director General of the Bureau of American Republics, a periodic leave of absence brought Hippisley to the United States on his way home to England. From about the middle of June to the end of July the Englishman visited his wife's family in Baltimore. He was pleased to renew his acquaintance with Rockhill, whom he had not seen for over ten years. "Naturally," he remembers, "I went over as frequently as I could to Washington to discuss the conditions in China with him and especially what could be done to maintain the 'open door' or equality of opportunity for all nations in that country." On one of these occasions Rockhill, deeply impressed by his friend's ideas, introduced him to the Secretary of State. Hay heard him expound, in outline, the scheme ultimately comprehended by the open door notes.

Throughout the informal negotiations of that summer, Hippisley was clearly the prime mover. Hay, though disposed to cooperate with England, was waiting for Rockhill to find a way to do it. Rockhill, who had been absent from China for seven years, was rusty on China. Hippisley came fresh from the scene, his mind brimming with images and theories of the concessions-scramble and how to deal with it. It was he who took the initiative, who supplied the concrete plans; nor did he lack encouragement. "China is, and will remain, the one absorbing subject," Rockhill told him, "so I am awfully anxious to have all the data you can give me on the subject, that I may not make any mistake, and that my conclusions shall be practicable."

When, about August first, Hay left Washington for his summer home in New Hampshire, and Hippisley departed Baltimore on a leisurely journey, *via* Lenox and Bar Harbor to Quebec (whence he would sail for England September seventh), Hippisley opened an active correspondence with Rockhill. "As I shall not now have an opportunity of seeing you before we start for Europe," he wrote July 25, "I write these lines to ask you to use your influence towards, if possible, inducing the govt. to do what it can to maintain the open door for ordinary commerce in China."

. . . Rockhill passed Hippisley's recommendations on to Hay after adding to their weight his own authoritative *imprimatur*. The same day he replied to Hippisley:

> You know what my views are about the position the United States should take in China; I would like to see it make a declaration in some form or other, which would be understood by China as a pledge on our part to assist in maintaining the integrity of the Empire. I fear, however, that home politics and next year's elections will interfere with this, for it might be interpreted by a large part of the voting population of the United States, especially the Irish and the Germans, as an adoption of the policy advocated by England, and any leaning towards England on the part of the administration would, at this time and for the next year to come, be dangerous, and might lose the President his nomination. I consequently fear that he will do absolutely nothing either on the lines you indicate, and which are clearly those most beneficial to our interests in China, or in any other which will commit us. We will simply continue drifting along.

Hay confirmed these doubts. "I thank you for your letter inclosing Mr. Hippisley's," he wrote, August 7. "I am fully awake to the great importance of what you say, and am more than ready to act. But the senseless prejudices in certain sections of the 'Senate and people' compel us to move with great caution."

Hippisley did not give up hope. His reason for "urging *prompt* action" along the lines of his last note was, he explained, "precisely to forestall any suggestion likely to prove injurious to the Administration that it was following the lead of or leaning towards England by inducing it to take the initiative itself; then if England took similar action, she would follow America's lead." The Englishman had developed a remarkable solicitude for the welfare of the United States. "I think it would be suicidal for America to drift and do nothing for another year," he warned.

> My latest advices from Peking say: "the activity of the Russians in Manchuria is simply wonderful. . . . The Russification of Peking and of North China will proceed as rapidly as has that of Manchuria." These are precisely the districts which are the great consumers of American textile fabrics, and I don't for a moment believe that American manufacturers will sit by with folded hands and see these districts closed without making an effort to retain them. Pressure will therefore be brought to bear upon the Administration and it may then have no option but to take such action as I have suggested, with possibly however the difference of following instead of leading England.

This time Rockhill's response was more encouraging. He had received "today," he wrote on the eighteenth, "pretty clear assurances from the State Department that it may take some action sooner than could be anticipated from the position it held until within a few weeks and which I gave you in my last letter." But Rockhill was not over-sanguine. Once more he showed himself to be in advance of Hippisley: he favored securing "tangible" assurances from the powers "as to their desire to maintain and insure the integrity of the Chinese Empire. . . ." This, he still believed the Administration was unwilling to consider; the best he and Hippisley could do was to "keep pegging away at it." The next day he submitted to Adee long extracts from Hippisley's last two letters.

Meanwhile two things had come to Hippisley's support. Almost simultaneously came the news of the return to the United States of Dr. Jacob Gould Schurman, Chairman of the President's Philippine Commission, and the Czar's ukase of August 15 declaring Talienwan a free port. All that restrained Hay from embarking on the policy advocated by Hippisley, apparently, was the opposition to it of the President himself. Whatever the true source of this opposition—respect for tradition, the lingering influence of Sherman, sincere conviction or mere partisan expediency—it had tied the Secretary's hands since his assumption of office. Undoubtedly Hay had been converted as early as June, 1898, when he had written McKinley a personal letter from the London embassy, urging him to reconsider the first Pauncefote overture. More lately he had professed to be "more than ready to act" and lamented the "senseless prejudices" that restrained him. It is probable that, for the past year, whenever the occasion had offered, he had urged on the President some such policy as that now in the making. Dr. Schurman and the Czar seem to have knocked the last props from under McKinley's resistance. . . .

The Rockhill memorandum (dated August 28, 1899) appears to have been the final instrument of McKinley's conversion. For, on September 5, Rockhill composed the actual drafts of the open door notes themselves, which, after a few corrections by Adee, were despatched the following day, over the signature of the Secretary of State, to the American ambassadors in London, Berlin and St. Petersburg. The notes, like the memoranda from which they were written, and as their authors had privately agreed, eschewed the subject of China's territorial integrity. This Rockhill felt to be "still such a complex question that I do not think we have it in anything like a shape to discuss it advantageously . . . so awfully big, that I think for the time being we had better not broach it over here." But, he believed, the notes would have the desired effect of giving China breathing space, of promoting "a general line of policy which may be favorable to the maintenance and the strengthening of the Peking Government."

The notes were carefully worded. Their authors were aware of the exigencies of American politics that restrained their own personal desires. Accordingly they recognized the spheres of influence as existing facts, omitted any reference to mining and railway concessions, and the whole perplexing problem of capital investment, and specifically asked only for equal commercial opportunity within each sphere. Each power addressed was requested to give its formal assurances that it would observe the regulations presented by the notes *mutatis mutandis*. But that is not all the notes requested. In addition to its own assurances, each power was urged to co-operate with the United States in obtaining the assurances of all the other powers concerned. Thus the notes invoked not only the time-honored American principle of the open door, but also the so-called "co-operative policy." The combination of the two, applied to the current situation in China, made the notes something more than a mere iteration of the traditional Far Eastern policy of the United States. It made them a foray into

World politics, an attempt to influence the foreign policies of the European powers in such a way as to establish free commercial competition in the region of Eastern Asia. It was an unusual thing for the United States to seek to influence the dispensations of international politics in regions outside its own hemisphere. . . .

A careful perusal of the replies to the open door notes shows Rockhill's assumptions, both as to the influence of the United States in the Far East and the effectiveness of the notes themselves, to have been unfounded. The replies to the notes were uniformly evasive and non-committal. The first and most satisfactory reply was the British, but even this left much to be desired. Though Lord Salisbury professed his enthusiasm for the open door principle, he was loath to apply it either to Hongkong or to Weihaiwei, contending that the former was a colony, the latter a leased territory, and opposing the application of the principle to areas in either of these categories.

The Prime Minister's attitude was "rather disappointing in view of his first reception of your proposition," Ambassador Choate wrote Hay. Moreover, Salisbury was of the opinion that "we are a little too sanguine in our expectations of obtaining Declarations from the other Powers." Nearly three months elapsed before Salisbury was willing to compromise, which he did grudgingly. Great Britain agreed to the application of the open door principle to Weihaiwei, and to all British leased territory and spheres of interest in China, present or future, the United States acquiesced in the exemption of Hongkong from this rule. The entire British declaration was then emasculated by the proviso that it was "to be considered as dependent on similar assent by the other Powers in like circumstances."

The replies of the other powers were full of loopholes, Russia's amounting to a thinly disguised rejection of the whole proposition. Each of them, like the British, made its acceptance contingent upon the acceptance of all the others, which reduced everyone to the least common denominator, the Russian. Rockhill and Hay realized the situation perfectly and tried to meet it with bluff. Rockhill privately admitted to Hippisley that the Russian reply "has what we call in America a string attached to it"; but he thought it "prudent" to accept it none the less. "Our object," Hay wrote Tower, "is now to give the widest significance to the Russian reply of which it is capable. Without running the risk of bringing upon ourselves a contradiction of our assumptions, we want to take it for granted that Russia has acceded to our proposals without much qualification." At length, on March 20, the Secretary of State cavalierly announced that he had received satisfactory assurances from all the powers addressed, and that he regarded each as "final and definitive."

Hay had not long to wait to discover just how "final and definitive" they were. In June, not three months after his expression of satisfaction, a Chinese patriotic society known to the West as the "Boxers" stirred up an armed rebellion against foreign missionaries and concession-hunters and the Manchu Government that had truckled with them. Ripping up portions of the Tientsin-Peking Railway and destroying telegraph lines, the rebels cut off Peking from the outside world, murdered the secretary of the Japanese legation, and the German minister, and besieged the foreign legations in the city. An allied military force was hastily despatched to the relief of the legations. From June 20 until August 14, the day the siege was lifted, the foreigners in Peking lived under fire in the legation compound, menaced by starvation and disease, their fate unknown either to their governments or to the troops marching to their rescue.

It was apparent to Hay from the outset that the disorders had provided certain of the powers not unwelcome pretexts for enlarging their spheres and extending their influence in China. Russia and Germany were on the march. Hay sensed the need—or opportunity—for more extensive measures than mere participation in the allied relief expedition. "We have no policy in China except to protect with energy American interests, and especially American citizens, and the legation," he had wired Conger, June 10. "There must be nothing done which would commit us to future action inconsistent with your standing instructions. There must be no alliances." When the Boxers moved on Peking he showed his hand more fully. On July 3, with the approval of McKinley, he despatched to the powers another circular defining American policy. Unlike the notes of the previous September, this circular asked for no assurances and, indeed, elicited none; it was merely submitted to the consideration of each of the powers addressed. Taking cognizance of the "virtual anarchy" existing in China it set forth the purpose of the United States to "act concurrently with the other powers" in restoring order and protecting the lives and property of its nationals and "all legitimate American interests." In its concluding sentence, however, it added to this purpose a momentous new objective, namely, "to seek a solution which may bring about permanent safety and peace to China, *preserve Chinese territorial and administrative entity*, protect all rights guaranteed to friendly powers by treaty and international law, and safeguard for the world the principle of equal and impartial trade with all parts of the Chinese Empire."

The United States had always stood for the "territorial and administrative entity" of China but in a purely subjective way. It had observed the principle itself; it had not assumed the function of persuading others to observe it. The notes of September 6, as we have seen, had accepted the impairment of China's territorial integrity as a *fait accompli*. They had taken it for granted that foreign spheres of influence and territorial concessions in China would continue to exist, and even to expand, as is proved by the fact that the notes asked for most-favored-nation treatment for American commerce in all future as well as present spheres and leased territories. But the circumstances attending the Boxer Rebellion, following the unfavorable reception of the September notes, led Hay to the conclusion that the maintenance of the open door in China depended on the maintenance of China's complete sovereignty over her own territories. In his circular of July 3, 1900, therefore, he went further than reiterating America's traditional policy of respect for China's integrity, further than asking the powers to observe the principle of equal commercial opportunity. He suggested a collective guarantee of both these conditions. To "preserve" Chinese integrity was something different from merely respecting it. Assuming, as did Hay himself, that the chief end of America's Far Eastern policy remained commercial, the circular of July 3 and the subsequent adherence of the United States to the principles it contained, appreciably altered the means to that end. He had committed the United States to the policy of striving to deter its competitors for the Chinese market from violating the territorial and administrative integrity of the Chinese nation.

Only Great Britain made response to Hay's circular, and this in the most casual manner. The other powers proceeded with their independent plans for obtaining satisfaction from, or taking advantage of, China. Russia continued to pour troops into Manchuria. That England had no faith in the Hay policy, and had decided to reply on means other than American note-writing to defend her interests in China, seems obvious. She had never banked wholly on American co-operation in the Far East, but had used this only as one of three instruments, the other two being outright participation in the concessions-scramble, and bilateral agreements with her rivals.

Hay need not have been puzzled (as he was) by Pauncefote's uncommunicative attitude during the summer of 1900; by Salisbury's intrigues with the other powers to permit Japan to send an expeditionary force into northern China; by the Anglo-German declaration of October 16, 1900, in favor of the open door and the territorial integrity of China. What these signs indicated was that Great Britain had turned to Japan as her partner in the Far East, her ally against Russia, and had resorted to bilateral negotiations to stay the advance of Germany.

It was in this manner that the partitioning of China was halted, temporarily, in 1900. The Boer War, the German navy, the maneuverings of the hostile European coalitions, the Czar, the Kaiser, Delcassé and Salisbury—these were the factors and agents that called the halt, not the diplomacy of John Hay. It was a case of political stalemate rather than conversion to principle. No power dared move further for fear of precipitating the universal *débâcle* that was destined to come a decade later, and so China was granted a brief respite.

Experience was disillusioning to the authors of the open door notes, as it was to Roosevelt in the case of the Philippines. No sooner had the rescue of the legations been effected than McKinley began to press for the withdrawal of the American troops from China. He feared their continued residence there as a political liability at home. Rockhill, who had done so much to launch the United States on its new policy, and who, in July, 1900, was sent to China as special commissioner to investigate the rebellion and represent his country at the peace settlement, readily confessed his discouragement. So did Hippisley. The excessive indemnities demanded of China, the latter wrote, after a long silence, in March, 1901, would have to be "liquidated by territorial concessions leading to partition and so ultimately to war among the Powers.

> The soldiers have committed atrocities horrible beyond description, and the Ministers of their nationals are all engaged in looting. While [*sic*] Russia working independently on her own account places Manchuria, Mongolia and Turkestan under a protectorate, and throws the treaty rights of other nations into the dustbin. Right and reason disappear, and we return to the ethics of the Dark Ages. To an outsider it is all very sad and shows utter demoralisation."

Rockhill replied in the same gloomy vein. He was, he said, "sick and tired of the whole business and heartily glad to get away from it.

> I have been able to do something for commercial interests, and in a number of points have been able to carry out the Secretary's views, but have been practically alone in the negotiations. England has her agreement with Germany, Russia has her alliance with France, the Triple Alliance comes in here, and every other combination you know of is working here just as it is in Europe. I trust it may be a long time before the United States gets into another muddle of this description."

Hay's disillusionment, though less outspoken, was if anything more complete. For in November, 1900, under pressure from the War and Navy Departments, he executed the surprising *volte face* of instructing Conger to endeavor to obtain for the United States a naval base and territorial concession at Samsah Bay in the Chinese maritime province of Fukien. The erstwhile champion of Chinese integrity, still outwardly loyal to the policy of his notes, had actually forsaken that policy and tried to enter the concessions-scramble. As it happened Fukien had already been pre-empted as a sphere of influence by Japan, whose treaty right in the province would be infringed by the American venture. Japan had to be consulted. It must have been embarrassing for Hay to read the Japanese reply, reminding him of his own admonitions against using the Boxer Rebellion as the opportunity for territorial aggrandizement, and reaffirming the Imperial Government's adherence to that principle.

Thereafter the Secretary of State trimmed the sails of his Far Eastern policy ever more closely to the wind. As Russia strengthened her hold on Manchuria, he gradually retreated to the position of his first open door notes, accepting the fact that Manchuria was no longer an integral part of the Chinese Empire, but rather a Russian province, in which open door treatment was to be bargained for with the Czar. "I take it for granted," he told Roosevelt in April, 1903, "that Russia knows as we do that we will not fight over Manchuria, for the simple reason that we cannot. . . . If our rights and interests in opposition to Russia in the Far East were as clear as noonday, we could never get a treaty through the Senate, the object of which was to check Russian aggression." To all intents and purposes Hay had abandoned the doctrine of the territorial integrity of China, at least to the extent of recognizing Manchuria as beyond the Chinese pale.

What, then, had the open door notes accomplished? They had not invented, or even promoted, a "co-operative" policy. There never had been a co-operative policy in Eastern Asia that rose above joint military expeditions, such as the Shimonoseki and Boxer, or identic notes of protest at anti-foreign riots. Only in common defense of their nationals did the powers stand together. As for co-operating among themselves, in the interest of collective security, fair play, free competition, equal opportunity, there was none of that; there never had been any. Japanese, Russian, British, German, French and American soldiers could all march together to Peking. But once the siege was raised and the diplomats had taken charge, every semblance of co-operation vanished.

It has been suggested that the Hay notes were part of a diplomatic trade by which the United States gained supremacy in the Caribbean, in return for co-operating with England in the Far East. But, in spite of intensive search, no evidence has been discovered that would remove the idea from the realm of conjecture. Chronology alone makes it plausible. By the Hay-Pauncefote Treaty of 1900 the United States gained from England the right to construct and maintain a canal across the Isthmus of Panama. At approximately the same time, America came to England's assistance in China. History abounds, however, with examples of the *post hoc* fallacy. Rockhill and Hippisley, at pains to exhaust every possible argument that might further their designs, never mentioned the connection between the Caribbean and the Far East, which Hippisley has since called "the product of lively but ill-balanced imagination."

England was scarcely in a position to exact any such price as that supposed to have been paid by Hay for her strategic retreat from the Caribbean. The Boer War, the growing power of the United States, not to recapitulate more of the many international factors already reviewed, were sufficient to account for that. Months before the open door notes were written, Salisbury had informed Hay (through Henry White) in so many words that he realized the United States would build the canal, that he approved, and that "the canal is of comparatively little importance to England now that they have the Suez Canal. . . ." Pauncefote and Salisbury did not receive the open door notes or the circular on China's territorial integrity as if they were collecting payment for value received.

Hay's claim that he had "accomplished a good deal in the East, but thus far without the expense of a single commitment or promise" is no less difficult to validate. Hay was technically correct: nothing had been "put in writing." Legally the United States was no more bound to pursue the policy of the notes than the powers which had, in varying degrees, evaded their demands. It was the style of the notes, the fact that they were promulgated in a manner deliberately contrived to mobilize public opinion and create the impression of an international commitment, and most important of all, the way Hay's successors practiced what he preached that molded American policy. It may be conceded that the Secretaries of State who followed John Hay did not adhere to the principles of the open door and the preservation of China's territorial integrity solely because he had done so, and at the same time, that tradition and precedent exert a powerful influence on foreign policy.

One thing is clear: Hay had not secured anything approaching an international guarantee of the open door or the "territorial and administrative entity" of China. He had merely oriented American policy toward a more active participation in Far Eastern politics in support of those principles. In so doing he had kept pace with the expansionist forces (of which he was as much product as cause) that had propelled the United States into the conquest and annexation of the Philippines.

3. *"China's Illimitable Markets"*

The following article does not deny the role of altruism in the Hay "Open-Door" policy but does reveal that powerful economic groups in America were involved in China and were partly responsible for the two notes. Many in the United States believed that unless foreign markets could be found for the ever-increasing surplus of American agricultural and industrial goods, the results would be contraction and economic depression. China's hundreds of millions of people offered a most attractive market solution to the "Bogey of the Surplus." Charles S. Campbell, Jr., is the author of a major study on Anglo-American relations at the turn of the 20th century.

American Business Interests and the Open Door in China

CHARLES S. CAMPBELL, JR.

One of the basic aims of American foreign policy has been to maintain the right of all countries to trade with China on an equal basis. The first formal declaration of this aim came with the sending of the Open Door notes in September, 1899. The origin of these notes has received much attention from historians in recent years, and certain aspects of their origin, particularly the part played by W. W. Rockhill and the Englishman, Alfred Hippisley, have become very well known. At least one aspect, however, has been entirely overlooked: namely, that special business interests in the United States were concerned over the possible loss of the Chinese market; were eager to have the government take just the sort of action which it did take; and were active in bringing pressure to bear on the government. It is the thesis of this article that they were partly responsible for the sending of the notes and, consequently, for America's Open Door policy.

It should be emphatically stated, however, that this article does not pretend to give a complete account of the origins of the Open Door policy. Not only does the author not believe that such an account can be given merely in terms of business pressure on Washington, but the article does not even consider business in general; it is limited almost exclusively to two groups of special interests, which might, indeed, be called one, so closely did they overlap. The almost complete absence of reference to many of the well-known aspects of the origin of the policy does not mean that the author considers these factors unimportant, but simply that he is confining himself to what has not been elaborated elsewhere. Numerous writers have attempted to give a rounded account of the matter; a very

Charles S. Campbell, Jr., "American Business Interests and the Open Door in China," *The Far Eastern Quarterly,* I (1941), 43–58. Reprinted with permission.

few have gone deeply into the part played by business; but no writer has dealt specifically with the special interests here under consideration. Yet the influence of these interests appears to have been so great that any complete history of the origins of the Open Door policy should include some mention of them.

One of these special interests was the American-China Development Company, a corporation founded in 1895 for the purpose of getting railroad concessions in China. Its sixty shares of stock were held by forty-nine shareholders, of whom the best known were the following: the Carnegie Steel Company; Thomas C. Platt, Senator from New York; Levi P. Morton, vice-president of the United States under President Harrison; Frederick P. Olcott, president of the Central Trust Company of New York; John I. Waterbury, president of the Manhattan Trust Company; James Stillman, president of the National City Bank; George F. Baker, president of the First National Bank of New York; Charles Coster, member of J. P. Morgan and Company; Jacob Schiff, member of Kuhn, Loeb, and Company; E. H. Harriman, chairman of the executive committee of the Union Pacific Railway; and G. R. Hegeman, president of the Metropolitan Life Insurance Company. Three officials of the Development Company were also important shareholders: A. W. Bash, its representative in China; General William Barclay Parsons, its chief engineer; and Clarence Cary, its legal adviser. With seven shares of stock, Cary was the company's chief shareholder.

Shortly after the formation of the American-China Development Company, Bash was sent to China to try to get a concession. In May, 1895, he called on Charles Denby, the American minister in Peking, and asked for his assistance. Since Denby had for years been trying to persuade Americans to do business in China, he was anxious to do what he could for Bash; but in view of the State Department's traditional caution about supporting private business interests, he thought it prudent to ask for instructions from Washington.

About this time Richard Olney became Secretary of State. As an advocate of more vigorous support for American enterprise in foreign countries than most of his predecessors, it is not surprising to find him advising Denby "to employ all proper methods for the extension of American commercial interests." It was perhaps as a result of this note that Bash secured shortly afterwards a preliminary contract for a railway concession between Peking and Hankow. But Bash was not empowered to conclude the contract; it was, therefore, necessary to wait until authorized agents of the company should arrive in China. When the agents, one of whom was Clarence Cary, did arrive, they found the Chinese refusing to continue negotiations. Accordingly, they complained to Denby. The minister called on the Chinese foreign office and told the officials that it would be "a breach of good faith" not to go through with the contract. Taking a strong line, he succeeded in persuading the Chinese to resume negotiations.

Meanwhile Olney had been succeeded by John Sherman, a man who did not believe in government support for such ventures as the Development Company. When the new Secretary of State read Denby's official report about the above incident, he was not pleased. "You should be cautious," he warned the minister, "in giving what might be understood as this Government's indorsement of the financial standing of the persons seeking contracts with that of China." It is not wholly surprising, therefore, that two months later a Belgian syndicate, instead of the American-China Development Company, was awarded the contract.

Despite the turn of events the Americans continued their efforts to obtain a concession somewhere in China; but the year closed with no success to report. Did the officials and the powerful shareholders of the Development Company know of Sherman's warning to Denby? Whether they did or not, they must have found little to their liking in the negative policy of the State Department under its new Secretary; and some of them took part in the organized attempt, as will be noted in what follows, to persuade the government to adopt a different policy.

A second group of special interests was the American exporters of cotton goods. Cotton goods were America's chief export to China, and that country provided by far the largest market for American cotton mills. In 1899 this country exported $24,852,691 worth of cotton goods, of which almost half, $10,290,981, went to China alone. No other country came close to this, the second largest importer taking only about one-fourth as much.

At that time England was the leading exporter of cotton goods to China, the United States was second, and far in the rear were Japan and the Netherlands. Although the annual value of the American exports was only about half that of the English, it had increased over 120 per cent from 1887 to 1897; while English exports had declined almost 14 per cent. Americans attached considerable importance to this rapid growth of exports. They believed that the United States was capturing the Chinese market and that it was a market well worth acquiring. Even those with little or no business in China were impressed, for they had great hopes for the future. In those times, as still today, China was considered in wide circles to be potentially the greatest market in the world.

We have, then, in the case of cotton, an American industry vitally concerned with the Chinese market. As many members of the industry were almost altogether dependent on that market, anything which the government might do to preserve it would be to their direct interest. The same, of course, was true of the American-China Development Company. The men connected with this company, along with the cotton exporters, were those who had the greatest financial interest in China, and it was they who were most active in bringing pressure to bear on the American government. Of course, business anxiety over the Chinese market was by no means limited to these two groups, but as they had so much more at stake than any other group, it would be misleading not to give them special treatment.

The first step taken by these special interests occurred at the beginning of 1898. At that time considerable anxiety arose out of developments in China. The previous March, France had made the island of Hainan a sphere of influence; in November, German troops had landed at Kiaochow; and shortly afterwards a Russian fleet had dropped anchor at Port Arthur. It looked to many businessmen as though something which they had been fearing for several years—the partition of China—might be on the verge of realization. The threat to Port Arthur was particularly disturbing to Americans, for it was a key city of Manchuria, which, together with the adjoining provinces of China proper, was the chief market for American cotton goods. It was widely expected that, should Russia get control, discriminatory tariffs would be introduced, and an important market would be lost to the United States.

Business opinion was also aroused by the attitude of the State Department. Despite what seemed to be so obviously a dangerous situation in China, responsible officials were giving no sign of alarm; in fact, they seemed almost to welcome the situation. Interviewed by the Philadelphia *Press*, Secretary Sherman stated that he did not see any likelihood of partition—at least, not for some time. Even if China should be partitioned, he said, "the powers would gladly seize the opportunity to trade with us. Our commercial interests would not suffer, as far as I can see, in the least —quite the contrary."

This expression of opinion was most disturbing to those with financial interests in China. In an article which he wrote apparently just after Sherman's statement, Clarence Cary, back from his unsuccessful trip to China in behalf of the American-China Development Company, denounced what he termed the Secretary's "quaint and dangerous view that the interests of the citizens of the United States are not threatened by a possible partition of China." In a similar vein, the New York *Journal of commerce and commercial bulletin,* a newspaper which often expressed the point of view of many cotton exporters, spoke in a strongly worded editorial of the "generally admitted necessity of prompting the Administration to give notice to the world that the United States will suffer no interference with the commercial rights it now possesses in China."

This combination of encroachment on Chinese soil and evidence of what they took to be disinterestedness on the part of the State Department so alarmed some of those with financial interests in China that they determined to take action. On January 6, 1898, three days after Sherman's statement to the *Press,* they held a meeting in the office of Clarence Cary in New York City. At the meeting a "Committee on American Interests in China" was founded. It was instructed to confer, first with the New York Chamber of Commerce, and then, if it should seem desirable, with other commercial organizations throughout the country, regarding "the methods to be adopted to conserve the rights of citizens of the United States in the Chinese Empire."

There were five members of the Committee: Clarence Cary, Everett Frazer, S. D. Brewster, John Foord, and E. L. Zalinski. Cary has been mentioned before; Frazer was the head of an American firm in Shanghai; Brewster, a partner in one of the large firms handling the export of cotton to China; Foord, a contributing editor of the *Journal of commerce and commercial bulletin;* and Zalinski, a member of the Bethlehem Iron Company. It should be noted that men connected with both the American-China

Development Company and with the cotton interests were on the committee. The committee became the channel through which men like Cary, interested in China as a field of investment, and others, anxious to preserve a market for their cotton, could and did attempt to divert the government from the negative attitude characteristic of it while Sherman was Secretary of State. Through it they were able to organize and co-ordinate their efforts to bring about a new policy.

Just a week after its founding the committee submitted to the New York Chamber of Commerce a petition signed by a large number of important firms. The petition urged the chamber to take such action as would direct the attention of the government to the threatening situation in China and would ensure "that the important commercial interests of the United States" be safeguarded. As a result of the petition the chamber adopted the following memorial on February 3 and forwarded it to President McKinley the same day:

> That there are important changes now going on in the relations of European powers to the Empire of China . . . affecting the privileges enjoyed under existing treaty rights by American citizens trading in and with China. That the trade of the United States to China is now rapidly increasing, and is destined, with the further opening of that country, to assume large proportions unless arbitrarily debarred by the action of foreign governments. . . . That, in view of the changes threatening to future trade development of the United States in China, the Chamber of Commerce . . . respectfully and earnestly urge that such proper steps be taken as will commend themselves to your wisdom for the prompt and energetic defence of the existing treaty rights of our citizens in China, and for the preservation and protection of their important commercial interests in that Empire.

Secretary Sherman, to whom the President had referred the memorial, informed the New York Chamber that the matter was being given the "most careful consideration." As a matter of fact, the same day that he wrote to the chamber he instructed the ambassador in Berlin to inform the authorities in that country of "the interest which this Government must necessarily feel in conserving and expanding the volume of trade which it has built up with China." If, as seems probable, this step was in part the result of the above memorial, it was the first success of the special interests in influencing the policy of the government.

During the first four months of 1898 there were several further developments which originated in the Committee on American Interests in China. The committee had communicated with the commercial organizations of Philadelphia, Boston, San Francisco, and Cleveland, as well as with that of New York, and during this period all except the Cleveland Chamber sent to Washington memorials similar to the one quoted above. Not quite so directly attributable to the committee were memorials received by the government from the Chambers of Commerce of Baltimore and Seattle. That they were inspired, at least indirectly, by the Committee on American Interests is evident in the fact that they were almost identical in wording with the memorial from the New York Chamber. It might also be mentioned that a number of American businessmen in China sent a telegram to the New York body, endorsing its memorial and stating that "immediate action" was necessary for the protection of American interests. This message was forwarded to the State Department.

The adoption of these memorials of early 1898 is doubtless to be attributed not only to the Committee on American Interests but also to events taking place in China during these same months. In February, China was forced to promise Great Britain that the rich Yangtze provinces would never be alienated to another power. This came as something of a shock to Americans, for Britain was commonly regarded as one of the bulwarks of the Open Door in China. Two months later a similar agreement regarding some of the southern provinces was made with France. Most alarming of all were the settlements with Germany and Russia in March—settlements which wound up the Kiaochow and Port Arthur affairs, the beginnings of which have been referred to. Germany succeeded in obtaining a ninety-nine-year lease of the land around Kiaochow Bay, along with extensive economic rights in Shantung province. Russia, after an acute crisis which almost led to war with Great Britain, secured a twenty-five-year lease of the southern tip of the Liaotung peninsula, with the right of building a railway to its principal city, Port Arthur. A more direct threat to the North China market could hardly have been imagined.

Despite both the ominous developments in the Far East and the memorials urging action, the State Department was not pursuing a forceful line. Apart from the mild warning to Germany mentioned above, the only positive step taken during the first part of 1898 was the sending of a telegram by the Secretary of State to Ambassador Hitchcock in St. Petersburg. Hitchcock was instructed to sound out Russia's intentions and to inform the Russian government that the United States was anxious to "maintain open trade in China." Although it was not at all the strong kind of move desired by the special interests, this *démarche* represented a further step in the evolution of the State Department away from the extreme indifference of Sherman earlier in the year. Together with the telegram to Germany it suggests that the memorials originating in the Committee on American Interests were having some effect in Washington.

Not only the government, but also the public in general, was becoming more conscious of the China market; and here too, part of the change must be attributed to the Committee on American Interests in China. Since the memorials inspired by it had been widely discussed in the press, they had reached a larger audience than government circles, and they had not been without effect on public opinion. Evidence for this is to be found in an article by John Foord, stating that because of the memorials the whole question of American business interests in China "began to assume a position of national prominence." As a member of the Committee on American Interests and as an editor of the *Journal of commerce,* Foord, it would seem, was in a position to assess the situation accurately.

The war with Spain, which began in April, 1898, brought with it a rising tide of imperialistic sentiment in the United States. Caught up in this tide and modified by it was the American attitude toward the complex situation in China. To be sure, there was no widespread thought of China as a possible colony, or even of a sphere-of-influence there, but, as Professor Pratt has shown, the foothold which the triumph at Manila Bay gave us in the Philippines was considered by many to be important chiefly because it might help us to hold open the door in the Far East. Then too the fact that America seemed to be suddenly growing up into a great power probably had the effect of making Americans more insistent that treaty rights, including those in China, be upheld.

During the war one of the most important developments in the history of the origins of the Open Door policy took place. The Committee on American Interests had come to the decision that a more permanent form of organization was needed, and to meet that need the committee was transformed in June, 1898, into the American Asiatic Association. The association had the same general aim as its predecessor. As stated in its constitution, this was "to secure the advantage of sustained watchfulness and readiness for action . . . in respect of . . . Asiatic trade, as well as in matters of legislation, or treaties affecting the same." All the members of the original committee became members of the Asiatic Association, and four of them became leading officials. Everett Frazer was the president; S. D. Brewster, the vice-president; John Foord, the secretary; and Clarence Cary, a member of the executive committee.

The reader will have noticed how often the names of two of these officials, Clarence Cary and John Foord, have occurred in the above pages. Both of them were intimately associated with the campaign to influence the policy of the government. Consider the strategic position of each: Cary, counsel for the American-China Development Company and member of the executive committee of the American Asiatic Association; Foord, secretary of the Asiatic Association, editor of its magazine, *Asia*, and contributing editor of the *Journal of commerce.* Although these men were influential only in indirect ways, it is entirely possible that they had as much to do with the sending of the September notes as had such well-known figures as W. W. Rockhill and Alfred Hippisley.

Four days after its founding the Association had just under fifty members. Among them were the General Electric Company; the Guaranty Trust Company; the New York Central and Hudson River Railroad Company; Charles Denby; W. W. Rockhill; Calvin Brice and W. D. Washburn, both officials of the American-China Development Company; and a large number of men in the cotton business.

In order to reach as wide an audience as possible, the association undertook the publication of a periodical entitled *Asia: journal of the American Asiatic association,* the editor of which, as has been said, was John Foord. But propaganda by the association did not become particularly widespread at this time; for, like its predecessor, the association devoted its attention chiefly to the State Department.

The American Asiatic Association was the principal channel through which the special interests made their influence felt in Washington and in the country at large. It was strongly supported by the *Journal of commerce and commercial bulletin,* which devoted an extraordinary amount of editorial and news space to questions of the Chinese market and consistently advocated energetic action by the government to safeguard that market. Co-operation between the association and the journal was doubtless facilitated by the fact that John Foord occupied an important position in each of these guardians of American interests in the Far East.

The founding of the Asiatic Association was the chief event concerned with the origins of the Open Door policy which took place during the war with Spain. However, a few other developments of the same time, though of comparatively minor importance, may also be mentioned.

Perhaps the outstanding of these was a recommendation to Congress by Sherman's successor in the State Department, William R. Day, that a trade commission be sent to China to investigate possibilities for greater exports to that part of the world. Although Congress took no action at the time, the incident has some significance as marking a further step in the evolution of the government toward the point of view of the special interests.

Also of significance was the appointment of John Hay to the position of Secretary of State. In view of the memorials of the early part of the year and such a further indication of the opinion of influential businessmen as the establishment of the Asiatic Association, it is quite possible that Hay's well-known propensity for the Open Door in China was one of the reasons for his appointment. Hardly had he assumed office when the new Secretary showed that his Far Eastern policy was going to be stronger than that of his two predecessors. Perhaps as a result of a memorial from one of the American establishments in China, stating that there was a "probability of serious interference [by Russia] with America's important trade in cotton . . . unless immediate steps are taken in Pekin to insist that our treaty rights with China be maintained," Hay ordered two gunboats to proceed to North China. The New York Chamber of Commerce, incidentally, expressed its "high appreciation" of the act. For the time being, however, nothing further came of the Russian threat.

The last event we need mention which occurred during the war was the annual message to Congress of President McKinley. Repeating Day's recommendation of a trade commission, the President stated that the United States was not an "indifferent spectator" of what was going on in China but that it would preserve its "large interests in that quarter by all means appropriate to the constant policy of our Government." This strong declaration was naturally hailed with delight by those with business interests in China.

When the war with Spain formally came to an end early in 1899 with the ratification of the peace treaty by the Senate, the government was able to turn its attention from military matters to such peacetime considerations as trade with China. In January it received an important memorial. Coming from a large number of cotton manufacturers, the memorial stated that the Chinese market would be lost to American cotton exporters "unless a vigorous policy is pursued on the part of the . . . Government"; it requested that the American diplomatic representatives at Peking and St. Petersburg "be instructed to give special attention to the subject." This memorial seems to have impressed Secretary Hay even more than the memorial of the preceding January had impressed Sherman. Referring to the "high character and standing of the signers," he ordered the envoys to give the "special attention" requested of them; and about a month later, apparently afraid he had not been sufficiently emphatic, he wrote a second time to the ambassador to Russia, asking him to continue "to act energetically in the sense desired by the numerous and influential signers of the petition."

Another episode of early 1899 worth mentioning was the Asiatic Association's strong support of a protest by the United States against an attempt by France to extend her concession in Shanghai. The association wrote to McKinley and Hay, urging that "all available means" be used "towards preserving for the world's commerce an 'open door' in the Far East." In sharp contrast with this was the association's viewpoint regarding an attempt to obtain an extension of the combined British and American concession. Negotiations with China had been going on for some time but without success. Angered and alarmed, the association informed Secretary Hay of "the necessity of . . . vigorous action . . . in order to obtain a definite solution." Sending a copy of this letter to the minister to China, Hay instructed him to devote his efforts to obtaining the extension. Two months later China gave way.

In March the campaign for the Open Door took a more decisive turn. It became known at that time that Italy was endeavoring to secure from the Chinese government a lease of Sanmen Bay, a bay located not far from Shanghai, the center of foreign business in China. Fears of partition once again rose quickly to the surface. There was widespread suspicion that Italy had the backing of Great Britain; if true, it would mean that the only remaining great power opposed to the partition of China was the United States.

The situation disturbed the American Asiatic Association to an extent which might seem surprising today. Today we know that the Sanmen Bay affair turned out to be a comparatively insignificant incident. But to those who lived at the time of the crisis itself this knowledge was lacking, and to them, fearful as they were that it would take very little indeed to start off the process of dismembering China, the spring of 1899 was a time of grave anxiety. So disturbing was the situation to the officials of the Asiatic Association that they held a series of meetings in order to discuss the possibility of a fundamental modification of the policy they had been pursuing.

As has been shown, this policy was to concentrate on the Department of State. True, there had been a certain amount of propaganda directed at the public in general through the periodical, *Asia: journal of the American Asiatic association,* and true it is also that this propaganda had been meeting with some success. As early as January the *Journal of commerce,* that close observer of anything pertaining to the Open Door, had pointed to the "new attitude of this country towards its commercial interests in China" and had stated that it was "partly the result of the American Asiatic Association." Nevertheless, greater success had been gained with the State Department. Secretary Sherman and Secretary Day had moved closer to the viewpoint of businessmen who were eager to see the Chinese market safeguarded. John Hay had not once failed to carry out any formal request regarding Far Eastern policy, and, indeed, the department under Hay had shown itself so willing to co-operate that there could be no doubt about its desire to maintain the Open Door in China.

Because of these facts the *Journal of commerce* and the Asiatic Association appear to have realized that pressure upon the State Department had become much less necessary than before. But this did not suggest to them that their usefulness was at an end. For although it was clear that many of the high officials in Washington were convinced that the Chinese market was of considerable value to the United States, it was equally clear that the general public was not convinced. Consequently, what had become desirable in place of so much attention to the State Department was, as the journal said, "education of the people, the press, and the politicians by those who see the vital necessity of the Chinese market"—in short, "active propaganda in the country at large." The Asiatic Association, as a faithful ally of the journal, came to the same conclusion. At the series of meetings which its officials were holding it was decided to embark upon "a campaign of public education in regard to the magnitude of the commercial interests of the United States in China." A committee to take charge of the campaign was appointed.

The writer has not been able to discover many details about the ensuing campaign. It is known that it was carried on in the press—the *Journal of commerce* presumably being the chief organ—and in publications of the association itself. It is also known that by the end of 1899 the association had at its disposal a fund for propaganda purposes amounting to several thousand dollars and that among the contributors to this fund were many of the exporters of cotton goods. Not much additional material, however, is available.

Did the campaign have any success in persuading the public of the importance of the market in China? No conclusive answer can be given to this question; for not only is it foolish to make too definite claims about the effects of any bit of propaganda, no matter how much one may know its nature, but also we have here a propaganda compaign concerning which relatively little is known.

It is worth while, however, to point out that both the American Asiatic Association and the *Journal of commerce* were convinced that their propaganda did have very considerable success. The statement of the journal in January, 1899, regarding the influence of the Asiatic Association in moulding public opinion has been mentioned above. Ten months later, in November, the propaganda of the Association had had more time to make itself felt. At that time the *Journal of commerce* reported that "there has never been a more remarkable advance of public sentiment in this country than that which has taken place . . . in regard to the responsibilities to be faced by our Government in the Far East." The journal boasted that "to the stage of public education which has been reached on this subject [the necessity of the Open Door to the United States] this journal may fairly claim to have largely contributed." The vice-president of the Asiatic Association said that the work of his organization would "take its place in history as part of one of the most memorable chapters in the annals of the American people. . . . You have only to compare," he said, "the state of public sentiment which we found existing in regard to the responsibilities of our country in Eastern Asia with the feeling which exists on that subject to-day to appreciate what the influence of the Association has been."

Moreover, at least one contemporary observer supported their claims. James S. Fearon, one of the leading exporters of cotton to China and for years chairman of the Shanghai Municipal Council—presumably a man whose opinions regarding American relations with China are worthy of respect—stated that much of the credit for the changed attitude of the American people toward the Chinese market was due to the American Asiatic Association and to the *Journal of commerce*.

The propaganda compaign was the outstanding feature of the months just before the sending of the Open Door notes, but this period was also marked by further pressure brought to bear on the State Department by the special interests. Although they initiated no more memorials at this time, the officials of the Asiatic Association are known to have corresponded with Secretary Hay and to have called upon him frequently regarding the country's Far Eastern policy.

The activity of the special interests during these months of 1899 was of such a nature as to make it extremely difficult to evaluate its significance. It is, of course, quite understandable that no records exist stating explicitly whether or not the administration was influenced by the propaganda campaign, and it is equally understandable that Secretary Hay never wrote down anything which would enable us to judge whether or not his thinking was affected by the letters from the officials of the Asiatic Association and by the visits these men paid him. It is far easier to trace the effects of the memorials of 1898 than of the propaganda and informal contacts of 1899.

But it would be a great mistake to overlook the possibility that these later activities too were of considerable importance. It may well have been that the *Journal of commerce* and the Asiatic Association were quite correct in their belief that the propaganda campaign was successful. If it was successful, if it did in fact make the public more conscious of America's stake in the Far East, it doubtless made it easier for the administration to take action designed to preserve the Chinese market. As for the letters and visits from the Asiatic Association to Hay, it is highly probable that such frequent reminders of the desires of certain businessmen had at least the effect of bolstering up the Secretary's own inclinations with respect to China. At any rate, it is clear that these activities of the special interests during the spring and summer of 1899 must have, along with the memorials of 1898, a place in any complete history of the origins of the Open Door policy.

On September 6, 1899, the first group of Open Door notes was dispatched. This was just the kind of step for which the special interests had been hoping and for which they had been working. To the cotton exporters the notes meant that their market appeared to be far more secure; and to the American-China Development Company they meant that there was much to be hoped for from a grateful China—and, indeed, a few months later the company at last secured the contract which it had so long been seeking.

The sending of these notes resulted from a great many factors, one of which was the organized attempt of certain business interests, particularly the men connected with the American China Development Company and the cotton exporters, to persuade the government to take just such a step. It has been shown how these interests, fearful lest the turn of events in China should result in financial loss to themselves, took measures designed to persuade the government to safeguard the Chinese market. First of all, they established the Committee on American Interests in China; later on, when this proved to be too weak an organization, they transformed it into the American Asiatic Association. This association, consistently supported by the *Journal of commerce and commercial bulletin*, was influential in persuading the administration (and very possibly the general public as well) that a particular line of policy would be of benefit to the nation as a whole. In these facts lies part of the explanation for the formulation of America's Open Door policy.

Additional Reading

Charles S. Campbell, Jr., *Anglo-American Understanding, 1898–1903* (1957).
———, *Special Business Interests and the Open Door Policy* (1951).
Tyler Dennett, *John Hay* (1933).
A. L. P. Dennis, *Adventures in American Diplomacy, 1896–1906* (1928).
L. M. Gelber, *The Rise of Anglo-American Friendship* (1938).
Pauline Tompkins, *American-Russian Relations in the Far East* (1949).
Paul A. Varg, *Open Door Diplomat: The Life of W. W. Rockhill* (1952).
E. H. Zabriskie, *American-Russian Rivalry in the Far East, 1895–1914* (1946).

12 *CARIBBEAN POLICY: Dollars or Security?*

As the year 1898 began, the United States was without naval bases and influence in the vital Caribbean area. Yet by 1917, the Caribbean Sea had been transformed into an American-controlled "lake." A canal route through the Central American isthmus had been acquired, five protectorates had been established (Cuba, Panama, Santo Domingo, Nicaragua, Haiti), the Danish West Indies were purchased, and European influence had been largely supplanted. Theodore Roosevelt made great strides by incorporating the Platt Amendment in a treaty with Cuba, leasing a canal zone from Panama, and proclaiming an international policeman's role for the United States in the Caribbean. President Taft assumed a financial protectorate in Nicaragua and launched a small-scale armed intervention there as well. The Wilson administration, although entering office pledged to end the alleged "dollar imperialism" of the past, was soon constrained by national exigencies and by benevolent impulses to undertake extensive armed interventions in Haiti and Santo Domingo.

In the aftermath of World War I, with its disillusionment with noble crusades and the revelation of unpleasant details in the armed occupations of Santo Domingo and Haiti, it became fashionable in "liberal" circles to denounce the Caribbean policies of the United States as dollar imperialism. American actions were viewed as undertaken primarily for crass economic reasons, to protect and promote private investments in the republics in the Central American area. The approach of World War II, however, with its external dangers to the Western Hemisphere, caused a reappraisal of past American policies in the Caribbean in terms of security requirements and benevolent impulses.

DOCUMENTS

1. Cuba and Panama: American Protectorates

Although Cuba obtained independence as a result of the Spanish-American War, it was kept under the tutelage of the United States. The Platt Amendment to the army appropriation bill in 1901 provided for a protectorate arrangement and the substance of this measure was subsequently incorporated in the 1903 treaty with Cuba. American troops withdrew from the island in 1902, but returned briefly in 1906–09 and 1917–22 to help preserve order in the republic. The 1903 Treaty with Panama in effect also made that state a satellite and illustrates the process of converting the Caribbean into an American sphere of control and influence.

Treaty between the United States and Cuba, signed, 1903

Article I. The Government of Cuba shall never enter into any treaty or other compact with any foreign power or powers which will impair or tend to impair the independence of Cuba, nor in any manner authorize or permit any foreign power or powers to obtain by colonization or for military or naval purposes, or otherwise, lodgment in or control over any portion of said island.

The Government of Cuba shall not assume or contract any public debt to pay the interest upon which, and to make reasonable sinking-fund provision for the ultimate discharge of which, the ordinary revenues of the Island of Cuba, after defraying the current expenses of the Government, shall be inadequate.

Article III. The Government of Cuba consents that the United States may exercise the right to intervene for the preservation of Cuban independence, the maintenance of a government adequate for the protection of life, property, and individual liberty, and for discharging the obligations with respect to Cuba imposed by the Treaty of Paris on the United States, now to be assumed and undertaken by the Government of Cuba.

Article V. The Government of Cuba will execute, and, as far as necessary, extend the plans already devised, or other plans to be mutually agreed upon, for the sanitation of the cities of the island, to the end that a recurrence of epidemic and infectious diseases may be prevented, thereby assuring protection to the people and commerce of Cuba, as well as to the commerce of the Southern ports of the United States and the people residing therein.

Article VII. To enable the United States to maintain the independence of Cuba, and to protect the people thereof, as well as for its own defense, the Government of Cuba will sell or lease to the United States lands necessary for coaling or naval stations, at certain specified points, to be agreed upon with the President of the United States. . . .

Convention between the United States and Panama, signed 1903

Article I. The United States guarantees and will maintain the independence of the Republic of Panama.

Article II. The Republic of Panama grants to the United States in perpetuity the use, occupation and control of a zone of land and land under water for the construction, maintenance, operation, sanitation and protection of said Canal of the width of ten miles extending to the distance of five miles on each side of the center line of the route of the Canal to be constructed. . . .

Article III. The Republic of Panama grants to the United States all the rights, power and authority within the zone mentioned and described in

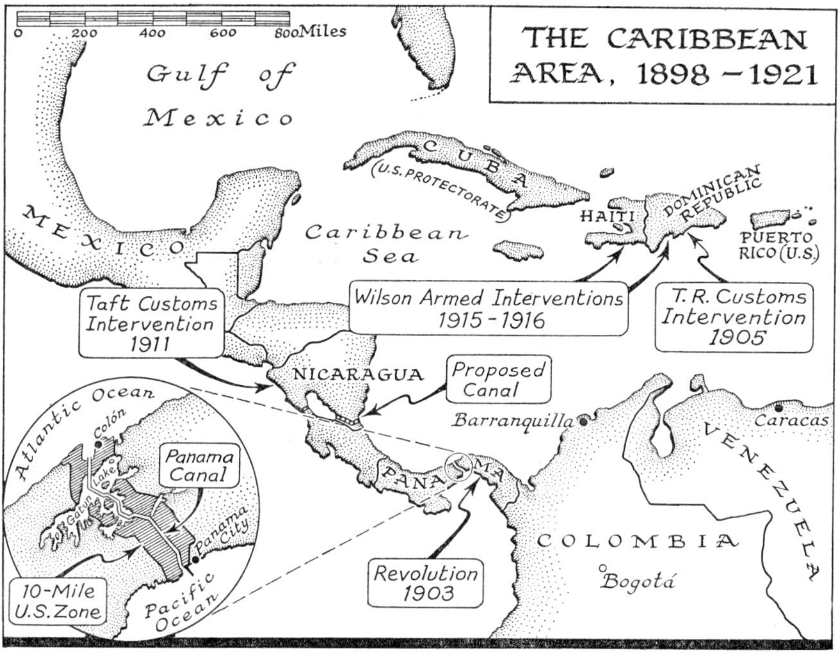

Article II of this agreement and within the limits of all auxiliary lands and waters mentioned and described in said Article II which the United States would possess and exercise if it were the sovereign of the territory within which said lands and waters are located to the entire exclusion of the exercise by the Republic of Panama of any such sovereign rights, power or authority.

Article XIV. As the price or compensation for the rights, powers and privileges granted in this convention by the Republic of Panama to the United States, the Government of the United States agrees to pay to the Republic of Panama the sum of ten million dollars ($10,000,000) in gold coin of the United States on the exchange of the ratification of this convention and also an annual payment during the life of this convention of two hundred and fifty thousand dollars ($250,000) in like gold coin, beginning nine years after the date aforesaid. . . .

Article XVIII. The Canal, when constructed, and the entrances thereto shall be neutral in perpetuity, and shall be opened upon the terms provided for by Section I of Article three of, and in conformity with all the stipulations of, the treaty entered into by the Governments of the United States and Great Britain on November 18, 1901. . . .

Article XXIII. If it should become necessary at any time to employ armed forces for the safety or protection of the Canal, or of the ships that make use of the same, or the railways and auxiliary works, the United States shall have the right, at all times and in its discretion, to use its police and its land and naval forces or to establish fortifications for these purposes. . . .

Article XXV. For the better performance of the engagements of this convention and to the end of the efficient protection of the Canal and the preservation of its neutrality, the Government of the Republic of Panama will sell or lease to the United States lands adequate and necessary for naval or coaling stations on the Pacific coast and on the western Caribbean coast of the Republic at certain points to be agreed upon with the President of the United States. . . .

2. *The Roosevelt Corollary*

With a new-found sense of the strategic importance of the seas bordering on the Panama Canal, the American "imperial life-line," President Theodore Roosevelt was acutely aware of the dangers of European armed intervention and financial influence in the Caribbean area. Venezuelan defaulting on its foreign debts had resulted in tripartite armed retaliation by Great Britain, Germany and Italy in 1902. Similar Dominican difficulties in 1904 threatened further European intervention. Anxious to preclude such dangerous lodgments and yet to safeguard foreign lives and property in the disorderly Caribbean states, President Roosevelt announced an extension of the Monroe Doctrine to an international police role for the United States. A financial overlordship in Santo Domingo ensued in 1905 and set the pattern for comparable arrangements later in Nicaragua, Santo Domingo, and Haiti.

Roosevelt's Annual Message to Congress, December 1904

. . . It is not true that the United States feels any land hunger or entertains any projects as regards the other nations of the Western Hemisphere save such as are for their welfare. All that this country desires is to see the neighboring countries stable, orderly, and prosperous. Any country whose people conduct themselves well can count upon our hearty friendship. If a nation shows that it knows how to act with reasonable efficiency and decency in social and political matters, if it keeps order and pays its obligations, it need fear no interference from the United States. Chronic wrongdoing, or an impotence which results in a general loosening of the ties of civilized society, may in America, as elsewhere, ultimately require intervention by some civilized nation, and in the Western Hemisphere the adherence of the United States to the Monroe Doctrine may force the United States, however reluctantly, in flagrant cases of such wrongdoing or impotence, to the exercise of an international police power. If every country washed by the Caribbean Sea would show the progress in stable and just civilization which with the aid of the Platt amendment Cuba has shown since our troops left the island, and which so many of the republics in both Americas are constantly and brilliantly showing, all question of interference by this Nation with their affairs would be at an end. Our interests and those of our southern neighbors are in reality identical. They have great natural riches, and if within their borders the reign of law and justice obtains, prosperity is sure to come to them. While they thus obey the primary laws of civilized society they may rest assured that they will be treated by us in a spirit of cordial and helpful sympathy. We would interfere with them only in the last resort, and then only if it became evident that their inability or unwillingness to do justice at home and abroad had violated the rights of the United States or had invited foreign aggression to the detriment of the entire body of American nations. It is a mere truism to say that every nation, whether in America or anywhere else, which desires to maintain its freedom, its independence, must ultimately realize that the right of such independence can not be separated from the responsibility of making good use of it. . . .

3. Wilsonian Caribbean Diplomacy

Although repeatedly proclaiming a new approach to Latin America, which disavowed imperialism and advocated harmonious and cooperative relations, President Woodrow Wilson approved more armed interventions than had his two predecessors in office. The reasons were in part the security requirements of defending the Panama Canal but also involved his determination to inculcate habits of good government in the Caribbean. Secretary of State William Jennings Bryan's instructions to the American minister in Santo Domingo, on September 9, 1913, reveal these purposes.

Wilson's Declaration of Policy with Regard to Latin America

One of the chief objects of my administration will be to cultivate the friendship and deserve the confidence of our sister republics of Central and South America, and to promote in every proper and honorable way the interests which are common to the peoples of the two continents. I earnestly desire the most cordial understanding and cooperation between the peoples and leaders of America and, therefore, deem it my duty to make this brief statement.

Cooperation is possible only when supported at every turn by the orderly processes of just government based upon law, not upon arbitrary or irregular force. We hold, as I am sure all thoughtful leaders of republican government everywhere hold, that just government rests always upon the consent of the governed, and that there can be no freedom without order based upon law and upon the public conscience and approval. We shall look to make these principles the basis of mutual intercourse, respect, and helpfulness between our sister republics and ourselves. We shall lend our influence of every kind to the realization of these principles in fact and practice, knowing that disorder, personal intrigues, and defiance of constitutional rights weaken and discredit government and injure none so much as the people who are unfortunate enough to have their common life and their common affairs so tainted and disturbed. We can have no sympathy with those who seek to seize the power of government to advance their own personal interests or ambition. We are the friends of peace, but we know that there can be no lasting or stable peace in such circumstances. As friends, therefore, we shall prefer those who act in the interest of peace and honor, who protect private rights, and respect the restraints of constitutional provision. Mutual respect seems to us the indispensable foundation of friendship between states, as between individuals.

The United States has nothing to seek in Central and South America except the lasting interest of the peoples of the two continents, the security of governments intended for the people and for no special group or interest, and the development of personal and trade relationships between the two continents which shall redound to the profit and advantage of both and interfere with the rights and liberties of neither.

From these principles may be read so much of the future policy of this Government as it is necessary now to forecast, and in the spirit of these principles I may, I hope, be permitted with as much confidence as earnestness to extend to the Governments of all the Republics of America the hand of genuine disinterested friendship, and to pledge my own honor and the honor of my colleagues to every enterprise of peace and amity that a fortunate future may disclose.

Secretary of State William Jennings Bryan's Instructions to the American Minister in Santo Domingo

DEPARTMENT OF STATE,
Washington, September 9, 1913

The President directs me to say for your instruction that the influence of this Government will be exerted for the support of lawful authorities in Santo Domingo, and for the discouragement of any and all insurrectionary methods. You will carry with you a copy of the President's statement of last March which sets forth fully, and in such a way as to leave no doubt, his position on two important points, namely: First, that we can have no sympathy with those who seek to seize the power of government to advance their own personal interests or ambition; and, second, that the test of a republican form of government is to be found in its responsiveness to the will of the people, its just powers being derived from the consent of the governed.

It is not to be expected that those in power will be able to avoid mistakes but mistakes should be corrected by constitutional means. Neither is it to be supposed that reforms will in all cases be brought about as soon as they ought to be, but the remedy for this is agitation—not insurrection.

Say to any who may feel aggrieved or who may be disposed to resort to violence that the good offices of this Government can be counted upon at all times to assist in the establishment of justice, in the remedying of abuses, and in the promotion of the welfare of the people. We must depend, therefore, upon all the people of Santo Domingo, of whatever party or faction, to join together in securing justice through law and in the election by free and fair ballot of officials whom the people desire. You will make it known to those now in insurrection that this Government will employ every legitimate means to assist in the restoration of order and in the prevention of further insurrections, holding itself open at all times to advise with the government in behalf of those who feel that they have a grievance.

I am sure that when the disinterestedness of our Government is fully understood, its friendship will be appreciated and its advice sought.

READINGS

1. Dollar Diplomacy in the Caribbean

Charles A. Beard, noted in American historiography for an economic interpretation of history, explains the Caribbean policies of the United States from 1901 through World War I as an example of economic and political imperialism. Most diplomatic historians view his explanation as too sweeping and oversimplified in the emphasis on economic motives as the main cause of interventions.

Imperial America

CHARLES AND MARY BEARD

The annexation of Porto Rico and absorption of Cuba under Republican auspices had been merely a prelude to the transformation of the Gulf of Mexico and the Caribbean into an inland sea of the United States. In the nature of things, to use the language of diplomacy, the region was a part of the American empire; for a lion's share of the commerce with nearly all the islands scattered between the Bahamas and Trinidad had been readily gathered into American hands. Even British and French traders could not resist the pull of the powerful market in the United States; while the combined efforts of Britain and Canada could not make water run up hill. On the mainland also, in Mexico, Central America, Colombia, and Venezuela, American business enterprise marched from one victory to another.

Political as well as economic processes favored the development of American hegemony. In those places where European powers did not keep order, there were periodic uprisings against the titular governments, revolts often purely factious, sometimes the efforts of honest men to oust corrupt and tyrannical adventurers, occasionally the outcome of a failure to appreciate the merits of foreign investors. Regardless of their source, they were always disturbing to business interests, particularly to the holders of local bonds. As a rule the outstanding obligations of Latin-American republics were large for the pertinent revenues. In fact they were generally inflated to a high pressure; for each uprising the debts of the defeated party were added to those of the victors, thereby preventing any such magnificent repudiation as had occurred when the government of Abraham Lincoln triumphed over that of Jefferson Davis in the Second American Revolution. It required, accordingly, no sweeping derangement of the social order in a Latin-American country to fetch down a high structure of finance.

In every crisis the government of the United States was involved, and given new occasions for assimilation. Besides being pledged under the Monroe Doctrine to prevent European powers from occupying more territory in the western hemisphere, even in the honest performance of collecting debts, it was continually besieged by American bankers and business men to help them save endangered revenues. At no time did it feel inclined to say that it would neither allow European governments to succor their nationals among the bondholders nor make any movement itself on their behalf. If the duties imposed by the necessity for action were slight, the mere presence of American battleships in the offing might enable bankers to take possession of customs houses and effect amicable settlements of debts by negotiations. If, however, local leaders refused to listen to the voice of warning and forced the landing of American marines, a limited warfare sometimes had to be waged on the basis of presidential orders to the Navy Department. And yet in no case did the parties of interest feel constrained to invoke the constitutional provision vesting the power to declare war in the Congress of the United States. As things turned out, American economic and political sovereignty was steadily advanced in the Caribbean without breaking the legal peace of the western hemisphere or disturbing the party of pacific intentions in the domestic hinterland.

A brief illustrative chronology hints at the process. In 1903, Germany was compelled by a threat of force from President Roosevelt to withdraw from Venezuela and submit certain financial claims to arbitration. In 1905, Roosevelt, by executive action, took over the customs houses of Santo Domingo and stationed war vessels in Dominican waters to give point to the argument. Under the Platt amendment, he interfered in Cuba in 1906, giving the natives a convincing proof that American warnings against disorder were to be respected. By a formal treaty ratified by the Senate of the United States, the pecuniary protectorate over Santo Domingo was made regular in 1907. The next year Secretary Knox broke off relations with the President of Nicaragua; a little later an American warship served notice on local contestants for power that there was to be no fighting in Bluefields—"thus protecting the preponderating American and other foreign interests," as the State Department in Washington put it. In 1911, on the suggestion of New York bankers, a treaty was negotiated with Honduras, extending American authority over that republic; though ratified by the United States Senate, it was rejected by the native authorities.

During the same year an American warship was sent to Nicaragua, a loan arranged, and a treaty drawn, reciting "the benevolent intentions" of the United States and putting the customs into the hands of a presidential appointee. When, in spite of three urgent messages from President Taft, the Senate declined to ratify the agreement, marines were landed in Nicaragua and business was restored to a normal course. In 1914–16, a treaty with Nicaragua was at last adopted ceding a canal strip and naval bases to the United States in return for three million dollars in cash to be expended largely for American goods in coöperation with American authorities. In 1915, the marines carried the flag into Haiti and established American suzerainty there after killing more than two thousand natives who, for one reason or another, got in the way of the operation. In 1916, Admiral Knapp—"to maintain domestic tranquillity"—took possession of Santo Domingo and declared that "republic" subject to the military government of the United States. In 1917, the Virgin Islands were purchased from Denmark. In 1920, the American navy was employed in helping to stabilize Guatemala. In 1921, after some American marines had smashed the office of the *Tribuna* in Managua, for printing critical articles, the minister of the United States requested the local Nicaraguan government to set apart adequate space outside the capital for drill grounds, a dance hall, and a moving picture theater to be used by American forces and also to designate special liquor saloons for their convenience. In 1923, the national assembly of Panama approved a large loan for highway construction to be secured by investments correctly placed in New York City. In 1924, the American marines once more came to the aid of public order in Honduras. In 1927, the marines were again in Nicaragua. Such was in brief a partial chronicle of what Secretary Knox called "dollar diplomacy."

The series of events here recited were accompanied by no expressions of ill-will on the part of the American government. On the contrary, Roosevelt, Taft, Wilson, Harding, and Coolidge all agreed that, in this connection, there was nothing either sinister or ungenerous in the purposes of the United States. Wilson was especially emphatic on this point. Speaking cordially of the Latin-American countries, he said: "We must prove ourselves their friends and champions upon terms of equality and honor. . . . We must show ourselves friends by comprehending their interests whether it squares with our interests or not." . . .

In fact, each of the numerous incidents in the extension of American authority over the Caribbean was marked by colors and episodes peculiar to the occasion. For that reason, the bare chronicle of the forward movement as a whole fails to give a correct impression of the higher law in its specific application. To gain an insight into that phase it is necessary to examine somewhat minutely an entire chapter of contingencies, and for the purpose of illustration the case of Haiti offers a sufficient revelation. That little island republic became the scene of revolutions and assassinations as soon as it cast off the yoke of France in 1803 and at all times thereafter showed an evident need for law, order, good roads, sanitation, education, and industrial progress. But the southern planters who ruled the United States in the middle period of national expansion, although they were ready to raise the flag over good land fit for cotton culture, shrank from relations too cordial with a spot where slaves had made a successful revolution and were trying to govern themselves. Moreover, their successors at Washington, the masters of business, were also largely indifferent to the requirements of Haiti as long as domestic enterprise—even farm mortgages—yielded ten or fifteen per cent or happy negotiations with the federal land office brought larger returns on smaller risks. But at the end of the century, when the southern slavocracy had moldered in its grave and the pecuniary equipment of the United States had been well rounded out, there arose a marked solicitude about the welfare of Haiti.

In 1902, one of the periodical rebellions that had plagued that small republic sent it swimming within the range of American kinetics. Turning for aid to the United States, the Haitian government floated a loan in New York at twelve per cent and invested large sums in ammunition at two or three times the usual price. Unabashed by these commitments, American munition makers showed an equal interest in the revolutionary forces fighting for "liberty" and sold them instruments of destruction, also on profitable terms. Observing the scrimmage from afar, European capitalists tendered their good offices with the same devotion to both parties, everyone of them knowing, as the American minister on the spot remarked with casual directness, that the civilized powers concerned would make the Haitians pay all bills no matter which side won in the civil war. Now, among the countries involved in this crisis, none was more anxious than the German Empire. German merchants controlled about nine-tenths of Haiti's foreign trade and showed a concern in local affairs that was artistically proportioned to the flow of goods. In the press of things, they were able to place a loan of half a million at thirty-five per cent interest and later they managed to float a smaller issue of three hundred thousand dollars which yielded a net sum of about half that amount to the Haitian treasury.

Naturally vexed by this precocity on the part of the Germans and fearing utter discomfiture at the hands of their rivals, American business men began to display great consternation, the State Department sharing their fear. Although an American company had got important railway and land concessions and although the National City Bank of New York had gathered in much of the Haitian debt on terms presumably not adverse, it was thought that the American share of the local proceeds was entirely too small. Moreover, there were irritations connected with an affront to national honor; open discrimination was shown by Haitians against some American citizens of Syrian origin who had been very active in bringing local trade into American hands. And this annoyance was augmented by an untoward incident, arising from an attempt of the Haitian president to seize the gold reserve in the local national bank, a design foiled by the intervention of American marines, and the transfer of the treasure on an American war vessel to New York, where it was safely deposited at a low rate of interest, leaving the Government of Haiti to clamor loudly for a return of the funds.

Since it was now evident that the friendly concern of the State Department in Washington must take a more practical form, President Wilson sent commissioners to Haiti charged with the task of persuading Vilbrun Guillaume Sam, president of the republic, to accept the benevolent protection of the United States. At the same time American bankers served notice on him that no more loans were to be expected without adequate guarantees, placing him in a real dilemma. Procuring aid from Berlin was out of the question, for Germany, in the toils of war, was blockaded by an invincible sea power. Neither was assistance from France forthcoming; that country, far from indicating a desire to help President Sam out of his pinch, dispatched a naval force to his republic to protect French lives and property.

Given this signal for action, the government of the United States, in the summer of 1915, ordered Admiral Caperton, in command of the good ship, *Washington,* to Haitian waters, just in time to learn that President Sam, enraged by the turn of events, had ordered the murder of more than a hundred prisoners and had been himself assassinated in retaliation. Visibly disturbed by such cruel deeds, the Admiral directed his marines to seize the local political theater and some blood was shed in the operation, but not enough to cause a declaration of war by Congress. Competent directors now being in charge, martial law was instituted under American auspices and the Haitian national assembly was permitted to elect as president, General Dartiguenave, a candidate acceptable to Admiral Caperton and apparently disposed to cooperate with American representatives on the ground.

At all events, as soon as he was installed, the General signed a treaty with his new friends. In the preamble, the document stated that it was the desire of the "High contracting parties . . . to confirm and strengthen the amity existing between them by the most cordial cooperation in measures for their common advantage." According to the terms of the bond the United States was to use its good offices in developing the agricultural, mineral, and commercial resources of the little republic, to name engineers whose advice was to bc binding in the management of the said resources, to take over and administer the customs of the republic, and to select the financial adviser charged with directing the fiscal affairs of the local government.

Thus, in a single stroke, the United States undertook to promote private enterprise and safeguard the public finances upon which large bond issues afloat in the United States rested for security. With the restraint that characterized Clive's course in India, the American administration refrained from annexing Haiti; indeed this would have been inconsistent with Wilson's lofty declaration of two years before to the effect that this country would "never again seek one additional foot of territory by conquest." In this spirit the Senate ratified the Haitian treaty of amity in the spring of 1916.

2. *Securing the Approaches to the Panama Canal*

Samuel F. Bemis rejects economic explanations and, correctly in the view of the majority of American historians, assigns great weight to strategic factors in the Caribbean. Dangerous foreign interpositions to protect their nationals and property could not be permitted in the zone of the vital Panama Canal. The only alternative envisioned by Roosevelt and Taft was to have the United States itself intervene to preserve order and encourage stability in the area.

The Roosevelt Corollary and Dollar Diplomacy

SAMUEL FLAGG BEMIS

. . .The day before the Senate of the United States advised the ratification of the Hay-Bunau-Varilla Treaty with the new republic of Panama, a most significant juridical verdict was announced on the other side of the Atlantic. The Hague Court of Permanent Arbitration on February 22, 1904, rendered its decision on the issue of preferential rights of the intervening powers to the designated Venezuelan assets for satisfaction of the adjudicated claims of foreign nationals. Unequivocally it decided that Germany, Great Britain, and Italy, the powers which had resorted to force to secure justice, had a right to payment ahead of the powers who had been content with a peaceful solution.

There is no question but that this decision placed a premium, in international law, upon forceful intervention against a delinquent state. In so doing, it put to American diplomacy a very serious dilemma. Within the strategic radius of the Panama Canal there were other Latin American republics, in the Caribbean and in Central America, whose irresponsibility toward their just obligations to foreigners was almost as confirmed as in Venezuela, and whose political stability was continually uncertain. Either the United States must recognize this sanctioned right of European intervention—now juridically sanctioned—and the contingent possibilities of foreign danger to the Monroe Doctrine in the neighborhood of the Panama Canal or it must itself vicariously assume responsibility for justice to the foreign nationals so that their governments would not have to intervene. The assumption of such responsibility entailed intervention by the United States itself. This was the dilemma, then: should the United States stand by with folded arms while non-American powers, backed in principle by a Hague Court decision, intervened and perhaps ensconced themselves in strategic positions from which in the future they might cut the Panama life-line and the security of the Continental Republic; or should it intervene itself to guarantee justice and responsibility in strategically located countries whose condition invited foreign intervention, and thereby run the risk of incurring by its own intervention the misunderstanding and animosity of the neighboring republics?

These questions were not new. Before the Civil War, Senator Sam Houston of Texas had advocated a protectorate over Mexico which would

From *The Latin American Policy of the United States*, copyright, 1943 by Samuel Flagg Bemis. Reprinted by permission of Harcourt, Brace & World, Inc. Pp. 151–158, 161–166.

include a service on her foreign bonds. He urged it as a means of extricating Mexico from the British lion's mouth, and thought that Great Britain might even welcome it. John Forsyth, United States minister to Mexico, had negotiated a treaty in 1857, by which the United States would have loaned money to Mexico to pay off British bondholders, the loan to be secured by a portion of that republic's customs revenues. Secretary of State Seward, in an effort to stave off European intervention, had negotiated a loan with the Juarez Government to enable it to pay the interest—at only 3 per cent—on its foreign debt for five years at least, but he never ventured to submit it to the Senate. The French intervention in Mexico was an historic example of how such European loans could lead to political and military intervention, to loss of independence itself. Secretary Hamilton Fish in 1869 favored collection of Venezuelan customs by United States officials in order to service that nation's defaulted foreign bonds—with a priority in payment to United States nationals. Except for this last condition, Fish's proposal anticipated the "dollar diplomacy" of the twentieth century. Again in 1881 Secretary of State James G. Blaine had suggested that the United States might place an agent in charge of the pledged customs of Venezuela to pay off foreign creditors pro rata in a secure and orderly way.

On all these occasions since the Civil War, British creditors, at least, expressed themselves favorable to such a collection by the United States. After the Venezuelan boundary controversy the British Government frequently hinted that if the United States expected to assume authority in the Caribbean region, it ought also to assume responsibility for the foreign debts of those states. Before the intervention in Venezuela in 1902 the German *chargé* in Caracas had asked the United States Minister there whether his Government would participate in a joint intervention. The latter, Herbert W. Bowen, said no: his Government could scarcely join in any forceful measures with European powers against an American republic; if any policing were to take place it ought to be by the United States alone, who could take care competently of the concerns of the European powers. As the Venezuela crisis of December, 1902, eased off, by the agreement in principle to arbitrate, the British Prime Minister, A. J. Balfour, had intimated that his government would be glad to see the United States take the troublesome republics of South America in hand; it had no objection to the Monroe Doctrine—on the contrary. "If the United States could see their way," declared a government spokesman in the debates on the Venezuelan affair in the House of Commons, "to the adoption of some effective course by which these almost periodical difficulties arising between the great powers and some of the states of South America could be prevented, I think I may say it would meet with cordial concurrence in this country." The London press chimed in with the same note. It was a welcome contrast to Great Britain's attitude at the beginning of the American Civil War. Then on the occasion of threatened Spanish invasion of the Dominican Republic, the British Ambassador at Washington had told Secretary Seward that he could not "allow" him to assert the Monroe Doctrine without reminding him that Great Britain repudiated it altogether!

Thus there was adequate reason to believe that Great Britain would welcome intervention by the United States alone, to clean up the bad finances of these shaky republics in case of another lapse of justice, and that Germany would not object to it. It proved that France and Belgium, too, were ready to acquiesce in such a procedure. To the United States such a course was preferable to participation in a joint receivership as proposed at various times by representatives of the European powers, which would have meant an "ottomanization" of the strategic Caribbean area. The events of the previous five years, together with the European situation, had induced—we will not say reconciled, unless in the case of Great Britain—the powers tacitly to accept the hegemony of the United States in that region.

The decision of the Hague Tribunal had hardly been announced when the Venezuela claims situation with all its implications for the Monroe Doctrine, implications so sharpened by that decision, repeated itself in the Dominican Republic. Anarchy, confusion and disaster had there become the order of the day. In April, 1904, the United States Minister in Santo Domingo reported—what was subsequently denied to the American Ambassador at Rome by the Italian Minister for Foreign Affairs—that Italy was about to intervene with naval forces to secure the rights of Italian nationals, fixed by a protocol of 1903. "I understand," he said, "that the action of the Italian Government is based upon the recent decision at the Hague."

The total Dominican debt in default was $32,000,000. Various national revenues had been hypothecated to Belgian, French, German, Italian, and Spanish creditors. Amidst alternating dictatorships and revolutions, the Santo Domingo Improvement Company, a New York corporation, had refunded some of the older defaulted foreign loans and floated new ones for public construction work. The United States Government was unwilling to intervene diplomatically to support this American corporation or importunate individual citizens until it became evident that it was more than a question of securing justice for the financial contracts of a national: it was a matter of defending by diplomatic arrangements the independent status of the island republic against *justifiable* forceful interventions *à la* Venezuela, justifiable interventions that might grow into more or less permanent occupations for other purposes, as in Egypt; that would menace the safety of the canal, the security of the two-ocean republic.

During the Venezuelan imbroglio the Department of State in 1903 peaceably arranged a diplomatic settlement by which the Santo Domingo Improvement Company ceded to the Dominican Government its holdings in the National Bank and the Central Dominican Railway, and accepted $4,500,000 in acquittal of a total credit claimed of $11,000,000. By this agreement a mixed commission of arbitration laid down (July 14, 1904) a schedule of payments, secured by stipulated customs revenues, to be made to an agent appointed by the United States Government and paid over to the creditor. At the first default the agent should have full power and authority to step in and to fix and collect customs and port dues of Puerto Plata, Sánchez, Samaná, and Montecristi, and apply them, after expenses of collection, to the scheduled liquidation of the debt.

Straightway the Dominican Government defaulted, and the agent took over collection (October, November, 1904). To this the other foreign creditors, with their colliding special hypothecations, quite naturally objected. They clamored for the support of their governments. President Roosevelt had to look forward to a foreign intervention or take the responsibility for intervention by the United States. He had little choice other than to intervene to secure justice for all the foreign creditors. Public opinion, as evidenced by the recent Venezuelan imbroglio, would not have tolerated an European intervention, nor would it have accepted participation by the United States in a joint intervention in an island that dominated so strategically the Caribbean Sea and the Atlantic approaches to the Panama Canal.

The Hague Court decision of February 22, 1904, significant as it was, was not necessary to convince President Roosevelt of the need of intervention by the United States. "San Domingo is drifting into chaos," he wrote to his eldest son, at the outbreak of the Russo-Japanese war, "for after a hundred years of freedom it shows itself utterly incompetent for governmental work. Most reluctantly I have been obliged to take the initial step of interference there. I hope it will be a good while before I will have to go further. But sooner or later it seems to me inevitable that the United States should assume an attitude of protection and regulation in regard to all these little states in the neighborhood of the Caribbean. I hope it will be deferred as long as possible but I think it is inevitable."

The first step in dealing with this dangerous Dominican dilemma had been to send Admiral Dewey and Assistant Secretary of State F. B. Loomis to investigate conditions in the Dominican Republic. Loomis's confidential report of March, 1904, stressed the chaotic situation there and the cross-claims of the foreign governments, and suggested an American receivership. Despite repeated importunities of successive Dominican Governments, and none more insistent than that which was temporarily and precariously in power in 1904, Theodore Roosevelt had no idea of annexing the island republic, or its neighbor Haiti, or even of establishing a naval base there. None was necessary between the United States naval base at Guantánamo, on the eastern tip of Cuba, and the United States island of Puerto Rico to the east of Hispaniola. The President went out of his way to repudiate in the most explicit manner, by personal statements, and by a note from the Secretary of State to the Haitian Minister in Washington, any thought of annexation. What he wanted was to accept, with the implied mandate of the European creditor powers, and at the request of the tottering Dominican Government, responsibility for the efficient and honest collection of the customs—pledged and cross-pledged as they already were—and a pro rata payment by an United States receivership of the foreign debt within the capacity of the island government. The reason for this, we cannot repeat too emphatically, was to remove any justification for intervention by foreign powers, after the fashion of Venezuela, within this strategic area so vitally related to the new Atlantic-Pacific life-line of the United States.

Diplomacy sealed the arrangement in the form of a protocol with the Dominican Government calling for a receivership in the hands of an agent appointed by the President of the United States, who would collect the customs under the protection of the United States Government if necessary, and pay out 45 per cent of the proceeds to the creditors pro rata, after satisfying the expenses of the receivership, and turn the remaining funds over to the Dominican Government. It does not seem, from the manner in which the negotiations were carried on, that the President had intended any more than an executive agreement; but apparently on mature consideration he decided that it was his duty to submit the document to the Senate for advice and consent as to formal ratification. At first the protocol contained a guaranty of the territorial integrity of the Dominican Republic. Since the Senate might stick at a guaranty, there was substituted in the final treaty a pledge to respect the territorial integrity of the Dominican Republic. Even so, the Senate postponed for two years its acceptance of the arrangement. A partisan minority resented Roosevelt's original intention not to consult it at all. But the strategic significance of the island was too vital to be neglected. In 1907 the Senate approved a new treaty, somewhat modified by dropping the territorial pledge and all references to the danger of foreign intervention, retaining the essential financial provisions. Meanwhile President Roosevelt had been executing its terms under a *modus vivendi* based on executive agreement. Controlling forces of the United States navy hovered in Dominican waters, if only to overawe the presence of Italian, French, and German units, but there was no occupation of the island, no interference (before 1912) with its internal affairs beyond the receivership of customs. An expert appointed by President Roosevelt was able in 1905 to scale down the debt, with the agreement of the creditors, from $32,000,000 to $17,000,000, and start a scheduled payment of new 50-year 5 per cent bonds issued, at the request of the Department of State, by New York banks to refund the adjusted debt. The result was a novel prosperity for the republic accompanied by a frustration of revolutionary habits hitherto confirmed.

Theodore Roosevelt confused the Latin American policy of the United States by identifying intervention in the Dominican Republic with the Monroe Doctrine, thus making that Doctrine, which had said "hands off" to Europe, seem to say "hands on" for the United States. Actually, as many a responsible statesman has pointed out since Woodrow Wilson's time, the Monroe Doctrine did not give to, nor did it withhold from the United States a right or policy of intervention. But President Roosevelt honestly and resolutely thought that because the Monroe Doctrine prohibited European intervention to secure justice, it ought to follow as a logical corollary that it sanctioned intervention by the United States in order to prevent it by Europe. In presenting the "protocol" to the Senate (February 15, 1905), he said:

> An aggrieved nation can without interfering with the Monroe Doctrine take what action it sees fit in the adjustment of its disputes with American States, provided that action does not take the shape of interference with their form of government or of the despoilment of their territory under any disguise. But, short of this, when the question is one of a money claim, the only way which remains, finally, to collect it is a blockade, or bombardment, or the seizure of the customhouses, and this means what is in effect a possession, even though only a temporary possession, of territory. The United States then becomes a party in interest, because under the Monroe doctrine it can not see any European power seize and permanently occupy the territory of one of these republics; and yet such seizure of territory, disguised or undisguised, may eventually offer the only way in which the power in question can collect any debts, unless there is interference on the part of the United States.

This was the well-intended but withal portentous "Roosevelt Corollary" to the Monroe Doctrine, the so-called policy of the "Big Stick": benevolent United States intervention to prevent non-American intervention, a bit of necessary diplomacy—at that time—but bad logic, which has required a generation to cast off.

Thoughtful scholars, like Professor Rippy, have wondered why it never occurred to Roosevelt to let all alien investors shift for themselves in the Dominican Republic. As a matter of fact, Roosevelt did announce in 1905 that his Government had always refused resort to the use of force for the collection of contract debts, and Secretary of State Root later repeated this in South America. Indeed, the United States had just ratified the inter-American convention of 1902 for the arbitration of pecuniary claims, and was preparing to support the Drago Doctrine at the coming Hague Peace Conference.

The obvious answer to the question just noted is that the other great powers would not renounce the right of intervention to secure justice, including contract debts; it had proven impossible in Venezuela a year previously for the United States to leave alien investors to shift for themselves. The European powers had intervened, and the Hague Court had just put an impressive sanction of international law on the justice of their use of force. If Roosevelt had stood aside in 1904, another intervention would almost certainly have followed and the control of the United States over the Panama Canal might have been checkmated at the very start of construction. Certainly the danger of this was sufficiently imminent to cause grave concern. Roosevelt was acting upon the traditional motive of security for the Continental Republic as he, and his compatriots, sensed it at the time. Not until the menace of European intervention had temporarily disappeared as a result of the First World War could a President of the United States safely think of liquidating the protective imperialism that had been established in the vital Caribbean area at the beginning of the century; not until then could there be a reasonable expectation, during the period between the two great wars, that the non-American powers would refrain from intervention in the New World to secure justice denied to their nationals.

This Dominican receivership does not appear to have awakened contemporaneously any appreciable resentment or distrust of other governments, even of the Latin American republics, although the press of France and Germany was caustic. The Latin American literary Yankeephobia that flamed up later was fanned to life in the intellectual foyers of the very European nations whose governments, under the circumstances of 1904–1907, had been so willing, even anxious, to have the rights of their nationals secured by the United States. . . .

Discerning students have blamed Taft and more particularly his Secretary of State, Philander C. Knox, for carrying the Roosevelt Corollary toward a more active and less disinterested intervention, notably in Nicaragua. They have stigmatized this action with the derogatory phrase of "dollar diplomacy," taking their cue from some frank avowals of the President that he considered it a most useful function of government to advance and protect the legitimate trade and investments of United States citizens in foreign countries, particularly in areas of competition like China, where they served to chaperon or neutralize imperialistic designs. In the course of this study we shall have more to say of dollar diplomacy. It was not designed to profit private interests. It was intended rather to support the foreign policy of the United States; in the instance of Latin America to support the Roosevelt Corollary to the Monroe Doctrine. In these interventions in Central America and the Caribbean there was also a certain characteristic missionary impulse to help the people themselves, willy-nilly, by stabilizing their governments and economies.

Zelaya resented the diplomatic intrusion of the United States and Mexico because it interfered with his own ambition to unify all Central America under his mastery by overturning governments in the neighboring states and putting in his puppets. He had consistently opposed the whole movement toward Central American solidarity by diplomatic and by constitutional processes. In his resentment he had also been very hostile to American private capital legally invested in Nicaragua. For example, he wished to cancel the United States-Nicaragua Concession, a mining property owned by a Pittsburgh corporation which represented the principal American private capital in the Isthmian republic. He wanted to take back this concession and sell it over again to somebody else for better terms. As a Pennsylvania lawyer and counsel to the corporation, Philander C. Knox, before he became Secretary of State, had himself passed upon the validity of the contract. It became clear that the Nicaraguan dictator was the greatest single menace to the whole treaty structure, as well as to American private contracts; that the Washington conventions would have little effect in stabilizing and uniting the five republics as long as Zelaya remained President of Nicaragua. There is no evidence to show that President Taft and Secretary Knox were more charitable toward the ambitious Isthmian general because of the latter's high-handed violation of these concessions, like Castro in Venezuela; on the contrary! Nor did reports of Zelaya's plans to make secret advances to Japan for a canal treaty ingratiate the dictator with the United States Government.

United States intervention in Nicaragua followed a revolution which broke out in 1909 against Zelaya in Bluefields and had at least the sympathy of the company which operated the United States-Nicaragua Concession. Zelaya's forces captured two United States citizens, named Cannon and Groce, professional dynamiters, who were laying mines in the San Juan River for the revolutionists, and executed them after court martial. They held commissions in the revolutionary army and considered themselves prisoners of war. President Taft made this the occasion for dismissing Zelaya's representative at Washington and landing marines to protect foreign nationals and property at Bluefields. Secretary Knox declared that the United States was convinced "that the revolution represented the ideals and will of a majority of the Nicaraguan people more truthfully than does the government of President Zelaya." As a result of this intervention Zelaya was overthrown. President Porfirio Díaz of Mexico, who had cooperated throughout with the United States to bring stability to Central America, advised Zelaya to quit. Soon a revolution in Mexico dethroned Díaz himself and left the United States as the sole sponsor of the precarious regional peace structure.

After a confusing interlude of shifting personnel in the revolutionary Nicaraguan government, Adolfo Díaz, who had been secretary of the United States-Nicaragua Concession emerged in 1911 with the assistance of American diplomacy as "constitutional" President, recognized by the United States. Secretary Knox negotiated with the new Government a treaty (the Knox-Castrillo convention), signed June 6, 1911, generally similar to the treaty of 1907 with the Dominican Republic, and identical to one that had just been signed with Honduras (January 10, 1911), for the purpose of refunding the debt of Nicaragua through new loans from New York bankers (Brown Brothers, J. and W. Seligman & Co.). This would have taken the old debt entirely out of the hands of an English syndicate, and put the new loan in a schedule of payment under an American receivership like that in the Dominican Republic. A separate executive agreement provided for a mixed commission to arbitrate the claims of American citizens against Nicaragua.

The Senate of the United States rejected both of these treaties, but the bankers, at the request of the Department of State and with its assistance, put through private contracts with Nicaragua which set up much the same sort of regime without treaty guaranties. On this basis they made a much smaller loan, $1,500,000 instead of $15,000,000, upon condition of securing control of the contemporaneously established National Bank of Nicaragua and the Nicaraguan state railways. Knox may have felt that he had the precedent behind him of Theodore Roosevelt's *modus vivendi* with the Dominican Republic after the Senate had first rejected the "protocol" of 1905; but unlike the Dominican example, the Senate never ratified the Knox treaties.

A new revolution against Adolfo Díaz's regime threatened to drift into the control of Zelaya's followers. If they should have gained control of the government, "all of the efforts of the State Department [says an historian of Central America] to place Nicaragua on her feet politically and financially would have been useless, and the interests of the New York bankers, who had undertaken their operations in the country at the express request of the United States Government, would be seriously imperiled." Accordingly, at the request of the Díaz Government the United States landed some 2,700 marines in 1912 and occupied the principal cities of the interior after a sharp engagement at Leon. From 1912 to 1933 (except for a brief interval following a trial withdrawal in 1925) a small force of United States marines maintained the Government of Nicaragua in office, supervised and policed elections, and trained up a Nicaraguan constabulary.

Thus fortified the government kept up payments on the old loans by the London bankers and the new loans of the New York bankers. Meanwhile, continued political agitation, crime, periodic revolts, disease, grasshopper plagues, and earthquakes worried, robbed, harassed, ravaged, devoured, and shook the already impoverished country and its people. The intervention of the United States was barely adequate to maintain elected governments in power and thus keep the pledged finances in order; it was not enough to regenerate Nicaragua as an effective protectorate had done in Cuba. Light as the intervention was, it was sufficient to arouse the animosity of other Latin American countries to whom Nicaraguan dissidents made their appeal. A full protectorate would not have been more hateful, and could have benefited the people much more.

After the failure of his financial treaties, Secretary Knox, alarmed at rumors of German interest in the Nicaraguan waterway, signed another treaty agreeing to pay Nicaragua $3,000,000 for an exclusive right of way for a canal, a naval base on the Gulf of Fonseca, and a ninety-nine-year lease of Great Corn and Little Corn Islands in the Caribbean near the Atlantic terminus of the route. This treaty was submitted to the Senate too late to get ratification before the end of the Taft Administration, but President Wilson took up the idea, with some modifications, and put it through, as we shall see in a later chapter.

It was one thing to build up, by cooperative measures short of actual military intervention, a structure of preventive diplomacy, designed to remove any justification for intervention by a non-American power in the Caribbean region. So Roosevelt and Root had done in Cuba and the Dominican Republic, in the latter instance with the implied mandate of the European powers, and this Roosevelt had rested on his famous Corollary. It was another step that Taft had taken under Knox's legal guidance: outright military intervention to safeguard the strategical interest of the United States in the Isthmian region. This smacked more of Roosevelt's intervention in Panama than it did of his diplomatic intervention in the Dominican Republic carried through under Root's guidance. By the same token, and other appearances (that of serving private interests), it created greater resentment both in Latin America and at home than did the Dominican receivership.

Intervention in Nicaragua and the occupation of that republic were certainly high-handed, uncalled for by any immediate exigency of foreign policy or national security, and actually contrary to the principles of the Washington conventions of 1907. Its effect, after the Senate rejected the Knox treaties of 1911, was to place the finances of that Isthmian country in the hands of private bankers for the next eight years. Their strict measures, alleviated by the Bryan-Chamorro Treaty ratified in 1916, and terminated by the Financial Plan of 1917, achieved the fiscal redemption of the country, but it is doubtful whether the local governments thus supported by United States marines furthered the concept of Central American confederation and union.

Knox would have imposed financial receiverships on Honduras and Guatemala too, if the Senate would have stood for it.

The Taft Administration took great pains to justify the Nicaraguan intervention constitutionally before Congress. Mr. J. Reuben Clark, Jr., Solicitor of the Department of State, compiled a long memorandum on *The Right to Protect Citizens in Foreign Countries by Landing Forces,* as established in international law and by United States precedent. Even after these arguments, the candid historian may be critical of the whole episode, but it certainly would be most unjust to attribute even the occupation of Nicaragua—cited so profusely as the standard illustration of the evils of dollar diplomacy—to the controlling power of private vested interests over the United States Government. Back of that intervention was an honest intent, at least, to stabilize and strengthen the international relations of Central America by substituting for Zelaya's focus of revolution and wars a truly representative and independent government and to further a union of all the Central American states on the foundation of the Washington conventions. The United States was interested in promoting this regional peace structure principally in order to remove any conceivable danger, even a remote one, of ultimate foreign intervention that might give military lodgment in the neighborhood of the Panama Canal, then advancing toward completion, or any possibility of a rival canal route falling under non-American influence.

Unfriendly foreign critics used the phrase "dollar diplomacy" to suggest a deliberate design by the United States to dominate the nearest Latin American republics, even the whole Western Hemisphere, for the private profit of "Wall Street." While not losing sight for one moment of the mistakes of foreign policy in the hands of the blundering Knox and Taft —and it is fortunate that the United Sates did not have to confront under their leadership any major crisis of diplomacy during the years 1909–1913—it is only fair to say that dollar diplomacy was more an easily misusable journalistic alliteration, alliterative unfortunately in all the principal languages of the New World and western Europe, that easily lent itelf to hateful propaganda and exaggerated Yankeephobia, than it was a truthful characterization of the protective foreign policy of the United States.

In their own uniquely inept way Taft and Knox were also following the instinct and traditions of continental security rather than the lead of selfish private interests. Nicaragua, like the Dominican Republic, like

Panama, like Haiti (where Woodrow Wilson was soon to send marines as well as to Santo Domingo), was one of the states of the New World, indeed of the entire world, where the least American capital was invested. It is a well-known fact that before the First World War indigenous capital found more lucrative employment in the United States than outside of its boundaries, that it was only with difficulty that the Department of State was able to persuade bankers to invest their funds for political purposes in foreign countries. The larger holdings of capital invested abroad in the New World were in Cuba, where "big business" had opposed intervention in 1898, in Mexico, where the United States Government and public opinion have certainly been averse to intervention for nearly a century; in Canada, and in the larger and more stable republics of South America.

It seems to be an historical fact that the more capital a country of the New World has accepted from private investors in the United States the less danger there has been of intervention. Such investments have brought a wealth of good to Latin American countries, but in the large it is doubtful whether they have been profitable to the economy of the United States, not to mention the investors. This is because they have not been wholly safe. They represented an overflow of luxury that the United States, unlike the great powers of the Old World, had not been willing, with its deep continental instincts of nonintervention, to guarantee and to secure by the use of force. But American diplomacy has always been sensitive to the strategical requirements of continental security. This, and not selfish private interests, really explained both the Roosevelt Corollary and the dollar diplomacy of Taft. It also explains in large measure the Latin American policy of Woodrow Wilson.

Additional Reading

W. H. Callcott, *The Caribbean Policy of the United States, 1890–1920* (1942).
H. C. Hill, *Roosevelt and the Caribbean* (1927).
Arthur S. Link, *Woodrow Wilson and the Progressive Era, 1910–1917* (1954).
——, *Wilson: the New Freedom* (1956).
Dana G. Munro, *The United States and the Caribbean Area* (1934).
E. T. Parks, *Colombia and the United States, 1765–1934* (1935).
J. Fred Rippy, *The Caribbean Danger Zone* (1940).
Charles C. Tansill, *The Purchase of the Danish West Indies* (1932).

13 *THE GREAT CRUSADE: American Involvement in World War I*

Much heat and some light have resulted from the controversy over the causes of the American entry into World War I. That this event should have occasioned an often impassioned debate is not surprising, in view of the psychological shock which the war dealt to older popular assumptions and beliefs.

The outbreak of the European war in August of 1914 came as a disheartening surprise to most Americans. Nurtured on the belief that the world was becoming economically interdependent and more civilized, educated Americans assumed that Western society had outgrown the barbaric warfare of the unhappy past. Peace societies flourished here and in Europe—both President Woodrow Wilson and William Jennings Bryan, his first secretary of state, had joined the American Peace Society—and two Hague conferences had attempted to humanize warfare through codifications of so-called international law. In this condition of shock, and despite the initial tendency to sympathize with the cause of the Entente Powers led by Great Britain and France, the people heartily approved President Wilson's proclamation of neutrality. The United States need not and should not become involved in the holocaust in Europe. The American tradition of isolation, stemming from Washington's Farewell Address and adhered to during the 19th century, assured citizens that the nation should remain aloof from the quarrels of the Old World.

A few realistic students of world affairs realized that isolation was no longer possible for a great power in the 20th century—indeed, that it had not really worked before, for the peace and prosperity of 19th century America was less the result of its deliberate policy of abstention and more the fortuitous and unearned security made possible by a century of general peace in Europe (1815–1914) and the benevolent role of Great Britain, the unchallenged mistress of the seas. Such persons were, as a consequence, greatly alarmed at the possibility of a German victory over British sea power, which might redouble Teutonic competition in Latin America and threaten the security of the United States in the Western Hemisphere.

Most Americans were not accustomed to realistic appraisals of the national interests, however, and reacted to the war largely on emotional and traditional grounds. Consequently, when events did pull the United States actively into the conflict in April, 1917, it was generally understood to be simply on the grounds of German violations of American neutral rights and honor. To justify the war, both to the nation and to himself, Wilson turned it into a crusade for universal democracy and perpetual peace. Inevitably there was an emotional letdown after the war, which was worsened by the Allied haggling over the spoils at the Paris Peace Conference and the subsequent Senate rejection of the treaty of peace and League of Nations. The disillusionment of the 1920's with crusades deepened into a resurgence of isolationist feeling as the rise of aggressive totalitarian states in Europe and the Far East in the 1930's threatened another world conflict. It was in this atmosphere that the historical debate over the origins of the first world war occurred.

DOCUMENTS

1. Belligerent Threats to Freedom of the Seas

In the agony of war, both sides undertook measures which affected American neutral rights on the presumably "free" seas. The British mining of the North Sea threatened neutral shipping and lives in that area—yet the United States declined to join other neutrals in protest. On the other hand, when Germany subsequently proclaimed a submarine zone around the British Isles, the American response was to enter a firm and vigorous unilateral protest.

The British North Sea Mining Zone, November 3, 1914

. . . During the last week the Germans have scattered mines indiscriminately in the open sea on the main trade route from America to Liverpool via north of Ireland. Peaceful merchant ships have already been blown up with loss of life by this agency. . . .

These mines can not have been laid by any German ship of war. They have been laid by some merchant vessels flying neutral flags which have come along the trade route as if for purposes of peaceful commerce and while profiting to the full by immunity enjoyed by neutral merchant ships have wantonly and recklessly endangered the lives of all who travel on the sea regardless of whether they are friend or foe, civilian or military in character.

Mine laying under neutral flag and reconnaissance conducted by trawlers, hospital ships, and neutral vessels are the ordinary features of German naval warfare.

In these circumstances, having regard to the great interests entrusted to the British Navy, to the safety of peaceful commerce on high seas, and to the maintenance within limits of international law of trade between neutral countries, the Admiralty feel it necessary to adopt exceptional measures appropriate to the novel conditions under which this war is being waged.

They therefore give notice that the whole of the North Sea must be considered a military area. Within this area merchant shipping of all kinds, traders of all countries, fishing craft, and all other vessels will be exposed to the gravest dangers from mines which it has been necessary to lay and from warships searching vigilantly by night and day for suspicious craft.

All merchant and fishing vessels of every description are hereby warned of the dangers they encounter by entering this area except in strict accordance with Admiralty directions. Every effort will be made to convey this warning to neutral countries and to vessels on the sea, but from the 5th of November onwards the Admiralty announce that all ships passing a line drawn from the northern point of the Hebrides through Faroe Islands to Iceland do so at their own peril. . . .

The United States Declines to Protest the Mining Zone
The Secretary of State to Minister in Norway

WASHINGTON, *November 10, 1914*

You may inform the Minister for Foreign Affairs that this Government does not see its way at the present time to joining other governments in protesting to the British Government against their announcement that ships entering the North Sea after November 5 do so at their own peril.

"Strict Accountability" Toward German Submarine Warfare
The Secretary of State to the Ambassador in Germany

WASHINGTON, *February 10, 1915*

Please address a note immediately to the Imperial German Government to the following effect:

The Government of the United States, having had its attention directed to the proclamation of the German Admiralty issued on the 4th of February, that the waters surrounding Great Britain and Ireland, including the whole of the English Channel, are to be considered as comprised within the seat of war; that all enemy merchant vessels found in those waters after the eighteenth instant will be destroyed, although it may not always be possible to save crews and passengers; and that neutral vessels expose themselves to danger within this zone of war because, in view of the misuse of neutral flags said to have been ordered by the British Government on the thirty-first of January and of the contingencies of maritime warfare, it may not be possible always to exempt neutral vessels from attacks intended to strike enemy ships, feels it to be its duty to call the attention of the Imperial German Government, with sincere respect and the most friendly sentiments but very candidly and earnestly, to the very serious possibilities of the course of action apparently contemplated under that proclamation.

The Government of the United States views those possibilities with such grave concern that it feels it to be its privilege, and indeed its duty in the circumstances, to request the Imperial German Government to consider before action is taken the critical situation in respect of the relations between this country and Germany which might arise were the German naval forces, in carrying out the policy foreshadowed in the Admiralty's proclamation, to destroy any merchant vessel of the United States or cause the death of American citizens.

It is of course not necessary to remind the German Government that the sole right of a belligerent in dealing with neutral vessels on the high seas is limited to visit and search, unless a blockade is proclaimed and effectively maintained, which this Government does not understand to be proposed in this case. To declare or exercise a right to attack and destroy any vessel entering a prescribed area of the high seas without first certainly determining its belligerent nationality and the contraband character of its cargo would be an act so unprecedented in naval warfare that

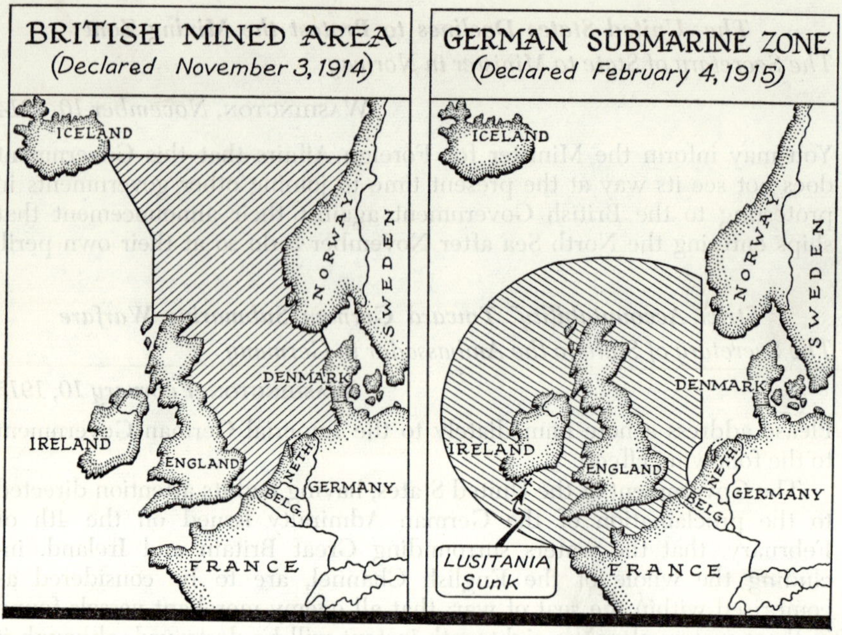

this Government is reluctant to believe that the Imperial Government of Germany in this case contemplates it as possible. The suspicion that enemy ships are using neutral flags improperly can create no just presumption that all ships traversing a prescribed area are subject to the same suspicion. . . .

If the commanders of German vessels of war should act upon the presumption that the flag of the United States was not being used in good faith and should destroy on the high seas an American vessel or the lives of American citizens, it would be difficult for the Government of the United States to view the act in any other light than as an indefensible violation of neutral rights which it would be very hard indeed to reconcile with the friendly relations now so happily subsisting between the two Governments.

If such a deplorable situation should arise, the Imperial German Government can readily appreciate that the Government of the United States would be constrained to hold the Imperial German Government to a strict accountability for such acts of their naval authorities and to take any steps it might be necessary to take to safeguard American lives and property and to secure to American citizens the full enjoyment of their acknowledged rights on the high seas. . . .

2. *The British "Blockade" and American Acquiescence*

In contrast to the insistence that Germany adhere strictly to the demands of international law, the British "blockade" of March, 1915 received only a long but mild protest.

The British "Blockade," March 11, 1915

WHEREAS the German Government has issued certain orders which, in violation of the usages of war, purport to declare the waters surrounding the United Kingdom a military area, in which all British and allied merchant vessels will be destroyed irrespective of the safety of the lives of passengers and crew, and in which neutral shipping will be exposed to similar danger in view of the uncertainties of naval warfare; and . . .

WHEREAS such attempts on the part of the enemy give to His Majesty an unquestionable right of retaliation; . . .

His Majesty is therefore pleased, by and with the advice of his Privy Council, to order and it is hereby ordered as follows:

1. No merchant vessel which sailed from her port of departure after the 1st March 1915 shall be allowed to proceed on her voyage to any German port. . . .

2. No merchant vessel which sailed from any German port after the 1st March 1915 shall be allowed to proceed on her voyage with any goods on board laden at such port. . . .

3. Every merchant vessel which sailed from her port of departure after the 1st March 1915 on her way to a port other than a German port, carrying goods with an enemy destination, or which are enemy property, may be required to discharge such goods in a British or allied port. Any goods so discharged in a British port shall be placed in the custody of the marshal of the Prize Court, and, unless they are contraband of war, shall, if not requisitioned for the use of His Majesty, be restored by order of the Court, upon such terms as the Court may in the circumstances deem to be just to the person entitled thereto. . . .

4. Every merchant vessel which sailed from a port other than a German port after the 1st March 1915 having on board goods which are of enemy origin or are enemy property may be required to discharge such goods in a British or allied port. Goods so discharged in a British port shall be placed in the custody of the marshal of the Prize Court, and, if not requisitioned for the use of His Majesty, shall be detained or sold under the direction of the Prize Court. The proceeds of goods so sold shall be paid into Court and dealt with in such manner as the Court may in the circumstances deem to be just. . . .

The American Reaction to the Blockade

The Secretary of State to the Ambassador in Great Britain

WASHINGTON, *March 30, 1915*

You are instructed to deliver the following to His Majesty's Government. . . .

The Government of the United States has given careful consideration to the subjects treated in the British notes of March 13 and March 15, and to the British order in council of the latter date.

These communications contain matters of grave importance to neutral nations. They appear to menace their rights of trade and intercourse not only with belligerents but also with one another. They call for frank comment in order that misunderstandings may be avoided. The Government of the United States deems it its duty, therefore, speaking in the sincerest spirit of friendship, to make its own view and position with regard to them unmistakably clear.

The order in council of the 15th of March would constitute, were its provisions to be actually carried into effect as they stand, a practical assertion of unlimited belligerent rights over neutral commerce within the whole European area, and an almost unqualified denial of the sovereign rights of the nations now at peace. . . .

A belligerent nation has been conceded the right of visit and search, and the right of capture and condemnation, if upon examination a neutral vessel is found to be engaged in unneutral service or to be carrying contraband of war intended for the enemy's government or armed forces. It has been conceded the right to establish and maintain a blockade of an enemy's ports and coasts and to capture and condemn any vessel taken in trying to break the blockade. It is even conceded the right to detain and take to its own ports for judicial examination all vessels which it suspects for substantial reasons to be engaged in unneutral or contraband service and to condemn them if the suspicion is sustained. But such rights, long clearly defined both in doctrine and practice, have hitherto been held to be the only permissible exceptions to the principle of universal equality of sovereignty on the high seas as between belligerents and nations not engaged in war.

It is confidently assumed that His Majesty's Government will not deny that it is a rule sanctioned by general practice that, even though a blockade should exist and the doctrine of contraband as to unblockaded territory be rigidly enforced, innocent shipments may be freely transported to and from the United States through neutral countries to belligerent territory without being subject to the penalties of contraband traffic or breach of blockade, much less to detention, requisition, or confiscation. . . .

The note of His Majesty's Principal Secretary of State for Foreign Affairs which accompanies the order in council, and which bears the same date, notifies the Government of the United States of the establishment of a blockade which is, if defined by the terms of the order in council, to include all the coasts and ports of Germany and every port of possible access to enemy territory. But the novel and quite unprecedented feature of that blockade, if we are to assume it to be properly so defined, is that it embraces many neutral ports and coasts, bars access to them, and subjects all neutral ships seeking to approach them to the same suspicion that would attach to them were they bound for the ports of the enemies of Great Britain, and to unusual risks and penalties.

It is manifest that such limitations, risks, and liabilities placed upon the ships of a neutral power on the high seas, beyond the right of visit and search and the right to prevent the shipment of contraband already referred to, are a distinct invasion of the sovereign rights of the nation whose ships, trade, or commerce are interfered with.

The Government of the United States is, of course, not oblivious to the great changes which have occurred in the conditions and means of naval warfare since the rules hitherto governing legal blockade were formulated. . . .

The possibilities of serious interruption of American trade under the order in council are so many, and the methods proposed are so unusual and seem liable to constitute so great an impediment and embarrassment to neutral commerce that the Government of the United States, if the order in council is strictly enforced, apprehends many interferences with its legitimate trade which will impose upon His Majesty's Government heavy responsibilities for acts of the British authorities clearly subversive of the rights of neutral nations on the high seas. It is, therefore, expected that His Majesty's Government, having considered these possibilities, will take the steps necessary to avoid them, and, in the event that they should unhappily occur, will be prepared to make full reparation for every act, which under the rules of international law constitutes a violation of neutral rights.

As stated in its communication of October 22, 1914, "This Government will insist that the rights and duties of the United States and its citizens in the present war be defined by the existing rules of international law and the treaties of the United States, irrespective of the provisions of the Declaration of London, and that this Government reserves to itself the right to enter a protest or demand in each case in which those rights and duties so defined are violated, or their free exercise interfered with, by the authorities of the British Government."

In conclusion you will reiterate to His Majesty's Government that this statement of the views of the Government of the United States is made in the most friendly spirit, and in accordance with the uniform candor which has characterized the relations of the two Governments in the past, and which has been in large measure the foundation of the peace and amity existing between the two nations without interruption for a century.

READINGS

1. Unneutrality and American Involvement

Critics of the American involvement in the great 1914–1918 conflict styled themselves "revisionists," meaning those who sought to probe behind the official explanations to the actual underlying causes of the war.* These writers challenged the generally accepted view that hostilities had resulted in 1917 only because of ruthless German submarine warfare affecting neutral trade and lives. Revisionist writers not only reflected the postwar mood of cynicism toward the war but also revealed strong inclinations toward an economic interpretation of history and a Freudian-produced awareness of mass psychology and the role of propaganda. The revisionists generally have agreed that the country had not really been neutral in thought or deed in 1914–1917. Instead,

* For an excellent historiographical article, consult Richard W. Leopold, "The Problem of American Intervention, 1917: An Historical Retrospect," *World Politics*, II (1950), 405–425.

most citizens had been pro-Ally from the beginning, a sentiment shared by President Wilson and most of his top officials. American policies toward the belligerents were benevolent toward the Allies and grudgingly strict toward Germany. Economically and financially, the nation through the one-sided war trade and private loans became virtually a silent partner of the Entente. Astute British propaganda capitalized on the situation to promote widespread condemnation of Germany as autocratic, militaristic and aggressive. A combination of pro-Ally policies and economic ties eventually pulled the United States into the war. The submarine, therefore, was not the basic cause of hostilities but simply the excuse. Harry Elmer Barnes was a pioneer revisionist and this selection has the virtue of being a bold and concise statement of that point of view.

The Entry of the United States into the World War

HARRY ELMER BARNES

. . . The approach to any interpretation of the entry of the United States into the World War must rest upon a review of the relations between Germany and the United States in the generation before the World War. The change in our sentiment towards Germany between 1870 and 1914 has been made the subject of an illuminating book by Dr. Clara E. Schieber. In 1870 we were overwhelmingly on the side of Prussia in the Franco-Prussian War, and were very friendly with the German states. Prussia was also the first European country to accept the sacrifices involved in the Bancroft treaties recognizing American naturalization as a renunciation of German citizenship. By 1914 there was more adverse sentiment towards Germany in this country than was directed against any other European state. The reasons for this transformation are numerous.

There was unquestionably some development of antipathy on account of the Bismarckian autocracy and militarism. The Kaiser's utterances on these and other matters were of striking character, much like those of Mr. [Theodore] Roosevelt in this country, and hence made good copy for the newspapers. Very important was the growth of trade rivalry. Both Germany and the United States underwent a tremendous economic and commercial development prior to the World War, and this led to competition for the markets of the world. Many believe this to be the most important and deep-seated cause of the growing coolness between the two countries. The imperialism associated with this commercial expansion brought numerous clashes in foreign policy. There was some trouble over Samoa between 1872 and 1889. The conduct of Admiral von Diederichs in the Philippines in 1898 was distinctly unfriendly to this country, and in marked contrast to that of the commander of the British fleet in these waters at the time. The procedure of Germany in China at the time of the occupation of the Shantung peninsula and in the Boxer Revolt alarmed the representatives of American interests in China. Germany was also making a notable economic conquest of Latin American markets in

Reprinted from *The Genesis of the World War* by Harry Elmer Barnes, by permission of Alfred A. Knopf, Inc. Pp. 587–589, 593–596, 598–600, 600–601, 604–607, 607–612, 614–615, 632–633, 634.

the decade before the War, and stirred the envy of American merchants and investors. Then there was a definite clash over Venezuela during Roosevelt's administration.

Another very important factor lay in the fact that few American papers had competent foreign correspondents in Germany, and, hence, relied for most of their material on German affairs upon the Harmsworth papers in England which were even notoriously anti-German. By the opening of the present century the anti-German current was definitely setting in in this country, and the various efforts to counteract it through the visit of Prince Henry in 1902, the gift of the statue of Frederick the Great in 1905, the exchange professorships, and the interpretation of German culture by Hugo Münsterberg were inadequate to the task. In other words, we were already very strongly pro-Entente before Printsip began his target-practice in the spring of 1914. . . .

The alleged reason why the United States entered the War was, of course, the resumption of unlimited German submarine warfare, but to have any understanding of the deeper causes we must get at the causes for the German submarine warfare in general, as well as its resumption in January, 1917. Here we are on firm ground. There is no doubt that the German submarine warfare was developed as a counter movement against the English violation of international law in regard to blockade, contraband and continuous voyage. By practically destroying, in these respects, the rights of neutrals, which had been worked out in a century of the development of international law, Great Britain was virtually able to shut off all imports into Germany from foreign countries, not only directly but also through neutral ports. It was to retaliate against this that Germany initiated her submarine warfare, which certainly cannot be regarded as in any sense more atrocious in fact or law than those English violations of neutral rights which had produced the submarine campaign. By practically acquiescing in these British violations of international law we not only lost most of what we had gained in the past in the way of establishing neutral rights on the seas, but also set a precedent which will prove an extremely nasty and embarrassing stumbling-block in the course of future negotiations in the event of war.

In addition to these English violations of international law which vitally affected Germany as well as neutrals, there were many other examples of British lawlessness, such as the interception of our mails, the use of the American flag on British ships, the seizure and search of United States officials below the rank of minister while traveling to and from their continental posts, and the capture of ships like the Dacia (by the French at the instigation of Page and the British), which had been legally transferred from enemy countries to American owners. If the United States had held England strictly to international law upon the threat of severance of diplomatic relations or even war, as we did in the case of Germany and as we unquestionably should have done in the case of England, the German submarine warfare would not have been necessary and probably would not have been utilized. So we may say with absolute certainty that it was the unneutrality, lack of courage, or maladroitness of the Washington authorities in regard to English violations of international law which produced the German submarine warfare that actually led us into war. It must be remembered, however, that the resumption of German submarine warfare, like the Belgian question in England, was the excuse and not the real reason for our entering the War. President Wilson and Colonel House had decided that we would come in at least a year before the submarine warfare was resumed by Germany.

The gist of the whole matter, then, appears to be that Mr. Wilson failed himself to observe the neutrality he enjoined upon his country at the outbreak of the War. By permitting England but not Germany to violate international law promiscuously he inevitably invited those reprisals which occurred. He then found in the action which he thus stimulated those ostensible causes for the war which he idealized after April, 1917. . . .

On the point that the failure of the United States to deal with both belligerents in identical fashion helped to bring on the War, Germany stated her position in the note of February 18, 1915, in which she said that "They (the Germans) rely on the neutrals who have hitherto tacitly or under protest submitted to the consequences, detrimental to themselves, of England's war of famine to display no less tolerance toward Germany, even if the German measures constitute new forms of maritime war, as has hitherto been the case with the English measures." This demand for impartiality of treatment was proper, but that the State Department did not consider it so is evident from Secretary Lansing's note to the German Government on May 8, 1916, as follows: "In order, however, to avoid any possible misunderstanding the Government of the United States notifies the Imperial Government that it cannot for a moment entertain, much less discuss, a suggestion that respect by German naval authorities for the rights of citizens of the United States upon the high seas should in any way or in the slightest degree be made contingent upon the conduct of any other Government affecting the rights of neutrals and non-combatants. Responsibility in such matters is single, not joint; absolute, not relative." This position of Secretary Lansing was unsound and improper. He could hardly demand that one belligerent obey the laws of war and tolerate repeated violations by the other. The toleration of British violation induced and made necessary the German departure. At an earlier stage in the war, our State Department seems to have admitted some such doctrine, but as we gradually departed from neutrality, the view changed and it was deemed proper to hold one belligerent to strict compliance with the laws governing neutrality and to permit the other widely to depart therefrom. At one time Lansing denounced the British measures as "illegal and indefensible" but he did nothing to support the use of these harsh words.

In considering the problem as to why Mr. Wilson and his associates were unwilling to intervene to coerce England and restrict her lawlessness on the seas, we can be sure that there were many and varied factors involved. Unquestionably the most powerful influence was the virulent pro-English attitude of Ambassador [Walter Hines] Page, who persistently and openly fought against Mr. Bryan and Mr. Lansing in the efforts of the latter to protect American rights against the arrogance and maritime anarchy of Great Britain. . . .

The following is a fair sample of Mr. Page's "patriotic" procedure as the accredited representative of the United States at the Court of St. James, entrusted with the responsibility of protecting the rights of his country. Our government had mildly protested against the flagrant violation of international law by the English, but Page, instead of presenting a forceful case to Sir Edward Grey, went through the form of reading it to Grey and then asked Grey to cooperate with him in formulating an effective reply *to our own State Department.* The offense of Benedict Arnold seems highly comparable. Both worked earnestly and directly to promote the cause of Anglo-American unity. This astonishing conduct of Page is revealed by Sir Edward Grey in his recently published memoirs. . . .

Added to Page's primary responsibility were the Anglo-mania of Secretary [of Agriculture, David F.] Houston, who had great influence with Mr. Wilson as an individual and as a member of his cabinet, and finally the very real pro-British sentiments of Mr. Wilson. Though Mr. Wilson's Anglo-mania was relatively slight and benign as compared with that of Mr. Page, it was unquestionably robust, and all of his writings from his youth onward reveal the fact that Mr. Wilson knew little or cared little about the culture of any other European country save that of England. All of his great heroes in literature and political science were English authors. These diverse facts and influences prevented Mr. Wilson from ever sending the strong note he had drafted in protest against English violations of our rights, and also prevented him from thoroughly backing up Mr. Lansing in his struggle against Mr. Page and the British authorities in the vain effort to defend American rights against Great Britain.

Our attitude as to the settlement of claims against the Entente and against Germany has been as lacking in impartiality as our conduct in enforcing the recognition of international law as between these two groups. Mr. Lansing announced in April, 1917, that our claims against Germany demanded immediate intervention and reprisal, and he added that our claims against the Allies for property losses in violation of American neutrality would be settled immediately after the close of the War. The claims against Germany, even when judged by standards entirely outside of international law, boil down to $180,000,000. In part to vindicate these claims we entered a war that cost us about $30,000,000,000. The claims against the Entente, even when based strictly on international law, greatly exceed $180,000,000. Nevertheless, though eight years have passed since the termination of hostilities, our Department of State has never made the slightest move to bring about a settlement of these large claims against the Entente.

Next we should note the powerful pressure of the great American financial interests and their subsidized press. From the beginning the international banking houses of the United States had taken a distinctly unneutral attitude, favoring investment in the bonds of the Allied countries, and discouraging or refusing investment in the paper of the Central

Powers. This immediately gave us a strong financial stake in the cause of the Entente, and this stake grew larger with each year of the war. Likewise, American industry inevitably became violently pro-Ally. This was due to the fact that the British illegal blockade unlawfully cut off our sales of war materials to the Central Powers and made our enormous war profits dependent upon the purchases made by Great Britain, France, Russia and Italy. Upon the prospects of their success in the War and their ability to prolong the conflict depended the relative amount of American profits and the probability of our receiving payment for the goods we sold to these Entente powers.

The writer is no fervent believer in the universal validity of the economic interpretation of history or in the correctness of the attempts which have been made to demonstrate that the United States went into the World War solely because of our investments in and sales to the Allied countries, but unquestionably from 1915–1918 the enormous power of American finance and industry was directed wholly toward the defense of the Allied powers and the support of their subtle propaganda. In most cases this did not rest upon any original sympathy with these countries, but upon the actual nature of the economic realities of the moment. Had we invested primarily in the bonds of the Central Powers, and had we been selling most of our goods to these same powers, there is no doubt that American finance and industry would have been as flagrantly pro-German as it was pro-English and pro-French in 1915, 1916 and 1917. . . .

The problem of the American bankers in regard to Allied credit became acute at the close of 1916. The ability to raise further loans for the Entente countries from private credit was practically at an end by January, 1917, and the Wall Street bankers were in despair. Their only hope of relief lay in the possibility of shifting the burden from their own shoulders to the back of the United States treasury. This feat could only be achieved by having the United States abandon the pretense of technical and formal neutrality and enter the conflict as a co-belligerent. The German submarine note of January 31, 1917, was therefore a veritable god-send to the international bankers of this country. It crowned with success their earlier efforts to bring about American intervention. One does not have to adopt the theory of diabolic possession in interpreting this aspiration or this conduct on the part of the leading bankers, many of whom were high-minded and pacifically inclined individuals. They had simply become very heavily involved in a complex net of international finance which seemed likely to disintegrate with disastrous results to themselves and their clients if we did not enter the World War. As is usual in the business world, they put their professional interests and commitments ahead of their personal opinions, preferences and convictions. It should be pointed out in passing that in one important way the entry of the United States proved a disaster to the bankers. By prolonging the War it brought on the Russian Revolution and the consequent loss of the loans to Russia.

One does not have to follow Upton Sinclair in every phase of his argument to be aware that American newspapers follow the dictates of American finance and industry very closely and very faithfully. Hence, the

American press had become by 1915 and 1916 almost uniformly and intolerantly pro-Ally, and in its editorials and its handling of the news scathingly attacked Mr. Wilson's neutral efforts. The favoritism of the press went so far that in some cases Englishmen actually took over the control of some of the leading dailies. Northcliffe spent vast sums of money to secure extensive control over the sentiment of the American press. In the case of the Providence *Journal,* the propaganda efforts of the editor were so extreme and flagrant, that in the case of faked material prepared for *World's Work,* the government had to intervene, and force moderation.

This favorable attitude of the American press toward the Entente Powers was an enormous advantage to them as compared with Germany in regard to the spreading of propaganda before the American people. We had no means of knowing that Germany would not have invaded Belgium or attacked the French Channel ports if England had agreed to remain neutral, or that Grey had made the decision for war before Belgium was invaded. We were ignorant of the fact that England had repudiated the cause of Serbia, and that France and Russia had been on the lookout for a Balkan dispute of an appropriate sort to be utilized as the basis for provoking a European war. Hence we felt that the Entente was fighting the cause of the small and weak nations against the ruthlessness of a great bully. We, of course, were led to believe that the war had been started through the deliberate determination of Germany to initiate her alleged long cherished plan to dominate the planet, while the Entente had proposed diplomatic settlement from the beginning and had only taken up arms in self-defense with the utmost reluctance. This theory of the German provocation of the War and the German lust for world dominion was played up in the newspapers and distributed in pamphlets of the National Security League and the American Defense Society until the danger from Germany struck terror into the hearts of Americans, and citizens of Peoria, Illinois, and Council Bluffs, Iowa, lived in daily dread of a German submarine attack; as a few years later they searched under their beds nightly for the Bolshevik there secreted.

Then, the United States was peculiarly at the mercy of the falsified atrocity pictures and other propaganda poured into this country by the Allies, who were at the same time able to keep from public knowledge the German counter-propaganda as well as German proofs of the falsity of these atrocity pictures, recently so conclusively demonstrated by Ferdinand Avenarius. These circumstances made it much easier for the pro-Ally groups to inflame American opinion and swing the country for war.

Further, the Germans were singularly awkward and unhappy in their utterances. The more exuberant among them openly voiced their aspirations as to territorial aggression and aggrandizement, while the Allies carefully restricted their similar plans to closely hidden secret treaties, and concentrated their publicity upon their unselfish and disinterested struggle for ideals and the peace of the world.

Finally there is the question of the *Lusitania,* one of the matters most exploited by friends of the Entente in their efforts to drive Mr. Wilson into the War. We now know that the *Lusitania* was carrying munitions of war—5400 cases of ammunition—as well as passengers, mail and express. It is a debatable point as to whether the *Lusitania* was violating international law by carrying these munitions of war. But it is beyond question that as a naval auxiliary, as a British ship warned of her danger in the war zone, and as a warship carrying munitions, she lost about all of her immunities as a merchant ship. Her passengers likewise assumed the risks inherent to their danger in accepting passage on the boat. If, in addition, she was armed she unquestionably lost all of her privileges as a peaceful merchant ship, and was not even entitled to a warning before being attacked. While any humane person would naturally deplore the loss of life incidental to the sinking of the *Lusitania,* it is necessary to insist here that the sinking of a score of ships such as the *Lusitania* in no way compared as an inhuman atrocity to the illegally produced British blockade of Germany which brought disease or starvation to tens of thousands of innocent German non-combatants. . . .

The case of Woodrow Wilson is singularly like that of Sir Edward Grey [British Foreign Secretary], namely, that of a man who loved peace but was drawn into war by a false conception of the facts and issues involved. There is no doubt that he was a pacifist at heart, but he viewed the conflict as one in which England was upholding the cause of civilization. This led to his determination to enter the conflict if the entry of the United States should become essential to a British victory and it was possible to put the country in as a unit. His policy, then, was one of combining a hope for an Entente victory with the preparation of the country for war in the event that England could not win without our assistance. There is no doubt that Wilson was as determined to enter the conflict as was Roosevelt, but he was far more subtle and adroit in his method of getting the country ready to support him in that move. When Wilson put the country into the War he had given the impression of having been a long-suffering and much abused pacifist who had resolutely stood out against war until no other alternative presented itself. This made the country convinced that it was really fighting in self-defense, something far different from what would have been the case if we had followed Roosevelt's advice and jumped headlong into the conflict after the sinking of the *Lusitania*. . . .

After the [1916] election, Germany, convinced, quite correctly, that the United States had in practice given up the pose of neutrality and intended to get into the War as soon as possible, decided to resort to a revival of unrestricted submarine warfare as a last hope and expedient. This decision was taken quite as much through a popular demand for such action in Germany as through any sinister and secret plotting of von Tirpitz [Navy Minister] or other officials. A starving people were demanding an early release from their suffering and despair through a rapid termination of the War. Having been the victims of illegal starvation and cut off from even neutral foodstuffs, they assented to the necessity of unrestricted submarine warfare which Tirpitz and others had assured them would bring the War to a speedy close. The United States had helped along this step in that our unwillingness to restrain Allied illegality forced Germany to seek reprisal and relief through the pursuit of desperate methods. Many believe that joy reigned in the White House when the German note of January 31, 1917, announcing the resumption of submarine warfare, reached this country. Whether this is true or not, there can be no doubt of the universal and complete rejoicing in Wall Street. . . .

Some have held that a powerful factor affecting Mr. Wilson's decision was his conviction by 1916 that he could not lead world policy through pacific methods but might assume world leadership if he threw the United States into the War and was thereby able to dominate the war aims of the Allied powers and the United States. Many of the facts in his conduct in the spring of 1916 and thereafter lend much plausibility to this hypothesis. The writer believes, however, that it was his pro-British sympathy more than anything else which led Mr. Wilson into his decision by the close of 1915 that we must enter the World War unless the English objectives could be realized through a negotiated peace. . . .

2. *"The War Was Made in Berlin"*

Opposed to the revisionists is the school of interpretation most fittingly described as the "submarine thesis." Adhering to the wartime explanations, this group of writers has maintained that hostilities resulted primarily from Germany's practice of underseas warfare. The American government had proclaimed official neutrality in 1914 and thereafter pursued impartial policies toward both belligerent sides. Neutral rights were diligently defended against the infractions of Great Britain and Germany, although the fact that the submarine threatened not merely property but lives as well made the deeds of the Berlin government far more serious than those of London. Wilson would not abandon the right of neutral citizens to travel the high seas subject only to the normal challenges of belligerents, a right which the U-boat violated by the sinking of merchant ships without warning and without providing for the safety of passengers and crew. As for the one-sided war trade with the Allies, this merely reflected the fact of British control of the seas and hence of access to the American market. Sentiment and economic ties no doubt helped explain why war with the Allies over their actions was improbable but they did not explain satisfactorily why the nation went to war with Germany. Only the ruthless use of the submarine against neutral lives and property forced a reluctant America to abandon its peaceful course and enter the war. Charles Seymour, a Wilsonian supporter during the war and professor of history at Yale University, in the following selection vigorously counters revisionist arguments and charges resulting from the then current Nye Committee congressional investigation into the activities of the bankers and munitions makers during the neutrality period 1914–17.

The Experience of 1914–1917

CHARLES SEYMOUR

Recent discussions of the causes of American intervention in the World War have stirred emotions; but they have failed to suggest conclusively measures that might have served to keep us at peace. There is talk of

Charles Seymour, *American Neutrality 1914–1917* (New Haven: Yale University Press, 1935), 1–26. Reprinted with permission.

the intrigues of munitions makers and the greed of capitalists. Less fantastic is the revival of the thesis that if we had treated Germany and the Allies with an even hand in meeting their attacks upon American neutral rights, we might have avoided intervention. A popular outline of the years 1914–17, by Mr. Walter Millis, implies that as we had permitted infractions of our rights by the Allies we had no right to protest to the point of war against Germany's use of the submarine. But he suggests no practicable alternatives to the policy followed by President Wilson. The country slithered into war, he evidently feels, much as Lloyd George once remarked that Europe had slithered into war in 1914. "Among them all," Mr. Millis writes of the Americans of 1917, "none quite knew how it had happened, nor why. . . ."

There was at least one American who was acutely aware of why the United States was brought into the World War. This was the President of the United States, who for nearly three years struggled to maintain neutrality in the face of difficulties that finally proved uncontrollable. Whether as a basis for future policy, or merely to set the historical record straight, it is worth while to review Woodrow Wilson's fight to avoid intervention.

Any inquiry into the causes of American participation in the war must begin with the personality of Wilson. His office conferred upon him a determining influence in foreign policy which was heightened by the troubled state of affairs abroad. His character was such that he never let this influence slip into other hands. He was his own foreign secretary. Conscious of the power and character of public opinion, "under bonds," as he put it, to public sentiment, he nevertheless made the major decisions on his own responsibility. He delivered his "too proud to fight" speech and he sent Bernstorff home without stopping to ask what the man in the street would say. Dominant sentiment in the United States was certainly pro-Ally. American economic prosperity, furthermore, depended upon the maintenance of our trade with the Allies. But it is a far cry from these facts to the assumption that because of them we adopted a policy that pointed toward intervention. It would be necessary to show that emotional sympathy and material interests overcame the strong pacifistic sentiment of Congress and people. It would especially be necessary to show that because of them Wilson first adopted a discriminatory attitude toward Germany and then surrendered his determination to keep the country out of war.

Ample evidence is now available regarding Wilson's sentiments toward the belligerents. If it reveals an underlying personal sympathy with the Allies, it also reveals a studied insistence not to permit that feeling to affect national policy. He was so far successful that he was attacked in turn by each belligerent group as being favorable to the other. There can be no question that he regarded the maintenance of peace as his first duty. Always he held to the double principle he formulated at the moment he was smarting under the news of the *Arabic's* sinking in August, 1915: "1. The people of this country count on me to keep them out of the war; 2. It would be a calamity to the world at large if we should be actively drawn into the conflict and so deprived of all disinterested influence over the settlement." He maintained this attitude in the face of what he regarded as gross affronts by Germany. "The country is undoubtedly back of me in the whole matter," he wrote privately in September, 1915, "and I feel myself under bonds to it to show patience to the utmost. My chief puzzle is to determine where patience ceases to be a virtue."

But across the determination to preserve peace ran the equally strong determination to preserve the neutral rights of the country. There was a higher principle which the President placed above peace: the honor of the United States. The outcome of this contradiction would be determined not by Wilson's policy but by that of the belligerents. . . .

Against both groups of belligerents Wilson steadily maintained American neutral rights. It is by no means a fact that he accepted British and Allied infractions of what he described as "hitherto fixed international law." The notes of protest which he sponsored and which so greatly annoyed those who, like Ambassador Page, frankly favored the Allied cause, made clear that the United States did not, and would not, recognize the legality of the Allied pseudo-blockade. In the late summer of 1916 the President secured from Congress wide powers permitting him to prohibit loans and to impose embargoes if retaliatory measures appeared advisable. A few weeks later he asked House to warn Sir Edward Grey "in the strongest terms" that the American people were "growing more and more impatient with the intolerable conditions of neutrality, their feeling as hot against Great Britain as it was first against Germany. . . ."

That he did not actually exercise the pressure of embargoes against the British and French resulted from two factors. The first was that the conflict over Allied interference with neutral trade was pushed into the background at critical moments by the more immediate and intense conflict with Germany over the submarine campaign. "If Germany had not alienated American sympathies," wrote Colonel House, "by her mode of warfare, the United States would not have put up with Allied control of American trade on the high seas." The fact has been emphasized by Winston Churchill: "The first German U-boat campaign," he writes, "gave us our greatest assistance. It altered the whole position of our controversies with America. A great relief became immediately apparent."

The second reason for not pushing the diplomatic conflict with the Allies to the point of retaliatory measures lay in the economic interests of America. Any practicable measures designed to enforce our interpretation of international law would have ruined the interests they meant to safeguard. By our formal protests we protected our ultimate property rights and built up a case for future damages to be proved before an international tribunal. Through private negotiations we secured in large measure the protection of immediate commercial interests. Whatever the inconvenience and delays experienced in our trade with the northern European neutrals, American foreign commence was deriving rich profits. Allied command of the sea did not touch our pockets so much as our pride. As [British] Ambassador Spring Rice cabled to Grey, it seemed "objectionable not because it is what it is, but because it is so all-pervading." Thus, if Wilson had destroyed the basis of our prosperity in order to compel immediate acceptance of the American interpretation of international law, which very few Americans understood and which even now is not entirely clear, he would have provoked something like a revolt against his administration. "If it came to the last analysis," wrote House to Wilson in the summer of 1915, "and we placed an embargo upon munitions of war and foodstuffs to please the cotton men, our whole industrial and agricultural machinery would cry out against it." Wilson's policy was designed not to favor the Allies but to protect the immediate interests of the nation and at the same time to preserve our ulimate legal rights. He yielded no principle and surrendered no claim.

The German attack upon American rights Wilson believed to be of an entirely different nature and one that must be met by different methods. The intensive submarine campaign was the answer to the system of Allied maritime control; logically, an excuse might be found for it. But its effects upon neutral rights were far more disastrous. For technical reasons and to operate effectively, the submarines must make their attack without warning, destroy blindly, escape as speedily as possible, leaving the sinking merchant ship, which might be neutral or belligerent, which might or might not carry contraband, with no assurance of what would happen to passengers and crew. To Wilson and to dominant American opinion, such wholesale methods of destroying enemy and neutral commerce were shocking. This was no question of "juridical niceties." The submarine campaign, unlike the Allied blockade, involved undiscriminating destruction of American property rights. It permitted no distinction between contraband and free goods. The Allied system gave to the American shipper reasonable assurance of safe passage after he had complied with certain formalities. Under the threat of the submarine the shipper faced the risk of losing his entire cargo. The Allied system did not involve the loss of American ships; if held in a British prize court the owner could find protection for them in legal procedure. The German submarine threatened the loss of the ship and the death of the crew and passengers as well.

Thus, from the point of view of material interests, there could be no comparison between the damage resulting to Americans from the Allied blockade and that from the intensive submarine campaign. If the latter were permitted, under protests comparable to those sent to the Allies, the result would be an almost complete blockade of American commerce, since shippers would not dare send cargoes and crew out to destruction. A clear illustration of the effect of the submarine campaign on American commercial, industrial, and agricultural interests was given by the congestion of our ports that followed the threat of submarine attacks in February and March, 1917. Freights were snarled, goods were spoiled, business was menaced with a complete tie-up.

Even so, Wilson might not have taken his firm stand against the submarine if merely property rights had been threatened. He was always careful not to interpret national policy in terms of purely material interests. Despite the difficulties involved, the economic aspects of the diplomatic conflict with Germany might have been adjudicated. But the submarine warfare involved attacks upon American lives, whether sailors on merchant ships or passengers. To Wilson it seemed a war on humanity. Between property interests and human rights there lay a clear distinction. It was brought home to all America when, on May 7, 1915, the *Lusitania* was sunk without warning, over eleven hundred persons drowned, men, women, and children, among them more than one hundred and twenty Americans. . . .

It has been frequently suggested that since the submarine campaign was designed to interrupt the flow of munitions from the United States to the Allies, Wilson might have imposed embargoes upon the export of munitions as a diplomatic bribe to Germany to give up the intensive use of the submarine. There is no indication that the President ever seriously considered this course. He was willing to utilize embargoes, if necessary as measures of retaliation against the Allies in the defense of American rights. But he was not willing to penalize ourselves in order to redress the inherent disadvantage of Germany resulting from Allied command of the seas. He agreed with Lansing that such a policy ran counter to the neutral duties of the United States. It would certainly have ruined not merely the "war babies" of industry, but the cotton and wheat growers, the copper producers, the iron and steel workers, and have thrown the country back into the bleak depression and unemployment from which it had just emerged.

There is no evidence that even the broadest sort of American embargo would have induced the Germans to forego the intensive use of the submarine. They meant to stop British imports of all raw materials, especially foodstuffs, not merely from the United States but from South America, India, and the Dominions. The purpose of the submarine campaign was far wider than the interruption of the Allied "munitions" trade with America; it was, according to the testimony given to the Reichstag investigating committee, designed to throw over the British the deadly fear of complete starvation and thus to compel them to sue for peace on German terms. [Field Marshal] Hindenburg and Ludendorff made quite plain that, in the winter of 1916–17, nothing but the prospect of immediate peace on such terms could have prevented the resumption of the submarine campaign.

Wilson, of course, might have avoided a break with Germany by surrendering the right to send American ships and citizens out on the high seas. Thus they would not be sunk by submarines. Such a policy was suggested by Mr. Bryan and was later embodied in the Gore-McLemore resolutions brought before Congress. The President believed that no government was justified in making this surrender. Through his protests to the Allies he had secured, without yielding any principle, a working arrangement that gave reasonable protection to American commercial interests. Now if, under the threat of the German submarine, he withdrew protection on the seas from American goods, sailors, and passengers, he would sacrifice interests that no protests could compensate and yield principles that nothing in the future could make good. . . .

It was all very well, Wilson pointed out, to argue that the material value of these rights could not be compared with the cost of a war. But if you begin to surrender accepted rights, where do you stop?

> If in this instance we allowed expediency to take the place of principle, the door would inevitably be opened to still further concessions. Once accept a single abatement of right, and many other humiliations would certainly follow. . . . What we are contending for in this matter is of the very essence of the things that have made America a sovereign nation. She cannot yield them without conceding her own impotency as a Nation and making virtual surrender of her independent position among the nations of the world.

Such was Wilson's position, written for all the world and especially for Germany to read. He maintained it consistently from the first declaration of submarine warfare in February, 1915, two years before the final break, when he warned the German Government that it would be held to "a strict accountability" for acts endangering American lives and property, and that the American Government would take any necessary steps to "secure to American citizens the full enjoyment of their acknowledged rights on the high seas." This warning was translated into specific terms a year later, after the sinking of the *Sussex*, taking the form of an ultimatum which left no further room for negotiation. . . .

The Germans yielded, if only for the moment, as a result of this definite warning. During the course of 1915 they had taken [Ambassador] Von Bernstorff's warnings not too seriously, and heeded them largely because they had not yet themselves realized what a powerful weapon they possessed in the submarine. After Wilson's *Sussex* note they were under no illusions. "There was no longer any doubt in Berlin," wrote the German Ambassador, "that persistence in the point of view they had hitherto adopted would bring about a break with the United States." But in the early autumn Hindenburg and Ludendorff threw their influence in favor of a resumption of the submarine campaign. The discussions in Berlin were clearly based upon the assumption of war with the United States. . . .

The one chance of preventing the resumption of the submarine campaign, and thus keeping the United States out of war, lay in peace negotiations. Bernstorff judged correctly that neither Wilson nor public opinion would permit America to enter the war on any issue other than the submarine, and that it was vital to secure a postponement of the intensive campaign. . . . Hence the eagerness with which he pressed upon Colonel House the importance of peace action by Wilson before it was too late. Hence also the determination with which Wilson, who realized the approaching danger, prepared his peace note of December 18, 1916. He wanted to make it, he wrote House, "the strongest and most convincing thing I ever penned."

In the circumstances the effort was bound to fail. Its effect was confused by the issuance of Bethmann's peace statement on December 12, which made Wilson's note appear to the Allies as part of a plan to rescue the Central Powers from defeat. The Allies were quite unwilling to negotiate with an unbeaten Germany. The Germans were determined to insist upon terms which the Allies would not have accepted until all hope of victory had faded. Neither side wished the mediation of Wilson. The British, according to Sir William Wiseman, felt that Wilson merely talked about ideals for which the Allies were dying. "We entertain but little hope," [Foreign Minister] von Jagow had written to Bernstorff, "for the result of the exercise of good offices by one whose instincts are all in favor of the English point of view, and who in addition to this, is so naïve a statesman as President Wilson." The new German Foreign Secretary, Zimmermann, said to the budget committee of the Reichstag: "The good thing about the break with the United States is that we have finally gotten rid of this person as peace mediator."

Wilson was not discouraged by the failure of the December peace notes. He worked all through January to secure a private statement of German terms, equipped with which he could start negotiations with the Allies. He was determined to save American neutrality. On January 4, 1917, in reply to House's suggestion of the need of military preparation "in the event of war," the President insisted: "There will be no war. This country does not intend to become involved in this war. We are the only one of the great white nations that is free from war today, and it would be a crime against civilization for us to go in." On January 22 he delivered before the Senate the address which he hoped would serve as a general basis for a negotiated peace, a settlement that would leave neither the one side nor the other crushed and revengeful, "a peace without victory." It opened, as British writers later insisted, the "last opportunity of ending the war with a real peace. For America was still pacific and impartial. . . . But unhappily for mankind, the British and Prussian war machines had by then taken charge."

It is possible that if Germany had then held her hand Wilson might have been able to force negotiations. The Allies were beginning to scrape the bottom of the money chest and the time was approaching when they would be dependent upon American credits. He could soon have exercised strong pressure upon them. On the other side the Kaiser, Bethmann, and Bernstorff had no profound confidence in the submarine and were inclined toward compromise. But the decision had already been taken in Germany. On January 9 Hindenburg and [Admiral] Holtzendorf insisted that all chance of peace had disappeared and forced approval of the intensive submarine campaign. On January 31 Bernstorff gave notice that from the following day the engagements of the pledge given after the sinking of the *Sussex* would no longer be observed.

Thus ended Wilson's last effort to achieve a compromise peace, and the rupture between Germany and the United States became inevitable. The President saw no escape from the fulfilment of the warning he had given the previous April. The shock was the worse for Wilson inasmuch as it came just as he hoped to initiate mediation. He said "he felt as if the world had suddenly reversed itself: that after going from east to west, it had begun to go from west to east and he could not get his balance."

Resentment against Germany, with whom he had been working for peace, was strong. He felt with House that Germany "desires some justification for her submarine warfare and thought she could get it by declaring her willingness to make peace." Bernstorff himself insists that it was the German declaration of submarine warfare and nothing else that mattered with Wilson. . . .

Even after the diplomatic rupture Wilson waited long weeks, to give every opportunity to the Germans to avoid war. Only actual overt acts would persuade him that they would carry their policy into effect. He was willing to negotiate everything except the sinking of passenger and merchant ships without warning. The Germans showed no sign of weakening. When it was suggested that America might be kept neutral if the submarines "overlooked" American boats, the Kaiser wrote on the margin of the memorandum which disapproved the suggestion on technical grounds: "Agreed, reject. . . . Now, once for all, an *end* to negotiations with America. If Wilson wants war, let him make it, and let him then have it." On March 27, following the sinking of four American ships, the President took the decision, and on April 2 he asked Congress to declare the existence of a state of war with Germany.

So far as tests can be applied, Wilson's position was approved by the American people. Like him they were determined to stay at peace so far as the exercise of their acknowledged rights could keep them at peace, but they regarded the submarine attacks as acts of war. They were by no means prepared to sacrifice American rights on the seas and adopt a policy of nonintercourse with European belligerents and neutrals which would have resulted in economic depression or disaster in the United States. So much is indicated by the votes in Congress on the Gore-McLemore resolutions and the armed shipping bill which gave overwhelming endorsement to Wilson's policy. On the other hand, whatever the emotional sympathy for the Allied cause in the United States and however close Allied and American commercial interests, the prevailing sentiment of the people was indelibly for peace until the submarines sank American ships. They rewarded the patience with which Wilson carried on long negotiations over the *Lusitania* as well as the firmness with which he issued the *Sussex* ultimatum by reëlecting him President in the autumn of 1916. He owed his victory to the pacifists. So far from being accused of chauvinism because of the stand he had taken against the submarine campaign, he was presented and elected on the basis of having "kept us out of war." But when on April 2, following the destruction of American ships, he declared that peace was no longer consistent with honor, Congress voted for war by tremendous majorities.

It frequently happens that the occasion for an event is mistaken for its cause. Sometimes, however, the occasion and the cause are the same. There is every evidence that the sole factor that could have driven Wilson from neutrality in the spring of 1917 was the resumption of the submarine campaign. On the very eve of his war speech he was seized by his hunger for peace.

> For nights, he said, he'd been lying awake over the whole situation . . . He said he couldn't see any alternative, that he had tried every way he knew to avoid war . . . had considered every loophole of escape, and as fast as they were discovered Germany deliberately blocked them with some new outrage.

In the circumstances there was no escape, for the point had been reached which he had long foreseen and dreaded, where he could not preserve both the peace and honor of the United States. "There is one choice we cannot make, we are incapable of making," he told Congress on April 2. "We will not choose the path of submission."

3. *The National Interests and the War*

A new trend in interpretation began to emerge during and after World War II. Denoting it, for lack of a better title, as the "national interest" school, this point of view reflected the increasing consciousness by Americans of their inextricable involvement in international politics. The journalists Walter Lippmann and Forest Davis advanced the provocative view that the United States had gone to war in 1917 primarily to protect the national security against a threatened German victory over the Allies. Since 1945 scholars have further explored this thesis and have found some supporting evidence. Edward H. Buehrig, a political scientist, in the next selection very subtly denotes the elements of realistic thinking behind Wilsonian policies and evaluates the President as not lacking in an awareness of balance of power considerations but as moving beyond that by 1917 to espouse the idealistic plan of perpetual peace through a league of nations organization.

Wilson and the Balance of Power

E. H. BUEHRIG

Foreword

The central theme of American foreign relations in the nineteenth century was the mutual accommodation progressively achieved between ourselves and Great Britain. The main theme in the present century is quite different, offering a melancholy contrast. At the turn of the century Germany and the United States had already emerged as great powers, and Japan was in process of attaining that status. Presently Russia took on new form and vigor, and Italy was to entertain high political ambition. Later still, India began to emerge, as did China. Coincident with this revolutionary change in the old order, the United States has come to blows twice with Germany and once each with Japan and Italy. Moreover, we have fought China and must consider the danger of war with the Soviet Union. At the halfway mark, the new century has witnessed serious conflict between ourselves and all our rising contemporaries save India.

Such a vast change of fortune suggests the presence of general causes, overshadowing the specific causes attending each of the successive crises.

Edward H. Buehrig, *Woodrow Wilson and the Balance of Power* (Bloomington: Indiana University Press, 1955), vii–ix, 268–275. Reprinted with permission.

How shall we characterize these broad movements of history, and what is the connection between them and our involvement in the first World War?

We can see today, what was much less clearly visible at the time, that the first World War signalized the decline of Europe from its former preeminence in world politics. With it, indeed, the Columbian era, that brilliant period of European expansion of which we ourselves are lasting evidence, was drawing to a close. Sooner or later such a decline was bound to occur. But the manner of its occurrence is a matter of particular interest. In the actual event, Europe did not succumb to superior alien forces but to her own internecine strife. German ambition, beyond the capacity of Continental Europe to cope with, engaged the energies of Great Britain. In fact, Anglo-German rivalry became a major point of tension, and Britain was no longer able to remain detached from Continental politics. Absorbed in the compelling necessities of European politics, Britain also ceased to serve effectively as a buffer between Europe and the United States.

Had it been accustomed to acting on power considerations, the United States might have based a policy forthrightly on Germany's attempt to supplant Great Britain. But the United States was not habituated to viewing international politics in such harsh terms. Moreover, it did not desire a future different from the past, nor was it covetous of either the glory or the responsibilities of world power. There was, consequently, no head-on collision with Germany. Rather German-American relations entered a legalistic maze in the perplexing intricacies of which the two countries eventually came to blows. It seems unlikely that the lawyers, by taking paths other than those actually chosen, might have significantly altered the outcome. Nor was commercial, any more than legal policy, the truly basic factor. The United States and Germany became embroiled because of their differing attitudes toward British control of the seas. Germany felt that she must challenge that control in the interest of her own future freedom of action. The United States, for its part, regarded British power benevolently, as a factor contributing to American security.

This is the state of affairs which the probing of the submarine revealed. Unwittingly, it was the instrument which laid bare the political connection with Europe which most Americans had ceased to believe existed, and which they were disposed to act on instinctively, rather than face the full implications of what was disclosed. . . .

A New Mold for American Policy

Our earliest experiences with foreign relations, in the period beginning with the American Revolution, required hard decisions and provided for the nation only a narrow margin of safety. In this respect the diplomacy of the Founding Fathers was not unlike today's. What came to be regarded as the traditional pattern of American policy, however, is of nineteenth-century origin. The announcement of the Monroe Doctrine in

1823 coincided with the beginning of an extraordinary period for the United States, in which the demands of security progressively relaxed. The Doctrine was a carefully considered response to a situation containing some elements of menace; but, oddly enough, the subsequent security of the nation was not attributable to its enforcement. For, as things turned out, there was no need to enforce it. This lack of serious occasion (except for the French intervention in Mexico during the American Civil War) for invoking the Doctrine, rather than the fact of its existence, underlay the unprecedented freedom of action of the United States in the nineteenth century; and this in turn gave rise to the isolationist tradition.

If we look for an explanation of so extraordinary a situation, we will find it in a circumstance not fully appreciated at the time, the character of our relations with Great Britain. Britain was herself a North American power—indeed at the end of the Napoleonic wars the dominant power in the Western Hemisphere. It followed that Great Britain was the main factor in our nineteenth-century situation, and the New World was the testing ground of Anglo-American relations. Fortunately accommodation rather than rivalry emerged as the dominant feature of Anglo-American relations. The achievement of this harmony between the two great English-speaking peoples is a lesson in statesmanship. Yet, because of its very completeness, accommodation exacted a price. In the United States it fostered indifference toward foreign policy which hampered the nation in responding with alert realism to the vastly altered conditions of world politics confronting it in the present century.

The first half of the twentieth century has been a transitional period in American history marking the end of one era and beginning of another. We had on the eve of the new century engaged in a small war of our own choosing. The imperial fruits of the ensuing peace treaty with Spain were regarded with considerable uneasiness. Events, however, soon pushed us into the main stream of international politics quite without regard to our own desires in the matter. Unwilling voyagers, we steered an erratic course. It required a second World War, the postwar pressure of Soviet Communism, and the new weapons of mass destruction to make us begin to exert our full influence in world affairs.

The war of 1914–18 presented the first major challenge to the pattern of our foreign relations as established in the nineteenth century; it also produced a response which even today continues to condition American policy. Already fully fashioned by April 1917, the response consisted of a league of nations with a universal guarantee of territorial integrity and political independence. This was a far cry indeed from adherence to the law of neutrality which in 1914 had been the automatic policy of the United States.

By what path did Woodrow Wilson arrive at the position of 1917, based on assumptions so radically different from those of traditional American policy? Speaking before the Senate in January 1917, Wilson contended that the United States, if it joined other nations in "guaranteeing the permanence of peace," would not break with tradition but actually fulfill "all that we have professed or striven for." He said he was proposing that the nations should with one accord adopt the doctrine of President Monroe as the doctrine of the world: that no nation should seek to extend its polity over any other nation or people, but that every people should be free to determine its own polity, its own way of development, unhindered, unthreatened, unafraid, the little along with the great and powerful. . . . There is no entangling alliance in a concert of power. When all unite to act in the same sense and with the same purpose all act in the common interest and are free to live their own lives under a common protection.

But we must judge this attempt to relate the new policy to the old a failure, for actually the historical record does not support the suggestion of an unbroken line of development from the Monroe Doctrine to the League of Nations. To be sure the Monroe Doctrine was designed to preserve the territorial integrity and political independence of the nations of the Western Hemisphere, but it had an obverse side: an attitude of aloofness toward Europe which had crystallized into a sort of permanent neutrality toward European politics. Essentially the United States, without full awareness, had in the nineteenth century sought a relationship to Europe not unlike that of neutralization attained by Switzerland. However, less undemanding than Switzerland, we had staked out a vast hemispheric area of primary interest. Moreover, much of the Western Hemisphere was economically underdeveloped and politically unstable, and it could not, therefore, escape the consequences of a major shift in the European balance of power. It was inevitable that with the first disturbance of such a nature the United States would drop its indifference toward European politics. The first World War was that occasion, and American policy responded in the halting, devious way that we have described.

We have seen that neutrality in 1914 was no mere personal preference of Wilson's. Its adoption was determined by history, whose molds are not easily broken and never so by intellectual processes alone. In fact, until the character and course of the war had emerged, it was unclear whether neutrality was the right or wrong policy. But as the war's true nature unfolded, American policy, adapting to the fact of a cataclysmic European and world struggle for power, early became a policy of benevolent neutrality strongly favoring the Allies. Yet, though the spirit of American neutrality departed increasingly from the letter until the discrepancy was wide indeed, Wilson steadfastly refused to acknowledge the divergence. Undoubtedly Wilson entertained a lingering regard for neutrality, the more so as a base from which to seek mediation, but his failure to characterize his policy openly for what it was—in such terms as House, for instance, employed privately—was due above all to a divided and clamorous public opinion, always on the verge of paralyzing disunity. No longer a private citizen in 1914–17, Wilson was the head of a great Government, and frankness appeared not a simple virtue and not always expedient.

Seeking the flexibility denied to a policy tied to the tactics of the submarine, Wilson endeavored to deemphasize the rules of maritime warfare and to take the ultimate political effects of the European struggle as the gauge of American action. It was in consequence of this endeavor that the league of nations became the dominant feature of his policy. The idea had been much abroad in the public mind, but as official policy the league emerged laboriously out of Anglo-American diplomacy, stemming from the efforts of House and Wilson on behalf of a negotiated peace. The initial attempts to mediate studiously avoided any commitment concerning future use of American power. Yet, as one observer expressed it, England was fighting for the nursery; as indeed was Germany also—with the difference that the latter was seeking to overturn the *status quo* which the former was determined to maintain. The war was not a mere quarrel over relative advantage but a struggle in which the future of great nations was at stake. Any attempt to mediate, therefore, had to take into account the dominating passion for security. In keeping with this characteristic of the war, Sir Edward Grey reacted to American proposals for mediation by advancing an idea of future concerted action against aggression. The foreign secretary was looking at the European situation, and saw the league as a device for bringing American power to bear in a Europe no longer capable of controlling itself. In a manner even more direct than that employed by George Canning in 1823, Grey was endeavoring through the New World to redress the balance of the Old.

Wilson's incorporation of the league idea into American policy was in response to Grey's initiative, but the idea did not have the same connotation for both men. Grey's thinking was empirical, in terms of the European problem; Wilson's idealistic, and of universal application. Grey saw the league as an elaboration of the traditional pattern of diplomacy; Wilson saw it as a new and independent force in the world capable of overriding the animosities and conflicts. To Grey the league was a means of channeling American power; to Wilson it was more the rallying point of world opinion.

Such in any event was the guise in which Wilson eventually depicted the league, though we have noted occasions when the President assessed the problem of American foreign policy in different terms. Not always had he regarded justice as a goal directly accessible through good will and rationality. In the debate with Lansing over the implications for American policy of the ideological aspect of the war, in the candid expression of misgivings to Frank I. Cobb on the eve of the War Message, and concealed in the January 22, 1917 address to the Senate—indeed underlying Wilson's whole policy of peace without victory—was an appreciation of the balance of power point of view: namely, that stability is to be found in an equilibrium of forces no less than in moral excellence.

Recognizing that these points of view are logically incompatible but that neither is exclusive of the other, we must ask why the idealistic element in Wilson's policy was finally so preponderant. To answer that this outcome accorded with Wilson's philosophical and temperamental leanings would not seem to cover the whole ground. Wilson, whether consciously or not, adapted his arguments to the requirements of public opinion, and nostalgic for the nineteenth century, the American nation wished to minimize the very exertion which Sir Edward Grey deemed the essential thing. Unaccustomed to the risk and burden of international responsibility, Americans were above all responsive to expressions of hope, pride, and sentiment. Thus the league was depicted in a fashion reflecting the very isolationism to which it was the supposed antithesis.

Additional Reading

Edwin Borchard and W. P. Lage, *Neutrality for the United States* (1937).
C. H. Grattan, *Why We Fought* (1929).
A. S. Link, *Woodrow Wilson and the Progressive Era, 1910–1917* (1954).
———, *Wilson: The Struggle for Neutrality, 1914–1915* (1960).
———, *Wilson the Diplomatist* (1957).
Ernest R. May, *The World War and American Isolation, 1914–1917* (1959).
Walter Millis, *Road to War: America, 1914–1917* (1935).
Alice M. Morrissey, *The American Defense of Neutral Rights, 1914–1917* (1939).
Harley Notter, *The Origins of the Foreign Policy of Woodrow Wilson* (1937).
H. C. Peterson, *Propaganda for War* (1939).
Daniel M. Smith, *Robert Lansing and American Neutrality, 1914–1917* (1958).
Charles C. Tansill, *America Goes to War* (1938).

14 THE DEFEAT IN THE SENATE OF THE VERSAILLES TREATY

As President Wilson in Paris was completing the fastening of the Covenant of the League of Nations to the treaty of peace with Germany, he received from America indications of mounting criticism of his handiwork. The Republican party had captured control of both houses of Congress in the 1918 elections and Henry Cabot Lodge of Massachusetts became chairman of the powerful Foreign Relations Committee in the new Senate. Under Lodge's direction, the committee was organized with a large number of opponents of the league concept. Made aware of growing political criticism during a quick return to the United States in February, 1919, Wilson upon resuming his labors in Paris secured a number of changes in the league charter which he hoped would allay the fears of critics. His efforts were to prove of little avail.

After the formal signing of the peace treaty at Versailles, the triumphant President bore the document with its precious covenant back to the United States and on July 10, 1919, formally laid the treaty before the Senate for its approval. Referred to the Lodge committee, there ensued a delaying process of protracted hearings and often irrelevant testimony before the treaty was reported back to the Senate burdened with 45 amendments and 4 reservations. These Republican-sponsored changes were subsequently reduced to the 14 "Lodge reservations," to be attached to the treaty as conditions of ratification.

Opposed to encumbering modifications of the treaty, President Wilson undertook an extensive speaking tour in September in the hope of bringing popular pressures to bear on recalcitrant senators. Never in robust health and now weakened by the tensions of war-waging and peace-making, the exhausted President was compelled to cancel the tour in late September and to return to the White House for rest. There, early in the following month, he suffered a severe stroke which rendered him partially paralyzed. Isolated in his sickroom, the seriously-ill Wilson was not active politically until November and in fact he made only a very limited recovery during the remainder of his term of office.

It was under these circumstances that the peace treaty came to a vote before the Senate on November 19, 1919, and was defeated. The feeble President continued to oppose the Lodge reservations and he urged loyal Democratic senators to vote against the treaty with reservations. Yet because of the Republican majority and the nature of the opposition in the Senate, the only hope for approval of the treaty was with the reservations. Consequently, the vote was 41 ayes to 50 nayes for the treaty with reservations, and 38 ayes to 53 nayes without. Revived for another vote on March 19, 1920, the treaty with the Lodge reservations—now 15 in number, after the addition of a clause advocating Irish independence—was again rejected by the vote of 49 ayes to 35 nayes. As the final tabulation was only 7 votes short of the necessary two-thirds majority, it was clear that Wilson himself had defeated the treaty by persuading 23 Democratic senators to join 12 "irreconcilables" in voting negatively.

Though Wilson hoped to make the treaty the key issue in the 1920 presidential campaign, the March vote in fact signified the death of the League in so far as American participation was concerned.

Questions raised by scholars about the defeat of the peace treaty and league have centered around the motives and actions of Lodge and Wilson. How seriously would the Lodge Reservations have affected the treaty and the operations of the league? If very little, and this has been the conclusion of most students of the period, why did the two antagonists attach so much importance to the reservations that Lodge and his supporters would not approve the treaty without the reservations and Wilson would not accept it with the changes? Was the Massachusetts senator motivated in his course by high principle, or was he following an obstructionist course merely for narrow partisan and personal purposes? Why did not Wilson, presumably aware of the innocuous if personally objectionable character of the reservations, rise above petty considerations to accept the treaty in the only way it could pass the Senate?

DOCUMENTS

1. *The Capstone of the Versailles Treaty: the League Covenant*

The focus of the public debate on the Treaty of Versailles was on Part I, the Covenant of the League of Nations. Within the Covenant, the key articles were numbers 10 through 16, involving the mutual guarantee and containing provisions for settlement of disputes and punishment of aggressors.

From the Covenant of the League of Nations

Article 1 [*3*]. Any Member of the League may, after two years' notice of its intention so to do, withdraw from the League, provided that all its international obligations and all its obligations under this Covenant shall have been fulfilled at the time of its withdrawal.

Article 2 The action of the League under this Covenant shall be effected through the instrumentality of an Assembly and of a Council, with a permanent Secretariat.

Article 3 [*3*]. The Assembly may deal at its meetings with any matter within the sphere of action of the League or affecting the peace of the world.

[*4*]. At meetings of the Assembly each Member of the League shall have one vote, and may have not more than three Representatives.

Article 4 [*1*]. The Council shall consist of Representatives of the Principal Allied and Associated Powers, together with Representatives of four other Members of the League. These four Members of the League shall be selected by the Assembly from time to time in its discretion. . . .

Article 5 [*1*]. Except where otherwise expressly provided in this Covenant or by the terms of the present Treaty, decisions at any meeting of the Assembly or of the Council shall require the agreement of all the Members of the League represented at the meeting.

Article 6 [*1*]. The permanent Secretariat shall be established at the Seat of the League. The Secretariat shall comprise a Secretary General and such secretaries and staff as may be required.

[*2*]. The first Secretary General shall be the person named in the Annex; thereafter the Secretary General shall be appointed by the Council with the approval of the majority of the Assembly.

Article 8 [*1*]. The Members of the League recognise that the maintenance of peace requires the reduction of national armaments to the lowest point consistent with national safety and the enforcement by common action of international obligations.

[*2*]. The Council, taking account of the geographical situation and circumstances of each State, shall formulate plans for such reduction for the consideration and action of the several Governments.

[*6*]. The Members of the League undertake to interchange full and frank information as to the scale of their armaments, their military, naval and air programmes and the condition of such of their industries as are adaptable to war-like purposes.

Article 10 The Members of the League undertake to respect and preserve as against external aggression the territorial integrity and existing political independence of all Members of the League. In case of any such aggression or in case of any threat or danger of such aggression the Council shall advise upon the means by which this obligation shall be fulfilled.

Article 11 [*1*]. Any war or threat of war, whether immediately affecting any of the Members of the League or not, is hereby declared a matter of concern to the whole League, and the League shall take any action that may be deemed wise and effectual to safeguard the peace of nations. In case any such emergency should arise the Secretary General shall on the request of any Member of the League forthwith summon a meeting of the Council.

[*2*]. It is also declared to be the friendly right of each Member of the League to bring to the attention of the Assembly or of the Council any circumstance whatever affecting international relations which threatens to disturb international peace or the good understanding between nations upon which peace depends.

Article 12 [*1*]. The Members of the League agree that, if there should arise between them any dispute likely to lead to a rupture, they will submit the matter either to arbitration or judicial settlement or to inquiry by the Council, and they agree in no case to resort to war until three months after the award by the arbitrators or the judicial decision, or the report by the Council.

Article 13 [*1*]. The Members of the League agree that, whenever any dispute shall arise between them which they recognize to be suitable for submission to arbitration or judicial settlement, and which cannot be satisfactorily settled by diplomacy, they will submit the whole subject matter to arbitration or judicial settlement.

[2]. Disputes as to the interpretation of a treaty, as to any question of international law, as to the existence of any fact which, if established, would constitute a breach of any international obligation, or as to the extent and nature of the reparation to be made for any such breach, are declared to be among those which are generally suitable for submission to arbitration or judicial settlement. . . .

[*4*]. The Members of the League agree that they will carry out in full good faith any award or decision that may be rendered, and that they will not resort to war against a Member of the League which complies therewith. In the event of any failure to carry out such an award or decision, the Council shall propose what steps should be taken to give effect thereto.

Article 14 The Council shall formulate and submit to the Members of the League for adoption plans for the establishment of a Permanent Court of International Justice. The Court shall be competent to hear and determine any dispute of an international character which the parties thereto submit to it. The Court may also give an advisory opinion upon any dispute or question referred to it by the Council or by the Assembly.

Article 15 [*1*]. If there should arise between Members of the League any dispute likely to lead to a rupture, which is not submitted to arbitration or judicial settlement in accordance with Article 13, the Members of the League agree that they will submit the matter to the Council. Any party to the dispute may effect such submission by giving notice of the existence of the dispute to the Secretary General, who will make all necessary arrangements for a full investigation and consideration thereof.

[*8*]. If the dispute between the parties is claimed by one of them, and is found by the Council, to arise out of a matter which by international law is solely within the domestic jurisdiction of that party, the Council shall so report, and shall make no recommendation as to its settlement.

Article 16 [*1*]. Should any Member of the League resort to war in disregard of its covenants under Articles 12, 13 or 15, it shall *ipso facto* be deemed to have committed an act of war against all other Members of the League, which hereby undertake immediately to subject it to the severance of all trade or financial relations, the prohibition of all intercourse between their nationals and the nationals of the covenant-breaking State, and the prevention of all financial, commercial or personal intercourse between the nationals of the covenant-breaking State and the nationals of any other State, whether a Member of the League or not.

[2]. It shall be the duty of the Council in such case to recommend to the several Governments concerned what effective military, naval or air force the Members of the League shall severally contribute to the armed forces to be used to protect the covenants of the League.

[3]. The Members of the League agree, further, that they will mutually support one another in the financial and economic measures which are taken under this Article, in order to minimise the loss and inconvenience resulting from the above measures, and that they will mutually support one another in resisting any special measures aimed at one of their number by the covenant-breaking State, and that they will take the necessary steps to afford passage through their territory to the forces of any of the Members of the League which are co-operating to protect the covenants of the League. . . .

Article 21 Nothing in this Covenant shall be deemed to affect the validity of international engagements, such as treaties of arbitration or regional understandings like the Monroe doctrine, for securing the maintenance of peace.

Article 22 [*1*]. To those colonies and territories which as a consequence of the late war have ceased to be under the sovereignty of the States which formerly governed them and which are inhabited by peoples not yet able to stand by themselves under the strenuous conditions of the modern world, there should be applied the principle that the well-being and development of such peoples form a sacred trust of civilisation and that securities for the performance of this trust should be embodied in this Covenant.

[2]. The best method of giving practical effect to this principle is that the tutelage of such peoples should be entrusted to advanced nations who by reason of their resources, their experience or their geographical position can best undertake this responsibility, and who are willing to accept it, and that this tutelage should be exercised by them as Mandatories on behalf of the League.

2. *Republican Objections: the Case for a "Little" America*

The Lodge Reservations to the Treaty of Peace, in the view of many Republicans and critics of the Covenant, were designed merely to safeguard legitimate American interests and rights. In his speeches, Senator Lodge disclaimed hostility to the idea of a league as such, but obviously he wanted one which was safe for the United States to join.

The Lodge Resolution of Ratification of the Treaty of Peace, November 19, 1919

Resolved . . . That the Senate advise and consent to the ratification of the treaty of peace with Germany . . . subject to the following reservations and understandings . . . which ratification is not to take effect or bind the United States until the said reservations and understandings . . . have been accepted by . . . at least three of the four principal allied and associated powers. . . .

1. . . . in case of notice of withdrawal from the league of nations, as provided in said article [Article 1], the United States shall be the sole

judge as to whether all its international obligations . . . have been fulfilled, and notice of withdrawal . . . may be given by a concurrent resolution of the Congress of the United States.

2. The United States assumes no obligation to preserve the territorial integrity or political independence of any other country . . . under the provisions of article 10, or to employ the military or naval forces of the United States under any article of the treaty for any purpose, unless in any particular case the Congress, which . . . has the sole power to declare war . . . shall . . . so provide.

3. No mandate shall be accepted by the United States under article 22 . . . except by action of the Congress of the United States.

4. The United States reserves to itself exclusively the right to decide what questions are within its domestic jurisdiction. . . .

5. The United States will not submit to arbitration or to inquiry by the assembly or by the council of the league of nations . . . any questions which in the judgment of the United States depend upon or relate to . . . the Monroe doctrine; said doctrine is to be interpreted by the United States alone and is . . . wholly outside the jurisdiction of said league of nations. . . .

6. The United States withholds its assent to articles 156, 157, and 158 [Shantung clauses]. . . .

7. The Congress of the United States will provide by law for the appointment of the representatives of the United States in the assembly and the council of the league of nations, and may in its discretion provide for the participation of the United States in any commission. . . . no person shall represent the United States under either said league of nations or the treaty of peace . . . except with the approval of the Senate of the United States.

9. The United States shall not be obligated to contribute to any expenses of the league of nations . . . unless and until an appropriation of funds . . . shall have been made by the Congress of the United States.

10. If the United States shall at any time adopt any plan for the limitation of armaments proposed by the council of the league . . . it reserves the right to increase such armaments without the consent of the council whenever the United States is threatened with invasion or engaged in war.

14. The United States assumes no obligation to be bound by any election, decision, report, or finding of the council or assembly in which any member of the league and its self-governing dominions, colonies, or parts of empire, in the aggregate have cast more than one vote. . . .

From a Speech by Henry Cabot Lodge in the Senate, August 12, 1919

. . . In article 10 the United States is bound on the appeal of any member of the league not only to respect but to preserve its independence and its boundaries, and that pledge if we give it, must be fulfilled.

There is to me no distinction whatever in a treaty between what some persons are pleased to call legal and moral obligations. A treaty rests and must rest . . . upon moral obligations. No doubt a great power impossible of coercion can cast aside a moral obligation if it sees fit and escape from the performance of the duty which it promises. The pathway of dishonor is always open. I, for one, however, cannot conceive of voting for a clause of which I disapprove because I know it can be escaped in that way. Whatever the United States agrees to, by that agreement she must abide. . . .

If China should rise up and attack Japan in an effort to undo the great wrong of the cession of the control of Shantung to that power, we should be bound under the terms of article 10 to sustain Japan against China. . . . I do not like the prospect. It shall not come into existence by any vote of mine. . . .

Let me now briefly point out the insuperable difficulty which I find in article 15. It begins: "If there should arise between members of the league any dispute likely to lead to a rupture." "Any dispute" covers every possible dispute. It therefore covers a dispute over tariff duties and over immigration. . . .

Immigration . . . cannot escape the action of the league by any claim of domestic jurisdiction; it has too many international aspects.

. . . So far as immigration is concerned, and also so far as tariff duties . . . are concerned, I deny the jurisdiction. There should be no possibility of other nations deciding who shall come into the United States, or under what conditions they shall enter. The right to say who shall come into a country is one of the very highest attributes of sovereignty. If a nation cannot say without appeal who shall come within its gates and become a part of its citizenship it has ceased to be a sovereign nation. . . .

If other nations are willing to subject themselves to such a domination, the United States, to which many immigrants have come and many more will come, ought never to submit to it for a moment. . . .

Let me now deal with the article [21] itself. . . . the Monroe doctrine is no more a regional understanding than it is an "international engagement." The Monroe doctrine was a policy declared by President Monroe. . . . It rested firmly on the great law of self-preservation, which is the basic principle of every independent State. . . .

The instant that the United States . . . ceases to be the sole judge of what it means, that instant the Monroe doctrine ceases and disappears from history and from the face of the earth. I think it is just as undesirable to have Europe interfere in American affairs now as Mr. Monroe thought it was in 1823, and equally undesirable that we should be compelled to involve ourselves in all the wars and brawls of Europe. . . .

Article 10 I have already discussed. There is no question that the preservation of a State against external aggression can contemplate nothing but war. In article 11, again, the league is authorized to take any action which may be necessary to safeguard the peace of the world. "Any action" includes war. . . . Article 16 embodies the boycott and also, in the last paragraph, provides explicitly for war. . . . Taken altogether, these provisions for war present what to my mind is the gravest objection to this league in its present form. We are told that of course nothing will be done . . . without the assent of Congress. If this is true, let us say so in the covenant. But as it stands there is no doubt whatever in my mind that American troops and American ships may be ordered to any part of the world by nations other than the United States, and that is a proposition to which I for one can never assent. It must be made perfectly clear that no American soldiers, not even a corporal's guard . . . can ever be engaged in war or ordered anywhere except by the constitutional authorities of the United States.

3. Wilson Appeals to the People

To President Wilson, on the other hand, the Lodge reservation strategy revealed doubts and hesitations unworthy of America and indicated a less than enthusiastic shouldering of the obligations of a great power. In addition, he asserted that the suggested alterations actually weakened the League and would cause other powers to insist on further changes.

Speech of President Wilson, Auditorium, San Francisco, September 17, 1919

. . . It is my purpose, fellow citizens, to analyze the objections which are made to this great League, and I shall be very brief. In the first place, you know that one of the difficulties which have been experienced by those who are objecting to this League is that they do not think that there is a wide enough door open for us to get out. For my own part, I am not one of those who, when they go into a generous enterprise, think first of all how they are going to turn away from those with whom they are associated. I am not one of those who, when they go into a concert for the peace of the world, want to sit close to the door with their hand on the knob and constantly trying the door to be sure that it is not locked. If we want to go into this thing—and we do want to go into it—we will go in it with our whole hearts and settled purpose to stand by the great enterprise to the end. Nevertheless, you will remember—some of you, I dare say—that when I came home in March for an all too brief visit to this country, which seems to me the fairest and dearest in the world, I brought back with me the first draft of the Covenant of the League of Nations. I called into consultation the Committees on Foreign Affairs and on Foreign Relations of the House and Senate of the United States, and I laid the draft of the Covenant before them. One of the things that they proposed was that it should be explicitly stated that any member of the League should have the right to withdraw. I carried that suggestion back to Paris, and without the slightest hesitation it was accepted and acted upon; and every suggestion which was made in that conference at the White House was accepted by the conference of peace in Paris. There is not a feature of the Covenant, except one, now under debate upon which suggestions were not made at that time, and there is not one of those suggestions that was not adopted by the conference of peace.

The gentlemen say, "You have laid a limitation upon the right to withdraw. You have said that we can withdraw upon two years' notice, if at that time we shall have fulfilled all our international obligations and all our obligations under the Covenant." "Yes," I reply; "is it characteristic of the United States not to fulfill her international obligations? Is there any fear that we shall wish to withdraw dishonorably? Are gentlemen willing to stand up and say that they want to get out whether they have the moral right to get out or not?" I for one am too proud as an American to debate that subject on that basis. The United States has always fulfilled its international obligations, and, God helping her, she always will. There is nothing in the Covenant to prevent her acting upon her own judgment with regard to that matter. The only thing she has to fear, the only thing she has to regard, is the public opinion of mankind, and inasmuch as we have always scrupulously satisfied the public opinion of mankind with regard to justice and right, I for my part am not afraid at any time to go before that jury. It is a jury that might condemn us if we did wrong, but it is not a jury that could oblige us to stay in the League, so that there is absolutely no limitation upon our right to withdraw.

One of the other suggestions I carried to Paris was that the committees of the two Houses did not find the Monroe Doctrine safeguarded in the Covenant of the League of Nations. I suggested that to the conference in Paris, and they at once inserted the provision which is now there that nothing in the Covenant shall be construed as affecting the validity of the Monroe Doctrine. What is the validity of the Monroe Doctrine? The Monroe Doctrine means that if any outside power, any power outside this hemisphere, tries to impose its will upon any portion of the Western Hemisphere the United States is at liberty to act independently and alone in repelling the aggression; that it does not have to wait for the action of the League of Nations; that it does not have to wait for anything but the action of its own administration and its own Congress. This is the first time in the history of international diplomacy that any great government has acknowledged the validity of the Monroe Doctrine. Now for the first time all the great fighting powers of the world except Germany, which for the time being has ceased to be a great fighting power, acknowledge the validity of the Monroe Doctrine and acknowledge it as part of the international practice of the world.

They are nervous about domestic questions. They say, "It is intolerable to think that the League of Nations should interfere with domestic questions," and whenever they begin to specify they speak of the question of immigration, of the question of naturalization, of the question of the tariff. My fellow citizens, no competent or authoritative student of international law would dream of maintaining that these were anything but exclusively domestic questions, and the Covenant of the League expressly provides that the League can take no action whatever about matters which are in the practice of international law regarded as domestic questions. We did not undertake to enumerate samples of domestic questions for the very good reason, which will occur to any lawyer, that if you made a list it would be inferred that what you left out was not included. Nobody with a thoughtful knowledge of international practice has the least doubt as to what are domestic questions, and there is no obscurity whatever in this Covenant with regard to the safeguarding of the United States, along with other sovereign countries, in the control of domestic questions. I beg that you will not fancy, my fellow citizens, that the United States is the only country that is jealous of its sovereignty. Throughout these conferences it was necessary at every turn to safeguard the sovereign independence of the several governments who were taking part in the conference, and they were just as keen to protect themselves against outside intervention in domestic matters as we were. Therefore the whole heartiness of their concurrent opinion runs with this safeguarding of domestic questions.

It is objected that the British Empire has six votes and we have one. The answer to that is that it is most carefully arranged that our one vote equals the six votes of the British Empire. Anybody who will take the pains to read the Covenant of the League of Nations will find out that the assembly—and it is only in the assembly that the British Empire has six votes—is not a voting body. . . .

Not a single affirmative act or negative decision upon a matter of action taken by the League of Nations can be validated without the vote of the United States of America. We can dismiss from our dreams the six votes of the British Empire, for the real underlying conception of the assembly of the League of Nations is that it is the forum of opinion, not of action. It is the debating body; it is the body where the thought of the little nation along with the thought of the big nation is brought to bear upon those matters which affect the peace of the world, is brought to bear upon those matters which affect the good understanding between nations upon which the peace of the world depends; where this stifled voice of humanity is at last to be heard, where nations that have borne the unspeakable sufferings of the ages that must have seemed to them like æons will find voice and expression, where the moral judgment of mankind can sway the opinion of the world. That is the function of the assembly. The assembly is the voice of mankind. The council, where unanimous action is necessary, is the only means through which that voice can accomplish action.

You say, "We have heard a great deal about Article X." I just now said that the only substitute for the League of Nations which is offered by the opponents is a return to the old system. What was the old system? That the strong had all the rights and need pay no attention to the rights of the weak; that if a great powerful nation saw what it wanted, it had the right to go and take it; that the weak nations could cry out and cry out as they pleased and there would be no hearkening ear anywhere to their rights. . . .

READINGS

1. The Case against Lodge

Some scholars have answered the question of who killed the treaty by attaching primary responsibility to Senator Lodge. The mastermind of Republican senatorial strategy, Lodge is depicted as motivated by an intense personal dislike of President Wilson and by a desire to embarrass the Democrats and win political advantages for the Republican party. Representative of this point of view is the following selection, utilizing psychological insights, by historians A. L. and J. L. George.

Battle with the Senate

A. L. AND J. L. GEORGE

All the time President Wilson was in Paris spending himself to the utmost first to secure the League Covenant and then to amend it, his enemies at home, led by Senator Lodge, plotted his defeat. When Lodge read the revised Covenant in the newspapers on April 28, 1919, he immediately concluded that Wilson's Herculean effort to amend the Covenant satisfactorily had been in vain. ". . . It is obvious," he stated to the press the next day, "that it will require further amendments . . ." Thereafter, he took the position that, so far from being an improvement over the original, the revised Covenant was "much worse than it was before." The Senate, he indicated, would have to save the country from the perils into which the President's feckless leadership, unless checked, would lead it.

Lodge, indeed, did not even have to examine the Covenant to be certain that it was a dangerous proposition. He had long since decided that while it would be "a mistake" to reject the *idea* of a league of nations—everyone, after all, favored the preservation of world peace—it would be possible to confound any practical plan, no matter what its terms. . . .

Throughout the battle over Senate ratification of the Treaty of Versailles, Lodge piously maintained that his position was dictated by an overriding concern for safeguarding the interests of the United States, and that he favored American entry into the League of Nations if only the Covenant could be so changed that basic American interests would be protected. It was widely suspected at the time, and frequently has been suggested since, that Lodge was out first and foremost to humiliate President Wilson, and that he had no use whatever for Wilson's League in any form. Since a policy of outright rejection would surely fail because of widespread public endorsement of the League, Lodge shrewdly feigned a more moderate position. He did so, according to this theory, the better ultimately to kill Wilson's creation or, at the very least, to change it and force the proud President to bow to the Republican-controlled Senate, thus yielding prestige, both personal and political.

In the light of Lodge's maneuvers throughout the Treaty fight, this interpretation is persuasive. It gains all but irresistible plausibility from the fact that when at last the Senate rejected the Treaty, League and all, Lodge felt, as he declared in a letter, that he and his colleagues had done very well. To one of his Senate colleagues, he referred to the outcome of the controversy as a "victory." Further, at the Republican Convention of 1920, Lodge refused to urge ratification of the Treaty with the reservations he had so vociferously advocated but preferred, instead, to leave the way open for a complete repudiation of the League. And when, indeed, the Republicans won the election of 1920, Lodge exultantly declared that so far as the United States was concerned, the League of Nations was dead.

Lodge personally detested Wilson, a fact to which his letters and papers eloquently testify. Quite apart from this highly personal consideration, however, as a Republican political leader Lodge had his eye upon the next presidential election, an event which has seldom failed to magnify the partisan component of issues before Congress for long months before its occurrence.

Whatever complex combination of personal, partisan and patriotic motives animated Lodge, certain it is that as soon as the Germans sued for peace in October, 1918, he turned all the resources of a cunning mind to the task of publicly embarrassing Wilson at every turn. He who had once proclaimed that where questions of foreign policy were concerned his politics always stopped at the water's edge, attempted, via Henry White,* to furnish Allied diplomats at the Peace Conference a memorandum suggesting that the President's ideas misrepresented the real sentiments of the people and Senate of the United States. His purpose, he stated frankly, was to strengthen the hands of these foreign diplomats in their dealings with Wilson. Lodge organized the Round Robin, which struck Wilson's prestige a mighty blow at just the moment the President needed all his authority to induce the Allies to moderate some of their demands. At the height of the Italian crisis, while Wilson was standing foursquare against the Italian claim to Fiume, Lodge issued a statement to the Italians of Boston upholding the Italian position. The Shantung settlement, the justice of which was indeed debatable, provided Lodge and his cohorts with a splendid excuse to heap further abuse upon their favorite villain.

As the *George Washington* bearing the President home from the Peace Conference coursed toward American shores, Senator Lodge was deep in plans to bring to his knees the man he hated more, he once confessed, than he had ever expected to hate anyone in politics, the man whom, James Buchanan perhaps excepted, he judged to be the worst President in the nation's history. The great alarum which he and his friends were spreading the length and breadth of the land was that Wilson's League was fraught with dire danger for the United States and that the Senate must now change the Covenant to make it safe.

Almost any man who was confronted with opponents as intelligent and resourceful as Lodge and his cohorts would be distressed and angered. A more detached leader than Wilson, however, might have been capable of

* A member of the American Peace Commission to Paris.

dispassionately countering Lodge's tactical maneuvers and of taking practical steps to mobilize all possible Senate support for the Treaty. Wilson's particular anxieties rendered him incapable of meeting Lodge's challenge with such equanimity. Because he was so peculiarly vulnerable to them, Lodge's barbs affected him as the proverbial red flag affects the proverbial bull.

Wilson had deep-seated doubts, which originated in his early years, of his intellectual competence, his moral worth and his strength. He had tried to overcome these self-doubts by rigorous training and ceaseless self-vindicating demonstrations through accomplishment that he was indeed of superior intelligence, of good and "unselfish" character, and of sufficient strength to escape the degradation of capitulating to anybody. With an unerring sense of where his adversary's weak points lay and with an air of patronizing superiority, Lodge peppered him with just those personal attacks which intensified Wilson's inner anxieties.

Did Wilson, after suffering much mortification for his "slowness" as a child, joyfully discover in his adolescence that he "had a mind" and thereafter take especial pride in his intellectual attainments? Lodge was not at pains to conceal his contempt for Wilson's "mind." In a Senate speech on February 28, 1919, it will be recalled, Lodge had derided Wilson as one whose intellect and position in the world he found something less than overpowering. As for being the "scholar in politics"—until Wilson's star eclipsed his own, Lodge had enjoyed that popular appellation—why, Wilson was no scholar at all, Lodge maintained. (As evidence of this, in a book he subsequently wrote, the learned Senator cited the fact that in making a classical allusion, Wilson had once confused Hercules with Antaeus, a blunder which Lodge considered "incredible.")

Did Wilson, trained by a father obsessed with the importance of proper use of the English language, take great pains with his style and inordinately value mellifluous phrases and graceful expression? "As an English production," Lodge once remarked of the Covenant, "it does not rank high. It might get by at Princeton but certainly not at Harvard."

Did Wilson secretly fear his "selfish" motives in exercising leadership and continually proclaim his own disinterestedness and, by extension, the disinterestedness of the nation in dealing with other nations? Lodge thought Wilson self-seeking, unprincipled, egotistical, timid, narrow-minded, a demagogue interested exclusively in his own aggrandizement —and he made no secret of his opinion.

Did Wilson, desperately eager to undercut Lodge's position, make the most painful compromises during the latter half of the Peace Conference in order to obtain amendments to the Covenant which would meet the major objections which had been raised against it? Lodge, so far from being nonplussed by Wilson's coup, summarily dismissed the revisions as worthless and served notice that the Senate would have to make further changes. Unless the President accepted these changes, he warned repeatedly, the Treaty would be defeated.

Not only was the substance of Lodge's thrusts unbearable to Wilson: the Senator's manner stung him to the quick. Even one of Lodge's life-long friends, William Lawrence, in summing up Lodge's career regretfully noted that "Cabot" had "a certain quality of voice in making his brightest and most penetrating remarks" which could mortally offend. . . .

Lodge trained all this capacity for sneering sarcasm against Wilson. There was something contemptuous in the very calmness of the man: it was as though he felt the objects of his scorn unworthy even of his enmity.

Once before, long ago, Wilson had had to endure barbed criticism. Once before, long ago, he had been sent in humiliation to revise and re-revise some carefully wrought composition. And long ago, overwhelmed by his masterful father, he had submitted to sarcastically made demands and to aspersions on his moral and intellectual worth. He had submitted in seeming docility. Perhaps the rage that he had suppressed then emerged in full force against those he encountered in later years who re-awakened the disagreeable sensations of half a century and more before.

Wilson's emotional commitment to the League was, as we have seen, of surpassing intensity. Even in connection with projects of far less personal significance to him, he habitually experienced any interference in his exercise of power as an intolerable threat. Small wonder, given the very real menace Lodge presented both to the League and to Wilson's inner equilibrium, that the mere mention of the Senator's name caused Wilson to clench his teeth in rage.

President Wilson arrived home from Europe on July 8, 1919. Two days later he appeared before the Senate to lay the Treaty before it for ratification. Shortly before leaving the White House to address the Senate, Wilson held a press conference. One of the reporters inquired whether the Treaty would pass if the Senate attached reservations to it. "I do not think hypothetical questions are concerned," Wilson flashed back. "*The Senate is going to ratify the treaty.*"

If his address to the Senate had a somewhat less peremptory tone, its plain implication was the same: the Senate *must* ratify the Treaty—it was God's will. It was not a perfect instrument, the President conceded. Many "minor compromises" had been made but, he declared euphemistically, the settlement "squares, as a whole, with the principles agreed upon as the basis of the peace. . . ." The Treaty's most important accomplishment was the creation of the League of Nations. "Dare we reject it and break the heart of the world?" Rejection was unthinkable. America, as had been universally recognized, "entered the war to promote no private or peculiar interest of her own but only as the champion of rights which she was glad to share with free men and lovers of justice everywhere." Now the world looked to America for moral leadership, and it was our duty to accept the responsibility of providing it. "The stage is set, the destiny disclosed," the President concluded. "It has come about by no plan of our conceiving, but by the hand of God who led us into this way. We cannot turn back. We can only go forward, with lifted eyes and freshened spirit, to follow the vision. It was of this that we dreamed at our birth. America shall in truth show the way. The light streams upon the path ahead, and nowhere else."

Unfortunately, as their immediate comments disclosed, many of the Senators saw "the light" streaming upon a number of alternative paths that the zealous President did not espy; and they regarded the destiny for America which Wilson envisaged more as a product of the plans of Woodrow Wilson than as a manifestation of the "hand of God." What about reservations, a number of them demanded. The President had not even mentioned the subject, which was uppermost in the minds of the Senators. Instead he had treated them to, as Senator Brandegee (R., Conn.) put it, "soap bubbles of oratory and soufflé of phrases."

The Treaty having been formally placed before the Senate, it was immediately referred to the Senate Foreign Relations Committee. The chairman of this Committee, of course, was Henry Cabot Lodge.

Though chairman of the Foreign Relations Committee and leader of the majority party in the Senate—there were 49 Republicans and 47 Democrats in the Senate newly organized in accordance with the results of the 1918 elections—Lodge was in an extremely difficult position. The nub of his dilemma was that public opinion overwhelmingly favored *a* league and, after Wilson succeeded in amending the Covenant in Paris to eliminate most of the dangers its opponents professed to see in it, the public plainly favored *the* League. Several polls testified to that fact. So did the tidal wave of favorable comment in the press and in lecture halls and pulpits throughout the land, of resolutions of endorsement by farm and labor organizations and by state legislatures.

Senator Lodge was greatly concerned over this state of affairs. He was shrewd enough to realize that, given the temper of the country and even of a goodly number of his Republican colleagues in the Senate, any immediate showdown between the supporters of the League and its opponents would result in a rout of the latter. To A. J. Beveridge he wrote in February, 1919:

> The situation . . . practically must be treated with great care. I have no doubt that a large majority of the people of the country are very naturally fascinated by the idea of eternal preservation of the world's peace. . . . Now I do not think it would be wise for us at this stage to make it a party issue, nor to confront it with a blank negative. I think what is necessary for us to do is to begin to discuss it and try to get what it involves and what it means before the American people. . . . I think the second thought is going to be with us, but the first thought is probably against us. Therefore, we must proceed with caution . . .

Lodge accordingly felt that it was necessary to gain time to influence opinion against the Treaty as it stood. The thing to do, Lodge thought, was to proclaim the supposed dangers inherent in Wilson's League from the Atlantic to the Pacific, from Canada to Mexico. Money aplenty was available for this enterprise. Speeches by Lodge and other critics of the League were printed and distributed by the hundreds of thousands. Meetings were held at which speakers warned that Wilson's League impaired American sovereignty, surrendered the Monroe Doctrine, entangled us in European and Asiatic intrigues, thus flouting George Washington's time-honored advice, and subjected American boys to the authority of a foreign agency which might at any time order them into battle for remote causes in remote parts of the world. Worse still, our boys might be ordered to fight in causes which would be plainly repugnant to any freedom-loving American, such as the quelling of Irish revolutionists for the benefit of their English oppressors.

Several minority groups were highly susceptible to these arguments. First, there were the Irish-Americans, bitterly resentful of Wilson because he had not fought for Irish self-determination at the Peace Conference. Then there were the German-Americans, some seven million strong, and in varying degrees incensed at Wilson for his role in the ignominious defeat of the Fatherland. Too, there were the Italian-Americans, up in arms against Wilson for his implacable opposition to awarding Fiume to Italy.

Other groups, based on mutually shared viewpoints rather than national origins, opposed the Treaty. There were, for example, the liberals, who were deeply disillusioned at what they considered Wilson's betrayal of his own principles at the Peace Conference. One of the leading liberal weeklies, *The Nation*, referred to the League of Nations as, to quote the title of one of its articles on the subject, "A Colossal Humbug," and analyzed one of the President's attempts to depict the disadvantages of rejecting the Treaty under the heading, "Mr. Wilson Rants."

More numerous and an even greater stumbling block to the League were the isolationists—those who still thought America could be a land unto herself and exist without sullying her hands in the endless broils of the rest of the world. To them, the League represented a dangerous departure from the principle, which had served so well in the past, of avoiding foreign entanglements. Once enter the League, they cried, and the United States would find that she had surrendered her sovereignty to a mongrel superstate. The isolationists drew strength from the fact that theirs was the hallowed national tradition. Their predictions of the dire consequences of venturing into new international relationships gave their more forward-looking compatriots many sober second thoughts.

All of these groups were natural targets for anti-League propaganda. Lodge and his political friends tirelessly fanned the flames of their various fears and resentments. The resultant cacophony of anti-League and anti-Wilson invective made many a citizen, not associated with any special group, wonder whether there must not be a kernel of truth in all the criticisms of the League; whether, after all, it would not be wise to "Americanize" the Treaty as so many people so loudly and so urgently recommended. By the time Wilson returned from Paris, there was still a widespread disposition to accept the Treaty and enter the League, but it was qualified by the growing feeling that perhaps the Treaty ought to be changed to further protect American interests.

If opinion throughout the country was growing more confused by the day as the result of the anti-League campaign, opinions in the Senate were in confusion twice compounded. For not only were the Senators prey to all the intellectual cross-currents abroad in the land: in addition, they were swayed by two other factors. First, it was in the nature of the case that the Senators, as politicians, should have politics on their minds—and the 1920 presidential election was little over a year away. Second, many a

Senator, on both sides of the aisle, welcomed the opportunity to settle old personal scores with Wilson, now that the war was over and they no longer felt obliged to suppress their antagonism. They would give Wilson an object lesson in respect for the legislative branch of government, using his beloved Treaty as the text. . . .

From a strictly partisan point of view, it would never do to allow Wilson, singlehanded, the great accomplishment of which he dreamed. On the heels of such a success, the Republicans feared, he might seek a third term—and might even win it. From the Republican point of view, Wilson's League must either be defeated or, at the very least, so "Republicanized" that the GOP could claim credit for some of its good features. That the Treaty would be ratified and the United States would enter the League, however, seemed a foregone conclusion. A large proportion of Republican Senators were willing to content themselves with making only minor changes in the Treaty. They, together with the Democrats, constituted a majority of the Senate and could probably attract sufficient additional votes to make up the necessary two-thirds for ratification.

It was into this complex situation that Lodge entered as majority leader of the Senate. It was a situation which filled the enemies of the Treaty with despair, for it seemed inevitable that, with some minor alterations, the Treaty would pass. One evening, Senator James E. Watson of Indiana dined with Lodge to discuss means for meeting the challenge posed by the Treaty. "Senator," Watson declared, "I don't see how we are ever going to defeat this proposition. It appears to me that eighty percent of the people are for it."

Lodge replied, "Ah, my dear James, I do not propose to try to beat it by direct frontal attack, but by the indirect method of reservations."

Watson was puzzled and asked Lodge to elaborate. Lodge did so, for two hours, until Watson, as he later wrote, "became thoroughly satisfied that the Treaty could be beaten in that way." For sheer brilliance of conception Lodge's strategy stands without parallel in American history. For the finesse with which he applied it, Lodge stands without peer as a master tactician and psychologist.

Lodge's whole plan of action was based upon his estimate that Wilson would never consent to accepting Senate reservations to the Treaty. To Lodge, as he later wrote, Wilson "was simply an element to be calmly and coolly considered in a great problem of international politics." It was the Senator's "calm" and "cool" judgment that Wilson would do all he could to "prevent the acceptance of the treaty with reservations. . . ."

Given this conviction and the intrepidity to stake his whole strategy on it, Lodge was able to map out a plan of action at once beautifully simple and subtle. All he had to do was tack reservations onto the Treaty, and most particularly onto the League Covenant, which Wilson held so dear. Then, if his theory was correct, Wilson could be counted on himself to destroy what he had invested his lifeblood to create. Lodge's first problem, therefore, was to make certain that a majority vote could be commanded for his reservations.

Of the forty-nine Republican Senators, fifteen, who came to be known as "irreconcilables" and "bitter-enders," were opposed to the Treaty in any way, shape or form. Led by William Borah of Idaho, a man of incorruptible conviction so fiercely determined to keep this nation out of the League that it was commonly believed he would bolt the Party in 1920 if dissatisfied with Republican leadership on the Treaty issue, the "irreconcilables" had unequivocally announced their intention of voting against the Treaty, amended or unamended, with reservations or without.

On April 29, 1919, three weeks before the new Congress was to convene, Lodge conferred with Borah for the purpose of enlisting his support for amendments and reservations. Lodge told Borah that in his judgment "the great mass of the people, the man in the street, to use a common expression" favored Wilson's League, and that "the vocal classes of the community"—clergymen, educators, newspaper editors, and opinion leaders generally—were also advocating the League as it stood. "With these conditions existing, I said to Senator Borah, it seemed perfectly obvious to me that any attempt to defeat the treaty of Versailles with the League by a straight vote in the Senate, if taken immediately, would be hopeless, even if it were desirable." There was only one thing to do, Lodge argued, and that was to attach amendments and reservations to the Treaty. If the Treaty then failed of ratification, Borah and his colleagues would be satisfied. If it passed, it would at least bear Republican improvements. Borah agreed with Lodge's analysis of the situation and pledged himself to vote for amendments and reservations with the understanding, of course, that on the final vote he would vote against ratification of the Treaty. Lodge was greatly pleased with this outcome—it "confirmed me in the opinions which I had formed as to the proper way of dealing with the treaty when it came before us."

Next, Lodge turned his attention to the organization of the Committee on Foreign Relations, the composition of which would be, as he later wrote, of unusual consequence. Lodge loaded the Committee with "irreconcilables," deliberately rejecting such middle-grounders as Senator Kellogg, because Kellogg declined to commit himself blindly to Lodge's leadership. Of the ten Republicans on the Committee, six were "irreconcilables" and three were strong reservationists. The Republican "mild reservationists" were appalled. It could be seen immediately, Lodge later blandly recorded, that it was a "strong" committee of the kind the situation required.

The dozen or so "mild reservationists" in the Senate, as their name implies, favored reservations, though of a generally minor character. Lodge could count on them to support *some* program of reservations. He would have to feel his way along to see how broad a one they would swallow. He could also count for support on three or four Democrats, who stood ready to defy Wilson and work for the interment of the Treaty.

By the time Wilson returned to Washington in July, 1919, Lodge could be certain that the one condition upon which his hopes rested—that Wilson would be confronted with the necessity of accepting reservations on pain of seeing the whole Treaty go down in defeat—would be fulfilled.

The arithmetic of the problem was inescapable. No matter what he did, Wilson was caught by it. There was only one exit from the trap: compromise on reservations. The possibility that the President would bow to the realities of the situation and accept reservations, either those of the "mild reservationists" or, if need be, Lodge's own, was the great vulnerability of the anti-Treaty strategy, the waking nightmare of those interested in defeating the Treaty during the nine months that it was before the Senate. Lodge remained imperturbable.

On one occasion, Senator Watson said to him, "Senator, suppose that the President accepts the Treaty with your reservations. Then we are in the League, and once in, our reservations become purely fiction."

Lodge smiled. "But, my dear James, you do not take into consideration the hatred that Woodrow Wilson has for me personally. Never under any set of circumstances in this world could he be induced to accept a treaty with Lodge reservations appended to it."

"But that seems to me to be rather a slender thread on which to hang so great a cause," Watson replied.

"A slender thread!" exclaimed Lodge. "Why, it is as strong as any cable with its strands wired and twisted together."

In later years, Lodge was able to write with some satisfaction that he had made no mistake in his estimate of what President Wilson would do under certain conditions.

Once in the hands of the Foreign Relations Committee, the Treaty was at the mercy of Lodge and the "strong" colleagues he had so carefully selected to assist in the contemplated operation upon Wilson's brain child. First, however, the patient had to be very, very carefully examined—and no one could hurry Dr. Lodge, for he and his fellow Republicans controlled the Committee.

Lodge began by reading the entire Treaty aloud—all two hundred sixty-eight pages of it. It took him two weeks. Much of his performance was witnessed only by the Committee clerk. On one occasion, even this captive audience departed. Undaunted, Lodge soliloquized. The reading finally completed, the Committee began hearings. Representatives of numerous groups which had failed to satisfy their aspirations at Paris gave vent to their spleen before the sympathetic Senators. Their complaints furnished excellent publicity for the alleged inequities of the Treaty. The hearings also served to give the Treaty's opponents, both in and out of the Senate, further time in which to educate public opinion to the dangers which they claimed would envelop the United States were the League Covenant to be allowed to stand unchanged.

Critics of the Covenant heaped abuse on it from its first word to its last, but major fire was concentrated on four points. First it was alleged that the Covenant as it stood gave the League the right to meddle in the domestic affairs of its members. Did we want to authorize a foreign superstate to interfere with our immigration policies, to tell us, for example, that we must admit Orientals into this country on an unrestricted basis? Or, to take another example, to authorize the League to dictate our tariff policy? Wilson's supporters pointed out that it was to meet this very criticism that the President, when he had returned to Paris in March, had secured an amendment to the Covenant providing that if a dispute between contending parties "is claimed by one of them, and is found by the Council, to arise out of a matter which by international law is solely within the domestic jurisdiction of that party, the Council shall so report, and shall make no recommendation as to its settlement." This formulation, Wilson's critics retorted, left it to the Council of the League to decide whether or not a dispute fell within the domestic jurisdiction of one of the parties. The United States should have this decision in its own hands where any question involving this country arose.

Second, it was alleged that the Covenant endangered the Monroe Doctrine. Wilson's supporters drew attention to a second amendment to the Covenant he had obtained while still in Paris stipulating that "nothing in this Covenant shall be deemed to affect the validity of international engagements, such as treaties of arbitration or regional understandings like the Monroe Doctrine, for securing the maintenance of peace." To this Wilson's critics replied that the Monroe Doctrine was *not* an "international engagement" or a "regional understanding." It was a unilateral policy of the United States, and must be expressly exempted from interpretation by foreign powers.

Third, it was alleged that the provision for withdrawal from the League was unsatisfactory. A third amendment to the Covenant which Wilson had secured in Paris in response to criticism at home provided that "any Member of the League may, after two years' notice of its intention so to do, withdraw from the League, provided that all its international obligations and all its obligations under this Covenant shall have been fulfilled at the time of its withdrawal." But who would decide whether a withdrawing nation had fulfilled all its obligations, it was demanded. Obviously, declared Wilson's supporters, the withdrawing nation would, since the League was nowhere empowered to decide such a question. This answer failed to satisfy Wilson's detractors. To them, the provision was, at best, ambiguous, and there must be no ambiguity in such a matter: the world must know that the United States alone would decide whether or not her obligations had been fulfilled and would expect the unconditional right to withdraw.

Fourth, having been uncertain for a time whether to regard Wilson's League as a powerless debating society or a dangerous superstate, Lodge and his friends took the latter position and fell upon Article X of the Covenant. Article X read:

> The Members of the League undertake to respect and preserve as against external aggression the territorial integrity and existing political independence of all Members of the League. In case of any such aggression or in case of any threat or danger of such aggression the Council shall advise upon the means by which this obligation shall be fulfilled.

This provision plainly overrode the United States Constitution, Wilson's critics charged. Under it, the League could order American boys into battle, or order the United States to impose economic boycotts on other nations. The Constitution, however, provides that only Congress can declare war, and all bills to raise revenue or affecting revenue must be passed by Congress and signed by the President. Wilson's defenders pointed out that since the Council's decisions required unanimity, it could not act without the assent of its United States delegate. This would prevent the Council from taking actions obnoxious to the United States. Further, the Council's action in any case was only *advisory*. It had no power to issue a legally binding order. Its advice created a moral, rather than a legal obligation, the point being that a moral obligation left room for the exercise of discretion and judgment. It would be up to Congress to decide whether to accept the Council's advice, and to determine what action to take in any particular case. If there were only a moral obligation, the anti-Wilsonites retorted, then what avail Article X? Every nation could construe the Council's advice as it pleased and the Council would then amount to nothing more than a toothless forum, after all. Wilson and his supporters replied that in such matters, there is a national good conscience. Nations generally attempt to fulfill solemn obligations, moral as well as legal. The mere acceptance of a moral obligation by nations toward each other was an excellent step forward in international relations.

There had been a time, not so many years before, when Lodge had cordially endorsed this very idea. . . .

In May, 1916, speaking at a meeting of the League to Enforce Peace, Lodge had reiterated the view that the only hope for future world peace lay in the creation of an international league with force at its disposal. "I know the obstacles," Lodge then had said:

> I know how quickly we shall be met with the statement that this is a dangerous question which you are putting into your agreement, that no nation can submit to the judgment of other nations, and we must be careful at the beginning not to attempt too much. I know the difficulties that arise when we speak of anything which seems to involve an alliance. But I do not believe that when Washington warned us against permanent alliances he meant for one moment that we should not join with the other civilized nations of the world if a method could be found to diminish war and encourage peace.

A man can change his opinions, however, and when his earlier views materialized in Wilson's Covenant, Lodge invoked the Founding Fathers to vindicate his opposition to Wilson's League in general and Article X in particular.

Wilson's adherents complained that the League's critics spoke as though the Covenant's provisions applied exclusively to the United States; as though the League were nothing but a gigantic conspiracy against the sovereignty of the United States. Britain, France, Italy and other nations were as concerned as we were to preserve their freedom of action and to keep control of their domestic problems in their own hands. All members would be bound by the same rules, these Wilsonians asserted. That being the case, and the other nations being as jealous of their prerogatives as the United States, in practice no great sacrifice of sovereignty would be required. Therefore, the safeguards which so many people were demanding in the form of changes in the Covenant were unnecessary because they were already clearly implicit and tacitly accepted by the other powers.

It will be obvious to the reader, even from this abbreviated account of some of the points of contention, that many arguments could be mustered to support a variety of views concerning each of them. Many were. The newspapers carried column after column of intricate legal discussions, with opinions and counteropinions, with accounts of complicated parliamentary maneuvers in the Senate and of a dizzying variety of views on a dizzying number of the Treaty's provisions. The public was rapidly becoming thoroughly confused, though through it all it remained clear that most people and most Senators wanted the League and the Treaty in some form. Why not, then, attach reservations, even if only to still groundless fears, and get the whole bothersome business out of the way once and for all? This feeling grew, both in and out of the Senate, as the dispute wore on.

Faced with this tangled situation, President Wilson struck an attitude which is as simple to describe as it is difficult to analyze. He would not consent to the embodiment of reservations or amendments of the Treaty in the resolution of ratification. He would consider, however, the possibility of issuing a separate statement of "reasonable interpretation(s)" simultaneously with the resolution of ratification. He took this position on the day he presented the Treaty to the Senate. He reaffirmed it when he met with the Senate Foreign Relations Committee on August 19. From start to finish, he did not deviate one jot from this position. It was on this issue of the *form* of the reservations, as well as of the content of the final version of the reservation to Article X, that the whole Treaty foundered. . . .

2. *Wilson Dooms His Own Handiwork*

Although aware of Lodge's motives and role, other historians have attributed the defeat of the Versailles Treaty largely to the stubborn pride and uncompromising course of President Wilson. By his failure to conciliate moderate critics of the League and his refusal to accept the Lodge Reservations, Wilson doomed his own creation to senatorial rejection. Professor Bailey concludes that Wilson must bear the major onus for the killing of the treaty in the United States.

The Supreme Infanticide

T. A. BAILEY

. . . Is it true that the invalid in the White House really strangled the treaty to death with his own enfeebled hands?

It is seldom that statesmen have a second chance—a second guess. They decide on a course of action, and the swift current of events beats them downstream from the starting point. Only rarely does the stream reverse itself and carry them back.

In November, Wilson had decided that he wanted deadlock, because he reasoned that deadlock would arouse public opinion and force the Senate to do his bidding. The tidal wave of public opinion did surge in, and Wilson got his second chance. But he threw it away, first by spurning compromise (except on his terms), and then by spurning the Lodge reservations.

There had been much more justification for Wilson's course in November than in March. In November [1919] he was sick, secluded, was fed censored news, and was convinced by Hitchcock that the strategy of deadlock was sound. In March, [1920] he was much improved in health, far less secluded, more in touch with the press and with the currents of opinion, though probably still not enough. He consulted even less with the Senate, presumably because he had made up his mind in advance to oppose the Lodge reservations. In November, there was a fair possibility of reconsideration; in March, it was clear that the only possibility lay in making the League an issue in the coming campaign. Wilson, with his broad knowledge of government and politics, should have seen that this hope was largely if not completely illusory. Perhaps he would have seen it had he not been blinded by his feeling for Lodge.

The evidence is convincing that Wilson wanted this issue cast into the hurly-burly of politics. He could not accept Lodge's terms; Lodge would not accept his terms. The only possible chance of beating the senator—and this was slim indeed—was to win a resounding mandate in 1920.

Yet this strategy, as already noted, meant further delay. At Paris, the feeling at times had been, "Better a bad treaty today than a good treaty four months hence." Europe was still in chaos, and increasingly in need of America's helping hand. Well might the Europeans cry, "Better a treaty with the Lodge reservations today than a probable treaty without reservations after the election." Or as Dr. Frank Crane wrote in *Current Opinion*, "It is vastly more needful that some sort of League be formed, *any sort*, than that it be formed *perfectly*." (Italics Crane's.)

Yet Wilson, for the reasons indicated, could not see all this clearly. Four days after the fatal vote he wrote Hitchcock, praising him for having done all in his power to protect the honor of the nation and the peace of the world against the Republican majority.

Mrs. Wilson, no doubt reflecting her husband's views, later wrote, "My conviction is that Mr. Lodge put the world back fifty years, and that at his door lies the wreckage of human hopes and the peril to human lives that afflict mankind today."

To the very end Wilson was a fighter. When the Scotch-Irish in him became aroused, he would nail his colors to the mast. He said in 1916 that he was "playing for the verdict of mankind." His conception of duty as he saw it was overpowering. He once remarked that if he were a judge, and it became his duty to sentence his own brother to the gallows, he would do so—and afterwards die of a broken heart.

It is well to have principles; it is well to have a noble conception of duty. But Wilson, as he became warmed up in a fight, tended to get things out of focus and to lose a proper sense of values.

The basic issue in 1920 was the Hitchcock reservations or the Lodge reservations. Wilson accepted those of Hitchcock while rejecting those of Lodge, which, he said, completely nullified the treaty and betrayed his promises to the Allies and to the American dead.

This, as we have seen, was a gross exaggeration. Minds no less acute than Wilson's, and less clouded with sickness and pride, denied that the Lodge reservations completely nullified the treaty. To the man in the street—in so far as he gave the dispute thought—there was little discernible difference between the two sets of reservations. How could one decry statements which merely reaffirmed the basic principles of the Constitution and of our foreign policy? To a vast number of Americans the Lodge reservations, far from nullifying the treaty, actually improved it. This was so apparent to even the most loyal Democrats in the Senate that Wilson could barely keep them in line.

In the final analysis the treaty was slain in the house of its friends rather than in the house of its enemies. In the final analysis it was not the two-thirds rule, or the "irreconcilables," or Lodge, or the "strong" and "mild reservationists," but Wilson and his docile following who delivered the fatal stab. If the President had been permitted to vote he would have sided with Borah, Brandegee, Johnson, and the other "bitter-enders"—though for entirely different reasons.

Wilson had said that the reservation to Article X was a knife thrust at the heart of the Covenant. Ironically, he parried this knife thrust, and stuck his own dagger, not into the heart of the Covenant, but into the entire treaty.

This was the supreme act of infanticide. With his own sickly hands Wilson slew his own brain child—or the one to which he had contributed so much.

This was the supreme paradox. He who had forced the Allies to write the League into the treaty, unwrote it; he who had done more than any other man to make the Covenant, unmade it—at least so far as America was concerned. And by his action, he contributed powerfully to the ultimate undoing of the League, and with it the high hopes of himself and mankind for an organization to prevent World War II.

The preceding dogmatic observations are of course qualified by the phrase, "in the last analysis."

Many elements enter into a log jam. Among them are the width of the stream, the depth of the stream, the swiftness of the current, the presence of boulders, the size of the logs, and the absence of enough lumberjacks. No one of these factors can be solely responsible for the pile-up.

Many elements entered into the legislative log jam of March, 1920.

Among them were isolationism, partisanship, senatorial prerogative, confusion, apathy, personal pride, and private feuds. No one of them was solely responsible for the pile-up. *But as the pile-up finally developed, there was only one lumberjack who could break it, and that was Woodrow Wilson.* If at any time before the final vote he had told the Senate Democrats to support the treaty with the Lodge reservations, or even if he had merely told them that they were on their own, the pact would almost certainly have been approved. So "in the last analysis" the primary responsibility for the failure in March rested with Wilson.

What about Lodge? If the treaty would have passed by Wilson's surrendering, it is not equally true that it would have passed by Lodge's surrendering?

The answer is probably "Yes," but the important point is that Lodge had far less responsibility for getting the treaty through than Wilson. If Lodge had yielded, he probably would have created a schism within his ranks. His ultimate responsibility was to keep the party from breaking to pieces, and in this he succeeded. Wilson's ultimate responsibility was to get the treaty ratified, and in this he failed. With Lodge, as with any truly partisan leader, the party comes before country; with the President the country should come before party, though unhappily it often does not.

It is possible that Wilson saw all this—but not clearly enough. He might have been willing to compromise if his adversary had been any other than Lodge. But so bitter was the feeling between the two men that Wilson, rather than give way, grasped at the straw of the election of 1920.

Lodge did not like Wilson either, but he made more of a show of compromising than the President. He actually supported and drove through amendments to his original reservations which were in line with Wilson's wishes, and he probably would have gone further had the "irreconcilables" not been on his back. He fought the crippling Irish reservation, as well as others supported by the "bitter-enders." Finally, he gave the Democrats a fair chance to reconsider their vote and get on the bandwagon, but they spurned it.

If Lodge's words mean anything, and if his actions were not those of a monstrous hypocrite, he actually tried to get the treaty through with his reservations. When he found that he could not, he washed his hands of the whole business in disgust.

The charge is frequently made that, if Wilson had yielded to his adversary, Lodge would have gleefully piled on more reservations until Wilson, further humiliated, would have had to throw out the whole thing.

The strongest evidence for this view is a circumstantial story which Secretary [of Agriculture] Houston relates. During a Cabinet meeting Wilson was called to the telephone, and agreed to make certain concessions agreeable to Lodge. Before adjournment the telephone rang again, and word came that Lodge would not adhere to his original proposal.

This story is highly improbable, because Wilson attended no Cabinet meetings between September 2, 1919, and April 13, 1920. By the latter date, all serious attempts at compromise had been dropped; by the earlier date the treaty was still before the Senate committee, and the Lodge reservations, though in an embryonic stage, were yet unborn. But, even if the story is true, it merely proves that Lodge veered about, as he frequently did under "irreconcilable" pressure.

In March, as in November, all Wilson had to do was to send over Postmaster General Burleson to the Senate a few minutes before the final vote with the quiet word that the Democrats were to vote "Yea." The treaty would then have passed with the Lodge reservations, and Lodge could hardly have dared incur for himself or his party the odium of moving to reconsider for the purpose of screwing on more reservations. Had he tried to do so, the "mild reservationists" almost certainly would have blocked him.

A few days after the disastrous final vote, Wilson's only comment to Tumulty was, "They have shamed us in the eyes of the world." If his previous words said what he really meant, he was hardly more shamed by the defeat of the treaty than by the addition of the Lodge reservations. In his eyes it all amounted to the same thing.

If the treaty had passed, would the President have been willing to go through with the exchange of ratifications? Would he not have pocketed it, as he threatened to do prior to the November vote?

Again, if Wilson's words may be taken at their face value, this is what he would have done. He had not backed down from his pre-November position. His Jackson Day message and his letter to Hitchcock made it unmistakably clear that he preferred the uncertainties of a political campaign to the certainties of ratification with the Lodge reservations. The addition of the indefensible Irish reservation provided even stronger justification for pocketing the entire pact.

It is probable that some of the loyal Democrats voted as they did partly because they were convinced that Wilson was going to pigeonhole the treaty anyhow. From their point of view it was better that the odium for defeat should seemingly rest on Lodge rather than on their President. It also seems clear that Wilson preferred, as in November, to have the blood of the treaty on the Senate doorstep rather than on his. As he wrote to Secretary [of State] Colby, on April 2, 1920, the slain pact lay heavily on the consciences of those who had stabbed it, and he was quite willing to have it lie there until those consciences were either awakened or crushed.

Yet it is one thing to say, just before Senate action, "I will pocket the treaty." It is another, after the pact is approved and sent to the White House, to assume this tremendous responsibility. The eyes of the world are upon the President; he is the only man keeping the nation out of the peace which it so urgently needs; he is the one man standing in the way of the rehabilitation which the world so desperately demands. Public pressure to ratify in such a case would be enormous—probably irresistible.

Some years later Senator Hitchcock said that in the event of senatorial approval Wilson would possibly have waited for the November election. If he had won, he would have worked for the removal of the Lodge reservations; if he had lost, then the compulsion to go through with ratification would have become overpowering. By November more than six months would have passed, and by that time Wilson might have developed a saner perspective.

But this is all speculation. Wilson gave orders that the treaty was to be killed in the Senate chamber. And there it died.

One other line of inquiry must be briefly pursued. Is it true, as some writers allege, that the thirty-odd Allied signatories of the original treaty would have rejected the Lodge reservations when officially presented? We recall that under the terms of the preamble these nations were privileged to acquiesce silently or file objections.

One will never know the answer to this question, because Wilson denied the other signatories a chance to act. But it seems proper to point to certain probabilities.

One or more of the Latin American nations might have objected to the reservation regarding the then hated Monroe Doctrine. Yet the Monroe Doctrine would have continued to exist anyhow; it was already in the Covenant; and these neighboring republics might well have swallowed their pride in the interest of world peace.

Italy probably would have acquiesced, and the evidence is strong that France would have done likewise. The Japanese could not completely overlook the Shantung reservation, but it was generally recognized in their press as meaningless, and for this reason it might have been tolerated, though not without some loss of face. It is noteworthy that the most important Japanese newspapers regretted the Senate stalemate as an encouragement to world instability, particularly in China.

Great Britain probably would have been the chief objector. The reservation on Ireland was highly offensive but completely innocuous, for the British lion had long endured Irish-American tail-twistings in pained but dignified silence. The reservation on six-to-one was a slap at the loyal and sacrificing Dominions, but it did not mean that their vote was to be taken away. Moreover, the contingency envisaged by this proviso was unlikely to arise very often, and in the long run would doubtless have proved inconsequential.

In sum, there were only two or three reservations to which the outside powers could seriously object. If they had objected, it is probable that a satisfactory adjustment could have been threshed out through diplomatic channels. For when it became clear that only a few phrases stood between the United States and peace, the dictates of common sense and the pressure of public opinion probably would have led to an acceptable compromise. If the Senate had refused to give ground in such a case, then the onus would have been clearly on it and not on Wilson. . . .

3. *Wilson Defended*

Arthur S. Link, author of a multi-volume biography of Wilson, recognizes the President's mistakes and defects but points out that Wilson had serious and defensible objections on high policy grounds to many of the Lodge Reservations.

Wilson the Diplomatist

ARTHUR S. LINK

. . . Virtually all historians now agree that Wilson's refusal to permit his followers in the Senate to approve the treaty with the Lodge reservations was an error of tragic magnitude. Having built so grandly at Paris, having fought so magnificently at home for his creation, he then proceeded by his own hand to remove the cornerstone of his edifice of peace. Why? Were there inner demons of pride and arrogance driving him to what one historian has called "the supreme infanticide"? Did his illness and seclusion prevent him from obtaining a realistic view of the parliamentary situation, or so disarrange him emotionally that he became incompetent in the tasks of statesmanship? Or was he simply an idealist who would make no compromises on what he thought were fundamental principles?

The historian, who sees through a glass darkly when probing the recesses of the mind, is not able to give final answers to questions like these. Wilson, for all his high-mindedness and nobility of character, was headstrong and not much given to dealing graciously or to compromising with men whom he distrusted and disliked. Once before, in a violent dispute at Princeton over control of the graduate school, he had revealed these same traits and suffered defeat because he could not work with men whom he did not trust. The sympathetic biographer would like to believe that it was his illness, which aggravated his bitterness and his sense of self-righteousness, that drove Wilson to his fatal choice. Perhaps this is true. He had not always been incapable of compromise; perhaps he would have yielded in the end if disease had not dethroned his reason.

These attempts to extenuate ignore the fact that there were fundamental and vital issues at stake in the controversy over the treaty—whether the United States would take leadership in the League of Nations without hesitations and reservations, or whether it would join the League grudgingly and with no promises to help maintain universal collective security. To Wilson the difference between what he fought for and what Lodge and the Republicans would agree to was the difference between the success or failure and the life or death of man's best hope for peace. This he had said on his western tour, at a time when his health and reasoning faculties were unimpaired. This he believed with his heart and soul. It is, therefore, possible, even probable, that Wilson would have acted as he did even had he not suffered his breakdown, for it was not in his nature to compromise away the principles in which he believed.

If this is true, then in this, the last and greatest effort of his life, Wilson spurned the role of statesman for what he must have thought was the nobler role of prophet. The truth is that the American people were not prepared in 1920 to assume the world leadership that Wilson offered them, and that the powers of the world were not yet ready to enforce the worldwide, universal system of collective security that the President had created.

Arthur S. Link, *Wilson the Diplomatist* (Baltimore: the Johns Hopkins Press, 1957), 153–156. Reprinted with permission.

Collective security failed in the portentous tests of the 1930's, not because the League's machinery was defective, but because the people of the world, not merely the American people alone, were unwilling to confront aggressors with the threat of war. As a result a second and more terrible world conflict came, as Wilson prophesied it would, and at its end the United States helped to build a new and different league of nations and took the kind of international leadership that Wilson had called for. But events of the past decade have not fully justified Wilson's confidence in international organization; the only really promising systems of collective security, the regional ones like NATO, have been of a kind that Wilson fervently denounced; and only the future can reveal whether his dream of a universal system can ever be made a reality.

And so it was Wilson the prophet, demanding greater commitment, sacrifice, and idealism than the people could give, who was defeated in 1920. It is also Wilson the prophet who survives in history, in the hopes and aspirations of mankind and in whatever ideals of international service that the American people still cherish. One thing is certain, now that men have the power to sear virtually the entire face of the earth: The prophet of 1919 was right in his larger vision; the challenge that he raised then is today no less real and no less urgent than it was in his own time.

Additional Reading

Selig Adler, *The Isolationist Impulse: Its Twentieth Century Reaction* (1957).
R. J. Bartlett, *The League to Enforce Peace* (1944).
Dana F. Fleming, *The United States and the League of Nations, 1918–1920* (1942).
John A. Garraty, *Henry Cabot Lodge* (1953).
W. Stull Holt, *Treaties Defeated by the Senate* (1933).
Rayford W. Logan, *The Senate and the Versailles Mandate System* (1945).

15 *THE TWENTIES: Isolationist?*

Senatorial rejection of the Versailles Peace Treaty and the subsequent Republican victory in the 1920 presidential election has usually been interpreted by historians as the beginning of a long period of isolationist foreign policies by the United States. Some have drawn graphic pictures of Uncle Sam, ostrich-like, burying his head in the sand and turning his back on world affairs in order to concentrate on the feverish boom of domestic prosperity. The period 1920–1933 thus seemed almost a disgraceful interlude between the earlier internationalism of Wilson and the later era of Franklin D. Roosevelt.

Yet study of the decade after 1920 reveals contradictory phenomena. On the one hand, the United States refused to join the League of Nations, raised its tariff rates to astronomical heights, refused to recognize a connection between German reparations and Allied ability to repay the war debts, and attached reservations disavowing any enforcement responsibility to most of the international agreements it approved. Conversely, the American government participated in several arms limitation conferences, cooperated increasingly in various League specialized functions and projects, helped launch the multilateral Pact of Paris denouncing aggressive warfare, and proclaimed during the depression a moratorium on collection of intergovernmental debts.

Perhaps the most satisfying interpretation of this rather confused period has been offered by Selig Adler, *The Isolationist Impulse* (1957). He sees the decade as neither isolationist by 19th-century standards nor as fully internationalist as were the eras of Wilson and F.D.R. Instead, it was characterized by "neo-isolationism," marked on the governmental level by limited international participation and the avoidance of binding political-military obligations. On the public level, most Americans were increasingly disillusioned and determined to avoid embroilments abroad, while a minority of devoted Wilsonians continued to struggle for the assumption of a larger role in international affairs.

DOCUMENTS

1. *Economic Isolationism*

The mixed character of the period is indicated by the following two documents. Wilson vetoed in 1921 the first of the high postwar tariffs, on the grounds that it would make repayment of the war debts difficult and would adversely affect world free trade. After his departure from office, and despite the warnings of many economists, the tariff was successfully raised in 1922 and again in 1930. Yet in 1931, as the world depression was deepening, President Herbert Hoover recognized a degree of American economic responsibility in proposing a "holiday" on payments of intergovernmental debts.

Wilson's Tariff Veto Message, March 3, 1921

I return herewith without my approval H. R. 15275, an act imposing temporary duties upon certain agricultural products to meet present emergencies, to provide revenue, and for other purposes. . . .

One does not pay a compliment to the American farmer who attempts to alarm him by dangers from foreign competition. The American farmers are the most effective agricultural producers in the world. Their production is several times as great for each worker as that of their principal foreign rivals. This grows out of the intelligence of the American farmer, the nature of his agricultural practices and economy, and the fact that he has the assistance of scientific and practical agencies which in respect to variety of activity, of personnel, and of financial support exceed those of any other two or three nations in the world combined. There is little doubt that the farmers of this Nation will not only continue mainly to supply the home demand but will be increasingly called upon to supply a large part of the needs of the rest of the world.

What the farmer now needs is not only a better system of domestic marketing and credit, but especially larger foreign markets for his surplus products. Clearly measures of this sort will not conduce to an expansion of the foreign market. . . .

I imagine there is little doubt that while this measure is temporary it is intended as a foundation for action of a similar nature of a very general and permanent character. It would seem to be designed to pave the way for such action. If there ever was a time when America had anything to fear from foreign competition, that time has passed. I can not believe that American producers, who in most respects are the most effective in the world, can have any dread of competition when they view the fact that their country has come through the great struggle of the last few years, relatively speaking, untouched, while their principal competitors are in varying degrees sadly stricken and laboring under adverse conditions from which they will not recover for many years. Changes of a very radical character have taken place. The United States has become a great creditor Nation. She has lent certain Governments of Europe more than $9,000,000,000, and as a result of the enormous excess of our exports there is an additional commercial indebtedness of foreign nations to our own of perhaps not less than $4,000,000,000. There are only three ways in which Europe can meet her part of her indebtedness, namely, by the establishment of private credits, by the shipment of gold, or of commodities. It is difficult for Europe to discover the requisite securities as a basis for the necessary credits. Europe is not in a position at the present time to send us the amount of gold which would be needed, and we could not view further large imports of gold into this country without concern. The result, to say the least, would be a larger disarrangement of international exchange and disturbance of international trade. If we wish to have Europe settle her debts, governmental or commercial, we must be prepared to buy from her, and if we wish to assist Europe and ourselves by the export either of food, of raw materials, or finished products, we must be prepared to welcome commodities which we need and which Europe will be prepared, with no little pain, to send us.

Clearly, this is no time for the erection here of high-tariff barriers. It would strike a blow at the large and successful efforts which have been made by many of our great industries to place themselves on an export basis. It would stand in the way of the normal readjustment of business conditions throughout the world, which is as vital to the welfare of this country as to that of all the other nations. The United States has a duty to itself as well as to the world, and it can discharge this duty by widening, not by contracting, its world markets. . . .

The Hoover Debt Moratorium, 1931

The American Government proposes the postponement during one year of all payments on intergovernmental debts, reparations and relief debts, both principal and interest, of course, not including obligations of governments held by private parties. Subject to confirmation by Congress, the American Government will postpone all payments upon the debts of foreign governments to the American Government payable during the fiscal year beginning July 1 next, conditional on a like postponement for one year of all payments on intergovernmental debts owing the important creditor powers. . .

The purpose of this action is to give the forthcoming year to the economic recovery of the world and to help free the recuperative forces already in motion in the United States from retarding influences from abroad.

The world-wide depression has affected the countries of Europe more severely than our own. Some of these countries are feeling to a serious extent the drain of this depression on national economy. The fabric of intergovernmental debts, supportable in normal times, weighs heavily in the midst of this depression.

From a variety of causes arising out of the depression such as the fall in the price of foreign commodities and the lack of confidence in economic and political stability abroad there is an abnormal movement of gold into the United States which is lowering the credit stability of many foreign countries. These and the other difficulties abroad diminish buying power for our exports and in a measure are the cause of our continued unemployment and continued lower prices to our farmers.

Wise and timely action should contribute to relieve the pressure of these adverse forces in foreign countries and should assist in the reestablishment of confidence, thus forwarding political peace and economic stability in the world. . . .

I wish to take this occasion also to frankly state my views upon our relations to German reparations and the debts owed to us by the allied Governments of Europe. Our government has not been a party to, or exerted any voice in determination of reparation obligations. We purposely did not participate in either general reparations or the division of colonies or property. The repayment of debts due to us from the Allies for the advance for war and reconstruction were settled upon a basis not contingent upon German reparations or related thereto. Therefore, reparations is necessarily wholly a European problem with which we have no relation.

I do not approve in any remote sense of the cancellation of the debts to us. World confidence would not be enhanced by such action. None of our debtor nations has ever suggested it. But as the basis of the settlement of these debts was the capacity under normal conditions of the debtor to pay, we should be consistent with our own policies and principles if we take into account the abnormal situation now existing in the world. I am sure the American people have no desire to attempt to extract any sum beyond the capacity of any debtor to pay and it is our view that broad vision requires that our government should recognize the situation as it exists. . . .

2. *Limited Participation*

Internationalists did win a limited victory in the 1920's in persuading a majority of Americans that it was safe to join the World Court. Yet the Senate attached reservations to its approval in 1926 which other signatories would not accept, particularly the fifth reservation concerning advisory opinions. Presidents Hoover and Roosevelt also failed in attempts to get favorable senatorial action, despite indications that a majority of citizens and members of the Senate were in approval. The Kellogg-Briand Pact or Treaty of Paris of 1928, condemning aggressive warfare but containing no enforcement provisions, thus represented the outer limits of participation in world affairs and the assumption of international responsibilities in the 1920's. Even so, in granting its approval the Senate Foreign Relations Committee attached interpretations safeguarding the right of self-defense and disavowing any obligation to enforce the pact against transgressors.

Reservations by the Senate to Joining the World Court, January 27, 1926

Resolved (*two-thirds of the Senators present concurring*), That the Senate advise and consent to the adherence on the part of the United States to the said protocol of December 16, 1920, and the adjoined statute for the Permanent Court of International Justice (without accepting or agreeing to the optional clause for compulsory jurisdiction contained in said statute), and that the signature of the United States be affixed to the said protocol, subject to the following reservations and understandings, which are hereby made a part and condition of this resolution, namely:

1. That such adherence shall not be taken to involve any legal relation on the part of the United States to the League of Nations or the assumption of any obligations by the United States under the treaty of Versailles. . . .

4. That the United States may at any time withdraw its adherence to the said protocol and that the statute for the Permanent Court of Inter-

national Justice adjoined to the protocol shall not be amended without the consent of the United States.

5. That the court shall not render any advisory opinion except publicly after due notice to all states adhering to the court and to all interested states and after public hearing or opportunity for hearing given to any state concerned; nor shall it, without the consent of the United States, entertain any request for an advisory opinion touching any dispute or question in which the United States has or claims an interest.

The signature of the United States to the said protocol shall not be affixed until the powers signatory to such protocol shall have indicated, through an exchange of notes, their acceptance of the foregoing reservations and understandings as a part and a condition of adherence by the United States to the said protocol.

Resolved further, As a part of this act of ratification that the United States approve the protocol and statute hereinabove mentioned, with the understanding that recourse to the Permanent Court of International Justice for the settlement of differences between the United States and any other state or states can be had only by agreement thereto through general or special treaties concluded between the parties in dispute; and

Resolved further, That adherence to the said protocol and statute hereby approved shall not be so construed as to require the United States to depart from its traditional policy of not intruding upon, interfering with, or entangling itself in the political questions of policy or internal administration of any foreign state; nor shall adherence to the said protocol and statute be construed to imply a relinquishment by the United States of its traditional attitude toward purely American questions.

The Kellogg-Briand Pact, August 27, 1928

Article I. The High Contracting Parties solemnly declare in the names of their respective peoples that they condemn recourse to war for the solution of international controversies, and renounce it as an instrument of national policy in their relations with one another.

Article II. The High Contracting Parties agree that the settlement or solution of all disputes or conflicts of whatever nature or of whatever origin they may be, which may arise among them, shall never be sought except by pacific means.

Article III. The present Treaty shall be ratified by the High Contracting Parties named in the Preamble in accordance with their respective constitutional requirements, and shall take effect as between them as soon as all their several instruments of ratification shall have been deposited at Washington. . . .

READINGS

1. The Return to Normalcy: Isolationism

John D. Hicks, a respected authority on Populism and recent American history, portrays the diplomacy of prosperous and isolationist America as ranging from restrictive immigration laws and an insistence on full repayment of the war debts to conclusion of that innocuous international gesture of good-will, the Pact of Paris.

The Diplomacy of Isolation

JOHN D. HICKS

Coolidge prosperity and American isolationism were in a sense two sides of the same coin. Whatever the American people might have thought about the subject during the debate on the Treaty of Versailles, most of them as the years wore on tended to accept as right and proper a minimum of American involvement in foreign affairs. American prosperity seemed to vindicate Harding's decision to turn his back on the League and the world, and Coolidge was not the man to embark upon any dangerous changes of direction.

There is reason to believe that Secretary Hughes accepted the return to isolation with considerable misgivings, but he was wise enough to know that the President, whatever his shortcomings, makes American foreign policy, not the Secretary of State. At first Hughes even failed to acknowledge the communications the United States received from the League of Nations, but when he saw that this gave offense, he corrected the error. Also, he arranged that the United States, through unofficial observers, should keep in touch with League affairs. When the American Bar Association met in London in July, 1924, as guests of the British bar, Hughes, who attended as president of the visiting group, took advantage of the opportunity to spell out American foreign policy, as he saw it, in precise detail. The United States, he said in a public address, was a nonaggressor nation devoted to peace; it would co-operate fully with other nations in the promotion of public health and other humanitarian enterprises, such as checking the trade of narcotics; it would give its support to institutions of international justice; and it would help with the economic rehabilitation of Europe, but by means other than direct governmental aid. Hughes's efforts to maintain international good manners worried some of the extreme isolationists, among them Senator Hiram Johnson of California, who privately questioned the Secretary's good faith, and as a member of the Senate Committee on Foreign Relations gloomily expressed his hope to delay, even if he could not prevent, "our going into Europe in one form or another."

The new immigration policy of the postwar years served to emphasize the wish of the American people to cut as completely as possible the ties that bound them to the Old World. During the war the double loyalties of certain "hyphenate" groups had aroused much criticism, and after the war the "red hysteria" undoubtedly contributed further to the conviction that the American nation had taken in about as many foreigners as it could digest. Organized labor had long expressed disapproval of letting in immigrants to compete in the American job market, and industry, with a steady backlog of unemployed from which to draw, offered little more than token objection to restriction. One of the first acts of the Harding administration was the Emergency Quota Act, signed May 19, 1921, which limited the number of aliens of any nationality who might be admitted in any fiscal year "to 3 per centum of the number of foreign-born persons of such nationality resident in the United States as determined by the United States census of 1910." The Act was originally designed to last for one year only, but it was later extended until 1924.

By that time experience had shown that the assigned quotas were permitting far more immigrants to enter the United States than Congress had intended—the total for 1924 exceeded 700,000; also, the law failed to discriminate as much as its proponents had hoped against immigrants from southern and eastern Europe. The Immigration Act of 1924, therefore, reduced the annual quota of each nationality to 2 per cent, and for the next three years shifted the computation of quotas to the census of 1890. The law stated that after 1927, however, the annual quota for each nationality was no longer to be computed from the number of foreign-born in the United States at any given time, but from "the number of inhabitants in 1920 whose origin by birth *or ancestry*" could be attributed to a given national area. And the annual quota of any nationality was to be a number which would bear "the same relationship to 150,000 as the number of inhabitants in continental United States in 1920 having that national origin" bore to the total number of inhabitants for the same year. To the Secretaries of State, Commerce, and Labor fell the thankless task of fixing quotas, but they found "national origins" so difficult to determine that the application of this aspect of the law was postponed from 1927 to 1929. The effect of the Act of 1924 was to hold immigration from 1925 to 1930 down to an annual average of about 300,000; and for the next ten years after that, with the help of the depression, to an annual average of about 50,000. The new Immigration Act thus marked the end of an era. The United States was no longer the refuge of the world's poor and oppressed; the Statue of Liberty now lifted her lamp only for a favored few.

The Act of 1924 made certain other innovations. Quotas established under the Act of 1921 applied only to Europe, the Near East, Africa, and Australia; for the Western Hemisphere there were no restrictions, and for certain Asiatic countries, notably Japan, other and special arrangements provided for virtual exclusion. The new law still permitted free access to the United States for immigrants from Canada, Newfoundland, and all the independent American republics, but it extended the quota system to the rest of the world, allowing to each nation a minimum of 100 immigrants, with this notable exception, that "No alien ineligible to citizenship shall be admitted to the United States." It was obvious that this clause was aimed directly at Japan, although the Gentlemen's Agreement of Theodore Roosevelt's administration was accomplishing the same end without a direct prohibition. But anti-Japanese sentiment on the Pacific Coast was strong, and Congress yielded to it the more readily when the Japanese ambassador announced that such a direct affront would have grave consequences. Japan, some congressmen implied, was threatening the United States. Secretary Hughes did his best to persuade Congress that this wanton insult to a supersensitive nation would destroy much of the good will achieved by the Washington Conference and by the generous American response to Japan's needs after the great earthquake of 1923. But Congress was not to be deterred, and Coolidge weakly signed the bill into law. Since the Supreme Court in *Ozawa* v. *the United States* (1922) had already decided that persons of Japanese birth were ineligible for naturalization, the effect of the law was crystal clear, and the reaction in Japan was extremely unfavorable. Congress by its thoughtless action had handed another weapon—popular hatred of the United States—to the Japanese militarists who plotted expansion in the Far East, even at the cost of war.

The Immigration Act of 1924 aroused much resentment also in Europe, particularly in Italy, where under the new quotas emigration to the United States dropped off by about nine-tenths. Because of the increased population pressure from which Italy suffered, Mussolini, whose attainment of power showed how unsafe the world was becoming for democracy, felt the freer to proceed with his program of colonial empire. Not only in Italy, but in many other countries also, the United States lost friends as the cruelties implicit in the law began to make themselves felt —wives denied permission to join their husbands in America, children separated from their parents, long quota waits for those who could go, detention and return for the ill-advised. Furthermore, the void left by the drop in European immigration tended to be filled in part by entrance into the United States of equally alien peoples from the Western Hemisphere, especially from Mexico, French Canada, and Puerto Rico. Also, there was a serious problem of enforcement, and the "bootlegging" of ineligibles into the United States, together with their occasional enforced return to their own country, added further to the international strain. Yet for the great majority of Americans there was no sign of regret over the policy of exclusion; the inequities in the law, most people agreed, should be ironed out, but the United States must never again open its portals to the Old World's "huddled masses yearning to breathe free."

There was something of this same spirit in the refusal of the United States to recognize the new government of Soviet Russia; if the actions of a given nation varied too much from what Americans regarded as proper, then its existence could simply be ignored. This policy, which the Harding administration inherited from its predecessor was by no means universally approved in the United States. Two senators, William E. Borah of Idaho and Joseph I. France of Maryland, took a particularly firm stand in favor of recognition. Borah was much influenced by Raymond Robins and other outstanding liberals, who believed that as long as the Russian problem remained unsettled the peace of Europe would remain unsettled, while France had visited Russia in the summer of 1921, had met the Bolshevik leaders, and had returned to the United States convinced that American recognition would help advance the conservative trend he thought he had seen in the Soviet Union. But Borah's Senate resolution favoring recognition was merely laid on the table, while France was ridiculed in the press as an "innocent abroad," or worse. On behalf of the administration, Secretary Hughes denied that the form of government adopted by Soviet Russia had anything to do with the official American attitude. The trouble, he said, was that the Soviet government had refused in three ways to accept its international obligations: (1) it had repudiated the debt it owed to the government of the United States, (2) it had confiscated the private property of American nationals, and (3) it had promoted propaganda in the United States that had as its object the overthrow of the American government. Borah, France, and others returned to the attack time after time, but Russian recognition was delayed until after the Roosevelt administration took office in 1933.

Nor was the American government disposed to promote in any way the resumption of normal trade relations between the United States and Soviet Russia. It had no objection to the mobilizing of American charity to help battle starvation during the Russian famine of 1921; according to Secretary Hoover the American Relief Administration spent $50 million for this purpose, and for the purchase of seed to be used in the 1922 planting. Nor was there any prohibition against individuals risking their property in trade with Russia, or even lending money to Russia if they so desired. But all Russian overtures for assistance from the United States government in reviving trade between the two nations were sternly discountenanced. The power of Russia to buy, Hughes maintained, depended on its ability to produce something to sell, and both he and Secretary Hoover implied in public statements that Russia could not hope to revive production until the Soviet government was ready to recognize the rights of private property.

Senator France argued for an American loan to Russia, the proceeds of which would enable the Soviets to pay claims against them and to buy American goods. But Hughes was adamant in his insistence that the Soviet government must demonstrate its willingness to guarantee within its borders the safety of life and property, the sanctity of contracts, and the rights of free labor before the United States would negotiate. The Russians made some effort to satisfy these conditions. At the Genoa Conference, which the nations of Europe held in the spring of 1922, a Russian representative told the American ambassador to Italy that, while Russia was unwilling to admit any such obligations as Hughes stipulated, it would in fact observe them with reference to Americans, if only the United States would recognize Russia. But again the United States was unresponsive. Whatever else the Department of State may have had in mind, it is obvious that it had no intention of doing anything that might in any way serve to perpetuate the Soviet system of government.

The United States also pursued an uncompromising policy, as long as it could, in its attempt to collect the intergovernmental debts due it from its former associates in the war, and from the succession states that the Peace of Paris had created in central and eastern Europe. Of the more than $10.3 billion so lent, only about $7 billion net was actually borrowed during the war, and not less than nine-tenths of this sum was used to pay for American goods purchased in the United States by the Allies. After the war was over the American government lent the war-torn nations of Europe an additional $3.3 billion in money and supplies for use in rehabilitation and relief. The American public should have distinguished between the war debts and these "peace debts," but it seldom did so; most Americans assumed that the European nations had borrowed the entire $10.3 billion for war purposes, and that ultimately they would repay these sums with interest—the rate, pending a postwar settlement, being set at 5 per cent.

The war was not long over before European nations began to take a very different view of debt repayment. To Americans the problem seemed simple: the United States had lent vast sums; the nations that had borrowed the money should pay back their loans. In Coolidge's words, "They hired the money, didn't they?" But to Europeans it was not that easy. In their view the war was fought for a common objective, and the victory was as essential for the safety of the United States as for their own. The United States had entered the struggle late, and had poured forth no such contribution in lives and losses as the Allies had made. It had paid in dollars, not in death and destruction, and now it wanted its dollars back—Uncle Shylock. Many Americans saw in this attitude only an attempt to defraud. A correspondent who had toured Europe wrote to Senator Johnson: "All of the peoples abroad look upon us as an international sucker from whom should be obtained by wheedling or otherwise part of our ill-gotten gains, but whom, during the process of relieving us of our funds, they regard with contempt, and about whom they laugh among themselves."

The real trouble was that the European nations had not the means with which to pay. Their gold had flowed in great quantity to the United States during the period of neutrality in payment for American goods; they could not send more without completely wrecking their currencies. Equally distressing was the American tariff policy; European nations could never hope to sell enough to the United States over its high tariff wall to enable them to build up the American balances they would need to liquidate their debts. The problem was further complicated by the debts that European nations owed each other, debts mainly due to loans the stronger Allies had made to the weaker before the United States became the chief banker for them all. Indeed, the British government had made loans comparable in face value to those made by the United States, and had actually lent more to the other Allies by many billions of dollars than it had borrowed from the United States. Protected by these mitigating circumstances, Great Britain took the lead as early as February, 1920, in broaching to the American government the subject of a general cancellation of war debts, pointing out the political and economic advantages that the adoption of such a policy would ensure.

Whatever the merits of the case, the American government showed no slightest disposition to accept the British overtures. Nor would it ever concede that the capacity of the Allies to repay the United States depended upon their ability to collect corresponding reparations from Germany. During the campaign of 1920, the Republicans denounced the Wilson administration for its failure to begin collections, and promised that as soon as they took office they would do better. When Secretary Mellon attempted to deliver on this promise, he found existing legislation inadequate to authorize the funding policy he had in mind, and asked Congress for plenary powers to deal with the problem. But Congress thought the matter too important for the Secretary of the Treasury to handle alone, and by an act of February 9, 1922, set up instead a World War Debt Funding Commission, consisting at first of five and by a later amendment of eight members, with the Secretary of the Treasury as chairman and the other members to be appointed by the President and confirmed by the Senate. (Among the appointive members, Harding chose Secretaries Hughes and Hoover.) The law also stipulated that loans should be repaid in twenty-five years, that the rate of interest charged should not be less than 4.25 per cent, and that there should be no cancellation of debts "except through payment thereof."

Smarting under the necessity, but consoled by the hope of collecting reparations from Germany, all the major debtors and most of the others—thirteen in all—eventually negotiated agreements with the Commission. In the negotiations the American representatives departed considerably from the instructions Congress had given them. While in each case they required ultimate payment in full of the principal, they spread the amortization over a period of sixty-two years instead of twenty-five, and they disregarded at will the high interest rate set by Congress. This policy meant that each agreement would have to be submitted to Congress for approval, but the commissioners realized, even if Congress did not, that the alternative would be no agreements at all. Throughout the negotiations the commissioners kept one eye on the capacity of each debtor nation to pay and the other on what minimum terms Congress would be willing to accept. They reached their first settlement with Great Britain in July, 1923, after six months of negotiation. The British representatives were shocked at the interest rates the American negotiators demanded, for the prewar borrowing rates in England had been much lower, and the American ambassador to Great Britain, Colonel George Harvey, had given them reason to expect a 2 per cent rate instead of the 3.3 per cent that the American commissioners demanded. Eventually the British government accepted the sixty-two year, 3.3 per cent terms as the best it could get.

The British agreement served as a model for the others, but Great Britain was the only wartime borrower to be charged so high a rate of interest. The other nations that agreed to pay 3.3 per cent on their loans were Czechoslovakia, Estonia, Finland, Hungary, Latvia, Lithuania, Poland, and Rumania, none of whom had borrowed from the United States until after the signing of the armistice, and all of whom owed comparatively small sums. For the remaining borrowers there were greatly reduced interest rates, for Belgium 1.8 per cent, for France 1.6 per cent, for

Italy 0.4 per cent, and for Yugoslavia 1 per cent. The terms of payment also differed considerably from country to country—Belgium, for example, was charged no interest on her pre-armistice debt, while France and Italy were not required to pay interest for the first five years of their indebtedness. But had the debts been paid in accordance with the agreements, the interest rates would have averaged out about as indicated. The life of the Commission expired by law on February 9, 1927; thereafter the Treasury Department worked out such agreements with other borrowers as were deemed necessary and possible. Among the impossible was the settlement of the Russian debt to the United States, which, however, was only $192 million, a small sum in comparison with Russia's debt to Great Britain of $4.3 billion.

Whatever the United States chose to pretend regarding the divorcement of war debts and reparations, in actual practice the two subjects were closely intertwined. By the much-debated war guilt clause, the Treaty of Versailles had required Germany to accept for herself and her allies the responsibility "for causing all the loss and damage to which the Allied and Associated Governments and their nationals have been subjected as a consequence of the war imposed upon them by the aggression of Germany and her allies." This clause in itself aroused great resentment, for few Germans believed that the Central Powers alone were responsible for the outbreak of war in 1914. Allied reliance upon the war-guilt thesis as the sole reason for demanding reparations made matters even worse. Had the victors merely assumed that they had the right to make the vanquished pay because they had lost the war, there would have been less room for argument. As it was, Germans could maintain with reason that the demand for reparations had no more validity than the charge of war guilt. Partly on this account neither the German government nor the German people ever really accepted the obligation of reparations payments; lacking any will to pay, their goal became instead the avoidance of payment. As Germans saw it, the Treaty of Versailles, by trimming Germany's borders at many vital spots, and by dividing her colonies among the victors, had gone far enough; the demand for reparations in addition was both unjust and unrealistic. Some Americans agreed. "I should like to see the 'sole guilt' fallacy rejected once and for all," wrote Senator Borah a few years later. "It is to the benefit of no one to maintain a false contention which serves only to keep alive resentment and retard the good faith and amity which we ought in every way to seek to foster and maintain. There was no 'sole guilt' as to that war."

Since the negotiators at Paris were unable to agree upon the total reparations bill, they put off for a period of two years the determination of the final figure; during this interval, however, they required Germany to pay nearly $5 billion in cash or in goods. The rest of the debt was to be determined by a Reparations Commission consisting of representatives from Great Britain, the United States, France, Italy, and, in alternation, Japan and Belgium. Failure of the United States to ratify the treaty cost Germany its only possible friend on the Commission; the other members differed only as to how much they thought they could get. When the

Commission reported in the spring of 1921, it proposed the colossal sum of $33 billion to be paid during a period of still undetermined length, but with an expectation of about $375 million each year from 1921 to 1925, and about $900 million each year thereafter. The Commission might reduce either the debt or the interest charges, but the Allied governments could punish by the armed invasion of German territory any willful defaults. Efforts to collect the huge sums expected proved to be singularly fruitless, but such payments as were made, together with the disruptions that the war had bequeathed to the German economy, led to a runaway inflation in Germany that virtually destroyed the middle class and undermined the authority of the new Weimar Republic. In January, 1923, over the opposition of Great Britain, the Reparations Commission declared Germany in willful default, and the troops of France and Belgium occupied the Ruhr Valley, the greatest industrial district left to Germany. But the military demonstration solved no problems, and made more; passive resistance in the Ruhr cut down on German production, while in France inflation began to mount ominously.

However much the United States might wish to remain isolated from Europe, there was no escaping the fact that the economic collapse of Germany would be a matter of almost as grave concern to Americans as to Europeans. Not only were the problems of war debts and reparations involved but also the economic health of Europe as a whole. American trade with Europe was vital to American prosperity; with the reparations problem unsolved that trade could not follow its natural lines. Secretary Hughes, who well understood that American isolation was a myth, began even before the invasion of the Ruhr to take a hand in the diplomatic game. Speaking before the American Historical Association in New Haven, Connecticut, he suggested on December 29, 1922, the creation of an international commission of experts to determine how much Germany was able to pay, and how the payments were to be made. "I have no doubt," he added, "that distinguished Americans would be willing to serve in such a commission." But the French were unwilling to accept this arrangement until the fall of 1923, when it became evident that the Ruhr invasion would accomplish nothing. They then joined with the other Allies in devising a plan whereby the Reparations Commission should appoint two committees, one to concentrate principally on problems of the German currency and budget, and the other on the recovery of German holdings from abroad. To head the first committee the choice fell upon an American, Charles Gates Dawes, and the agreements the committees reached became known as the Dawes Plan. Most Americans acquiesced readily in this limited degree of American participation in European affairs, but to a few extreme isolationists anything of the kind remained a base betrayal.

Whether Hughes was "the real author and spiritual father of the Dawes Plan," as a German journalist claimed, or Dawes himself, the program that the experts devised seemed to make sense. It recognized that there were two separate problems involved, (1) the attainment of solvency by the German government, with an annual excess of receipts over expenditures, and (2) the actual transfer to the Allies of surplus sums so accumulated. First of all Germany had to have a stable currency. To this end the Dawes Plan proposed an international loan of $200 million in gold, the reorganization of the Reichsbank under Allied supervision, and the issuance of a new monetary unit, the reichsmark, with a gold value of 23.8 U.S. cents. As for reparations, the plan set no precise figure, but, on the basis of careful study of Germany's capacity to pay, it proposed a graduated schedule of annuities, beginning at $250 million the first year and rising over a period of five years to a normal expectation of $625 million; this sum, however, could be increased or reduced as German prosperity rose or fell. During the first two years the German government might meet its obligations in part from the international loan, but it was also required to bond and mortgage its railways and principal industries, and to use the proceeds along with taxes to make the stipulated payments. The Dawes Plan also provided safeguards to prevent reparations payments from "threatening the stability of the German currency." While the German government must make all payments as scheduled, these funds would remain in Germany until such a time as the exchange market justified their transfer. An Agent General for Reparations Payments, to be appointed by the Reparations Commission, was to co-ordinate and supervise these activities.

The Dawes Plan, after acceptance by both Germany and the Allies, went into effect September 1, 1924, and for a time seemed to work reasonably well. It carried with it a separate agreement for the withdrawal of foreign troops from the Ruhr, a process that began at once and ended on July 31, 1925. The international loan was readily subscribed, with over half the money coming from American investors, and other measures that the Plan called for were gradually effected. For a time the revival of the German economy seemed assured. The choice of S. Parker Gilbert of Morgan and Company as Agent General proved to be singularly felicitous, and the German government profited greatly from his advice. It was Gilbert's opinion, however, that Germany must eventually be left "to perform on her own responsibility," while with the fulfillment of the German disarmament program it also seemed reasonable that the foreign troops still stationed in the Rhineland should be removed.

Eventually another committee of experts, headed by another American, Owen D. Young, produced a new set of agreements even more favorable to Germany than those of the Dawes Plan. The representatives of fifteen nations, including Germany, signed the preliminary terms at The Hague, August 31, 1929, in the presence of an American observer. This time Germany's total liability was set definitely at a little more than $8 billion, with interest at 5.5 per cent, the payments to be distributed over a period of 58.5 years. The new plan required "unconditional" annuities of only $153 million, much less than the payments required by the Dawes Plan, but, oddly enough, about equal to the total sums the Allied nations had agreed to pay each year on their war debts to the United States. "Conditional" payments, which depended on German prosperity, and ran much higher, were secured by a mortgage on the German railways. The problem of turning German marks into foreign currencies now became the responsibility of the German government, which would work through a new Bank of International Settlements set up by the Allies at Basel, Switzerland. Whereas the Dawes Plan was meant to be merely temporary, the Young Plan was regarded as "final and definitive." As further evidence that the Allies now regarded Germany as trustworthy, they withdrew the rest of their troops from German soil.

During the five years of the Dawes Plan and the first two of the Young Plan the German government met its reparations payments regularly, although it was usually forced to borrow in order to balance its budget. But confidence in German recovery was high, and there were plenty of investors who were ready to purchase German securities, both within and without Germany. It was the outside borrowing that enabled Germany to keep up with its reparations payments. Not only the various German governmental units, federal state and municipal, borrowed heavily from foreign investors, but German business firms, banks, and public utilities also followed this course. Precise figures on the amount of outside capital that flowed into Germany during these years are hard to get, but undoubtedly the American loans alone were not less than the $2.6 billion that the United States collected from the Allies prior to July 1, 1931, on their war debts. The direct relation between German reparations and Allied payments to the United States on war debts could hardly have been more obvious. What happened in effect was that Germany used the credits provided by outside investors, at least in part, to pay its reparations bills, while the Allies used that portion of these credits furnished by American investors to meet their war-debt payments to the United States. Thus the sums that the American Treasury collected from European debtor nations came in reality from the American people. More than that, the export of American capital to foreign borrowers, regardless of nationality, did much to support the business boom of the 1920's in the United States. Few people seemed to realize that the American nation was not only sending American goods abroad in gratifying volume, but that it was also sending along the money with which to pay for them. When finally American investors cut down on their foreign loans, the resulting decline in foreign purchases added materially to the economic gloom that settled down over the United States in the early 1930's.

American participation in the settlement with Germany indicated that the involvement of the United States in world affairs ran far deeper than many Americans realized. The United States, try as it might, could not simply concentrate on its own prosperity, and let the rest of the world "stew in its own juice"; it could not even permit Germany to collapse. Above all, the American nation must somehow share in the task of preserving world peace, for war anywhere in the world was certain to affect the United States, however determined its neutrality. A convinced minority of the American people still adhered to the conviction that the United States should have entered the League of Nations, and hoped that eventually this end might be achieved.

Numerous societies made this their goal, among them the League of

Nations Non-Partisan Association, headed by John H. Clarke, a former Justice of the United States Supreme Court, whose book on *America and World Power* (1925) well summarized the pro-League position. The World Peace Foundation, generously endowed many years before by Edwin Ginn, the Boston publisher; the Carnegie Endowment for International Peace, headed by the indefatigable Nicholas Murray Butler; and the Institute of International Relations, operating from Geneva with both British and American backing, all undertook the wide distribution of pro-League literature.

Such prominent individuals as Walter Lippmann, William Allen White, Hamilton Holt, Manley O. Hudson, and Raymond B. Fosdick gave the cause their earnest support. The Woodrow Wilson Foundation presented in 1924 the first of a series of $2,500 awards to individuals who had in some outstanding way contributed to world peace; Elihu Root, recipient of the second such award, rebuked the United States in his acceptance statement for its faithlessness in failing to enter the League. But the implacable opposition of the Republican party to the League, coupled with the indifference toward it of too many leading Democrats, foredoomed the pro-League advocates to failure. By the end of the 1920's they tacitly accepted as a substitute goal the greater co-operation of the United States with the League, pointed with pride to the important parts that American observers took in League meetings, and noted pleasurably the numerous League agreements that the United States had accepted. According to Charles A. Beard, the United States was in actual fact a member of the League, whatever its pretenses.

But Beard was wrong; the United States was not only not a member of the League, it refused so much as to give its adherence to the World Court, although during the Roosevelt and Taft administrations Republicans and Democrats alike had regarded the creation of such a body as a matter of primary importance. In accordance with Article 14 of the League Covenant, plans for the establishment of a Permanent Court of International Justice began to take form as early as June, 1920, and by January, 1922, the Court was able to hold its first session. Among the distinguished jurists who had framed the protocol under which it was to operate was Elihu Root, elder statesman of the Republican party, and during the deliberations he had had as his legal adviser James Brown Scott, a distinguished American authority on international law. The protocol left the way open for American adherence to the World Court, as it was commonly called, and undoubtedly the overwhelming majority of the American people favored such a course. But the extreme isolationists in the Senate had driven themselves into such a frenzy of opposition to anything that savored of "Wilsonism" or the League that the Harding administration moved cautiously on the subject. Finally Hughes, who strongly favored American adherence, persuaded the President to advocate such a course in a message to the Senate, February 24, 1923. Four reservations drawn by Hughes were designed to protect the United States against any slightest League involvement. But the Senate Committee on

Foreign Relations was still dominated by the intransigents, Harding's support proved to be only lukewarm, and the Senate failed to act.

President Coolidge in his first annual message, December, 1923, also commended the Court to the favorable consideration of the Senate, and the evidence that public opinion still favored adherence could hardly have been stronger. The Senate obstructionists, lacking any real arguments to justify their position, finally hit upon the right of the Court to give "advisory opinions" as somehow dangerous to the independence of signatory powers. The result, arrived at after a maximum of delay and debate, was a fifth reservation, insisting that the Court should not render any such opinion without giving due notice in advance to all interested states and providing them an opportunity for public hearings if they so desired; also, that it should not, "without the consent of the United States, entertain any request for an advisory opinion touching any dispute or question in which the United States has an interest." Finally on January 27, 1926, nearly three years after Harding's original message on the subject, the Senate voted for adherence to the Court, 76 to 17, conditioned upon acceptance of the reservations it had adopted. But the end was not yet. When the Council of the League of Nations sought to clarify the meaning of the American reservations, President Coolidge took the position that they had been rejected. Under the circumstances, he said, he could see "no prospect of this country adhering to the Court." Twice later, once during Hoover's administration and once during Roosevelt's, the Senate had a chance to ratify the World Court protocol on terms carefully drawn to meet American objections, but twice more the Senate failed to approve. . . .

Before his term of office ended, Coolidge consented to one more effort on behalf of world peace. Two Americans, a Chicago lawyer named Salmon O. Levinson and a Columbia University professor, James T. Shotwell, had for several years advocated, quite separately from each other, that the true approach to world peace was through an international agreement that would officially condemn war. As matters stood, international law accepted war as legal; why should war not be made to bear instead the stigma of illegality? Levinson believed that if the nations of the world would only outlaw war formally, that might be enough, but Shotwell regarded sanctions as a necessity; there must be force behind the agreement. Among the many Americans who took up with the "outlawry of war" idea, as the concept came generally to be called, was William E. Borah, chairman of the Senate Committee on Foreign Relations. The notion that some positive action should be taken toward the abolition of war also crossed the Atlantic, where it was deliberately planted in the mind of Aristide Briand, French Foreign Minister, by Professor Shotwell himself. And Briand, a master politician, used it in an address to the American people, April 6, 1927, which announced that "France would be ready publicly to subscribe, with the United States, to any mutual engagement tending, as between those two countries, to outlaw war." Since France did not see eye to eye with the United States on such important matters as the Geneva Conference and war debts, Briand perhaps thought this gesture of good will might not be amiss. Secretary Frank B. Kellogg, who had succeeded Hughes in 1925, was at first annoyed at Briand's move, while President Coolidge was piqued that the French Foreign Minister had gone over the head of the American government to the American people directly. Just at this juncture, Charles A. Lindbergh flew the Atlantic in his *Spirit of St. Louis* and landed at Paris; the general enthusiasm that this exploit awakened seemed somehow to call for appropriate action. Both the Levinson and the Shotwell groups made the most of this situation, public opinion soon began to veer strongly their way, and Kellogg at length invited Briand to submit his proposal through normal diplomatic channels, which was done.

Both Borah and the American State Department were quick to see the hazards of the Briand proposal in its original form. It would not do for the United States to sign a special treaty outlawing war between the United States and France without signing similar treaties with many other powers. A bilateral treaty might, by itself, even imply an alliance; for if France went to war with some other nation, then the United States would be bound in advance not to fight against France, come what might. The only tolerable procedure would be to expand the Briand proposal into a general agreement. Finally on December 28, 1927, Kellogg wrote Briand that the United States would favor, instead of the two-power treaty, "an effort to obtain the adherence of all the principal powers of the world to a declaration renouncing war as an instrument of national policy." This was more than Briand had bargained on, and for a time he stalled. Could such a treaty, he questioned, be reconciled with the commitments to other powers that France had already made? But Kellogg's enthusiasm for the idea grew; he even circulated a draft agreement among the great powers that was accepted without hesitation by Germany, Italy, and Japan. Great Britain and France, after the best American tradition, insisted on wordy reservations, but at length they also agreed. Kellogg would have preferred to sign the treaty in Washington, but as part of the price necessary to win French approval, he yielded to Briand's desire that it be signed in Paris. There on August 27, 1928, fifteen nations affixed their signatures to a pact renouncing war "as an instrument of national policy," and promising to solve all disputes of "whatever nature or whatever origin" by "pacific means." Thereafter the pact remained open "for adherence by all the other powers of the world." The first such adherent was the Soviet Union, whose presence at Paris the United States had not desired, lest it might imply recognition.

By the time the Pact of Paris reached the United States Senate, public opinion throughout the nation had so firmly endorsed the document that ratification came easily. Instead of the customary reservations, the Committee on Foreign Relations provided the Senate with an interpretative report. The pact, declared the committee, did not in any way curtail the right of the United States to self-defense, of which the Monroe Doctrine was an essential part; nor did it provide for sanctions, either express or implied, which would in any way oblige the United States to take action against a violator of the pact; nor did it in any respect change or qualify "our present position or relation to any pact or treaty existing between other nations or governments." So interpreted, the Pact of Paris received the approval of the Senate by a vote of 85 to 1, the lone objector being Senator John J. Blaine of Wisconsin. Not every senator who voted for it, however, believed in its value. Senator Carter Glass of Virginia, for example, pointed out that unless the signatory powers stood behind the treaty with force it could never amount to anything, and voted for it as "worthless, but perfectly harmless." Senator Hiram Johnson of California asserted that, like the characters in a Henry James novel, it had been "analyzed by its proponents practically into disintegration." "The explanations and interpretations," he wrote to his sons, "have made its nothingness complete." But Borah noted in rebuttal that treaties with sanctions had usually only led to war, and that the mobilization of world opinion against war was in itself a considerable victory. By the time the treaty was officially declared in force at Washington, July 24, 1929, thirty-one nations, in addition to the original fifteen, had adhered to it, and they were later followed by eighteen others, a total of sixty-four. Only four nations, all Latin American (Argentina, Bolivia, El Salvador, and Uruguay), failed to adhere. Mere gesture that it was, the Kellogg-Briand Peace Pact expressed eloquently the earnest hope of the world for peace.

2. *Economic Internationalism*

In a provocative essay, William A. Williams dissents from the accepted version of the 1920's and instead depicts it as a decade of forceful American economic international expansion and of vigorous diplomacy. Sweeping aside what he describes as stereotyped definitions of "internationalists" and "isolationists," Williams asserts that the foreign policies of the Harding-Coolidge era were aimed at promoting a world-wide community of interest by persuading other powers to accept the internationalizing of business methods and techniques: by limiting the Soviet Russian influence, preventing colonial clashes and rebellion, integrating Japan and Germany into the new system, and persuading Great Britain to accept American leadership.

The Legend of Isolationism in the 1920's

W. A. WILLIAMS

The widely accepted assumption that the United States was isolationist from 1920 through 1932 is no more than a legend. Sir Francis Bacon might have classed this myth of isolation as one of his Idols of the Market-Place. An "ill and unfit choice of words," he cautioned, "leads men away into innumerable and inane controversies and fancies." And certainly the application of the terms *isolation* and *isolationism* to a period and a policy that were characterized by vigorous involvement in the affairs of the world with consciousness of purpose qualifies as an "ill and unfit choice of words." Thus the purpose of this essay: on the basis of an investiga-

William Appleman Williams, "The Legend of Isolationism in the 1920's" *Science & Society*, XVIII (1954), 1–20. Reprinted with permission.

tion of the record to suggest that, far from isolation, the foreign relations of the United States from 1920 through 1932 were marked by express and extended involvement with—and intervention in the affairs of—other nations of the world.

It is both more accurate and more helpful to consider the twenties as contiguous with the present instead of viewing those years as a quixotic interlude of low-down jazz and lower-grade gin, fluttering flappers and Faulkner's fiction, and bootlegging millionaires and millionaire bootleggers. For in foreign policy there is far less of a sharp break between 1923 and 1953 than generally is acknowledged. A closer examination of the so-called isolationists of the twenties reveals that many of them were in fact busily engaged in extending American power. Those individuals and groups have not dramatically changed their outlook on foreign affairs. Their policies and objectives may differ with those of others (including professors), but they have never sought to isolate the United States.

This interpretation runs counter to the folklore of American foreign relations. Harvard places isolationism "in the saddle." Columbia sees "Americans retiring within their own shell." Yale judges that policy "degenerated" into isolation—among other things. Others, less picturesque but equally positive, refer to a "marked increase of isolationist sentiment" and to "those years of isolationism." Another group diagnoses the populace as having "ingrained isolationism," analyzes it as "sullen and selfish" in consequence, and characterizes it as doing "its best to forget international subjects." Related verdicts describe the Republican party as "predominantly isolationist" and as an organization that "fostered a policy of deliberate isolation."

Most pointed of these specifications is a terse two-word summary of the diplomacy of the period: "Isolation Perfected." Popularizers have transcribed this theme into a burlesque. Their articles and books convey the impression that the Secretaries of State were in semi-retirement and that the citizenry wished to do away with the Department itself. Columnists and commentators have made the concept an eerie example of George Orwell's double-think. They label as isolationists the most vigorous interventionists.

The case would seem to be closed and judgment given if it were not for the ambivalence of some observers and the brief dissents filed by a few others. The scholar who used the phrase "those years of isolationism," for example, remarks elsewhere in the same book that "expansionism . . . really was long a major expression of isolationism." Another writes of the "return to an earlier policy of isolation," and on the next page notes a "shift in policy during the twenties amounting almost to a 'diplomatic revolution.'" A recent biographer states that Henry Cabot Lodge "did not propose . . . an isolationist attitude," but then proceeds to characterize the Monroe Doctrine—upon which Lodge stood in his fight against the League of Nations treaty—as a philosophy of "isolation." And in the last volume of his trilogy, the late Professor Frederick L. Paxton summed up a long review of the many diplomatic activities of the years 1919–1923 with the remark that this was a foreign policy of "avoidance rather than of action."

But a few scholars, toying with the Idol of the Market-Place, have made bold to rock the image. Yet Professor Richard Van Alstyne was doing more than playing the iconoclast when he observed that the "militant manifest destiny men were the isolationists of the nineteenth century." For with this insight we can translate those who maintain that Lodge "led the movement to perpetuate the traditional policy of isolation." Perhaps William G. Carleton was even more forthright. In 1946 he pointed out that the fight over the League treaty was not between isolationists and internationalists, and added that many of the mislabeled isolationists were actually "nationalists and imperialists." Equally discerning was Charles Beard's comment in 1933 that the twenties were marked by a "return to the more aggressive ways . . . [used] to protect and advance the claims of American business enterprise." All these interpretations were based on facts that prompted another scholar to change his earlier conclusion and declare in 1953 that "the thought was all of keeping American freedom of action."

These are perceptive comments. Additional help has recently been supplied by two other students of the period. One of these is Robert E. Osgood, who approached the problem in terms of *Ideals and Self-Interest in American Foreign Relations.* Though primarily concerned with the argument that Americans should cease being naive, Osgood suggests that certain stereotypes are misleading. One might differ with his analysis of the struggle over the Treaty of Versailles, but not with his insistence that there were fundamental differences between Senators Lodge and William E. Borah—as well as between those two and President Woodrow Wilson. Osgood likewise raises questions about the reputed withdrawal of the American public. Over a thousand organizations for the study of international relations existed in 1926, to say nothing of the groups that sought constantly to make or modify foreign policy.

Osgood gives little attention to this latter aspect of foreign relations, a surprising omission on the part of a realist. But the underlying assumption of his inquiry cannot be challenged. The foreign policy issue of the twenties was never isolationism. The controversy and competition were waged between those who entertained different concepts of the national interest and disagreed over the means to be employed to secure that objective. Secretary of State Charles Evans Hughes was merely more eloquent, not less explicit. "Foreign policies," he explained in 1923, "are not built upon abstractions. They are the result of practical conceptions of national interest arising from some immediate exigency or standing out vividly in historical perspective."

Historian George L. Grassmuck used this old-fashioned premise of the politician as a tool with which to probe the *Sectional Biases in Congress on Foreign Policy.* Disciplining himself more rigorously in the search for primary facts than did Osgood, Grassmuck's findings prompted him to conclude that "the 'sheep and goats' technique" of historical research is eminently unproductive. From 1921 to 1933, for example, the Republicans in both houses of Congress were "more favorable to both Army and Navy measures than . . . Democrats." Eighty-five percent of the same Republicans supported international economic measures and agreements. As for the Middle West, that much condemned section did not reveal any "extraordinary indication of a . . . tendency to withdraw." Nor was there "an intense 'isolationism' on the part of [its] legislators with regard to membership in a world organization." And what opposition there was seems to have been as much the consequence of dust bowls and depression as the product of disillusioned scholars in ivory towers.

These investigations and correlations have two implications. First, the United States was neither isolated nor did it pursue a policy of isolationism from 1920 to 1933. Second, if the policy of that era, so generally accepted as the product of traditional isolationist sentiment, proves non-isolationist, then the validity and usefulness of the concept when applied to earlier or later periods may seriously be challenged.

Indeed, it would seem more probable that the central theme of American foreign relations has been the expansion of the United States. Alexander Hamilton made astute use of the phrase "no entangling alliances" during the negotiation of Jay's Treaty in 1794, but his object was a *de facto* affiliation with the British Fleet—not isolation. Nor was Thomas Jefferson seeking to withdraw when he made of Monticello a counselling center for those seeking to emulate the success of the American Revolution. A century later Senator Lodge sought to revise the Treaty of Versailles and the Covenant of the League of Nations with reservations that seemed no more than a restatement of Hamilton's remarks. Yet the maneuvers of Lodge were no more isolationist in character and purpose than Hamilton's earlier action. And while surely no latter-day Jefferson, Senator Borah was anything but an isolationist in his concept of the power of economics and ideas. Borah not only favored the recognition of the Soviet Union in order to influence the development of the Bolshevik Revolution and as a check against Japanese expansion in Asia, but also argued that American economic policies were intimately connected with foreign political crises. All those men were concerned with the extension of one or more aspects of American influence, power, and authority.

Approached in this manner, the record of American foreign policy in the twenties verifies the judgments of two remarkably dissimilar students: historian Richard W. Leopold and Senator Lodge. The professor warns that the era was "more complex than most glib generalizations . . . would suggest"; and the scholastic politician concludes that, excepting wars, there "never [was] a period when the United States [was] more active and its influence more felt internationally than between 1921 and 1924." The admonition about perplexity was offered as helpful advice, not as an invitation to anti-intellectualism. For, as the remarks of the Senator implied, recognition that a problem is involved does not mean that it cannot be resolved.

Paradox and complexity can often be clarified by rearranging the data around a new focal point that is common to all aspects of the apparent contradiction. The confusion of certainty and ambiguity that characterizes most accounts of American foreign policy in the twenties stems from the fact that they are centered on the issue of membership in the League of Nations. Those Americans who wanted to join are called internationalists. Opponents of that move became isolationists. But the subsequent action of most of those who fought participation in the League belies this simple classification. And the later policies of many who favored adherence to the League casts serious doubts upon the assumption that they were willing to negotiate or arbitrate questions that they defined as involving the national interest. More pertinent is an examination of why certain groups and individuals favored or disapproved of the League, coupled with a review of the programs they supported after that question was decided.

Yet such a re-study of the League fight is in itself insufficient. Equally important is a close analysis of the American reaction to the Bolshevik Revolution. Both the League Covenant and the Treaty of Versailles were written on a table shaken by that upheaval. The argument over the ratification of the combined documents was waged in a context determined as much by Nikolai Lenin's *Appeal to the Toiling, Oppressed, and Exhausted Peoples of Europe* and the Soviet *Declaration to the Chinese People* as by George Washington's Farewell Address.

Considered within the setting of the Bolshevik Revolution, the basic question was far greater than whether or not to enter the League. At issue was what response was to be made to the domestic and international division of labor that had accompanied the Industrial Revolution. Challenges from organized urban labor, dissatisfied farmers, frightened men of property, searching intellectual critics, and colonial peoples rudely interrupted almost every meeting of the Big Four in Paris and were echoed in many Senate debates over the treaty. And those who determined American policy through the decade of the twenties were consciously concerned with the same problem.

An inquiry into this controversy over the broad question of how to end the war reveals certain divisions within American society. These groupings were composed of individuals and organizations whose position on the League of Nations was coincident with and part of their response to the Bosheviks; or, in a wider sense, with their answer to that general unrest, described by Woodrow Wilson as a "feeling of revolt against the large vested interests which influenced the world both in the economic and the political sphere." Once this breakdown has been made it is then possible to follow the ideas and actions of these various associations of influence and power through the years 1920 to 1933.

At the core of the American reaction to the League and the Bolshevik Revolution was the quandary between fidelity to ideals and the urge to power. Jefferson faced a less acute version of the same predicament in terms of whether to force citizenship on settlers west of the Mississippi who were reluctant to be absorbed in the Louisiana Purchase. A century later the anti-imperialists posed the same issue in the more sharply defined circumstances of the Spanish-American War. The League and the Bolsheviks raised the question in its most dramatic context and in unavoidable terms.

There were four broad responses to this reopening of the age-old dilemma. At one pole stood the pure idealists and pacifists, led by William Jennings Bryan. A tiny minority in themselves, they were joined, in terms of general consequences if not in action, by those Americans who were preoccupied with their own solutions to the problem. Many American business men, for example, were concerned primarily with the expansion of trade and were apathetic toward or impatient with the hullabaloo over the League. Diametrically opposed to the idealists were the vigorous expansionists. All these exponents of the main chance did not insist upon an overt crusade to run the world, but they were united on Senator Lodge's proposition that the United States should dominate world politics. Association with other nations they accepted, but not equality of membership or mutuality of decision.

Caught in the middle were those Americans who declined to support either extreme. A large number of these people clustered around Woodrow Wilson, and can be called the Wilsonites. Though aware of the dangers and temptations involved, Wilson declared his intention to extend American power for the purpose of strengthening the ideals. However noble that effort, it failed for two reasons. Wilson delegated power and initiative to men and organizations that did not share his objectives, and on his own part the president ultimately "cast in his lot" with the defenders of the status quo.

Led by the Sons of the Wild Jackass, the remaining group usually followed Senator Borah in foreign relations. These men had few illusions about the importance of power in human affairs or concerning the authority of the United States in international politics. Prior to the world war they supported—either positively or passively—such vigorous expansionists as Theodore Roosevelt, who led their Progressive Party. But the war and the Bolshevik Revolution jarred some of these Progressives into a closer examination of their assumptions. These reflections and new conclusions widened the breach with those of their old comrades who had moved toward a conservative position on domestic issues. Some of those earlier allies, like Senator Albert J. Beveridge, continued to agitate for an American century. Others, such as Bainbridge Colby, sided with Wilson in 1916 and went along with the president on foreign policy.

But a handful had become firm anti-expansionists by 1919. No attempt was made by these men to deny the power of the United States. Nor did they think that the nation could become self-sufficient and impregnable in its strength. Borah, for example, insisted that America must stand with Russia if Japan and Germany were to be checked. And Johnson constantly pointed out that the question was not whether to withdraw, but at what time and under what circumstances to use the country's influence. What these men did maintain was that any effort to run the world by establishing an American system comparable to the British Empire was both futile and un-American.

In this they agreed with Henry Adams, who debated the same issue with his brother Brooks Adams, Theodore Roosevelt, and Henry Cabot Lodge in the years after 1898. "I incline now to anti-imperialism, and very strongly to anti-militarism," Henry warned. "If we try to rule politically, we take the chances against us." By the end of the first world war another generation of expansionists tended to agree with Henry Adams about ruling politically, but planned to build and maintain a similar pattern of control through the use of America's economic might. Replying to these later expansionists, Borah and other anti-expansionists of the nineteen-twenties argued that if Washington's influence was to be effective it would have to be used to support the movements of reform and colonial nationalism rather than deployed in an effort to dam up and dominate those forces.

For these reasons they opposed Wilson's reorganization of the international banking consortium, fearing that the financiers would either influence strongly or veto—as they did—American foreign policies. With Senator Albert B. Cummins of Iowa they voted against the Wilson-approved Webb-Pomerene Act, which repealed the anti-trust laws for export associations. In the same vein they tried to prevent passage of the Edge Act, an amendment to the Federal Reserve Act that authorized foreign banking corporations. Led by Borah, they bitterly attacked the Versailles Treaty because, in their view, it committed the United States to oppose colonial movements for self-government and to support an unjust and indefensible status quo. From the same perspective they criticized and fought to end intervention in Russia and the suppression of civil liberties at home.

Contrary to the standard criticism of their actions, however, these anti-expansionists were not just negative die-hards. Senator Cummins maintained from the first that American loans to the allies should be considered gifts. Borah spoke out on the same issue, hammered away against armed intervention in Latin America, played a key role in securing the appointment of Dwight Morrow as Ambassador to Mexico, and sought to align the United States with, instead of against, the Chinese Revolution. On these and other issues the anti-expansionists were not always of one mind, but as in the case of the Washington Conference Treaties the majority of them were far more positive in their actions than has been acknowledged.

Within this framework the key to the defeat of the League treaty was the defection from the Wilsonites of a group who declined to accept the restrictions that Article X of the League Covenant threatened to impose upon the United States. A morally binding guarantee of the "territorial integrity and existing political integrity of all members of the League" was too much for these men. First they tried to modify that limitation. Failing there, they followed Elihu Root and William Howard Taft, both old time expansionists, to a new position behind Senator Lodge. Among those who abandoned Wilson on this issue were Herbert Hoover, Calvin Coolidge, Charles Evans Hughes, and Henry L. Stimson.

Not all these men were at ease with the vigorous expansionists. Stimson, for one, thought the Lodge reservations "harsh and unpleasant," and later adjusted other of his views. Hoover and Hughes tried to revive their version of the League after the Republicans returned to power in 1920. But at the time all of them were more uneasy about what one writer has termed Wilson's "moral imperialism." They were not eager to identfy themselves with the memories of that blatant imperialism of the years 1895 to 1905, but neither did they like Article X. That proviso caught them from both sides, it illegalized changes initiated by the United States, and obligated America to restore a status quo to some aspects of which they were either indifferent or antagonistic. But least of all were they anxious to run the risk that the Wilsonian rhetoric of freedom and liberty might be taken seriously in an age of revolution. Either by choice or default they supported the idea of a community of interest among the industrialized powers of the world led by an American-British entente as against the colonial areas and the Soviet Union.

This postwar concept of the community of interest was the first generation intellectual off-spring of Herbert Croly's *Promise of American Life* and Herbert Hoover's *American Individualism.* Croly's opportunistic nationalism provided direction for Hoover's "greater mutuality of interest." The latter was to be expressed in an alliance between the government and the "great trade associations and the powerful corporations." Pushed by the Croly-Hoover wing of the old Progressive Party, the idea enjoyed great prestige during the twenties. Among its most ardent exponents were Samuel Gompers and Matthew Woll of the labor movement, Owen D. Young of management, and Bernard Baruch of finance.

What emerged was an American corporatism. The avowed goals were order, stability, and social peace. The means to those objectives were labor-management co-operation, arbitration, and the elimination of waste and inefficiency by closing out unrestrained competition. State intervention was to be firm, but moderated through the cultivation and legalization of trade associations which would, in turn, advise the national government and supply leaders for the federal bureaucracy. The ideal was union in place of diversity and conflict.

Other than Hoover, the chief spokesmen of this new community of interest as applied to foreign affairs were Secretaries of State Hughes and Stimson. In the late months of 1931 Stimson was to shift his ground, but until that time he supported the principle. All three men agreed that American economic power should be used to build, strengthen, and maintain the co-operation they sought. As a condition for his entry into the cabinet, Hoover demanded—and received—a major voice in "all important economic policies of the administration." With the energetic assistance of Julius Klein, lauded by the National Foreign Trade Council as the "international business go-getter of Uncle Sam," Hoover changed the Department of Commerce from an agency primarily concerned with interstate commerce to one that concentrated on foreign markets and loans, and control of import sources. Hughes and Stimson handled the political aspects of establishing a "community of ideals, interests and purposes."

These men were not imperialists in the traditional sense of that much abused term. All agreed with Klein that the object was to eliminate "the old imperialistic trappings of politico-economic exploitation." They sought instead the "internationalization of business." Through the use of economic power they wanted to establish a common bond, forged of similar assumptions and purposes, with both the industrialized nations and the native business community in the colonial areas of the world. Their deployment of America's material strength is unquestioned. President Calvin Coolidge reviewed their success, and indicated the political implications thereof, on Memorial Day, 1928. "Our investments and trade relations are such," he summarized, "that it is almost impossible to conceive of any conflict anywhere on earth which would not affect us injuriously."

Internationalization through the avoidance of conflict was the key objective. This did not mean a negative foreign policy. Positive action was the basic theme. The transposition of corporatist principles to the area of foreign relations produced a parallel policy. American leadership and intervention would build a world community regulated by agreement among the industrialized nations. The prevention of revolution and the preservation of the sanctity of private property were vital objectives. Hughes was very clear when he formulated the idea for Latin America. "We are seeking to establish a *Pax Americana* maintained not by arms but by mutual respect and good will and the tranquillizing processes of reason." There would be, he admitted, "interpositions of a temporary character"—the Secretary did not like the connotations of the word intervention—but only to facilitate the establishment of the United States as the "exemplar of justice."

Extension to the world of this pattern developed in Latin America was more involved. There were five main difficulties, four in the realm of foreign relations and one in domestic affairs. The internal problem was to establish and integrate a concert of decision between the government and private economic groups. Abroad the objectives were more sharply defined: circumscribe the impact of the Soviet Union, forestall and control potential resistance of colonial areas, pamper and cajole Germany and Japan into acceptance of the basic proposition, and secure from Great Britain practical recognition of the fact that Washington had become the center of Anglo-Saxon collaboration. Several examples will serve to illustrate the general outline of this diplomacy, and to indicate the friction between the office holders and the office dwellers.

Wilson's Administration left the incoming Republicans a plurality of tools designed for the purpose of extending American power. The Webb-Pomerene Law, the Edge Act, and the banking consortium were but three of the more obvious and important of these. Certain polishing and sharpening remained to be done, as exemplified by Hoover's generous interpretation of the Webb-Pomerene legislation, but this was a minor problem. Hoover and Hughes added to these implements with such laws as the one designed to give American customs officials diplomatic immunity so that they could do cost accounting surveys of foreign firms. This procedure was part of the plan to provide equal opportunity abroad, under which circumstances Secretary Hughes was confident that "American business men would take care of themselves."

It was harder to deal with the British, who persisted in annoying indications that they considered themselves equal partners in the enterprise. Bainbridge Colby, Wilson's last Secretary of State, ran into the same trouble. Unless England came "to our way of thinking," Colby feared that "agreement [would] be impossible." A bit later Hughes told the British Ambassador that the time had come for London's expressions of cordial sentiment to be "translated into something definite." After many harangues about oil, access to mandated areas, and trade with Russia, it was with great relief that Stimson spoke of the United States and Great Britain "working together like two old shoes."

Deep concern over revolutionary ferment produced great anxiety. Hughes quite agreed with Colby that the problem was to prevent revolutions without making martyrs of the leaders of colonial or other dissident movements. The despatches of the period are filled with such expressions as "very grave concern," "further depressed," and "deeply regret," in connection with revolutionary activity in China, Latin America, and Europe. American foreign service personnel abroad were constantly reminded to report all indications of such unrest. This sensitivity reached a high point when one representative telegraphed as "an example of the failure to assure public safety . . . the throwing of a rock yesterday into the state hospital here." Quite in keeping with this pattern was Washington's conclusion that it would support "any provisional government which gave satisfactory evidence of an intention to re-establish constitutional order."

Central to American diplomacy of the twenties was the issue of Germany and Japan. And it was in this area that the government ran into trouble with its partners, the large associations of capital. The snag was to convince the bankers of the validity of the long range view. Hoover, Hughes and Stimson all agreed that it was vital to integrate Germany and Japan into the American community. Thus Hughes opposed the French diplomacy of force on the Rhine, and for his own part initiated the Dawes Plan. But the delegation of so much authority to the financiers backfired in 1931. The depression scared the House of Morgan and it refused to extend further credits to Germany. Stimson "blew up." He angrily told the Morgan representative in Paris that this strengthened France and thereby undercut the American program. Interrupted in the midst of this argument by a trans-Atlantic phone call from Hoover, Stimson explained to the president that "if you want to help the cause you are speaking of you will not do it by calling me up, but by calling Tom Lamont." Stimson then turned back to Lamont's agent in Europe and, using "unregulated language," told the man to abandon his "narrow banking axioms."

Similar difficulties faced the government in dealing with Japan and China. The main problem was to convince Japan, by persuasion, concession, and the delicate use of diplomatic force, to join the United States in an application of its Latin American policy to China. Washington argued that the era of the crude exploitation of, and the exercise of direct political sovereignty over, backward peoples was past. Instead, the interested powers should agree to develop and exercise a system of absentee authority while increasing the productive capacity and administrative efficiency of China. Japan seemed amenable to the proposal, and at the Washington Conference, Secretary Hughes went a great distance to convince Tokyo of American sincerity. Some writers, such as George Frost Kennan and Adolf A. Berle, claim that the United States did not go far enough. This is something of a mystery. For in his efforts to establish "cooperation in the Far East," as Hughes termed it, the Secretary consciously gave Japan "an extraordinarily favorable position."

Perhaps what Kennan and Berle have in mind is the attitude of Thomas Lamont. In contrast to their perspective on Europe, the bankers took an extremely long range view of Asia. Accepting the implications of the Four and Nine Power Treaties, Lamont began to finance Japan's penetration of the mainland. Hughes and Stimson were trapped. They continued to think in terms of American business men taking care of themselves if given an opportunity, and thus strengthening Washington's position in the world community. Hughes wrote Morgan that he hoped the consortium would become an "important instrumentality of our 'open door' policy." But the American members of the banking group refused to antagonize their Japanese and British colleagues, and so vetoed Washington's hope to finance the Chinese Eastern Railway and its efforts to support the Federal Telegraph Company in China.

In this context it is easy to sympathize with Stimson's discomfort when the Japanese Army roared across Manchuria. As he constantly reiterated to the Japanese Ambassador in Washington, Tokyo had come far along the road "of bringing itself into alignment with the methods and opinion of the Western World." Stimson not only wanted to, but did in fact give Japan every chance to continue along that path. So too did President Hoover, whose concern with revolution was so great that he was inclined to view Japanese sovereignty in Manchuria as the best solution. Key men in the State Department shared the president's conclusion.

Stimson's insight was not so limited. He realized that his predecessor, Secretary of State Frank B. Kellogg, had been right: the community of interest that America should seek was with the Chinese. The Secretary acknowledged his error to Senator Borah, who had argued just such a thesis since 1917. Stimson's letter to Borah of February 23, 1932, did not say that America should abandon her isolationism, but rather that she had gone too far with the wrong friends. The long and painful process of America's great awakening had begun. But in the meantime President Hoover's insistence that no move should be made toward the Soviet Union, and that the non-recognition of Manchuko should be considered as a formula looking toward conciliation, had opened the door to appeasement.

Additional Reading

Selig Adler, *The Isolationist Impulse* (1957).

Joseph Brandes, *Herbert Hoover and Economic Diplomacy: Department of Commerce Policy, 1921–1928* (1962).

Robert P. Browder, *The Origins of Soviet-American Diplomacy* (1953).
Richard W. Current, *Secretary Stimson: A Study in Statecraft* (1954).
L. Ethan Ellis, *Frank B. Kellogg and American Foreign Relations, 1925–1929* (1961).
Herbert Feis, *The Diplomacy of the Dollar: First Era, 1919–1932* (1950).
Robert H. Ferrell, *American Diplomacy in the Great Depression: Hoover-Stimson Foreign Policy, 1929–1933* (1957).
———, *Peace in Their Time: The Origins of the Kellogg-Briand Pact* (1952).
E. E. Morison, *Turmoil and Tradition: A Study of the Life and Times of Henry L. Stimson* (1960).
Dexter Perkins, *Charles Evans Hughes and American Democratic Statesmanship* (1956).
J. Chalmers Vinson, *William E. Borah and the Outlawry of War* (1957).
B. H. Williams, *Economic Foreign Policy of the United States* (1929).

16 THE WASHINGTON ARMS CONFERENCE:
Statesmanship or Illusion?

The 1920's have been described as the era of the disarmament illusion. Optimism then seemed justified as the civilized world voiced a realization of the destructive futility of war and significant progress apparently was made toward large-scale arms reductions and the pacific settlement of international disputes. Peace societies in Europe and America redoubled efforts in behalf of peace and disarmament and carried on extensive educational and lobbying activities. A series of naval arms conferences were held, the Pact of Paris condemning war as an instrument of national policy was adopted by most nations of the world, and in 1932, after years of preparation, the League of Nations sponsored a World Disarmament Conference in Geneva attended by 60 countries. Alas, it was destined for failure, as the rise of Adolf Hitler to power in Germany and the march of an expansionist Japan in the Far East ushered in a decade of crises and another global war.

The American people in the hopeful twenties were proud that their government was playing a vigorous role in the great movement for world peace. For in addition to a vital part in initiating the "outlawry of war" in the Pact of Paris, the United States sponsored a series of apparently epochal naval arms limitation conferences. The Harding Administration began in 1921 when, anxious to avert an expensive arms race and to balance rejection of the League with a positive gesture at international cooperation and peace, a conference of major naval powers and states interested in the problems of the Pacific was called at Washington. The resultant Washington treaties ostensibly stabilized the Far East and curtailed naval establishments. It was hailed as a great achievement for the United States, the Republican administration, and world peace. Later efforts to extend limitations to naval craft below the capital warship class, after suffering a check at the Geneva Conference in 1927, scored a victory at the London Conference in 1930. The structure collapsed shortly thereafter, however, as Japan demanded parity with Great Britain and the United States in all warship categories. The Japanese government denounced the naval agreements in 1934 and the second London Conference of 1935 failed to bridge the disagreement. The United States once more found itself in a naval construction race, woefully lagging behind a now aggressive Japan.

The value of the Washington agreements was questioned even at the time by some sceptical Americans. Later, the whole movement seemed to many to have been a costly illusion. The questions raised by the many efforts at arms limitations in the 1920's, which no doubt have applicability in the present Cold War period as well, are several: What causes wars—arms races *per se* or underlying political tensions and conflicting goals? Can there be successful arms reductions without adequate prior provisions for the security of the involved nations? Are limited efforts at stabilization of an area, such as the Washington conference undertook, more feasible than the large-scale efforts sponsored by the League of Nations and later by the United Nations?

DOCUMENTS

"The Parchment Peace"

In the pretentious and vague rhetoric for which he was renowned, President Warren G. Harding in an annual message hailed the successes of the recent Washington Conference. Besides confidently predicting that the pacts had ended all chance of war in the Pacific, he made clear that the United States would not assume any binding obligations in world affairs but would confine its role to "moral influence." To underscore that point, the Senate in approving the consultative Four Power Pact, attached a reservation disavowing any commitment to support the agreement by use of force. The Five Power Pact compensated Japan for the short end of the capital ship ratio by prohibiting further naval fortifications by Great Britain and the United States in the western Pacific while Japan was left free to strengthen bases in its home islands. The Nine Power Pact gave the Open Door in China international treaty status for the first time but contained no enforcement provisions. Little wonder that a later historian has aptly described the achievements as "The Parchment Peace."

President Harding's Annual Message, December 8, 1922

. . . I bring you no apprehension of war. The world is abhorrent of it, and our own relations are not only free from every threatening cloud, but we have contributed our larger influence toward making armed conflict less likely.

Those who assume that we played our part in the World War and later took ourselves aloof and apart, unmindful of world obligations, give scant credit to the helpful part we assume in international relationships.

Whether all nations signatory ratify all the treaties growing out of the Washington Conference on Limitation of Armament or some withhold approval, the underlying policy of limiting naval armament has the sanction of the larger naval powers, and naval competition is suspended. Of course, unanimous ratification is much to be desired.

The four-power pact, which abolishes every probability of war on the Pacific, has brought new confidence in a maintained peace, and I can well believe it might be made a model for like assurances wherever in the world any common interests are concerned.

We have had expressed the hostility of the American people to a super-government or to any commitment where either a council or all assembly of leagued powers may chart our course. Treaties of armed alliance can have no likelihood of American sanction, but we believe in respecting the rights of nations, in the value of conference and consultation, in the effectiveness of leaders of nations looking each other in the face before resorting to the arbitrament of arms. . . .

After all there is less difference about the part this great Republic shall play in furthering peace and advancing humanity than in the manner of playing it. We ask no one to assume responsibility for us; we assume no responsibility which others must bear for themselves, unless nationality is hopelessly swallowed up in internationalism. . . .

The Four Power Pact between the United States of America, the British Empire, France, and Japan, Signed December 13, 1921

I

The High Contracting Parties agree as between themselves to respect their rights in relation to their insular possessions and insular dominions in the region of the Pacific Ocean.

If there should develop between any of the High Contracting Parties a controversy arising out of any Pacific question and involving their said rights which is not satisfactorily settled by diplomacy and is likely to affect the harmonious accord now happily subsisting between them, they shall invite the other High Contracting Parties to a joint conference to which the whole subject will be referred for consideration and adjustment.

II

If the said rights are threatened by the aggressive action of any other Power, the High Contracting Parties shall communicate with one another fully and frankly in order to arrive at an understanding as to the most efficient measures to be taken, jointly or separately, to meet the exigencies of the particular situation.

III

This Treaty shall remain in force for ten years from the time it shall take effect, and after the expiration of said period it shall continue to be in force subject to the right of any of the High Contracting Parties to terminate it upon twelve months' notice. . . .

The Five Power Pact between the United States of America, the British Empire, France, Italy, and Japan, Signed February 6, 1922

Article II. The Contracting Powers may retain respectively the capital ships which are specified in Chapter II, Part 1. On the coming into force of the present Treaty, but subject to the following provisions of this Article, all other capital ships, built or building, of the United States, the British Empire and Japan shall be disposed of as prescribed in Chapter II, Part 2. . . .

Article III. Subject to the provisions of Article II, the Contracting Powers shall abandon their respective capital ship building programs, and no new capital ships shall be constructed or acquired by any of the Contracting Powers except replacement tonnage which may be constructed or acquired as specified in Chapter II, Part 3. . . .

Article IV. The total capital ship replacement tonnage of each of the Contracting Powers shall not exceed in standard displacement, for the United States 525,000 tons (533,400 metric tons); for the British Empire 525,000 tons (533,400 metric tons); for France 175,000 tons (177,800 metric tons); for Italy 175,000 tons (177,800 metric tons); for Japan 315,000 tons (320,040 metric tons).

Article V. No capital ship exceeding 35,000 tons (35,560 metric tons) standard displacement shall be acquired by, or constructed by, for, or within the jurisdiction of, any of the Contracting Powers.

Article VI. No capital ship of any of the Contracting Powers shall carry a gun with a calibre in excess of 16 inches (406 millimetres).

Article VII. The total tonnage for aircraft carriers of each of the Contracting Powers shall not exceed in standard displacement, for the United States 135,000 tons (137,160 metric tons); for the British Empire 135,000 tons (137,160 metric tons); for France 60,000 tons (60,960 metric tons); for Italy 60,000 tons (60,960 metric tons); for Japan 81,000 tons (82,296 metric tons).

Article IX. No aircraft carrier exceeding 27,000 tons (27,432 metric tons) standard displacement shall be acquired by, or constructed by, for or within the jurisdiction of, any of the Contracting Powers.

However, any of the Contracting Powers may, provided that its total tonnage allowance of aircraft carriers is not thereby exceeded, build not more than two aircraft carriers, each of a tonnage of not more than 33,000 tons (33,528 metric tons) standard displacement, and in order to effect economy any of the Contracting Powers may use for this purpose any two of their ships, whether constructed or in course of construction, which would otherwise be scrapped under the provisions of Article II. . . .

Article XII. No vessel of war of any of the Contracting Powers, hereafter laid down, other than a capital ship, shall carry a gun with a calibre in excess of 8 inches (203 millimetres).

Article XIX. The United States, the British Empire and Japan agree that the *status quo* at the time of the signing of the present Treaty, with regard to fortifications and naval bases, shall be maintained in their respective territories and possessions specified hereunder:

(1) The insular possessions which the United States now holds or may hereafter acquire in the Pacific Ocean, except (*a*) those adjacent to the

coast of the United States, Alaska and the Panama Canal Zone, not including the Aleutian Islands, and (*b*) the Hawaiian Islands;

(2) Hongkong and the insular possessions which the British Empire now holds or may hereafter acquire in the Pacific Ocean, east of the meridian of 110° east longitude, except (*a*) those adjacent to the coast of Canada, (*b*) the Commonwealth of Australia and its Territories, and (*c*) New Zealand;

(3) The following insular territories and possessions of Japan in the Pacific Ocean to wit: the Kurile Islands, the Bonin Islands, Amami-Oshima, the Loochoo Islands, Formosa and the Pescadores, and any insular territories or possessions in the Pacific Ocean which Japan may hereafter acquire.

The maintenance of the *status quo* under the foregoing provisions implies that no new fortifications or naval bases shall be established in the territories and possessions specified; that no measures shall be taken to increase the existing naval facilities for the repair and maintenance of naval forces, and that no increase shall be made in the coast defenses of the territories and possessions above specified. This restriction, however, does not preclude such repair and replacement of worn-out weapons and equipment as is customary in naval and military establishments in time of peace. . . .

The Nine Power Pact between the United States of America, Belgium, the British Empire, China, France, Italy, Japan, the Netherlands, and Portugal, February 6, 1922

Article I. The Contracting Powers, other than China, agree:

(1) To respect the sovereignty, the independence, and the territorial and administrative integrity of China;

(2) To provide the fullest and most unembarrassed opportunity to China to develop and maintain for herself an effective and stable government;

(3) To use their influence for the purpose of effectually establishing and maintaining the principle of equal opportunity for the commerce and industry of all nations throughout the territory of China;

(4) To refrain from taking advantage of conditions in China in order to seek special rights or privileges which would abridge the rights of subjects or citizens of friendly States, and from countenancing action inimical to the security of such States.

Article II. The Contracting Powers agree not to enter into any treaty, agreement, arrangement, or understanding, either with one another, or, individually or collectively, with any Power or Powers, which would infringe or impair the principles stated in Article I.

Article VII. The Contracting Powers agree that, whenever a situation arises which in the opinion of any one of them involves the application of the stipulations of the present Treaty, and renders desirable discussion of such application, there shall be full and frank communication between the Contracting Powers concerned. . . .

READINGS

1. A Victory for Peace and Trade

In 1931 it was still possible to be optimistic about the prospects for further arms reductions and the maintenance of peace. Benjamin H. Williams, a political scientist and author of a treatise on American economic foreign policies, concluded that substantial progress had been made in the Twenties and at the American initiative, and he confidently anticipated further gains at the World Disarmament Conference scheduled for 1932. He noted the close alliance between American business groups interested in foreign trade and the State Department, manifested in the calling of the Washington Conference to halt a costly naval race and thereby to allay world tensions and rivalries harmful to the international business community.

The Washington Conference

BENJAMIN H. WILLIAMS

The conference method of dealing with international questions has almost unlimited possibilities. In the solution of problems of mutual interest among nations it represents the substitution of intelligent direction for disorganization and chance. The use of this method in attempting to bring rational order into world affairs has been given great stimulus in the years following the war, and in no field has it been used more strikingly than in that of naval limitation. Before 1914, as has been shown, the efforts to stop the growth of armaments were sporadic and ineffectual. Since the war there has been hardly a year in which there has not been a notable meeting of an international conference or commission to give serious and prolonged consideration to the matter. And a continuation of the series of important gatherings to grapple with the question is definitely upon the program for the future. Some of these meetings have accomplished real gains and others have been unable to achieve any concrete or immediate results. Practically every discussion has, however, helped to clarify the subject, and has made a later solution easier. The whole movement bears unmistakable marks of progress. Only by comparison with the past can we judge the trend of the movement. The present situation is certainly far more encouraging than was that at the time of the Second Hague Conference in 1907 when the subject could not be placed on the agenda for fear of breaking up the conference. . . .

The Washington Conference was an epochal event in international politics, for it reached the first important agreement among the great powers for the limitation and reduction of armaments. It established the method and set the standard for practically all the immediately effective work on this subject for a decade, and its precedent will probably influence the movement for many years to come.

From the beginning the Washington Conference was dominated by the personality of Secretary of State Charles Evans Hughes. Mr. Hughes was fairly well in tune with the sentiments of the large business groups

Benjamin H. Williams, *The United States and Disarmament* (New York & London: McGraw-Hill, 1931, 140–160, 304–310. Reprinted with permission.

centered in New York City. As has been said, one of the guiding principles of the international bankers is friendship between the United States and the greater powers. . . .

At Washington, Mr. Hughes was desirous of removing certain particular causes of friction which were pregnant with danger, and he wished, in general, to build up the intangible asset of good will. To do this he was willing to sacrifice the large capital ships which were in the process of construction, for he felt that because of the bitterness which they were certain to promote they were a liability to the expanding American economy. Realistic thinking was necessary to grasp this proposition which runs decidedly counter to the older systems of thought.

Doubtless the great climax of Mr. Hughes' successful career came at the opening of the Washington Conference. In a speech delivered on November 12, 1921, he outlined in detail practically all that was to be accomplished in the way of naval tonnage limitation. He offered to abandon the American program of capital ship construction in return for concessions from Great Britain and Japan on a somewhat smaller scale. . . .

Secretary Hughes then presented a specific and practical program for reduction, the main points of which were as follows:

1. That all capital ship building programs, either actual or projected should be abandoned;
2. That further reduction should be made through the scrapping of certain of the older ships;
3. That, in general, regard should be had to the existing naval strength of the powers concerned;
4. That the capital ship tonnage should be used as the measurement of strength for navies and a proportionate allowance of auxiliary combatant craft prescribed.

Becoming more concrete, he detailed a program for the scrapping of American, British, and Japanese capital ships and further specified which ships each of the three powers should retain. The limitations on the French and Italian navies were reserved for later consideration. Here, indeed, was a departure from the grandiose generalities and meaningless professions of good will which had been the bane of previous disarmament discussions. Nor was there the resort to bickerings over minor technicalities in guns and characteristics of ships which is often the defense of the unwilling technician. The method of disarmament was freehanded and sweeping. The British writers, Kenworthy and Young, said about it: "He was sinking in a few sentences more tonnage in battleships than all the battles of the world had sunk in a century." Ichihashi, who was present and attached to the Japanese delegation, wrote: "It electrified the calm session; some were shocked, some were even alarmed, but others were pleased. It made the day a memorable one in history." Seasoned journalists, whose lives have been devoted to dramatizing political events for their newspaper readers, have sought to depict the effect of the speech. Mark Sullivan in his book, *The Great Adventure at Washington*, has devoted many pages to describing the reaction to "that inspired moment" of various personalities in the plenary session. According to his description, Admiral Beatty of the British Navy "came forward in his chair with the manner of a bulldog, sleeping on a sunny porch, who has been kicked in the stomach by the foot of an itinerant soap-canvasser." Lord Lee reached around excitedly for pencil and paper. Miss Tarbell testifies that the Japanese "took it without a flicker of an eyelash," while Louis Seibold wrote: "There was no discounting the surprise of Prince Tokugawa, Baron Kato, and Ambassador Shidehara. The Italian, Portuguese, and Belgian envoys appeared to be greatly pleased if a trifle startled." Well might these veteran writers wax enthusiastic, if slightly at variance, for they had lived through a climax in the drama of history.

The Hughes plan for reducing the capital ships of the three powers to the ratios of 5 : 5 : 3 was adopted. The tonnage figures which were first suggested by the Secretary of State were scaled slightly upwards to make it possible for the Japanese to retain the newly completed *Mutsu*, a ship which, it was stated, had been constructed partially from contributions of Japanese school children. Japanese naval officers had taken great pride in this modern 16-inch gun battleship. Accordingly, the *Mutsu* was retained and the feelings of the Japanese school children were spared, but the other powers were given compensation in additional tonnage.

The ratios for France and Italy, after some heavy pressure upon the French delegates, were finally set at 1.67 each as compared with 5 : 5 : 3 for the United States, Great Britain, and Japan. Hereafter, for convenience, the ratios of the five powers will be referred to as 10 : 10 : 6 : 3.33 : 3.33. The numbers and tonnage of capital ships to be retained by each of the powers were eventually fixed as follows:

Country	*No.*	*Tonnage*
United States	18	525,850
Great Britain	20	558,950
Japan	10	301,320
France	10	221,170
Italy	10	182,800

It will be noted that the tonnage left to the powers did not correspond entirely to the ratios agreed upon. Thus the American tonnage was 33,100 tons below that of Great Britain. The reason for this discrepancy was that the British vessels retained were slightly older than those left to the United States. With the larger tonnage given to Great Britain it was estimated that the two fleets of capital ships were of about the same strength.

The tons in which the fleets were measured were not the same but varied somewhat according to systems in use in the different navies. The treaty included a definition of standard displacement as that of the ship complete, fully manned, engined and equipped ready for sea, including all armament and ammunition, equipment, outfit, provisions and fresh water for crew, miscellaneous stores and implements of every description that are intended to be carried in war, but without fuel or reserve feed water on board. The ton agreed upon was the long ton of 2,240 pounds.

When this standard ton was later applied to measure the existing fleet it was found that the older British method of measurement had included fewer items than the treaty definition of displacement while the American method had included more. The British ships, when translated into standard tonnage, accordingly ran somewhat higher than the treaty figures and the American ships ran somewhat lower. The revised figures as of December 31, 1929, which were accepted as correct by the American delegates to the London Conference, showed 532,400 tons of capital ships for the United States. This included some 30,000 tons that had been added through the modernization of ten American ships since the Washington Conference. The British capital ship strength was set down as 608,650 tons. Thus, even with the increase from modernization, the American ships were 76,250 tons behind the British.

The discrepancy, however, was of only temporary importance. After the year 1931, when replacements of capital ships were to be permitted, the tonnage of the various powers was expected to fall in line with their respective ratios until in 1942 they would be exactly in accord with their allotments. Measured in treaty tons the 1942 strength would be as follows:

Country	*No.*	*Tonnage*
United States	15	525,000
Great Britain	15	525,000
Japan	9	315,000
France	5	175,000
Italy	5	175,000

All of this reduction required the destruction of many capital ships. American critics of the Washington Conference have pointed out that the United States gave up much more than did the other powers. This is true. A comparison of the tonnage destroyed is difficult to reduce to exact mathematical terms because of the variation in the definition of displacement which then existed in the different navies, and because of other variable factors such as the age and gun power of the existing vessels which were destroyed and the percentage of completion of the doomed ships which were in process of construction. The following figures set forth the number of the scrapped ships and their tonnage, but, because of the difference in definition of tons involved, the statistics are only approximately accurate.

Country	*No. of capital ships destroyed*	*Tonnage*
United States	28	845,740
Great Britain	24	583,000
Japan	16	435,328
Total	68	1,864,068

Of the sixteen powerful capital ships of the 1916 program, eleven were scrapped, or, if you include the *Lexington* and *Saratoga*, battle cruisers which were not destroyed but were converted into aircraft carriers, the number is thirteen. Senator Hale, chairman of the Senate Committee on Naval Affairs, estimated that of these ships, which were all in process of construction, the battleships were 43 per cent and the battle cruisers were 16 per cent complete. This is what is referred to when critics of the Washington Conference speak of the sinking by the United States of the most powerful fleet afloat.

In addition to limitations upon capital ships, the tonnage for aircraft carriers was restricted as follows:

United States	135,000
Great Britain	135,000
Japan	81,000
France	60,000
Italy	60,000

Auxiliary combat craft, including cruisers, destroyers, submarines, and other smaller types of ships, were not limited at the Washington Conference. In his opening speech, Secretary Hughes had suggested figures of limitations for auxiliary vessels as well as for capital ships, but this part of the program met with little enthusiasm from the other powers. The most apparent reason for the failure of this proposal was the inability to agree regarding the submarine.

The people of Great Britain, remembering the lessons of the World War, were desirous of abolishing the submarine. The prospect of starvation in a future war, because of the blocking of trade routes and the stoppage of food importation, had created a bitter antagonism in the British Isles against this instrument of commerce destruction. Seeking to capitalize the great moral indignation against the U-boat which continued as a hang-over from the days of the war, the British delegation asked that the submarine be abolished. Lord Lee, the principal spokesman of the delegation on the subject, advanced an elaborate argument to prove that the submarine was not of much value in coastal defense or in attack against naval vessels. The destruction of commerce was the only use to which it could be put, he alleged, and in this work it could not be employed except in violation of the rules of international law. The only solution to the problem, according to his reasoning, was to do away with the nefarious craft altogether. His argument fell upon deaf ears, for all of the four other powers were able to see great possibilities for the submarine outside of the field of commerce destruction. They, accordingly, refused to agree to abolition.

Another conflict arose over the tonnage in submarines which was to be allotted under the treaty. Mr. Hughes had proposed 90,000 tons for Great Britain and the United States, 54,000 tons for Japan, and it was his intention that the French and Italian submarine quotas should be fixed in accordance with their capital ship ratios, which would have given them 30,000 tons each. When the British protested that the tonnage figures were too large, Mr. Hughes suggested that the United States and Great Britain should reduce their strength to 60,000 tons and that Japan, France, and Italy should retain their existing tonnage which he understood to be 31,452 for Japan, 31,391 for France, and about 21,000 tons for Italy.

The French, who are the chief admirers of the submarine, now came forth to block further progress in this direction. They had been displeased with the low ratio awarded to them in capital ships and were not disposed to yield further ground. After receiving instruction from Paris, M. Sarraut of the French delegation announced that the cabinet and Supreme Council of National Defense had fixed 90,000 tons as the absolute minimum below which France could not go in submarines "without imperiling the vital interests of the country and of its colonies and the safety of their naval life." Mr. Balfour, the cold and cynical leader of the British delegation, replied bitingly to the effect that

> this constituted a somewhat singular contribution to the labors of a conference called for the diminution of armament . . . It was perfectly obvious that the proposed 90,000 tons of submarines were intended to destroy commerce. They could not be intended for any other purpose . . . It was perfectly clear that if at Great Britain's gates a fleet of 90,000 tons of submarines (60,000 tons of which were to be of the newest type) was to be constructed, no limitation of any kind of auxiliary vessels capable of dealing with submarines could be admitted by the Government which he represented.

The British thereupon refused to accept limitations as to destroyers, which are the swift surface vessels used to hunt down and annihilate the submarine. The limitation of cruisers, which are the nemesis of the destroyer, was in turn impossible. Perhaps the British delegates were secretly glad that there was to be no limitation of auxiliary combat craft; but it was far better for their purposes that the breakdown should be laid to the French submarine program rather than to the needs of the British for commerce destroyers. The latter necessity might have been difficult to defend in the atmosphere of Washington. It may be that similar sentiments were held by Italy and Japan, but their delegates openly regretted that auxiliary craft were not included in the restricted classes. At any rate the failure to limit these vessels, as will be seen, left an opening for another naval race.

The conference made one final attempt to restrict the submarine. The sentiment on the part of the British delegation against that vessel was too strong to be utterly ignored. Accordingly, a draft treaty was drawn up which prohibited the employment of submarines as commerce destroyers by the five powers and invited all other nations to adhere to the prohibition. The treaty failed, however, owing to the fact that France neglected to ratify it. The French are much like other people, and when it comes to naval bickerings they are very reluctant to give up any prospective advantages. Furthermore, their moral indignation, as in other countries, runs strangely enough along the lines of self-interest. During the war the use of the submarine by the Germans against commercial vessels was widely deprecated as inhuman and barbarous. But when it came to ratifying an agreement denying themselves the right to do the same thing, the French were negligent. And so, in the final result, the submarine was not limited at Washington.

Another matter as serious as the competition in capital ships was the growing menace of fortifications in the Pacific. The lines of attack in a conflict between the United States and Japan were gradually moving closer. Prior to the conference there had been much talk of increasing the American fortifications in Guam and the Philippines. Japan had rather hurriedly completed the naval works at the Bonin Islands and Amami-Oshima. Hector Bywater, who has studied the Far Eastern situation carefully, says that the evidence of these serious naval preparations had led many observers in the Far East to believe that Japan would have made the beginning of work on the American bases in Guam and Manila a cause for war. Few people in the United States realized that American peace was thus threatened. These minor policies in the Far East which were comparatively unimportant to the American people, so far as prospective benefits were concerned, were of immence importance to Japan, who regarded her very existence as in jeopardy.

When Japan came to the conference, therefore, her delegates were firmly prepared to seek a *status quo* limitation on fortifications in the Pacific. In fact, if such limitation had not been forthcoming it is very doubtful if the Japanese would have been willing to agree to capital ship limitation on the 10 : 10 : 6 basis. On the other hand American naval officers who had long laid plans for the extension of the fortifications and fleet facilities in both Guam and the Philippines raised objections to the Japanese demand for limitation. Secretary Hughes was in a difficult situation. If he listened to the Japanese demand he would offend the American naval group. If he listened to the American naval advice he would wreck the conference. He chose to give success to the conference through an agreement to the *status quo* on naval bases.

The treaty finally provided for the maintenance of the *status quo* with regard to the following Pacific fortifications and naval bases:

Those of the United States: The insular possessions in the Pacific except (*a*) those adjacent to the coast of the United States, Alaska, and the Panama Canal Zone (not including the Aleutian Islands), and (*b*) the Hawaiian Islands. The possessions to which the restriction applies are the Philippines, Guam, American Samoa, and the Aleutian Islands. Henceforth the United States must depend upon Hawaii for its furthest fortified western base.

Those of Great Britain: Hongkong and the insular possessions in the Pacific, east of the meridian of 110 degrees east longitude, except (*a*) those adjacent to the coast of Canada, (*b*) the Commonwealth of Australia and its territories, and (*c*) New Zealand. The line drawn at 110 degrees east longitude excluded Singapore from the operation of the treaty.

Those of Japan: The following insular possessions in the Pacific: the Kurile Islands, the Bonin Islands, Amami-Oshima, the Loochoo Islands, Formosa and the Pescadores, and any insular territories or possessions in the Pacific Ocean which Japan may hereafter acquire. This leaves the Japanese free to fortify Japan proper.

The effect of this limitation is admirably summarized by Bywater who states that before the conference the possible bases of war between Japan and the United States were about to be extended to within easy striking distance of each other. If the United States had carried out its plans to fortify Guam and the Philippines, the distance between the base at Cavite and the Japanese coast would have been 1,700 miles while the American stronghold at Guam would have been but 1,360 miles from Japan and 800 miles from the Bonin Islands. The wide waste of water which had served so well to isolate the United States in the past was to be eliminated. Now with the *status quo* decided upon at Washington the ocean barrier has been maintained. The distance from the Hawaiian Islands to Yokosuka, the most easterly base in Japan proper, is 3,375 miles; and thus a great stretch of ocean continues to intervene between the American base of naval operations and that of a prospective foe. . . .

One of the major results of the conference, which helped to clear the air of international suspicion, was the termination of the Anglo-Japanese Alliance. The alliance had been first formed in 1902, and in the original form it related to the questions of equal opportunity and territorial integrity in China and Korea. If either party to the alliance should engage in war with another power regarding its interests in these questions and should be attacked by a third power, then the other party to the alliance would come to the assistance of its doubly beleaguered ally. Thus, in the Russo-Japanese War, if either France or Germany had entered the war on the side of Russia, Great Britain would have been obligated to come to the assistance of Japan. The purpose of the Japanese in entering the alliance was to secure support against Russia, which country was at that time bearing down upon Manchuria. The Japanese also realized that an alliance with Great Britain would greatly enhance their prestige. On the part of Great Britain the alliance was intended to secure the benevolent neutrality of Japan in case of trouble with either Russia or Germany, and the assistance of Japan in case of war with both over the eastern question. . . .

In 1911 the alliance was again renewed with an amendment to the effect that it should not be operative as against a third power which should conclude a general arbitration treaty with one of the parties to the alliance. By this amendment Great Britain hoped to allay the fears of the United States, for a general arbitration treaty had just been negotiated between the two Anglo-Saxon powers. Later, however, the arbitration treaty received the customary death blow in the Senate.

In 1921, the treaty, which was to run for ten years, would have been terminated if denounced by either party. If neither party took action, it was to continue indefinitely. There was at that time much speculation as to the fate of the alliance. Germany had disappeared from the scene even more completely than Russia. The only common danger which faced the two countries in the Far East was the United States with its expanding fleet. The menace of American battleships and prospective bases in the Philippines and Guam gave Japan a strong reason for desiring the continuation of the alliance. British interests were divided. A war with the United States, even with Japan as an ally, would have been exceedingly disastrous to British commerce; and it might likewise have divided the empire. The Pacific dominions regarded the United States as a lesser evil than Japan, and definitely showed their hostility to the alliance in the Imperial conference of 1921. On the other hand, a ruthless and crushing competition in shipbuilding on the part of the United States which would have compelled the British to accept naval inferiority would not have left them in a satisfactory position to terminate the alliance. Baffled for financial reasons in maintaining her position on the sea, Great Britain might conceivably have felt such indignation that she would have been moved to combine her naval strength with that of Japan. When, however, the United States at the opening of the Washington Conference showed a willingness to scrap her mammoth capital ship program, the last important reason from the standpoint of Great Britain for continuing the compact with Japan was gone. Great Britain took the initiative in the abandonment of the alliance. Mr. Balfour submitted to Mr. Hughes a tentative suggestion for a triple or quadruple entente in the Pacific. The Japanese were then bluntly told of this action which meant the passing of the alliance.

In place of the alliance the Four-power Pacific Treaty was signed by the United States, Great Britain, Japan, and France. The treaty obliges the four parties to respect the rights of one another relating to their insular possessions and insular dominions in the Pacific. The obligation of consultation in a conference in case of disputes arising from any Pacific question which cannot be diplomatically adjusted is imposed. If the rights of the parties in the Pacific are threatened by the aggressive action of any outside power, the parties have agreed to communicate with one another as to the best measures to be taken.

The treaty marks a departure from the separate policy of the United States in the Pacific. If Great Britain and Japan should have a dispute over Japanese economic claims in Manchuria, the United States would be bound to meet with the treaty powers to consult as to a solution of the matter. The consultation agreement is the mildest form of joint action for the prevention of war. The slender obligations imposed upon the United States under it are, after all, to the best interests of this country, as a war in the Pacific region could not but prove a danger to all of the larger powers in that area. Furthermore, an exceedingly valuable consideration which the United States received for signing the treaty was the cancellation of the Anglo-Japanese Alliance.

The Four-power Treaty together with the other acts of the conference went far to make the great ocean off our western coast pacific in fact as well as in name.

The conference marks a turning point in international relations. By 1921, the western world had at last been convinced that heavy naval armaments were unprofitable and dangerous. At that point the United States, because of its wealth and on account of the building program already under way, held the key position in much the same way as did Germany in 1899. For certain understandable reasons the United States was willing to forego its leadership in naval building. These reasons were a lack of strong militarist tradition and the fact that business leaders in this country were not convinced of the economic necessity of sea supremacy. Fortunately at that moment there was in the office of Secretary of State a clear-headed man who could see with realistic vision the true self-interest of his country and who was competent to enact that interest into policy. The Washington Conference deservedly stands as one of the most commendable achievements in post-war diplomacy.

2. *Naval Arms Limitations in the Twenties: Immediate Successes and Eventual Failures*

From the perspective of another world war and the beginnings of the Cold War with Russia, Dr. Merze Tate, an historian of disarmament diplomacy, sketches the movement for arms limitations and thoughtfully evaluates the successes and failures of the 1920's and 1930's. She carefully relates arms proposals to national policies and security requirements, and concludes that while the Washington Conference was a notable achievement for the times, it later proved to have been a costly failure. The entire structure of naval limitations, so painfully erected at the Washington Conference in 1921 and the London Conference in 1930 was destroyed by 1935 because underlying assumptions of continuing stability in Europe and the Far East proved erroneous.

Naval Conferences between the Wars

MERZE TATE

. . . The Washington Conference of 1921, despite its failure to limit auxiliary naval craft and land and air forces, was a memorable occasion, for it was the first successful attempt to restrict and reduce armaments. All earlier parleys had failed because concrete plans had been avoided and only general views had been exchanged. In this conference the United States had proposed a definite program for the limitation of naval armaments. The nature of the plan and the source from which it came arrested the attention of the war-weary world. No ulterior motives, such as those attributed to the Czar and his ministers in 1898, and to the British Liberal Government in 1907, could be ascribed to the United States government. Our country with its enormous financial and natural resources occupied a position of commanding advantage in any armament race; therefore, as initiator of the conference, the United States was in a peculiarly strong and unassailable position to take the lead. While asking others to make some sacrifices, Washington seemed ready to make even larger ones. In a sense the United States was practicing self-denial in accepting a position of theoretical parity with her closest rival.

At the conference, the naval limitation provisions were avowedly aimed at giving Great Britain, the United States, and Japan maritime superority in their own waters. But Japanese control of the Far East was buttressed by the nonfortification agreement. This removed the chance of England's and America's having the use of either Corregidor or Hong Kong as naval

Reprinted by permission of the publishers from Merze Tate, *The United States and Armaments.* Cambridge, Mass.: Harvard University Press, Copyright, 1948, by The President and Fellows of Harvard College. Pp. 138–140, 254–265.

bases in the event of war in the Pacific. Under the established 5–5–3 ratio, Japan, in addition, was given an absolute naval mystery in all Asiatic waters between the Aleutian Islands and Indo-China, because distance more than counterbalanced the numerical advantage of the Anglo-American fleets. Raymond Leslie Buell summarized the Pacific situation created at Washington as follows:

> As a result of the Naval Treaty, adopting the 5–5–3 ratio and the non-fortification agreement, it is now impossible for any power to intervene successfully in the Orient by force, if acting alone. By the Four-Power Treaty, it is now impossible for Great Britain and the United States to combine their fleets in order to intervene jointly. Moreover, by the Four-Power Treaty the freedom of the United States and Great Britain to bring diplomatic pressure against Japan is also probably limited. Consequently, as long as these Treaties are adhered to, Japan is absolutely supreme in the eastern Pacific and over Asia.
>
> At the same time, the Naval Treaty has made a successful Japanese attack on the Pacific Coast impossible, because Japan, as far as capital ships are concerned, will have a fleet forty per cent inferior to the American fleet; because Japan has no real bases or fortifications in the Pacific this side of the Bonins; and because the United States retains the right to increase the fortifications in Hawaii. As a result of this Treaty, it has become a physical impossibility for the United States successfully to attack Japan and Japan to attack the United States.

Concerning the other points that were treated at the Washington Conference, the territorial integrity and the independence of China were guaranteed. This guarantee was in the form of the Nine-Power Treaty, signed by all the Pacific powers except the Soviet Union.

The Washington settlement, through the abrogation of the Anglo-Japanese Alliance, resulted in a sweeping adjustment of the political alignment in the Pacific region; it freed the United States, especially the west coast area, from apprehension of a Japanese attack; it also relieved the Japanese of uneasiness about naval bases in the Pacific, and so, temporarily, reduced the tension in the Far East. No action, however, was taken to revise American immigration and tariff policies, both deep sources of irritation to the Japanese.

Today, considering in retrospect the history of the intervening twenty-six years since the Washington Treaties were signed, it is difficult to hail the conference as a diplomatic victory for the United States. Instead of securing our national interest vis-á-vis Great Britain and Japan, we made a double surrender. In consenting in advance to scrap our excess tonnage in capital ships, the United States relinquished the most effective means of obtaining British consent to parity in all other categories. Likewise, in pledging ourselves not to add to the existing fortifications on Guam, Tutuila, the Aleutians, and the Philippines, we surrendered our power to act in the Far East not only to preserve the "open door" and the territorial integrity of China but to protect our own outlying possessions. When war with Japan came, the Philippines, Guam, and Wake were hers. Even Hawaii was at her mercy had Japan realized it. Air power, which has profoundly altered the strategy and use of naval strength, was left out of consideration. Nor was real progress in limitation or reduction of naval armaments achieved, for the restrictions in the treaty extended only to dreadnoughts and aircraft carriers. As a consequence, the naval race was transferred from capital ships to big crusiers, and in this category a new competition ensued.

. . . The Washington, Geneva, and two London naval conferences brought into bold relief the clash in national policies of the parties concerned, and illustrated that arms can be limited only when states feel secure. Thus, deliberations at Washington were dominated by the conviction that the greatest threat to world peace lay in the disturbed conditions and international rivalries in the Pacific. The United States, in calling that conference, was anxious to stabilize the Far Eastern situation in a way favorable to American interests. In persuading Great Britain and Japan to give up their alliance we eliminated a powerful combination which might have thwarted or frustrated American policies in the Orient.

Limitation of battleships and aircraft carriers was realized at Washington because of a combination of several circumstances. These were:

1. The policies of the three great naval powers apparently were not in conflict. Not one appeared to covet the territory of the other or to have any political reason for establishing naval superiority over others in their homewaters. At the same time, all had an economic interest in stabilizing armament.

2. The initiator of the conference was in a superior economic position and under a system of unbridled competition could easily outstrip its rivals.

3. The same country, nevertheless, was willing to make the greatest sacrifices to achieve a satisfactory understanding at a level which would represent economy and security for all.

4. This potentially superior state was at the same time satisfied with its territorial and political position, and enjoyed the greatest national security.

5. There were no political disputes outstanding between the English-speaking powers, so Anglo-American agreement on naval parity was possible. Thus the conference established the psychological—but not the technical—basis for a future understanding.

6. The agreement was restricted to two types of vessels—capital ships and aircraft carriers. Thus the conference did not have to consider the defense of the lines of communication of the British Empire and the naval forces of the minor powers, or to raise the question of the interdependence of armaments generally. An attempted solution of any one of these problems would have wrecked the conference. Moreover, quantitative and qualitative limitations of battleships were achieved, perhaps, not only because this type of ship was extremely costly but also because certain technical experts doubted its fighting value.

7. The American proposal was an attempt to apply the total or "global" tonnage method of limitation; consequently, France and Italy could adhere to some features of it, thus making a five-power agreement possible.

8. The Washington Treaty provided for a limitation of capital ships based on the approximate *status quo.* Acceptance of this principle, unfortunatly, led to competition in other categories of vessels.

9. Japan accepted a position of capital ship inferiority in accordance with the 5–5–3 ratio on condition that Great Britain and the United States agree not to build new fortifications in the Pacific during the life of the treaty. Thus Japan temporarily abandoned naval equality with her most powerful competitors in exchange for security, indeed supremacy, in her home waters and the seas of the Far East. But in return for that naval supremacy in the western Pacific, she promised to evacuate Siberia, restore Shantung, and respect the sovereignty of China.

10. Finally, no attempt was made to provide machinery for the prevention or settlement of international disputes in the Pacific. Both Great Britain and the United States were willing to accept and trust Japan's word, which was the only sanction of the agreements.

The Washington treaties, taken together, were based on certain assumptions which in the long run proved fallacious. Thus, according to George E. Taylor:

> They assumed that there would not be any serious changes in Europe; this was correct enough for a decade but not for two decades. They assumed that China would put her house in order without the aid of Soviet Russia, without a strong anti-imperialist movement, and without popular revolution. They assumed that constitutional government would prosper in Japan, and that expansive tendencies would get weaker rather than stronger. The Washington Treaties, if these assumptions had been at all correct, would have written into international law the structure of a stable Pacific. There was every reason to think that the balance of power had been restored in America's favor.

These Washington agreements concerned, in their substantive effect, the three great sea powers, and the negative results of this lack of a real basis of accord between the ocean powers and the naval powers of Europe were seen in the succeeding conferences. Although no understanding was reached with regard to land and air armaments, submarines, and auxiliary craft, the limitation of capital ships produced a favorable psychological effect, and led members of the Congress and the House of Commons to request another conference to deal with those categories of vessels left unlimited at Washington.

Accordingly, in 1927 President Coolidge invited the naval powers to consider the extension of the Washington ratios to auxiliary craft. At the Geneva Three-Power Naval Conference, although Great Britain and the United States were agreed on accepting parity, no formula could be found to achieve it. At Washington the plan of Charles Evans Hughes had provided for a flat tonnage system of measurement. American and British fleets were to be equal, or approximately so, ship for ship and ton for ton. But this method was too inflexible to meet the problems of cruiser limitation. Great Britain could not see why the United States should want parity in 6-inch-gun cruisers, since our defense needs were far less than hers. Consequently England decided that if our country desired equality for its prestige value, the American fleet would have to be expanded to match Great Britain's, since reduction to the American level would have endangered the safety of the Empire.

On the other hand, the United States could not understand why Great Britain should object to American construction of 10,000-ton cruisers so long as the total mathematical tonnage did not exceed that of the British. We contended that parity in all classes had been agreed upon at Washington, while the British insisted that they had accepted the principle of equality only in battle fleets—not in those vessels required for trade route protection. Each side argued for a definition of "equality" or "parity" which, if accepted, would give it superiority.

The reason for the special difficulties in applying the principle of mutual limitation to cruisers could, however, be traced further back than the Washington Conference. One was the peculiarly unbalanced composition of the American fleet. For fifteen years prior to the conference, speed had been of secondary consideration in planning our battle fleet. We had not constructed enough cruisers to perform the duties of advance guards, outposts, or eyes of the battleships. Money appropriated by Congress had gone mainly into the construction of capital ships. Moreover, the undiscussed problems of capture at sea and the convertibility of merchant ships into cruisers were other underlying difficulties which prevented an understanding.

The Three-Power Conference approach to disarmament was purely technical, and naval experts were in charge of the proceedings. No proposal was advanced like that Secretary Hughes made at Washington, which went beyond numerical calculations of ratios of tons and guns, which translated idealism into practical propositions. At Geneva the United States had no concessions to make, no offering of vessels as in the conference of 1921. There was a difference between the actual scrapping of ships built and building and the threat to construct if agreement were not reached. Even the ordinary layman could see the dramatic sacrifices made at Washington. But the British proposition to limit the 8-inch-gun cruiser at the Geneva Conference was viewed with skepticism and could not be interpreted as a concession. Great Britain had been the first to initiate extensive construction of these super-cruisers and had, therefore, set the pace in a new, dangerous, and expensive form of competition. Her action could be interpreted in a fashion similar to her proposal to limit dreadnoughts at the second Hague Conference—a desire to force a halt in competition at the moment of her own great preponderance.

Failure of the British and Americans to reach an agreement in 1927 was more unfortunate than was realized at the time and of greater import for its effects on the Far Eastern situation than the temporary misunderstanding between the two nations. Viscount Cecil observes:

> In fact, it was even more serious than we knew, for up to that time Japanese policy had been essentially pacific and accommodating. A very few years later it changed its character and became unscrupulously adventurous, resulting in the Manchurian policy which began the series of international aggressions leading ultimately to the Polish war. It is at

> least possible that, if we had settled the cruiser question, as Japan was most anxious to do, we should have helped to strengthen the peace party in that country and the invasion of Manchuria might never have taken place. The fact that the break arose from Anglo-American differences was another serious feature, not only because any injury to our relations with the United States is to be deplored, but because such a difference is especially harmful in the Far East. It was the want of hearty co-operation between the two countries which encouraged Japan to attack Manchuria, and added greatly to the difficulty of stopping her.

With the American invention of a flexible yardstick, an agreement was possible which would permit Great Britain and the United States to have the type of fleet each required. The adoption of such a criterion, the change of governments in both countries with the resultant willingness of each nation to make concessions to the other's point of view, and the signing of the Kellogg-Briand Pact created an atmosphere in which discussions of naval limitation could be resumed. If that agreement was to help maintain international peace, armaments could not longer be employed for the furtherance of national policies. If the United States and Great Britain were sincere in their adherence to the Pact, the principle of "offensive power parity" or "combat parity" had lost its meaning. With political differences settled, the problems of the "offensive" 8-inch-gun cruiser versus the "defensive" 6-inch-gun cruiser, and the arming of merchant ships—problems which had been insoluble at Geneva in 1927—were easily resolved at London. The London Conference of 1930 demonstrated that all classes of naval vessels could be limited by diplomacy.

In the years following the Washington settlement, and especially after the Geneva Three-Power Conference, when attention was focused on the Anglo-American controversy over equality, Japan was regarded of secondary importance in naval considerations. She made no impossible demands and was ready to accept almost any arrangement on which Great Britain and the United States would agree so long as she secured about the same ratios as at Washington. Nevertheless, during the twenties Japan quietly engaged in a building program which gave her, in both cruisers and submarines, an actual ratio somewhat in excess of 5–3. Thus, when the first London Conference met she had achieved virtual parity in cruisers with the United States and tonnage superiority in submarines. While the United States and Great Britain debated the problem of naval "equality," the conflict between our country and Japan arose from the endeavor on the part of the United States to extend the 5–3 ratio to auxiliary categories, which the oriental power countered with an increasingly persistent effort to gain recognition of a higher ratio. At London, Japan secured a slightly higher ratio in cruisers and parity in submarines. But far more portentous was her announcement that five years later she might demand parity in all categories.

Between the signing of the London Treaty of 1930 and the London Conference of 1935, there were increased political tension in the Mediterranean and undeclared wars in Ethiopia and Asia. Japan's conquest of Manchuria and her threat of hegemony in the Far East conflicted with both American and British interests. Fearing that the United States and Great Britain might some day challenge her imperialistic ventures, Japan demanded parity, for equality from her point of view would only mean a 10–5 ratio in the face of a combined Anglo-American force.

In such a charged international atmosphere, the conference of 1935 seemed doomed to failure. The chief difficulty arose over the question whether disarmament should rest on the principle of equality of armament or equality of security. Japanese demands for a so-called "upper limit" amounted to changing the 5–5–3 ratio to 5–5–5. Neither English-speaking power was willing to accede to this proposal, for it would have given their rival more than equality of security, which she already had in the China Sea and the Pacific Ocean. Thereupon Japan withdrew from the conference, and the system of combined quantitative and qualitative limitation of naval armaments ended. Although the United States preferred a combination of the two methods, she was forced to the conclusion that qualitative even without quantitative restriction would offer distinct advantages, and would certainly be better than no limitation at all. Thus the London Treaty of 1936 differed from its predecessors by giving more prominence to restrictions upon the size of ships and the caliber of their guns.

By 1936 the United States and Great Britain were firmly resolved they should have no competitive building. Those two powers, which had maintained an unbroken peace for over a century, were able to agree because their national policies coincided. On this point Simonds and Emeny write:

> If American policy envisaged the annexation of Canada or of the corridor separating Alaska from the United States, or if British policy contemplated the seizure of Alaska to anticipate such annexation, no Anglo-American agreement in the matter of naval strength would have been possible. For parity would have conferred such decisive superiority upon the United States in American waters that Canada would be completely cut off from British aid, while the superiority Great Britain would demand for the defense of Canada would constitute a threat to the security of the United States.

Why should Anglo-American relations have been disturbed for a decade over "parity," and for what reason was that term ever applied to naval limitation? So far as the United States was concerned, equality with Great Britain was not based upon any potential danger, but was a matter of national pride and prestige. If parity with Great Britain required a naval tonnage far in excess of what our country wanted to construct and greater than it needed for national security, why should this nation have insisted upon it? Why could we not accept British superiority? On the other hand, what danger did Great Britain face in granting superiority in 8-inch-gun cruisers to the United States if the total British tonnage guaranteed the security of the Empire? If war between the two English-speaking countries was out of the question, should one of them have worried whether the other built 8-inch-gun or 6-inch-gun cruisers? The answer to this question was complicated by the fact that Britain was most directly concerned with the navies of other powers. The effect of the increase of American naval strength on the relations of Great Britain with other states worried British statesmen. Although Britain might not notice what ships were constructed on this side of the Atlantic, other nations would; with these countries Great Britain was concerned.

Furthermore, why were the two great sea powers able to agree upon parity in 1929? Finally, why were they firmly opposed to granting parity to Japan? And why did Japan insist upon it when parity meant an unassailable supremacy in the Far East? The answers to the foregoing questions are to be found in the national policies of the states concerned. The arguments over parity, equality, minimum requirements, "offensive" 8-inch-gun cruisers, submarines, etc., were simply political difficulties dressed in technical garb.

The approach to disarmament based on purely technical grounds, on an attempt to fix a ratio of the relative military and naval strengths to be allotted the different states, was bound to fail because it presupposed that nations would still go on fighting each other. The technical justification of military and naval requirements rested upon the experience of past battles and upon the anticipation of future wars. And every nation defined "requirements" to suit its own particular situation. So long as the approach to the problem was based upon old fears and old suspicions there could be little hope of disarmament. No country could obtain security for itself by a fixed minimum or maximum of armaments which it might create.

Hence the Washington, Geneva, and London naval conferences taken together achieved no general limitation of armaments and thus contributed little to permanent peace. The Washington Treaty ensured Great Britain, the United States, and Japan absolute superiority in the regions of primary interest to each of them. Of the three powers, Japan made the greatest gains in security for herself, and at the same time removed all possibility of interference with her national policies. When, in pursuance of an aggressive nationalism and in total disregard of the Nine-Power Treaty to respect Chinese territory, that oriental power invaded Manchuria, Britain and America lacked the means to make an effective protest. At Washington they had surrendered the right to maintain adequate naval bases in the Far East and had agreed to a naval ratio that rendered successful intervention impossible. Even more disastrous for them, as subsequent events demonstrated, the two English-speaking nations underestimated the overwhelming significance and striking power of airplanes, and they neglected to prepare an adequate defense against that weapon for their treaty fleets.

Twentieth century development of aircraft has presented the world with a revolutionary means of transportation, communication, and destruction. The invention of Wilbur and Orville Wright should have operated to improve the distribution of resources and to increase goodwill among peoples. Actually, it has operated principally to make war most efficient and more devastating.

Representatives at the postwar naval conferences, however, practically ignored this new weapon. They argued and debated for days and weeks over naval ratios, parity, caliber of guns, and tonnage of ships, thinking and scheming in terms of Jutland or Skagerrak. Within two decades after the Washington Conference, and only five years after the second London Conference, sea power had been shorn of much of its effectiveness when used without air support. In World War II the battleship had to face as an adversary the airplane, which had lifted "striking force into a third dimension, into a medium which the surface vessel cannot penetrate." In the battle for Crete, where there was a "clear-cut confrontation of overwhelming sea power and overwhelming air power," air power triumphed. At the outbreak of the Pacific war the United States was particularly deficient in modern land-based fighters and in carriers. In the first phase of that war, therefore, the Japanese, because of their initial air superiority, won one success after another in the Philippines, Malaya, the Netherlands East Indies, the Islands of the Pacific, Burma, and in the Bay of Bengal.

The officials of the United States Strategic Bombing Survey were of the opinion that "one thousand planes in the Philippines, at least equal in performance to the best then available to the Japanese, including types effective against shipping, well-manned, equipped and supplied, and dispersed on some 50 airfields, would have seriously impeded the original Japanese advance if knowledge of their existence had not entirely dissuaded the Japanese from making the attempt."

The destructive aërial blows Japan dealt Pearl Harbor on December 7, 1941, put out of commission 18 vessels, 177 planes, and a large floating dry-dock, as well as other essential piers and dockyards. That attack crippled the United States Pacific air and naval forces for the first year of the war, and prevented them from operating to save the Philippines. The supremacy of the air arm was again clearly demonstrated by the fact that airplanes sank the *Prince of Wales*, the *Repulse*, the *Haruna*, and the *Arizona*. Naval experts had given assurance that the first-named vessel was unsinkable. Moreover, in the decisive Battle of the Bismarck Sea, March 3–5, 1943, United Nations' land-based air power scored such a complete victory that to the Japanese it assumed the proportion of a major disaster.

Upon entering the war, the United States was deficient not only in the numbers but in the quality of many of its aircraft types. We were forced thereafter into hasty and costly modification and technical development programs to raise the performance of our aircraft to acceptable standards. These programs could have been conducted more efficiently and economically during prewar years. But, "in the actual conduct of the war we more quickly grasped the strategic revolution brought about by the capabilities of air power than did the Japanese. By the end of 1943 we had achieved through combat and the augmentation of our forces, such clear-cut superiority over the Japanese in all elements of air power that eventual victory was assured."

Japan, more than any other ocean power, watched the growth of air armaments with ill-concealed alarm, and made concessions on naval ratios only after having prevented the further construction of naval and air bases within striking distance of her shores. In the conversations preliminary to the London Conference of 1935 Admiral Yamamoto contended that developments in aviation had upset the equilibrium established in the

Pacific by the Washington Treaty, to the advantage of an attacking fleet. At this second London Conference the Japanese delegates proposed the abolition of what they termed the "aggressive" aircraft carrier, realizing, of course, its potential menace to their teeming, lightly-built cities, all of which were within bombing range of planes from large carriers. With few British and American bastions in the Far East, with Singapore and Pearl Harbor 3000 and 3400 miles respectively from Japan, the aircraft carrier has served as a floating base from which planes have operated directly against the Japanese cities and fleet.

The Japanese contention of the increased danger to their Empire from air power was certainly justifiable and their fears of modern aviation were realized in World War II. During that war American naval aviation in the Pacific won both success and distinction in its basic purpose of destroying hostile air and naval forces, in amphibious warfare involving attacks in support of landing operations, in reconnaisance over the sea, and in challenging and defeating land-based planes over positions held in force by the Japanese. Moreover, because of its mobility and the striking power and long range of its weapons, the aircraft carrier proved itself a major and vital element of naval strength. The epic Battle of the Coral Sea demonstrated how devastating a modern carrier could be. Within a period of eleven hours, on May 4, 1942, American pilots, gunners, and carrier crews damaged or destroyed more warships, transport, and auxiliary vessels than ever before had been wrecked by airplanes in a single sustained bombardment. Finally, the first bombs to fall on Tokyo were launched from carrier-based planes, while Japan's dramatic capitulation followed the dropping from the air of two small atomic bombs on Hiroshima and Nagasaki.

This study has emphasized and reiterated that armies, navies, and air fleets are the most important instruments of national policy. A country's armaments must, therefore, be adequate to sustain its commitments, and its preparedness must coincide with and be sufficient to support its foreign policies. To this simple and cardinal principle the United States government failed to adhere throughout the twenties and thirties and the American people have paid dearly for the mistake.

Certain of our foreign policies, namely, the maintenance of the Open Door and the territorial integrity and political entity of China, could not be enforced by our warships and airplanes. An attempt by Great Britain and the United States to stabilize and protect China and to police the Orient was bound to lead to a war with Japan, a struggle which the English-speaking powers would find difficult to win.

Therefore, the questions naturally arise: If our treaty fleet and bases were inadequate to enforce certain of our Far Eastern policies, should not those policies have been revised or abandoned? Or should we have built more battleships and airplanes and fortified more bases?

Building overwhelming navies and air fleets and maintaining large imperial forces would not have proved a satisfactory solution of the Far Eastern question. Nor was conceding ships and granting security ratios the proper approach. The concessions that Great Britain and the United States should have made would have cost little and would have held no danger for anyone. Only two years after the Washington Conference, the American Congress in 1923 largely undid the work and destroyed the spirit created there by terminating the Gentlemen's Agreement, and by passing an "unwise, impolitic and dangerous" exclusion law, which for thirty years the United States and Japanese governments had tried to avoid. In 1925 the United States declined Japan's offer of a draft treaty which would have given American authorities complete control over Japanese immigration upon a basis of reciprocity. Thus the first blow at the spirit of the Washington treaties was struck, not by Japan, but by the United States. Also irritating to the leading oriental power was the British Commonwealth policy of prohibiting immigration to Australia, New Zealand, and Canada to all but Caucasians. As though these acts were not sufficient, the Smoot-Hawley tariff of 1930 and the British imperial preference policy did further damage.

Actually, what was needed in the twenties and thirties was not a series of disarmament conferences to palaver over such terms and questions as war potential, budgetary limitation versus limitation of material, displacement and replacement of ships, caliber of guns, parity, and naval ratios among nations—problems which will never be resolved permanently so long as primary sources of friction are not removed. Instead of carrying on discussions about the foregoing subjects, the states should have established a system of collective security against aggression, and then proceeded to the gradual removal of the causes of war, peaceful reconsideration of treaties which had become inapplicable, recognition of the right of defeated countries to equality in armaments, readjustment of distorted boundary lines, liberalization of immigration and tariff policies, redefinition or abrogation of the Open Door policy, redistribution of colonial territories and raw materials, and reëxamination and revision of imperialism.

Military preparations are the visible signs of national passions and international unrest, and so long as the utility of armaments as instruments of policy is not reduced, limitation will not be achieved. Disarmament, both by the direct method of restriction and by the indirect process of organizing collective security, has failed tragically because all peoples have coveted national security but have envisioned different means of achieving it. The supreme desire of Great Britain was peace—that peace in Europe and throughout the world which would bring prosperity to the British Empire. To attain that end the United Kingdom advocated land disarmament, for large standing armies were not essential to her security. Moreover, they might disturb the peace of Europe and involve England in another Continental war. Britain was determined, however, to maintain naval superiority in all regions vital to her. At the same time, the primary concern of the United States was peace and noninvolvement in European quarrels. Security for the homeland had long since been attained and was no grave problem. No population pressures disturbed the country, and self-sufficiency in the economic field, which removed the menace of blockade, reconciled the American people to the *status quo.* Great Britain and the United States, although satisfied with their territorial possessions and sincere in their acceptance of the world *status quo,* were not prepared to defend it in regions where their interests were not vital. France, too, desired peace, but peace based upon either Anglo-American guarantees of French security or an effective League of Nations. The Soviet Union, likewise, was ready to respect the *status quo* and the territorial integrity of other nations. Each of these powers was fairly satisfied with its geographic boundaries. On the other hand, Germany, Italy, and Japan found the *status quo* intolerable because it restricted them to limits they considered incompatible with their future national development.

The post-World War I peoples were therefore divided into two classes: those satisfied and those dissatisfied with the *status quo*. The French, British, and Americans were in the first group. They had already secured what they wanted, did not intend to expand further, and consequently believed expansion to be generally wrong. The Germans, Japanese, and Italians sought security through the revision of the existing frontiers; they intended to expand because some important principle seemed to make it right in their particular cases. The determination of the dissatisfied or "renovating" states to expand endangered the peace of the world even more than did the imperialism of those powers of the nineteenth century which believed that expansion was the "white man's burden," the "*mission civilisatrice*," or "manifest destiny.". . .

Additional Reading

R. L. Buell, *The Washington Conference* (1922).
R. H. Ferrell, *American Diplomacy in the Great Depression* (1957).
D. F. Fleming, *The United States and World Organization, 1920–1933* (1938).
A. W. Griswold, *The Far Eastern Policy of the United States* (1938).
Y. Ichihashi, *The Washington Conference and After* (1928).
Raymond G. O'Connor, *Perilous Equilibrium: The United States and the London Naval Conference of 1930* (1962).
Harold and Margaret Sprout, *Toward a New Order of Sea Power* (1940).
J. Chalmers Vinson, *The Parchment Peace: the United States Senate and the Washington Conference, 1921–1922* (1955).

17 *PEARL HARBOR: F.D.R., War Monger or Statesman?*

The 1930's were years of deepening isolationist sentiment in America. Disillusionment with the 1917 Great Crusade, the menace of new aggression in the Far East and Europe, and the problems of depression at home made the majority of citizens increasingly determined not to become involved again in an overseas war. The Nye Committee investigations of the connection between munitions makers, bankers, and war in 1917 suggested means of avoiding another unnecessary entanglement. The result of these factors was passage of neutrality legislation in 1935–1937, designed to prevent a future involvement by abandoning much of America's traditional defense of neutral rights. In future wars, American citizens would be prohibited from loaning money or selling arms to belligerents, and from traveling on belligerent passenger ships.

President Franklin D. Roosevelt and a growing number of influential citizens became convinced that isolationist policies would not adequately safeguard the nation's interests against the Axis threat in Europe and the Japanese expansionist drive in the Far East. Efforts were made to re-educate the American public and to use American influence on the side of the resistors of aggression. After the European War began in September, 1939, the Roosevelt administration moved from making the American market available to Great Britain and her allies to the extension of material aid and a posture just short of formal hostilities with Germany. In the Pacific, efforts to check Japan's drives in China and in southeastern Asia took the form of repeated warnings and moral condemnations and tightening economic coercion: the restrictive licensing of exports of petroleum and scrap metals in July, 1940, and the embargoing of the exportation of aviation gasoline outside the Western Hemisphere; in September, 1940, in reaction to the signing of the Rome-Berlin-Tokyo Tripartite Alliance, exports of scrap iron and steel were also prohibited; and in July, 1941, in response to the ominous Japanese occupation of southern Indo-China, all Japanese assets in the United States were frozen, which meant that all trade including vital oil shipments was halted. War came in December, 1941, as the result of Japanese attacks in the Pacific; Germany and Italy responded to their ally's actions by also declaring war on the United States.

Since 1945, both political and scholarly debate has raged about the causes and wisdom of the American involvement in World War II. In a very real sense, this was merely a continuation of the pre-Pearl Harbor political controversies on foreign policy, temporarily silenced by the need for wartime unity, and of the historical dialogue on the Great Crusade in World War I. Historians naturally sought to relate as fully as possible the events culminating in the second global holocaust in the 20th century. In addition, many Americans were soon dismayed at the shape of the postwar world, in which the United States and its friends seemed even more insecure than in 1939–1941, in the face of a worldwide Communist drive for empire. Frustration, disillusionment, and weariness with the costs of the Cold War intermingled with domestic politics to lead to a frantic search of the historical record for convenient scapegoats on which to blame the nation's plight. Among scholars, critics of F.D.R.'s foreign policies and the war entry have again been styled "revisionists," while defenders are best described as "internationalists." Although the exchanges have been marked by impassioned charges of blunders and plots, some accomplishments have resulted from the academic battle. Official and private papers have become available more rapidly than after the First World War; the story has therefore been more completely related, and several noteworthy scholarly volumes have been published.*

DOCUMENTS

1. Steps toward a "Shooting War" in the Atlantic

With the Nazi attack on Poland and the formal beginning of World War II in September, 1939, President Roosevelt successfully sought to amend the neutrality laws to permit Allied arms purchases. The Fourth Neutrality Act on November 4, 1939, repealed the arms embargo and permitted "cash and carry" sales to the belligerents. The fall of France in June of 1940 indicated that more had to be done if Great Britain was to survive, which Roosevelt believed American interests required. In response to urgent British requests, fifty World War I destroyers were exchanged, on executive authority only, for defense bases from Newfoundland to the Caribbean. Following the presidential election, Roosevelt reluctantly decided that even more aid was mandatory, and after a fireside chat urging that the United States should be an "arsenal of democracy," he proposed the Lend-Lease scheme to Congress. It was approved on March 11, 1941. These measures, although patently unneutral and scathingly condemned by non-interventionists, received the support of the majority of Americans. Patrolling and then convoying followed passage of Lend-Lease and eventually clashes resulted between American naval vessels and German submarines. In justifying "shoot on sight" orders because of German U-boat attacks, Roosevelt neglected to tell the American people that the destroyer *Greer* had been trailing the underseas craft before being fired upon.

The Destroyer-Bases Swap: Message of President Roosevelt to the Congress, September 3, 1940

I transmit herewith for the information of the Congress notes exchanged between the British Ambassador at Washington and the Secretary of State on September 2, 1940, under which this Government has acquired the right to lease naval and air bases in Newfoundland, and in the islands of Bermuda, the Bahamas, Jamaica, St. Lucia, Trinidad, and Antigua, and in British Guiana; also a copy of an opinion of the Attorney General dated August 27, 1940, regarding my authority to consummate this arrangement.

The right to bases in Newfoundland and Bermuda are gifts—generously given and gladly received. The other bases mentioned have been acquired in exchange for fifty of our over-age destroyers.

* See Wayne S. Cole, "American Entry in World War II: A Historiographical Appraisal," *Mississippi Valley Historical Review, XLIII* (1957), 595–617.

This is not inconsistent in any sense with our status of peace. Still less is it a threat against any nation. It is an epochal and far-reaching act of preparation for continental defense in the face of grave danger.

Preparation for defense is an inalienable prerogative of a sovereign state. Under present circumstances this exercise of sovereign right is essential to the maintenance of our peace and safety. This is the most important action in the reinforcement of our national defense that has been taken since the Louisiana Purchase. Then as now, considerations of safety from overseas attack were fundamental.

The value to the Western Hemisphere of these outposts of security is beyond calculation. Their need has long been recognized by our country, and especially by those primarily charged with the duty of charting and organizing our own naval and military defense. They are essential to the protection of the Panama Canal, Central America, the Northern portion of South America, The Antilles, Canada, Mexico, and our own Eastern and Gulf Seaboards. Their consequent importance in hemispheric defense is obvious. For these reasons I have taken advantage of the present opportunity to acquire them.

Lend-Lease Aid to the Allies: Speech by President Roosevelt to the Congress, January 6, 1941

I address you, the Members of the Seventy-seventh Congress, at a moment unprecedented in the history of the Union. I use the word "unprecedented," because at no previous time has American security been as seriously threatened from without as it is today.

Our national policy is this:

First, by an impressive expression of the public will and without regard to partisanship, we are committed to all-inclusive national defense.

Second, by an impressive expression of the public will and without regard to partisanship, we are committed to full support of all those resolute peoples, everywhere, who are resisting aggression and are thereby keeping war away from our hemisphere. By this support, we express our determination that the democratic cause shall prevail; and we strengthen the defense and security of our own Nation.

Third, by an impressive expression of the public will and without regard to partisanship, we are committed to the proposition that principles of morality and considerations for our own security will never permit us to acquiesce in a peace dictated by aggressors and sponsored by appeasers. We know that enduring peace cannot be bought at the cost of other people's freedom.

In the recent national election there was no substantial difference between the two great parties in respect to that national policy. No issue was fought out on this line before the American electorate. Today, it is abundantly evident that American citizens everywhere are demanding and supporting speedy and complete action in recognition of obvious danger.

Therefore, the immediate need is a swift and driving increase in our armament production.

To change a whole nation from a basis of peacetime production of implements of peace to a basis of wartime production of implements of war is no small task. And the greatest difficulty comes at the beginning of the program, when new tools and plant facilities and new assembly lines and shipways must first be constructed before the actual matériel begins to flow steadily and speedily from them.

The Congress, of course, must rightly keep itself informed at all times of the progress of the program. However, there is certain information, as the Congress itself will readily recognize, which, in the interests of our own security and those of the nations we are supporting, must of needs be kept in confidence.

New circumstances are constantly begetting new needs for our safety. I shall ask this Congress for greatly increased new appropriations and authorizations to carry on what we have begun.

I also ask this Congress for authority and for funds sufficient to manufacture additional munitions and war supplies of many kinds, to be turned over to those nations which are now in actual war with aggressor nations.

Our most useful and immediate role is to act as an arsenal for them as well as for ourselves. They do not need man power. They do need billions of dollars worth of the weapons of defense.

The time is near when they will not be able to pay for them in ready cash. We cannot, and will not, tell them they must surrender, merely because of present inability to pay for the weapons which we know they must have.

I do not recommend that we make them a loan of dollars with which to pay for these weapons—a loan to be repaid in dollars.

I recommend that we make it possible for those nations to continue to obtain war materials in the United States, fitting their orders into our own program. Nearly all of their matériel would, if the time ever came, be useful for our own defense.

Taking counsel of expert military and naval authorities, considering what is best for our own security, we are free to decide how much should be kept here and how much should be sent abroad to our friends who by their determined and heroic resistance are giving us time in which to make ready our own defense.

For what we send abroad, we shall be repaid, with a reasonable time following the close of hostilities, in similar materials, or, at our option, in other goods of many kinds which they can produce and which we need.

Let us say to the democracies: "We Americans are vitally concerned in your defense of freedom. We are putting forth our energies, our resources, and our organizing powers to give you the strength to regain and maintain a free world. We shall send you, in ever-increasing numbers, ships, planes, tanks, guns. This is our purpose and our pledge."

In fulfillment of this purpose we will not be intimidated by the threats of dictators that they will regard as a breach of international law and as an act of war our aid to the democracies which dare to resist their aggression. Such aid is not an act of war, even if a dictator should unilaterally proclaim it so to be.

When the dictators are ready to make war upon us, they will not wait for an act of war on our part. They did not wait for Norway or Belgium or the Netherlands to commit an act of war.

Their only interest is in a new one-way international law, which lacks mutuality in its observance, and, therefore, becomes an instrument of oppression.

The happiness of future generations of Americans may well depend upon how effective and how immediate we can make our aid felt. No one can tell the exact character of the emergency situations that we may be called upon to meet. The Nation's hands must not be tied when the Nation's life is in danger.

We must all prepare to make the sacrifices that the emergency—as serious as war itself—demands. Whatever stands in the way of speed and efficiency in defense preparations must give way to the national need. . . .

In the future days, which we seek to make secure, we look forward to a world founded upon four essential human freedoms.

The first is freedom of speech and expression—everywhere in the world.

The second is freedom of every person to worship God in his own way—everywhere in the world.

The third is freedom from want—which, translated into world terms, means economic understandings which will secure to every nation a healthy peacetime life for its inhabitants—everywhere in the world.

The fourth is freedom from fear—which, translated into world terms, means a world-wide reduction of armaments to such a point and in such a thorough fashion that no nation will be in a position to commit an act of physical aggression against any neighbor—anywhere in the world.

That is no vision of a distant millennium. It is a definite basis for a kind of world attainable in our own time and generation. That kind of world is the very antithesis of the so-called new order of tyranny which the dictators seek to create with the crash of a bomb.

To that new order we oppose the great conception—the moral order. A good society is able to face schemes of world domination and foreign revolutions alike without fear. . . .

Roosevelt's "Shoot on Sight" Address, September 11, 1941

The Navy Department of the United States has reported to me that on the morning of September fourth the United States destroyer *Greer*, proceeding in full daylight towards Iceland, had reached a point southeast of Greenland. She was carrying American mail to Iceland. She was flying the American flag. Her identity as an American ship was unmistakable.

She was then and there attacked by a submarine. Germany admits that it was a German submarine. The submarine deliberately fired a torpedo at the *Greer*, followed later by another torpedo attack. In spite of what Hitler's propaganda bureau has invented, and in spite of what any American obstructionist organization may prefer to believe, I tell you the blunt

fact that the German submarine fired first upon this American destroyer without warning, and with deliberate design to sink her.

Our destroyer, at the time, was in waters which the Government of the United States had declared to be waters of self-defense—surrounding outposts of American protection in the Atlantic. . . .

This was piracy—legally and morally. It was not the first nor the last act of piracy which the Nazi Government has committed against the American flag in this war. Attack has followed attack. . . .

The important truth is that these acts of international lawlessness are a manifestation of a design which has been made clear to the American people for a long time. It is the Nazi design to abolish the freedom of the seas and to acquire absolute control and domination of the seas for themselves.

For with control of the seas in their own hands, the way can become clear for their next step—domination of the United States and the Western Hemisphere by force. Under Nazi control of the seas, no merchant ship of the United States or of any other American republic would be free to carry on any peaceful commerce, except by the condescending grace of this foreign and tyrannical power. The Atlantic Ocean which has been, and which should always be, a free and friendly highway for us would then become a deadly menace to the commerce of the United States, to the coasts of the United States, and to the inland cities of the United States.

The Hitler Government, in defiance of the laws of the sea and of the recognized rights of all other nations, has presumed to declare, on paper, that great areas of the seas—even including a vast expanse lying in the Western Hemisphere—are to be closed, and that no ships may enter them for any purpose, except at peril of being sunk. Actually they are sinking ships at will and without warning in widely separated areas both within and far outside of these far-flung pretended zones.

This Nazi attempt to seize control of the oceans is but a counterpart of the Nazi plots now being carried on throughout the Western Hemisphere —all designed toward the same end. For Hitler's advance guards—not only his avowed agents but also his dupes among us—have sought to make ready for him footholds and bridgeheads in the New World, to be used as soon as he has gained control of the oceans.

His intrigues, his plots, his machinations, his sabotage in this New World are all known to the Government of the United States. Conspiracy has followed conspiracy. . . .

To be ultimately successful in world-mastery, Hitler knows that he must get control of the seas. He must first destroy the bridge of ships which we are building across the Atlantic, over which we shall continue to roll the implements of war to help destroy him and all his works in the end. He must wipe out our patrol on sea and in the air. He must silence the British Navy.

It must be explained again and again to people who like to think of the United States Navy as an invincible protection, that this can be true only if the British Navy survives. That is simple arithmetic.

For if the world outside the Americas falls under Axis domination, the shipbuilding facilities which the Axis powers would then possess in all of Europe, in the British Isles, and in the Far East would be much greater than all the shipbuilding facilities and potentialities of all the Americas—not only greater but two or three times greater. Even if the United States threw all its resources into such a situation, seeking to double and even redouble the size of our Navy, the Axis powers, in control of the rest of the world, would have the man-power and the physical resources to outbuild us several times over.

It is time for all Americans of all the Americas to stop being deluded by the romantic notion that the Americas can go on living happily and peacefully in a Nazi-dominated world. . . .

We have sought no shooting war with Hitler. We do not seek it now. But neither do we want peace so much that we are willing to pay for it by permitting him to attack our naval and merchant ships while they are on legitimate business.

I assume that the German leaders are not deeply concerned by what we Americans say or publish about them. We cannot bring about the downfall of Nazism by the use of long-range invective.

But when you see a rattlesnake poised to strike, you do not wait until he has struck before you crush him.

These Nazi submarines and raiders are the rattlesnakes of the Atlantic. They are a menace to the free pathways of the high seas. They are a challenge to our sovereignty. They hammer at our most precious rights when they attack ships of the American flag—symbols of our independence, our freedom, our very life. . . .

It is no act of war on our part when we decide to protect the seas which are vital to American defense. The aggression is not ours. Ours is solely defense.

But let this warning be clear. From now on, if German or Italian vessels of war enter the waters the protection of which is necessary for American defense they do so at their own peril.

The orders which I have given as Commander-in-Chief to the United States Army and Navy are to carry out that policy—at once.

The sole responsibility rests upon Germany. There will be no shooting unless Germany continues to seek it. . . .

2. *Who Served an Ultimatum, Japan or the United States?*

Revisionists have emphasized that the American government knew through the Magic code intercepts that the Japanese offer of the *modus vivendi* on November 20, 1941, was final and if it failed would be followed by hostilities. The Hull reply six days later, therefore, has been described by these writers as an ultimatum. Secretary Hull later stated that he and the President believed that to accept the Japanese plan would have been an abandonment of Nationalist China; they viewed the American reply of November 26 as merely a formal restating of the American position for the sake of the historical record.

Draft Proposal Handed by the Japanese Ambassador (Nomura) to the Secretary of State, November 20, 1941

1. Both the Governments of Japan and the United States undertake not to make any armed advancement into any of the regions in the Southeastern Asia and the Southern Pacific area excepting the part of French Indo-China where the Japanese troops are stationed at present.

2. The Japanese Government undertakes to withdraw its troops now stationed in French Indo-China upon either the restoration of peace between Japan and China or the establishment of an equitable peace in the Pacific area.

In the meantime the Government of Japan declares that it is prepared to remove its troops now stationed in the southern part of French Indo-China to the northern part of the said territory upon the conclusion of the present arrangement which shall later be embodied in the final agreement.

3. The Governments of Japan and the United States shall cooperate with a view to securing the acquisition of those goods and commodities which the two countries need in Netherlands East Indies.

4. The Governments of Japan and the United States mutually undertake to restore their commercial relations to those prevailing prior to the freezing of the assets.

The Government of the United States shall supply Japan a required quantity of oil.

5. The Government of the United States undertakes to refrain from such measures and actions as will be prejudicial to the endeavors for the restoration of general peace between Japan and China.

Document Handed by the Secretary of State to the Japanese Ambassador (Nomura)

WASHINGTON, NOVEMBER 26, 1941

OUTLINE OF PROPOSED BASIS FOR AGREEMENT BETWEEN THE UNITED STATES AND JAPAN

SECTION I

Draft Mutual Declaration of Policy

The Government of the United States and the Government of Japan both being solicitous for the peace of the Pacific affirm that their national policies are directed toward lasting and extensive peace throughout the Pacific area, that they have no territorial designs in that area, that they have no intention of threatening other countries or of using military force aggressively against any neighboring nation, and that, accordingly, in their national policies they will actively support and give practical application to the following fundamental principles upon which their relations with each other and with all other governments are based:

(1) The principle of inviolability of territorial integrity and sovereignty of each and all nations.
(2) The principle of non-interference in the internal affairs of other countries.
(3) The principle of equality, including equality of commercial opportunity and treatment.
(4) The principle of reliance upon international cooperation and conciliation for the prevention and pacific settlement of controversies and for improvement of international conditions by peaceful methods and processes.

The Government of Japan and the Government of the United States have agreed that toward eliminating chronic political instability, preventing recurrent economic collapse, and providing a basis for peace, they will actively support and practically apply the following principles in their economic relations with each other and with other nations and peoples:

(1) The principle of non-discrimination in international commercial relations.
(2) The principle of international economic cooperation and abolition of extreme nationalism as expressed in excessive trade restrictions.
(3) The principle of non-discriminatory access by all nations to raw material supplies.
(4) The principle of full protection of the interests of consuming countries and populations as regards the operation of international commodity agreements.
(5) The principle of establishment of such institutions and arrangements of international finance as may lend aid to the essential enterprises

and the continuous development of all countries and may permit payments through processes of trade consonant with the welfare of all countries.

SECTION II

Steps to Be Taken by the Government of the United States and by the Government of Japan

The Government of the United States and the Government of Japan propose to take steps as follows:

1. The Government of the United States and the Government of Japan will endeavor to conclude a multilateral non-aggression pact among the British Empire, China, Japan, the Netherlands, the Soviet Union, Thailand and the United States.

2. Both Governments will endeavor to conclude among the American, British, Chinese, Japanese, the Netherland and Thai Governments an agreement whereunder each of the Governments would pledge itself to respect the territorial integrity of French Indochina and, in the event that there should develop a threat to the territorial integrity of Indochina, to enter into immediate consultation with a view to taking such measures as may be deemed necessary and advisable to meet the threat in question. Such agreement would provide also that each of the Governments party to the agreement would not seek or accept preferential treatment in its trade or economic relations with Indochina and would use its influence to obtain for each of the signatories equality of treatment in trade and commerce with French Indochina.

3. The Government of Japan will withdraw all military, naval, air and police forces from China and from Indochina.

4. The Government of the United States and the Government of Japan will not support—militarily, politically, economically—any government or regime in China other than the National Government of the Republic of China with capital temporarily at Chungking.

5. Both Governments will give up all extraterritorial rights in China, including rights and interests in and with regard to international settlements and concessions, and rights under the Boxer Protocol of 1901.

Both Governments will endeavor to obtain the agreement of the British and other governments to give up extraterritorial rights in China, including rights in international settlements and in concessions and under the Boxer Protocol of 1901.

6. The Government of the United States and the Government of Japan will enter into negotiations for the conclusion between the United States and Japan of a trade agreement, based upon reciprocal most-favored-nation treatment and reduction of trade barriers by both countries, including an undertaking by the United States to bind raw silk on the free list.

7. The Government of the United States and the Government of Japan

will, respectively, remove the freezing restrictions on Japanese funds in the United States and on American funds in Japan.

8. Both Governments will agree upon a plan for the stabilization of the dollar-yen rate, with the allocation of funds adequate for this purpose, half to be supplied by Japan and half by the United States.

9. Both Governments will agree that no agreement which either has concluded with any third power or powers shall be interpreted by it in such a way as to conflict with the fundamental purpose of this agreement, the establishment and preservation of peace throughout the Pacific area.

10. Both Governments will use their influence to cause other governments to adhere to and to give practical application to the basic political and economic principles set forth in this agreement.

READINGS

1. F.D.R.: War Monger

Charles C. Tansill has written for World War II, as earlier for World War I, the most scholarly account from the revisionist point of view. The revisionists are agreed that the Axis was not a threat to the United States and that there was no imperative need for America to enter the conflict. Yet for reasons of his own—perhaps ambition or love of the British—President Roosevelt deliberately embarked on a course which he knew would probably lead to war. At the same time, he carefully concealed his true purposes from the American people and justified his policies on the grounds that they would keep the nation at peace. When Adolf Hitler refused to be baited into declaring war in the Atlantic, the United States entered via the "backdoor," by provoking Japan into the Pearl Harbor assault. Most historians decline to accept as valid such revisionist views.

Backdoor to War

CHARLES C. TANSILL

Roosevelt Regards Neutrality as an Outmoded Concept

While the President was pleading with Mussolini to remain neutral in the great conflict that was wrecking Europe, he himself was pushing America down the road to war. On April 16 it was reported that the Anglo-French Purchasing Commission could obtain planes of almost any type then being produced for the armed forces of the United States. This news encouraged the French Premier, Paul Reynaud, to send to Washington (May 14) the startling request that the American Government arrange for the "sale or lease of old destroyers." On the following day Winston Churchill, who displaced Chamberlain as Prime Minister on May 10, sent a more ambitious request that was quite breath-taking:

> All I ask now is that you [President Roosevelt] should proclaim non-belligerency, which would mean that you would help us with everything short of actually engaging armed forces. Immediate needs are: First of all, the loan of forty or fifty of your older destroyers; . . . Secondly, we want several hundred of the latest types of aircraft; . . . Thirdly, anti-aircraft equipment and ammunition. . . . Fourthly, the fact that our ore supply is being compromised from Sweden, from North Africa and perhaps from Northern Spain, makes it necessary to purchase steel in the United States. . . . I should like to feel reasonably sure that when we can pay no more, you will give us the stuff all the same. Fifthly, . . . the visit of a United States Squadron to Irish ports . . . would be invaluable.

The President replied that he could not make a deal concerning the destroyers "without authorization from Congress." Moreover, America "needed the destroyers" for its "own defences." Churchill greatly regretted this negative answer but he still hoped to get "at the earliest possible date" the "largest possible number of Curtiss P-40 fighters." In conclusion he

Charles Callan Tansill, *Backdoor to War: The Roosevelt Foreign Policy, 1933–1941*. Pp. 586–589, 595–599, 602–606, 611–615, 616, 639–642, 645–652.

sounded a loud note of alarm that he knew would profoundly affect the President. If Britain were "left by the United States to its fate," there was a definite danger that the British fleet might be turned over to the Germans as a bargaining point.

We have already noted that in 1939, while Chamberlain was still Prime Minister, Churchill began his momentous personal correspondence with President Roosevelt. It has been stated that one of the first cablegrams sent by Churchill to Roosevelt was phrased in a most grandiloquent manner. The gist of it has been given as follows: "I am half American and the natural person to work with you. It is evident we see eye to eye. Were I to become Prime Minister of Britain we could control the world."

Churchill states that he sent "nine hundred and fifty" of these cablegrams to the President and received "about eight hundred in reply." His relations with the American Chief Executive "gradually became so close that the chief business between our two countries was virtually conducted by these personal interchanges between him and me. . . . As head of the State as well as Head of the Government, Roosevelt spoke and acted with authority in every sphere."

It is obvious that Churchill regarded Roosevelt as an American dictator who had little concern for the opinions of Congress and the American people. With reference to the matter of war the Churchill cablegrams reveal that he believed that Roosevelt could plunge America into the conflict in Europe at any time he desired. The French Cabinet apparently had the same viewpoint.

The urgency of Churchill was translated into hysteria by Premier Reynaud. On May 18, Bullitt was informed by Alexis Léger, Secretary-General of the French Foreign Office, that Reynaud was about to request President Roosevelt to ask Congress for a declaration of war against Germany. Bullitt frankly informed Léger that such a request would be worse than useless: Congress would almost unanimously vote against such a declaration. The President then talked to Bullitt over the telephone and instructed him to say that "anything of this nature was out of the question." But Reynaud continued to press for the impossible. On May 22 he told Bullitt that the German tide was growing more menacing every minute. There was grave danger that the French public would insist upon a separate peace with Germany. In that event a German victory over Britain "would follow in a few weeks." After this dire event the Panama Canal would be destroyed by air bombardment and the "American Army would be able to offer little resistance." Prompt action by the American Government was "the only real guarantee that Hitler would not some day be in the White House."

A week later the Reynaud appeals grew more frantic. On May 28 he warned Bullitt that he had convincing evidence that "if France and England were conquered, Hitler would move almost immediately against the United States." The American fleet should be sent at once to the Mediterranean so as to exert pressure upon Mussolini to stay out of the war.

The President did not send the fleet to the Mediterranean but he decided to permit American pilots to fly planes, ordered by the Allies, to

Halifax and other ports in the Canadian maritime provinces. Before this decision the Dominion had been designated as a combat area and American nationals had not been allowed to enter it in aircraft belonging to belligerent nations. The President then urged Churchill to send additional planes to France but he was told that Britain needed all available aircraft for defense against expected German attack. Ambassador Bullitt became furious over this negative reply from Britain and he confided to Secretary Hull his belief that the British Cabinet "might be conserving their air force and fleet so as to use them as bargaining points in negotiations with Hitler."

Both the President and Secretary Hull discounted these observations of Bullitt. They were certain that while France "was finished," Britain, with the aid of American supplies, could withstand a German assault. It was imperative, therefore, that these supplies be rushed at once to British ports. Joseph C. Green, chief of the Division of Controls, brought to Secretary Hull's attention an old statute of May 12, 1917. The language of this statute could be interpreted so as to authorize the exchange of army and navy aircraft for new models of a more advanced type. Arrangements were made with a Buffalo concern to deliver to them fifty planes belonging to the Naval Reserve squadrons in exchange for planes of a "superior type." These planes were then rushed to Britain. But Churchill wanted more than planes. In order to meet his importunate requests, the President turned to the Acting Attorney General, Francis Biddle, who conveniently ruled that the Secretary of War had the right to sell surplus war supplies to "any corporation or individual upon such terms as may be deemed best."

General George C. Marshall, as Chief of Staff, now came to the front and directed his chief of Ordnance and his Assistant Chief of Staff to survey the entire list of American reserve ordnance and munitions stocks. On June 3 he approved these lists. The first list was a lengthy one. . . .

The Destroyer Deal

The fall of France imparted a sense of urgency to the Administration's program for aiding Britain by the sale or lease of war matériel. The President's qualms about constitutional limitations slowly disappeared under the drumfire of repeated requests from Churchill. Moreover, he brought into his Cabinet certain new members who were not averse to a prowar inclination. This was particularly true of the new Secretary of War, Henry L. Stimson, who was a notorious war hawk. It is apparent that after June 1940 the Administration embarked upon a phony bipartisan policy that pointed directly to American intervention in the European conflict.

This policy was given a green light on June 10 when Senator Sheppard offered an amendment to a pending defense bill authorizing the War Department to exchange unserviceable or surplus materials for others of which there was a scarcity. Senator Clark, of Missouri, declared that the purpose of the amendment was "an evasion of international law and of the Neutrality Act." But the amendment was adopted by a large majority and the measure finally became law on July 2, 1940.

In the meantime Senator David I. Walsh had sponsored legislation that would provide against any "limitation or reduction in the size of our Navy." The Act of June 28, 1940, embodied the ideas of Senator Walsh. It was not long, however, before the fertile mind of Benjamin Cohen, special assistant to the Attorney General, found several loopholes in this act. The President still had wide powers he could use without previous consultations with Congress. This opinion of Mr. Cohen was shrewdly argued but the Chief Executive "frankly doubted" if it would "stand up." He also feared that Congress was "in no mood at the present time to allow any form of sale."

These doubts were dissolved under the impact of pressure from Churchill. On June 24 he wrote to Mackenzie King and once more emphasized the danger that if England fell there was the possibility that Hitler would get the British fleet. Four days later, in a letter to Lord Lothian in Washington, he repeated this disturbing thought which should be repeated to Roosevelt. He also complained that Britain had "really not had any help worth speaking of from the United States so far." After more than a month of silence he wrote again to the President (July 31) to inform him that the need for destroyers had "become most urgent." The whole fate of the war might rest upon the speed with which these destroyers were delivered. He was confident that the President would not "let this crux of the battle go wrong" for want of the much-needed warships. When Lord Lothian spoke of an exchange of naval bases for destroyers, Churchill indicated his preference was for an indefinite lease and not an outright sale.

Churchill's cablegram to the President (July 31) had led to a Cabinet meeting in the White House on August 2. There was immediate agreement that "the survival of the British Isles under German attack might very possibly depend on their getting these destroyers," but there was also recognition that legislation would be "necessary" to authorize any deal concerning the destroyers. If the British Government would give positive assurances that the British fleet "would not under any conceivable circumstances fall into the hands of the Germans," the opposition in Congress would be "greatly lessened." Perhaps William Allen White would work upon Wendell Willkie, Joseph Martin, and Charles McNary and thus divide the Republican ranks! When the President talked with White over the telephone he elicited a promise from the famous editor to get in touch with Willkie at once.

There was no doubt in Churchill's mind that any transfer of American destroyers to Britain would be a "decidedly unneutral act by the United States." It would justify a declaration of war by Hitler. Such action would be eminently agreeable to Churchill who would ardently welcome American help in the struggle against the dictatorships. But the situation had to be handled carefully. When Lord Lothian (August 6) cabled that the President was exceedingly anxious for a pledge that the British fleet would not be turned over to the Germans in the event that Britain fell, Churchill refused to give one. The British nation would "not tolerate any discussion of what we should do if our island were overrun." It would be best to couple the transfer of destroyers with the lease of naval and air bases in Newfoundland and on some British islands in the Caribbean.

On August 13 the essential paragraphs in this agreement were worked out during a conference between the President, Secretaries Knox, Morgenthau, and Stimson, and Sumner Welles. In the meantime William Allen White had received assurances from Wendell Willkie that he would "not make a campaign issue of the transfer." The services of General Pershing were next enlisted. The old warrior warned the American public in a broadcast that Britain needed immediate aid. This could best be given by placing at the disposal of the British and Canadian governments "at least fifty over-age destroyers which are left from the days of the World War." Admirals Yarnell, Standley, and Stirling supported this viewpoint.

On August 16, President Roosevelt issued a statement that he was negotiating with the British Government for the acquisition of naval and air bases. Nothing was said about a deal for destroyers. Senator David I. Walsh was still showing strong opposition to such a transaction. With the hope of changing the Senator's opinion in this regard the President wrote him a letter with the familiar salutation, "Dear Dave." He assured the Senator that the British islands were "of the utmost importance to our national defence as naval and operating bases." After reminding him that Jefferson in 1803 had purchased Louisiana "without even consulting Congress," the President then expressed the hope that there would be no further opposition to a deal that would be the "finest thing for the nation that has been done in your lifetime and mine."

"Dear Dave" did not fall for this bait so he was later smeared as a loose character. But even so staunch a New Dealer as Secretary Hull had doubts about a destroyer deal and he regretfully informed Lord Lothian that in order "to meet the wishes of your Government an amendment to these provisions of law [the United States Code and the Act of June 28, 1940] may be necessary." But this would take time and Britain's need was immediate. In the meantime Churchill on August 20 had announced in Parliament that negotiations were in progress for leasing air and naval bases in Newfoundland and on British islands in the Caribbean to the United States. Two days later he explained to President Roosevelt the difficulties that would attend any exchange of letters that would admit "in any way that the munitions which you send us are a payment for the facilities." The dispatch of war matériel to Britain should seem to be "a separate spontaneous act on the part of the United States, arising out of their view of the world struggle." But Sumner Welles informed Lord Lothian that under existing legislation it was "utterly impossible" for the President to send destroyers to Britain as a spontaneous gift; they could be sent only as a *quid pro quo*.

On August 23 the President confessed to Secretary Hull that the negotiations with Britain "on the bases and destroyers have bogged down. Please see what you can do." In an extended conference among the President, Secretary Hull, and Lord Lothian the matter was further explored. Secretary Hull made it clear to the British Ambassador that the President "had no authority whatever to make a gift of public property to any Government or individual." But Attorney General Jackson had no trouble finding convenient loopholes in existing legislation. His assistant, Ben Cohen, had also discovered them some months previously. The Act of June 15, 1917, made it unlawful to send any ship out of the United States that was "built, armed or equipped as a vessel of war, with any intent or under any agreement or contract . . . that such vessel shall be delivered to a belligerent nation." This restriction did not apply "to vessels like the over-age destroyers which were not built, armed, equipped as, or converted into, vessels of war with the intent that they should enter the service of a belligerent."

Mr. Jackson blandly pushed aside the pertinent provisions of the Treaty of Washington (May 8, 1871) and Article 8 of the Hague Convention XIII of 1907 which required that a neutral government take measures to prevent the departure from its jurisdiction of any vessel intended to engage in belligerent operations, if the vessel was specially adapted within the neutral's jurisdiction to warlike use. The one precedent that Mr. Jackson adduced to support his contention concerning the transfer of destroyers was a most dubious one. Indeed, the opinion of the Attorney General was distinctly "phony" and was based upon the familiar dictum: "What's the Constitution between friends."

The way was now prepared for the destroyer deal. On September 2 notes were exchanged between Secretary Hull and Lord Lothian which first recited that the British Government, freely and without consideration, granted to the United States a lease for the "immediate establishment and use of naval and air bases and facilities" on the Avalon Peninsula and on the southern coast of Newfoundland, and on the east coast and on the Great Bay of Bermuda. The second item dealt with the establishment by the United States of air and naval bases on certain British territory in the Caribbean (Bahamas, Jamaica, Saint Lucia, Trinidad, Antigua, and British Guiana) in exchange "for naval and military equipment and material which the United States Government will transfer to His Majesty's Government." The leases would run for a period of 99 years. At the same time Churchill also gave an assurance that the British fleet would not be scuttled or surrendered. This assurance was not to be published.

From the viewpoint of international law the destroyer deal was definitely illegal. As Professor Herbert Briggs correctly remarks: "The supplying of these vessels by the United States Government to a belligerent is a violation of our neutral status, a violation of our national law, and a violation of international law." Professor Edwin Borchard expressed a similar opinion: "To the writer there is no possibility of reconciling the destroyer deal with neutrality, with the United States statutes, or with international law." The whole matter was correctly described by the *St. Louis Post-Dispatch* in a pertinent headline: "Dictator Roosevelt Commits an Act of War."

Lend-Lease—Back Door to Intervention in World War II

It was entirely fitting that lend-lease legislation should have a prelude of promises by the President that American boys would not be sent abroad to die along far-flung frontiers. It had been evident to the President in the summer of 1940 that American involvement in World War II might be just around the corner of the next year. Senator Wheeler had read between the lines of the President's pronouncements and when he saw the word *war* written in bold letters he tried to block such a contingency by a strongly-worded plank in the Democratic platform. But the pledge to keep out of "foreign wars" was nullified by the pregnant phrase—"except in case of attack." It would not be difficult for an Administration seeking war to push one of the Axis powers to the point where an attack was inevitable.

But the American people, like William Allen White, had to be fooled by pacific phrases. When the election currents in the fall of 1940 appeared to be making a turn towards Wendell Willkie, the President made some new pledges at Philadelphia on October 23: "To every man, woman and child in the nation I say this: Your President and your Secretary of State are following the road to peace. . . . We are arming ourselves not for any purpose of conquest or intervention in foreign disputes." A week later, in Boston, his pledge became more specific: "While I am talking to you mothers and fathers, I give you one more assurance. I have said this before, but I shall say it again and again and again: Your boys are not going to be sent into any foreign wars."

Robert Sherwood who helped to prepare this Boston speech had some qualms of conscience in later years: "For my own part, I think it was a mistake for him [the President] to go so far in yielding to the hysterical demands for sweeping reassurance, but, unfortunately for my own conscience, I happened at the time to be one of those who urged him to go the limit on this. . . . I burn inwardly whenever I think of those words 'again—and again—and again.'"

In the spring of 1941 these fires of conscience were burning very low in the President's entourage. Under the impact of appeals from Churchill in England the entire structure of American neutrality was finally demolished by the legislative bomb of lend-lease. This bomb was many months in the making. On November 6, 1940, Churchill wrote to Roosevelt to express his profound relief at the election results: "I feel you will not mind my saying that I prayed for your success and that I am truly thankful for it. . . . I must avow my sure faith that the lights by which we steer will bring us all safely to anchor." Those lights would lead America into the war.

On December 8, 1940, Churchill sent another long letter in which he outlined in great detail the pressing needs of Britain. In Churchill's eyes these needs were also America's needs because Britain was fighting our war as well as hers. The safety of the United States was "bound up with the survival and independence of the British Commonwealth of Nations." Therefore, America should rush to Britain war matériel of specified kinds together with the gift or loan "of a large number of American vessels of war." It was useless to expect Britain to pay for these loans. The moment was approaching when the British Government would "no longer be able to pay cash for shipping and other supplies." The few dollars Britain had left were badly needed for domestic requirements. It would be wrong "in principle" for Britain to be "divested of all saleable assets, so that after the victory was won with our blood, civilisation saved, and the time gained for the United States to be fully armed against all eventualities, we should stand stripped to the bone." America should bear a large part of the financial burden for a new crusade in Europe.

Roosevelt received this communication while he was cruising in the Caribbean. When he returned on December 16 he signified his ardent approval of aid to Britain at America's expense. On the following day, at a press conference, he recited an interesting parable:

> Suppose my neighbor's house catches fire and I have a length of garden hose four or five hundred feet away. If he can take my garden hose and connect it up with his hydrant, I may help him to put out the fire. Now what do I do? I don't say to him before that operation, "Neighbor, my garden hose cost me fifteen dollars; you have to pay me fifteen dollars for it." No! What is the transaction that goes on? I don't want fifteen dollars— I want my garden hose back after the fire is over. . . . What I am trying to do is to eliminate the dollar sign.

What he really meant to say was that he was trying to eliminate the dollar sign so far as Britain was concerned. The American taxpayers would have it before their anxious eyes for the next generation. But before they had time to make any estimates, a lend-lease bill was introduced in the House of Representatives. It bore the significant number H.R. 1776. In that year we declared our independence from Britain; in 1941 we put it into grave peril by giving Britain a blank check which Churchill filled in with great gusto and then sent back to Washington for Roosevelt's indorsement. Harry Hopkins was the contact man in this regard and while still in Britain he heard Churchill's famous broadcast in which the following dangerous nonsense was beamed to rapt American listeners:

> It seems now to be certain that the Government and the people of the United States intend to supply us with all that is necessary for victory. In the last war the United States sent two million men across the Atlantic. But this is not a war of vast armies, firing immense masses of shells at one another. We do not need the gallant armies which are forming throughout the American Union. We do not need them this year, nor next year, nor any year that I can foresee.

These assurances of Churchill were of the same stripe as the Roosevelt assurances during the last days of his campaign for re-election. He probably remembered Lord Northcliffe's sharp indictment of the American masses during the World War: "What sheep!" They could be sheared once more for British benefit by constant repetition of the old propaganda line about Britain fighting America's fight. Roosevelt repeated this line on December 29 in a "fireside chat" to the American people. Aid to Britain was now a question of "national security." If Britain were conquered, "all of us in the Americas would be living at the point of a gun."

On the following day the President summoned to the White House, Secretary Morgenthau and Arthur Purvis, head of the Anglo-French Purchasing Commission, to discuss the details of lend-lease legislation. On January 2, 1941, Edward Foley, Morgenthau's general counsel, and his assistant, Oscar Cox, began the arduous task of drafting the bill. When opposition to the bill developed in certain circles in the State Department, Secretary Knox remarked to Morgenthau in his best serio-comic manner: "Let's organize a hanging bee over there someday and hang the ones that you and I pick out." Some of the clique around the President probably would have regarded the matter of a hanging bee very seriously when Senator Wheeler began a series of blasts against lend-lease legislation. On January 4, 1941, he asked some very pertinent questions: "If it is our war, how can we justify lending them stuff and asking them to pay us back? If it is our war, we ought to have the courage to go over and fight it, but it is not our war." A week later, in a radio broadcast, he feathered a shaft that evoked an immediate cry of pain from the sensitive President. He regarded the lend-lease program as "the New Deal's 'triple A' foreign policy—to plow under every fourth American boy." The President deeply resented these prophetic words and denounced the Wheeler comment upon lend-lease as the "rottenest thing that has been said in public life in my generation."

Although Admiral Stark expressed on January 13 the opinion that "we are heading straight for this war," the lend-lease program was sold to the American people as a form of peace insurance. On March 11, 1941, the lend-lease bill was signed by the President. . . .

In the meantime the Führer was showing a strong determination to adhere to his policy of keeping out of war with the United States. In May 1941 the German attitude was summed up at a meeting between Hitler and his naval advisers:

> Whereas up to now the situation confronting submarines and naval forces on operations was perfectly clear, naval warfare in the North Atlantic is becoming increasingly complicated as the result of the measures taken by the U.S.A. In order to help Britain, the American neutrality patrol, which was hitherto confined to the area within the American neutrality zone, has been reinforced and considerably extended toward the east to about 38° W., i.e. as far as the middle of the Atlantic. The true character of the American neutrality patrol is shown by the fact that vessels on patrol have also been instructed to report by radio any battleships encountered. . . .
>
> We have laid down the following rules for naval warfare in order to comply with German political aims with regard to the U.S.A.:
>
> No attack should be made on U.S. naval forces and merchant vessels.
>
> Prize regulations are not to be applied to U.S. merchant ships.
>
> Weapons are not to be used, even if American vessels conduct themselves in a definitely unneutral manner.
>
> Weapons are to be used *only if U.S. ships fire the first shot.*
>
> As a result of these instructions and of the constant endeavors on the

part of Germany not to react to provocation, incidents with the U.S.A. have been avoided up to the present time.

It is unmistakable that the U.S. Government is disappointed about this cautious attitude on the part of Germany, since one of the most important factors in preparing the American people for entry into the war is thus eliminated. The U.S. is therefore continuing its attempt to obliterate more and more the boundary line between neutrality and belligerency, and to stretch the "short of war" policy further by constantly introducing fresh measures contrary to international law.

The next naval incident involving German-American relations was the sinking of the American merchant ship (May 21, 1941) *Robin Moor,* New York to Cape Town, by a German submarine. There was no visit or search but the crew and passengers were allowed to take to open lifeboats. As the sinking occurred outside the blockade zone it is evident that the submarine commander disregarded orders concerning American ships. Admiral Raeder immediately issued orders to prevent further incidents of this nature, and Hitler, after confirming these instructions, remarked that he wished to "avoid any incident with the U.S.A." On June 20 the President sent a message to Congress in which he bitterly criticized Germany as an international outlaw. He followed this message with another move in the direction of war. On July 7 he ordered American occupation of Iceland. Two days later Secretary Knox gave a statement to the press which implied that the American patrol force in the North Atlantic had the right to use its guns when the occasion arose.

This occasion arose on September 4, 1941, when the destroyer *Greer,* bound for Iceland, was informed by a British plane that a submerged U-boat lay athwart her course some ten miles ahead. The *Greer* at once laid a course for the reported submarine, and after having made sound contact with it, kept it on her bow for more than three hours. During this period a British plane dropped four depth charges in the vicinity of the submarine without effect. Finally, the submarine commander grew tired of this game of hide-and-seek and launched a torpedo which the *Greer* was able to dodge. When the *Greer* counterattacked with depth charges, the submarine launched another torpedo which was avoided. When sound contact with the submarine could not be reestablished, the *Greer* resumed course for Iceland.

On September 11 the President gave a broadcast which presented a distorted version of the *Greer* incident. He conveniently forgot to tell that the initiative had been taken by the *Greer:* "She [the *Greer*] was flying the American flag. Her identity as an American ship was unmistakable. She was then and there attacked by a submarine. Germany admits that it was a German submarine. . . . We have sought no shooting war with Hitler. . . . The aggression is not ours. Ours is solely defense." American vessels would now shoot at sight.

In the face of this serious incident that clearly showed the aggressive character of American naval patrolling, Hitler maintained his policy of avoiding difficulties with the United States. On September 17 orders concerning American merchant vessels exempted them from attack, even when in convoy, in all zones except that immediately surrounding the British Isles. In the Pan-American safety belt "no warlike acts" were to be carried out on German initiative.

The American answer to these pacific gestures was to authorize escort duty for American destroyers. It was arranged that an American escort group, based on Argentia, should take over from a Royal Canadian Navy escort at a designated place off Newfoundland and hand over the convoy to a Royal Navy escort at an agreed mid-ocean meeting place. Convoying was now an established practice, and it should be kept in mind that Secretary Knox, during the lend-lease hearings, had frankly admitted that he regarded convoying as an "act of war."

This *de facto* war in the Atlantic soon produced another incident. On October 16 five American destroyers rushed from Reykjavik, Iceland, to the help of a convoy that was being attacked by submarines. On the following day, while in the midst of the fighting, the destroyer *Kearny* was struck by a torpedo and slowly made its way back to Iceland. It had deliberately moved into the center of a pitched battle between German submarines and British and Canadian warships and had taken the consequences. It was not long before President Roosevelt gave to the American people a twisted account of the incident. On October 27 he recounted the happenings on October 16 and 17 and asserted that he had "wished to avoid shooting." America had "been attacked. The U.S.S. *Kearny* is not just a Navy ship. She belongs to every man, woman, and child in this Nation. . . . Hitler's torpedo was directed at every American." In order to give additional overtones of villainy to his description of Nazi wickedness he then stated that he had a secret map made in Germany which disclosed Hitler's plan to put all the continent of South America under his domination. But that was not all. He had in his possession another document made in Germany that revealed Hitler's intention, if he was victorious, to "abolish all existing religions." It should be evident that the "forward march of Hitlerism" should be stopped. . . . We are pledged to pull our own oar in the destruction of Hitlerism." The American Navy had been given orders to "shoot on sight." The Nazi "rattlesnakes of the sea" would have to be destroyed.

This declaration of war was confirmed by the *Reuben James* incident. On October 31, while the *Reuben James* was escorting a convoy to Iceland, some German submarines were encountered about 600 miles west of that island. The American destroyer was struck by a torpedo and rapidly sank. Only 45, out of a crew of about 160, were saved. When the news of the sinking of the *Reuben James* reached Germany, Hitler remarked: "President Roosevelt has ordered his ships to shoot the moment they sight German ships. I have ordered German ships not to shoot when they sight American vessels but to defend themselves when attacked." On November 13, 1941, the directives for conduct of German warships when encountering American naval vessels remained pacific: "Engagements with American naval or air forces are not to be sought deliberately; they are to be avoided as far as possible. . . . If it is observed before a convoy is attacked that it is being escorted by American forces, the attack is not to be carried out."

Germany was trying desperately to stay out of war with the United States. America's attitude was clearly stated by Sumner Welles at Arlington on November 11: "Beyond the Atlantic a sinister and pitiless conqueror has reduced more than half of Europe to abject serfdom. It is his boast that his system shall prevail even unto the ends of the earth. . . . The American people after full debate . . . have determined upon their policy. They are pledged . . . to spare no effort and no sacrifice in bringing to pass the final defeat of Hitlerism and all that which that evil term implies. . . . We cannot know, we cannot yet foresee, how long and how hard the road may be which leads to that new day when another armistice will be signed."

To the mind of Welles and to others in the White House group it was obvious that America was really in the war. But the American people did not realize that momentous fact, nor did they know that they were pledged "to spare no effort and no sacrifice in bringing to pass the final defeat of Hitlerism." It was easy for Mr. Welles to speak glibly of sacrifice. He had long enjoyed wealth and high social position. The word "sacrifice" had always been excluded from his dictionary. As the spokesman for the President he was suddenly breaking to the American people the dread news that they had become involved in a war they had ardently wished to avoid. The war hawks of 1941 were never tired of sneering at the majority of Americans as benighted isolationists who had tried to build a Chinese wall around the United States and thus cut it off from all foreign contacts. They knew their sneers were patent lies. America had never been isolated from the social, economic, religious, and cultural forces that shaped the modern world. Thanks to its geographical position it had escaped the recurring tides of conflict that had crumbled the walls of ancient civilizations and washed away the heritage men had earned through dauntless courage and high endeavor. Americans had been isolationists only against war and its evident evils, and their country had grown prosperous beyond the dreams of the founding fathers. But in 1915, President Wilson began to nurse the thought of sharing America's ideals and wealth with the rest of the world, and two years later he led us into a foreign war that he hoped would make the world safe for democracy. But this theme song turned sour in American ears when it led to the great parade of 1917 which ended for many men in the vast cemeteries in France. It gained new popularity after 1933, and with Roosevelt as maestro, the old macabre accents began to haunt every home. In 1941 his orchestra of death was anxiously waiting for the signal to begin the new symphony. He had hoped for a German motif but Hitler had refused to assist with a few opening martial notes. Perhaps some Japanese statesman would prove more accommodating. At any rate, after the *Reuben James* incident had fallen flat he turned his eyes towards the Orient and sought new inspiration from the inscrutable East. He found it at Pearl Harbor when Japanese planes sounded the first awesome notes in a chorus of war that is still vibrating throughout the world. The story of how the first notes in the script of that chorus were written in by President Roosevelt is told in the next chapter.

When the President perceived that Hitler would not furnish the pretext for a war with Germany, he turned to the Far East and increased his pressure upon Japan. The path to Pearl Harbor had already been pointed out by Mr. Hornbeck in February 1939. After discussing how the American Government had tried to restrain the Japanese advance in North China by "moral and economic opposition," he stated his belief that in the long run the situation would so "develop that military opposition by this country will have to be offered."

But Herbert Feis, the adviser on International Economic Affairs, still favored economic pressure, so on July 26, 1939, Secretary Hull sent a note to Ambassador Horinouchi informing him that the Treaty of February 21, 1911, would terminate on January 26, 1940. The way was thus prepared for an all out economic offensive against Japan. . . .

The Atlantic Conference Pushes America Closer to a Break with Japan, 1941

For Japan there were very dark clouds along the Newfoundland horizon. On the evening of August 9, in the Newfoundland harbor of Argentia, Roosevelt and Churchill had their first conference. The British were particularly concerned about the danger of a Japanese thrust into the southwest Pacific area, and Sir Alexander Cadogan had drafted parallel Anglo-American declarations designed to halt this possible advance. America was to state very frankly that "any further encroachment by Japan in the Southwestern Pacific" would compel the United States to take measures that might lead to war. In order to implement this declaration the President was to "seek authority from Congress" to employ American armed forces as he thought best. The President at once rejected any thought of consulting with Congress. On his own initiative and responsibility he would let the Japanese Government know that if her armed forces moved southward, "various steps would have to be taken by the United States notwithstanding the President's realization that the taking of such further measures might result in war between the United States and Japan." But Sumner Welles thought that the United States should play the role of policeman in a much wider area than the southwest Pacific. America should be ready to repel any Japanese thrust whether it was directed "against China, against the Soviet Union or against the British Dominions or British colonies, or the colonies of the Netherlands in the Southern Pacific area." Churchill and Roosevelt were in hearty agreement with this wider formula, but the President was too cautious to broadcast it to the American public. It had better remain a secret understanding.

Churchill had failed to secure a parallel declaration that pointed straight to war, but the Roosevelt pledges of support relieved most of his fears. This fact was revealed in his speech to Parliament on January 27, 1942: "The probability, since the Atlantic Conference . . . that the United States, even if not herself attacked, would come into a war in the Far East, and thus make final victory sure, seemed to allay some of these anxieties. . . . As time went on, one had greater assurance that if Japan ran amok in the Pacific, we should not fight alone."

Roosevelt Refuses to Meet Prince Konoye

In a statement he handed to the Japanese Ambassador on August 17, Roosevelt carried out his pledge to Churchill. It was phrased in language that was not unduly provocative, but its meaning was very clear:

> If the Japanese Government takes any further steps in pursuance of a policy or program of military domination by force or threat of force of neighboring countries, the Government of the United States will be compelled to take immediately any and all steps which it may deem necessary toward safeguarding the legitimate rights and interests of the United States and American nationals and toward insuring the safety and security of the United States.

With reference to a meeting between Prince Konoye and President Roosevelt, the Japanese Ambassador was informed that if his Government was ready "to suspend its expansionist activities" and embark upon a "peaceful program for the Pacific," the government of the United States "would be glad to endeavor to arrange a suitable time and place to exchange views."

Before this Roosevelt statement could reach Tokyo, Foreign Minister Toyoda had a conference with Ambassador Grew and once more strongly pushed the idea of a meeting at Honolulu between Konoye and Roosevelt. He ardently hoped that at such a meeting it would be possible "to reach a just and equitable agreement." Grew was so deeply impressed with the sincerity of Toyoda's plea that he immediately sent a dispatch to Secretary Hull and urged, "with all the force at his command, for the sake of avoiding the obviously growing possibility of an utterly futile war between Japan and the United States, that this Japanese proposal not be turned aside without very prayerful consideration. . . . The opportunity is here presented . . . for an act of the highest statesmanship . . . with the possible overcoming thereby of apparently insurmountable obstacles to peace hereafter in the Pacific."

On August 28, Ambassador Nomura delivered to President Roosevelt a personal message from Konoye pleading for a meeting which could "explore the possibility of saving the situation." In his remarks to Nomura with reference to a possible meeting with Konoye, the President appeared to think that it would be difficult for him to go as far as Hawaii. Possibly Juneau, Alaska, would be more suitable.

As the President vacillated as to what course to pursue about this proposed meeting with Konoye, an Imperial conference was held on September 6. It was finally decided that Japanese preparations for war would have to be continued so "that they be completed approximately toward the end of October." At the same time, the Foreign Office should "endeavor by every possible diplomatic means to have our demands agreed to by America and England." If these negotiations did not lead to favorable results by the early part of October, then the government should "get ready for war against America."

The position of Japan was very clear. It was insisting upon American recognition of Japan's dominance in the Far East. In the Root-Takahira Agreement of November 30, 1908, we had given Japan a green light to move ahead in Manchuria. Japan had taken advantage of President Theodore Roosevelt's friendly suggestions and had strongly intrenched herself in large areas in North China. In the face of rapidly expanding Russian power in the Far East, this action had been regarded as a national imperative. In the Far East the future belonged either to Japan or Russia, not to a China that had been exhausted by an endless cycle of war, revolution, and war. The policy of President Franklin D. Roosevelt and Secretary Hull in giving strong support to a gravely weakened China was highly unrealistic, and the later collapse of the American position in China stems straight back to the decisions taken in September and October 1941.

During the eventful weeks of September, President Roosevelt seemed unable to make up his mind concerning a meeting with Konoye. In order to dispel this sense of uncertainty, the Division of Far Eastern Affairs (Mr. Ballantine) prepared a long memorandum which was highly critical of Japan. In conclusion, Mr. Ballantine remarked: "The holding of the meeting between the President and the Japanese Prime Minister on the basis of the present status of the discussions between this country and Japan would result in more of disadvantage than of advantage as regards this country's interests and policies." From Tokyo, Ambassador Grew spoke from an entirely different angle. He would not stand inflexibly upon certain principles and demand that Japan agree to accept every one of them. Political differences can be expressed in subtle shades that need not affront nations involved in serious controversy; one does not have to insist upon the conventional pattern of black and white. If America would show some slight spirit of compromise, this concession might evoke concessions on the part of Japan and some path to understanding might be found. There was no real point in insisting that Konoye agree in advance to a long agenda which would awaken instant opposition in Japan. During the sessions of a conference between Konoye and Roosevelt it was highly possible that a spirit of reciprocity might arise which would turn thoughts from war to peace. The situation required statesmanship of the highest order. There seemed no reason to doubt that it could be found in Washington.

Unfortunately, at this time of national crisis, President Roosevelt did not measure up to the demands of the hour. Without the courage to make a decision in the matter of meeting Konoye, he pushed the responsibility upon the shoulders of Secretary Hull. Hull did not hesitate. He was always "wound-up" for such occasions. On October 2 he handed to Ambassador Nomura a statement that contained all the Hull clichés about high moral principles being the directing force in international relations. Dubious American practices in the Caribbean were not mentioned. After a long rehearsal of the reasons why the Hull-Nomura conversations had been a flat failure, he sonorously remarked that before there could be a meeting between the President and Prince Konoye, there would first have to be an agreement upon basic principles of policy. He knew that such an agreement was not possible. He had cleared the decks of the American ship of state for war at any time. It would not be long in coming. . . .

Japan Is Maneuvered into Firing the First Shot at Pearl Harbor

In the second week in November 1941 tension began to mount in Tokyo. On November 10 the Japanese Foreign Minister expressed to Grew the opinion that the "preliminary and exploratory conversations" in Washington had proceeded long enough. It was time for both countries to "enter into formal and official negotiations." The Japanese Government had "repeatedly made proposals calculated to approach the American point of view, but the American Government . . . had taken no step toward meeting the Japanese position." On this same day (November 10), Ambassador Nomura presented to President Roosevelt a further explanation of his Government's proposals. In the meantime the Japanese Foreign Office instructed Nomura that November 25 was the deadline. All negotiations would have to be concluded by that date. This deadline was repeated from Tokyo on November 11. Under pressure from the Foreign Office, Nomura was extremely anxious to secure an early answer to the Japanese proposals of November 7 and 10. While he was awaiting this answer, he noted the military preparations that were being rushed by the Roosevelt Administration: "They are contriving by every possible means to prepare for actual warfare." Tokyo replied to this cablegram by insisting that the deadline of November 25 was "an absolutely immovable one."

Secretary Hull knew of this deadline through intercepted Japanese instructions to Nomura, so on November 15 he handed to Nomura a long oral statement setting forth the bases of an agreement. He knew they would not be acceptable to Japan. Complete control over "its economic, financial and monetary affairs" should be restored to China, and Japan should abandon any thought of preserving in China, or anywhere else in the Pacific area, a "preferential position."

The abrupt tone of this note was a challenge that could easily lead to a break in diplomatic relations. Japan had long feared that such a break was inevitable, but in a final attempt to stave off such an emergency it had been decided to send to Washington another diplomat who would assist Nomura in the delicate negotiations that were hanging by a very slender thread. The new appointee, Saburo Kurusu, had served as consul in Chicago and New York and had recently been in Berlin as ambassador. His happy marriage to an American girl gave him a personal interest in maintaining friendly relations between Japan and the United States.

On November 17, Nomura and Kurusu had a talk with President Roosevelt, and then long, inconclusive conversations with Hull were carried on. To Kurusu it seemed that the President was "very much in earnest in regard to effecting an understanding between Japan and the United States." With Hull, little progress was made. This was particularly true with reference to a solution of the difficulties between China and Japan. Roosevelt seemed to have taken a liking to his old naval acquaintance, Nomura, and was not ready to push things. One day Lowell Mellett and Max Lowenthal paid a visit to the office of Senator Burton K. Wheeler to convey the information that "the President does not want to push America into the war." The Senator took this statement with a large grain of salt, but he remembered that at times Secretary Hull had been more belligerent than the President. This fact had been particularly evident during the sessions of the Democratic National Convention in 1940. When Wheeler was putting up a strong fight to write an antiwar plank in such specific terms that the President could not disregard it, "Jimmy" Byrnes confided to him that Hull was strongly against such a plank. It would prevent him from exerting maximum pressure upon Japan.

In November 1941 the Hull policy of pressure upon Japan was being implemented at full strength. On November 20, Kurusu discussed with Hull the matter of bringing to a close the hostilities between China and Japan. The Japanese Foreign Office believed this could be arranged if the United States would stop sending supplies to China. After stressing this point, Nomura then remarked: "If the tension between Japan and the United States can be relaxed, be it ever so little, particularly in the southwestern Pacific, and quickly clear the atmosphere, then I think we could go on and settle everything else." Kurusu pushed the idea of a *modus vivendi,* and President Roosevelt responded by outlining one that might be accepted. The fourth item in this Presidential proposal read as follows: "U.S. to *introduce* Japs to Chinese to talk things over but U.S. to take no part in their conversations. Later on Pacific agreements."

Japan met this show of conciliation with a concession of her own. The deadline in the negotiations was now extended from November 25 to November 29. But this was the final concession: "This time we mean it, that the deadline absolutely cannot be changed. After that things are automatically going to happen."

On the same day that this deadline was extended (November 22), Nomura and Kurusu once more met Hull in conference. It was soon apparent from his tone that there was small chance that Japanese conditions for a truce would be accepted: (1) a revocation of the American order of July 26 freezing Japanese credits in the United States and thereby stopping all shipments of oil from American ports; (2) American consent to a program aimed at increasing the export of oil and other commodities from the Netherlands East Indies to Japan; (3) American mediation between China and Japan so as to initiate negotiations between the two powers and the cessation of American assistance to Chiang Kai-shek. American consent to these conditions was out of the question even if Japan made far-reaching concessions in return.

During the conference on November 22, Hull acidly complained of the "threatening tone" of the Japanese press and then asked why some Japanese statesman did not start "preaching peace?" When Nomura remarked that he "did not have the slightest doubt that Japan desired peace," Hull scoffed at this statement and lamented that it was a pity that Japan "could not do just a few small things to help tide over the situation." He was particularly critical of the Japanese attitude towards Chiang Kai-shek.

Two days later (November 24), Hull had a conference with the diplomatic representatives of Australia, Britain, China, and the Netherlands. He quickly discovered that the Chinese Ambassador, Dr. Hu Shih, was not enthusiastic about a three months' truce with Japan. But Hull went ahead and drafted a *modus vivendi* which President Roosevelt regarded as a "fair proposition" but he was "not very hopeful" and thought there might be "real trouble very soon."

On the following morning (November 25), Hull showed to Secretaries Knox and Stimson this draft that provided for a three months' truce with Japan. But its terms were so drastic that Stimson believed that Japan would not accept it. That afternoon Secretaries Hull, Knox, and Stimson, along with General Marshall and Admiral Stark, went to the White House for a long conference with the President. From intercepted Japanese cablegrams to Nomura, the President knew that the Japanese deadline for an end to the current negotiations was on November 29. He expressed a fear that Japanese armed forces might make an attack "as soon as next Monday." The main question was "how we should maneuver them into the position of firing the first shot without allowing too much danger to ourselves.

When Hull returned to the Department of State he had a long talk with the Chinese Ambassador who handed him a telegram from Chungking: "After reading your [Hu Shih's] telegram the Generalissimo showed rather strong reaction. He got the impression that the United States Government has put aside the Chinese question in its conversations with Japan instead of seeking a solution and is still inclined to appease Japan at the expense of China." This impudent telegram placed Hull on the defensive. He frankly admitted that the conversations he had been carrying on with the Japanese envoys were merely a delaying action: "The official heads of our Army and Navy for some weeks have been most earnestly urging that we not get into war with Japan until they have an opportunity to increase further their plans and methods and means of defense in the Pacific area."

On the afternoon of November 25 there were more cablegrams from China. Mr. T. V. Soong handed Secretary Stimson another cablegram from Chiang Kai-shek in which the Generalissimo urged the United States to be "uncompromising" in its attitude towards Japan. This pressure was increased by a communication from Owen Lattimore, the American adviser of Chiang Kai-shek, to Lauchlin Currie, administrative assistant to President Roosevelt: Any "*modus vivendi*" arrived at with

Japan "would be disastrous to Chinese belief in America." For a week Currie was "terribly anxious" because he feared that "Hull was in danger of selling China and America and Britain down the river." In Chungking, Madame Chiang Kai-shek became "unrestrainedly critical" of the American Government for its failure to "plunge into the war" and thus aid China.

On the morning of November 26, Hull saw a telegram from Churchill to the President: "There is only one point that disquiets us. What about Chiang Kai-shek? Is he not having a very thin diet?" It was not long before Hull was nearly hysterical. During a telephone conversation with Secretary Stimson he remarked that he had just about made up his mind about the *modus vivendi*—he "would kick the whole thing over." A few moments later Stimson phoned to the President and informed him that a Japanese expeditionary force was moving south from Shanghai. The President promptly "blew up" and exclaimed that this fact "changed the whole situation because it was an evidence of bad faith on the part of the Japanese." But the leading officers of the American armed forces still counseled caution. On this same morning (November 26) there was a meeting of the Army-Navy Joint Board and Admiral Ingersoll presented a series of arguments "why we should not precipitate a war."

But Hull was tired of carrying on negotiations with Japan. He was not a master of diplomatic double talk and he squirmed under the direct questions of the Japanese envoys. As far back as January 23, 1941, he had listened without any real interest to the proposals that Bishop Walsh and Father Drought had brought from Matsuoka: "(1) an agreement to nullify their [Japanese] participation in the Axis Pact; (2) a guarantee to recall all military forces from China and to restore to China its geographical and political integrity." If he had rejected these unusually conciliatory proposals why should he be deeply concerned about recent ones that did not go nearly so far!

On the afternoon of November 26 he abandoned all thought of a truce with Japan and put into final shape a ten-point proposal. Both he and the President knew this program would be rejected by Japan. There was no thought of compromise or conciliation: "The Government of Japan will withdraw all military, naval, air and police forces from China and from Indochina." When Kurusu read the ten-point proposal of Secretary Hull he immediately inquired if this was the American answer to the Japanese request for a *modus vivendi* or truce. Was not the American Government interested in a truce? Hull merely replied that "we have explored that" but had arrived at no real decision. Kurusu could only reply that the Secretary's attitude "could be interpreted as tantamount to meaning the end." It was obvious that the next step was war.

On the morning of December 4, the Navy radio receiving station at Cheltenham, Maryland, intercepted a Japanese overseas news broadcast from Station JAP in Tokyo, in which there was inserted a false weather report, "east wind rain." On November 19 the Japanese Government had instructed its ambassador in Washington that such a weather forecast would indicate imminence of war with the United States. After intercepting this Japanese instruction the radio receiving stations of the American armed forces were on the alert for the "east wind rain" message. As soon as it was translated, Lieutenant Commander Kramer handed it to Commander Safford with the exclamation: "This is *it*." Safford got in touch immediately with Rear Admiral Noyes who telephoned the substance of the intercepted message "to the naval aide to the President."

According to the testimony of Captain Safford [in 1941 a Commander], the

> "winds" message and the change of the [Japanese] naval operations code came in the middle of the week: two days to Saturday and three days to Sunday. It was unthinkable that the Japanese would surrender their hopes of surprise by delaying until the week-end of December 13–14. This was not crystal-gazing or "intuition"—it was just the plain, common sense acceptance of a self-evident proposition. Col. Sadtler saw it, and so did Capt. Joseph R. Redman, U.S.N., according to Col. Sadtler's testimony in 1944. . . . The Japanese were going to start the war on Saturday, December 6, 1941, or Sunday, December 7, 1941.

For the next three days Commander Safford and Lieutenant Commander Kramer tried in vain to get some action out of their superior officers with regard to the implications of the "east wind rain" message. When they induced Captain McCollum to exert some pressure upon Admiral Stark he was given a sharp rebuke which so infuriated him that he later poured the whole story into the receptive ears of Admiral Kimmel. This disclosure led Kimmel to press for the Pearl Harbor investigations.

The unaccountable failure of high naval officers to convey a warning to Honolulu about the imminence of war was given additional highlights on the evening of December 6 when the Japanese reply to the American note of November 26 was sent secretly to Ambassador Nomura. It was intercepted by Navy receiving stations and decoded. When the President read this message to Nomura he at once exclaimed: "This means war!" He tried to get in touch with Admiral Stark but was informed that the chief of naval operations was at the National Theatre enjoying the delightful strains of *The Student Prince*. The next day the Admiral's ears would be assailed by the crashing echoes of the attack upon Pearl Harbor.

It would ordinarily be assumed that the President, after reading this intercepted Japanese message, would hurriedly call a conference of the more important Army and Navy officers to concert plans to meet the anticipated attack. The testimony of General Marshall and Admiral Stark would indicate that the Chief Executive took the ominous news so calmly that he made no effort to consult with them. Did he deliberately seek the Pearl Harbor attack in order to get America into the war? What is the real answer to this riddle of Presidential composure in the face of a threatened attack upon some American outpost in the faraway Pacific? This problem grows more complicated as we watch the approach of zero hour. At 9:00 A.M. on December 7, Lieutenant Commander Kramer delivered to Admiral Stark the final installment of the Japanese instruction to Nomura. Its meaning was now so obvious that Stark cried out in great alarm: "My God! This means war. I must get word to Kimmel at once." But he made no effort to contact Honolulu. Instead he tried to get in touch with General Marshall, who, for some strange reason, suddenly decided to go on a long horseback ride. It was a history-making ride. In the early hours of the American Revolution, Paul Revere went on a famous ride to warn his countrymen of the enemy's approach and thus save American lives. In the early hours of World War II, General Marshall took a ride that helped prevent an alert from reaching Pearl Harbor in time to save an American fleet from serious disaster and an American garrison from a bombing that cost more than two thousand lives. Was there an important purpose behind this ride? This question looms constantly larger as we look further into the Pearl Harbor hearings.

When Colonel Bratton, on the morning of December 7, saw the last part of the Japanese instruction to Nomura he realized at once that "Japan planned to attack the United States at some point at or near 1 o'clock that day." To Lieutenant Commander Kramer the message meant "a surprise attack at Pearl Harbor today." This information was in the hands of Secretary Knox by 10:00 A.M., and he must have passed it on to the President immediately.

It was 11:25 A.M. when General Marshall returned to his office. If he carefully read the reports on the threatened Japanese attack (on Pearl Harbor) he still had plenty of time to contact Honolulu by means of the scrambler telephone on his desk, or by the Navy radio or the FBI radio. For some reason best known to himself he chose to send the alert to Honolulu by RCA and did not even take the precaution to have it stamped, "priority." As the Army Pearl Harbor Board significantly remarked: "We find no justification for a failure to send this message by multiple secret means either through the Navy radio or the FBI radio or the scrambler telephone or all three." Was the General under Presidential orders to break military regulations with regard to the transmission of important military information? Did he think that the President's political objectives outweighed considerations of national safety? Was the preservation of the British Empire worth the blood, sweat, and tears not only of the men who would die in the agony of Pearl Harbor but also of the long roll of heroes who perished in the epic encounters in the Pacific, in the Mediterranean area, and in the famous offensive that rolled at high tide across the war-torn fields of France? New cemeteries all over the world would confirm to stricken American parents the melancholy fact that the paths of military glory lead but to the grave.

But the President and Harry Hopkins viewed these dread contingencies with amazing equanimity. In the quiet atmosphere of the oval study in the White House, with all incoming telephone calls shut off, the Chief Executive calmly studied his well-filled stamp albums while Hopkins fondled Fala, the White House scottie. At one o'clock, Death stood in the doorway. The Japanese had bombed Pearl Harbor. America had suddenly been thrust into a war she is still fighting.

2. *F.D.R. and the Axis Threat*

Rooseveltian foreign policy was defended against revisionist charges by Basil Rauch of Columbia University, author of an early study of the New Deal. With other historians in the "internationalist school," he believes that Roosevelt correctly viewed Hitlerite Germany as a threat to American security and values. Consequently, F.D.R. rendered aid short of war to Britain and the other states resisting Hitler. He long believed, however, that the Axis could be checked without direct American involvement. As for Japan, although the Roosevelt administration condemned the Japanese invasion of China, dating from 1937, it was hoped that peace could be preserved, especially since Europe had top priority. The tortuous negotiations and the slowly tightening economic pressures were intended to check Japan without war; even when code intercepts indicated that the Japanese leaders were determined on hostilities unless America acquiesced in the Nipponese conquests, it was still hoped that the conflict could be delayed. The Pearl Harbor attack came as a complete surprise. (The Beard and Morgenstern volumes referred to by Rauch in the following selection are: Charles A. Beard, *President Roosevelt and the Coming of the War* [1948]; and George Morgenstern, *Pearl Harbor: The Story of the Secret War* [1947].)

From Munich to Pearl Harbor

BASIL RAUCH

During the decade 1933–1942, world events and President Franklin D. Roosevelt led the American people and their government to adopt collective security as the foreign policy of the United States. The late Dr. Charles A. Beard is the only historian who has written on the process by which the nation abandoned isolationism and turned to internationalism. His two books, *American Foreign Policy in the Making: 1932–1940: A Study in Responsibilities,* and *President Roosevelt and the Coming of the War: 1941. A Study in Appearances and Realities* frankly aim to destroy the faith of Americans in the honesty of President Roosevelt in planning the new foreign policy.

These books propose a revisionist interpretation of the causes of American entry into the Second World War. After the First World War, revisionist historians won over the American public to their view that the United States had entered that war not because Germany committed aggression against it, but because American bankers and munitions manufacturers plotted entry for their own profit. The thesis provided justification for the return to isolationism. Beard's purpose was to create a similar disillusionment regarding the reasons for American entry into the recent war, and a similar revulsion against the foreign policy of internationalism.

The villain in Beard's plot is not an economic group with a vested interest in war, but the President of the United States acting for motives which are not defined. The picture of President Roosevelt engaged in a colossal and profoundly immoral plot to deceive the American people into

Basil Rauch, *Roosevelt: From Munich to Pearl Harbor.* New York: Farrar, Straus and Cudahy, Inc. (Creative Age Press), 1950. Reprinted with permission. Pp. 1–6, 376, 388–390, 392–393, 455, 458–459, 460–461, 462–467, 468–472, 475–477.

participating in the war unnecessarily and contrary to their interests might be thought so overdrawn as to be unconvincing. But Beard relies upon the effects of the twelve and more years of widely publicized hatred of Roosevelt by a minority of the public and the majority of the press to make the familiarity of his characterization overcome its implausibility.

An indication of Beard's desire to capitalize on anti-Roosevelt feeling is that in his two books he almost completely ignores the part Secretary of State Hull played in the making of administration foreign policy. Hull's work was certainly second in importance only to that of the President himself, and in details it was more revealing than Roosevelt's. But, because Hull was generally regarded as an honest and safe leader, his presence on Beard's stage as Roosevelt's partner would have been an inartistic contradiction of Beard's image of Roosevelt pursuing a sinister plot.

This is only one of the many artful exclusions Beard practices. More important is his exclusion of any data on the objective course of world events which might suggest that the United States, confronted by rising Axis power, did actually face danger to its own security. In Beard's books, not policies of Hitler or Japan but the policies of Roosevelt created first the danger and then the fact of United States participation in the Second World War. In the early pages of *American Foreign Policy in the Making,* Beard shows admirable, perhaps even excessive, respect for the complexities of problems of historical causation, but only in order to justify his own failure to assess the part of the aggressor nations in causing the Second World War. Thereafter Beard proceeds in the remainder of that book and throughout his second one to make a masterpiece of oversimplification in order to lay responsibility for war upon Roosevelt.

Besides excluding material essential for the understanding of Roosevelt's foreign policy, Beard violently distorts the material he does use. His principal distortions are two: that internationalists, led by Roosevelt during the thirties, wanted the United States to go to war; and that Roosevelt practiced deception on the American people regarding the nature and aims of his foreign policy.

The first of these distortions depends upon a perverse definition of internationalism. Beard lifts his definition from the lexicon of isolationism and uses it in both his books as axiomatic truth. His complete definition follows:

> Here and in the following pages the term *internationalism* is used as meaning: World peace is desirable and possible; it is indivisible and can be secured for the United States only by entering into a positive connection with a league, or association, of nations, empowered to make pacific adjustments of international conflicts and to impose peace, by effective sanctions or by force, on aggressors or peace breakers; the United States cannot maintain neutrality in case of any major war among European and Asiatic powers.

This definition is fair enough up to the word "only," which, strengthened as it is by the word "positive," falsifies the program of American internationalists, especially of the time when President Roosevelt came to office, as if the *ultimate* step by the United States in the direction of collective security, that is, "a positive connection with a league, or association, of nations," was the "only" and therefore the *first* step they advocated. The Roosevelt administration never advocated United States entry into the League of Nations. It did advocate parallel action with the League in particular cases, after the United States should have first decided independently in each case that the action of the League corresponded to the interests and policy of the United States. Whether independent and parallel action with the League of Nations may be termed a "positive connection with a league" is debatable, but it is also beside the point.

The heart of the argument was that isolationists during the period between the two World Wars asserted the impossibility of the United States taking part in collective action against an aggressor without forming "entangling alliances" and making "prior commitments" which would destroy the sovereignty of the United States and permit other nations to determine its policy and even plunge it into war against its will. This was the chief argument against joining the League after the First World War. Henry L. Stimson, President Hoover's Secretary of State, President Roosevelt, and Secretary Hull were, nonetheless, internationalists even though they conceded to the power of this argument. Their statesmanship consisted in devising techniques which would permit the United States to take part in international action for collective security without forming entangling alliances or making prior commitments. One such was the technique of "parallel action"; another was "consultation," whereby the United States promised to consult with other nations when aggression occurred, but reserved the right to judge for itself in each case whether it should take action against the aggressor; a third was a discriminatory arms embargo against aggressors; a fourth was Lend Lease; a fifth was the "veto power" of the United States in the Security Council of the United Nations, which not only avoids prior commitment by the United States to take action in any particular case, but enables the United States to prevent the Security Council itself from taking action.

The development of such techniques is of supreme importance in the history of collective security as an American policy. It is sometimes argued that these techniques compromised the policy of collective security to the point of obliteration. In this view, the effective policy of the United States under Roosevelt shifted not from isolation to collective security but from isolation to participation in world politics to protect the United States and increase its power at the expense of other powers. Whether this is indeed a fair statement of the "inner meaning" or Roosevelt's policy will be discussed hereafter. In either case, Roosevelt's method was cooperation with some powers against others; the method was supported by internationalists and the development certainly marked a change in United States foreign policy. Whatever the "inner meaning" of this development, isolationists denied that national sovereignty could be preserved by any method except abstinence from cooperation with other governments; they asserted that the object of the new policy was not peace but war, and Beard perpetuates their distortions as "truths of history."

The new techniques enabled Roosevelt and other leaders to go before the country and plead for collective security, and at the same time promise in good faith that they did not contemplate entangling alliances or prior commitments and that they had as their greatest purpose avoidance of United States participation in war. Throughout his two books, Beard calls such promises "retreats" from the policy of collective security or "denials" of that policy and examples of how Roosevelt "misled" the people. Evidently parallel action, consultation, and a discriminatory arms embargo do not constitute for Beard a "positive connection with a league." Positive or not, these techniques constituted the program of American internationalism during the thirties, and Beard's definition of that word evades, as isolationists generally evaded, that fact, in order to make the false charge that internationalism did involve entangling alliances and prior commitments—and war.

Collective security, the isolationists charged, would involve the United States in war. It would be a most evil war because entangling alliances and prior commitments would make it an "offensive" war, one that was "none of our business," fought by the United States "against our will," "to pull other people's chestnuts out of the fire." The President was accused of advocating internationalism *because* it would involve the United States in war. Beard arranges his definition of internationalism to lead his readers into acceptance of the charge as truth. The central argument of internationalists, that collective security is precisely the only means whereby the United States can *avoid* war, he distorts into a charge that they believe in using force, not solely as a last recourse *after* peaceful moral, diplomatic, economic, and political sanctions have failed to halt an aggressor, but at the outset, as an *alternative* to other sanctions. The word "or" in Beard's definition ". . . impose peace, by effective sanctions or by force, . . ." mashes into one lump the series of measures, carefully graded from less to more coercive, with which internationalists believe an aggressor should be faced—those measures to be applied successively, with the hope and reasonable expectation that the threat of stronger measures would, at a stage short of war, stop the aggressor. No reasonable observer is likely to argue that, if all the allied and associated powers that ultimately combined to win the First and Second World Wars had combined before those wars began and faced Germany and its allies with the certainty of their collective action, those wars would have occurred.

A fair definition of internationalism must specify that the policy involves a series of collective measures, graded from less to more coercive, by a group of nations having a large share of world power, and the reasoned conviction of internationalists that the threat of these measures will stop aggression before the last one, force, is reached. Thus the central, simple fact may be understood: internationalists support collective measures against aggression as the best means of securing world peace.

Beard's other chief distortion—that Roosevelt practiced deception on the American people regarding the nature and aims of his foreign policy —depends upon his distorted definition of internationalism. Beard proves in great detail that Roosevelt repeatedly assured the American people that his policy was to avoid entangling alliances, prior commitments, and war. He finds deception in these assurances because an internationalist policy, in Beard's view, could not avoid entangling alliances, prior commitments, and war.

His thesis is maintained by butchering the record and throwing out its most vital parts. Roosevelt, from his first to his last days in office, not only repeatedly assured the American people that his policy was to avoid entangling alliances, prior commitments and war, but he devised and repeatedly urged upon the public and Congress techniques of collective security which, while avoiding entangling alliances and prior commitments, he as an internationalist was convinced were the best means of preventing United States involvement in war. . . .

Japan's Secret Program

[Japanese Foreign Minister] Matsuoka's statement afforded a public glimpse of the secret program of the Japanese government, which was fully exposed after the war by the International Military Tribunal for the Far East. It was adopted in October, 1940, and designated three objectives: early successful settlement of the China Incident; a nonaggression pact with Russia; and incorporation of the countries of southeast Asia and the southwest Pacific, including Malaya, India, Australia, and New Zealand, in the Greater East Asia Co-Prosperity Sphere. Singapore and the Philippines were regarded as the keys. If they were won, all the rest would fall easily to Japan.

Action to achieve the third objective was planned on two fronts: diplomatic and military. Britain would be offered Japanese mediation in the European war in return for recognition of the Co-Prosperity Sphere, including surrender of Singapore. In February, 1941, the Japanese leaders told the Germans that a military attack against Singapore was planned. Military bases were to be secured in Indo-China and Thailand. The United States was to be offered Japanese recognition of "Philippine independence" in return for American recognition of the Co-Prosperity Sphere. In January, 1941, the Japanese Commander of the Combined Fleets approved and transmitted to Imperial General Headquarters a plan for a surprise attack on Pearl Harbor while the two countries were at peace. In May, 1941, the Japanese Navy began training for the attack.

Thus it is now clear that when Matsuoka told the Japanese Diet in January, 1941, that he wanted the United States to agree to Japanese supremacy in the western Pacific, he actually demanded American cooperation with Japan to achieve its conquests as the price of American immunity from Japanese attack against the United States.

In the innumerable American-Japanese conversations of 1941, the Roosevelt administration never refused to discuss a Japanese proposal, it never issued an ultimatum, and it never offered or agreed to proposals which signified appeasement, that is, which gave consent or support to Japanese conquests of territories of third countries. . . .

Roosevelt and Hull Call a Halt

The Japanese-American conversations had all but broken down when Hitler invaded the Soviet Union on June 22. The Roosevelt administration became concerned that the Japanese would attack Russia or take advantage of Russia's preoccupation to launch the long-expected southward movement. The President sent a message to Premier Konoye on July 6 stating the earnest hope of the United States government that reports of Japan's decision to enter the war against the Soviet Union were not based on fact, because it would destroy the possibility of strenthening the peace of the Pacific area. Konoye answered with a copy of an oral statement Matsuoka had made to the Soviet Ambassador on July 2, declaring that Japan, in its present "awkward" position, hoped to preserve the spirit of mutual trust among the Axis allies while maintaining good relations with the Soviet Union. And Konoye turned about to ask the United States whether reports were true that the United States intended to intervene in the European war. The American answer to this was that United States policy was based solely on self-defense against the Germans, who were the chief threat to the security of the Western Hemisphere, and that American aid to Russia would "in no manner threaten the security of nations which have not joined the conflict on Hitler's side."

At the same time, the Roosevelt administration received alarming information of Japanese preparations for a major war. Ominous movements were made publicly, and Magic intercepts contained such signals as the following, in a message from Tokyo to Berlin on July 2, the day of an Imperial Conference:

> The Imperial Government shall continue its endeavor to dispose of the China incident, and shall take measures with a view to advancing southward in order to establish firmly a basis for her self-existence and self-protection.

Other intercepts named French Indo-China and Thailand as immediate targets. Matsuoka instructed Nomura:

> In the meantime, diplomatic negotiations shall be carried on with extreme care. Although every means available shall be resorted to in order to prevent the United States from joining the war, if need be Japan shall act in accordance with the three-Power pact and shall decide when and how force will be employed.

Matsuoka was not quite frank with Nomura. The Far East Tribunal later learned that the Imperial Conference of July 2 had decided to continue conversations with the United States as a cover while final preparations for military action were completed. Troops that later landed in Malaya and the Philippines now began practicing.

On July 18, Admiral Teijiro Toyoda replaced Matsuoka as Foreign Minister of Japan. This shift is called by Morgenstern proof that Japan was amenable to American criticisms of Matsuoka. But promptly after the change, on July 21, Japanese troops invaded southern Indo-China, and it is doubtful whether Roosevelt and Hull could, in the light of that act, sensibly interpret the fall of Matsuoka as a sign of a Japanese turn against the policy of aggression. In southern Indo-China the Japanese occupied and built up bases which gave them a strategic position pointing inexorably towards the Philippines, Malaya, Singapore, and the NEI. In short, the new aggression was proof that the program of southward advance was underway.

It made a farce of Nomura's pretense that his government wished a "peaceful settlement," that Matsuoka's belligerence was a matter of "politics" only for "home consumption." The conversations were broken off by the United States on July 23. It was Japan's new aggression, in contradiction of its professions in Washington, that led Roosevelt and Hull to call a halt. Morgenstern distorts the incident by avoiding mention of the crucial sequence of dates and by giving Japanese unwillingness to sign a blank check for the United States in Europe as the reason why negotiations "stalled." The Japanese, in Morgenstern's account, gave ample proof of good faith by dismissing Matsuoka from power. The Roosevelt administration was unreasonable in its demands and sought excuses to break off conversations in order to invoke economic sanctions with "clear understanding" that they "might easily precipitate war."

The possibility that Japanese invasion of southern Indo-China may have influenced the administration is carefully ignored by Morgenstern. On July 23, two days after that invasion, Sumner Welles told Nomura that Secretary Hull could see no basis for continuation of their conversations. He asserted that agreement with the United States would have given Japan an "infinitely greater amount of security, both military and economic," than it could obtain by conquest. He said the United States had to assume that the Japanese government was taking "the last step" before proceeding on a campaign of totalitarian expansion in the South Seas. Nomura pleaded for "patience" and against "hasty conclusions." He said an embargo on oil exports to Japan would undoubtedly "inflame Japanese public opinion." Welles assured him that Hull would wish to talk again with him. . . .

Economic Sanctions

On July 25 [1941] the administration froze Japanese assets in the United States to prevent their use in trade between the United States and Japan "in ways harmful to national defense and American interests." It also froze Chinese assets at the request of the Chinese government to prevent liquidation of those which were obtained by "duress or conquest." The purpose of the latter action was underlined in a statement of the President that the administration of the licensing system with respect to Chinese assets would be conducted with a view to strengthening the Chinese government and was "a continuation of this Government's policy of assisting China." Synchronization of British policy was apparent the next day when Britain froze Japanese assets and denounced its commercial agreements with Japan. Also on July 26, President Roosevelt nationalized the armed forces of the Philippines.

On the day the United States froze Japanese assets, Colonel Iwakuro told Joseph W. Ballantine, of the State Department, that if the United States took such action, he believed Japan would have no alternative but to go south to Malaya and the NEI to obtain essential supplies. He said such action would also prevent another attempt to reach an "understanding," which his government otherwise urged. Iwakuro said Nomura was too "gentle" to express these views as he did. Ballantine received the impression that the Japanese had no real expectation that conversations would be resumed and that no reply was called for beyond the statements of Welles and Roosevelt to Nomura.

In Tokyo, Ambassador Grew asked Toyoda to consider well how the President's offer to neutralize Indo-China met Japanese contentions. He said that if it were accepted it might establish a new basis for continuation of the Hull-Nomura talks looking towards a general agreement. Grew and Welles both told the Japanese the freezing order, like the earlier abrogation of the American-Japanese commercial treaty, would at first be interpreted liberally by the United States.

Thus doors were again left open by the Roosevelt administration for the Japanese government to achieve peacefully its legitimate ambitions. But immediately reports were received that the Japanese were making demands on Thailand of the same sort which had preceded invasion of southern Indo-China.

Roosevelt promptly on July 31 told the Japanese government through Welles and Nomura that in the judgment of the United States government "there was not the remotest threat of danger to Japan nor the slightest justification for Japan alleging" that concessions by Thailand were necessary as a means of assuring a Japanese source of raw materials or as a military precaution. But Roosevelt again offered Japan a constructive alternative: he said his offer to neutralize Indo-China should now be regarded as embracing Thailand in order to give Japan the same guarantees and security in that area.

Just as the offer regarding Indo-China had been backed up by the freezing order, so now the President's offer regarding Thailand was backed up on August 1 by an embargo against the export of aviation gasoline. The stated purpose was "in the interest of national defense," and merely on that ground the order was long overdue. In the opinion of most Americans it was also long overdue as an economic sanction against Japanese aggression, and the order was greeted with very wide public satisfaction. . . .

Roosevelt and Pearl Harbor

The fall of the Konoye government led Admiral Stark to send a war warning on October 16, 1941, to Admiral Husband E. Kimmel in command of the Pacific fleet and to Admiral Thomas C. Hart in Command of the Asiatic fleet. The first inference in this warning was that war between Japan and Russia was "a strong possibility." But, the warning continued:

> Since the United States and Britain are held responsible by Japan for her present desperate situation, there is also a possibility that Japan may attack these two powers. In view of these possibilities, you will take due precautions, including such preparatory deployments as will not disclose strategic intention nor constitute provocative actions against Japan.

This reflected the estimate of Washington authorities that Japan was most likely to attack Russia at the penultimate moment of Hitler's conquest, in like manner as Mussolini had attacked France. The Pacific commanders were given enough information regarding diplomatic developments to lead them to believe that they knew the situation, but not enough to judge it as effectively as the leaders in Washington. Magic intercepts, the best source of information regarding Japanese intentions, were not transmitted to the commanders. Copies went to only nine persons in Washington, including President Roosevelt, Secretaries Hull, Stimson and Knox, General Marshall and Admiral Stark. General Marshall later said this was necessary to guard a military secret of incalculable value. . . .

Foreign Minister Togo on November 3 sent Saburo Kurusu, former Japanese Ambassador to Germany, to Washington to "assist" Nomura. He had signed the Axis alliance in Berlin. In spite of this, Ambassador Grew saw no reason to believe that Kurusu was "any more friendly to the Nazis than to us."

Grew sent a report to Hull and Welles on November 3 which, as he wrote in his diary, he hoped history would not overlook if war occurred. He did not renew his September 29 proposal that "constructive conciliation" be the policy of the United States. Once more he ruled out appeasement of Japan. But he did give full credit to the sincerity of the Tojo government in "seeking conciliation with the United States." He reasoned that Japanese pro-Axis elements had gained power following the Fall of France. But after the signing of the Axis alliance, Germany's failure to invade Britain and its attack against the Soviet Union, coupled with the strong policy of the United States, had strengthened moderate elements and led the Japanese government to seek conciliation with the United States. If this effort failed, Grew wrote that he foresaw:

> a probable swing of the pendulum in Japan once more back to the former Japanese position or even farther. This would lead to what he has described as an all-out, do-or-die attempt, actually risking national hara-kiri, to make Japan impervious to economic embargoes abroad rather than to yield to foreign pressure. It is realized by observers who feel Japanese national temper and psychology from day to day that, beyond peradventure, this contingency not only is possible but is probable.

This turned out to be a correct prediction. But Grew offered no advice as to how the United States might fend off Japan's "do-or-die attempt." It was his opinion that strengthening economic sanctions would not avert war. But he believed the primary question was whether American national interests justified war in case the first line of national defense, diplomacy, failed.

Since appeasement of Japan, including the relaxation of economic sanctions, was ruled out, the only possibility Grew saw for a peaceful solution is found in his assertions that Japanese "moderate elements" were still in power, that the Japanese government actually sought conciliation with the United States.

If Hull could agree with this on November 3, his belief vanished two days later. A Magic intercept of Togo to Nomura read:

> "Because of various circumstances, it is absolutely necessary that all arrangements for the signing of this agreement be completed by the 25th of this month. I realize that this is a difficult order, but under the circumstances it is an unavoidable one. Please understand this thoroughly and tackle the problem of saving the Japanese-American relations from falling into a chaotic condition."

Secretary Hull observes in his *Memoirs* that this meant Japan had "already set in motion the wheels of her war machine. . . ." This and other signs Hull read as proof that Japan was turning to new aggressive advances in the South Seas, "including war with the United States if we did not sign the agreement she required."

Grew himself saw similar evidence in the Japanese press. On November 5 he noted in his diary a list of seven demands which the *Japan Times and Advertiser* said the United States should adopt to make "restitution" to Japan. Besides bald versions of demands already made officially by the Japanese government, this one was laid down:

> Acknowledge Japan's Co-Prosperity Sphere and leadership of the western Pacific, letting Manchuria, China, Indo-China, Thailand, the Netherlands Indies and other states and protectorates establish their own political and economic relations with Japan without interference of any kind.

This newspaper was known to be the organ of the Japanese Foreign Office. . . .

To Gain Time

To keep the door open in order to seize the last chance of tiding things over became the purpose of the Roosevelt administration in the last round of conversations with Japan. Hull warned the President and Cabinet on November 7 that "we should be on the lookout for a military attack by Japan anywhere at any time." This led to warning speeches to the public by Secretary Knox and Under Secretary Welles.

But Hull's warning to the Cabinet did not lead to a new warning by authorities in Washington to commanders in the Pacific for two more weeks. Secretary of War Stimson has written that since August, 1941, the General Staff had been developing an important new strategic concept regarding the Philippine Islands. Formerly the Islands had been regarded as an "unprotected pawn" certain to fall easily to Japan early in a war. But General Douglas MacArthur had been recalled in July to active duty in the United States Army after building up the Philippine Army for the Commonwealth, and he was highly optimistic that his forces could hold the Islands. Also, proponents of air power believed that if a force of the new B-17 heavy bombers, the Flying Fortresses, could be sent to the Philippines, the Islands could be defended and the Japanese could be prevented from moving south through the China Sea. Stimson on October 6 told Hull the Army needed three months to build up the Philippines.

Concentration on the task of building up defenses of the Philippines, as the point where the United States was most likely to be attacked by Japan, evidently preoccupied Washington authorities during the weeks following Hull's warning to the Cabinet. The Secretary of State set out to provide the commodity his colleagues demanded of him—time. . . .

Kurusu

Kurusu arrived in Washington on November 17 and was immediately presented to Hull and Roosevelt. Hull distrusted him and was convinced that he knew the plans of his government and played a double role of trying to press the United States to accept Japan's terms or, failing that, would try to lull the administration with talk until Japan was ready to strike. An oral statement to Hull by Nomura ignored the request that Wakasugi's October 13 statements be confirmed. An "explanation" declared that the escape clauses in the Japanese draft proposals for an agreement were used

> only in order to express the qualification which is due to and necessary for a sovereign state and were not intended to limit or narrow down in any way the peaceful intentions of the Japanese Government.

This was very different from Wakasugi's offer to withdraw the clauses.

The President told Kurusu that the policy of the United States in relation to Germany was one of self-defense. Kurusu said Germany had not "up to this time" asked Japan to fight; that Japan was serving "a desirable purpose" without fighting. This evidently meant that Japan was keeping large bodies of Soviet troops and large portions of the British and American Navies diverted from Europe and the Atlantic. The President and Hull found it necessary to explain that not the United States but Japan was the aggressor in the Pacific. Kurusu said he was not familiar with commercial policy and had not examined Hull's proposal on that issue. He repeated the perennial Japanese complaint that troops could not be withdrawn from China "at once." The President in turn repeated the American answer that "the question ought to be worked out in a fair way considering all of the circumstances. . . ." And he promised that "at a suitable stage," after Pacific questions had been determined, the United States might bring Japan and China together to settle remaining questions or details.

"East Wind Rain"

Secretary Hull wrote in his *Memoirs* that the situation now "could not have been more tense." The day before Kurusu arrived, a Magic intercept from Togo to Nomura rejected Nomura's suggestion that the Japanese government ought to "wait and see what turn the war takes and remain patient." Togo replied that he was "awfully sorry to say that the situation renders this out of the question. I set the deadline for the solution of these negotiations . . . and there will be no change." That deadline, November 25, was a week off. Nomura grasped at the President's mention on November 10 of a *modus vivendi* between Japan and the United States. In an intercepted message to Tokyo on November 19, Nomura stated: "I think that it would be better to fix up a temporary 'truce' now in the spirit of 'give and take' and make this the prelude to greater achievements to come later." Tokyo answered on November 20: "Under the circumstances here, we regret that the plan suggested by you . . . would not suffice for saving the present situation."

This interchange demonstrated two things about the *modus vivendi*, which was presently discussed in Washington: that even the "moderate" Nomura meant it to be preliminary not to peace but to "greater achievements," that is, conquest; and that his government was not interested in a truce which would require postponement of the attacks it had planned. If one speaks of the realities of the situation, as they were exposed to Roosevelt and Hull in the intercepted Japanese messages, it was Japan that issued an ultimatum, including demands, a deadline, and threat of aggression if the demands were not met in the specified time; and for the United States it was, in Hull's words, "a case of signing on the dotted line or taking the consequences."

Ambassador Grew, on the same day that Kurusu arrived in Washington, sent Hull another warning of "the need to guard against sudden Japanese naval or military actions in such areas as are not now involved in the Chinese theater of operations." He said that the intelligence activities of his Embassy were practically restricted to "what could be seen with the naked eye," and that Washington must not depend upon him for any advance information. Troop dispositions, however, indicated new operations either in the southwest Pacific, or Siberia, or both. Actually of course the Japanese were organizing the raiding force that attacked Pearl Harbor, as well as the other forces designated for points in the southwest Pacific, including the Philippines. But it is notable that Grew in Tokyo evidently saw no reason to warn Washington against more than the "normal" targets of Japan: the southwest Pacific and Siberia.

Nor did Magic intercepts give the administration leaders a more accurate picture of Japanese intentions. The most specific intercept was the famous "east wind rain" message of November 19 from Tokyo to the Japanese Embassy in Washington. In it a complete breakdown of the conversations was foreseen, and a code for future use was designated:

> In case of emergency (*danger of cutting off our diplomatic relations*), and the cutting off of international communications, the following warning will be added in the middle of the daily Japanese language short wave news broadcast:
>
> (1) In case of Japan-U.S. relations *in danger:* Higashi No Kazeame [east wind rain].
>
> (2) Japan-U.S.S.R. relations: Kitanokaze Kumori [north wind cloudy].
>
> (3) Japan-British relations: Nishi No Kaze Hare [west wind clear].

The prevailing expectation in Washington was that the Japanese would move into Thailand and southward towards Malaya and the NEI, with a possible attack against the Philippines to protect their flank; or, less likely than the southward move, they might move against Siberia. The words italicized in the message quoted above indicate that the code was to be used in a situation amounting to less than a Japanese surprise attack against one or more of the three great powers, that is, *danger*, not certainty, that *diplomatic relations* would end. In another message on the same day, Tokyo warned that if relations with the United States were "*becoming dangerous*," the word "Higashi" would be used at the beginning and end of Japan's intelligence broadcast."

It may be conjectured that the Japanese government used such "mild" terms out of caution, not wishing to reveal its actual plans in any message sent abroad. Furthermore, Admiral T. S. Wilkinson, Director of Naval Intelligence, believed that the Germans knew in October, 1941, that the United States had solved the Japanese code and had warned the Japanese government. It would be an obvious ruse of the Japanese to send plausible but misleading information in the useless code. If Washington officials were suspicious that the Japanese knew their code was broken, they would not accept intercepts at face value.

It seems doubtful that one may fairly base judgments of the actions of the Roosevelt administration upon the premise that the Magic intercepts gave leading officials accurate foreknowledge of Japanese actions. Not only was there no reference in the intercepts to an impending Japanese attack upon any American territory, but the intercepts were probably read with considerable skepticism. Responsible officials in Washington could be expected to rely chiefly on known Japanese military and naval movements and an estimate of "logical" probabilities. Both pointed to Japanese attack upon the Philippines as the most extreme probability, and Magic intercepts did not contradict this estimate.

The chief item used by Morgenstern to support the isolationist thesis that Washington officials knew beforehand Pearl Harbor would be attacked is a series of intercepts beginning September 24, 1941, of messages between Tokyo and the Japanese Consul General in Honolulu. These messages conveyed the anxiety of Tokyo for data regarding the exact locations of warships in Pearl Harbor, and the reports of the Consul General containing full information. Morgenstern neglects to mention that such information was well within the requirements of a Japanese plan of sabotage by Japanese agents. The authorities at Pearl Harbor were prepared against that danger. But Morgenstern himself does not claim to find in any message prior to one dated 7:22 P.M., December 6, and another of a few hours later, 12:42 A.M., December 7, material that "gave away" the secret of a bombing raid. In these messages the Consul General *for the first time* spoke of air defenses at Hawaii and observed: "I imagine that in all probability there is considerable opportunity left to take advantage for a surprise attack. . . ." Morgenstern then comments that after a December 4 intercept of an "east wind rain" execute message, and the long series of Japanese messages from Honolulu to Tokyo, "there could be no question where the attack would come."

This slurs over his own admission that, not the "long series of messages," but only those sent within the last twelve hours before the Japanese planes appeared over Pearl Harbor at dawn on December 7 actually pointed to raiding planes rather than sabotage. The fact that the two messages which did expose the secret were not decoded until December 8, Morgenstern calls "Washington's excuse. . . ." But Morgenstern himself makes this excuse seem extremely plausible. He describes how the "give-away" messages were intercepted in San Francisco and copies mailed to Washington. Hearing of this, Army Signal Intelligence Service ordered the messages to be sent to Washington on a new teletype machine which had been installed that day. When the messages arrived in Washington, translators were called to night duty. But the final and very lengthy Japanese diplomatic message was then being intercepted, and the translators worked on it instead. Other messages less indicative of Japanese attack were processed even more slowly.

Such is the best evidence Morgenstern can find that for Washington officials "there could be no question where the attack would come," with its implication that commanders at Pearl Harbor were not ordered to shift from preparations against sabotage to preparations against air attack because Roosevelt, Hull, Stimson, Knox, Marshall, and Stark preferred the more serious loss of life and damage to the fleet that would result from mistaken preparations. For such a terrible implication, Morgenstern at the crucial point can do no better than verify the plain reason why Washington officials did not receive the "give-away" messages in time, and call the reason an "excuse." . . .

The Modus Vivendi

The Japanese on November 20 offered a draft proposal for a "temporary agreement." In the light of the rejection by the Japanese government, on November 19, of Nomura's suggestion in favor of such an agreement, this proposal must be regarded as the sheerest of hypocrisies designed to occupy the time while the Japanese task force proceeded to Hawaii. Two of the chief issues on which the United States desired settlement, namely, Japan's obligation under the Axis alliance, and economic policy in China and the Pacific regions, were left for later consideration. On remaining issues, Japan offered to make one concession, withdrawal of Japanese troops from southern to northern Indo-China, in return for United States cooperation with Japan in securing the fruits of aggression in China. Japan asked the United States to stop giving aid to China and to restore economic relations with Japan, including delivery to Japan of a required quantity of oil, while Japan made "peace" with China. Kurusu had admitted to Hull that "peace" with China would involve the stationing of Japanese troops there for an indefinite period. Besides providing Japan with American oil to help it impose its will on China, the United States was asked to "cooperate" with Japan in obtaining for it oil and other materials in the NEI. Japan would promise to make no armed movement southward, but offered no guaranty against aggression northward.

Hull considered that the proposals called for "virtually a surrender" by the United States. He asked Kurusu and Nomura, as he later wrote:

> what they thought would be the public reaction in the United States if we were to announce tomorrow that we had decided to discontinue aid to Great Britain. There was no reply. "In the minds of the American people," I continued, "the purposes underlying our aid to China are the same as the purposes underlying aid to Great Britain. . . ."

Hull regarded the situation as virtually hopeless. But the military leaders pleaded with him for more time, and therefore Hull and State Department officials sought desperately to work out some counterproposal to keep the conversations going. For a few days a three-months' *modus vivendi* was considered. It is noteworthy that it was while Hull worked on this scheme, that the Japanese task force was ordered on November 22 to proceed eastward through the north Pacific to reach Hawaii by December 7. No inkling of this reached American observers or officials in Washington, but ominous movements of Japanese forces into positions where they were poised for attacks against Thailand, Malaya, the NEI, and possibly the Philippines or Guam, were known in detail. On November 24, Army and Navy commanders in the Pacific were warned that a Japanese "surprise aggressive movement in any direction including an attack on the Philippines or Guam is a possibility." This was interpreted in Hawaii to require no change in preparations against sabotage as the chief danger.

President Roosevelt, Secretary of the Treasury Morgenthau, and other officials helped Hull explore the possibility of a *modus vivendi*, and he consulted the representatives of Great Britain, China, the Netherlands, and Australia. A Magic intercept from Tokyo to Kurusu and Nomura on November 22 extended the deadline from November 25 to 29. One phrase in it provides the first reason why Hull in the end decided not to make a counterproposal for a *modus vivendi*. The Japanese Ambassadors were instructed: "Stick to our fixed policy. . . ." This could only mean that nothing but complete American surrender to the Japanese proposals would satisfy Tojo. It confirmed Hull's belief that no arrangement that the United States could accept would be acceptable to Japan. The intercepted message ended: "This time we mean it, that the dead line absolutely cannot be changed. After that things are automatically going to happen."

The second reason why Hull decided against the *modus vivendi* is that the government of China objected to it and obtained wide support for its objection, including that of Churchill. The final American draft of the *modus vivendi* called for mutual pledges that the United States and Japan would not advance in the Pacific area by force or threat of force; Japan would withdraw its troops from southern Indo-China, and also reduce its forces in northern Indo-China to 25,000—a number thought to preclude a campaign to close the Burma Road; the United States would allow limited quantities of American oil, cotton, and other commodities to go to Japan and it would buy Japanese goods; the United States would urge Britain, Australia, and the Netherlands to resume trade similarly with Japan; and the United States affirmed its fundamental position that any settlement between Japan and China must be based upon the principles of "peace, law, order, and justice." Attached to this three-months' *modus vivendi* was a ten-point proposal for a permanent agreement.

The *modus vivendi* drawn up by Hull meant temporary appeasement of Japan insofar as it would give temporary United States approval to Japanese conquests and relax the economic sanctions which the United States, Britain, Australia and the Netherlands had imposed against Japan during preceding months. The plan must be regarded as a product of the desperation of the Roosevelt administration in its fight for time. Had it been offered to Japan, it would have been a violation of the administration's principle of no compromise with aggression.

Only agreement by China, the government which would be the chief victim of this appeasement, that the time which might be gained would be worth the sacrifice, would have justified such an offer to Japan. China refused to agree. Churchill supported the Chinese view. After hectic discussions, the decision was reached on the night of November 25 to make no counterproposal of a *modus vivendi* but to answer the Japanese only with the ten-point proposal for a permanent settlement.

On the Rock of Principle

In this decision the Roosevelt administration met the supreme test of its statesmanship in service of the policy of collective security against aggression. Beard's statement that the decision was made "for reasons which are nowhere explicit" is nonsense; Beard himself recites the evidence that the Chinese government violently opposed the *modus vivendi*. He ignores another contributing factor, that is, the futility of offering to Japan, in the face of the intercepted instructions to the Ambassadors to "stick to our fixed policy," an American *modus vivendi* which would have required Japan to retreat from its "fixed policy," especially in the matter of the number of troops to be left in northern Indo-China. Beard does not wish to admit that the one thing which might have justified temporary appeasement of Japan was the consent of China. The Roosevelt administration refused to make a deal with Japan affecting China's fate without its consent. It refused to ignore the rights of China as Chamberlain had ignored those of Czechoslovakia at Munich.

On the rock of this principle, the last possibility of Roosevelt and Hull attempting to postpone the deadline in Japan's ultimatum collapsed. Actually, no such possibility existed. But the administration believed that a possibility still existed that Japan would only attack non-American territory, leaving room for a choice by the United States whether it should enter the war.

No one but an absolute pacifist would argue that the danger of war is a greater evil than violation of principle. It must be concluded that the isolationist thesis involves denunciation of the Roosevelt-Hull decision against the *modus vivendi* because of the nature of the principle involved. The isolationist believes that appeasement of Japan without China's consent violated no principle worth a risk of war. The internationalist must believe that the principle did justify a risk of war. In short, subjective and *a priori* attitudes ultimately determine judgment of the Roosevelt-Hull policy. If an observer can be imagined to exist who is "neutral" as between the attitudes of isolationists and internationalists, he might conclude that it did not matter whether or not the Roosevelt administration offered the *modus vivendi* because the Japanese government was certain to reject it. . . .

The Message of November 26

Hull's answer on November 26 was a refusal to surrender to the Japanese ultimatum. This was implicit in his rejection of the Japanese proposal for a *modus vivendi*. But he did not entirely reject that proposal, and he offered Japan a draft plan for an agreement on all points at issue as a basis for continued negotiations. This took away from his answer all character of a challenge to Japan to carry out its threat of war. Hull did not expect the Japanese government to accept his constructive proposal for an agreement, and he warned the armed service chiefs that Japan could be expected now to attack, but this was not, as the isolationists charge, proof that he regarded his answer as an "ultimatum." It was proof that he judged correctly that Japan would attack if the United States did not entirely surrender to Japan's ultimatum.

Hull's draft proposal for an American-Japanese agreement contained ten points. None of them was unacceptable or disadvantageous to a Japanese government mindful of the real interests of Japan: 1) a multilateral nonaggression pact among the governments principally concerned in the Pacific; 2) an agreement among the governments principally interested to respect the territorial integrity of Indo-China and equality of economic opportunity in that country; 3) no support of any Chinese government except the national government of Chiang Kai-shek; 4) relinquishment of extraterritorial rights in China by the United States as well as all other powers; 5) a liberal trade agreement between the United States and Japan; 6) mutual removal of freezing measures; 7) stabilization of currency values between the dollar and the yen; 8) an agreement that neither country would interpret an agreement with a third country in a way that would conflict with the fundamental purpose of establishing peace; 9) both governments would use their influence to lead other governments to accept and carry out the principles of this American-Japanese agreement; 10) Japan would withdraw its forces from China and Indo-China.

This draft proposal was accompanied by an explanation that the United States government regarded "some" but not all of the points in the Japanese *modus vivendi* of November 20 as in conflict with the fundamental principles to which each government had committed itself. The American draft proposal was not offered as the only terms of agreement the United States was willing to accept. Hull explained to Nomura and Kurusu that it was offered as "*one practical exemplification of a program which this Government envisages as something to be worked out during our further conversations.*"

To sum up: the American answer to Japan on November 26 did not reject *all* of the terms of Japan's proposed *modus vivendi;* the American draft proposal was not offered as the *only* terms of agreement the United States would accept; the United States made *no demands* upon Japan; the American draft proposal contained many offers that the Japanese had often admitted were advantageous to Japan because they would satisfy Japanese demands for security and prosperity—most significantly, an offer to end United States economic sanctions against Japan; it named *no deadline* for an answer by Japan; it contained *no threat of force or war* or other penalty if Japan refused to accept the American proposal; it specifically *invited* Japan to *continue negotiations;* it *promised to consider* new Japanese proposals, in the usual manner of a peaceful power, in the course of further negotiations.

To call such a proposal an "ultimatum" or an "ultimative notice" is to murder the meaning of the word. If, as the Minority Report asserts, the Japanese war lords "treated" this answer "as an ultimatum," evidence is available, in Togo's description of the Japanese terms of November 20 as an ultimatum, which proves that he, at least, had for some days already accepted the fact which American isolationists reject: that to the Japanese government belonged the responsibility for war that accrues to a government guilty of issuing an ultimatum. When the Japanese Foreign Minister admits responsibility, it seems excessive for Americans to find the Japanese innocent and their own government guilty. . . .

Additional Reading

Harry Elmer Barnes, ed., *Perpetual War for Perpetual Peace* (1953).
Charles A. Beard, *President Roosevelt and the Coming of the War, 1941* (1948).
Robert J. C. Butow, *Tojo and the Coming of the War* (1961).
W. H. Chamberlin, *America's Second Crusade* (1950).
Wayne S. Cole, *America First: The Battle Against Intervention, 1940–1941* (1953).
Robert A. Divine, *The Illusion of Neutrality* (1962).
Donald F. Drummond, *The Passing of American Neutrality, 1937–1941* (1955).
Herbert Feis, *The Road to Pearl Harbor* (1950).
William L. Langer and S. E. Gleason, *The Challenge to Isolation, 1937–1940* (1952).
———, *The Undeclared War, 1940–1941* (1953).
Walter Millis, *This Is Pearl!* (1947).
Paul W. Schroeder, *The Axis Alliance and Japanese-American Relations, 1941* (1958).
R. A. Theobald, *The Final Secret of Pearl Harbor* (1954).
Gerald E. Wheeler, *Prelude to Pearl Harbor: The United States Navy and the Far East, 1921–1931* (1963).
Roberta Wohtsletter, *Pearl Harbor: Warning and Decision* (1962).

18 *THE YALTA CONFERENCE: Unnecessary Concessions or the Price of Coalition Diplomacy?*

When Soviet Russia was suddenly attacked by its erstwhile ally Nazi Germany, on June 22, 1941, the American government promptly decided to extend Lend-Lease aid to the new recruit against the Axis. The flow of war supplies was substantially increased after the United States actively entered the war and by 1945 totaled approximately $11 billions. Roosevelt and Winston Churchill, the British Prime Minister, also made repeated efforts to assuage Soviet suspicions of the West and thus not only to facilitate the waging of war but to lay the basis for an enduring postwar collaboration and peace.

Russia seemed to undergo a fundamental change during the war, presaging Big Three cooperation in the post-Hitler world. The Communist International, instrument of world revolution, was disbanded; a measure of religious freedom was permitted within the Soviet Union; and the Declaration of the United Nations, a statement of liberal war goals, was subscribed to by Moscow. A series of major conferences among the Big Three powers appeared to have solidified cooperation and alliance: the Moscow Foreign Ministers' Conference in October, 1943; the Roosevelt-Churchill meeting with Premier Joseph Stalin at Teheran in December, 1943; and the summit conference at Yalta in the Crimea, February, 1945.

The Yalta Conference marked the apex of Big Three collaboration and was probably the most important of the conferences in its far-ranging decisions. The final stages of the war against Hitler were determined and Russia agreed to enter the Far Eastern phase against Japan. Important decisions affecting the map of postwar Europe were adopted and concessions were made in the Far East to Russia as the price of cooperation.

Even during the war, there were some vocal critics of the alliance with Soviet Russia. In the years of Cold War from 1947 on, this criticism mounted and often became bitter and hysterical in tone. The Cold War struggle was so different from the expected postwar world, so costly in money, manpower, and foreign commitments, that it caused a searching re-examination of wartime diplomacy and agreements. Domestic politics also were involved, as many Republicans were eager to belabor the Democratic New Deal–Fair Deal administration with charges of blunders at home and abroad. The Yalta Conference and agreements were especially singled out for scathing attacks and even for charges of treason and betrayals to the Communists.

DOCUMENTS

The Yalta Conference

The Big Three leaders, with their aides, met February 4–11, 1945 to make final military arrangements and begin the planning of the postwar world. Besides the public agreements, several secret accords were concluded regarding the kinds of reparations to be secured from defeated Germany, three votes for Russia in the projected United Nations, and the entry of the Soviet Union into the struggle with Japan. The following selections include extracts from the Protocol of the Proceedings of the conference, which was then a secret document.

Report of the Crimea Conference

For the past eight days, Winston S. Churchill, Prime Minister of Great Britain, Franklin D. Roosevelt, President of the United States of America, and Marshal J. V. Stalin, Chairman of the Council of Peoples' Commissars of the Union of Soviet Socialist Republics have met with the Foreign Secretaries, Chiefs of Staff and other advisors in the Crimea. . . .

The following statement is made by the Prime Minister of Great Britain, the President of the United States of America, and the Chairman of the Council of Peoples' Commissars of the Union of Soviet Socialist Republics on the results of the Crimean Conference:

I

The Defeat of Germany

We have considered and determined the military plans of the three allied powers for the final defeat of the common enemy. The military staffs of the three allied nations have met in daily meetings throughout the Conference. These meetings have been most satisfactory from every point of view and have resulted in closer coordination of the military effort of the three Allies than ever before. . . .

Nazi Germany is doomed. The German people will only make the cost of their defeat heavier to themselves by attempting to continue a hopeless resistance.

II

The Occupation and Control of Germany

We have agreed on common policies and plans for enforcing the unconditional surrender terms which we shall impose together on Nazi Germany after German armed resistance has been finally crushed. These terms will not be made known until the final defeat of Germany has been accomplished. Under the agreed plan, the forces of the Three Powers will each occupy a separate zone of Germany. Coordinated administration and control has been provided for under the plan through a central Control

Commission consisting of the Supreme Commanders of the Three Powers with headquarters in Berlin. It has been agreed that France should be invited by the Three Powers, if she should so desire, to take over a zone of occupation, and to participate as a fourth member of the Control Commission. The limits of the French zone will be agreed by the four governments concerned through their representatives on the European Advisory Commission.

It is our inflexible purpose to destroy German militarism and Nazism and to ensure that Germany will never again be able to disturb the peace of the world. We are determined to disarm and disband all German armed forces; break up for all time the German General Staff that has repeatedly contrived the resurgence of German militarism; remove or destroy all German military equipment; eliminate or control all German industry that could be used for military production; bring all war criminals to just and swift punishment and exact reparation in kind for the destruction wrought by the Germans; wipe out the Nazi party, Nazi laws, organizations and institutions, remove all Nazi and militarist influences from public office and from the cultural and economic life of the German people; and take in harmony such other measures in Germany as may be necessary to the future peace and safety of the world. It is not our purpose to destroy the people of Germany, but only when Nazism and Militarism have been extirpated will there be hope for a decent life for Germans, and a place for them in the comity of nations.

III

Reparation by Germany

We have considered the question of the damage caused by Germany to the Allied Nations in this war and recognized it as just that Germany be obliged to make compensation for this damage in kind to the greatest extent possible. A Commission for the Compensation of Damage will be established. . . .

IV

United Nations Conference

We are resolved upon the earliest possible establishment with our allies of a general international organization to maintain peace and security. We believe that this is essential, both to prevent aggression and to remove the political, economic and social causes of war through the close and continuing collaboration of all peace-loving peoples. . . .

We have agreed that a Conference of United Nations should be called to meet at San Francisco in the United States on April 25th, 1945, to prepare the charter of such an organization, along the lines proposed in the informal conversations at Dumbarton Oaks. . . .

V

Declaration on Liberated Europe

We have drawn up and subscribed to a Declaration on liberated Europe. This Declaration provides for concerting the policies of the three Powers and for joint action by them in meeting the political and economic problems of liberated Europe in accordance with democratic principles. The text of the Declaration is as follows:

The Premier of the Union of Soviet Socialist Republics, the Prime Minister of the United Kingdom, and the President of the United States of America have consulted with each other in the common interests of the peoples of their countries and those of liberated Europe. They jointly declare their mutual agreement to concert during the temporary period of instability in liberated Europe the policies of their three governments in assisting the peoples liberated from the domination of Nazi Germany and the peoples of the former Axis satellite states of Europe to solve by democratic means their pressing political and economic problems.

The establishment of order in Europe and the rebuilding of national economic life must be achieved by processes which will enable the liberated peoples to destroy the last vestiges of Nazism and Fascism and to creat[e] democratic institutions of their own choice. This is a principle of the Atlantic Charter—the right of all peoples to choose the form of government under which they will live—the restoration of sovereign rights and self-government to those peoples who have been forcibly deprived of them by the aggressor nations.

To foster the conditions in which the liberated peoples may exercise these rights, the three governments will jointly assist the people in any European liberated state or former Axis satellite state in Europe where in their judgment conditions require (*a*) to establish conditions of internal peace; (*b*) to carry out emergency measures for the relief of distressed people; (*c*) to form interim governmental authorities broadly representative of all democratic elements in the population and pledged to the earliest possible establishment through free elections of governments responsive to the will of the people; and (*d*) to facilitate where necessary the holding of such elections. . . .

VI

Poland

We came to the Crimea Conference resolved to settle our differences about Poland. We discussed fully all aspects of the question. We reaffirm our common desire to see established a strong, free, independent and democratic Poland. As a result of our discussions we have agreed on the conditions in which a new Poland Provisional Government of National Unity may be formed in such a manner as to command recognition by the three major powers.

The agreement reached is as follows:

A new situation has been created in Poland as a result of her complete liberation by the Red Army. This calls for the establishment of a Polish Provisional Government which can be more broadly based than was possible before the recent liberation of western Poland. The Provisional government ["Lublin" regime] which is now functioning in Poland should therefore be recognized on a broader democratic basis with the inclusion of democratic leaders from Poland itself and from Poles abroad. This new Government should then be called the Polish Provisional Government of National Unity.

M. Molotov, Mr. Harriman and Sir A. Clark Kerr are authorized as a Commission to consult in the first instance in Moscow with members of the present Provisional Government and with other Polish democratic leaders from within Poland and from abroad, with a view to the reorganization of the present Government along the above lines. This Polish Provisional Government of National Unity shall be pledged to the holding of free and unfettered elections as soon as possible on the basis of universal suffrage and secret ballot. In these elections all democratic and anti-Nazi parties shall have the right to take part and to put forward candidates.

When a Polish Provisional Government of National Unity has been properly formed in conformity with the above, the Government of the U.S.S.R., which now maintains diplomatic relations with the present Provisional Government of Poland, and the Government of the United Kingdom and the Government of the United States will establish diplo-

matic relations with the new Polish Provisional Government of National Unity, and will exchange Ambassadors by whose reports the respective Governments will be kept informed about the situation in Poland.

The three Heads of Government consider that the eastern frontier of Poland should follow the Curzon Line with digressions from it in some regions of five to eight kilometres in favor of Poland. They recognize that Poland must receive substantial accessions of territory in the north and west. They feel that the opinion of the new Polish Provisional Government of National Unity should be sought in due course on the extent of these accessions and that the final delimitation of the western frontier of Poland should thereafter await the Peace Conference. . . .

VIII

Meetings of Foreign Secretaries

Throughout the Conference, besides the daily meetings of the Heads of Governments and the Foreign Secretaries, separate meetings of the three Foreign Secretaries, and their advisers have also been held daily.

These meetings have proved of the utmost value and the Conference agreed that permanent machinery should be set up for regular consultation between the three Foreign Secretaries. They will, therefore, meet as often as may be necessary, probably about every three or four months. These meetings will be held in rotation in the three Capitals, the first meeting being held in London, after the United Nations Conference on world organization.

IX

Unity for Peace as for War

Our meeting here in Crimea has reaffirmed our common determination to maintain and strengthen in the peace to come that unity of purpose and of action which has made victory possible and certain for the United Nations in this war. We believe that this is a sacred obligation which our Governments owe to our peoples and to all the peoples of the world.

Only with continuing and growing co-operation and understanding among our three countries and among all the peace-loving nations can the highest aspiration of humanity be realized—a secure and lasting peace which will, in the words of the Atlantic Charter, "afford assurance that all the men in all the lands may live out their lives in freedom from fear and want."

Victory in this war and establishment of the proposed international organization will provide the greatest opportunity in all history to create in the years to come the essential conditions of such a peace.

WINSTON S. CHURCHILL
FRANKLIN D. ROOSEVELT
[I. STALIN]

FEBRUARY 11, 1945 [Released to the press February 12, 1945]

Protocol of the Proceedings of the Crimea Conference

The Crimea Conference of the Heads of the Governments of the United States of America, the United Kingdom, and the Union of Soviet Socialist Republics which took place from February 4th to 11th came to the following conclusions.

I. World Organization

It was decided:

(1) that a United Nations Conference on the proposed world organization should be summoned for Wednesday, 25th April, 1945, and should be held in the United States of America.

(2) the Nations to be invited to this Conference should be:

(*a*) the United Nations as they existed on the 8th February, 1945 and

(*b*) such of the Associated Nations as have declared war on the common enemy by 1st March, 1945. (For this purpose by the term "Associated Nation" was meant the eight Associated Nations and Turkey). When the Conference on World Organization is held, the delegates of the United Kingdom and the United States of America will support a proposal to admit to original membership two Soviet Socialist Republics, i.e., the Ukraine and White Russia. . . .

III. Dismemberment of Germany

It was agreed that Article 12 (*a*) of the Surrender Terms for Germany should be amended to read as follows:

> "The United Kingdom, the United States of America and the Union of Soviet Socialist Republics shall possess supreme authority with respect to Germany. In the exercise of such authority they will take such steps, including the complete disarmament, demilitarisation and the dismemberment of Germany as they deem requisite for future peace and security."

The study of the procedure for the dismemberment of Germany was referred to a Committee. . . .

V. Reparation

The following protocol has been approved:

1. Germany must pay in kind for the losses caused by her to the Allied nations in the course of the war. Reparations are to be received in the first instance by those countries which have borne the main burden of the war, have suffered the heaviest losses and have organised victory over the enemy.

2. Reparation in kind is to be exacted from Germany in three following forms:

> *a*) Removals within 2 years from the surrender of Germany or the cessation of organised resistance from the national wealth of Germany located on the territory of Germany herself as well as outside her territory (equipment, machine-tools, ships, rolling stock, German investments abroad, shares of industrial, transport and other enterprises in Germany etc.), these removals to be carried out chiefly for purpose of destroying the war potential of Germany.
>
> *b*) Annual deliveries of goods from current production for a period to be fixed.
>
> *c*) Use of German labour.

3. For the working out on the above principles of a detailed plan for exaction of reparation from Germany an Allied Reparation Commission will be set up in Moscow. It will consist of three representatives—one from the Union of Soviet Socialist Republics, one from the United Kingdom and one from the United States of America.

4. With regard to the fixing of the total sum of the reparation as well as the distribution of it among the countries which suffered from the German aggression the Soviet and American delegations agreed as follows:

> The Moscow Reparation Commission should take in its initial studies as a basis for discussion the suggestion of the Soviet Government that the total sum of the reparation in accordance with the points (*a*) and (*b*) of the paragraph 2 should be 20 billion dollars and that 50% of it should go to the Union of Soviet Socialist Republics.

The British delegation was of the opinion that pending consideration of the reparation question by the Moscow Reparation Commission no figures of reparation should be mentioned.

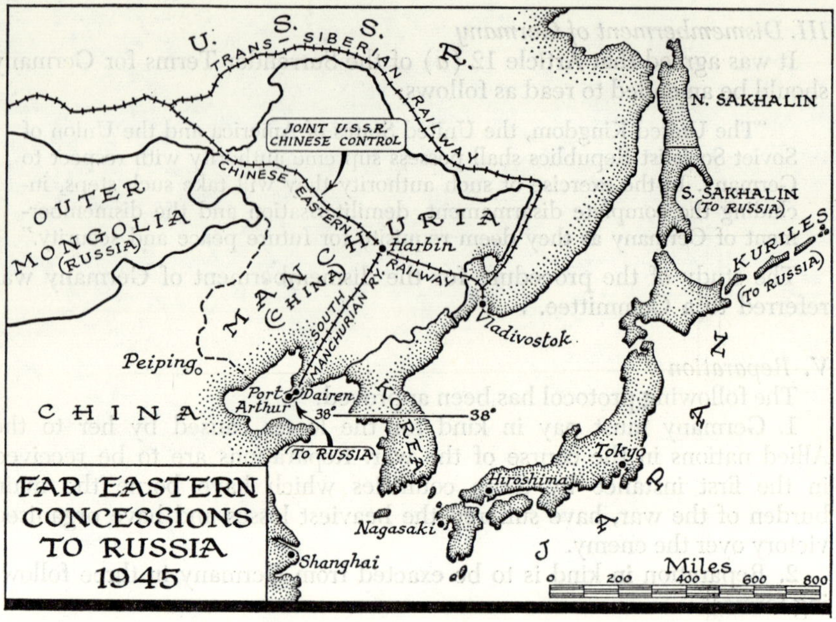

The above Soviet-American proposal has been passed to the Moscow Reparation Commission as one of the proposals to be considered by the Commission.

VI. Major War Criminals

The conference agreed that the question of the major war criminals should be the subject of enquiry by the three Foreign Secretaries for report in due course after the close of the Conference. . . .

[Released to the press by the State Department, March 24, 1947]

Agreement Regarding Entry of the Soviet Union into the War Against Japan

TOP SECRET

Agreement

The leaders of the three Great Powers—the Soviet Union, the United States of America and Great Britain—have agreed that in two or three months after Germany has surrendered and the war in Europe has terminated the Soviet Union shall enter into the war against Japan on the side of the Allies on condition that:

1. The *status quo* in Outer-Mongolia (The Mongolian People's Republic) shall be preserved;

2. The former rights of Russia violated by the treacherous attack of Japan in 1904 shall be restored, viz:

(*a*) the southern part of Sakhalin as well as all the islands adjacent to it shall be returned to the Soviet Union,

(*b*) the commercial port of Dairen shall be internationalized, the preeminent interests of the Soviet Union in this port being safeguarded and the lease of Port Arthur as a naval base of the USSR restored,

(*c*) the Chinese-Eastern Railroad and the South-Manchurian Railroad which provides an outlet to Dairen shall be jointly operated by the establishment of a joint Soviet-Chinese Company it being understood that the preeminent interests of the Soviet Union shall be safeguarded and that China shall retain full sovereignty in Manchuria;

3. The Kuril islands shall be handed over to the Soviet Union.

It is understood, that the agreement concerning Outer-Mongolia and the ports and railroads referred to above will require concurrence of Generalissimo Chiang Kai-Shek. The President will take measures in order to obtain this concurrence on advice from Marshal Stalin.

The Heads of the three Great Powers have agreed that these claims of the Soviet Union shall be unquestionably fulfilled after Japan has been defeated.

For its part the Soviet Union expresses its readiness to conclude with the National Government of China a pact of friendship and alliance between the USSR and China in order to render assistance to China with its armed forces for the purpose of liberating China from the Japanese yoke.

[I. STALIN]
FRANKLIN D. ROOSEVELT
WINSTON S. CHURCHILL

FEBRUARY 11, 1945 [Released to the press by the State Department, February 11, 1946]

READINGS

1. "Stalin's Greatest Victory"

Although the Yalta Conference occurred in the recent past, a number of pertinent public and private records have already been opened to scholarly use and several important studies have appeared. Among critics of Yalta, the outpouring ranges from hysterical charges of treason and conspiracy to balanced but critical evaluations. Chester Wilmot's account, written by an English writer close to British officials during the war, falls into the latter category. Wilmot is critical of Roosevelt's suspicions of alleged British imperialism, which he claims prevented closer Anglo-American diplomatic collaboration, and of the American President's naive belief that he could win Stalin's friendship through conciliation and concessions. The Far Eastern concessions to Russia gave Stalin a "moral cloak" for aggression in China.

The Struggle for Europe

CHESTER WILMOT

. . . Three days before he set out for Malta and the Crimea, Roosevelt took the oath for the fourth time as President of the United States, and, in the course of his inaugural address, declared, "We have learned to be citizens of the world, members of the human community. We have learned the simple truth, as Emerson said, 'the only way to have a friend is to be one.'"

This was the creed that Roosevelt carried to Yalta. There was, in his view, no fundamental conflict of national interest between the Soviet Union and the United States; the Russian and American peoples had so much in common that they would readily co-operate in the cause of peace and freedom if only there could be a real meeting of minds between their leaders. His trust in Stalin and his faith in his own ability to win the Soviet Union's lasting co-operation were still high, although the unhappy course of Russo-Polish relations during the past year might well have given him reason to doubt both his own personal influence and Russia's post-war intentions.

Three times since Teheran, Roosevelt had made a direct approach to Stalin in the hope of inducing him to reach a reasonable agreement with the Polish Government in London; each time he had been rebuffed and Stalin had shown no inclination whatever to allow the principles of the Atlantic Charter to apply to Poland. Nevertheless, Mikolajczyk [Premier of the Polish Government in Exile] reports—and there is no reason to disbelieve him—that, when he was in Washington in June 1944, Roosevelt told him, "Stalin is a realist, and we mustn't forget, when we judge Russian actions, that the Soviet régime has had only two years of experience in international relations. But of one thing I am certain, Stalin is not an Imperialist." Roosevelt explained to Mikolajczyk that he had not been able to take a public stand on the Polish question because it was election year, but "eventually," he said, "I will act as moderator in this problem and effect a settlement." Believing, as he had said after Teheran, that Stalin was "getatable," Roosevelt felt sure that when they met again across the conference table there would be no problem they could not solve on a "man-to-man" basis.

Roosevelt was not alone in thinking that Diplomacy by Friendship would bring a sympathetic response from Stalin. The most influential of his advisers—military and political alike—were agreed, as Hull says, that they "must and could get along with the Soviet Government," and that this would be possible if they were "patient and forbearing." The idea that they could "get along with" the Russians came more easily to the American leaders than to the British, for the United States is the great melting pot and the American people have shown an unparalleled capacity for absorbing into their own society a multitude of nationalities.

Perhaps the best exposition of Roosevelt's idea is to be found in a memorandum which Hopkins [Harry Hopkins, Roosevelt's personal adviser] wrote six months after Yalta. "We know or believe," he said, "that Russia's interests, so far as we can anticipate them, do not afford an opportunity for a major difference with us in foreign affairs. We believe we are mutually dependent upon each other for economic reasons. We find the Russians as individuals easy to deal with. The Russians undoubtedly like the American people. They like the United States. They trust the United States more than they trust any other power in the world . . . above all, they want to maintain friendly relations with us. . . . They are a tenacious, determined people who think and act just like you and I do."

Eisenhower endorsed this view of the Russian people when he wrote, "In his generous instincts, in his love of laughter, in his devotion to a comrade, and in his healthy, direct outlook on the affairs of workaday life, the ordinary Russian seems to me to bear a marked similarity to what we call an 'average American.'" Eisenhower believed too that there was a special bond between the United States and the Soviet Union, a bond that was inevitably lacking in the Anglo-American association. He felt, he says, that "in the past relations of America and Russia there was no cause to regard the future with pessimism." On the one hand, "the two peoples had maintained an unbroken friendship that dated back to the birth of the United States as an independent republic"; on the other, "both were free from the stigma of colonial empire building by force."

This remarkable statement stems straight from the Founding Fathers. It was the American way of saying that politically both peoples were free from original sin. That this was not true of either was irrelevant; it was believed, not merely by Eisenhower but also by many Americans who should have been better acquainted with their own history. This belief was implicit in Roosevelt's approach to the problems which were to be discussed at Yalta. In his eyes, Britain was an Imperial Power, bearing the "colonial stigma"; Russia was not. That assessment of his allies was a decisive factor in Roosevelt's readiness to make concessions to the Soviet Union both in Europe and Asia in order to ensure Stalin's entry into the Pacific War.

Roosevelt's intimates give two reasons for his determination to enlist the aid of Russia against Japan. His personal Chief of Staff, Admiral Leahy, says that the President was actuated by the belief that "Soviet participation in the Far East operation would insure Russia's sincere co-operation in his dream of a united, peaceful world." On the other hand, his Secretary of State, Stettinius, reports that "immense pressure [was] put on the President by our military leaders to bring Russia into the Far Eastern War. At this time the atomic bomb was still an unknown quantity and our setback in the Battle of the Bulge was fresh in the minds of all. We had not as yet crossed the Rhine. No one knew how long the European War would last nor how great the casualties would be." Stettinius adds that the American Chiefs of Staff had warned Roosevelt that "without Russia it might cost the United States a million casualties to conquer Japan" and that the Pacific War might not end until 1947.

The chief advocate of this view was Marshall [Army Chief of Staff], but Roosevelt's military advisers were by no means unanimous in the belief that it would be necessary to invade the Japanese home islands. Leahy says that at Pearl Harbour, in July 1944, both MacArthur and Nimitz (the two commanders directly concerned) had told the President that "Japan could be forced to accept our terms of surrender by the use of sea and air powers without the invasion of the Japanese homeland." Since then, at the Battle for Leyte Gulf in October, the Japanese Navy had suffered such a crushing defeat that well before Yalta Leahy considered that the war against Japan "had progressed to the point where her defeat was only a matter of time and attrition." This was also the opinion of Arnold, the Chief of the Air Staff, whose Super-Fortresses were already bombing Japan from island airfields. There was no longer any great need for air bases in the Maritime Provinces of the Soviet Union, and, after the unhappy experiment of "shuttle-bombing" in Europe, Arnold did not set much store by any facilities he might be granted in Asia. Nevertheless, the advice of Marshall and King prevailed.

The supporters of Russian intervention were considerably influenced by their estimate of the amount of help the United States would receive, or should accept, from Britain in the war against Japan. Here the colonial issue again entered American calculations. Virtually all the British and Imperial forces in the Far East were deployed in Admiral Lord Louis Mountbatten's South-East Asia Command (SEAC) for operations in Burma, and in due course Malaya and Sumatra. This deployment was dictated as much by geographical as political factors, but it was presumed in Washington that Churchill was more interested in regaining Britain's lost colonies than in bringing about the early defeat of Japan. Consequently, it came as a great surprise—to the British as much as to the American Chiefs of Staff—when at Quebec in September 1944 the Prime Minister suddenly offered to send a large part of R.A.F. Bomber Command and the main British Battle Fleet into the Central Pacific. This offer was promptly accepted by Roosevelt, but, when it was raised at the next meeting of the Combined Chiefs of Staff, "all hell broke loose"—Arnold's phrase—and King "hotly refused to have anything to do with it." Cunningham, the First Sea Lord, reports that King was sharply called to order by Leahy and "eventually gave way; but with a very bad grace."

Although there was no trace of King's Anglophobia in Marshall or Arnold, the American Chiefs of Staff had never allowed their British colleagues any voice in the conduct of the Pacific War, nor were they eager to have British forces play a major part in it lest this should give Britain the right to claim possession or trusteeship of some of the Japanese Empire. Further, they believed—and they so advised the President—that "in the interests of national defence, the Japanese mandated islands in the Pacific captured by our forces should be retained under the sovereignty of the United States and not delivered to the trusteeship of the United Nations." True to his principles, Roosevelt rejected this proposal, but those same principles made him distrustful of the activities and intentions of the British and French in South-East Asia.

Roosevelt was determined that Indo-China should not go back to France and he had refused to agree to any French military mission being accredited to SEAC. He was prepared to allow the Dutch to return to the Netherlands East Indies, because Queen Wilhelmina had promised to give them self-government, but he intended that these islands should be liberated by American forces so that he would be in a position to enforce fulfilment of this promise. Accordingly, the sole Dutch possession placed within the sphere of prospective British operations was Sumatra and this island only because of its geographical relation to Malaya. Moreover, the American Chiefs of Staff, on MacArthur's recommendation, decided that the British should not be allowed to take over the military control of the East Indies after their recapture. "The exact British intentions were not known," says Leahy, "but past experience indicated that if they did get control of some Dutch territory, it might be difficult to pry them loose." This view appears to have been shared by Roosevelt, for he told Stettinius that "the British would take land anywhere in the world even if it were only rock or a sandbar."

Roosevelt's eagerness to buy Stalin's aid in the war against Japan was principally due to his desire to save lives, but in the light of all the evidence it seems fair to say that he was also actuated by the hope that Russia's intervention would enable the United States to strike the decisive blow at Japan, and compel her surrender, before the British, French or Dutch could regain possession of their colonies. The United States would thus be able to demand that the colonies which had been liberated from the Japanese should now be liberated from the dominion of their original owners.

In due course, as it turned out, the Americans were able to achieve this purpose without the intervention of Russia. When the Japanese announced their readiness to capitulate, MacArthur, who was acting as co-ordinator of all the surrender arrangements, forbade Mountbatten to accept any local surrender in South-East Asia or to send any relief or reoccupation forces into Japanese-held areas until the overall surrender had been signed in Tokyo. Since this ceremony was not to take place for another twelve days, Mountbatten ignored his orders so far as missions of mercy were concerned, because, as he says in his dispatch, "if relief stores and personnel had not been sent in at once, the delay of twelve days imposed on me would have resulted in many more deaths each day among the prisoners [of war]."

The instructions regarding the movement of naval and military forces were observed, though these were already at sea, and the British were thus placed in the humiliating position of not being permitted to re-occupy their own colonies, until the Japanese High Command had formally acknowledged defeat to an American general on an American battleship in Tokyo Bay.

Although this particular manifestation of American anti-colonialism was not revealed until six months after Yalta, the attitude which inspired it was implicit in the policy Roosevelt pursued throughout the war.

The plenary sessions of the Yalta Conference were held at Livadia Palace overlooking the Black Sea. The ownership of this palace had changed since it was built by the Romanoffs, but the aims and ambitions of the new owners differed little from those of its former masters. The only significant difference was that the men who now sought to fulfil Russia's imperial destiny were more ruthless and more powerful.

At the opening session on Sunday, February 4th, Stalin made a gesture which was both tactful and tactical. He proposed, as he had at Teheran, that Roosevelt should take the chair, and thus once again he brought the President half-way to his side. Yet Stalin showed no early inclination to follow the chairman's lead, least of all with regard to the President's cherished plan for creating a world peace organisation based on the recognition of the sovereign rights of all nations. The first time the subject was raised, "Stalin made it quite plain," says Stettinius, "that the three Great Powers which had borne the brunt of the war should be the ones to preserve the peace." He declared, moreover, that he would "never agree to having any action of any of the Great Powers submitted to the judgment of the small powers." In reply to this argument Churchill spoke for all the Western World in saying, "The eagle should permit the small birds to sing and care not wherefor they sang." That evening, when Stettinius and Eden discussed the outlook, they agreed that "the trend . . . seemed to be more towards a three-power alliance than anything else."

Evidently sensing that the time was not opportune to pursue the question of the world peace organisation, Roosevelt, at the start of the second plenary meeting, turned the discussion to the future of Germany. At the Moscow Conference of Foreign Ministers in November 1943 it had been decided that Germany should be completely disarmed and should pay reparations for the physical damage she had inflicted on the Soviet Union and other Allied countries. Then, and at Teheran, the question of partitioning Germany had been debated without any conclusions being reached, but it had been assumed that in any case the three powers would occupy the country, and by November 1944 they had agreed upon the actual zones of occupation and upon their joint responsibility for Berlin. At Yalta the "Big Three" confirmed their determination to demand the "Unconditional Surrender" of Germany and, for the first time, there was detailed consideration by the Russian and Anglo-American Chiefs of Staff on the military measures necessary to bring about Hitler's final defeat. On the question of post-war Germany, however, there was no such unanimity and it was soon evident that there was a considerable divergence between the British and Russian attitudes, especially with regard to the principle of partition, the extent of reparations and the right of France to share in the occupation.

The Russian view was that there should be only three occupying powers; that they should decide at Yalta to partition the Reich into a number of separate states and to include a declaration to this effect in the surrender terms; and that Germany should be deprived of eighty per cent of her heavy industry and should pay reparations in kind to the value of twenty billion dollars, half of which should go to the Soviet Union.

Churchill was not slow to realise that, if these proposals were adopted, Germany would be rendered politically impotent and economically impoverished. Although determined to ensure that Germany should not again disturb the peace of Europe, he did not wish to see her entirely neutralised as a factor in the balance of power. Accordingly, he doubted the wisdom of partitioning the Reich unless the Soviet Union would agree to the creation of a strong Danubian Confederation—and this had already been rejected by both Stalin and Roosevelt. Moreover, he did not wish to make Germany pay such severe reparations that her economy would collapse unless it were sustained by the Western Powers as it had been after the First World War. Finally, the Prime Minister wanted the French to have an equal share in both the occupation and administration of Germany so that there would be a second European voice to support Britain's in the Allied Control Commission. He was the more emphatic on this point, for the President said that the American troops would be withdrawn from Europe in "two years at the outside." Whereupon Churchill commented, without indicating what threat he feared, "Great Britain alone will not be strong enough to guard the Western approaches to the Channel."

As the discussion developed—both in the plenary sessions and at meetings of the Foreign Ministers—Roosevelt and Stettinius endeavoured to take an intermediate stand on these issues. The result was that three distinct viewpoints emerged. With regard to partition, Stalin wanted a definite commitment both now and in the surrender terms; Churchill wished to make no commitments either way; and Roosevelt suggested that they should mention dismemberment in the terms without binding themselves to this policy. On the matter of reparations, Stalin demanded explicit acceptance in the Protocol of the overall figure of twenty billion dollars; Churchill opposed any mention of any figure even in a secret document; and Roosevelt inclined to the view that the Russian figure might be taken as "a basis for discussion." As for the occupation of Germany, Churchill insisted that France should have a seat on the Control Commission as well as a zone; Stalin argued against both suggestions; and Roosevelt proposed that France should have a zone but no seat.

On each of these questions the President was in fundamental agreement with the Prime Minister's stand (though not with all his reasons), but in public discussion Roosevelt played the mediator. He was not interested in upholding the balance of power concept, nor was he deeply concerned with the intrinsic merits of the German problem. To him Germany was not an issue in itself, but a bargaining point in the wider issue that was uppermost in his mind—the winning of Stalin's cooperation in the international peace organisation, and in the war against Japan.

To some extent the role of arbiter was thrust upon Roosevelt when he became chairman, but there is no doubt that he preferred it since he was thus able to preserve greater freedom of action and to avoid committing himself until he had heard the rival views. The results of the President's determination to act as mediator were twofold. On the one hand, the assertion of what were in reality Anglo-American views and principles was frequently left to the British alone—much to Churchill's annoyance; and on the other, as one of Roosevelt's closest advisers says, "the Soviet leaders did over-estimate the ultimate extent of the President's generosity and his willingness to compromise on principles."

The problem of Germany's future was still undecided when—at the third plenary session on February 6th—Roosevelt returned to the question of post-war peace and asked Stettinius to review the questions which had been in dispute at the Dumbarton Oaks Conference. There the Americans, British, Chinese and Russians had agreed on the principles and purposes of what was to become the United Nations, and had decided there should be a General Assembly, a Security Council and various other instrumentalities. The area of agreement had ended, however, when the Soviet Delegate, Gromyko, had proposed that all sixteen republics of the Soviet Union should have seats in the Assembly (a proposal which "left Stettinius and Cadogan breathless"), and had demanded that in the Security Council the Great Powers should have the right to veto any proposals, except those which related to points of procedure.

It has been alleged by some of Roosevelt's critics that the establishment of the veto power in the Security Council was a concession made by him at Yalta to induce Stalin to join the United Nations. This is not so. The basic principle of the veto was never in dispute. None of the Great Powers was prepared to submit itself and its interests unreservedly to the jurisdiction of an international security organisation. All were agreed that there must be "unqualified unanimity of the permanent members of the Council on all major decisions relating to the preservation of peace, including all economic and military enforcement measures." This was inevitable. The President, haunted by the ghost of Wilson, insisted on the veto power because he knew that the United States Senate would not surrender to an international body the right to commit American forces to military action. Churchill was equally insistent on this point because, as he said at Yalta, he would "never consent to the fumbling fingers of forty or fifty nations prying into the life's existence of the British Empire."

Although both Britain and America felt obliged to retain the right to veto any international "police action," they had no desire to curtail discussion or to prevent any small power bringing a cause of grievance to the notice of the Security Council. At Dumbarton Oaks, however, Gromyko had refused to accept this view and had told Stettinius, "The Russian position on voting in the Council will never be departed from!" Nevertheless, on December 5th, 1944, Roosevelt had sent to Stalin and

Churchill a compromise formula which, while recognising the need for unanimity on matters involving the application of sanctions, provided that on questions relating to the peaceful settlement of any dispute no member of the Council would cast its vote, or exercise its veto, if it were a party to that dispute.

Now, at Yalta, after Stettinius had re-stated this formula, Churchill declared Britain's acceptance of it, and added, "We see great advantage in the three Great Powers not assuming the position of rulers of all the rest of the world without even allowing them to state their case." When Stalin spoke, however, he again emphasised the importance of unanimity, declaring that the real problem was to preserve the unity of the Great Powers and to work out a covenant that would achieve this purpose. "The danger in the future," he said, "is the possibility of conflicts among ourselves." Apologising to the President, Stalin said that he was not yet ready to pass judgment on the voting formula, because he had had "no chance to study this question in detail." Yet he proceeded to give such a concise analysis of its implications that it was obvious he must have studied it rather carefully at some time during the two months since he had received Roosevelt's draft!

After this exchange Stettinius was more confident, believing that for the first time Stalin really understood the American point of view. Byrnes, on the other hand, felt that the Russians "could not be greatly interested in the United Nations organisation," and Leahy thought it "difficult to foresee on what grounds an agreement could be reached." This impression seemed to be confirmed when, at the next meeting of the Foreign Ministers, Molotov refused even to discuss the Security Council voting procedure.

Leaving this matter for the moment, Roosevelt brought up the Polish question. He announced his readiness to accept the Curzon Line, but proposed that Stalin might agree to leave within Poland the city of Lwow and the nearby oilfields. "He pointed out," says Stettinius, "that he was merely suggesting this for consideration rather than insisting on it." In fact, the main argument he advanced in its support was that "it would have a salutary effect on American public opinion," a consideration which was hardly likely to carry much weight with the Soviet dictator. Thus, although the President's expert advisers had warned him that these oilfields were essential to the Polish economy, he did not make an issue of it, so anxious was he to preserve the role of mediator, not only on the frontier question but also in the establishment of a new Polish government.

Churchill was already committed to the Curzon Line, but he declared that if Stalin were to accept the President's Lwow plan, it would be "a magnanimous gesture" which Britain would "admire and acclaim." The Prime Minister said, however, that he was more interested in the sovereignty and independence of Poland than in the matter of frontiers, and that he, like the President, wished to see established in Warsaw a "fully representative Polish government," pledged to the holding of free elections. For Britain, having risked so much in Poland's cause, this was a question of honour.

In reply, Stalin delivered an impassioned speech. "For the Russian people," he said, "Poland is not only a question of honour but also a question of security. Throughout history Poland has been the corridor through which the enemy has passed into Russia . . . It is in Russia's interests that Poland should be strong and powerful, in a position to shut the door of this corridor by her own force." Turning to the problem of frontiers, he said that the Soviet Union must have Lwow and could not accept anything but "the line of Curzon and Clemenceau." Stalin declared: "You would drive us into shame! What will be said by the White Russians and the Ukrainians? They will say that Stalin and Molotov are far less reliable defenders of Russia than are Curzon and Clemenceau . . . I prefer the war should continue a little longer . . . to give Poland compensation in the West at the expense of the Germans. . . . I am in favour of extending the Polish Western frontier to the Neisse River.

Stalin was equally unresponsive to Roosevelt's suggestion that a new Polish Government should be formed from members of the five main political parties, including representatives of the Government in London. He stated that he did not trust the London Poles and would not recognise any administration except that already established in Lublin. "We demand order," he said, "and we do not want to be shot in the back."

Churchill joined issue vigorously with Stalin, declaring that Britain could not accept the Lublin Committee, since it did not represent more than a third of the nation; nor could he agree to extend Poland's western frontier to the River Neisse, thus giving her virtually all Silesia. "It would be a pity," he said, "to stuff the Polish goose so full of German food that he will die of indigestion." On that discordant note the meeting adjourned.

That evening Roosevelt sent Stalin a conciliatory letter, in which he reaffirmed the American opposition to the Lublin Committee, but added the assurance, "The United States will never lend its support in any way to any provisional government in Poland which would be inimical to your interests." Although he regarded this letter as an act of mediation, Roosevelt compromised his own independence by telling Stalin, "I am determined there shall be no breach between ourselves and the Soviet Union." With that statement he admitted that, if Stalin made an issue of Poland, the United States would give way.

When the Big Three met again next afternoon (February 7th) Stalin acknowledged receipt of the President's letter, but stated that his own reply was not yet ready as it was being typed; in the meantime he would like to discuss the international peace organisation. Roosevelt agreed, and Molotov proceeded to say that the Soviet Union was "happy to accept the entire American proposal" about voting in the Security Council, and would not press for all sixteen Soviet Republics to be members of the United Nations. It would be satisfactory if seats were granted to the Ukraine and White Russia. As it had already been agreed that Britain, the four Dominions and India should have individual representation in the General Assembly, Churchill could not oppose this request, and, although Roosevelt did not give his consent immediately, he told Stettinius that he "did not believe there was anything preposterous about the Russian proposal." Indeed, he regarded it as a small price to pay for Soviet co-operation.

The President and the Prime Minister were delighted at this manifestation of Stalin's willingness to join the United Nations and they felt he had made substantial concessions on two vital issues about which he had previously been intractable. They had feared that Stalin was interested only in securing a Three-Power Alliance, but now Roosevelt, at any rate, believed he had persuaded Stalin not only to recognise the sovereign rights of small nations, but also to act in friendly concert with the other great Powers in maintaining peace and extending the frontiers of freedom.

This belief was confirmed when Stalin agreed that the Soviet Union would take part in the United Nations Conference to be held in San Francisco in April, and would support there the right of the United States to have three votes in the General Assembly, if the President desired to make such a claim. It seemed to Roosevelt that these concessions were an earnest of Stalin's good faith, for it could not be foreseen then that the Soviet Union would abuse the veto power, as it was to do in the years after the war, employing it to prevent discussion as well as decision and endeavouring to exercise it even on questions of procedure. That afternoon at Yalta it appeared that Anglo-American diplomacy had gained a considerable victory, and the President felt that the long and arduous journey had not been in vain.

During the brief adjournment which followed this discussion about the United Nations the prevailing opinion among the Western delegates was that the concessions Stalin had made represented a decided change of heart. Considered in relation to what followed, however, these concessions appear as a tactical manœuvre designed to make the Western delegations more receptive to the Soviet plan for Poland which Molotov put forward while the meeting still glowed with goodwill. This plan did little more than set out in formal terms the attitude Stalin had so forcibly proclaimed the day before. The only hint of any readiness to meet the Western view was contained in the statement that the present Provisional Government (i.e. the Lublin Committee) might be enlarged to include "some democratic leaders from Polish *émigré* circles." Since the Russians refused to regard even Mikolajczyk, the leader of the Peasant Party, as a "democrat," that concession meant nothing. The moral of this day's proceedings was that, while Russia was willing to join the United Nations, she was not prepared to rely on it entirely. She intended to safeguard her own security in any event by ensuring that she had subservient neighbours in Europe and a commanding position in Asia.

Stalin's Asiatic ambitions were revealed on the following afternoon during a private discussion with Roosevelt about the Soviet Union's entry into the Japanese War. This discussion was conducted on a strictly

Russo-American basis and in conditions of great secrecy. The only other persons present, apart from the two interpreters, were Molotov and Averell Harriman, the American Ambassador to the Soviet Union.

At the President's request, Churchill was not there and, when the negotiations were continued on the technical level by the Chiefs of Staff, the British did not take part. Even within his own entourage Roosevelt was most uncommunicative. Stettinius, though Secretary of State, was merely notified that talks were in progress. When he asked if the State Department should not be represented, Roosevelt replied that the problem was "primarily a military matter . . . and had best remain on a purely military level." This was a specious answer, for Stalin had long since committed himself on the basic military issue; the main point to be decided at Yalta was the political price of his participation.

It was in October 1943 that Stalin had first promised to join in the war against Japan after the defeat of Germany. He had made this offer to Cordell Hull, who says that it was "entirely unsolicited . . . and had no strings attached to it." At Teheran a month later, Stalin had repeated this promise virtually as a *quid pro quo* for the Second Front and for Lend-Lease. Nevertheless, Roosevelt had then volunteered to restore Russia's rights in the Manchurian port of Dairen and to ensure her free access to warm waters. Finding that the President was a "soft touch," Stalin proceeded to make this gesture his price with the paradoxical result that Soviet demands grew as the American need for Russian assistance in the Eastern War declined. During Churchill's visit to Moscow in October 1944, the Marshal said that "the Soviet Union would take the offensive against Japan three months after Germany's defeat, provided the United States would assist in building up the necessary reserve supplies and *provided the political aspects of Russia's participation had been clarified.*" During this Moscow meeting, as on five other separate occasions in 1944, Stalin gave an assurance that Russian air and naval bases in the Maritime Provinces would be made available to American forces. In December, however, this assurance was withdrawn, presumably with a view to strengthening the bargaining position of the Soviet Union at Yalta.

The course of the fateful discussions which took place behind closed doors in Livadia Palace on the afternoon of February 8th is not known in detail, for none of those who took part have publicly revealed what was said and the accounts given by Leahy, Sherwood and Stettinius, though authoritative, are second-hand. What was decided, however, is revealed only too clearly in the terms of the agreement which was subsequently signed by Stalin, Roosevelt and Churchill. This provided that "in two or three months after Germany has surrendered . . . the Soviet Union shall enter the war against Japan" on certain conditions: that "the status quo in Outer Mongolia" was to be preserved; that the Kurile Islands, north of Japan, were to be "handed over to the Soviet Union"; and that the rights Russia had lost after her defeat by Japan in 1904 were to be restored. Russia was thus to regain possession of Southern Sakhalin, the "international port" of Dairen and the naval base of Port Arthur. In addition, although China was to "retain full sovereignty in Manchuria," the principal Manchurian railways were to be "jointly operated by . . . a Soviet-Chinese Company" which was to safeguard "the pre-eminent interests of the Soviet Union." Apart from agreeing to enter the Pacific War, Stalin conceded nothing in writing. He promised Roosevelt that the United States could have bases in the Maritime Provinces, but this was not mentioned in the agreement, nor was there any reference to the one million tons of additional supplies that were to be provided by the Americans. These supplies were duly delivered, but the Russians made sure that the establishment of the bases never proceeded beyond discussions in Moscow.

The President's Chief of Staff (Admiral Leahy) says that, when the Russian terms were mentioned at a subsequent plenary session, there was "little discussion and no argument." It appears that Stalin blandly explained, "I only want to have returned to Russia what the Japanese have taken from my country"; and that Roosevelt replied, "That seems like a very reasonable suggestion from our ally. They only want to get back that which has been taken from them." Churchill must have listened a little incredulously to this exchange for he cannot have forgotten that Roosevelt had once said to him: "Winston . . . you have four hundred years of acquisitive instinct in your blood and you just don't understand how a country might not want to acquire land somewhere if they can get it. A new period has opened in the world's history and you will have to adjust yourself to it."

The British should have known, if the Americans did not, that Stalin's justification could not by any means cover all the Soviet claims. The Kuriles had never formally belonged to Russia. The reclaimed "rights" in Manchuria were those which in the nineteenth century had enabled Russia to exercise in this province a degree of dominion which seriously impinged upon Chinese sovereignty. These "rights" rested on no more substantial foundations than those extra-territorial privileges which the United States, Britain and other countries had given up in 1943 at Roosevelt's own instigation and in fulfilment of his pledge to restore and respect the independence of China. To accept the "status quo" in Outer Mongolia, which Moscow had been sedulously luring away from its allegiance to Chungking, was to acknowledge that the Soviet Union, not China, should enjoy political supremacy in that country. In short, by this agreement Russia was to become, with Anglo-American consent, the political heir of Japan in Manchuria, and thereby in North China.

No arrangement was made at Yalta with regard to the occupation of Korea and the post-war fate of that unhappy country appears to have been mentioned only incidentally. Stalin inquired whether it was to be occupied by any foreign troops. When Roosevelt replied that this was not intended, Stalin, no doubt thinking far into the future, "expressed his approval."

Upon learning the full extent of the Soviet terms, some of Churchill's advisers were deeply concerned, for they discovered that, although Stalin had made no further commitments whatever and although the most important of his claims had to be met by their ally, China, not by Japan, the President and the Prime Minister were required to declare that "these claims of the Soviet Union shall be unquestionably fulfilled after Japan has been defeated." Moreover, Stalin was insisting that for security reasons the Chinese Government should not even be informed until the Soviet Union was ready to attack. Roosevelt had undertaken to secure Chiang Kai-Shek's compliance in due course but, as Sherwood says, "if China had refused to agree to any of the Soviet claims, presumably the U.S. and Britain would have been compelled to join in enforcing them." To some of the British delegation it seemed rather incongruous that, while urging Churchill to hand Hong Kong over to China as "a gesture of good-will," Roosevelt was prepared to promise Stalin substantial concessions in Manchuria, and to do this without so much as consulting the Chinese. This point was appreciated by at least one of his staff, for Leahy reports that he warned Roosevelt, "Mr. President, you are going to lose out on Hong Kong if you agree to give the Russians half of Dairen"; and that Roosevelt replied, "Well, Bill, I can't help it."

Eden did all he could to dissuade the Prime Minister from setting his signature to the terms agreed upon by Roosevelt and Stalin. Churchill replied that he must sign, because he felt that "the whole position of the British Empire in the Far East might be at stake." The Prime Minister had good reason to fear that, since he had been excluded from the negotiations about the Japanese War, Britain might well be excluded from future discussions about the Far East if she did not stand by the United States now. Like Leahy, he may also have foreseen that, if these territorial concessions were made to Russia, Roosevelt would not be in a strong moral position to enforce his oft-repeated "threat" to reform the British Empire.

Of all the agreements reached at Yalta, this is the most controversial and would seem to be the least defensible. Yet it does not appear that the concessions, which Stalin obtained, were wrung from a reluctant Roosevelt. Sherwood records that the President had been "prepared even before the Teheran Conference . . . to agree to the legitimacy of most if not all of the Soviet claims in the Far East," although he expresses the opinion that "Roosevelt would not have agreed to the final firm commitment," if he had not been "tired and anxious to avoid further argument." Stettinius disagrees with this opinion and explains that "the Far Eastern agreement was carefully worked out and was not a snap decision made at Yalta." He endeavours to defend the concessions by asking: "What, with the possible exception of the Kuriles, did the Soviet Union receive at Yalta which she might not have taken without any agreement?"

That question does not pose the real issue which surely was: What did the Soviet Union receive at Yalta which she could not have taken without flagrantly violating the fundamental principles of the Atlantic Charter and the United Nations to which she had subscribed? The real issue for the world and for the future was not what Stalin would or could have taken but what he was given the right to take. This agreement provided Stalin with a moral cloak for his aggressive designs in Asia, and, more important, with almost a legal title enforceable at the Peace Conference to the territories and privileges which he demanded.

The President's surrender on this question is the more remarkable because it involved the sacrifice of those very principles which he had striven to uphold throughout his dealings with Churchill and Stalin. He had always insisted that he would not make any post-war commitments which would prejudice the peace treaties; he would recognise no spheres of influence, no territorial changes except those arrived at by mutual agreement, and no transfers of colonial territory except under conditions of international trusteeship. By making this agreement about the Japanese War, however, Roosevelt weakened both his mediating influence and his bargaining position in relation to problems arising out of the German War. He was not well placed to defend the sovereignty of Poland, once he had agreed to the infringement of China's sovereignty without her consent and in breach of the promise he had given to Chiang Kai-Shek at Cairo in 1943. He could not make any effective protest against the Russians' creating a sphere of influence in the Balkans, when he had acknowledged their sphere of influence in Mongolia and Manchuria. Having departed from his principles in Asia, he could not expect to be allowed to apply them in Europe; not against a realist like Stalin. Consequently, the President was now in a less favourable position than he had been at the start of the conference. Stalin's appetite had been whetted, not satisfied.

The records kept by those who were present at Yalta give the impression that the negotiations about Russia's part in the Pacific War on the Thursday afternoon marked the turning point in the week's discussions. If this was not realised by the Western delegations at the time, it seems to have been fully appreciated by Stalin. Thereafter, having gained the concessions which were to enable him to dominate China, he proceeded to consolidate politically the strategic advantages his armies had already secured in Europe. Stalin was better able to press his demands now, for he could play upon the sense of gratitude and co-operation he had built up in the Americans, and to a lesser extent in the British, by his agreement to help in the defeat of Japan and the creation of the international security organisation. The remaining negotiations were to prove the truth of the warning which had been sent to Washington two months earlier by the Head of the American Military Mission in Moscow (General Deane), an astute and not unsympathetic observer of the Soviet scene. In a letter to Marshall in December Deane had written, "We never make a request or proposal to the Soviets that is not viewed with suspicion. They simply cannot understand giving without taking, and as a result even our giving is viewed with suspicion. Gratitude cannot be banked in the Soviet Union. Each transaction is complete in itself without regard to past favours."

When the discussions about Poland were continued, as they were at each session on the last four days, the Russians gained their way on almost every point. Nothing more was heard of the President's suggestion that Poland should keep the Lwow region. The Curzon Line was accepted and this fact was duly recorded in the Protocol. With regard to Poland's western frontier, however, Stalin did not press for the formal recognition of a specific line, since he realised that neither Roosevelt nor Churchill were prepared to go beyond the Oder. He readily consented to the suggestion that "the final delimitation of the western frontier should await the Peace Conference," for in the meantime that left him free to make his own arrangements about the German territory between the Oder and the Neisse.

The negotiations about the future government of Poland were very much more protracted and involved. The essence of the argument was that the Western Powers advocated the formation of an entirely new administration representing "all democratic and anti-Fascist forces," whereas the Russians proposed merely to enlarge the Lublin Committee, and to do this in such a way that the Polish Communists could retain control. Churchill and Eden fought for four days against this proposal, insisting that Great Britain could not withdraw her recognition of the London Government unless there was "a completely new start . . . on both sides on equal terms." The British also demanded that the new government should be provisional and should be pledged to hold "free and unfettered elections as soon as possible on the basis of universal suffrage and secret ballot," and that these elections should be conducted under the supervision of the American, British and Soviet Ambassadors.

The Russians consented to the holding of free elections and Molotov told Roosevelt that these could be held "within a month." On the other hand, he bluntly rejected the supervision proposal, arguing that this would be "an affront to the pride and sovereignty of the independent people"! Eden endeavoured to insist on this safeguard, for he feared that any unsupervised elections would be a mockery, but at the final meeting of the Foreign Ministers Stettinius announced that "the President was anxious to reach agreement and that to expedite matters he was willing to make this concession." With regard to the setting up of a new administration, the three Ministers eventually decided upon a compromise formula which read: "The Provisional Government which is now functioning in Poland should be reorganised on a broader democratic basis with the inclusion of democratic leaders from Poland itself and from Poles abroad." To this end various Polish leaders from all non-Fascist parties were to be brought together in Moscow for consultations with Molotov and the British and American Ambassadors.

When this formula was adopted at the plenary session on February 10th the Western delegates, with few exceptions, believed that they had reached, as Sherwood says, "an honourable and equitable solution." They were acting in good faith and they presumed that Stalin was equally sincere, for he also set his hand to a "Declaration on Liberated Europe" which reaffirmed the principles of the Atlantic Charter. By this Declaration the three Powers bound themselves "to build . . . a world order under law, dedicated to peace, security and freedom and the general well-being of all mankind," and agreed to act in concert "in assisting the peoples liberated from the dominion of Nazi Germany and the peoples of the former Axis satellite states of Europe . . . to create democratic institutions of their own choice."

These fine phrases were to prove less important than the terms of the Polish formula, which was so loosely worded that it left the Russians ample room to manœuvre. Roosevelt certainly entertained some doubts on this score, for he concurred when Leahy said to him, "Mr. President, this is so elastic that the Russians can stretch it all the way from Yalta to Washington without ever technically breaking it." The essential fact was that, while the British and Americans started by refusing to accord any recognition whatever to the Lublin Committee, they ended by allowing it to be described in the communiqué as "the present Provisional Government of Poland." Moreover, although they had originally insisted that an entirely fresh administration should be formed, they finally agreed to the words "the Provisional Government now functioning in Poland should be reorganised." The only real difference between that formula and what Stalin had initially demanded was a change in verb; "enlarged" had become "reorganized."

Having secured virtually all he wanted in Poland, Stalin made a conciliatory gesture with regard to the occupation of Germany. When the President announced that he now believed France should have a seat on the Control Commission as well as a zone of occupation, Stalin replied simply, "I agree." So far as he was concerned, this was a minor concession, for it did not require any material sacrifice on the part of the Soviet Union. Where her interests and assets were directly concerned, however, as in the matter of reparations, he was both stubborn and persistent. On the one hand, he refused altogether to discuss the Soviet Union's right to use German manpower; on the other, he demanded that a firm agreement should be reached at Yalta on the amount of "reparations in kind" that Germany should be required to pay. Again and again, one or other of the Soviet delegates returned to their original figure of "20 billion dollars" arguing that, if this amount were accepted as "a basis for discussion," it "would not commit the Allies to that exact sum."

The Americans were inclined to accept that assurance, especially when it was repeated by Stalin, and to allow the figure to be mentioned in the Protocol. On this question, however, the British were absolutely adamant. Eden pointed out that they could not tell what Germany could afford to pay until they had discovered how much of the German economy survived the bombing and the general destruction of war. The settlement of the actual amount should be left to the Reparations Commission, which they had agreed to create. The Yalta Protocol should merely lay down principles to guide the Commission and should state that, "In establishing the amount of reparations account should be taken of arrangements made for the partitioning of Germany, the requirements of the occupying forces and Germany's need from time to time to acquire sufficient foreign currency from her export trade to pay for current imports." The British wanted it expressly stated that "Germany's industrial capacity would not be reduced to a point which would endanger the economic existence of the country." Eden argued that the Russians could not expect Germany to make large annual payments out of current production over a period of ten years, if German manufacturing capacity were reduced to the extent the Soviet Union demanded. These two objectives, he declared, were irreconcilable, as indeed they were to prove to be. "The British objective," said Eden, with marked prescience, "is to avoid a situation in which as a result of reparations we will have to finance and feed Germany." The logic of Eden's arguments was overwhelming and both Roosevelt and Stettinius agreed with it, but they did not think that the Soviet figure was unreasonable and they were strongly moved by sympathy for the terrible sufferings of the Russian people.

At the penultimate plenary session Stalin spoke with great emotion of the vast and wanton destruction which the Germans had caused in Russia and pleaded for due compensation. Churchill read a telegram from the British War Cabinet protesting that reparations to the value of 20 billion dollars was far more than Germany could afford. It seemed that a deadlock had been reached. The Russians would not accept the British principles, and the British would not accept the Russian figure, not even as "a basis for discussion." Thereupon, Roosevelt suggested that the whole problem should be left to the Reparations Commission in Moscow. Churchill and Stalin agreed, but that was not the end of the matter.

During this session Hopkins scribbled a note to Roosevelt saying, "Mr. President, the Russians have given in so much at this Conference that I do not think we should let them down. Let the British disagree if they want to—and continue their disagreement at Moscow." That night at a dinner given by the Prime Minister, Stalin tackled Churchill again, saying that he did not like to have to go back to Moscow and tell the Soviet people that owing to British opposition they would not receive adequate reparations. The combined effect of Stalin's persistence and Hopkins's intervention was that when the Protocol was signed next morning it contained the statement that "the Soviet and American delegations agreed" that the Reparations Commission "should take in its initial studies as a basis for discussion the suggestion of the Soviet Government that the total sum should be 20 billion dollars and that 50 per cent of it should go to the U.S.S.R." The British view that "no figure should be mentioned" was also recorded, but this was of little account. The figure was there—however hedged around with qualifying phrases—and it was linked to the names of the Soviet Union and the United States.

Although the very persistence of the Russians on this point might well have served as a warning, it is doubtful whether any member of the Western delegations foresaw then that, in spite of Stalin's repeated assurances, the Russians would soon be claiming that to "take as a basis for discussion" meant to "accept in principle." From this it was a short step to the claim subsequently made by Molotov that "President Roosevelt had agreed at Yalta that Soviet reparations should total at least ten billion dollars."

On that final Sunday morning at Livadia Palace neither the Americans nor the British suspected that the public communiqué and the secret protocol, so solemnly signed and endorsed with such expressions of mutual trust and good-will, would soon be distorted and violated by their Soviet Allies, and that this process of distortion and violation would begin before the Prime Minister and the President had been able to report to their respective legislatures on the conference at which, they both asserted, the Great Powers were "more closely united than ever before."

In the House of Commons on February 27th, the Prime Minister declared: "The impression I brought back from the Crimea . . . is that Marshal Stalin and the Soviet leaders wish to live in honourable friendship and equality with the Western democracies. I feel also that their word is their bond. I decline absolutely to embark here on a discussion about Russian good faith." That evening in Bucharest—despite the Yalta Declaration on Liberated Europe—Molotov's deputy (Andrei Vishinsky) issued to King Michael a two-hour ultimatum, demanding the dismissal of the Rumanian Prime Minister, General Radescu, the leader of an all-party Government.

Four days later, addressing a joint session of Congress, the President said: "The Crimea Conference . . . spells—and it ought to spell—the end of the system of unilateral action, exclusive alliances, and spheres of influence, and balances of power and all the other expedients which have been tried for centuries and have always failed. . . . I am sure that—under the agreement reached at Yalta—there will be a more stable political Europe than ever before." That evening in Bucharest, without any reference whatever to the Allied Control Commission, Vishinsky issued to King Michael a second ultimatum, demanding that he should appoint as Prime Minister Petru Groza, the leader of the Rumanian Communists.

2. *Yalta in Historical Perspective*

John L. Snell, an authority on recent European diplomatic history, has edited a stimulating volume on various aspects of the Yalta agreements. The following selection sums up his judgment that Yalta was a defensible attempt to assure continued Soviet cooperation through minimum concessions to Russian desires. Even the Far Eastern terms, perhaps indefensible on strictly moral grounds, were understandable from a military and political point of view. Yalta was the supreme effort at wartime and postwar cooperation; it also was an attempt to set outer limits to Soviet expansion. Its chief defect, therefore, was that Russia did not observe in the future the commitments made at the Crimea meeting.

Yalta in Retrospect

JOHN L. SNELL

The Yalta conference ended on February 11 on notes of friendship and good will. At the final banquet the evening before, Churchill declared hopefully in his toast to Stalin that the "fire of war had burnt up the misunderstandings of the past." But he more accurately summarized the

John L. Snell, editor, *The Meaning of Yalta* (Baton Rouge: Louisiana State University Press, 1956), 188–208. Reprinted with permission.

general meaning of Yalta later when, in writing of the agreements reached at the meeting, he concluded: "All now depended upon the spirit in which they were carried out."

PRAISE AND HOPE

Roosevelt and Churchill returned home by easy stages while communiqués summarizing some of their agreements were circulated throughout the world. The Far Eastern agreements could not be made known, of course, until after Russia actually entered the war against Japan. Similarly, the agreements to consider the dismemberment of Germany and the detailed statement on reparations for the Soviet Union could not be published, lest they give Nazi propagandists ammunition and thereby prolong the war in Europe. But the communiqué did make known all the Yalta agreements concerning Poland and summarized the essence of the Yalta agreements concerning the United Nations.

In the United States and Great Britain, the political leaders, press and public, on the basis of the Yalta communiqué, gave high praise to the work of the Crimea conference. *Time,* largest news magazine of the United States, spoke for many segments of public opinion in reporting that Yalta might turn out to be the most important conference of the century. It praised the special recognition by the conferees of the principle of free and unfettered elections in liberated territories and the reaffirmation of the Dumbarton Oaks principles, which would "reassure many a citizen that World War II was not being fought in vain." The magazine reported that Congress, in its first, informal reaction, "overwhelmingly" approved the results of the conference. *Time* drew attention to the special statement of the former isolationist leader, Senator Arthur H. Vandenberg, that Yalta reaffirmed "basic principles of justice to which we are deeply attached, and it undertakes for the first time to implement these principles by direct action." Herbert Hoover was quoted as saying that the conference offered "a great hope to the world," and Senator Alben W. Barkley, the majority leader of the Senate, declared that he regarded it "as one of the most important steps ever taken to promote peace and happiness in the world." These opinions, delivered before some of the Yalta agreements were known, emphasized those achievements which Roosevelt had put first at the Crimea conference, the effort to make effective the organization of the U.N. in accordance with the principles outlined at Dumbarton Oaks.

At first most of the western world rejoiced at Big Three agreement on the important issues of war and peace. Germany and Japan were to be defeated, peace to be restored, and Good was to reign in the world. The first protests were raised by the Polish leaders abroad. The Polish government in exile received the Yalta communiqué on the evening of February 12 and denounced it next morning as a violation of the principles of the Atlantic Charter and the right of every nation to protect itself. And when Prime Minister Churchill asked the House of Commons on February 27 to approve his actions at Yalta, he was attacked because of his concessions to the Russians on the Polish question. To his critics he spoke of Stalin's solemn pledges and declined "absolutely" to embark on a discussion of Russian good faith. He admitted that many imponderables lay ahead, but cautioned that it was a mistake to look too far into the future. "Only one link in the chain of destiny," he added, "can be handled at a time." A great majority in the House of Commons approved the Yalta decisions, but twenty-five members, most of them Conservatives, voted against Churchill, and eleven members of the government abstained.

Roosevelt on March 2 made his report on Yalta to a joint session of Congress. Sitting to avoid the use of heavy braces on his legs, he showed the exhaustion of his long trip and the exertions of twelve years in the Presidency in his haggard face, his almost unique reference to his infirmity, and in the thickness of his speech. He asked the support of Congress and the American people in carrying out the Yalta decisions, saying that without their backing the meeting would have produced no lasting results.

THE ONSET OF DISILLUSIONMENT

The initial praise for those Yalta agreements which were known in February, 1945, soon gave way to criticism of Russia in the American press. In the United Nations Conference for World Organization at San Francisco in April, 1945, and in pre-armistice negotiations in March and April, the U.S.S.R. began to empty the reservoir of good will which it had built up in the West in the last years of the war. At San Francisco in April, 1945, Molotov began the tactics of negation which were to make *nyet* a dirty word in Western lexicons. Before the war ended in Europe in May, Soviet activities in the Baltic states, Rumania, Hungary, and Poland caused uneasiness among the western Allies. By the end of 1945 it was apparent that Red Army occupation forces intended to despoil their area of Germany, reform its society in the Soviet image, and integrate it into the Soviet orbit. But for a time American soldiers who had seen their friends killed by German arms and who regretted their years spent in a war they had not wanted actually welcomed Russian occupation of Germany on the grounds that the Red forces would punish the Nazis as they deserved. Despite some alarm over Soviet activities in eastern and central Europe, the American people in the latter half of 1945 and the early part of 1946 were intent on getting the troops home as soon as possible.

Expansion of Russian Influence in Europe

Even before the German surrender was signed at Reims in May, 1945, the Soviet Union began the policy of creating satellite states on its borders. Old-time Communist agitators, deserters, expatriates, exiles, escaped prisoners, and apprentice conspirators began to find their way to power. Some emerged from resistance ranks, where they had served courageously during part of the war years, or were sent back from the Soviet Union to their former homes to organize or strengthen Communist cadres in key government ministries. In some cases they reached power directly; often they infiltrated labor or agrarian regimes and ultimately eliminated or won over those who initially opposed them. Some of the Communist-controlled countries invited Soviet military missions, which virtually ran the armed forces of the countries concerned and gave backing to the police forces of such states. In Hungary, Rumania, Yugoslavia, and the Russian zone of Austria, the Russians gained a strong foothold.

The China Deal Falls Through

The treaty agreements of August, 1945, between Nationalist China and the U.S.S.R. soon proved disappointing. Part of the troubles arose, however, because of the weakness and unfavorable location of Nationalist Chinese troops. At the war's end Chiang Kai-shek's troops were concentrated in southwest China, pushed there by the Japanese or sent there for possible use in Burma. Forces of Red China were in a better position to co-operate with the Soviet forces in the north and northeast. . . .

SUSPICION BEGINS AT HOME

In the five years between the end of World War II and the beginning of war in Korea, American distrust and fear of Soviet Russia increased as the Chinese Communists mastered all of continental China, Communist parties made election gains in France and Italy, and the U.S.S.R. imposed an "Iron Curtain" over most of central and eastern Europe. Greece, Turkey, and Iran were threatened and the western sector of Berlin was menaced with starvation by a Soviet blockade. Russian benediction was given to the North Korean attack in 1950 and to the later Chinese entry into the battle against the United Nations forces. The calling up of American troops for service in Korea intensified the sense of betrayal and frustration which had been created by the earlier aggression. To all Americans it was a forcible and sickening reminder that the war against totalitarianism had merely reached the intermission period in 1945, not the final curtain. Realization that years of war had brought only the briefest of respites from conflict created a mass anger which reached the point of hysteria when it was found that the Russians had the secret of that monstrous invention and "ultimate" weapon, the A-bomb.

Suspicion grew rapidly in the atmosphere of fear and anger and defeat, generated in the years 1945–50. When Whittaker Chambers, self-confessed former Russian agent, produced papers allegedly given him by Alger Hiss, a respected State Department official who had been at Dumbarton Oaks, at Yalta, and at San Francisco, it seemed that the Soviet plot ran everywhere. Political maneuvers for partisan advantage became intertwined with security measures. Liberals, who suspected that the Hiss case was a contemporary parallel of the "Dreyfus affair" intended to destroy the remaining architects of the New Deal and Fair Deal as well as to catch Communists, undertook to defend Hiss on the assumption that he could not be guilty because he *must* not be. When he was convicted of perjury, they were rendered speechless and virtually powerless for a season. The indictment or conviction of other officials increased the fear of the American public. When it was found that a number of atomic scientists, as Communists, or in the name of world science, or with a cosmic naïveté about the best means to keep the peace of the world, had handed over secrets to the Russians, it seemed that no one could be trusted.

It was in this period of unbridled suspicion that the Yalta conference commitments, known by 1946 to be more numerous than originally supposed, were wrenched out of historical perspective and blamed for most of the evils in world politics since February, 1945. As a result, Yalta's historical significance has been confused, its decisions exaggerated, and its effect on the course of subsequent events distorted. Above all, the historical context in which Yalta occurred was overlooked. Forgotten was the fact that the Soviet Union had borne the main brunt of the German attack in 1941 and 1942, while Britain and the United States were trying to hold on in the Pacific and were gathering their forces for a return to Europe. Forgotten were wartime fears in the West that Russia might succumb or that she might decide to let the western Allies and Germany fight a costly war of attrition. Forgotten also was the fact that in the years 1942–45 co-ordination of Anglo-American and Russian pressure against Germany had brought victory in Europe. As a result of this forgetfulness, all Soviet gains at Yalta seemed uncalled for or part of a conspiracy to aid Russia. Yalta became a symbol for betrayal and a shibboleth for the opponents of Roosevelt and of international co-operation.

Each year after 1945 thus brought increased demands for "the whole truth" about Yalta. The defeat of Chiang Kai-shek focused attention on the part the Yalta Far Eastern concessions supposedly played in his downfall. The beginning of the war in Korea raised the question of whether or not Yalta had been responsible for Communist influence in that country. The recall of MacArthur led his supporters to assert that his advice, had it been sought in 1945, would have prevented concessions to the Russians. The year 1955 saw the publication by the State Department of documents on the Crimea conference. These were followed by Department of Defense releases. Neither set of documents backed the thesis of "betrayal and sellout" presented so often in the halls of Congress and during the political campaigns of 1952.

NO BETRAYAL AT YALTA

The State Department and military advisers who drew up the briefing papers and memoranda for President Roosevelt's use at Yalta and the officials who accompanied him to the conference did not mislead him into making wrongful concessions to the Russians. On nearly every concession made at the Crimea conference State Department advisers were more anti-Russian than Roosevelt or Churchill. Secretary of State Stettinius and his staff stood firmly against the exaggerated Soviet demands and no one did more than Ambassador Harriman to warn the President against them. Papers written by Hiss before and during the Yalta conference opposed the Russian demand for unlimited veto power in the Security Council of the proposed U.N. and contested the Soviet claim to special representation in the U.N. It is clear from the Hiss notes on the conference and from Charles Bohlen's [State Department adviser and translator at Yalta] testimony before the Senate Foreign Relations Committee in 1953 that Hiss's role was confined almost exclusively to United Nations questions. The published record of everything that Hiss wrote and said on the subject fully reflects a concern for safeguarding American interests. Roosevelt's final approval of the extra seats for the Russians took Hiss by surprise and found him saying a few minutes before the President's approval that the Americans had not agreed to the Russian request. It is an extreme and unfounded application of the principle of guilt by association to argue that Hiss's presence at Yalta and San Francisco in some way tainted those conferences with perjury and subversion.

Yet, concessions were made to the Russians at Yalta, and the most significant thus far have been those concerning the Far East. For a variety of reasons these Far East concessions have given rise to the most pronounced denunciations of the Yalta conference. Among these reasons are the following: (1) attacks against Yalta by a coalition of proponents of Chiang Kai-shek, opponents of Roosevelt and Marshall, and the champions of MacArthur, (2) an uninformed assumption that it was Yalta that caused the downfall of Chiang Kai-shek, (3) a general prejudice against "secret diplomacy" among the American people and the fact that the agreements were reached privately by Roosevelt and Stalin, (4) the weakening of American and Japanese defenses which the concessions represented, and (5) a conviction that Roosevelt had no moral right to grant Chinese territory to the Russians.

Bohlen's arguments that Churchill was not present at the discussions on the Far East because the United States was largely responsible for that theater of the war and that China was excluded because Russia was then unwilling to be connected openly with arrangements dealing with the Far East are cogent but not conclusive. The fact that the agreement was quickly reached regarding territory belonging to neither of the conferees is hard to reconcile with Wilsonian ideals of "open covenants openly arrived at" and with the spirit of the Atlantic Charter and the Cairo Declaration.

But the suggestion that Roosevelt's promise to seek Chiang Kai-shek's agreement to concessions in the Far East brought the downfall of Nationalist China has been effectively denied by Harriman and Bohlen, and is not borne out by the facts of twentieth-century Chinese development. The willingness of Chiang to carry out these concessions in return for Russian recognition of his government has already been noted. Arguments that the United States did not properly back Chiang Kai-shek against Mao Tse-tung and that Marshall and his advisers weakened the Nationalists in insisting on compromises with the Chinese Communists should not be charged against the negotiators at Yalta, whatever their foundation in fact. Actually, in 1945 the Generalissimo thought he had a good arrangement with Stalin and for a time after the war his armies seemed to be strongly situated in parts of northern China. Overextension of supply lines, failure to get firm possession of the liberated territory, overconfidence, poor leadership, inflation, refusal to reform Kuomintang corruption, failure to satisfy the land hunger of the Chinese peasant, and, above all, the failure of Stalin to keep his promises to Chiang Kai-shek are the chief explanations for the Nationalist debacle of 1946–50. Strategically, the grant of the Kuriles and Southern Sakhalin to a potential enemy of the United States was unsound. In case of a future war between the United States and the U.S.S.R. the American position would be definitely weakened. But few Americans thought of such a war in 1945.

The moral aspects of the concessions have worried liberal supporters of Roosevelt and angered his opponents. To those who had observed the spread of late nineteenth- and early twentieth-century imperialism, concessions to the Soviet Union at the expense of China smelled of an ancient evil. The names Dairen, Port Arthur, and the South Manchurian Railway reminded the West of the Treaty of Shimonoseki, the Russo-Japanese struggle for power in Korea and Manchuria in 1904–1905, and the steady march of Japan toward control of the Far East. The 1945 grant of concessions which the czar's representatives had once won from a defenseless China smacked of a return to the breakup of China. In the disillusionment which came after 1946 many people forgot that the territory Russia gained in 1945 had not been in China's control since 1905. Within a few weeks after the war ended, the Russians held the various ports and possessions which had been promised them, without the Nationalists ever being in contact with the territory involved. Later, Stalin returned part of these areas to the technical control of the Chinese Communists, who in turn made concessions to the Russians.

Despite these extenuating arguments, and the explanations presented earlier, there is no real defense on *moral* grounds of the Far Eastern concessions to the Soviet Union. It is the one point at which Roosevelt openly went back to the type of arrangement which he and other western leaders had previously condemned. Morality and reality were in conflict; reality won. Defenders of the Far Eastern concessions can only justify them in terms of (1) the need of Russian aid against Japan to shorten the war in the Far East and save American lives, or (2) the need to prolong wartime co-operation with the U.S.S.R. into the postwar era.

WAS RUSSIAN AID NEEDED IN THE FAR EAST?

Many critics of the Yalta conference have insisted that Russian participation was not needed. One group points to possession of the A-bomb and overwhelming naval and air superiority in the Pacific to prove that the United States at the beginning of February, 1945, needed no assistance to defeat Japan.

Knowledge of the A-bomb at Yalta

Major General Leslie R. Groves, military head of the atomic bomb project, at the end of December, 1944, notified General Marshall, Secretary Stimson, and President Roosevelt that one atomic bomb, possessing enormous destructive power, would be ready for use about the first of August, 1945, that one more would be ready toward the end of 1945, and that others would follow, apparently at shortened intervals thereafter. Colonel William S. Considine, who was assigned to the Manhattan atomic project in 1944–45, testified in 1951 that he informed Secretary Stettinius at Yalta that a successful bomb would in fact be constructed, that it would be ready about the first of August, and that such a bomb would wreck a large-sized city. These facts might well have made the military and political advisers of the President far more sanguine about their prospects of an early victory than they were. However, in the absence of an actual explosion of a bomb, there was some ground for military advisers, who had to fight until the end of the year with one bomb, to proceed on the basis that the bomb would be a bonus and not the weapon which would bring early victory.

Furthermore, the military advisers of the President were less positive concerning the value of the A-bomb than was the head of the Manhattan project. Of these the least hopeful was Admiral Leahy, Chief of Staff to the President. Leahy has frankly admitted that although General Groves in September, 1944, had made the most convincing report on the possibilities of the atomic bomb he had heard up until that time, he still did not have "much confidence in the practicability of the project." Less than a week before the actual dropping of the bomb on Hiroshima, Leahy told King George VI that he did not think it would be as effective as expected. "It sounds," he added, "like a professor's dream to me." President Truman in his memoirs has confirmed the admiral's skepticism on the subject. So far as Leahy was concerned, the development of the bomb did not affect the question of Russian aid one way or the other. His faith in 1944 and in 1945 lay in the navy; he was convinced that the fleet could defeat the Japanese without ground force help.

The Navy Argument

Fleet Admiral Ernest J. King has written that he, Leahy, Fleet Admiral Chester W. Nimitz, and other naval officers felt that the defeat of Japan could have been accomplished by sea and air power alone, without the necessity of the actual invasion of the Japanese home islands by ground forces. According to King, he and Leahy reluctantly acquiesced in the decision to attack the home islands, feeling "that in the end sea power would accomplish the defeat of Japan." Yet, on June 21, 1951, Admiral King wrote Senator William Knowland that at the time of the Yalta conference he was "agreeable" to the entry of the U.S.S.R. into the war against Japan. "Our contention," he continued, "was that blockade and bombardment could bring about Japanese capitulation, and that in connection with this course of action, engagement of the Japanese armies in Manchuria would hasten that capitulation." This throws great light on the Far Eastern concessions. No one doubted at Yalta that the Japanese would be ultimately defeated, nor that a blockade might gradually starve the Japanese islands into submission. But Americans in the spring of 1945 had no desire to leave millions of soldiers, sailors, and airmen under arms, waiting for the ultimate surrender of the Japanese, eighteen months or more in the future.

The Air Force Story

Some critics have declared that air intelligence experts knew that Japan was finished and that if General Henry H. Arnold had been well enough to attend the Yalta conference, he could have made the President aware of this fact and thus have prevented concessions to Stalin. Such a statement apparently assumes that the air force was then engaged in massive operations of such a type that air bombardment could have ended the war in the Pacific quickly without ground action. This hopeful thesis has been refuted by the arguments of General Laurence S. Kuter, who represented General Arnold at Yalta:

> By March 9, 1945, only 22 small-scale B-29 strikes had been flown against Japan from the Marianas. Although the size of these strikes was steadily growing, the average number of airplanes to reach Japan from the Marianas at the time of the Yalta conference was eighty. The Yalta conference ended exactly one month before the first of the effective medium-altitude fire-bomb strikes on Japanese cities had been delivered. . . . It was sixty-five days before the first five-hundred-airplane strike could be delivered. . . .

The bad reputation now attached to Yalta, Kuter concluded in 1955, has arisen from subsequent political experience with Russia, and "to some extent from misinformation generated by partisan oratory and nourished by shaky memories."

The Army Wanted Help

While it was believed that American naval and air forces had gained superiority in the Pacific by February, 1945, military planners forecast that the war against Japan would likely last eighteen months after the defeat of Germany, with possible casualties, according to Secretary of War Stimson, of at least 500,000 and possibly as many as a million men. The first months of the 1945 campaigns had produced constantly mounting totals of dead and wounded. As has been noted (Chapter I), casualties at Iwo Jima and Okinawa confirmed the trend. In the spring General MacArthur himself favored Russian action in support of his offensives against the Japanese home islands. This notwithstanding, in October, 1955, General MacArthur declared that he was not consulted about concessions to the Russians and that he considered them fantastic. This argument is irrelevant. It is not the responsibility of the soldier to make political arrangements; rather it is to state what is necessary to accomplish his mission. MacArthur had only to notify Marshall of his needs, and the Chief of Staff had only to inform Roosevelt of army requirements in the Pacific. After that it was the President's duty to provide that aid on the best terms he could obtain. Had he refused to seek Soviet aid against Japan, he would almost certainly have been criticized by military commanders in 1945 instead of after his death.

It is interesting to note two contemporary reactions of Pacific veterans to the August, 1945, entry of the Russians into the war. General Robert L. Eichelberger, commander of the Eighth Army, declared: "Whether Japan surrenders in the near future or decides to fight on in a suicide finish, the entrance of Russia into the Pacific War has hastened the end of World War II." And the way the common soldier felt was revealed by the comment of Sergeant Hubert Eldridge of Kentucky, who told reporters: "I've been in the army four and a half years. Maybe those bombs and those Russians will help me get out now." The hope of getting home alive and quickly, clearly expressed in this statement, was the collective wish of the American soldiers in the Pacific; and that wish was one of the political realities that shaped the Yalta agreements.

What Would the Russians Have Done Without Concessions?

But the western Allies need not have promised the Russians anything, say the critics; Stalin would have fought Japan without concessions. Without Russian documents, one can not say positively what the Soviet Union would have done. Stalin had made a deal with an enemy in 1939; in 1945, he might conceivably have remained true to his 1941 treaty of neutrality with Japan, or even have converted it into a pact of alliance, if the Japanese had offered him concessions which he could not obtain from China with American help. Various roads were open to Stalin in the spring and summer of 1945. He might have made a deal with Japan in return for concessions in Manchuria and Korea; he might have remained neutral in the Far East until the United States suffered heavy casualties and then entered at peak strength into the Pacific war. Either of these policies would have enabled the Red Army to dominate Europe, while the United States and Britain withdrew their forces from Germany and Italy to the Pacific. Finally, Stalin might have attacked Japan without any agreement regarding the future terms of peace.

In view of the Russian ability to take what they wanted in 1945 without Allied agreement, in view of the additional aid the Allies needed in Europe and the Pacific, and in view of what Chiang Kai-shek was willing to give in August, 1945, for what he thought to be recognition by the Soviet government, one must conclude that the Far Eastern concessions at Yalta did not seem excessive in February, 1945. Even today it is difficult to avoid the conclusion that if Stalin had not received them from Roosevelt and Churchill he would have sought them—or even greater gains—from someone else or have taken them without Allied or Chinese consent. The terms of the Yalta agreements concerning the Far East were in the nature of a Roosevelt-Stalin contract and constituted not only concessions to Stalin but also restraining limitations. It was not Roosevelt's fault that Stalin later broke the contract.

THE MEANING OF YALTA

"It is a mistake," wrote Winston Churchill to Foreign Secretary Eden one month before the Yalta conference, "to try to write out on little pieces of paper what the vast emotions of an outraged and quivering world will be either immediately after the struggle is over or when the inevitable cold fit follows the hot." "These awe-inspiring tides of feeling," he added, "dominate most people's minds, and independent figures tend to become not only lonely but futile." The Prime Minister, with the prescience he so often showed, in these words pointed clearly to the problems which faced the Allies when they came to talk of the final victory and the beginnings of peace. The thirst for vengeance, the rapidly shifting desires of the public, and the unique difficulties of the democratic leader were thus graphically stated.

Churchill was aware that a responsible leader cannot escape the consequences of his acts. To mobilize the full support of the British and American people for war against Germany and Japan, he and Roosevelt had encouraged strong feelings against the aggressors. In order to maximize the war effort against the Axis states, Roosevelt and Churchill had often followed the rule of expediency in their dealings with the Soviet Union and other associated powers. Both leaders, perhaps mindful of the sneers of critics in the twenties at Wilson's World War I idealism, had tended to make their pleas at the level of self-preservation. Public demands for stern justice had been both acknowledged and spurred by the 1943 demand, which was never withdrawn, for unconditional surrender. At Yalta the free world still wanted punishment and reparation for Lidice, Rotterdam, Coventry, Nanking, Shanghai, Bataan, and Pearl Harbor. The story of the Malmedy massacre was still being circulated to troops in the field in Europe at the time of the Crimea conference. The full horrors of Buchenwald and Dachau were not yet known, but their stench was abroad.

Criticism of the actions of the Big Three at Yalta thus becomes in part an indictment of long-established Western assumptions about popular democracy. Roosevelt and Churchill were restricted in their actions at Yalta by the patterns of thought and action which their people demanded and which they themselves had laid down. As practical political leaders, they dared not go too far beyond what their followers would accept. One finds both a partial criticism and a partial explanation of the Yalta negotiations in one of the main theses of Walter Lippmann's thoughtful book, *Essays in the Public Philosophy*. "When the world wars came," Lippmann has written, "the people of the liberal democracies could not be aroused to the exertions and sacrifices of the struggle until they had been frightened by the opening disasters, had been incited to passionate hatred, and had become intoxicated with unlimited hope." The enemy had to be portrayed as evil incarnate, and the people told that when this particular opponent had been forced to unconditional surrender, "they would re-enter the golden age." Lippmann contends that the people of the western democracies have shown a compulsion to error which arises out of a time lag in democratic opinion and have compelled their governments "to be too late with too little, or too long with too much, too pacifist in peace and too bellicose in war, too neutralist or appeasing in negotiation or too intransigent."

The meaning of Yalta cannot be grasped unless the conditions under which the conference leaders worked are remembered. In February, 1945, the Allied peoples generally agreed that Germany and Japan must be severely punished and cured of aggressive tendencies. Agreement was widespread that Germany and Japan must be effectively disarmed and their heavy industries restricted in order to prevent them from making war in the future. The western powers generally acknowledged that the U.S.S.R. had suffered terribly in the war and should receive compensation from the common enemies. Thoughts of the postwar era were pervaded by a desire to counterbalance the power of Germany and Japan by the force of the "world policemen" who had co-operated to win the war. Roosevelt certainly hoped, and probably believed until the last weeks before his death, that he could sit down at a table with Stalin and Churchill and work out solutions to the problems of the world. The Big Three tended, as a result, to give smaller states little opportunity to shape their own futures. The President strongly believed that Soviet expansive tendencies would be allayed when the U.S.S.R. won security on its European and Asian frontiers.

Other assumptions likewise encouraged Roosevelt to overestimate the possibilities of postwar co-operation with the Soviet Union. Knowledge that Russia had been severely damaged in the early years of the war with Germany led him to surmise that the U.S.S.R. might require a generation to recover. Some Washington officials believed that the Soviet Union would be dependent upon postwar economic aid for her recovery, and that for this reason Stalin could be counted upon to maintain good relations with the United States. In short, one must remember both the war-born opportunism and the hopes and fears of 1945: concessions which would shorten the war and save lives would be acceptable to the people of the West; the formation of a workable United Nations organization held hope for the correction of any basic errors which might have been made in the various peace arrangements; and, more realistically, it was feared that the Soviet Union might become the center of opposition to the West unless bound as closely as possible to its wartime allies.

All these factors powerfully asserted themselves when the Big Three met in the Crimean palace of the czar in February, 1945. But yet another factor loomed large in the conference at Yalta. The disintegration of Germany meant that the force which had dominated central Europe since 1938 was gone and that its place in central-eastern Europe would be taken by the Soviet Union. A disarmed Italy and a weakened France could not be expected to balance the enormous power of the Red Army. Britain, seriously drained of her capital wealth by the heavy exactions of the war and lacking the manpower reserves to challenge a potential enemy of Russia's strength, could not hope to redress the balance of Europe as she had for two centuries. The people of the United States viewed their exertions in Europe as temporary and hoped for their early termination; they were in no state of psychological readiness to take up Britain's traditional role. The approaching defeat of Japan threatened to create a power vacuum in the Far East like that which Hitler's defeat would leave in Europe. Thus concessions at Yalta inevitably reflected the powerful position of the Soviet Union in Europe and its potential power in the Far East. Personal diplomacy at Yalta came to grips with the basic realities of a new balance of power in the world at large, and the freedom of action of the individual statesman was greatly restricted by these impersonal forces. Therein lies the overriding fact about the conference; without its comprehension, the meaning of Yalta is sure to be missed.

Several courses were open to the western leaders at Yalta in dealing with the new set of power relationships. It was possible to make minimum concessions to Stalin and hope for Russian co-operation and goodwill; it was possible to break off discussions at the first sign of demands which would ratify the new power relationships or create a greater imbalance in world politics than already existed; and it was possible to state certain moral positions in indignant and ringing Wilsonian phrases. Roosevelt and Churchill selected the first course, believing and hoping that it would bring victory and at the same time save the peace. They gained something by forcing the Russians to put their promises on record; but they could not make Stalin keep his word. The United States and Great Britain have at least the moral right and, technically, the legal right to use Soviet violations as the basis for repudiation of Allied concessions at Yalta, for it was the Soviet breach of contract that started the "Cold War."

After 1952 Eisenhower and Dulles faced the same alternatives which confronted Roosevelt and Stettinius in 1945: the Russians must be lived with, or they must be fought. There were elements of kinship between Roosevelt's belief that he could achieve real peace by sitting down with Churchill and Stalin and Eisenhower's attempt in 1955 to settle world problems in conferences at "the summit." And there were even clearer similarities between the "spirit of Geneva" of 1955 and the spirit of Yalta a decade earlier. Both were predicated upon the necessity of co-existence and both assumed a mutual desire for co-operation. In 1955, as in 1945, American efforts to co-operate "bumped, very hard indeed, against the great stone face of Communism." Thus the Geneva conferences of 1955 may in another day be as violently and as generally attacked as Yalta was assailed after 1946. If so, the result will be neither sound history nor wise politics.

The vitality of a democratic society certainly demands constant and well-informed criticism of leadership. But neither the free world nor the

United States can be made strong by irrational denunciations of its leaders and cries of treason which grow out of frustration and fear. It was from these manifestations of national immaturity that the myth of the Yalta "betrayal" arose. The western world justifiably looks today to the United States for rational leadership and an infusion of confidence, not for mass hysteria and symptoms of a national inferiority complex. The country which constantly tears at its vitals and heedlessly destroys the reputations of its loyal public servants cannot give the sane and courageous guidance so desperately needed to calm the fears and solve the problems of a troubled world. In its reflections on Yalta, as in its conduct in world affairs, the United States can scarcely do better than adopt for its guidance the words of Washington: "Let us raise a standard to which the wise and honest can repair."

Additional Reading

Winston Churchill, *Triumph and Tragedy* (1953).
Herbert Feis, *Churchill, Roosevelt, Stalin* (1957).
———, *Between War and Peace: The Potsdam Conference* (1960).
———, *Japan Subdued: the Atom Bomb and the End of the War in the Pacific* (1961).
George F. Kennan, *Russia and the West under Lenin and Stalin* (1961).
W. L. Neumann, *Making the Peace, 1941–1945* (1950).
E. J. Rozek, *Allied Wartime Diplomacy: A Pattern in Poland* (1958).
R. E. Sherwood, *Roosevelt and Hopkins* (1948).

19 ORIGINS OF THE COLD WAR

American foreign policy has undergone a veritable "revolution" since 1945. In startling contrast to the post-World War I period, this time the American people and government undertook long-term economic and military responsibilities in Europe and the Far East. It seemed that valuable lessons had been absorbed from the unfortunate results of American withdrawal after 1919.

During World War II, the willingness of the American people to join a world collective security organization, the United Nations Organization, indicated the shift toward a more responsible postwar foreign policy. It was hoped that creation of the U.N.O. and continuation of Anglo-American-Soviet cooperation after the war would ensure a peaceful and stable world community. A large reservoir of goodwill and admiration existed in America for the Russian people, the result of their heroic resistance to the Nazi invaders, and the American government redoubled efforts to remove Soviet suspicions and assure postwar harmony. But all proved of little avail, and both President Roosevelt and his successor Harry S. Truman experienced increasing difficulties in dealing with the Soviets during the final months of the war. 1946 was the year of transition. As signs of Soviet unilateral policies and apparent violations of wartime agreements multiplied, American attitudes began to harden. The creation of puppet Communist regimes in Poland and in the Balkan states, refusal to cooperate in a unified policy for occupied Germany, and Soviet pressures on Turkey and Iran convinced the Truman administration that all hope for postwar collaboration and friendship was gone.

The challenge, as American policy-makers viewed it, was accepted early in 1947 and the policy of "containment" was adopted to check Soviet imperialism. In January, Bizonia was formed from the American and British zones in Germany, which with the subsequent adhesion of the French zone created the basis for the West German Republic; in March, the Truman Doctrine of military aid to states threatened with aggression was proclaimed; economic aid to war-racked Western Europe was offered via the Marshall Plan in June; and by the end of the year discussions were underway which culminated in 1949 in the signing of the North Atlantic Treaty of defensive military alliance.

The Cold War was underway with a vengeance. Soviet responses to American moves took a variety of forms: the largely spurious Molotov Plan for economic aid to the satellites; the formation of the Cominform, successor to the old Comintern, to tighten Moscow control over foreign Communist parties and governments; and the military "defensive" alliance known as the Warsaw Pact. In the years since, the Cold War has spread to envelop the Far East, Near East, and Africa. The following documents and readings center on the origins of this global struggle and on the question of responsibility for its inauguration. Most scholars have accepted the popular and official American view that Russian intransigence and unilateralism were alone to blame for termination of wartime cooperation and the beginning of postwar tensions and conflicts. A minority, however, has viewed the United States as equally, or even primarily, responsible for initiation of the Cold War.

DOCUMENTS

1. The Truman Doctrine and Containment of Russia

President Truman's address to Congress on March 12, 1947, initiated what was subsequently christened the policy of "containment." Although the President specifically asked authorization for military aid only to Greece and Turkey, he proclaimed a readiness to aid nations anywhere who were threatened by "armed minorities or by outside pressures." In the July issue that year of *Foreign Affairs*, George F. Kennan, one of the State Department policy planners, enunciated the new approach in an anonymous article on "The Sources of Soviet Conduct." It would be American policy to check Russian threats by a counter application of power wherever and whenever required. In addition to halting Soviet imperialism, containment would put Russia under great pressure and in time would encourage major changes, whether evolutionary or by violence, within the Soviet empire.

Greek-Turkish Aid Program: Message of the President to the Congress, March 12, 1947

The gravity of the situation which confronts the world today necessitates my appearance before a joint session of the Congress.

The foreign policy and the national security of this country are involved.

One aspect of the present situation, which I wish to present to you at this time for your consideration and decision, concerns Greece and Turkey.

The United States has received from the Greek Government an urgent appeal for financial and economic assistance. Preliminary reports from the American Economic Mission now in Greece and reports from the American Ambassador in Greece corroborate the statement of the Greek Government that assistance is imperative if Greece is to survive as a free nation.

I do not believe that the American people and the Congress wish to turn a deaf ear to the appeal of the Greek Government. . . .

When forces of liberation entered Greece they found that the retreating Germans had destroyed virtually all the railways, roads, port facilities, communications, and merchant marine. More than a thousand villages had been burned. Eighty-five percent of the children were tubercular. Livestock, poultry, and draft animals had almost disappeared. Inflation had wiped out practically all savings.

As a result of these tragic conditions, a militant minority, exploiting human want and misery, was able to create political chaos which, until now, has made economic recovery impossible.

Greece is today without funds to finance the importation of those goods which are essential to bare subsistence. Under these circumstances the people of Greece cannot make progress in solving their problems of reconstruction. Greece is in desperate need of financial and economic assistance to enable it to resume purchases of food, clothing, fuel, and seeds. These are indispensable for the subsistence of its people and are obtainable only from abroad. Greece must have help to import the goods necessary to restore internal order and security so essential for economic and political recovery.

The Greek Government has also asked for the assistance of experienced American administrators, economists, and technicians to insure that the financial and other aid given to Greece shall be used effectively in creating a stable and self-sustaining economy and in improving its public administration.

The very existence of the Greek state is today threatened by the terrorist activities of several thousand armed men, led by Communists, who defy the Government's authority at a number of points, particularly along the northern boundaries. . . .

Meanwhile, the Greek Government is unable to cope with the situation. The Greek Army is small and poorly equipped. It needs supplies and equipment if it is to restore authority to the Government throughout Greek territory.

Greece must have assistance if it is to become a self-supporting and self-respecting democracy.

The United States must supply that assistance. We have already extended to Greece certain types of relief and economic aid, but these are inadequate.

There is no other country to which democratic Greece can turn. . . .

The British Government, which has been helping Greece, can give no further financial or economic aid after March 31. Great Britain finds itself under the necessity of reducing or liquidating its commitments in several parts of the world, including Greece.

We have considered how the United Nations might assist in this crisis. But the situation is an urgent one requiring immediate action, and the United Nations and its related organizations are not in a position to extend help of the kind that is required. . . .

No government is perfect. One of the chief virtues of a democracy, however, is that its defects are always visible and under democratic processes can be pointed out and corrected. The Government of Greece is not perfect. Nevertheless it represents 85 percent of the members of the Greek Parliament who were chosen in an election last year. Foreign observers, including 692 Americans, considered this election to be a fair expression of the views of the Greek people. . . .

Greece's neighbor, Turkey, also deserves our attention.

The future of Turkey as an independent and economically sound state is clearly no less important to the freedom-loving peoples of the world than the future of Greece. The circumstances in which Turkey finds itself today are considerably different from those of Greece. Turkey

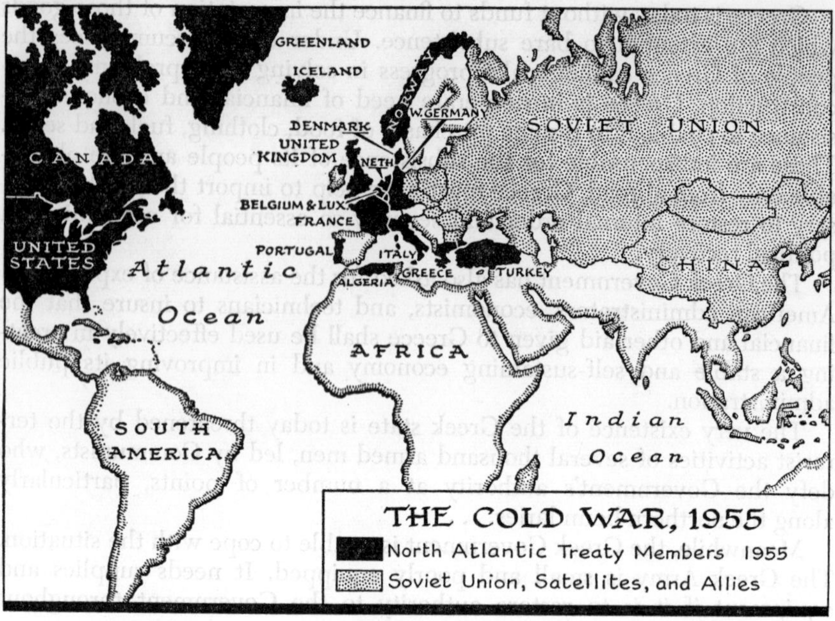

has been spared the disasters that have beset Greece. And during the war the United States and Great Britain furnished Turkey with material aid.

Nevertheless, Turkey now needs our support.

Since the war Turkey has sought additional financial assistance from Great Britain and the United States for the purpose of effecting that modernization necessary for the maintenance of its national integrity.

That integrity is essential to the preservation of order in the Middle East.

The British Government has informed us that, owing to its own difficulties, it can no longer extend financial or economic aid to Turkey.

As in the case of Greece, if Turkey is to have the assistance it needs, the United States must supply it. We are the only country able to provide that help.

I am fully aware of the broad implications involved if the United States extends assistance to Greece and Turkey, and I shall discuss these implications with you at this time. . . .

To insure the peaceful development of nations, free from coercion, the United States has taken a leading part in establishing the United Nations. The United Nations is designed to make possible lasting freedom and independence for all its members. We shall not realize our objectives, however, unless we are willing to help free peoples to maintain their free institutions and their national integrity against aggressive movements that seek to impose upon them totalitarian regimes. This is no more than a frank recognition that totalitarian regimes imposed upon free peoples, by direct or indirect aggression, undermine the foundations of international peace and hence the security of the United States.

The peoples of a number of countries of the world have recently had totalitarian regimes forced upon them against their will. The Government of the United States has made frequent protests against coercion and intimidation, in violation of the Yalta Agreement, in Poland, Rumania, and Bulgaria. I must also state that in a number of other countries there have been similar developments.

At the present moment in world history nearly every nation must choose between alternative ways of life. The choice is too often not a free one. . . .

I believe that it must be the policy of the United States to support free peoples who are resisting attempted subjugation by armed minorities or by outside pressures.

I believe that we must assist free peoples to work out their own destinies in their own way.

I believe that our help should be primarily through economic and financial aid which is essential to economic stability and orderly political processes.

The world is not static, and the *status quo* is not sacred. But we cannot allow changes in the *status quo* in violation of the Charter of the United Nations by such methods as coercion, or by such subterfuge as political infiltration. In helping free and independent nations to maintain their freedom, the United States will be giving effect to the principles of the Charter of the United Nations.

It is necessary only to glance at a map to realize that the survival and integrity of the Greek nation are of grave importance in a much wider situation. If Greece should fall under the control of an armed minority, the effect upon its neighbor, Turkey, would be immediate and serious. Confusion and disorder might well spread throughout the entire Middle East.

Moreover, the disappearance of Greece as an independent state would have a profound effect upon those countries in Europe whose peoples are struggling against great difficulties to maintain their freedoms and their independence while they repair the damages of war. . . .

Should we fail to aid Greece and Turkey in this fateful hour, the effect will be far-reaching to the West as well as to the East.

We must take immediate and resolute action.

I therefore ask the Congress to provide authority for assistance to Greece and Turkey in the amount of $400,000,000 for the period ending June 30, 1948. . . .

In addition to funds, I ask Congress to authorize the detail of American civilian and military personnel to Greece and Turkey, at the request of those countries, to assist in the tasks of reconstruction, and for the purpose of supervising the use of such financial and material assistance as may be furnished. I recommend that authority also be provided for the instruction and training of selected Greek and Turkish personnel. . . .

If further funds, or further authority, should be needed for purposes indicated in this message, I shall not hesitate to bring the situation before the Congress. On this subject the Executive and Legislative branches of the Government must work together.

This is a serious course upon which we embark.

I would not recommend it except that the alternative is much more serious. . . .

The seeds of totalitarian regimes are nurtured by misery and want. They spread and grow in the evil soil of poverty and strife. They reach their full growth when the hope of a people for a better life has died.

We must keep that hope alive.

The free peoples of the world look to us for support in maintaining their freedoms.

If we falter in our leadership, we may endanger the peace of the world —and we shall surely endanger the welfare of our Nation. . . .

2. *The Marshall Plan*

The offer of economic aid to facilitate European recovery from war damages launched a highly successful American policy based not on charity but on principles of enlightened self-interest. By 1952, when Marshall Plan aid ended and was succeeded by a Mutual Defense program, over $12 billions had been expended with the bulk concentrated on Great Britain, France, and Italy. The results were on the whole highly gratifying, for Communist inroads were checked and eventually the basis laid for a booming prosperity in Western Europe.

European Recovery Program: Remarks by the Secretary of State George C. Marshall at Harvard University, June 5, 1947

. . . In considering the requirements for the rehabilitation of Europe, the physical loss of life, the visible destruction of cities, factories, mines, and railroads was correctly estimated, but it has become obvious during recent months that this visible destruction was probably less serious than the dislocation of the entire fabric of European economy. For the past 10 years conditions have been highly abnormal. The feverish preparation for war and the more feverish maintenance of the war effort engulfed all aspects of national economies. Machinery has fallen into disrepair or is entirely obsolete. Under the arbitrary and destructive Nazi rule, virtually every possible enterprise was geared into the German war machine. Long-standing commercial ties, private institutions, banks, insurance companies, and shipping companies disappeared, through loss of capital, absorption through nationalization, or by simple destruction. In many countries, confidence in the local currency has been severely shaken. The breakdown of the business structure of Europe during the war was complete. Recovery has been seriously retarded by the fact that two years after the close of hostilities a peace settlement with Germany and Austria has not been agreed upon. But even given a more prompt solution of these difficult problems, the rehabilitation of the economic structure of Europe quite evidently will require a much longer time and greater effort than had been foreseen.

There is a phase of this matter which is both interesting and serious. The farmer has always produced the foodstuffs to exchange with the city dweller for the other necessities of life. This division of labor is the basis of modern civilization. At the present time it is threatened with breakdown. The town and city industries are not producing adequate goods to exchange with the food-producing farmer. Raw materials and fuel are in short supply. Machinery is lacking or worn out. The farmer or the peasant cannot find the goods for sale which he desires to purchase. So the sale of his farm produce for money which he cannot use seems to him an unprofitable transaction. He, therefore, has withdrawn many fields from crop cultivation and is using them for grazing. He feeds more grain to stock and finds for himself and his family an ample supply of food, however short he may be on clothing and the other ordinary gadgets of civilization. Meanwhile people in the cities are short of food and fuel. So the governments are forced to use their foreign money and credits to procure these necessities abroad. This process exhausts funds which are urgently needed for reconstruction. Thus a very serious situation is rapidly developing which bodes no good for the world. The modern system of the division of labor upon which the exchange of products is based is in danger of breaking down.

The truth of the matter is that Europe's requirements for the next three or four years of foreign food and other essential products—principally from America—are so much greater than her present ability to pay that she must have substantial additional help or face economic, social, and political deterioration of a very grave character.

The remedy lies in breaking the vicious circle and restoring the confidence of the European people in the economic future of their own countries and of Europe as a whole. The manufacturer and the farmer throughout wide areas must be able and willing to exchange their products for currencies, the continuing value of which is not open to question.

Aside from the demoralizing effect on the world at large and the possibilities of disturbances arising as a result of the desperation of the people concerned, the consequences to the economy of the United States should be apparent to all. It is logical that the United States should do whatever it is able to do to assist in the return of normal economic health in the world, without which there can be no political stability and no assured peace. Our policy is directed not against any country or doctrine but against hunger, poverty, desperation, and chaos. Its purpose should be the revival of a working economy in the world so as to permit the emergence of political and social conditions in which free institutions can exist. Such assistance, I am convinced, must not be on a piecemeal basis as various crises develop. Any assistance that this Government may render in the future should provide a cure rather than a mere palliative. Any government that is willing to assist in the task of recovery will find full cooperation, I am sure, on the part of the United States Government. Any government which maneuvers to block the recovery of other countries cannot expect help from us. Furthermore, governments, political parties, or groups which seek to perpetuate human misery in order to profit therefrom politically or otherwise will encounter the opposition of the United States.

It is already evident that, before the United States Government can proceed much further in its efforts to alleviate the situation and help start the European world on its way to recovery, there must be some agreement among the countries of Europe as to the requirements of the situation and the part those countries themselves will take in order to give proper effect to whatever action might be undertaken by this Government. It would be neither fitting nor efficacious for this Government to undertake to draw up unilaterally a program designed to place Europe on its feet economically. This is the business of the Europeans. The initiative, I think, must come from Europe. The role of this country should consist of friendly aid in the drafting of a European program and of later support of such a program so far as it may be practical for us to do so. The program should be a joint one, agreed to by a number of, if not all, European nations.

An essential part of any successful action on the part of the United States is an understanding on the part of the people of America of the character of the problem and the remedies to be applied. Political passion and prejudice should have no part. With foresight, and a willingness on the part of our people to face up to the vast responsibility which history has clearly placed upon our country, the difficulties I have outlined can and will be overcome.

3. *The North Atlantic Treaty Organization*

The "revolution" in American foreign policy was completed with the signing of the North Atlantic Pact in 1949. The United States thus engaged in the second binding military alliance of its history and the only one to be concluded in a period of nominal peace. The original membership of 12 has since been expanded to 15, with the inclusion of Greece, Turkey, and West Germany.

North Atlantic Treaty, April 4, 1949

Preamble

The Parties to this Treaty[1] reaffirm their faith in the purposes and principles of the Charter of the United Nations and their desire to live in peace with all peoples and all governments.

They are determined to safeguard the freedom, common heritage and civilization of their peoples, founded on the principles of democracy, individual liberty and the rule of law.

[1] Belgium, Canada, Denmark, France, Iceland, Italy, Luxembourg, Netherlands, Norway, Portugal, the United Kingdom, and the United States.

They seek to promote stability and well-being in the North Atlantic area.

They are resolved to unite their efforts for collective defense and for the preservation of peace and security.

They therefore agree to this North Atlantic Treaty:

Article 3. In order more effectively to achieve the objectives of this Treaty, the Parties, separately and jointly, by means of continuous and effective self-help and mutual aid, will maintain and develop their individual and collective capacity to resist armed attack.

Article 4. The Parties will consult together whenever, in the opinion of any of them, the territorial integrity, political independence or security of any of the Parties is threatened.

Article 5. The Parties agree that an armed attack against one or more of them in Europe or North America shall be considered an attack against them all; and consequently they agree that, if such an armed attack occurs, each of them, in exercise of the right of individual or collective self-defense recognized by Article 51 of the Charter of the United Nations, will assist the Party or Parties so attacked by taking forthwith, individually and in concert with the other Parties, such action as it deems necessary, including the use of armed force, to restore and maintain the security of the North Atlantic area.

Any such armed attack and all measures taken as a result thereof shall immediately be reported to the Security Council. Such measures shall be terminated when the Security Council has taken the measures necessary to restore and maintain international peace and security.

Article 6. For the purpose of Article 5 an armed attack on one or more of the Parties is deemed to include an armed attack on the territory of any of the Parties in Europe or North America, on the Algerian departments of France, on the occupation forces of any Party in Europe, on the islands under the jurisdiction of any Party in the North Atlantic area north of the Tropic of Cancer or on the vessels or aircraft in this area of any of the Parties.

Article 7. This Treaty does not affect, and shall not be interpreted as affecting, in any way the rights and obligations under the Charter of the Parties which are members of the United Nations, or the primary responsibility of the Security Council for the maintenance of international peace and security.

Article 9. The Parties hereby establish a council, on which each of them shall be represented, to consider matters concerning the implementation of this Treaty. The council shall be so organized as to be able to meet promptly at any time. The council shall set up such subsidiary bodies as may be necessary; in particular it shall establish immediately a defense committee which shall recommend measures for the implementation of Articles 3 and 5.

Article 10. The Parties may, by unanimous agreement, invite any other European state in a position to further the principles of this Treaty and to contribute to the security of the North Atlantic area to accede to this Treaty. . . .

Article 11. This Treaty shall be ratified and its provisions carried out by the Parties in accordance with their respective constitutional processes. . . .

Article 12. After the Treaty has been in force for ten years, or at any time thereafter, the Parties shall, if any of them so requests, consult together for the purpose of reviewing the Treaty. . . .

Article 13. After the Treaty has been in force for twenty years, any Party may cease to be a party one year after its notice of denunciation has been given to the Government of the United States of America, which will inform the Governments of the other Parties of the deposit of each notice of denunciation. . . .

READINGS

1. Containment: A Response to Soviet Imperialism

John Spanier, a political scientist interested in Cold War problems, shares the view that Soviet intransigence and expansionism compelled the United States to embark on a counter policy of military and economic containment. Russian actions after 1945 shattered American hopes for postwar harmony and tranquillity. Yet months of slow reassessment ensued before America accepted the challenge and, in the form of the Truman Doctrine, took a firm stand in behalf of the security of the free world.

The Beginning of the Cold War

JOHN SPANIER

Soviet Postwar Expansion

The American dream of postwar peace and Big Three cooperation was to be shattered as the Soviet Union expanded into Eastern and Central Europe, imposing its control upon Poland, Hungary, Bulgaria, Romania, and Albania. (Yugoslavia was already under the Communist control of Marshal Tito, and Czechoslovakia was living under the shadow of the

John Spanier, *American Foreign Policy Since World War II* (New York: Frederick A. Praeger, Publisher, 1962, revised edition), 19–27, 28–31, 32, 33. Reprinted with permission.

Red Army.) In each of these nations of Eastern Europe where the Russians had their troops, they unilaterally established pro-Soviet coalition governments. The key post in these regimes—the ministry of the interior, which usually controlled the police—was in the hands of the Communists. With this decisive lever of power in their grasp, it was an easy matter to extend their domination and subvert the independence of these countries. Thus, as the war drew to a close, it became clear that the words of the Yalta Declaration, in which the Russians had committed themselves to free elections and democratic governments in Eastern Europe, meant quite different things to the Russians than to Americans. To the Russians, "democratic governments" meant Communist governments, and "free elections" meant elections from which parties not favorable to the Communists were barred. The peace treaties with the former German satellite states (Hungary, Bulgaria, Romania), which were painfully negotiated by the victors in a series of Foreign Ministers' conferences during 1945 and 1946, could not reverse the tight Soviet grip on what were by now Russian satellite states. Democratic principles could not be extended beyond Western power. Russian dominance in the Balkans and Poland was, in short, firmly established, and Russian power now lapped the shores of the Aegean, the Straits of Constantinople, and—through its close relationship with Yugoslavia—the Adriatic.

Greece, Turkey, and Iran were the first states beyond the confines of the Red Army to feel the resulting expansionist pressure of the Soviet Union. In the period from the end of the war to early 1947, the Russians attempted to effect a major breakthrough into the Middle East. Every would-be world conqueror—Napoleon, Kaiser Wilhelm II, and Hitler, to mention only a few of the more recent ones—has tried to become master of this area. Napoleon called the Middle East the key to the world, and well he might, for the area links Europe, Africa, and Asia. The power that dominates the Middle East is in an excellent position to expand into North Africa and South Asia, and thereby gain control of the World-Island.

The pressure on Iran began in early 1946 when the Russians refused to withdraw their troops from that country. These troops had been there since late 1941, when Russia and Britain had invaded Iran in order to forestall increased Nazi influence and to use Iran as a corridor for the transportation of military aid shipped by the West to the Persian Gulf for transit to Russia. The Russians had occupied northern Iran, the British the central and southern sections. The Tripartite Treaty of Alliance signed in early 1942 by Iran, Britain, and Russia specified that within six months of the cessation of hostilities all troops would be withdrawn; the Allies also pledged themselves to respect Iran's sovereignty and territorial and political independence.

The final date set for evacuation from Iran was March 2, 1946. British and United States troops—the latter had arrived after America's entry into the war, to help move the lend-lease supplies to Russia—had already left. Only the Soviet troops still remained. Indeed, the Russians were sending in more troops and tanks. Their goal: to reduce Iran to a Soviet satellite.

The Russians had, in fact, begun their campaign in late 1944, when they demanded exclusive mineral and oil rights in northern Iran and offered to supply the Iranians with experts to help administer their government. When the Iranian Government rejected these demands, the Russians had organized a revolt by the Communist-controlled Tudeh Party in the north. The revolt began openly in November, 1945, and the Red Army prevented the Iranian Army from quelling it. The Tudeh Party, renamed the Democratic Party, then formed a government in Azerbaijan. The Russian game was clear: to force the Iranian Government to recognize the Soviet puppet regime in Azerbaijan, which would then send "elected representatives" to the legislature in Teheran. These would then exert pressure on the government to grant Russia the economic and political control it wanted in Iran. The result would have been the conversion of Iran into a Soviet satellite. It was imperative, therefore, that Soviet troops be forced to withdraw. Not until then could the national government and troops attempt to cope with the Communist government in the north.

During this period, the Soviet Union also put pressure on Turkey. Indeed, the Russians had begun to do this as early as June, 1945, when they suddenly demanded the cession of several Turkish districts lying on the Turkish-Russian frontier, the revision of the Montreux Convention governing the Dardenelles Straits in favor of a joint Russo-Turkish administration, Turkey's abandonment of her ties with Britain and the conclusion of a treaty with the Soviet Union similar to those which Russia had concluded with its Balkan satellites, and finally, the lease to the Soviet Union of bases for naval and land forces in the Straits for its "joint defense." In August, 1946, the Soviet Union renewed its demand, in a note to the United States and Britain, for a new administration of the Straits. In effect, this would have turned Turkey, like Iran, into a Soviet satellite.

In Greece, too, Communist pressure was exerted on the government through wide-scale guerrilla warfare, which began in the fall of 1946. Civil war in Greece was actually nothing new. During the war, the Communist and anti-Communist guerrillas fighting the Germans had spent much of their energy battling each other. When the British landed in Greece and the Germans withdrew from the country, the Communists had attempted to take over the capital city of Athens. Only after several weeks of bitter street fighting and the landing of British reinforcements was the Communist control of Athens dislodged and a truce signed in January, 1945. Just over a year later—in March, 1946—the Greeks held a general election in which right-wing forces captured the majority of votes.

The Greek situation did not improve, however. The country was exhausted from the Italian and German invasions, the four years of occupation, and the Germans' scorched-earth policy as they retreated. Moreover, Greece had always been dependent upon imports that were paid for by exports; but her traditional market in Central Europe was now closed. While the masses lived at a bare subsistence level, the black market flourished. The inability of any government to deal with this situation aroused a good deal of social discontent. And the large 100,000-man army which Greece needed to protect her from her Communist neighbors (Albania, Yugoslavia, and Bulgaria) had brought the country to near-bankruptcy. If Britain had not helped finance—as well as train and equip—the army and kept troops in the country to stabilize the situation, Greece would in all probability have collapsed. It was in these circumstances that in August, 1946, the Communists began to squeeze Greece by renewing the guerrilla warfare in the north, where the guerrilla forces could be kept well supplied by Greece's Communist neighbors.

In all these situations, the American Government was suddenly confronted with the need for action to support Britain, the traditional guardian of this area, against encroachment. In the case of Iran, the United States and Britain delivered firm statements which strongly implied that the two countries would use force to defend Iran. The Soviet response in late March, 1946, was the announcement that the Red Army would be withdrawn during the next five to six weeks. In the Turkish case, the United States sent a naval task force into the Mediterranean immediately after the receipt of the Soviet note on August 7. Twelve days later, the United States replied to the note by rejecting the Russian demand to share sole responsibility for the defense of the Straits with Turkey. Britain sent a similar reply. The Greek situation had not yet come to a head, and the need for American action could be postponed for a while longer. But it should be pointed out that the Administration's actions in Iran and Turkey were merely swift reactions to immediate crises. They were not the product of an over-all American strategy. Such a coherent strategy could only arise from a new assessment of Soviet foreign policy.

The Strategy of Containment

A period of eighteen months passed before the United States undertook that reassessment—from the surrender of Japan on September 2, 1945, until the announcement of the Truman Doctrine on March 12, 1947. Perhaps such a re-evaluation could not have been made any more quickly. Public opinion in a democratic country does not normally shift drastically overnight. It would have been too much to expect the American public to change suddenly from an attitude of friendliness toward the Soviet Union—inspired largely by the picture of Russian wartime bravery and endurance and by hopes for peaceful postwar cooperation—to a hostile mood. The American "reservoir of goodwill" for the Soviet Union could not be emptied that quickly. Moreover, the desire for peace was too strong. The United States wished only to be left alone to preoccupy itself once more with domestic affairs. The end of the war signaled the end of power politics and the restoration of normal peacetime harmony among nations. In response to this expectation, the public demanded a speedy demobilization. The armed forces were thus reduced to completely inadequate levels of strength. In May, 1945, at the end of the war with Germany, the United States had an army of 3.5 million men organized into 68 divisions in Europe, supported by 149 air groups. Our allies supplied another 47 divisions. By March, 1946, only ten months later, the United States had only 400,000 troops left, mainly new recruits; the homeland reserve was six battalions. Further reductions in Army strength followed. Air Force and Navy cuts duplicated this same pattern.

The Eightieth Congress, which convened in Washington in January, 1947, represented this postwar mood of withdrawal well. The Senate was divided into 51 Republicans and 45 Democrats, and the House into 245 Republicans and 118 Democrats. House Speaker Joseph Martin stated Republican intentions in his opening address to his colleagues: a reduction in government expenditures to allow for a 20 per cent income tax reduction. The Congress thereupon cut the President's budget from $41 billion to $31.5 billion. The Secretary of War denounced the cut and warned that the United States might have to withdraw its troops from Germany and Japan; and the Secretary of the Navy announced that the cut would render the Navy impotent. This deliberate and unilateral disarmament could not have failed to encourage Russian intransigence in Europe and increased Soviet pressure in southeast Europe and the Middle East. As this pressure increased in intensity and scope, however, American policy toward the Soviet Union began to be re-evaluated.

Three positions became clear during this period. At one extreme stood that old realist Winston Churchill. At the end of the European war, he had counseled against the withdrawal of American troops. He had insisted that they stay, together with British troops, in order to force the Soviet Union to live up to its Yalta obligations regarding free elections in Eastern Europe and the withdrawal of the Red Army from Eastern Germany. The United States had rejected Churchill's plea. In early 1946, at Fulton, Missouri, Churchill took his case directly to the American public. The Soviet Union, he asserted, was an expansionist state. "From Stettin in the Baltic to Trieste in the Adriatic, an iron curtain has descended across the continent. Behind that line lie all the capitals of the ancient states of Central and Eastern Europe. Warsaw, Berlin, Prague, Vienna, Budapest, Belgrade, Bucharest, and Sofia, all the famous cities and populations around them lie in the Soviet sphere and all are subject in one form or another, not only to Soviet influence but to a very high and increasing measure of control from Moscow." Churchill did not believe that the Russians wanted war: "What they desire is the fruits of war and the indefinite expansion of their power and doctrines." This could be prevented only by the opposing power of the British Commonwealth and the United States. Churchill, in short, said bluntly that the cold war had begun, that Americans must recognize this fact and give up their dreams of Big Three unity in the United Nations. International organization was no substitute for the balance of power. "Our difficulties and dangers will not be removed by closing our eyes to them. They will not be removed by mere waiting to see what happens; nor will they be relieved by a policy of appeasement." An alliance of the English-speaking peoples was the prerequisite for American and British security and world peace.

At the other extreme stood Secretary of Commerce Henry Wallace, who felt it was precisely the kind of aggressive attitude expressed by Churchill that was to blame for Soviet hostility. The United States and Britain had no more business in Eastern Europe than had the Soviet

Union in Latin America; to each, the respective area was vital for national security. Western interference in nations bordering on Russia was bound to arouse Soviet suspicion, just as Soviet intervention in countries neighboring on the United States would. "We may not like what Russia does in Eastern Europe," said Wallace. "Her type of land reform, industrial expropriation, and suspension of basic liberties offends the great majority of the people of the United States. But whether we like it or not, the Russians will try to socialize their sphere of influence just as we try to democratize our sphere of influence (including Japan and Western Germany)." The tough attitude that Churchill and other "reactionaries" at home and abroad demanded was precisely the wrong policy; it would only increase international tension. "We must not let British balance-of-power manipulations determine whether and when the United States gets into a war . . . 'getting tough' never bought anything real and lasting—whether for schoolyard bullies or world powers. The tougher we get, the tougher the Russians will get." Only mutual trust would allow the United States and Russia to live together peacefully, and such trust could not be created by an unfriendly American attitude and policy.

The American Government and public wavered between these two positions. The Administration recognized that Big Three cooperation had ended, and it realized that the time when the United States needed to demonstrate goodwill toward the Soviet Union in order to overcome the latter's suspicions had passed. No further concessions would be made to preserve the surface friendship with the Soviet Union. We had tried to gain Russia's amity by being a friend; it was now up to her leaders to demonstrate a similarly friendly attitude toward us as well. Paper agreements, written in such general terms that they actually hid divergent purposes, were no longer regarded as demonstrating such friendship. Something more than paper agreements was needed: Russian words would have to be matched by Russian deeds.

The American Secretary of State, James Byrnes, called this new line the "policy of firmness and patience." This phrase meant that the United States would take a firm position whenever the Soviet Union became intransigent, and that we would not compromise simply in order to reach a quick agreement. This change in official American attitude toward the Soviet Union was not, however, a fundamental one. A firm line was to be followed only on concrete issues. The assumption was that if the United States took a tougher bargaining position and no longer seemed in a hurry to resolve particular points of tension, the Soviet rulers would see the pointlessness of their obduracy and agree to fair compromise solutions of their differences with the United States and the West. In short, American firmness would make the Russians "reasonable." For they were regarded as "unreasonable" merely on particular issues; that this "unreasonableness" might stem from the very nature of the Communist regime had not yet occurred to American policy-makers. They did not yet agree with Churchill's position that the Soviet government was ideologically hostile to the West and that it would continue to expand until capitalism had been destroyed. The new American position, as one political analyst has aptly summed it up, "meant to most of its exponents that the Soviet Union had to be induced by firmness to play the game in the American way. There was no consistent official suggestion that the United States should begin to play a different game." The prerequisite for such a suggestion was that American policy-makers recognize the revolutionary nature of the Soviet regime.

This recognition came with increasing speed as the Greek crisis reached a peak. By early 1947, it was obvious that the United States would have to play a different game. It was George Kennan, the Foreign Service's foremost expert on the Soviet Union, who first presented the basis of what was to be a new American policy. Kennan's analysis began with a detailed presentation of the Communist outlook on world affairs. In the Soviet leaders' pattern of thought, he said, Russia had no community of interest with the capitalist states; indeed, they saw their relationship with the Western powers in terms of an innate antagonism. Communist ideology had taught them "that the outside world was hostile and that it was their duty eventually to overthrow the political forces beyond their borders. The powerful hands of Russian history and tradition reached up to sustain them in this feeling. Finally, their own aggressive intransigence with respect to the outside world began to find its own reaction. . . . It is an undeniable privilege for every man to prove himself right in the thesis that the world is his enemy; for if he reiterates it frequently enough and makes it the background for his conduct, he is bound to be right." According to Kennan, this Soviet hostility was a constant factor; it would continue until the capitalist world had been destroyed: "Basically, the antagonism remains. It is postulated. And from it flow many of the phenomena which we find disturbing in the Kremlin's conduct of foreign policy: the secretiveness, the lack of frankness, the duplicity, the war suspiciousness, and the basic unfriendliness of purpose." Kennan did suggest, however, that Soviet tactics might change, depending upon circumstances: "And when that happens, there will always be Americans who will leap forward with gleeful announcements 'that the Russians have changed,' and some who will even take credit for having brought about such 'changes.' But we should not be misled by tactical maneuvers. These characteristics of Soviet policy, like the postulates from which they flow, are basic to the *internal* nature of Soviet power, and will be with us . . . until the nature of Soviet power is changed. [Italics added.]" Until that moment, he said, Soviet strategy and objectives would remain the same.

The struggle would thus be a long one. Kennan stressed that Soviet hostility did not mean that the Russians would embark upon a do-or-die program to overthrow capitalism by a fixed date. They had no timetable for conquest. . . .

How could the United States counter such a policy—a policy that was always pushing, seeking weak spots, attempting to fill power vacuums? Kennan's answer was that American policy would have to be one of "long-term, patient, but firm and vigilant containment." The United States would find Soviet diplomacy both easier and more difficult to deal with than that of dictators such as Napoleon or Hitler. "On the one hand, it [Soviet policy] is more sensitive to contrary force, more ready to yield on individual sectors of the diplomatic front when that force is felt to be too strong, and thus more rational in the logic and rhetoric of power. On the other hand, it cannot be easily defeated or discouraged by a single victory on the part of its opponents. And the patient persistence by which it is animated means that *it can be effectively countered not by sporadic acts which represent the momentary whims of democratic opinion, but only by intelligent long-range policies on the part of Russia's adversaries—policies no less steady in their purpose, and no less variegated and resourceful in their application, than those of the Soviet Union itself.* [Italics added.]" Kennan thus envisaged containment as *the* test of American democracy, with our very survival as the stake. If the United States failed to meet the strict requirements of this test, it would suffer the same fate as previous civilizations, becoming no more than a name in history books.

On the other hand, if American society rose to the challenge, it could ensure its future. For containment could contribute to changes within the Soviet Union which might bring about a moderation of its revolutionary aims. The United States, Kennan emphasized, "has it in its power to increase enormously the strains under which Soviet policy must operate, to force upon the Kremlin a far greater degree of moderation and circumspection than it has had to observe in recent years, and in this way to promote tendencies which must eventually find their outlet in either the breakup or the gradual mellowing of Soviet power. For no mystical, messianic movement—and particularly not that of the Kremlin—can face frustration indefinitely without eventually adjusting itself in one way or another to the logic of that state of affairs." Kennan's theory was thus not so new. He was, in effect, asserting the old thesis that within an authoritarian or totalitarian society there are certain strains and stresses, and that these give rise to frustrations which can only be relieved by being channeled into an aggressive and expansionist foreign policy. Kennan's remedy was to prevent this expansion, thereby aggravating the internal tensions in such a way that they would either destroy the Soviet System or force the Soviet leaders to placate the domestic dissatisfaction. Assuming that the Soviet leaders preferred to remain in power and that they would therefore be compelled to adopt the second course, they would have no alternative but to moderate their foreign policy. For a relaxation of international tensions was the prerequisite for coping with their domestic problems. Thus, the Kremlin would have no choice but to surrender its revolutionary aims and arrange a *modus vivendi* with the Western powers—above all, with the United States.

The Truman Doctrine

Whether the United States could meet this Soviet challenge became a pressing question when, on the afternoon of February 21, 1947, the First Secretary of the British Embassy in Washington visited the State Department and handed American officials two notes from His Majesty's Government. One concerned Greece, the other Turkey. In effect, they both stated the same thing: that Britain could no longer meet its traditional responsibilities in those two countries. Since both were on the verge of collapse, the import of the British notes was clear: that a Russian breakthrough could be prevented only by an all-out American commitment.

February 21 was thus a historic day. On that day, Great Britain, the only remaining power in Europe, acknowledged her exhaustion. She had fought Philip II of Spain, Louis XIV of France, Kaiser Wilhelm II and Adolf Hitler of Germany. She had preserved the balance of power which protected the United States for so long that it seemed almost natural for her to continue to do so. But her ability to protect that balance had steadily declined in the twentieth century. Twice she had needed American help. Each time, however, she had fought the longer battle; on neither occasion had the United States entered the war until it became clear that Germany and its allies were too strong for her and that we would have to help her in safeguarding our own security. Now, all of a sudden, there was no power to protect the United States but the United States itself; no one stood between this country and the present threat to its security. All the other major powers of the world had collapsed—except the Soviet Union, which was the second most powerful nation in the world and was wedded to an expansionist ideology. The cold fact of a bipolar world suddenly faced the United States. The country could no longer shirk the responsibilities of its tremendous power.

The immediate crisis suddenly confronting the United States had its locale in the eastern Mediterranean. Direct Soviet pressure on Iran and Turkey had temporarily been successfully resisted. The Russians had now turned to outflanking these two nations by concentrating their attention on Greece. If Greece collapsed—and all reports from that hapless country indicated that it would fall within a few weeks—it would only be a question of time until Turkey and Iran would crumble before Soviet power. But the fall of Greece would not only affect its neighbors to the east; it would also lead to an increase of Communist pressure on Italy. Italy would then be faced with two Communist states to its east—Yugoslavia and Greece—and with the largest Communist party in Western Europe in its own midst. And to the northwest of Italy lay France, with the second largest Communist party in the West. Thus, the security of all of Western Europe would be endangered as well. The immediate danger, however, remained in the eastern Mediterranean; and the Soviet desire for control over this area was underlined by its demands that the city of Trieste at the head of the Adriatic be yielded to Yugoslavia and that Italy's former colonies of Tripolitania and Eritrea in North Africa be placed under Soviet trusteeship.

The United States had no choice but to act in this situation. The results of inaction were only too clear: the collapse of Europe's flank in the eastern Mediterranean, the establishment of Communist dominance in the Middle East, and a Soviet breakthrough into South Asia and North Africa. The psychological impact upon Europe of such a tremendous

Soviet victory over the West would have been disastrous. For Europeans already psychologically demoralized by their sufferings and fall from power and prestige, this would have been the final blow. In short, what was at stake in Greece was America's survival itself.

President Truman was quick to recognize this stark fact. On March 12, 1947, he went before a joint session of Congress and delivered a speech which must rank as one of the most important in American history. The President first outlined the situation in Greece: her lack of natural resources; the cruel German occupation, resulting in widespread destruction; her inability to import the goods she needed for bare subsistence, let alone reconstruction; the Communist efforts to exploit these conditions by spreading political chaos and hindering any economic recovery; and the guerrilla warfare in northern Greece, where the Communist forces were receiving aid from Yugoslavia, Albania, and Bulgaria.

Then Truman came to the heart of his speech. Here he spelled out what was to become known as the Truman Doctrine. The United States, he emphasized, could survive only in a world in which freedom flourished. . . .

Truman asked Congress to appropriate $400 million for economic aid and military supplies for both countries, and to authorize the dispatch of American civilian and military personnel in order to help the two nations in their tasks of reconstruction and provide their armies with appropriate instruction and training. Truman ended on a grave note:

> . . . I am confident that the Congress will face these responsibilities squarely.

The Congress and the American people did. History had once more shown that when a great and democratic people is given decisive and courageous leadership, the people will respond quickly and wisely. Under Truman's leadership, the American public had made a decisive commitment. The United States was now a full participant in the international arena. There could no longer be any retreat. The survival of freedom was dependent solely upon the United States. The only question was how responsibly and honorably this country would bear its new burden of world leadership.

2. *American Responsibility for the Cold War*

In the following selection, D. F. Fleming expresses a minority dissent among scholars in attributing the origins of the Cold War in large measure to allegedly misguided American policy and especially to the Truman Doctrine. Under the influence of Winston Churchill and others, Truman launched a dangerous and unwise policy of military alliances against Russia and a holy crusade against communism. Whatever the merits of Fleming's interpretation, the sensitive reader can appreciate the compelling earnestness of the author's plea for "co-survival." A political scientist at Vanderbilt University, Fleming has written extensively on American relations with the League of Nations and other international organizations.

The Cold War and Its Origins

D. F. FLEMING

Preface

This book is an account of the great continuing conflict of the twentieth century, the struggle which will determine whether our civilization is to disappear in the nuclear flames of a final war of annihilation or find essential unity in one family of organized nations.

The record here attempted was begun in 1947, when it seemed more than probable that we would go on into a third world war within one lifetime. It is the writer's effort to try to forestall what he has never doubted would be the end of both the American dream and Western civilization. . . .

It is my profound belief that nothing is so revolutionary as these world wars and that there is no rational alternative to relying chiefly on the irresistible force of evolution to modify communism, and all other systems, to bring them into closer harmony with the universal aspirations for a good life which all men share. I have never doubted that we can compete successfully with communism, if we place our main reliance on nonmilitary methods.

However, after World War II our leaders quickly swung all the way over from our isolationist refusal to accept any responsibility in the world and came close to assuming military responsibility for everything everywhere. We heavily and positively over-compensated for our negative failure after 1918.

We do not seem able to learn the lesson of each succeeding world crisis until it is too late. During World War II we repented of our tragic failure to lead the League of Nations and we took our place at the head of a new league.

The lesson of World War I, that we cannot resign from the world, was learned at a sadly late date but once again the mandate of a world war was disregarded. The lesson of World War II was that the losing side must not plunge the world into another world war in order to restore or improve its position. We had just permitted Germany to do that, with calamitous consequences.

Nevertheless, after 1945 we ourselves at once assumed the position of a loser. Though we were the mightiest nation which had ever stood upon this planet, and though our undamaged strength had increased prodigiously as a result of World War II, we said that we had "lost" East Europe and China, and we rebelled against these two main consequences of the war.

Knowing that world wars can grow out of great myths like this, I was appalled to see the United States move promptly into a new balance of

D. F. Fleming, *The Cold War and Its Origins, 1917–1960* (Garden City, N. Y.: Doubleday & Company, Inc., 1961), Vol. I, pp. xi–xiii, 334–337, 348–357, 436–450, 474–476. Reprinted with permission.

power conflict, while the embers of the last one were still hot, certain that the terribly wounded Soviet Union was out to take over the world.

This was done, also, in the light of the deadly flashes at Hiroshima and Nagasaki, which revealed clearly and with finality that another world war would complete the lethal progression of our time toward mutual extermination.

Since August 6, 1945, this process has advanced with relentless speed. Our decision that the Soviets should never possess an A-bomb if international control could prevent it; their prompt acquisition of the weapon; our drive for the H-bomb, with Russian success almost simultaneous; their plunge to leadership in intercontinental jet bombers and global guided missiles—these and other miracles of destruction tumbling on each other's heels leave us little time to make peace.

Yet for fifteen years after 1945 peace was not made and we proceeded doggedly along the same old cycle of international rivalry, crisis after crisis, and ever mounting arms burdens—just as if the most destructive weapon of war was still the machine-gun, and as if we were still in the springtime of 1914, ignorant of the enormous steps toward destroying civilization soon to be made in the two world wars.

Of course we say to ourselves that because it would be so horrible and so senseless it will not happen. Our Civil Defense Administrator has told us that in a surprise attack the Soviets could kill above 40,000,000 Americans, merely with bombers, and if the best possible shelters had been constructed. Yet soon thousands of ICBM's must be expected to stand triggered in the northern forests on both sides. It has been estimated, too, that we could mount a surprise thermonuclear attack on the Soviet Union which would cause deaths in the order of several hundred millions, depending on which way the winds blew.

It is an easy retreat from reality to say that no ruler of a great power would ever be mad or frightened enough to give the order, and no small nation turbulent or rebellious enough to touch off catastrophe. But humane men reasoned in the same way in early 1914, as well as in 1938, and no man can be safe until peace is made, and until some curbs are put upon the power of governments to assert their sovereign wills against each other once too often.

Yet we Americans are currently trying hard to devise new rules for victory, or at least stalemate, in "limited" nuclear wars, without using the city and nation killers. We strive assiduously to produce "clean" H-bombs and whole families of little ones, in an attempt to restore some shadow of rational possibility to the institution of war, and to the threat of its use as an instrument of diplomacy. These efforts may ease us into the final nuclear holocaust, but they can never take us back into the ages when major wars could be survived. The only way of escape lies forward; toward the elimination of great power wars. The inexorable procession of "ultimate" weapons leaves us no choice but to master them before they destroy us. . . .

It was under the shadow of this infinite and constantly darkening peril that this book was written. That is why I have sought at every stage to present the other side, how it looks to "the enemy," in the belief that this is essential to the avoidance of the final grand smash.

Of course this has been a difficult undertaking in a time when nearly all of the great organs of public opinion management have been massed to stress the iniquity and wickedness of our opponents. Yet it is only by striving constantly to see the other side that we can hope to survive, in the age of push-button ICBM's and beyond. . . .

Rising Tension: November 1945–July 1946

During the last weeks of 1945 long speeches began to be made in the United States Senate revealing the deepest aversion to the Soviet Union and a corresponding desire to deal with her sternly.

Stop Appeasing Russia. Senator Burton K. Wheeler, of Montana, led off, on November 27, with a speech filling twenty-three pages in the *Congressional Record,* less a moderate amount of interruption. Wheeler was one of the many isolationists who were catapulted into the war by Pearl Harbor. Now that the war was over they were ready to say "I told you so" with a vengeance. Wheeler declared that Truman had "inherited an almost insoluble situation—one which some of us foresaw was the inevitable consequence of policies pursued before Pearl Harbor." Now, "something terrible is happening to America and the world. . . . We confront the greatest crisis in human history."

Before explaining what the catastrophe was, Wheeler proclaimed triumphantly that the entire world was out of control. He read quotations describing bad conditions all over the globe. Then he launched into a long assault upon the Soviet Union, defining the issue as not communism, but "power—sheer, naked and unadulterated power." He listed all the territories annexed by Russia, from Finnish Karelia to Bessarabia. Then he called the roll of the satellite countries dominated by the Soviets, from Finland all the way around to the Far East.

Why had all this happened? "The only reason why, to this moment, Russia has had a free hand to liquidate all potential opposition, both among organized patriotic resistance groups and among the disorganized helplessly miserable masses, is because we have been willing not only to shield her and keep the facts from the American people but also because, by our abject appeasement for the sake of a specious unity, we have deliberately played her game for her."

Being a very able lawyer, Wheeler had chosen his point of attack shrewdly. The great bulk of the American people knew that Allied appeasement of the Fascist dictators had been an abysmal failure. Americans also hate being suckers, especially a second time. If therefore they could be convinced that they were starting down the slippery path of appeasement again, or already sliding rapidly down it, they would be certain to react sharply. It would, moreover, be relatively easy to make that charge stick. The great backlog of pre-war distrust and fear of Communist Russia could be stirred to red heat without too much effort.

Proceeding, Wheeler charged that "our appeasement, our betrayal of principles, our abandonment of human beings to a fate worse than death have made Europe and Asia a veritable chamber of horrors." He inserted dozens of quotations, many dealing with the raping of German women by Russian troops, to show how horrible conditions were, and asserted that "we dare not look for one moment longer with the blurred vision of hate, of revenge, of fear, upon an enemy whose predicament now threatens the greatest human catastrophe in history.

After further pages of material to create sympathy for Germany, and charging that "every step" which Russia had taken since the San Francisco Conference showed that she intended "to go her way for power, power and more power," he declared that "we must quit appeasing Russia and let her know once and for all that we did not fight this war to let her enslave the people of Europe."

The charge that Russia controlled Eastern Europe merely because we appeased her was, of course, without foundation. She was there because the pre-war Allied effort to turn Hitler to the East had backfired. Far from wanting to prevent her entry into East Europe we had been keenly afraid she might stop on her own borders, but myriads of Americans would forget their history and bristle at the idea of appeasing the Reds.

Russia a World Aggressor. On December 4 Senator James O. Eastland, of Mississippi, took up the cudgels in favor of Germany. He quoted five long rape stories from the Patterson press, *The Washington Times* and *The New York Daily News,* before asserting that "even communistic periodicals are admitting that ten to fifteen million Germans will die of starvation this winter."

Germany had served both as a neutralizing agent and a barrier between the Oriental hordes and the West for 2000 years. Now "we find in Czechoslovakia savage, barbarian Mongolian hordes stalking the streets of western civilization as conquerors" and thinking of engulfing Western Europe. We could not permit Germany to become a satellite of Russia. Germany was the keystone of Europe. We must hold Western Europe. He shuddered to think what a union of Russia and Germany under the banner of communism would mean. The American people "must realize that Russia is a predatory, aggressor nation, and that today she follows the same fateful road of conquest and aggression with which Adolph Hitler set the world on fire."

This speech came close to justifying the Nazi racial theories and very near to saying that we had backed the wrong horse in supporting the savage Russians against the civilized Germans. It implied also, as had Wheeler, that we should change sides and back the Germans against the Reds. Before long many Americans would be planning to arm Germany again. But the really pregnant part of Eastland's speech was the charge that Russia was another aggressor, just as bad as Hitler.

This was another analogy that would be widely accepted without examination, as it was repeated over and over again in coming months. Together the cry "No More Appeasement" and the slogan "Another

Aggressor" made a potent combination. The moral was perfectly plain. If another aggressor is on the march we must stop this thing now. Delay only makes matters worse. . . .

Eden's Appraisal. Contemporaneous with Eastland's charge that Russia was an aggressor, just as dangerous as Hitler, Anthony Eden discussed Russia's motives in the House of Commons, on November 22, 1945. Chiding the Russians for thinking that any plans for the organization of Western Europe must be aimed at them, he avowed his full belief that Russia's arrangements in East Europe were directed against a German resurgence. They were not aimed at Britain. He was "convinced it is the literal truth. We know that Russian arrangements are not aimed against us."

This was the testimony of one of the most responsible of all British statesmen. He knew, as did any student of the war, that Russian policy in East Europe was dominated by the most powerful and poignant defensive purposes and emotions. But the immensely powerful anti-Russian and anti-Communist influences in the United States, both lay and clerical, gave no recognition to history. Russia in East Europe was a brutal, barbaric aggressor, obviously out to conquer the world.

Atomic World Power. Opportunely, too, the atomic bomb had provided a weapon with which we could stop this new menace. It enabled us to defend the United States against Russian "aggression," easily, surely and cheaply. Senator Edwin Johnson, of Colorado, leading member of the Military Affairs Committee, explained it to the Senate on November 28. We had the blueprints for a new plane with a flying range of 10,000 miles. "Therefore, with the strategic location of airfields from the Philippines to Alaska, on the coast of Asia, from Alaska to the Azores in the South Atlantic, we can drop, on a moment's notice, atomic bombs on any spot on the earth's surface and return to our base."

We dared not contemplate a defense program of lesser scope, Johnson said. Would the world like it? He thought most of it would, but no matter: "With vision and guts and plenty of atomic bombs, ultra-modern planes, and strategically located air-bases the United States can outlaw wars of aggression. . . ." The courage to do it was also the price of survival.

And the United Nations? "The world organization which I am thinking of is one designed to stop war with the atomic bomb in the hands of the United States as the club behind the door, to be used only when a bandit nation goes berserk."

Evidently there was still such a nation loose in the world. Johnson strongly opposed the talk of inevitable war with Russia, but he admonished her: "Don't make the fatal mistake of pushing us around. We won't take it."

Senator Johnson meant well by the world. He did not mean to hurt anyone. All he asked was the power to atom bomb "on a moment's notice" any nation which misbehaved. The Russians would have nothing to worry about so long as they conducted themselves properly, according to his standards. . . .

Churchill's Fulton Speech

Preliminary Conference. The same could hardly be said of Winston Churchill's famous speech at Westminster College, Fulton, Missouri—in President Truman's home state—on March 5, 1946. During several weeks spent in Florida he carefully matured his blast, after flying to Washington on February 10 for a conference with President Truman which was reported to concern his speech. That the content of the speech was discussed hardly admits of doubt, since it was to be a world-shaking event.

As the momentous day approached, Churchill returned from Florida to Washington and the President journeyed with him to Fulton to present him to his audience and to bless the occasion. . . .

The Address. The urgency of the occasion was soon evident. In the grand prose cadences which had thrilled so many millions of Americans during the war, Churchill declared that "Opportunity is here now, clear and shining, for both our countries. To reject it or ignore it or fritter it away will bring upon us all the long reproaches of the aftertime." Constancy of mind was essential and persistency of purpose.

What for? "Our over-all strategic concept" was to protect the myriad cottages or apartment homes of the wage earners "from the two gaunt marauders—war and tyranny." The Missouri folk had not been conscious that these two monsters were about to attack them until Churchill described "the frightful disturbance in which the ordinary family is plunged when the curse of war swoops down upon the bread-winner and those for whom he works and contrives."

It was evident that the situation was serious, for Churchill went on to urge that the UN "must immediately begin to be equipped with an international armed force" and a certain number of air squadrons. He asserted that it would be "criminal madness" to cast the atomic bomb adrift "in this still agitated and ununited world." No one would be able to sleep so soundly if some Communist, or Neo-Fascist state had invented the bomb. God had willed that this should not be.

Then he came to the second danger which threatened "the cottage home," tyranny, the "police governments" of Eastern Europe. It was "not our duty at this time, when difficulties are so numerous, to interfere forcibly in the internal affairs of countries whom we have not conquered in war," but we must "never cease to proclaim in fearless tones the great principles of freedom. . . ."

The inference was clear that we could not go to war to drive the Communists out of Eastern Europe *at this time,* but we must keep the matter in mind and we must keep on insisting that "the people of any country have the right and should have the power" to exercise all the rights of Englishmen and to enjoy all of the governmental processes and freedoms of the Anglo-Saxon world, which Churchill enumerated in full.

Then "at this sad and breathless moment" he came to "the crux of what I have travelled here to say"—no prevention of war or successful UN without an alliance of the English-speaking peoples, continuance of the Joint Chiefs of Staff, joint use of all naval and air force bases all over the world, doubling our mobility.

Otherwise, "The Dark Ages may return, the Stone Age." "Beware, I say: Time may be short. Do not let us take the course of letting events drift along until it is too late." A shadow had fallen. Nobody knew "what Soviet Russia and its Communist international organization intends to do in the future, or what are the limits if any to their expansive and proselytizing tendencies." From Stettin to Trieste there was "an iron curtain." He saw enormous and wrongful inroads into Germany.

Turkey and Persia were profoundly alarmed. And in front of the iron curtain "Communist Fifth Columns" were everywhere, "a growing challenge and peril to civilization." In the Far East there was anxiety, especially in Manchuria.

Having built up this picture of a terrible juggernaut operating all over the world which had to be tamed, Churchill then repulsed "the idea that a new war is inevitable, still more that it is imminent." He did not believe that Russia desired war, only "the fruits of war and the indefinite expansion of their power and doctrines." Therefore "while time remains" he demanded the "establishment of conditions of freedom and democracy as rapidly as possible in all countries." Since nothing except overwhelming force could rapidly eliminate communism from East Europe and Russia herself, he did not explain how this was to be done. . . .

Then he drew on the great prestige which he had won before 1939. The last time he "saw it all coming and cried aloud," but "no one paid any attention." Surely we "must not let that happen again." There must be "a good understanding," that is, a showdown, with Russia "now, in 1946."

The old warrior and world strategist was off again, and with a terrifying start. He had waged war on the Reds in Russia to the limit of British tolerance during 1919 and 1920. Then throughout the twenties he had preached the menace of the Red revolution, never losing an opportunity to refer to the Bolshevik leaders "as murderers and ministers of hell."

Forced to welcome their aid in 1941 to save Britain, he had incessantly attempted the impossible feat of using them to beat Germany while denying them the fruits of victory. Now he would mobilize the might of the United States to achieve what he had never been able to do before.

A Master Stroke. If, too, there is a Third World War, Churchill's Missouri speech will be the primary document in explaining its origins. His was the first full-length picture of a Red Russia out to conquer the world. Backed by the immense authority of his war record, and by the charm of his great personality, it pre-conditioned many millions of listeners for a giant new *cordon sanitaire* around Russia, for a developing world crusade to smash world communism in the name of Anglo-Saxon democracy. In print Churchill's battle cry became the bible of every warmonger in the world. It said all they had wanted to say and with his great name behind it, it could be used endlessly with great effect.

At Fulton, Churchill also prevailed over Roosevelt and Hull, the great American leaders who had checkmated him in all the later stages of the war, preventing him from creating a gulf between East and West. At Fulton he did it. Had Roosevelt lived, Churchill would never have dared to propose that he come to the United States and issue a call for a world alliance to encircle the Soviet Union and establish Western democracy in Eurasia. If he had ventured to make such a speech in the United States he would have been sharply disavowed. But with Roosevelt dead he was able not only to do that, but to carry President Truman along in his baggage.

Whether the idea of the speech originated with Churchill or Truman is not yet known. In the light of Truman's strongly hardened determination to quit "babying" the Soviets, he was probably the originator. It seems a little odd that in his *Memoirs* there is only one casual reference to an event of such outstanding importance, one of the chief landmarks of the Cold War. . . .

Brooks Atkinson wrote from Moscow describing "the outburst of fury" which Churchill's speech had loosed. It had enormously raised the pitch of political feeling in Russia. The Russian people were kept aware generally of threats to their security, but here was something specific. Like all other peoples, the Russians did not want war. "They have had a bellyfull of carnage. They have not had time enough yet to recover from the deep poignant suffering of the fierce war years, when they lost more lives than both the British and Americans." They would therefore be slow to believe in the possibility of war again, without a bombshell such as Churchill's speech. It "had the effect of electrifying and depressing everyone" and it fell squarely into the familiar pattern of Soviet beliefs—capitalistic hostility, encirclement and the violent imperialism of a dying capitalist economy leading to war—this time against the Soviet Union.

In other words, few things could have convinced the Russian people of the reality of great danger ahead so effectively as Churchill's speech did. He could and did do it better and more easily than any other living person, binding the Soviet peoples to their leaders as nothing else could. . . .

Our Firm But Moderate Policy of Making Peace Condemned. The extent of the push which Churchill gave toward irreconcilable conflict stands out sharply by comparing his speech with those of Byrnes and Vandenberg a few days before. Reporting on the London UN sessions Vandenberg filled four columns with praise of UN, listing the credit items on the ledger of the London meetings. Then he asked "What is Russia up to now?" He named the places all around the world where she was pressing for advantage, and asserted his belief that the two great rival ideologies could "live together in reasonable harmony if the United States speaks as plainly upon all occasions as Russia does; if the United States just as vigorously sustains its own purposes as Russia does. . . ." The situation called for "patience and good will but not for vacillation." . . .

On February 28 Byrnes made a speech which also indicated a tougher line toward Russia. Still he stressed that there had always been ideological differences in the world, and that "in this world there is room for many people with varying views and many governments with varying systems." The United States wished "to maintain friendly relations with all nations and exclusive arrangements with no nation." "We will gang up against no state," Byrnes declared. "We will do nothing to break the world into exclusive blocs or spheres of influence." Only an "inexcusable tragedy of errors could cause serious conflict between this country and Russia."

This was the policy which Byrnes and Vandenberg had enunciated a few days before Churchill spoke. Neither had given the slightest indication of belief that an irreconcilable conflict existed, or that Russia had to be hemmed in and overawed with overwhelming power. Neither had suggested that democracy had to be enforced everywhere. Both had given every indication that they expected to make peace, though with difficulty.

It was this sensible attitude which Churchill contradicted completely. He taught that all civilization was in imminent peril of destruction by Russia. The time was terribly short and our lives and fortunes could be saved only by a swift mobilization of overwhelming power against her. He desired to gang up with a vengeance.

Toughness Prescribed. It was this policy which, backed by President Truman, prevailed. Byrnes had already felt strong presidential disapproval for the agreements with Russia which he had made at Moscow. Truman had been influenced by his military and Congressional advisers, Admiral William D. Leahy, Senators Connally and Vandenberg, all of whom thought Byrnes had not been tough enough. This was the view of British Foreign Secretary Bevin, who had "rather openly accused him of weakness and appeasement." Now after the supreme demand for toughness at Fulton our policy steadily hardened. Churchill's speech "marked the critical point where relations between the West and the East turned for the worse." . . .

Moderation Advised. The *démarche* at Fulton, Missouri, launched the United States openly upon a policy of dealing with Russia as an incorrigible menace. On March 10, Cordell Hull revealed his deep alarm over the turn in events. We who are living, he said, must not allow the human race to commit suicide through selfishness, impatience and provocation. Addressing all the members of the United Nations, Hull offered a five-point program for overcoming what he termed the spirit of impatience. He urged each government to: (1) examine with sympathy and patience the views of others; (2) ascertain the true facts; (3) avoid the assumption of adamant positions; (4) refrain from exaggerating and over-emphasizing one's own claims; and (5) refrain from making an appeal to prejudice.

This was the voice of true statesmanship. Of course it needed to be heard in Moscow. Yet the voice of reason and moderation, of firmness and patience, could no longer have much effect in the West. There the implacable Truman-Churchill spirit had seized control. It was their policy of alliance against Russia and restraining communism by military means which was to rule for many a day—until its bankruptcy was demonstrated, as it would be, or another global war came. . . .

Atomic Ultimatum. The practical certainty that such a war could not be ended did not deter some Americans from wanting to start it. Thus George H. Earle, former American Minister to Bulgaria, returned to make "America realize what a frightful menace we have in Russia." It was "the greatest danger that ever threatened America." Civilization's outlook was "the blackest in history." He urged that Russia be given an ultimatum to "get back to her own territory and if they refused I would use the atomic bomb on them while we have it and before they get it." He asserted that "If Russia had the atomic bomb there would be few Americans alive today."

Truman's Baylor Speech. On March 6, 1947, President Truman made a speech at Baylor University on foreign economic policy which was a virtual declaration of irreconcilable conflict against both communism and democratic socialism. He explained that freedom was more important than peace and that freedom of worship and speech were dependent on freedom of enterprise. Something "deeper than a desire to protect the profits of ownership" was involved.

Freedom of enterprise was limited when governments conducted foreign trade or when the governments planned the economy. In the latter case "Governments make all the important choices and he (the trader) adjusts himself to them as best he can."

This, said the President, "was the pattern of the seventeenth and eighteenth centuries" and "Unless we act, and act decisively, it will be the pattern of the next century. . . . If this trend is not reversed the Government of the United States will be under pressure, sooner or later, to use these same devices to fight for markets and for raw materials." It would find itself in the business of "telling every trader what he could buy or sell, and how much, and when, and where." This was "not the American way" and "not the way of peace." The implication was plain that state trading (in the U.S.S.R. and its satellites) and government control of trade (in Britain and much of West Europe) led to war.

This was serious enough, but even more ominous were the assumptions that "the whole world should adopt the American system" and that "the American system could survive in America only if it became a world system."

The Baylor speech was closely studied by every European government as a challenge by the strongest economic unit ever developed on earth, one which had just grown to gargantuan size on government orders. During the four war years, 1942 to 1946 inclusive, the American Government had poured 306 billion dollars into the coffers of American business, taking all the responsibility, building hundreds of new plants for business to operate, guaranteeing unlimited markets and immense profits.

The result of this exhibition of "free enterprise" was the growth of the great American corporations to such power that at the end of the war our Federal Trade Commission reported that the 62 largest manufacturing corporations had accumulated liquid capital sufficient "to purchase the assets of nearly 90 per cent of all the other manufacturing corporations in the United States." Many of these tremendous economic giants were more powerful than the entire national economies of dozens of nations, but the Baylor speech declared that they must not have the competition of state owned or state planned economies. If American freedom of worship and speech was to survive, the regimented economies of the world had to go.

Coming from a government which controlled three-fourths of the world's invested capital, and more than half of its industry, the Baylor speech was a statement which would give all other governments pause. It indicated how easy it would be for the world's economic colossus to decide that all other economic systems were un-American and threats to American freedom. It indicated that the representatives of American capitalism who had come into key posts in Washington after Roosevelt's death held the same view about the world that Lenin and other Communist zealots had. The world could not accommodate diverse systems. It must be one or the other: communism or free enterprise capitalism.

The Occasion for the Doctrine

Paralysis in Britain. The apparently well founded hopes for peace at the end of the year were suddenly upset by a great snow storm which whirled into a high pressure area above northern Russia and descended on the British Isles, late in January 1947, covering them from three to twenty feet deep with snow which promptly froze into ice after one day of thaw.

Britain was paralyzed. Her tired miners, mainly older men, could not get into their deep, narrow, hard-to-work coal seams. The scanty supplies above ground could be moved only with slow, heroic efforts. It was several weeks before anything like normal circulation could be restored to Britain's economic veins, and by then $800,000,000 of desperately needed export production had been lost and the world had seen clearly that Britain was too weak to resume her former role as a great power. Up to that time the illusion had persisted that the power which had dominated the world for more than a century before 1914, and which had recovered after 1918, would take her place as a fairly strong third in the new galaxy of great powers. Actually, this was impossible. Another huge bite had been taken from her overseas assets. Now they were overbalanced by far larger debts owed to all the dominions—even $4,000,000,000 to India, now emerging into independence. What was left could not support a great navy and 1,400,000 troops scattered around the world, particularly if the British people at home were to have a decent standard of living. . . .

British Failure in Greece. The parlous state of affairs in Greece had been known to our government for several months. The British had explained to Secretary Byrnes in the previous summer that they would have to cut their losses in Greece. Since the end of the war the British had poured $760,000,000 worth of supplies into Greece, without doing more than keep the country alive. Nothing was left over for reconstruction. This was due to three reasons: the thorough ruination of Greece by the Germans and Italians; the antagonisms and demoralization left by the civil war a year earlier; and the inability of the corrupt Rightist government to suppress a large scale communist-led guerrilla movement which ruled the mountains and controlled most of the country outside the big cities. The government turned Rightist bands loose in the country, and they did their best to crush the Left, but the net result was to drive to the hills many embittered men who were not communists. The majority of the rebels were "not communists."

The rebels also received aid from communist ruled Bulgaria, Yugoslavia and Albania, Greece's northern neighbors. Besides arms, munitions and medical help the rebels were permitted to retreat over the border when hard pressed, to rest and be re-outfitted, particularly in Yugoslavia. The Western powers had tried to stop this aid through the United Nations, by sending a commission to investigate, which was still in Greece in March 1947, along with an official American economic mission headed by Paul Porter, but there was not much chance of success by this method against the opposition of Russia and her satellites.

The Greek Problem Presented to Us. This was the general situation when on February 24, 1947, the British Ambassador orally informed Under Secretary of State Dean Acheson, that the British Government would evacuate its army and cease to look after Greece on March 31. . . .

The Preparation of the Doctrine. The first meeting of State Department experts with Under Secretary of State Dean Acheson left some concerned by the responsibility of challenging the Soviet Union, others elated by the prospect, and some filled with awe. Acheson was to lead in the epochal turning point, since Secretary of State George Marshall was being intensively briefed for the approaching Moscow Conference on the future of Germany and would shortly leave for the Conference.

At a meeting with the Congressional leaders of both parties, on February 27, Acheson left them all deeply impressed by his account of the persistent efforts of the Soviet Union to encircle Turkey, thus laying three continents open to Soviet domination, and Germany—through the communists in France, Italy, Austria and Hungary. The Soviet Union was "aggressive and expanding" and Russia and the United States were "divided by an unbridgeable ideological chasm." Not since Rome and Carthage had there been such a polarization of power and it was up to us to block the Soviets in Greece and Turkey.

None of the leaders of Congress questioned the assumption of protectorates over Greece and Turkey. Senator Vandenberg, supported by others, insisted that the President should explain the new policy in a message to the Congress and a radio address to the people, in the broad context which Acheson had made, and he reiterated this request later. The radio address was dropped only at the last minute, but on April 27 Acheson had an off-the-record conference with about twenty leading newspaper men, and other briefing sessions prepared the way for public support of the program. A Cabinet committee prepared "a program of communication with leaders throughout the country, particularly business people." . . .

On the same afternoon [February 28] a large meeting of State, War and Navy officials was held in which the view was unanimous that the new policy should be presented to the public in terms of "assistance to free governments everywhere" that needed help against Communist aggression or subversion. This view came from all parts of the assembly, which also wanted the world strategic situation to be explained to the people.

A paper written up after this discussion became the basic document for the President's address and it contained the statement that it should be "the policy of the United States to support free peoples who are resisting attempted subjugation by armed minorities or by outside pressures." . . .

Truman's Long Held Purpose. The President himself was ready to seize the occasion to quarantine Soviet communism. On March 23, 1947, an authoritative article was published in the *New York Times* by Arthur Krock, who stated that the Truman Doctrine had been in the President's mind a long time. . . .

In his article of March 23 Krock stated that after inquiry he had reached the conclusion that Moscow had better disabuse itself of the growing impression that Mr. Truman merely adopted the view of his counsellors. On the contrary, the President began to abandon hope of achieving peace and security by "a continued policy of appeasement and official treatment of Russia as a government friendly to the United States," as long ago as the London Conference of Foreign Ministers in September 1945. "He made up his mind then that, when a fitting opportunity arose and one which Congress and the people would recognize as such, he would proclaim the new doctrine. On several occasions he thought the time had come, but some of his important advisers talked him out of it." When the British note of February 24, 1947, announcing withdrawal from Greece, came it pointed to a situation which the President found suited to his "long held purpose." It only remained to put "Mr. Truman's now-matured policy" before the world suitably. The alternative of limiting the message to the immediate task in hand was rejected and Clark Clifford, "who must at first hand have heard the doctrine in its long period of oral formulation," was set to drafting "the global anti-Communist policy." The President insisted that the important word *must,* instead of "should," be inserted in the master-key paragraph of the message, to make it read: "I believe that it *must* be the policy of the United States to support free peoples who are resisting attempted subjugation by armed minorities or by outside pressure." When it was finally finished Mr. Truman "rehearsed its delivery several times with apparently growing satisfaction." It said what he wanted to say. . . .

In his *Memoirs* (II, 105) Mr. Truman relates that the first draft of the message presented by the State Department "was not at all to my liking." In spite of all the high purpose recorded above by its draftsman, Joseph E. Jones, it was full of "all sorts of background data and statistical figures," sounding like "an investment prospectus." So Truman sent it back asking for more emphasis on general policy and it was rewritten for that purpose, but it still seemed to him "half-hearted." Therefore in "the key sentence" he scratched out "should" and wrote "must" and did the same thing in several other places. He "wanted no hedging in this speech."

George Kennan's Dissent. From this concordance of agreement that the Soviet Union and communism must be publicly quarantined there was one strong and surprising dissent. From our embassy in Moscow George F. Kennan had sent long messages urging a stiffening of our responses to Russia in the post-war period. In March 1947 he was in Washington, already designated by Marshall as head of a new policy planning staff. At the moment he was occupied with lectures to the War College and he had no part in formulating the Truman Doctrine, though he knew it was in preparation.

On the afternoon of March 6 he came over to see how things were going and was shown the third draft, before the message had gone to the White House and been sharply stiffened. In its milder form the message disturbed Kennan deeply. "To say that he found objections to it is to put it mildly," said Joseph M. Jones. "He objected strongly both to the tone of the message and to the specific action proposed." He favored economic aid to Greece, but wanted to keep the military aid small. He was opposed to aid of any kind to Turkey, whereas the others regarded the defense of the Straits as the most vital consideration involved, though the Turkish end was softpedalled in the message.

It was the tone and ideological content of the message to which Kennan most objected, "the portraying of two opposing ways of life, and the open-end commitment to aid free peoples." Moreover, he felt so strongly that he voiced his objections to a number of people in the Department including finally Acheson, but "It was too late."

This first reaction by Kennan to the Truman-Churchill Doctrine of a global quarantine of the Soviet Union and communism would have astonished the world had it been known soon after 1947, for his famous article on "The Sources of Soviet Conduct," in the July 1947 issue of *Foreign Affairs* (which will be discussed later), caused him to be widely regarded as the father of the containment doctrine. Yet in the light of the revelation just quoted it would seem that Kennan was rationalizing and softening the doctrine rather than fathering or inventing it. On the contrary, his initial reaction was that the proclamation of a head-on collision between two ways of life and two great powers was much too sweeping, and that it was dangerous. . . .

Did the Republicans Require Conversion? It has often been said that a planetary declaration of conflict with communism and the Soviet Union was necessary to pry from the famous 80th Congress Republican majorities the $400,000,000 desired as a first instalment for Greece and Turkey. This Congress, which had just taken its seat in January, was undoubtedly bent on reducing the budget and taxes. For two months they had been debating whether to cut the President's 37 billion budget by 6 billion or somewhat less. They would not like a big appropriation for foreign aid.

Nor was helping the corrupt Greek Government an easy thing to sell to Congress. On February 23 Stewart Alsop cabled from Athens that the main characteristic of this government seemed to be "its total impotence." Most of the Greek politicians had "no higher ambition than to taste the profitable delights of a free economy at American expense." Senator Vandenberg was reported to have told the President that if he expected to get the money he would have to "scare hell out of the country"—an apt description of the technique which was employed. This motive may also have determined in part Vandenberg's requirement that the President lay it all down in global terms in both a Congressional message and a radio address. . . .

The Truman Doctrine and Its Reception

The President read the message to a joint session of the two Houses of Congress on March 12, in an even monotone. He received light applause at three points. For the most part the Congress listened grimly and silently. On the same morning the *New York Times* had predicted that Truman would "ring down the curtain on one epoch in America's foreign policy." As he read, there could be no doubt that this was the case. . . .

We could not "realize our objectives," unless we were "willing to help free people to maintain their free institutions and their national integrity against aggressive movements that seek to impose upon them totalitarian regimes." This had happened, in spite of our frequent protests and in violation of the Yalta Agreement, in Poland, Bulgaria, Rumania and other countries. The time had come when "nearly every nation must choose between alternative ways of life," one distinguished by free institutions and the other by terror and oppression. He believed "that *it must be the policy of the United States to support free peoples who are resisting attempted subjugation by armed minorities or by outside pressure.*" [Italics added.]

"If Greece should fall under the control of an armed minority," confusion and disorder might spread east throughout the entire Middle East and west through the countries of Europe. He therefore asked for four hundred million dollars for Greece and Turkey and authority to detail civilian and military personnel to them.

All Revolution Forbidden. No pronouncement could have been more sweeping. Wherever a communist rebellion developed the United States would suppress it. Wherever the Soviet Union attempted to push outward, at any point around its vast circumference, the United States would resist. The United States would become the world's anti-communist, anti-Russian policeman.

This, too, was not the full extent of the Doctrine, for its all inclusive language also forbade every kind of revolution, democratic or otherwise. It would be difficult to find a revolution anywhere which had not been the work of an armed minority. The people might later come to the support of the fighting rebels, but revolutions were notoriously made by comparatively small groups of determined armed men. According to the new doctrine this could not happen, if for no other reason because some communists would almost inevitably be mixed up in the revolution, or an alarmed government would allege they were. The President went on to say that the status quo was not sacred, but he had made it so. So far as the United States was concerned the method by which this nation was born was outlawed. There would be no more revolutions thereafter, in spite of the fact that many hundreds of millions of people lived a miserable existence under the misrule of a few. Revolution was finished. All of these peoples would have to stay put. If their rulers should decide to alleviate their condition somewhat, well and good, but they could not be coerced or subjected to "such subterfuges as political infiltration." . . .

Encirclement of the Soviet Union Proclaimed. The wheel had come to full circle with a vengeance. The isolationist United States, desiring only to be let alone, had become the world's policeman. Wherever public order was disturbed, we would be there. Wherever the Soviet Government or communism attempted an advance the United States would combat it. The most gigantic land power on the face of the globe, living on the opposite side of the earth from the United States, was to be fenced in at all points. Thus far and no farther! In the two previous balance of power struggles Germany had complained constantly that she was being encircled, but not one of her opponents ever dreamed of admitting that she was. Now Mr. Truman had proclaimed from one of the world's greatest rostrums the most gigantic encirclement ever conceived in the mind of man. . . .

Europe Amazed and Alarmed. From Paris Harold Callender wrote that the ablest diplomatic officials in Europe, of French and other nationalities, regarded Truman's message as certain to compel a showdown between the Soviet Union and the Western world. They read it "with amazement, since they expected nothing so stern or forthright." It was "a revolution in United States foreign policy more notable even than American participation in the United Nations." To a "striking extent professional diplomatic quarters, and other non-Communist or anti-Communist quarters, echoed in only slightly attenuated form the Moscow charge of a new and expanding American imperialism." French journals commented uneasily on the pessimism of our attitude and on the sharpening of the issue.

In London "rumbles of protest and ironical cheers from Labor M.P.s punctuated each effort by speakers in the House of Commons to describe President Truman's program of American aid for Greece and Turkey as a step toward world freedom and democracy." The *Daily Herald*, official Labor party newspaper, said: "Our first reaction to President Truman's speech on Wednesday was one of uneasiness. Our second thoughts are no happier."

There was no spontaneous enthusiasm in Britain. Mr. Churchill spoke only for a minority. Most people were distinctly disturbed, especially because the United States was tending toward individual rather than collective action in international affairs. . . .

Censure in Britain. On April 7 the Cooperative Party of Great Britain, one of the major arms of the Labor Party, and representing about 7,500,000 working people, "approved by a large majority" a resolution condemning Truman's program of aid to Greece and Turkey as "a menace to world peace and the negation of the democratic principles for the preservation of peace for which the grave sacrifices of the last war were made." The party executive opposed the resolution, but the delegates insisted on its passage. They felt that "this attempt to by-pass the United Nations Organization will seriously impair the authority of the organization and destroy the confidence and hopes of free peoples everywhere."

Simultaneously a poll of 83 diplomats, representing 38 countries, showed 82 per cent of them regretting as a matter of principle that the United States did not come before the UN with the Greek and Turkish problems. In France General Charles de Gaulle urged the unity of Western Europe, to provide a balance between the world's "two enormous masses, both expanding."

The Continent Shocked by the "Either-Or" Challenge. On March 30 Mallory Browne made a close survey of European opinion from London for the *New York Times*. In Britain he thought a vast majority welcomed the Truman Doctrine as evidence that the United States had come of age and would not withdraw into isolation again, but there was fear that Truman's "blunt challenge to Soviet Russia" might lead to a war in which Britain would be the first and worst victim. Many were afraid that another war would wipe out their island. In France and a number of other continental countries it appeared that "doubts prevailed over hopes." In Italy the enthusiasm of the favorable opinion was tempered by widespread fear that it meant war. The Czechs were equally fearful. In the Low Countries and Scandinavia, where some of the most politically mature peoples in the world live, most people appeared to have been "shocked by the strong language Truman used," and decidedly nervous over the consequences. Even the conservatives tended "to ask whether it was wise." From all the diversity of opinion one overwhelming impression emerged, that the United States had embarked on a course which would bring "either real peace or the annihilation of atomic war."

This contemporary judgment inescapably raises the question whether there was anything in the world situation in March 1947 which compelled the United States to stake the future of all humanity upon one world-shaking defiance of the Soviet Union. . . .

Was the Truman Doctrine a Declaration of War?

Formally and legally it was not. This could be asserted with a perfectly straight face, and with ample legal documentation. The Soviet Union was not mentioned, nor the Turkish Straits. We had a right to aid any friendly government that we wished to help. Turkey felt pressed and there was a crisis in Greece. We had as much right to proclaim an anti-communist crusade—or holding operation—as the Russian controlled press had to proclaim the inevitability of Western capitalism's collapse and the wickedness of Western "imperialism."

All this is incontrovertible and, given both our deep vexation over the communist organization of East Europe and the geopolitical argument, some action on our part in Greece was foreordained. Greece would not be allowed to fall into the Soviet orbit. Some anti-communist connotation was also advisable to secure quick congressional approval.

These considerations still leave the question whether it was wise and statesmanlike to issue a global declaration setting limits both to communist expansion and Soviet expansion. It can readily be argued that this was the straightforward thing to do, to draw a line around both. Yet strategically it was a rash and unenforceable commitment. The Soviet Union already occupied the Heartland of Eurasia to its full limits, and all of our sea and air power, plus the A-bomb could not indefinitely prevent her from pushing out if she chose. Worse still, an open direct proclamation of encirclement was one of the best means of causing her to choose to push out.

The global containment Doctrine committed the United States to standing guard, not only at the Straits but all around the vast perimeter of the Soviet Union and its satellites. It pledged the prestige and resources of the United States, and especially the prestige of Mr. Truman, at virtually all points on the earth which mattered, either militarily or politically, leaving the initiative to the Russians and to local communist movements. Wherever either chose to fight we would accept the battlefield, no matter how remote or unfavorable. This was clearly a self-defeating policy, one fitted to squander our resources on the way to an immeasurable, unmanageable war.

Turning Point. The defenders of the Truman Doctrine announced with satisfaction that it was the end of an era, the period of "appeasement," and the beginning of a new era of firm containment. However, a full appraisal indicated that a much more fateful turn had been made, the turn from a post-war period to a pre-war atmosphere. The Truman Doctrine and the X article both ignored the problem of settling the Second World War, giving the impression that no settlement could be reached, that it was to be hereafter a matter of pressure and counter pressure. Less than two years after the bombs stopped falling in Europe American diplomacy came close to abdicating. Its arguing powers were exhausted. Stronger measures would have to be taken.

In this sense the Truman Doctrine was an effective declaration of war, one which had formed in Mr. Truman's mind in the autumn of 1945, almost before the fumes of Hiroshima had drifted around the earth. It gave notice to both sides, and to innumerable millions of people all over the world who wanted no fresh conflict, that a new global struggle was joined. It started trains of fear and hatred and action in many millions of minds, centering around Washington and Moscow, which ran for many years. . . .

It is easy enough to declare cold war, draw lines and hurl thunderbolts. It requires statesmanship to make peace and draw the nations nearer together. . . .

There can be no real understanding of the Cold War unless chronology is kept in mind. What came first? What was action and what reaction? The later event could not be the cause of the earlier.

Especially is it necessary to consider what followed the Truman Doctrine. Not everything which came after it was an effect of the Doctrine, but its effects upon Soviet policy and action were bound to be profound.

There does not seem to be evidence of any sudden turn of Soviet policy to hostility toward the United States or toward the West after World War II. Frederick C. Barghoorn, a student of Soviet policy who works constantly with Russian language sources, speaks of "the gradual process by which the Politburo openly reverted to its pre-war line, and transferred the symbols of the 'reaction,' 'aggression,' and 'imperialism' from Germany and Japan to Britain and America." . . .

It was not until Andrei Zhdanov's speech of September 1947 that a postwar division of the world into two camps was proclaimed in Russia, "the anti-democratic and imperialist camp on the one side, and the anti-imperialist and democratic on the other." Attacking the Marshall Plan as a device for "the enslavement of Europe," Zhdanov accused the United States of seeking world domination. Because her "monopolists" feared the success of communism they had launched a world-wide crusade against communism, he charged.

This was undoubtedly political warfare, but it can hardly be considered remarkable after the enunciation of the Truman Doctrine, Kennan's elaboration of the American containment drive and the Marshall Plan—altogether the greatest peace time political-economic offensive on record. An offensive of this character was bound to bring replies, both ideological and actual.

Additional Reading

Norman A. Graebner, *Cold War Diplomacy, 1945–1960* (1962).
George F. Kennan, *American Diplomacy, 1900–1950* (1951).
Walter Lippmann, *The Cold War: A Study in U.S. Foreign Policy* (1947).
John Lukacs, *A History of the Cold War* (1961).
Joseph P. Morray, *From Yalta to Disarmament: Cold War Debate* (1961).
Harry B. Price, *The Marshall Plan and Its Meaning* (1955).
Hugh Seton-Watson, *Neither War nor Peace: The Struggle for Power in the Postwar World* (1960).
John L. Snell, *Wartime Origins of the East-West Dilemma over Germany* (1959).
———, "The Cold War: Four Contemporary Appraisals," *American Historical Review,* LXVIII (1962), 69–75.

20 THE KOREAN WAR AND AMERICAN FOREIGN POLICY:

Asia First or Europe?

The years of the Truman administration were probably the most creative in the history of American foreign relations. In bold and imaginative response to the Communist challenge, new policies were designed and put into effect: Truman Doctrine, Marshall Plan, N.A.T.O., and Point Four technical assistance to "backward" nations. The American people in approving these measures revealed that they had at last matured and were prepared to assume the burdens and responsibilities as *the* great non-communist world power.

But it was a reluctant assumption of responsibility for many Americans. During World War II, it had been expected that after crushing the Axis powers and the institution of a new collective organization, the United States could return to something close to prewar normality. Instead, the enormous costs and strains of the Cold War appeared destined to last into the indefinite future. Quite a few "conservatives" were also increasingly frustrated at the continued political predominancy of the Democratic party and certain social changes that were underway at home. A combination of unfortunate developments ignited this mixture of frustration and uneasiness into a fire-storm of public hysteria and hunts for scapegoats to blame for the national plight. Nationalist China fell by 1949 and was supplanted by a Communist regime allied to Moscow; Russia exploded its first atomic bomb in mid-1949, three to five years before expected by Western experts; the Korean War, begun in June, 1950, to halt the Red North Korean invasion, fluctuated dismayingly and without promise of speedy or complete victory; and at home, investigating committees unearthed evidence of considerable past Communist infiltration into government and of the loss of some military secrets.

The results were charges that America had been the victim of 20 years of Democratic blunder, plunder, and perhaps treason at home and abroad. Great public debates raged as to whether it was correct to continue to concentrate on the Communist menace primarily in Europe or to meet the challenges in the Far East by full involvement if necessary. The late Senator Joseph McCarthy, Republican from Wisconsin, used his subcommittee to launch a series of charges of treason and a "great conspiracy" to explain current ills. While he was by no means the only laborer in the vineyard of the domestic search for Communist infiltrators, McCarthy's name was attached as a label for the period 1950–1954. By the latter year, the hysteria was subsiding and American foreign policy remained essentially as before. Yet a considerable, if inestimable, damage had probably been wrought to the morale of the foreign service and in an increasing inflexibility of policy in the Far East.

The readings focus on the Korean War and General Douglas MacArthur's strategy differences with the Truman administration. The great public debate ignited by MacArthur's dismissal by Truman essentially involved whether basic American strategy in the Cold War should concentrate on the Soviet menace in Europe or should emphasize the Far East as the immediate area of concern. Many critics of administration commitments in Europe were apparently the "new isolationists of the 1950's," as Norman A. Graebner describes them, for at the same time they advocated vigorous military measures in Asia which probably would have led to a major war with Red China.

DOCUMENTS

A Limited War in Korea

In the following two documents, President Truman explained to the American people why he acted on his executive authority in June, 1950, to defend invaded South Korea; and why, in April, 1951, he declined to enlarge the Korean War and decided to recall General Douglas MacArthur from command of the American forces there. The primacy of the Soviet threat in Europe and the dangers of a major diversionary war in Asia required efforts to limit the war in Korea.

Initial Measures Taken by the United States in the Korean Crisis: Statement by the President, June 27, 1950

In Korea, the Government forces, which were armed to prevent border raids and to preserve internal security, were attacked by invading forces from North Korea. The Security Council of the United Nations called upon the invading troops to cease hostilities and to withdraw to the 38th Parallel. This they have not done but, on the contrary, have pressed the attack. The Security Council called upon all members of the United Nations to render every assistance to the United Nations in the execution of this resolution. In these circumstances, I have ordered United States air and sea [and subsequently land] forces to give the Korean Government troops cover and support.

The attack upon Korea makes it plain beyond all doubt that communism has passed beyond the use of subversion to conquer independent nations and will now use armed invasion and war. It has defied the orders of the Security Council of the United Nations issued to preserve international peace and security. In these circumstances, the occupation of Formosa by Communist forces would be a direct threat to the security of the Pacific area and to United States forces performing their lawful and necessary functions in that area.

Accordingly, I have ordered the Seventh Fleet to prevent any attack on Formosa. As a corollary of this action, I am calling upon the Chinese Government on Formosa to cease all air and sea operations against the Mainland. The Seventh Fleet will see that this is done. The determination of the future status of Formosa must await the restoration of security in the Pacific, a peace settlement with Japan, or consideration by the United Nations.

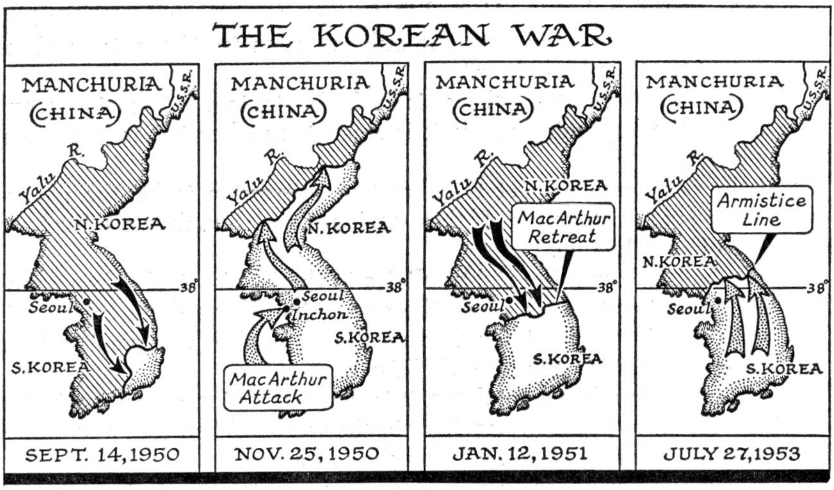

I have also directed that United States forces in the Philippines be strengthened and that military assistance to the Philippine Government be accelerated. . . .

I know that all members of the United Nations will consider carefully the consequences of this latest aggression in Korea in defiance of the Charter of the United Nations. A return to the rule of force in international affairs would have far-reaching effects. The United States will continue to uphold the rule of law.

I have instructed Ambassador Austin, as the representative of the United States to the Security Council, to report these steps to the Council.

United States Policy in the Korean Conflict
Address by the President, April 11, 1951

I want to talk plainly to you tonight about what we are doing in Korea and about our policy in the Far East.

In the simplest terms, what we are doing in Korea is this: We are trying to prevent a third world war.

I think most people in this country recognized that fact last June. And they warmly supported the decision of the Government to help the Republic of Korea against the Communist aggressors. Now, many persons, even some who applauded our decision to defend Korea, have forgotten the basic reason for our action.

It is right for us to be in Korea. It was right last June. It is right today.

I want to remind you why this is true.

The Communist Threat to Freedom

The Communists in the Kremlin are engaged in a monstrous conspiracy to stamp out freedom all over the world. If they were to succeed, the United States would be numbered among their principal victims. It must be clear to everyone that the United States cannot—and will not—sit idly by and await foreign conquest. The only question is: When is the best time to meet the threat and how?

The best time to meet the threat is in the beginning. It is easier to put out a fire in the beginning when it is small than after it has become a roaring blaze.

And the best way to meet the threat of aggression is for the peace-loving nations to act together. If they don't act together, they are likely to be picked off, one by one.

If they had followed the right policies in the 1930's—if the free countries had acted together, to crush the aggression of the dictators, and if they had acted in the beginning, when the aggression was small—there probably would have been no World War II.

If history has taught us anything, it is that aggression anywhere in the world is a threat to peace everywhere in the world. When that aggression is supported by the cruel and selfish rulers of a powerful nation who are bent on conquest, it becomes a clear and present danger to the security and independence of every free nation.

This is a lesson that most people in this country have learned thoroughly. This is the basic reason why we joined in creating the United Nations. And since the end of World War II we have been putting that lesson into practice—we have been working with other free nations to check the aggressive designs of the Soviet Union before they can result in a third world war.

That is what we did in Greece, when that nation was threatened by the aggression of international communism.

The attack against Greece could have led to general war. But this country came to the aid of Greece. The United Nations supported Greek resistance. With our help, the determination and efforts of the Greek people defeated the attack on the spot.

Another big Communist threat to peace was the Berlin blockade. That too could have led to war. But again it was settled because free men would not back down in an emergency.

The Communist Plan for Conquest

The aggression against Korea is the boldest and most dangerous move the Communists have yet made.

The attack on Korea was part of a greater plan for conquering all of Asia. . . .

They want to control all Asia from the Kremlin.

This plan of conquest is in flat contradiction to what we believe. We believe that Korea belongs to the Koreans, that India belongs to the Indians—that all the nations of Asia should be free to work out their affairs in their own way. This is the basis of peace in the Far East and everywhere else.

The whole Communist imperialism is back of the attack on peace in the Far East. It was the Soviet Union that trained and equipped the

North Koreans for aggression. The Chinese Communists massed 44 well-trained and well-equipped divisions on the Korean frontier. These were the troops they threw into battle when the North Korean Communists were beaten.

Stopping Short of General War

The question we have had to face is whether the Communist plan of conquest can be stopped without general war. Our Government and other countries associated with us in the United Nations believe that the best chance of stopping it without general war is to meet the attack in Korea and defeat it there.

That is what we have been doing. It is a difficult and bitter task.

But so far it has been successful.

So far, we have prevented World War III.

So far, by fighting a limited war in Korea, we have prevented aggression from succeeding and bringing on a general war. And the ability of the whole free world to resist Communist aggression has been greatly improved.

We have taught the enemy a lesson. He has found out that aggression is not cheap or easy. Moreover, men all over the world who want to remain free have been given new courage and new hope. They know now that the champions of freedom can stand up and fight and that they will stand up and fight.

Our resolute stand in Korea is helping the forces of freedom now fighting in Indochina and other countries in that part of the world. It has already slowed down the timetable of conquest.

In Korea itself, there are signs that the enemy is building up his ground forces for a new mass offensive. We also know that there have been large increases in the enemy's available air forces.

If a new attack comes, I feel confident it will be turned back. The United Nations fighting forces are tough and able and well equipped. They are fighting for a just cause. They are proving to all the world that the principle of collective security will work. We are proud of all these forces for the magnificent job they have done against heavy odds. We pray that their efforts may succeed, for upon their success may hinge the peace of the world.

The Communist side must now choose its course of action. The Communist rulers may press the attack against us. They may take further action which will spread the conflict. They have that choice, and with it the awful responsibility for what may follow. The Communists also have the choice of a peaceful settlement which could lead to a general relaxation of tensions in the Far East. The decision is theirs, because the forces of the United Nations will strive to limit the conflict if possible.

We do not want to see the conflict in Korea extended. We are trying to prevent a world war—not to start one. The best way to do that is to make it plain that we and the other free countries will continue to resist the attack.

The Best Course to Follow

But you may ask: Why can't we take other steps to punish the aggressor? Why don't we bomb Manchuria and China itself? Why don't we assist Chinese Nationalist troops to land on the mainland of China?

If we were to do these things we would be running a very grave risk of starting a general war. If that were to happen, we would have brought about the exact situation we are trying to prevent.

If we were to do these things, we would become entangled in a vast conflict on the continent of Asia and our task would become immeasurably more difficult all over the world.

What would suit the ambitions of the Kremlin better than for our military forces to be committed to a full-scale war with Red China?

It may well be that, in spite of our best efforts, the Communists may spread the war. But it would be wrong—tragically wrong—for us to take the initiative in extending the war.

The dangers are great. Make no mistake about it. Behind the North Koreans and Chinese Communists in the front lines stand additional millions of Chinese soldiers. And behind the Chinese stand the tanks, the planes, the submarines, the soldiers, and the scheming rulers of the Soviet Union.

Our aim is to avoid the spread of the conflict.

The course we have been following is the one best calculated to avoid an all-out war. It is the course consistent with our obligation to do all we can to maintain international peace and security. Our experience in Greece and Berlin shows that it is the most effective course of action we can follow.

First of all, it is clear that our efforts in Korea can blunt the will of the Chinese Communists to continue the struggle. The United Nations forces have put up a tremendous fight in Korea and have inflicted very heavy casualties on the enemy. Our forces are stronger now than they have been before. These are plain facts which may discourage the Chinese Communists from continuing their attack.

Second, the free world as a whole is growing in military strength every day. In the United States, in Western Europe, and throughout the world, free men are alert to the Soviet threat and are building their defenses. This may discourage the Communist rulers from continuing the war in Korea—and from undertaking new acts of aggression elsewhere.

If the Communist authorities realize that they cannot defeat us in Korea, if they realize it would be foolhardy to widen the hostilities beyond Korea, then they may recognize the folly of continuing their aggression. A peaceful settlement may then be possible. The door is always open.

Then we may achieve a settlement in Korea which will not compromise the principles and purposes of the United Nations.

I have thought long and hard about this question of extending the war in Asia. I have discussed it many times with the ablest military advisers in the country. I believe with all my heart that the course we are following is the best course.

I believe that we must try to limit the war to Korea for these vital reasons: to make sure that the precious lives of our fighting men are not wasted; to see that the security of our country and the free world is not needlessly jeopardized; and to prevent a third world war.

Avoiding Confusion over U.S. Policy

A number of events have made it evident that General MacArthur did not agree with that policy. I have therefore considered it essential to relieve General MacArthur so that there would be no doubt or confusion as to the real purpose and aim of our policy.

It was with the deepest personal regret that I found myself compelled to take this action. General MacArthur is one of our greatest military commanders. But the cause of world peace is more important than any individual.

The change in commands in the Far East means no change whatever in the policy of the United States. We will carry on the fight in Korea with vigor and determination in an effort to bring the war to a speedy and successful conclusion. . . .

We are ready, at any time, to negotiate for a restoration of peace in the area. But we will not engage in appeasement. We are only interested in real peace.

Real peace can be achieved through a settlement based on the following factors:

One: the fighting must stop.

Two: concrete steps must be taken to insure that the fighting will not break out again.

Three: there must be an end to the aggression.

A settlement founded upon these elements would open the way for the unification of Korea and the withdrawal of all foreign forces.

In the meantime, I want to be clear about our military objective. We are fighting to resist an outrageous aggression in Korea. We are trying to keep the Korean conflict from spreading to other areas. But at the same time we must conduct our military activities so as to insure the security of our forces. This is essential if they are to continue the fight until the enemy abandons its ruthless attempt to destroy the Republic of Korea.

That is our military objective—to repel attack and to restore peace.

In the hard fighting in Korea, we are proving that collective action among nations is not only a high principle but a workable means of resisting aggression. Defeat of aggression in Korea may be the turning point in the world's search for a practical way of achieving peace and security.

The struggle of the United Nations in Korea is a struggle for peace.

The free nations have united their strength in an effort to prevent a third world war.

That war can come if the Communist rulers want it to come. But this Nation and its allies will not be responsible for its coming.

We do not want to widen the conflict. We will use every effort to prevent that disaster. And in so doing we know that we are following the great principles of peace, freedom, and justice.

READINGS

1. "Asia First" Strategy

When South Korea was invaded on June 25, 1950, President Truman acted solely on his executive authority and ordered American forces to join in the defense. Subsequently, the Security Council of the United Nations called for collective resistance to the North Korean invasion, but the bulk of non-Korean troops committed were to come from the United States. Under General MacArthur's command the U.N. forces in Korea rallied and by October entered Communist North Korea in order to unify the entire peninsula. As troops neared the Yalu River and the Manchurian frontier, Red Chinese "volunteers" suddenly entered the fray in late November, 1950, and drove MacArthur's forces below the 38th parallel before they rallied and returned approximately to that line. General MacArthur understandably was frustrated by the administration's refusal to allow him to expand the scope of the war by bombing Chinese bases and supply routes to North Korea. Put simply, he advocated an "Asia First" strategy to do whatever was necessary to win full victory in Korea, while the Truman administration insisted that the main Soviet threat was in Europe and refused to risk involvement in a mainland full-fledged war with Red China. MacArthur's attempts to appeal his case to the American people caused his recall from command on April 11, 1951. The following selection in defense of MacArthur is by Major General (Ret.) Charles Willoughby, formerly an intelligence officer on MacArthur's Staff.

The Chinese Communist War

C. A. WILLOUGHBY & J. CHAMBERLAIN

. . . When General MacArthur succeeded in the spectacular landing at Inchon, in September 1950, the fate of the North Koreans was sealed—but the Chinese Reds chose to wait until the end of October, *i.e.*, at least six weeks, before they started crossing the Yalu. Why did they fail to come to the assistance of the North Koreans immediately? For the simple reason that after Inchon, they had to face the probability that the Yalu bridges and their adjacent bases would be bombed, which would have jeopardized successful intervention.

So for six weeks all they did was to hint that if UN troops crossed the 38th Parallel, they might enter the war. Communist supporters and dupes promptly yielded to this blackmail. The Korean War would have terminated if the U.S. had issued a warning to the effect that any entry of the Chinese Communists into Korea would be considered an act of hostility.

They would have stayed on the other side of the Yalu. Instead—through a weak policy and for fear of Russian intervention—information must have been relayed to the other side, guaranteeing that those bridges would enjoy sanctuary and their bases left intact. And so, Ho Shai-Lai concluded, the Communists were not only assured that there was no real intention to win—but they were also guaranteed against the risk of losing. No better assurance could have been furnished. They marched on that assurance. . . .

General MacArthur reiterated that he "planned the air-interdiction of the Yalu bridges and expected to slow down the Reds through this measure." As it turned out, the General was expressly forbidden all-out air bombardment, on Washington orders, and half a dozen American divisions were consequently exposed to the full onslaught of overwhelming numbers. Was this a calculated sacrifice to some obscure diplomatic motivation?

The withdrawals of the Eighth Army were made with consummate skill. MacArthur himself regarded the whole operation as one of his best . . . if not the best! He felt that the hard decisions he had made and the skill displayed by his field commanders in their implementation had saved not only the Eighth Army but Korea itself and, with it, our future hopes for the Far East. MacArthur was well aware that the entire situation would be misunderstood and misrepresented but merely said dryly: "I've always been able to take care of the enemy in my front—but have never been able to protect myself from shafts from the rear."

After the entry of China into the war, the American Army was compelled to take odds never before encountered in the entire military history of the nation. There is nothing even remotely comparable in recent wars. However, the impact of the disaster school of war reporting on public opinion in the fall of 1950 was such that it must now be driven home forcefully that the frightening stories of the time represent a distortion of history. We fought harder in Korea than in Europe, and, given the circumstances, just as successfully. A brief parallel shows this vividly, for the Allied campaign in Italy had some similarities to that in Korea. Topography and road net were similar. The Italian front was approximately 100 miles as compared with 140 miles in Korea. In Italy, however, the Allies employed two armies, the American Fifth and the British Eighth with thirty-one first-class divisions to fight against a variable twenty to twenty-seven Italo-German divisions somewhat battered and usually half the Allied troop strength. Italy was a strategic sideshow. Nothing vital was at stake. The war could not conceivably be won there. One need not strain one's imagination to guess what thirty-one Anglo-American divisions, instead of only nine, would have done to the Chinese in Korea, at any stage of the war.

Nevertheless the Allied high command, the Joint Chiefs of Staff, the American and British "brass" in Italy threw in a great superiority of means. It is a point of historical importance that the same "brass," still powerful in Washington during 1950 and 1951, apparently changed the basis of their military calculations between the Anzio and the Yalu. It is impossible to understand on a professional basis how the General Staff in Washington could placidly accept the staggering odds piled on the Eighth Army in Korea. Instead of a pat on the back for our teen-age draftees of a few months' training who were fighting rather forlornly in an alien land, an inexplicable wave of defeatist reports engulfed the Eighth Army with wide repercussions at home and abroad. Here is a cross section of some characteristic comments of the period:

> The flight of our troops before Chinese peasant soldiers was the most shameful disgrace suffered by American arms since the first Battle of Bull Run in 1861. . . .
>
> It was America's worst licking since the battle of the Bulge and maybe even Pearl Harbor. Barring a military miracle, the Army might have to be evacuated in a new Dunkerque, from being lost in a new Bataan. . . .

An explosion of white-hot wrath was spontaneous throughout the rank and file of the Eighth Army. Petitions were circulated by enlisted men of the 2d Division, demanding a retraction and denouncing these reports as "vicious lies and slander upon thousands of American war dead."

A cold statistical comparison of dead, wounded, and missing with battle-action losses of World War II is a complete refutation of the deadly nonsense which was fed to an anxious and bewildered public. A reference to the Tenth Army in the Ryukus during World War II is enlightening, since some of the divisions involved in the three months' fight for Okinawa also appeared in the Yalu operations, *viz.*, the 1st Marine and the 7th Infantry Division.

COMPARISON OF LOSSES

TENTH ARMY (RYUKUS) AND EIGHTH ARMY (YALU)

Ryukus Operations	*1945*	*Yalu Operations*	*1950*
XXIVth Corps	34,736	Eighth Army	7,337
7th Division	*10,893*	2d Division	*4,131*
27th Division	*5,224*	1st Cav. Div.	*443*
77th Division	*7,126*	24th Division	*146*
96th Division	*10,247*	25th Division	*1,606*
Corps Troops	*1,246*	Other U.N.	*1,011*
III Amph. Corps.	26,724	Xth Corps	5,638
1st Mar. Div.	*13,002*	1st Mar. Div.	*2,891*
2d Mar. Div.	*95*	3d Division	*650*
6th Mar. Div.	*12,815*	7th Division	*2,097*
Corps Troops	*812*		
Tact. Air Force	520		
Tenth Army Troops	1,015		
Army Garrisons	2,636		
Total	65,631		12,975

On the average, individual divisions on Okinawa sustained from *two to five times the losses incurred in the withdrawal from the Yalu* five years later. The Eighth Army in 1950 took on extraordinary numerical odds, facing from twenty-four to thirty-nine Chinese divisions; the Tenth Army in the Ryukus was involved with only one Japanese corps of three divisions. Bastogne in Belgium was not unlike Anju in Korea, and Anzio in Italy was not unlike Inchon.

In the Bulge operations in 1944, the 108th Division, directly in the line of advance of the German penetration, lost 8,490 men of its total strength of 14,032 in a period of fourteen days.

In the Anzio campaign in the spring of 1943, American losses for the four-month period amounted to an aggregate of 43,000. Casualties of the 3d Division alone were 3,131 during an eight-day period. That same division was in the Hamhung-Wonson withdrawal in Korea eight years later: it lost 650 men.

The evacuation of the X Corps from the port of Hungnam, with the 1st Marine, 3d and 7th Divisions fighting heroic rear-guard actions that stopped three Chinese corps in their tracks, was exposed to unwarranted comments. This remarkably smooth and efficient amphibious operation was loudly proclaimed "a second Dunkerque." The absurdity of this classification is self-evident:

	Ships		*Personnel*	*Equipment*
	Total	*Sunk*	*Evacuated*	*Salvaged*
Dunkerque	841	163	338,000	—
Hungnam	163	—	205,000	350,000 tons 17,500 vehicles

About Dunkerque, Churchill said:

> More than 300,000 British and French troops scrambled for boats and ships of the rescue fleet. An estimated 2,000 men were lost at sea, as well as over 200 ships and most of the Army equipment, including 120,000 vehicles, 2,700 artillery pieces and 90,000 rifles. Our armies at home were almost unarmed except for rifles. There were hardly five hundred field guns of any sort and hardly 200 tanks in the whole country. Months must pass before our factories could make good even the munitions lost in Dunkerque. . . .

Compare this tragic description of real disaster with the terse radio from General Almond, commander of the American X Corps, on December 24:

> The Xth Corps, reinforced, has completed evacuation by air and sea from Hungnam at 14:36 Hrs. 350,000 tons of supplies and equipment have been withdrawn. Nothing has been left to the enemy. 105,000 troops, including S. Korean units and approximately 100,000 refugees, have been evacuated to safety in South Korea. Structures of possible military value to the enemy have been destroyed. The enemy paid heavily for his attempt to interfere with our operations. The losses of our forces were comparatively light.

When General MacArthur, during his visit with General Almond at Yonpo Airport (near Hamhung) on December 8, asked, "How long can the X Corps maintain its position in this area with Hungnam Port as the base of supply?" General Almond replied:

For as long as you desire; the X Corps is now established in a tactically strong position with a secure base and line of supply by sea; we can stay here as a threat to the enemy's flank and should do so, unless there are no other troops available to support the Eighth Army from the U.S.

But higher authority had decreed that sufficient forces should not be sent from the United States and General MacArthur had to bow to the inevitable. He was forced to use the X Corps to strengthen the badly used Eighth Army in the south instead of maintaining it as a dagger in the enemy's flank at Hungnam and Hamhung.

MacArthur stabilized his lines early in January at a position midway in South Korea. General Walker had been killed in an accident and the Eighth Army was now under command of Gen. Matthew B. Ridgway. MacArthur flew to Korea on January 20, nullified any suggestion that the enemy might drive our forces into the sea, and issued orders for the counteroffensive.

His field strategy had involved breaking contact with the enemy and a rapid withdrawal to lengthen and expose the latter's supply lines. What resulted was a pyramiding of logistic difficulties for the Reds and an almost astronomical increase in the destructiveness of our air power. Soon the balance was restored between the opposing forces. MacArthur's objective was again to be the enemy's supply lines.

For psychological as well as other reasons MacArthur proposed by constant thrusts to regain the Seoul line for a base of operation from which to clear North Korea of enemy forces. This could be accomplished through the air destruction of enemy concentration and installations, the closing of major lines of enemy supply and communication through the sowing of defensive fields of suitable radioactive materials available as by-products of atomic manufacture, and simultaneous amphibious landings at the upper ends of both coasts of North Korea. For these amphibious landings, he would employ the new divisions just ordered to the Far East and picked veteran troops from Formosa which had been offered. It was to be Inchon again—only on a larger scale!

In frequent visits to the front, General MacArthur made his own lucid appraisal of the chronology of the fighting and accurately forecast the slow deterioration and eventual defeat of the Chinese hordes:

February 13: I am entirely satisfied with the situation at the front. The enemy has suffered a tactical reverse. His losses are amongst the bloodiest in modern times.

February 20: The enemy is finding it an entirely different problem fighting 350 miles from his base than when he had sanctuary in his immediate rear. He is paying now for the illusion so falsely but effectively propagandized that he had defeated our Eighth Army decisively. I note that Marshal Stalin has just predicted the annihilation of our forces in Korea—but his Comrades will have to do lots better than they have yet done, to prove him a prophet.

March 24: It is increasingly evident that the heavy destruction of the enemy's lines of supply, caused by our round-the-clock air and naval bombardment, left his troops in forward areas deficient in requirements.

> The enemy's human-wave tactics have failed. He is showing less stamina than our own troops under the rigours of climate, terrain and battle. Of even greater significance has been the revelation that this new enemy, Red China, of such exaggerated and vaunted military power, lacks the industrial capacity essential to modern war.
>
> Expansion of our operations to the enemy coastal areas and interior bases would doom Red China to imminent military collapse. These basic facts established, there should be no insuperable difficulty in arriving at decisions on the Korean problem if the issues are resolved on their own merits. . . .

To the very moment of General MacArthur's dismissal, Washington was informed of the fluctuating situation in Korea and the enormous potential of victory inherent in the last two months. As early as March, a blueprint was drawn: expansion of our operations to the enemy coastal and interior bases; the threat of aerial reprisal—a concept which was new to Truman but has since become a commonplace item, under Eisenhower, as a deterrent for war. MacArthur personified this threat. Somehow MacArthur had to be eliminated. The enemy made one last convulsive, bloody effort to discredit him in the field and so to convince the Western world that the fiction of military power that they and their stooges had established was real.

The enemy staged an abortive offensive in April. The Eighth Army anticipated it by fifteen days and was ready; our troops "rolled with the punch" and then counterattacked with brilliant success. The Reds tried again in May—and for the last time. They suffered crippling losses. Of twenty-one Chinese divisions which started the attack, sixteen lost half or more of their effectives and were *hors de combat;* the XII, XV, XXVII, and LX Corps had disappeared; only one corps, the XX was able to continue in action. It must be realized that the Chinese Third and Fourth Armies were the best they had; the seventy to eighty divisions, stuck in Korea and literally consumed in this holocaust, were the best divisions they had; in all of China, from Tibet to Siberia, there remained about 120 second-rate divisions of variable quality, from fair to poor—and the Korean drain was endless, relentless, and killing.

The Chinese recognized the implications: just short of collapse, they called for a truce for the sole purpose of physical recovery, and they obtained it through the crafty, superbly timed intervention of the Soviets in the gullible and lukewarm United Nations. President Truman added the final touch by relieving his ablest field commander on the eve of another victory. The effect of these incongruous measures coalesced to eliminate the one man in the Far East whom communism had reason to fear. Truman had played right into the Communists' evil hands. . . .

MacArthur recognized the symptoms of weakness of the Reds, drew common-sense conclusions, and pressed for a military decision through attack on the Chinese sanctuary. He recommended to Washington that he be permitted air-bombardment in due course of military installations north of the Yalu then actively employed against us, naval blockade of the coast of China to cut off enemy supplies, and renewed his request for the utilization of Nationalist Chinese troops available on Formosa. These recommendations were actually approved by the Joint Chiefs of Staff, but somewhere between the offices of the Secretary of Defense, Gen. George C. Marshall, the Secretary of State Dean G. Acheson, and President Truman, they were pigeonholed; and we took the course leading to the stalemate of positional warfare, by all odds the most costly and least productive method of waging war.

To his staff, General MacArthur said:

> The overriding deficiency incident to the conduct of the war in Korea by the United Nations lies in its lack of will for victory. Underlying the whole problem has always been the indeterminate question as to whether or not the Soviet contemplates the conquest of the world by military means rather than by those of more peaceful persuasion.
>
> If it intends to use force, the time and place will be at its own initiative and could not fail to be influenced by the fact that in the atomic area, the lead of the United States is being steadily diminished with the passage of time. So likewise is the great industrial potential of the United States as compared with the Communist world.
>
> In short, it has always been my own belief that any action we might take to resolve the Korean problem could not in itself be a controlling factor in the precipitation of a world conflict. It is quite probable that the Soviet masses are just as eager for peace as are our own people. They probably suffer the delusion that there are aggressive intentions against them on the part of the capitalist world and that they would welcome an imaginative approach which would allay this false impression. . . .

On January 14, 1951, President Truman sent a personal message to General MacArthur finishing with these words: "The entire nation is grateful for your splendid leadership in the difficult struggle in Korea and for the superb performance of your forces under most difficult circumstances." Less than three months later, on the eve of another victory, he suddenly, without warning, relieved MacArthur of his command in a most savage and brutal way. The peremptory order did not permit him even to bid good-by to his troops. Superbly trained, they carried on under other generals, one of whom, James A. Van Fleet, was fully as certain as MacArthur himself that victory over the Chinese Communists could have been had if the politicians had simply given the soldiers the word.

The Dismissal

As far as MacArthur's own knowledge of its circumstances is concerned, his dismissal is still shrouded in considerable mystery. His first information of it came over the public radio. But in summarizing, ex post facto, the possible reasons for it, MacArthur has listed three things which members of the Truman Administration seized upon to prepare a case for ridding themselves of their foremost general.

> The decision [said MacArthur] was arbitrary. I warned of the dangers of Formosa falling under Communist control. This was said to be contrary to existing policy. The Secretary of State has since declared that it was long-standing policy of the United States.

The second reason given was my readiness to meet the enemy commander to discuss terms. This identical proposal was received enthusiastically when made by the Soviets.

The third reason was my reply to a Congressman. There is a law that no member of the Armed Forces shall be restricted from communicating with members of Congress.

In retrospect, it must seem that all of the Administration's "reasons" masked something deeper. General Bradley, presumably speaking for the Joint Chiefs of Staff, said on one occasion that MacArthur "was not in sympathy with the decision to try to limit the conflict in Korea. The J.C.S. had decided to try to avoid a third war." Yet MacArthur desired only to destroy the enemy where he had chosen to attack, in Korea. His proposals to bomb the Yalu bridges, to avail himself of the right of "hot pursuit" of enemy aircraft, and to utilize his own air and naval forces to carry the war to the enemy's supply and communications, were hardly a prescription for a third *world* war. They were merely the prescription for ending the war he had been ordered to fight. In no case was he in favor of sending American troops to fight on Chinese soil. "Anybody who advocates that," so MacArthur said, "should have his head examined."

The first inkling of trouble with the Administration came when MacArthur made a reply to an inquiry by the Veterans of Foreign Wars about the strategic value of Formosa. The letter, written on August 27, 1950, is hardly startling, for its contents are today an accepted part of our Far Eastern strategy. But it constitutes an interesting footnote to history, by a military commander of the first rank who has spent many years in the Far East:

> Any appraisal of Formosa's strategic potential, requires an appreciation of the changes wrought in the course of the past war. Prior thereto the Western strategic position of the United States lay on the littoral line of the Americas with an exposed island salient extending out through Hawaii, Midway, and Guam to the Philippines. That salient was not an outpost of strength but an avenue of weakness along which the enemy could and did attack us. The Pacific was a potential area of advance for any predatory force intent upon striking at the bordering land areas.
>
> All of this was changed by our Pacific victory. Our strategic frontier then shifted to embrace the entire Pacific Ocean, which has become a vast moat to protect us as long as we hold it. Indeed it acts as a protective shield for all of the Americas and for all lands of the Pacific Ocean area. We control it to the shores of Asia by a chain of islands extending in an arc from the Aleutians to the Marianas held by us and our former allies. *From this island chain we can prevent any hostile movement into the Pacific.* Our line of defense is a natural one and can be maintained with a minimum of military effort and expense. It envisions no attack against anyone, nor does it provide the bastions essential for offensive operations, but properly maintained would be an invincible defense against aggression. If we hold this line we may have peace. If we lose it, war is inevitable.
>
> The geographic location of Formosa is such that in the hands of a power unfriendly to the United States, it constitutes an enemy salient in the very center of this defense perimeter. There is on Formosa a con-

centration of operational air and naval bases which is potentially greater than any similar concentration on the Asiatic mainland. Our air supremacy at once would become doubtful. Formosa in the hands of a hostile power could be compared to an unsinkable aircraft carrier and submarine tender. Submarine blockade by the enemy would become a virtual certainty.

As a routine courtesy to journalists, copies of this letter were sent to the press some days before it was scheduled to be read at the Veterans of Foreign Wars annual convention in Chicago. To MacArthur, the letter seemed sheerest common sense about geographical factors as they relate to strategy. But the President, for reasons that are still inexplicable, took violent exception to the letter and ordered it withdrawn. MacArthur complied with the order. It was too late, however, to keep its contents from reaching the public; *Life* magazine and David Lawrence's *U.S. News and World Report,* for example, had already printed it and committed it to the mails. *Life,* in fact, had made it its editorial for the week.

Within twenty-four hours of the "withdrawal" that failed to withdraw the letter's contents, Truman summoned Louis Johnson, his Secretary of War, to discuss ways and means for the relief of MacArthur "as Korean commander." Johnson revealed this in testimony before the Joint Senate Investigating Committee on June 14, 1951. After discussion, however, the conclusion was reached not to do anything "at that time." MacArthur did not have the slightest suspicion of what was going on.

Considering that Formosa was a touchy subject with both State Department and White House, MacArthur's previous staff visit to Formosa and brief consultation with Chiang Kai-shek in 1950 must be considered a contributory cause to the smoldering hostility in Washington.

There was no real cause for resentment, however. MacArthur had no plenary power to arrive at political understandings. He was not an ambassador charged with negotiating for the State Department. On the other hand, it was well within his prerogatives as a regional commander in the Far East to visit adjacent strategic areas for purposes of obtaining firsthand impressions of their military and geographic potentials. When he could not go himself, he habitually sent senior staff officers or commanders. General Stratemeyer of the Air Force, accompanied by General Willoughby, made just such an exploratory staff journey to Hong Kong, Hai-phong, Bangkok, and Singapore.

MacArthur thus flew to Formosa. Washington was advised and made no objections. The General met Chiang and his principal civil and military staff. He attended a briefing of the map-room variety which outlined the Nationalist Chinese concept of the situation. He attended a ceremonial dinner—and then returned to Tokyo: *Tant de fruit pour une omelette?*

The Inchon victory followed MacArthur's temporary "reprieve" by Truman and Louis Johnson—and naturally nothing much could be done to push immediately for the removal of a commander who had just won a decisive battle. But on March 20 of the following year, when the fighting in Korea had reached the "accordion" stage, Washington plucked up its nerve. The occasion for moving decisively against MacArthur presented itself on the 20th when MacArthur wrote a mild enough answer to a letter from Joe Martin, leader of the House Republicans. It read:

> Dear Congressman Martin:
>
> I am most grateful for your note of the 8th forwarding me a copy of your address of February 12th. The letter I have read with much interest, and find that with the passage of years you have certainly lost none of your old-time punch.
>
> My views and recommendations with respect to the situation created by Red China's entry into war against us in Korea have been submitted to Washington in most complete detail. Generally these views are well known and clearly understood, as they follow the conventional pattern of meeting force with maximum counter-force as we have never failed to do in the past. Your view with respect to the utilization of the Chinese forces on Formosa is in conflict with neither logic nor this tradition.
>
> It seems strangely difficult for some to realize that here in Asia is where Communist conspirators have elected to make their play for global conquest, and that we have joined the issue thus raised on the battlefield; that here we fight Europe's war with arms while the diplomats there still fight it with words; that if we lose the war to Communism in Asia the fall of Europe is inevitable, win it and Europe most probably would avoid war and yet preserve freedom. As you point out, we must win. There is no substitute for victory.
>
> With renewed thanks and expressions of most cordial regard, I am
>
> Faithfully yours,
> Douglas MacArthur

MacArthur had been saying the same sort of thing for months, in both letters and statements. But this time it was "different" for one simple reason: Truman had decided to act. The Administration was making ready for its great "peace" play; Acheson was even then busy circulating peace proposals to the UN nations which had troops in Korea. It was at this point that MacArthur called upon the Chinese Communist commander in Korea to surrender—"or else." MacArthur offered the Chinese commander an opportunity to meet with him for a discussion in the field. He stressed the reserve strength which the United Nations could bring to bear upon the enemy if he insisted upon continuing the war.

MacArthur construed his own "peace" offer as (*a*) a smart stroke of psychological warfare and (*b*) an effort to back up the peace campaign that was being waged in the United Nations. To Truman, however, it was an impertinence. Two days after the Martin letter had been published, Truman conferred with Acheson, Bradley, Marshall, and Averell Harriman. The generals were uneasy at first about touching a soldier who was a popular idol, but Acheson and Truman carried the day. After sounding out the Joint Chiefs of Staff, who formulated some "military considerations" which made the firing of MacArthur desirable, Bradley was in a position to tell Truman that the high brass "concurred" with his decision to relieve MacArthur. Truman's own reasons for taking the step were subsequently summed up as (*a*) the letter about Formosa, (*b*) the Martin letter and (*c*) the offer to deal with the Chinese in the field.

As a fitting irony, Truman then turned over to the "European-minded" Marshall the job of drafting a dismissal message for the Presidential signature.

> I deeply regret [the message said] that it becomes my duty as President . . . to replace you as Supreme Commander. . . . You will turn over your commands, effective at once, to Lieut. Gen. Matthew B. Ridgway. . . . My reasons for your replacement will be made public concurrently with the delivery to you of the foregoing order, and are contained in the next following message.
>
> Harry S. Truman

It was originally planned to let Secretary of War Frank Pace, Jr., who was then in the Far East, deliver the dismissal note to MacArthur at the Tokyo Embassy. But the April 12 radio got there ahead of Pace. MacArthur and his wife were entertaining visitors at luncheon when Sid Huff, the General's aide, picked the dismissal notice from a news broadcast. With tears in his eyes he called Mrs. MacArthur from the table. She returned to break the news.

Not a flicker of emotion stirred MacArthur's face. When the General subsequently read the official confirmation, he turned to his wife and said serenely, "Jean, we're going home at last." To the press, Gen. Courtney Whitney said: "I have just left the General. He received the word magnificently. He never turned a hair. His soldierly qualities were never more pronounced. I think this has been his finest hour."

The Communists reveled in the news when they heard it. In a "Proclamation of the Japanese Communist Party concerning General MacArthur's Dismissal," they said:

> MacArthur's dismissal most plainly reveals that due to the strongly growing discrepancy and divergence of opinion amongst the imperialistic nations, a cornerstone of their war-provocative policy seeking world control has crumbled before the peace-loving masses composed of over a billion people.
>
> One of Premier Stalin's great predictions, that "all meddlers will no doubt meet with certain failure," has come true.
>
> It is also clear that as a result of this dismissal the separatist peace group [pro U.S.] is now in a state of confusion, and the Yoshida cabinet and their clique have lost their staunch supporter of the past several years.
>
> We now have an opportune moment. By taking advantage of the confusion, an all-out peace and antiwar preparation movement can be strengthened.
>
> In co-ordination with a poll of 40,000,000 [Japanese] voters on the general peace issue, efforts will be made to expose thoroughly the maladministration of the Yoshida cabinet, sweeping from local autonomy the Liberal party influence advocating a separate peace [with the U.S.] at the same time bringing about the downfall of the Yoshida cabinet.

The plain people of Japan, however, spoke with a different voice. The dismissal dominated news and editorial columns in Tokyo and other Japanese cities more completely than any world event since the surrender.

The initial reaction was shock and disappointment, regret and fear. The final phase was one of resolutions of national gratitude and sincere editorial tributes to MacArthur's efforts in behalf of Japan. Said *Mainichi Shimbun* (circulation 3,970,000):

> MacArthur's dismissal is the greatest shock since the end of the war. He dealt with the Japanese people not as a conqueror but a great reformer. He was a noble political missionary. What he gave us was not material aid and democratic reform alone—but a new way of life, the freedom and dignity of the individual. . . . We shall continue to love and trust him as one of the Americans who best understood Japan's position.

Said *Asahi Shimbun* (circulation 4,074,000):

> The removal is a great disappointment to the Japanese, especially when the peace settlement is so near. Japan's recovery must be attributed solely to his guidance. We feel as if we had lost a kind and loving father.

On the day of MacArthur's departure the 20-mile roadway to Haneda Airfield was lined by thousands of Japanese, of every social class, bearing American and Japanese flags. People wept as the General's car rolled past them. And *Mainichi Shimbun* provided the final commentary:

> We wanted your further help in nurturing our green democracy to fruition. We wanted your leadership at least until a signed peace treaty had given us a send-off into the world community.

The citizens of Kanagawa Prefecture, embracing the great port city of Yokohama, put into words what was latent in many Japanese hearts. On the base of a bronze bust which Japan's leading sculptor had been commissioned to create, the words foretold the judgment of history: "General Douglas MacArthur—Liberator of Japan."

The reaction of America to the General's homecoming was no less affecting than that of Japan to his departure. When he landed in San Francisco, he had spent twenty-five years on foreign service, longer than any officer or man of the U.S. Army. On Friday afternoon, in Japan, he had first heard the news of the dismissal. He was gone on Monday to receive at home the greatest welcome ever accorded an American. His staff thrilled to the echo of his closing words as he said farewell in the halls of Congress:

> I have just left your fighting sons in Korea. They have met all tests there and I can report to you without reservations, they are splendid in every way.
>
> It was my constant effort to preserve them and end this savage conflict honorably and with the least loss of time and a minimum sacrifice of life. Its growing bloodshed has caused me the deepest anguish and anxiety. Those gallant men will remain often in my thoughts and in my prayers always.
>
> I am closing my fifty-two years of military service. When I joined the Army, even before the turn of the century, it was the fulfillment of all my boyish hopes and dreams.
>
> The world has turned over many times since I took the oath on the

plain at West Point, and the hopes and dreams have long since vanished, but I still remember the refrain of one of the most popular barracks ballads of that day, which proclaimed, most proudly, that "Old soldiers never die. They just fade away."

And like the old soldier of that ballad, I now close my military career and just fade away—an old soldier who tried to do his duty as God gave him the light to see that duty.

Goodbye.

2. *MacArthur's Recall, A Necessary Reassertion of Civilian Authority*

The defense of the administration was that the main enemy was Soviet Russia and that the area of principal threat was in Western Europe. MacArthur's recommendations would thus have led to war in a secondary area and would have opened the way for a possible Soviet thrust in Europe. Dismissal of MacArthur came because his insubordination required a reassertion of civilian control of foreign policy and the military.

Truman Versus MacArthur: Achilles Rebound

JOHN W. SPANIER

Prior to the North Korean attack in June 1950, the Administration's foreign policy was based upon the fundamental assumption that the Soviet Union presented the chief threat to American security; Moscow's leaders were committed to the elimination of all non-Communist nations. George Kennan compared Soviet expansion to

> a fluid stream which moves constantly, wherever it is permitted to move, toward a given goal. Its main concern is to make sure that it has filled every nook and cranny available to it in the basin of world power. But if it finds unassailable barriers in its path, it accepts these philosophically and accommodates itself to them. The main thing is that there should always be pressure, unceasing constant pressure, toward the desired goal. There is no trace of any feeling in Soviet psychology that the goal must be reached at any given time.

The American task was, therefore, to erect "unassailable barriers" in the path of Soviet power to contain its further spread. The Truman Doctrine, the Marshall Plan, the Berlin Airlift, NATO, were all part of this policy.

The principal aim of this "long-term, patient but firm and vigilant containment of Russia's expansive tendencies" was not the destruction of the Soviet Union and its satellites, but the creation of a balance of power to effect this "containment." The objective of this policy was to deter the Kremlin from attempting to achieve world domination by resort to total war, lead it instead to the negotiating table, and to settle the principal cold war issues. A second characteristic of containment was its

Reprinted by permission of the publishers from John W. Spanier, *The Truman-MacArthur Controversy and the Korean War*. Cambridge, Mass.: The Belknap Press of Harvard University Press. Copyright, 1959, by The President and Fellows of Harvard College. Pp. 257–277.

assumption that such a "situation of strength" could be attained by the United States only in association with its principal NATO allies. American independence and security had traditionally required a balance of power in the interior of Europe to check any nation which possessed ambitions to conquer the sea-bordering states as a prerequisite to first eliminating England and then proceeding to world conquest. Consequently, the collapse of NATO could not be tolerated.

The military heart of this containment policy was the almost complete reliance upon strategic air power to deter or win World War III. The Western armies stationed in Europe were not sufficiently large to prevent the Russian army from reaching the English Channel. The NATO army was primarily a "plate-glass" which would set off the burglar alarm and send the United States Strategic Air Command flying toward its Soviet targets. The assumption was that the only kind of war possible was a total war which would begin the moment the Soviet Union struck a surprise blow at either the United States or America's "first line of defense" in Western Europe.

It was this reliance upon a strategy of total war which had been responsible for the Joint Chiefs' recommendation to withdraw American troops from South Korea and for Secretary Acheson's and General MacArthur's exclusion of the Republic from the Pacific defense perimeter. For in an all-out war South Korea would indeed be neither strategically vital to the United States nor defensible; its fate would be determined by the results of the conflict fought in other theaters. The limited war with which the North Koreans faced the President and his advisers on June 25, 1950, therefore presented the Administration with an agonizing dilemma.

On the one hand, the Communist invasion of South Korea struck at the basic presuppositions of American policy. If the primary purpose of containment was to prevent further Soviet expansion, American inaction in the face of Soviet aggression could only encourage further such acts in the future. The appetites of dictators were insatiable; one meal only whetted their palates and increased their hunger. If the aim of containment was also to hold together the Western powers, American refusal to rescue a friend in distress would disintegrate NATO. Our European allies would have believed that in a similar crisis they would be abandoned in a similar manner; consequently, they would have dismissed American treaty pledges as valueless, turned to neutralism for safety, isolated the United States, and deprived the Strategic Air Command of a large measure of its deterrent power.

On the other hand, the limited Soviet challenge in Korea did not fit our strategic doctrine. South Korea was certainly not "worth" the price of total war; massive retaliation upon Moscow was not the answer to the shrewd Russian exploitation of the government's one-sided concentration upon air-atomic striking power. A more limited response was needed. Fortunately, the United States had several undermanned and "undertrained" divisions in near-by Japan. Ironically, therefore, the Administration was compelled to fight a limited war to preserve its total-war policy; it was forced to respond by less than total means to a Soviet satellite in order to prevent the disintegration of a policy predicated upon massive retaliation as the principal means of deterring or winning a total war with the Soviet Union.

The price for American unpreparedness to fight a less than total war was strategic improvisation. Administration officials, still deeply imbued with the belief that the main contest would be with the Soviet Union and fought over the possession of Western Europe, thought of the Korean War only as a strategic diversion cleverly planned by the Kremlin as a means to weaken American power and divert it from Europe. Thus, while the government's political and military leaders knew that the limited Soviet attack in Korea left the United States with no alternative but to respond to it, they were determined that the fighting in the "far-off" Asian peninsula be kept as limited as possible. The Korean War was a necessary war: to teach the Soviet leaders that aggression would not pay; to hold together the Western alliance; and to preserve the military basis of containment. Nevertheless, it remained a "peripheral" war.

During the first stage of the conflict the objective was the restoration of the Republic of Korea to its prewar status. General MacArthur's magnificent amphibious operation at Inchon transformed the character of the war; his military victory changed it from a defensive war seeking only to re-establish the *status quo* to an offensive war attempting to affect a permanent change in the *status quo*. The North Koreans had been defeated; the military situation favored the fulfillment of an American goal of several years' standing: the unification of the whole of Korea. The Administration thereupon shifted its emphasis from containing the expansion of Soviet power to the forceful liberation of a Soviet satellite.

At the same time, the Administration abandoned the two assumptions upon which it had based its strategy in previous clashes with the Soviet Union: first, that the United States had to limit its efforts to contain Soviet expansionist moves to the restoration of the *status quo;* and second, that if the United States managed to re-establish the old equilibrium, the Russian leaders broke off the engagement and accepted the pre-crisis situation. After Inchon, however, the United States government made no attempt, as it had, for instance, after its successful resistance in Berlin, to negotiate an end to the hostilities through diplomatic channels. The Administration offered the Soviets only the total elimination of their satellite; in accordance with its own conclusion that it was dangerous to extend its reaction to Russian moves beyond the re-establishment of the *status quo,* the government must have expected the rejection of its demand for North Korea's unconditional surrender. Secretary Acheson had himself stated that governments do not negotiate their own survival. American insistence upon the military unification of Korea thus assured the continuation of hostilities.

This objective was officially proclaimed on October 7, 1950. Prior to that day the aim of the campaign had been only the restoration of the *status quo:* since a non-Communist South Korea had existed before the outbreak of the Korean War, the threat to Communist China of a liberated Republic of Korea was no greater than that before June 25, 1950.

But on October 7, as American-led forces surged northwards toward the Manchurian border, the threat to Communist China's industrial center became one of far greater magnitude. But the Administration believed that it was politically safe to drive into North Korea and free the Soviet satellite from Communist domination. The Chinese Communists were believed to be Chinese first and Communist second; moreover, they were allegedly already involved in such an intense struggle with the Soviet Union to prevent the latter from detaching Northern China, Manchuria, and Sinkiang, that Peking's anxious eyes were turned to the Northern provinces, not to Korea; China's traditional enemy was Russia, not the United States.

The resulting attempt of the Democrats to practice in October and November 1950 what the Republicans were only to preach two years later, led Communist China to intervene in order to redress the balance. The rapid change in the resulting military situation quickly led the Administration to deny its revisionist objective and revert once more to its *status quo* guise. The continued division of Korea was inherent in the Administration's rejection of MacArthur's military proposals to counter China's intervention.

One of the reasons for this rejection was the Administration's concern lest the Soviet Union might precipitate World War III. The government insisted that the United States must not offer the Russians any pretext for intervention. "Every decision I made in connection with the Korean conflict," the President wrote later, "had this one aim in mind: to prevent a third world war and the terrible destruction it would bring to the civilized world. This means that we should not do anything that would provide the excuse to the Soviets and plunge the free nations into full-scale all-out war . . . The points that appeared most critical [in the middle of December 1950] were Berlin, Western Germany, Indo-China, Yugoslavia, and Iran. In each of these areas a minor incident could easily be created which would give the Russians an excuse for open intervention . . . and the Kremlin might not be bluffing and might have decided that the time was in fact ripe for a general war with the United States." In the Administration's opinion, MacArthur's strategy to bomb Communist China, blockade her ports, and sanction Chinese Nationalist attacks upon the mainland would provide the Kremlin with just such an excuse.

But even if the Soviet Union should remain a spectator, the United States could not extend the war; it had to avoid becoming engaged in a "war of attrition" with Chinese manpower. Korea would "bleed us dry" and make it impossible to build a strong military defense in Europe. A large-scale commitment of American power in Asia would not only expose Europe to Soviet armies; it might incite such an attack at a moment of maximum American weakness on the continent. Nothing, General Bradley asserted, would delight the Kremlin more than the "enlargement of the war in Korea to include Red China . . . It would necessarily tie down additional forces, especially our sea power and air power, while the Soviet Union would not be obliged to put a single man into the conflict . . . A 'limited war' with Red China would increase the risk we are taking by engaging too much of our power in an area that is not the critical strategic prize. Red China is not the powerful nation seeking to dominate the world . . ." It was for this reason that MacArthur's strategy would involve us in the wrong war, at the wrong place, at the wrong time, and with the wrong enemy. The President stressed the same point: ". . . I never allowed myself to forget that America's principal enemies were sitting in the Kremlin, or that we could not afford to squander our reawakening strength as long as that [of] the enemy was not committed in the field but only pulling the strings behind the scenes." The United States had, therefore, to conserve its strength to check the main danger—Soviet Russia which *was* "the powerful nation seeking to dominate the world"—and not waste its power in a peripheral area.

This view was shared by Britain and France. America's chief allies were reluctant to see American power directed to the Far East before Europe was secure against Russian assault; they had no desire to risk the outbreak of World War III so soon after the second had ended for an area that was to them of minor strategic significance; and they hoped that their friendly attitude would hasten the split between the Chinese Communists and the Kremlin, as well as identify at least Britain and France with the new trends in Asia, social progress and national independence. Thus, if the United States decided to carry the war to Communist China, it would have to "go it alone." But the premise of creating "situations of strengths" and balancing Soviet might or winning a total war was NATO's unity and combined strength. It "is of transcendent importance," Secretary Acheson stressed, "that in our policies in all parts of the world, where danger may be created, we work absolutely in hand with our allies."

For these reasons, American policy-makers were willing to settle the war on the 38th Parallel. The Communists had attempted to erase the parallel and expand their power by incorporating South Korea into the Communist bloc; neither the north Koreans nor the Chinese Communists had achieved this objective. The Communists had also hoped to destroy the Western alliance and isolate the United States; in this too they had failed. NATO had been preserved and greatly strengthened by the new rearmament program and the addition of four American divisions. And Korea's primary purpose, to put the Communists on notice that the Western Powers would not tolerate Communist expansion by military force, had been achieved. The wisest course was thus to end this strategic diversion, to conclude this peripheral war, and once again concentrate on the main task: the strengthening of air-atomic striking power to deter the Soviet Union from precipitating total war and the building of a "situation of strength" in Western Europe.

MacArthur's fundamental charge against the Administration was that its restrictions kept him from achieving "victory" in the field. Inherent in this accusation was MacArthur's repudiation of the Administration's basic assumptions, above all the supposition that the Soviet Union might be ready and willing to fight a total war, and that the United States, therefore, must not provide an eager Kremlin with any excuse for attack.

MacArthur contended that the Administration divorced theory from practice. In theory, American foreign policy was based upon the assumption that the United States held sufficient power, above all air-atomic striking power, to deter the Soviet Union from launching an all-out war; in practice, American policy-makers acted upon the assumption that a limited extension of the war would hand the Soviets an excuse for precipitating World War III. On the one hand, the Kremlin was allegedly reluctant to engage in global hostilities with the United States because of America's greater retaliatory strength, inherent primarily in the destructive power of the Strategic Air Command; on the other hand, the Kremlin regarded our purported deterrent power with so little respect that it would deliberately risk total war rather than suffer a limited defeat of Communist China (a limited defeat would preclude the unconditional surrender and overthrow of Peking, and leave it weakened but nevertheless in control of the Chinese mainland).

MacArthur failed to see any consistency between the Administration's rationale of its foreign policy, based upon the atomic impact of massive retaliation, and its failure to act upon its own premise. If it were true that the United States held the atomic balance—as he believed and the Administration professed—then his recommendations for air attacks and a naval blockade of Communist China could be safely executed. SAC would continue to deter the Soviet Union and ensure that the limited hostilities, although somewhat extended, would remain confined to the Chinese-Korean theater; our superior strategic air power would provide the umbrella under which this expanded limited war could be fought. It was sheer fantasy, MacArthur charged, to suppose that American air attacks upon Manchuria would provide an eager Kremlin the opportunity to enter the battle. The Soviet Union possessed far inferior retaliatory power (the Russians did not begin to develop their long-range air force until 1954); why should it, therefore, be allowed to handcuff American strength? The United States possessed the superior atomic sanction; why should it not take advantage of this greater power? MacArthur pointed to the paradox that the side with the smaller strategic strength had paralyzed the will to act of the side which possessed the more effective striking force. The Administration's fear to act upon his recommendations to attack across the Yalu and the resultant impasse on the Korean battlefield was not a military stalemate, but a stalemate between the Soviet leaders *militarily incapable* of destroying the center of free world power and American policy-makers *psychologically reluctant* to exploit the advantage of the very atomic balance which they claimed was the primary safeguard of peace.

If the Russian leaders were really militarily capable of winning a total war and were merely seeking a convenient pretext to launch World War III, they would hardly need the United States to furnish the excuse; they were perfectly capable of manufacturing their own. If they were, however, restrained by American air power, they would rather tolerate a limited defeat of their chief ally than risk suicide. North Korea was no more "worth" the cost of an all-out conflict to the Soviet Union than

South Korea had been to the United States; nor was Communist China's position in North Korea "worth" that price as long as American objectives remained confined to the Korean peninsula.

MacArthur also dissented from the Administration's assumption that even if an attack upon Communist China would not precipitate World War III, this country must not become engaged in a "war of attrition" lest this course would weaken NATO and provoke a Soviet attack. The General denied that the Korean War was a Russian maneuver to draw American strength away from Europe and dissipate it against Chinese manpower, a strategic diversion which must be ended as soon as possible at minimum cost to the central effort to strengthen our total-war deterrent.

Not only was the "real" challenge against the enemy's number-one team in Europe hypothetical, for it was "Russia's policy . . . not to sacrifice its own troops but to use those of friends," but:

> Mr. Truman failed abysmally to comprehend the Soviet Strategy in the latter's continuing and relentless effort to control the world . . . He failed to understand that the global panorama has long encompassed three great areas of potential struggle: In the center, Europe; on the flanks, Asia to the north and Africa to the south. Mr. Truman apparently thought of the center as the area of supreme interest and potential struggle, believing that if it could be held safely all else would fall into place . . .
>
> What the Soviets sought were the economic frontiers of the world—Asia to the north, Africa to the south—frontiers which possessed such a mighty reservoir of the world's potential wealth in raw resources. The center represented little in economic advance, the flanks everything. The Soviet strategy was merely to defend in Europe but to advance by way of the flanks; to cause the free world to concentrate its resources at the center to the neglect of the vital ends.

Korea was, therefore, the right war at the right place at the right time, and above all else, with the right enemy. For Communist China was Soviet Russia's chief ally and most powerful friend in Asia. Therefore, a defeat inflicted upon Communist China, however limited that defeat might be, would affect both Soviet strength in Asia and the global balance of power between the Western and Communist blocs. The defeat of the Chinese Communists in Korea would strengthen the friendship and support of the Asian peoples, particularly the Japanese and Filipinos, for the United States; the loss of American prestige in an acceptance of the stalemate would alienate their sympathies. Conversely, Communist China's status would be recognized as "the military colossus of the East"; America's fear to demonstrate its superior strength would make our friends feel less secure and drive the neutral nations deeper into neutralism; for they would feel more threatened as a result of Peking's unchallenged recognition as a strong and menacing neighbor and therefore look upon the Communist states with a more friendly, if also a more apprehensive, eye. The destruction of Communist China's industrial complex, military depots, and communication network would gravely weaken Sino-

Soviet offensive strength in the Far East and deter Moscow and Peking from initiating any further aggressive adventures; confining hostilities to the Korean peninsula and concluding the war on the basis of the *status quo* would leave Sino-Soviet power intact and encourage it to exploit the West's weakness and lack of determination in other areas. Indeed, if the war in Korea were "lost"—by MacArthur's definition—the Western democracies would have suffered such a first-class political and psychological defeat that the Soviets could not but be emboldened to new efforts to undermine Western Europe. But to drive the Chinese Communists out of Korea in accordance with his strategy, MacArthur asserted, would demonstrate to the Western nations that even the Sino-Soviet alliance shrank from certain risky steps; victory would raise Europe's self-confidence by showing the limits of Communist power and the superior strength of the United States. It is for this reason that MacArthur insisted that Korea was *the* test of NATO and that Europe's first line of defense was not in Germany but in Korea.

His war in Korea was not, therefore, a sideshow; it was at the center of the world-wide struggle. The war, to be sure, contained its risks, but this was inherent in the nature of international politics and the original decision to fight in Korea; the conflict also presented a great opportunity to inflict a limited yet severe defeat upon the Sino-Soviet bloc, demonstrate American determination and power, raise Western resolution and self-assurance, and forestall the disaffection of friendly Asian nations. This opportunity outweighed all the risks, particularly since these risks were minimized by the deterrent power of America's superior atomic air-striking power.

MacArthur also emphasized that an alliance could act decisively only if its members were agreed on the nature of the danger facing them. If they were not animated by such a common realization, they not only did not add to the security of the United States; they detracted from it by restraining the United States from taking the steps necessary to safeguard its interests. The argument that the Administration could not accept his recommendations because it could not afford to isolate itself in the face of the Soviet threat toward Europe, was invalid; it was not the existence of the alliance which would deter the enemy's aggression, but the resolution which bound it together in concrete instances which called for vigorous action. When such determination and will-power were lacking, the United States must protect its own interests. The Administration's unwillingness to risk the loss of its allies allowed American policy to be dictated by the weaker members of the alliance. Under these circumstances, the achievement of allied unity became self-defeating; for the price of continued cooperation was the substance of action. In MacArthur's opinion, this price was too high and was paid upon the false assumption that unilateral action by the United States in Asia would undermine NATO, isolate this country, and encourage a Soviet attack in Europe. MacArthur believed that this prejudged the issue because it presumed that the United States was more dependent for its security upon its European allies than they upon the United States.

Since he was unwilling to accept formal unity for inaction or half-hearted effort, MacArthur advised that in order to forestall the disastrous effects he foresaw from an acceptance of a Korean stalemate, the United States "go it alone." European reluctance to become involved in major hostilities in the Far East ought not to prevent the Administration from taking actions which were in America's interest; the Administration could not give global scope to an alliance whose conflict of interests in areas outside of Europe paralyzed it.

The United States was sufficiently strong to fight the Korean War by herself; she had to act unilaterally if necessary, and pursue alone those policies which aimed at the preservation of a favorable balance of power. The United States must not allow this balance to be overturned by subordinating her strategy to allied fears; for in the final analysis, the security of Europe depended upon this country's ability to maintain this equilibrium. After the North Korean invasion, the United States had not first asked its allies whether they would approve of American intervention; the American government had acted in accordance with the dictates of national security. Allied consent had subsequently been extended, but it had not been a precondition for action. The Administration ought now to act upon its own precedent.

Communist China's appearance on the battlefield thus brought into the open the almost total disagreement between the Administration and its Commander in Chief, Far East, a disagreement which had, of course, never lain far below the surface and had irritated the relationship between Washington and Tokyo from the beginning of the war. Since shortly after the outbreak of hostilities, MacArthur had openly advocated that the United States maximize its commitment to Chiang Kai-shek and take a strong stand against Communist China; and his repeated "military" criticisms of the Administration's preoccupation with Europe and alleged neglect of American interests in the Far East were hardly new.

But these frequent and vigorous challenges of Administration policy after China's intervention were, however, incompatible with the President's continuing civilian supremacy and authority as chief diplomat and Commander in Chief to formulate and implement the policies the Chief Executive considered necessary to ensure the nation's self preservation. MacArthur embarrassed the Administration by giving the world the impression that the United States spoke with two voices—one civilian, one military—on foreign policy; he confused our allies and increased their reluctance to follow American policy because they feared that the government could not control him; and his March 24 statement actually forestalled the execution of Presidential policy. This situation was intolerable and left Mr. Truman no choice but to dismiss his field commander. But the price the President paid included, among other things, the adoption of a stronger anti-Mao and pro-Chiang policy along the lines advocated by the "old soldier" who refused to fade away.

The Administration's political weakness and vulnerability in Congress was a further cause for the Truman-MacArthur controversy; the President's lack of strength was particularly noticeable in the Senate. The reason for this was that in early 1950 the leadership of the Republican party in Congress on matters of foreign policy returned from the liberal eastern wing of the party to the traditional and predominantly middle-western conservatives, who constitute the majority of Republicans in Congress. These conservative Republicans rejected "bipartisan" cooperation. They believed that partisanship in foreign policy was politically expedient; "me-tooism" in international affairs, as in domestic affairs, resulted in defeat at the polls. Policies stamped with the Administration trade-mark were credited by the electorate to the party in power, and not to the "loyal" opposition which had supported them. In addition, Taft Republicans were convinced that the Democratic party, aided by the "heretical" eastern wing of their own party, were destroying the foundations of the American political and economic system, and that this process could be halted only by the restoration to power of the heirs and custodians of the "true" Republican tradition with its belief in a strong legislature, a balanced budget, and a minimum of government intervention in business. Thus partisanship in foreign policy was also an ideological necessity.

The conservative Republicans focused their criticisms upon the New Dealers. The latter's crimes were many: they had fathered "Socialism" and the Welfare State in America; they had involved the United States in World War II; they had "sold out" China and Eastern Europe at the wartime conferences with Stalin; and they had allowed Communist agents and "sympathizers" to infiltrate the American government. In short, the New Dealers were responsible for altering the traditional libertarian American system, entangling the United States in the complications of the international world, and aiding, either unwittingly or deliberately, the forces of World Communism. This conspiratorial interpretation of American domestic and foreign politics could not have been advanced at a more appropriate moment in American postwar history. Popular frustration with the cold war was widespread.

Republican mid-term election successes appeared to prove to orthodox party strategists that opposition *per se* was good politics, and that their pre-election estimate that attacks upon foreign policy were politically profitable was correct. As a result, after November 7, 1950, they no longer confined their broadsides to Yalta, Teheran, and Potsdam; Alger Hiss and other cases of espionage; the Administration's "loss" of China and responsibility for the war in Korea; they now attacked the whole scope of American foreign policy, particularly the European policy. General MacArthur's close link to this group, among whom such leaders as Taft, Wherry, Bridges, and Knowland were largely oriented toward Asia, lent it great prestige and strengthened its criticisms.

These attacks had even before June 25, 1950, imposed an increasing inflexibility upon American Far Eastern policy; they had prevented the Administration from initiating its Mao Tse-tito policy and forestalled the complete abandonment of Chiang Kai-shek. The Administration's protection of Formosa after the outbreak of North Korean aggression satisfied the opposition only temporarily. As the war progressed, their assaults became increasingly vociferous in their demands for a stronger anti-Mao and pro-Chiang policy; and their electoral gains, together with Communist China's intervention, added to the pressure exerted upon the Administration to adopt General MacArthur's proposal to extend the war and hit across the Yalu River.

These attacks were not, however, powerful enough to achieve this aim; but they were sufficiently strong to place American diplomacy in a domestic political straightjacket which foreclosed negotiations as a means to end hostilities, brought the Administration to endorse a large-scale military-aid program for Chiang, to announce a rather doubtful enthusiasm for his regime, and even to issue a call for a revolution within Communist China. Thus, in May and June 1951, during the Senate inquiry into MacArthur's dismissal, the extraordinary and ridiculous situation arose in which, on the one hand, the Administration was defending its limitation of the war and its dismissal of General MacArthur for advocating the opposite course, and at the same time renouncing its acceptance of the *status quo* and the implicit recognition of Peking's existence which this implied, and presenting the key issue as the survival of the Chinese Communist regime itself. Since regimes do not, however, negotiate about their own survival, this issue could only have been settled by the total war with Communist China—and perhaps with the Soviet Union—which the Administration had already rejected as too dangerous a course. Thus, if the government's call for an internal revolt within Communist China had been taken seriously by Peking, it would have committed the United States to an interminable war with no possibility of ending it through negotiations or a cease-fire.

Walter Lippmann subsequently wrote that the situation had been so serious that President Truman

> was not able to make peace, because politically he was too weak at home. He was not able to make war because the risks were too great. This dilemma of Truman's was resolved by the election of Eisenhower . . . President Eisenhower signed an armistice which accepted the partition of Korea and a peace without victory because, being himself the victorious commander in World War II and a Republican, he could not be attacked as an appeaser. President Truman and Secretary Acheson, on the other hand, never seemed able to afford to make peace on the only terms which the Chinese would agree to, on the terms, that is to say, which Eisenhower did agree to. The Democrats were too vulnerable to attack from the political followers of General MacArthur and of the then powerful Senator McCarthy, and indeed to attack from the whole right wing of the Republican party.

Thus the separation of powers exaggerated the peculiar American tendency to define foreign policy objectives in abstract and ideological terms; for to gain congressional and popular support for their policies, presidents must oversell their policies. This they do, not by presenting the key issues as enlightened—yet nevertheless, "selfish"—national interests, but as the highest moral principles and aims.

Whereas interests can, however, be compromised, principles cannot.

Their integrity, indeed their survival, can be guaranteed only by the total destruction of the enemy and the complete elimination of the evil which threatens to contaminate, if not to abolish, them. Anything less than the full application of "righteous power," and the achievement of complete victory, creates an embarrassing discrepancy between expectation and reality, and leaves in its wake widespread disillusionment.

The Administration's political weakness was evident, however, not only in its acceptance of much of its critics' policy and its apparent inability to sign an armistice on or near the 38th Parallel, but also in its failure to take effective measures to restrict MacArthur's discretionary powers. Nowhere was this more vividly demonstrated than in North Korea after the first signs of Chinese Communist intervention. MacArthur believed that boldness and a show of force would convince Peking that Korea's fate had already been settled; any hesitation would be interpreted as weakness and an invitation to full-scale intervention. The Administration proposed that only South Korean troops be sent into the area along the Manchurian frontier and northeastern provinces bordering the Soviet Union; by this means it expected to reassure Peking that American troops would not invade Manchuria. But MacArthur advanced the proper "purely military" considerations which he claimed necessitated his advance to the Yalu, and the government surrendered meekly. The reason it later advanced for its laxness was the American tradition granting generals great latitude in determining the tactical means to gain their objectives. This was primarily a rationalization; American policy-makers could hardly have been blind to the interrelationship of tactical means on the one hand and strategic concepts and political consequences on the other. A more reasonable explanation would attribute their paralysis to the Administration's fear of being accused of "softness" toward Communism, its uncertainty that MacArthur could not again carry off a "tremendous gamble" as at Inchon, its field commander's heightened prestige since that brilliant victory and Republican mid-term victories.

This is not to say that MacArthur's determination to launch his "end of the war" offensive, or the Administration's failure to stop him, were responsible for Communist China's full-scale intervention. The key decision determining the intervention was probably the crossing of the parallel; this is not, however, to excuse Washington's relaxation of political control as MacArthur advanced into North Korea. In seeking allied support for the crossing of the parallel, the Administration had given assurances that it would direct its military operations in North Korea with circumspection, that it would conduct itself with caution and avoid all acts which might provoke either Russia or China. MacArthur's operations, in the view of the allies, hardly supported this understanding; in their opinion, MacArthur's "belligerent" statements, together with his advance to the Yalu, gave Peking reasonable grounds for suspicion of American intentions and at least a partial justification for its intervention. Consequently, London and Paris refused to sanction an extension of the war beyond the Yalu, and slowed down and later eviscerated the Administration's condemnation of Communist

China. This one incident, they believed, had shown both MacArthur's liberal—perhaps more appropriately, unwarranted—interpretation of his orders, and the Administration's inability to exert effective control over him. Thus Truman's domestic weakness was one of the principal causes for the lack of allied confidence and insistence upon restraint.

The intensity of the executive-legislative battle not only allowed MacArthur to inject himself into this conflict and exploit his strong legislative support, but made it incumbent upon the Administration to invoke the Joint Chiefs' public support for its policies. Thus, ironically, the President's main reason for dismissing MacArthur, the necessity to preserve the principle of civilian control of the military, had to rely for its defense almost completely upon General Bradley and his three colleagues. The Joint Chiefs, widely regarded as a strictly professional and disinterested body, could command senatorial attention, for they combined the roles of World War II heroes and technical experts; consequently, they bore the chief burden of explaining to the inquiring senators the relationship of military strategy to political objectives, the respective contribution of Europe and Asia to our national security, and the value and role of allies in American policy. Secretary Acheson, despite the articulate, organized, and persuasive presentation of his testimony, could command no such reception; his Congressional audience received him in a more hostile and skeptical mood.

If the Administration's political vulnerability left the Joint Chiefs little choice but to lend their glamor to the government's policies, it also squandered much of their wartime prestige and reputation for political neutrality. Senator Taft's announcement, shortly after General MacArthur's dismissal, that he no longer possessed any confidence in General Bradley's professional judgment—as if "purely military" evaluations were ever without political implications!—is symptomatic of this change of attitude. Apparently the Senator believed that Bradley's opinions were warped by a purported pro-Democratic bias. Taft's criticism, however, even if it were true—and all the evidence belies it—would hardly be germane; for he is not disputing the fact that military men speak for or against national issues of a highly controversial nature in public, but the fact that General Bradley agreed with the President's policy, and disagreed with his, Senator Taft's, views. His point was not that a criticism of his and former President Hoover's almost exclusive reliance on air and sea power for the defense of the American Gibraltar should have been the task of the military's civilian superiors; his point was that General Bradley had found his strategy wanting. His concern was not, therefore, with the problem that partisan alignment of generals implied for the future of civilian supremacy; he was merely incensed that there were also "Democratic Generals," like the chairman of the Joint Chiefs, not just "Republican Generals," like MacArthur.

Nonetheless, the Senator's hostility to General Bradley does draw attention to the manner in which the separation of powers between the President and Congress draws military leaders into political conflict. The danger in this is not that military officers belong, as Senator

Taft seemed to believe, to one or the other of the two principal parties. The real threat lies elsewhere; that the generals' independent judgment lends itself to exploitation by both parties; and that this will signal, as Walter Lippmann has written, "the beginning of an altogether intolerable thing in a republic: namely a schism within the armed forces between the generals of the Democratic Party and the generals of the Republican Party"; and that the result will considerably weaken civilian control and presidential direction of foreign policy.

Our study of the Truman-MacArthur controversy has shown that the preservation of civilian control is not merely a simple matter of maintaining a number of appropriate constitutional and institutional safeguards. Indeed, the word "control" is in itself somewhat vague, for it implies that to avert a threat from the professionals of the sword restraints need be applied only to them; this is not necessarily true. At a time of high international tension, such as 1950–1951, during which the population and their elected officials are intensely preoccupied with security, the dominance of the military and "military" attitudes among civilians both in and out of government may become overriding. This is particularly true if such a period of crisis should last a relatively long time, or be followed rapidly by successive crises. Under such circumstances, American democracy may be transformed into a "garrison state" in which all power is concentrated in the Executive, authority flows downward, and democratic liberties are merely memories. This state of affairs, as Louis Smith has emphasized, may come "not by willful usurpation by the military but by successive adaptations for defense having the support of public opinion. It may be ushered in, not by conspiracy, but by plebiscite. It may come into power, not over the wreckage of the civil organs traditionally expected to repress it, but with their respective support."

This points to what is thus the principal as well as the most easily perceptible factor determining the effectiveness of civilian control: the quality of the nation's civilian leadership, that is, the ability of the politically responsible officials to recognize threats to their supremacy and their courage to act in order to preserve their control, no matter how unpopular their steps.

> Only to the extent that civilian leaders are committed to democratic values and procedures and the necessity for a civilian point of view can the requisite supremacy be maintained. Their intelligence and understanding, their clarity of purpose and direction, and their courage and confidence in the face of various anxieties and exigencies of a "cold war" and even full-scale war itself seem to be crucial . . . civilian apathy and ignorance may as effectively subvert civilian supremacy as a deliberate attempt by the military to augment their supremacy.

Another factor of key importance during a period of war is a field commander who is not violently opposed to the policies he is expected to execute, at least not so violently that he will refuse to restrict his objections to constitutionally authorized channels. No government can allow a military officer to challenge its whole foreign policy publicly; such toleration would undermine its authority to determine the nation's policy, divide the domestic support it needs, and alienate the allies it desires.

This need for a field commander more in sympathy with official strategy becomes even more urgent in view of the latitude the United States has traditionally granted its military officers. Since it is not customary for an Administration to issue specific orders to a military executive thousands of miles away, the latter can, owing to poor judgment or deliberate design, make decisions whose political and strategic consequences may well prevent the achievement of the government's objectives, if not undermine them. Necessity may, therefore, compel a re-examination of the tradition of military freedom lest it excuse us into disaster. In limited warfare not only military strategy, but on occasions even military tactics, have important political repercussions.

Imposing such restrictions on the man in the field will require a change in the traditional American attitude that war is a purely military instrument. The military, as well as their civilian superiors, will have to recognize that Clausewitz' definition of war as a political tool means that military operations are not only subordinate to political aims, but that there is no such thing as an autonomous sphere in which military operations are conducted in a strictly military manner unencumbered by "outside interference." None of the other generals who directed the Korean War, with the sole exception of General Ridgway, understood war in any broader sense than their own narrow professional definition. James Van Fleet, Mark Clark, Turner Joy, all took MacArthur literally and echoed his calls for a military victory; after all, was MacArthur not voicing merely the obvious?

Not until military men as a whole accept the need for close political direction will they be less likely to issue public statements voicing their displeasure at the "political interference" with their conduct of a limited war; indeed, until they abandon their notion that war is a military tool they will find it difficult wholly to accept the concept of limited warfare. Military men seem sometimes to forget that they are servants of the state and that they will not be judged by the nature of the policies they implement, only by how well they implement these policies. Their civilian superiors are responsible for the actual formulation of political strategy, not they. It is not their function to take their disagreements into the public forum for national debate.

Indeed, unless the soldier observes more carefully the limitations imposed upon him by his professional obligations and responsibilities, he will in fact be helping to undermine the control his civilian superiors exercise over him. For the separation of powers provides, as one writer has aptly phrased it, "a perpetual invitation, if not an irresistible force, drawing military leaders into political conflicts." In these circumstances, it will be a rare political opposition that will resist taking the field commander's criticisms (or the criticisms of one or more members of the Joint Chiefs) to the nation in order to capture political power by exploiting the American public's temperamental inability or unwillingness to fight anything less than total war. As it is, the institutional and psychological jealousies between the President and Congress, the irresponsible opposition which profits politically from Administration weaknesses and failures, the weak party discipline, and the possibility of a mid-term upset, seriously limit even a strong chief executive's degree of "peacetime" diplomatic freedom and ability to carry on his own foreign policy without succumbing, at least to some degree, to his opponent's program. The link between the opposition party and the general in the field, particularly a popular general, will intensify this tendency.

But basically the problem of preserving effective civilian control and minimizing the possibilities of the soldier–opposition party liaison is a question of how rapidly the American people adjust their traditional approach to foreign policy under the pressures and tensions of the cold war: how quickly they learn that they cannot at one moment preoccupy themselves with domestic affairs to the almost complete neglect of foreign policy, and at the next moment, when the enemy menace has become clear, focus all their attention and energies upon his utter destruction; how soon they accept the constantly recurring limited challenges, even limited wars, without the kind of intense and desperate frustration which might spill over either into total war or isolation. The process of learning is necessarily a slow one. "Taken as a whole," Robert Osgood has said, "the American record in foreign policy since 1945 is a remarkable adaptation to novel and challenging circumstances." Nevertheless, this record "does not show a real adjustment, either in its underlying conceptions of force and politics or in its concrete policies, to the imperatives of a strategy capable of resisting limited aggression by limited means. Such adaptation is bound to be encumbered by the weight of traditional habits of mind resisting the pressure of unprecedented events."

The time of such adaptation can, however, be shortened in the armed forces through education. Officers should receive a broader training than they have in the past so that they become aware of the wider context in which military policies have to be decided. Some civilians may fear that military men with a fuller understanding of the political and economic conditions that affect military strategy will be able to present their military points of view more effectively and thereby undermine civilian authority. In fact, such officers, precisely because they are aware of the broader framework of policy, are least likely to threaten civilian supremacy. The MacArthur case, to be sure, might prove otherwise; but the MacArthurs, who are willing to challenge their governments openly in an effort to change official policy to one more in accordance with their own political predilections, are a rarity. The Mark Clarks, Van Fleets, and Turner Joys, with their strong belief that war is a nonpolitical instrument and that wars can only be won if the politicians and diplomats do not "interfere" in them are not a rarity. It is for them that Clausewitz wrote that "the art of war in its highest point of view becomes a policy, but, of course, a policy which fights battles instead of writing notes. According to this view, it is an unpermissible and even harmful distinction, according to which a great military event or the plan for such an event should admit a *purely military judgment;* indeed, it is an unreasonable procedure to consult professional soldiers on the plan of war, that they may give a *purely military opinion* . . . [For] war is an instrument of policy; it must necessarily bear the character of policy; it must measure with policy's measure. The conduct of war, in its great outlines, is, therefore, policy itself, which takes up the sword in place of the pen, but does not on that account cease to think according to its own laws." The traditional American belief in the separation of military and nonmilitary factors may not have been harmful during a period of isolation; it cannot, unless revised, fail to be harmful, even disastrous, at a time of global involvement.

Additional Reading

Herbert Agar, *The Price of Power: America Since 1945* (1955).
Eric F. Goldman, *The Crucial Decade and After: America, 1945–1960* (1961 ed.).
Norman A. Graebner, *The New Isolationism* (1956).
Trumbull Higgins, *Korea and the Fall of MacArthur* (1960).
Walter Johnson, *1600 Pennsylvania Avenue: Presidents and the People, 1929–1959* (1960).
G. F. Kennan, *Realities of American Foreign Policy* (1954).
Harry S. Truman, *Memoirs* (2 vols., 1956).
Allen S. Whiting, *China Crosses the Yalu* (1960).

21 *CURRENTS IN AMERICAN FOREIGN POLICY SINCE 1952*

The readings in this chapter do not focus on a specific historical problem but were selected to illustrate the main thrust and tenor of the Eisenhower-Dulles era and the early years of the Kennedy administration. The Republicans triumphed in the 1952 presidential election by concentrating on a growing public unhappiness with the Korean War in particular and the Cold War in general, plus the issues of domestic corruption and alleged Communist infiltration in government. Secretary of State John Foster Dulles, until his retirement and death in 1959, played an unusually large role in shaping American foreign policies and an attempt was made under his guidance to effect a new departure promising dramatic successes at lower costs. Yet by the end of the Eisenhower period, most scholars and observers were agreed that the Republicans had been compelled to continue the essentials of the Truman-Acheson containment policy. The administration of President John F. Kennedy, succeeding in 1960, has not achieved any major changes in containment either, but in contrast to the Eisenhower administration it has greatly increased military spending for conventional and strategic nuclear weapons and has launched a new economic aid program for Latin America.

1. Dynamic Liberation and the New Look

The Republican platform in 1952 in effect promised to reverse the containment policy, allegedly immoral because it accepted the status quo and left millions of people in the satellite countries behind the Iron Curtain, and to seize the initiative with a new dynamic policy capable of putting Russia on the defensive and slowly pushing back Soviet power. In his pre-confirmation testimony before the Senate committee, the moralistic Dulles spoke of substituting "Peaceful Liberation" for containment. Subsequently, a new approach to Soviet aggressive thrusts on the periphery of the "free world" was announced. Instead of meeting attacks wherever they occurred and perhaps having American power drained by a number of Koreas in the future, the United States would reserve the right to retaliate instantly and massively with its atomic-hydrogen forces directly at the heart of Communist power in Soviet Russia. This approach led to a "New Look" in military policy: in contrast to the previous emphasis on balanced military forces armed both with conventional and atomic weapons, the new policy stressed expenditures on the atomic deterrent, or as a Secretary of Defense put it, the getting of a "bigger bang for the buck."

Senate Hearings on Dulles' Appointment to the State Department

Communist Enslavement of Free Peoples

. . . The CHAIRMAN. I am particularly interested in something I read recently, to the effect that you stated you were not in favor of the policy of containment. I think you advocated a more dynamic or positive policy.

Can you tell us more specifically what you have in mind? This, of course, is subject always to your own objections, if you think the question goes beyond a matter of qualifications.

Mr. DULLES. There are a number of policy matters which I would prefer to discuss with the committee in executive session, but I have no objection to saying in open session what I have said before: namely, that we shall never have a secure peace or a happy world so long as Soviet communism dominates one-third of all of the peoples that there are, and is in the process of trying at least to extend its rule to many others.

These people who are enslaved are people who deserve to be free, and who, from our own selfish standpoint, ought to be free because if they are the servile instruments of aggressive despotism, they will eventually be welded into a force which will be highly dangerous to ourselves and to all of the free world.

Communist Defection

Therefore, we must always have in mind the liberation of these captive peoples. Now, liberation does not mean a war of liberation. Liberation can be accomplished by processes short of war. We have, as one example, not an ideal example, but it illustrates my point, the defection of Yugoslavia, under Tito from the domination of Soviet communism.

Well, that rule of Tito is not one which we admire, and it has many aspects of despotism, itself; but at least it illustrates that it is possible to disintegrate this present monolithic structure which, as I say, represents approximately one-third of all the people that there are in the world.

Soviet Russian-Chinese Alliance

The present tie between China and Moscow is an unholy arrangement which is contrary to the traditions, the hopes, the aspirations of the Chinese people. Certainly we cannot tolerate a continuance of that, or a welding of the 450 million people of China into the servile instruments of Soviet aggression.

Policy of Containment

Therefore, a policy which only aims at containing Russia where it now is, is, in itself, an unsound policy; but it is a policy which is bound to fail because a purely defensive policy never wins against an aggressive policy.

If our only policy is to stay where we are, we will be driven back. It is only by keeping alive the hope of liberation, by taking advantage of that wherever opportunity arises, that we will end this terrible peril which dominates the world, which imposes upon us such terrible sacrifices and so great fears for the future. But all of this can be done and must be done in ways which will not provoke a general war, or in ways which will not provoke an insurrection which would be crushed with bloody violence, such as was the case, for example, when the Russians instigated the Polish revolt, under General Bor, and merely sat by and watched them when the Germans exterminated those who were revolting.

Peaceful Liberation

It must be and can be a peaceful process, but those who do not believe that results can be accomplished by moral pressures, by the weight of propaganda, just do not know what they are talking about.

I ask you to recall the fact that Soviet communism, itself, has spread from controlling 200 million people some 7 years ago to controlling 800 million people today, and it has done that by methods of political warfare, psychological warfare and propaganda, and it has not actually used the Red Army as an open aggressive force in accomplishing that.

Surely what they can accomplish, we can accomplish.

Surely if they can use moral and psychological force, we can use it; and, to take a negative defeatist attitude is not an approach which is conducive to our own welfare, or in conformity with our own historical ideas. . . .

Speech of John Foster Dulles before the Council on Foreign Relations, January 12, 1954

It is now nearly a year since the Eisenhower administration took office. During that year I have often spoken of various parts of our foreign policies. Tonight I should like to present an overall view of those policies which relate to our security.

First of all, let us recognize that many of the preceding foreign policies were good. Aid to Greece and Turkey had checked the Communist drive to the Mediterranean. The European Recovery Program had helped the peoples of Western Europe to pull out of the postwar morass. The Western powers were steadfast in Berlin and overcame the blockade with their airlift. As a loyal member of the United Nations, we had reacted with force to repel the Communist attack in Korea. When that effort exposed our military weakness, we rebuilt rapidly our military establishment. We also sought a quick buildup of armed strength in Western Europe.

These were the acts of a nation which saw the danger of Soviet communism; which realized that its own safety was tied up with that of others; which was capable of responding boldly and promptly to emergencies. These are precious values to be acclaimed. Also, we can pay tribute to congressional bipartisanship which puts the nation above politics.

But we need to recall that what we did was in the main emergency action, imposed on us by our enemies.

Let me illustrate.

1. We did not send our army into Korea because we judged in advance that it was sound military strategy to commit our Army to fight land battles in Asia. Our decision had been to pull out of Korea. It was Soviet-inspired action that pulled us back.

2. We did not decide in advance that it was wise to grant billions annually as foreign economic aid. We adopted that policy in response to the Communist efforts to sabotage the free economies of Western Europe.

3. We did not build up our military establishment at a rate which involved huge budget deficits, a depreciating currency, and a feverish economy because this seemed, in advance, a good policy. Indeed, we decided otherwise until the Soviet military threat was clearly revealed.

We live in a world where emergencies are always possible, and our survival may depend upon our capacity to meet emergencies. Let us pray that we shall always have that capacity. But, having said that, it is necessary also to say that emergency measures—however good for the emergency—do not necessarily make good permanent policies. Emergency measures are costly; they are superficial; and they imply that the enemy has the initiative. They cannot be depended on to serve our long-time interests.

The Need for Long-Range Policies

This "long time" factor is of critical importance.

The Soviet Communists are planning for what they call "an entire historical era," and we should do the same. They seek, through many types of maneuvers, gradually to divide and weaken the free nations by overextending them in efforts which, as Lenin put it, are "beyond their strength, so that they come to practical bankruptcy." Then, said Lenin, "our victory is assured." Then, said Stalin, will be "the moment for the decisive blow."

In the face of this strategy, measures cannot be judged adequate merely because they ward off an immediate danger. It is essential to do this, but it is also essential to do so without exhausting ourselves.

When the Eisenhower administration applied this test, we felt that some transformations were needed.

It is not sound military strategy permanently to commit U.S. land forces to Asia to a degree that leaves us no strategic reserves.

It is not sound economics, or good foreign policy to support permanently other countries; for in the long run, that creates as much ill will as good will.

Also, it is not sound to become permanently committed to military expenditures so vast that they lead to "practical bankruptcy."

Change was imperative to assure the stamina needed for permanent security. But it was equally imperative that change should be accompanied by understanding of our true purposes. Sudden and spectacular change had to be avoided. Otherwise, there might have been a panic among our friends and miscalculated aggression by our enemies. We can, I believe, make a good report in these respects.

We need allies and collective security. Our purpose is to make these relations more effective, less costly. This can be done by placing more reliance on deterrent power and less dependence on local defensive power.

This is accepted practice so far as local communities are concerned. We keep locks on our doors, but we do not have an armed guard in every home. We rely principally on a community security system so well equipped to punish any who break in and steal that, in fact, would-be aggressors are generally deterred. That is the modern way of getting maximum protection at a bearable cost.

What the Eisenhower administration seeks is a similar international security system. We want, for ourselves and the other free nations, a maximum deterrent at a bearable cost.

Local defense will always be important. But there is no local defense which alone will contain the mighty landpower of the Communist world. Local defenses must be reinforced by the further deterrent of massive retaliatory power. A potential aggressor must know that he cannot always prescribe battle conditions that suit him. Otherwise, for example, a potential aggressor, who is glutted with manpower, might be tempted to attack in confidence that resistance would be confined to manpower. He might be tempted to attack in places where his superiority was decisive.

The way to deter aggression is for the free community to be willing and able to respond vigorously at places and with means of its own choosing.

So long as our basic policy concepts were unclear, our military leaders could not be selective in building our military power. If an enemy could pick his time and place and method of warfare—and if our policy was to remain the traditional one of meeting aggression by direct and local opposition—then we needed to be ready to fight in the Arctic and in the Tropics; in Asia, the Near East, and in Europe; by sea, by land, and by air; with old weapons and with new weapons.

The total cost of our security efforts, at home and abroad, was over $50 billion per annum, and involved, for 1953, a projected budgetary deficit of $9 billion; and $11 billion for 1954. This was on top of taxes comparable to wartime taxes; and the dollar was depreciating in effective value. Our allies were similarly weighed down. This could not be continued for long without grave budgetary, economic, and social consequences.

But before military planning could be changed, the President and his advisers, as represented by the National Security Council, had to take some basic policy decisions. This has been done. The basic decision was to depend primarily upon a great capacity to retaliate, instantly, by means and at places of our choosing. Now the Department of Defense and the Joint Chiefs of Staff can shape our military establishment to fit what is *our* policy, instead of having to try to be ready to meet the enemy's many choices. That permits of a selection of military means instead of a multiplication of means. As a result, it is now possible to get, and share, more basic security at less cost. . . .

2. *Criticisms of Eisenhower's Foreign Policies*

Long before the end of Eisenhower's second term it was obvious that (1) the chief diplomatic contribution of the Eisenhower period was merely the further extension of defensive alliances around the globe to contain Communist expansion; and (2) that the tragic aftermath of the 1956 Hungarian Revolution had revealed the bankruptcy of "liberation" policies. The United States had to a degree encouraged this type of revolt against Communist masters but when it occurred feared to intervene lest World War III be precipitated. A "balance of terror" in the new weapons had been reached between the United States and Soviet Russia which precluded dramatic changes in favor of either side.

In October of 1957, Soviet Russia scored a technological and psychological triumph in launching the first earth satellite (Sputnik) and thereafter indicated that it possessed a decisive lead over the United States in the ballistics missiles field. When the American Defense Secretary in 1959 admitted that if Russia built to capacity it might have a 3 to 1 missile lead over the United States by the early 1960's, a number of alarmed critics, Democrats and Republicans, began to speak of imminent national danger and to urge heavy defense spending to overcome the "missile gap." Subsequently, revised intelligence estimates of actual Soviet production and increased American procurement largely eliminated the alleged gap.

In the following selection, Democratic Senator J. William Fulbright of Arkansas, Chairman of the Senate Foreign Relations Committee, criticized the Eisenhower administration for a general failure to respond creatively to foreign policy challenges.

Speech by Senator Fulbright, March 5, 1960

Mr. FULBRIGHT. Mr. President, the Congress of the United States has been in session for 2 months. During that period we have heard the President in his report on the state of the Union assure the American people that all is right with the world, and that our freedoms and our place in the world are secure.

We have received his budget message and been assured again that all is well—indeed, very good, because we look forward to a budget surplus, albeit we must do without new schools and better missiles. . . .

We have debated the state of our defenses and argued whether by 1962 the Soviet superiority in missiles would be 3 to 1 or maybe only 2 to 1. . . .

Where do we stand today?

A nation with a gross national product that will soon hit a peacetime high of $500 billion and with a per capita income of over $2,500—nearly double that of any other nation—is debating the extent to which our Armed Forces may be inferior to those of the Soviet Union.

If there is confusion about the facts, some things are clear. It is humiliating that the debate should have to occur. Its occurrence is evidence of our failures. It is a revelation of our lack of foresight of possessing great riches yet failing to use them to make ourselves, and keep ourselves, the world's strongest power, although to do less is to invite national extinction.

Mr. Khrushchev, having outrun us, is not one to let our grass grow under his feet. "It would be naive to think," he has said, "that we are going to sit with arms folded" while the Americans "make every effort to raise their rocketry from the state it is now in and reach a better position." But before considering this let us place the problem in perspective.

Men have anciently yearned for a universal commonwealth. Now we have it of sorts. But it is a commonwealth of fear kept going by a precarious balance of terror, a chilling oscillation between negotiation and incineration.

We endure in an era of total crisis. The great truths are denied. Black becomes white, the horizontal vertical. Whole states—as Estonia, Latvia, Lithuania and lately Tibet—sink from sight. Whole countries—as Hungary—languish behind bars. An ancient culture such as China's is shattered and remade overnight into the largest anthill slave state men have ever known. . . .

We have never faced an antagonist quite like this one. The Soviet Union swiftly leaped from the oxcart to the moon. It rose from a second-rate underdeveloped country to loom menacingly over the world.

Master of complex technologies, primitive and advanced, her soldiers march with black bread in their hands and the awful secrets of nuclear fission in their minds. Their leaders are obsessed by a dedicated sense of mission to dominate all mankind. . . .

Elsewhere, a colossal specter rises in the Far East. It commands the world's largest labor force. At this time 100 million people—a group exceeding half of our total population—are building the world's greatest network of hydroelectric stations, irrigation canals, and dams. Red China is attempting within one generation an enterprise greater than any undertaken by man: that of catching up, in this short time, with the most advanced industrialized nations. Many experts believe she will become a major industrial power during the late 1960's.

China's vast population grows. Soon 1 in 3, or 1 in 4, of all men will be Chinese. Awesomely industrious, tough, inured to hardship, China's millions are as the fingers of the hand manipulated by their determined and ruthless masters. They direct a revolution unparalleled in its dimensions which in its pitilessness, has swiftly destroyed a culture ancient when Christ was born.

We may expect that within foreseeable time the fingers will become a clenched fist prepared to smash all that stands in the path of China's domination of the Asian reaches, their resources, and the nearly three-quarters of a billion people who inhabit them.

Returning to the Soviet Union we find that Mr. Khrushchev even as he

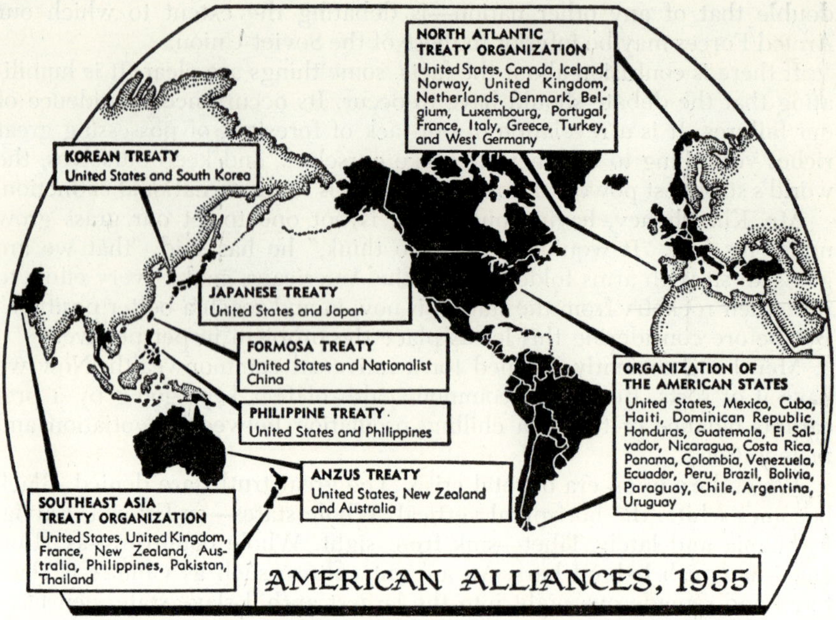

bade goodby to his American hosts,* repeated what he has often said: Communism would take us over. Given communism's unrelenting objective—world domination—this goal is logical. We must be the first to go by one means or another. For when the free world's shield is broken those whom it shelters become defenseless.

We have been warned, but have we heard? If we should perish it will not be for lack of warning but for lack of the will to survive.

In this context there is something new under the sun. It is a newness illuminated by the fact that the sun itself is no longer inviolate and unattainable. For the first time a would-be conqueror could win the world; win it in perhaps 30 minutes. He might succeed where others, from Genghis Khan to Hitler, had failed.

How almost overwhelming, then, must be the temptation to such a one to act? How nearly irresistible the compulsion to use his ocean-spanning, catastrophic weapons? How intoxicating the vision that, winning, the world would be one state to do his bidding with its people as his puppets, its continents as his provinces, and its seas as his lakes?

How must the aspirant conqueror be moved when he contrasts the position of his country and ours at the end of the war—only 15 years ago—and today? For among nations, as among individuals, what ultimately counts is not being but becoming.

At the war's end we were, incomparably, the world's strongest power, commanding the mightiest fighting force ever assembled, and a monopoly of atomic weapons. Our wartime casualties had been small, our homeland was untouched, our farms and factories had hugely expanded. The world's

* Khrushchev toured the United States in September 1959.

gold flowed to us. The world's trade fell to us as former rivals were removed from competition. We stood upon the heights of power, prestige, riches. We had arrived.

What of the Soviet Union in 1945? She did not announce her casualties lest they reveal her grave weakness. But they were on the order of 20 million people. She suffered an enormous loss of houses, factories, powerplants, domestic animals. Many thought that for years to come her energies would be absorbed by domestic reconstruction.

But she quickly repaired her war damages. Then she built a giant heavy industry, created new cities, opened vast new lands to cultivation. Above all she advanced education in a mighty surge of passionate and determined effort. . . .

Forty-four years ago communism was confined to a rented room in Zurich, Switzerland. Today it dominates one-third of the earth containing 40 percent of the population and a third of the industrial power. . . .

Surprisingly to the West, the Soviet Union exploded an atomic bomb only 4 years after the war's end. Four years later she exploded a hydrogen bomb. Now abreast of us in this field she forged ahead of us in the conquest of space as she launched man's first satellite and was first to the moon.

She maintains vast armies, and a navy second to ours. No power has ever had, in peacetime, so many submarines. They number 450; two-thirds of them long-range ocean patrol types. In 1956 alone Soviet shipyards built 100 submarines, or one every third or fourth day during the year. This is as many submarines as we have in our entire fleet.

In addition the Soviet Union is mounting a worldwide trade offensive aimed primarily at us. Hence the challenge to us is total. It involves the military, the political, the intellectual, and the industrial. The measures of our antagonist cannot be countered by half-measures or by halfhearted competition.

If, Mr. Khrushchev must reason, his country has come so far so fast, how much will it forge ahead of us in the future unless we greatly step up our pace in education, weapons, foreign aid, and foreign trade? But how shall we excel in these fields if we are more concerned with keeping up with the Joneses than surpassing the challenges of Khrushchevs?

How shall others appraise us—to consider only one phase of the struggle—in the light of Dr. Wernher von Braun's remarks about the conquest of space?

Last year he said the Russians disregarded our efforts. "The Russians appear so sure of their technological leadership," he observed, "and their ability to retain the initiative that they do not even consider the possibility someone else might beat them to the moon."

They were right. They got there first.

Only the other day Dr. von Braun said we cannot overtake the Soviet Union in the space race "for several years." It is "still moving faster than us," and he would "not be surprised" if it placed the first man in orbit this year.

President Eisenhower denies we are in a space race. But ordinary men believe we are in the race and are behind the pacesetter. Mr. Eisenhower also denies that our prestige has been lowered by our poor showing in space.

Here he is contradicted by an administration member, Mr. George V. Allen, head of the U.S. Information Agency. He says that the effect of Sputnik I was to "plunge the U.S. scientific prestige far below that of the Soviet Union" in critical India, Italy, Turkey, and elsewhere.

Many, in a world dominated by science, regard us as occupying a second-rate position in science. How long will it be before they fatally downgrade us to the status of second-rate power?

Mr. Eisenhower is also in sharp conflict with critics of our defenses. He treats them contemptuously. He was not disturbed, he said, "because anyone with a parochial viewpoint says the bosses know nothing about it."

Generals are not to reason why. Their Commander in Chief complains that "too many generals have all sorts of ideas." . . .

Yet this is the somber reality. Mr. Eisenhower, by virtue of his powers as President of the United States and Commander in Chief of its Armed Forces is the only man alive whose decisions about our armaments, if faulty, could cause the free world to be lost in an afternoon.

But he has dubbed those who disagree with his judgments as "noisy extremists"; men unpatriotic because they have "the tendency to disparage our country," while they are also dishonest because their assertions are "spurious"; that is, they are fake.

The group so condemned includes such distinguished soldiers as former Army Chiefs of Staff Generals Ridgway and Taylor, Gen. James M. Gavin, former Chief of Army Research and Development, and General Power, present Chief of the Strategic Air Command; such distinguished journalists as Joseph Alsop and Walter Lippmann, and such research organizations as the Rand Corp. and the Rockefeller Bros. Fund. . . .

Perhaps more disturbing is the President's assertion to a press conference that he knows more than "almost anyone" about military matters. This is dangerous because the President's attitudes foreclose discussion while precluding reason; deter military men, fearful of their careers, from speaking up; encourage the dominance of yes-men, and tend to drive superior men from the service. Such men are repelled by assumptions of omniscience this side of heaven. . . .

These men believe that our survival is imperiled; that we are not doing enough to assure our security to the greatest degree possible; that we should do more; and if it costs more to do more we ought to pay for it in the spirit of "damn the torpedoes, go ahead."

But let there be no mistake about this. If we are to have peace we must have a high degree of discipline at home. We must understand—and the President is the only man among us who can bring this forcibly to the Nation—that waging peace in our times is a task of formidable proportions second only to waging war.

The successful waging of peace requires a vigorous national administration, an informed people, and a mature people who know that you cannot be adult without being willing to pay for what you want. It is only in heaven that you can eat your cake and have it too.

This is the melancholy pass to which we have come. It is like the common story of the rich, miserly recluse found starving in a garret. There has never been a time when we did not have the resources of men, money, and access to knowledge that might have given us a wide lead over any aggressor and made attack upon us suicidal. Yet we have apparently believed we could not afford to spend enough to secure our liberties.

Let us again hear from *Life* magazine, a longtime, devoted supporter of this administration. In its issue of February 15, 1960, *Life* says editorially:

> President Eisenhower's defense budget is dangerously deficient. He has great military experience and deep confidence his $41 billion program is adequate. But harsh facts argue it isn't.
>
> The harshest fact is that by the President's own intelligence estimates, the Soviets by 1963 will have twice as many ICBM's as we—enough by SAC Commander Thomas Power's warning, to wipe out all our bases and retaliatory planes in one salvo.
>
> In order to do all that needs to be done we are convinced that the United States must spend on defense, at the very least, $2 billion more than it is now planning.

3. *Kennedy: A More Vigorous Foreign Policy*

A few days after taking office, President John F. Kennedy outlined to Congress and the nation the more energetic policies he intended to pursue in defense and foreign affairs. The "New Frontier" in military policy was in essence a return to the Truman program of maintaining adequate conventional as well as nuclear arms; in foreign policy, it meant a de-emphasis on military pacts as the way to halt the spread of Communism and a renewed program of economic aid to underdeveloped countries via governmental grants and loans, in conjunction with the cooperation of the prosperous countries of Western Europe.

President Kennedy's 1961 State of the Union Message

. . . But all these problems pale when placed beside those which confront us around the world. No man entering upon this office, regardless of his party, regardless of his previous service in Washington, could fail to be staggered upon learning—even in this brief 10-day period—the harsh enormity of the trials through which we must pass in the next four years. Each day the crises multiply. Each day their solution grows more difficult. Each day we draw nearer the hour of maximum danger, as weapons spread and hostile forces grow stronger. I feel I must inform the Congress that our analyses over the last 10 days make it clear that—in each of these principal areas of crises—the tide of events has been running out and time has not been our friend.

In Asia, the relentless pressures of the Chinese Communists menace the security of the entire area—from the borders of India and South Viet Nam to the jungles of Laos, struggling to protect its newly won independence. We seek in Laos what we seek in all Asia, and, indeed, in all the world—freedom for the people and independence for their government. This Nation shall persevere in our pursuit of these objectives. . . .

In Latin America, Communist agents seeking to exploit that region's peaceful revolution of hope have established a base on Cuba, only 90 miles from our shores. Our objection with Cuba is not over the people's drive for a better life. Our objection is to their domination by foreign and domestic tyrannies. Cuban social and economic reform should be encouraged. Questions of economic and trade policy can always be negotiated. But Communist domination in this hemisphere can never be negotiated. . . .

Our greatest challenge is still the world that lies beyond the cold war—but the first great obstacle is still our relations with the Soviet Union and Communist China. We must never be lulled into believing that either power has yielded its ambitions for world domination—ambitions which they forcefully restated only a short time ago. On the contrary, our task is to convince them that aggression and subversion will not be profitable routes to pursue those ends. Open and peaceful competition—for prestige, for markets, for scientific achievement, even for men's minds—is something else again. For if freedom and communism were to compete for man's allegiance in a world at peace, I would look to the future with ever increasing confidence.

To meet this array of challenges—to fulfill the role we cannot avoid on the world scene—we must reexamine and revise our whole arsenal of tools.

One must not overshadow the other. On the Presidential coat of arms, the American eagle holds in his right talon the olive branch, while in his left is held a bundle of arrows. We intend to give equal attention to both.

First, we must strengthen our military tools. We are moving into a period of uncertain risk and great commitment in which both the military and diplomatic possibilities require a free world force so powerful as to make any aggression clearly futile. Yet in the past, lack of a consistent, coherent military strategy, the absence of basic assumptions about our national requirements and the faulty estimates and duplication arising from interservice rivalries have all made it difficult to assess accurately how adequate—or inadequate—our defenses really are.

I have, therefore, instructed the Secretary of Defense to reappraise our entire defense strategy—our ability to fulfill our commitments—the effectiveness, vulnerability, and dispersal of our strategic bases, forces, and warning systems—the efficiency and economy of our operation and organization—the elimination of obsolete bases and installations—and the adequacy, modernization, and mobility of our present conventional and nuclear forces and weapons systems in the light of present and future dangers. I have asked for preliminary conclusions by the end of February—and I shall then recommend whatever legislative, budgetary, or executive action is needed in the light of these conclusions.

In the meantime, I have asked the Defense Secretary to initiate immediately three new steps clearly needed now:

(*a*) I have directed prompt action to increase our airlift capacity. Obtaining additional air transport mobility—and obtaining it now—will better assure the ability of our conventional forces to respond, with discrimination and speed, to any problem at any spot on the globe at any moment's notice. In particular it will enable us to meet any deliberate effort to avoid or divert our forces by starting limited wars in widely scattered parts of the globe.

(*b*) I have directed prompt action to step up our Polaris submarine program. Using unobligated shipbuilding funds now (to let contracts originally scheduled for the next fiscal year) will build and place on station—at least 9 months earlier than planned—substantially more units of a crucial deterrent—a fleet that will never attack first, but possess sufficient powers of retaliation, concealed beneath the seas, to discourage any aggressor from launching an attack on our security.

(*c*) I have directed prompt action to accelerate our entire missile program. . . . If we are to keep the peace, we need an invulnerable missile force powerful enough to deter any aggressor from even threatening an attack he would know could not destroy enough of our own force to prevent his own destruction. For as I said upon taking the oath of office: "Only when our arms are sufficient beyond doubt can we be certain beyond doubt that they will never be employed."

Secondly, we must improve our economic tools. Our role is essential and unavoidable in the construction of a sound and expanding economy for the entire non-Communist world, helping other nations build the strength to meet their own problems, to satisfy their own aspirations, and to surmount their own dangers. The problems in achieving this goal are towering and unprecedented—the response must be towering and unprecedented as well, much as lend-lease and the Marshall plan were in earlier years, which brought such fruitful results.

(*a*) I intend to ask the Congress for authority to establish a new and more effective program for assisting the economic, educational, and social development of other countries and continents. That program must stimulate and take more effectively into account the contributions of our allies, and provide central policy direction for all our own programs that now so often overlap, conflict, or diffuse our energies, and resources. Such a program, compared to past programs, will require—

more flexibility for short-run emergencies;

more commitment to long-term development;

new attention to education at all levels;

greater emphasis on the recipient nations' role, their effort and their purpose, with greater social justice for their own people, with broader distribution and participation of their people, and more efficient public administration and more efficient tax systems of their own.

and orderly planning for national and regional development instead of a piecemeal approach. . . .

(*c*) To our sister Republics to the south, we have pledged a new alliance for progress—alianza para progreso. Our goal is a free and prosperous Latin America, realizing for all its states and their citizens a degree of economic and social progress that matches their historic contributions of culture, intellect, and liberty. To start this Nation's role at this time in that alliance of neighbors, I am recommending the following:

That the Congress appropriate in full the $500 million fund pledged by the Act of Bogotá, to be used not as an instrument of the cold war, but as a first step in the sound development of the Americas.

That a new Inter-Departmental Task Force be established under the leadership of the Department of State, to coordinate at the highest level all policies and programs of concern to the Americas.

That our delegates to the OAS, working with those of other members, strengthen that body as an instrument to preserve the peace and to prevent foreign domination anywhere in the hemisphere.

That, in cooperation with other nations, we launch a new hemispheric attack on illiteracy and inadequate educational opportunities at all levels; and, finally,

That a food-for-peace mission be sent immediately to Latin America to explore ways in which our vast food abundance can be used to help end hunger and malnutrition in certain areas of suffering in our own hemisphere.

(*d*) This administration is expanding its new food-for-peace program in every possible way. The product of our abundance must be more effectively used to relieve hunger and help economic growth in all corners of the globe. I have asked the director of this program to recommend additional ways in which these surpluses can advance the interests of world peace—including the establishment of world food reserves.

(*e*) An even more valuable national asset is our reservoir of dedicated men and women—not only on our college campuses but in every age group—who have indicated their desire to contribute their skills, their efforts, and a part of their lives to the fight for world order. We can mobilize this talent through the formation of a National Peace Corps, enlisting the services of all those with the desire and capacity to help foreign lands meet their urgent needs for trained personnel.

(*f*) Finally, while our attention is centered on the development of the non-Communist world, we must never forget our hopes for the ultimate freedom and welfare of the eastern European peoples. In order to be prepared to help reestablish historic ties of friendship, I am asking the Congress for increased discretion to use economic tools in this area whenever this is found to be clearly in the national interest. This will require amendment of the Mutual Defense Assistance Control Act along the lines I proposed as a member of the Senate, and upon which the Senate voted last summer. Meanwhile, I hope to explore with the Polish Government the possibility of using our frozen Polish funds on projects of peace that will demonstrate our abiding friendship and interest in the people of Poland.

Third, we must sharpen our political and diplomatic tools—the means of cooperation and agreement on which an enforceable world order must ultimately rest.

(*a*) I have already taken steps to coordinate and expand our disarmament effort—to increase our programs of research and study—and to make arms control a central goal of our national policy under my personal direction. The deadly arms race, and the huge resources it absorbs, have too long overshadowed all else we must do. We must prevent that arms race from spreading to new nations, to new nuclear powers, and to the reaches of outer space. We must make certain that our negotiators are better informed and better prepared—to formulate workable proposals of our own and to make sound judgments about the proposals of others.

I have asked the other governments concerned to agree to a reasonable delay in the talks on a nuclear test ban—and it is our intention to resume negotiations prepared to reach a final agreement with any nation, that is equally willing to agree to an effective and enforceable treaty.

(*b*) We must increase our support of the United Nations as an instrument to end the cold war instead of an arena in which to fight it. . . .

(*c*) Finally, this administration intends to explore promptly all possible areas of cooperation with the Soviet Union and other nations "to invoke the wonders of science instead of its terrors." Specifically, I now invite all nations—including the Soviet Union—to join with us in developing a weather prediction program, in a new communications satellite program, and in preparation for probing the distant planets of Mars and Venus, probes which may someday unlock the deepest secrets of the universe.

Today this country is ahead in the science and technology of space, while the Soviet Union is ahead in the capacity to lift large vehicles into orbit. Both nations would help themselves as well as other nations by removing these endeavors from the bitter and wasteful competition of the cold war. The United States would be willing to join with the Soviet Union and the scientists of all nations in a greater effort to make the fruits of this new knowledge available to all—and, beyond that, in an effort to extend farm technology to hungry nations—to wipe out disease—to increase exchanges of scientists and their knowledge—and to make our own laboratories available to technicians of other lands who lack the facilities to pursue their own work. Where nature makes natural allies of us all, we can demonstrate that beneficial relations are possible even with those with whom we most deeply disagree—and this must someday be the basis of world peace and world law. . . .

4. *Cuba: the "Eyeball to Eyeball" Confrontation*

The revolutionary regime of Fidel Castro in Cuba increasingly manifested Marxian Communist overtones in 1960 and continued its violent denunciation of alleged Yankee imperialism in the Western Hemisphere. The harassment caused President Eisenhower to break diplomatic relations with Cuba in January, 1961. President Kennedy continued his anti-Castro policy, although the attempted invasion of Cuba at the Bay of Pigs by Cuban exile forces

in April, 1961 was a fiasco. When Soviet Russia not only underwrote Cuba financially and sent numerous technicians to help stabilize its chaotic economy, but also sought to establish a missile base there, President Kennedy met the challenge firmly. In October, 1962, he offered Khrushchev the alternative of a withdrawal or an armed confrontation. After a brief hesitation, Khrushchev agreed to remove the missiles and bombers.

The Castro regime remained, however, and Republican critics early in 1963 charged that Kennedy had failed to ensure by land inspection that the threat had been completely removed, and that inadequate measures had been taken to eliminate Castroism from the Caribbean.

The Soviet Threat to the Americas: Address by President Kennedy, October 22, 1962

Good evening, my fellow citizens. This Government, as promised, has maintained the closest surveillance of the Soviet military buildup on the island of Cuba. Within the past week unmistakable evidence has established the fact that a series of offensive missile sites is now in preparation on that imprisoned island. The purpose of these bases can be none other than to provide a nuclear strike capability against the Western Hemisphere. . . .

The characteristics of these new missile sites indicate two distinct types of installations. Several of them include medium-range ballistic missiles capable of carrying a nuclear warhead for a distance of more than 1,000 nautical miles. Each of these missiles, in short, is capable of striking Washington, D.C., the Panama Canal, Cape Canaveral, Mexico City, or any other city in the southeastern part of the United States, in Central America, or in the Caribbean area.

Additional sites not yet completed appear to be designed for intermediate-range ballistic missiles capable of traveling more than twice as far—and thus capable of striking most of the major cities in the Western Hemisphere, ranging as far north as Hudson Bay, Canada, and as far south as Lima, Peru. In addition, jet bombers, capable of carrying nuclear weapons, are now being uncrated and assembled in Cuba, while the necessary air bases are being prepared.

This urgent transformation of Cuba into an important strategic base—by the presence of these large, long-range, and clearly offensive weapons of sudden mass destruction—constitutes an explicit threat to the peace and security of all the Americas, in flagrant and deliberate defiance of the Rio Pact of 1947, the traditions of this nation and hemisphere, the Joint Resolution of the 87th Congress, the Charter of the United Nations, and my own public warnings to the Soviets on September 4 and 13.

Soviet Contradictions Cited

This action also contradicts the repeated assurances of Soviet spokesmen, both publicly and privately delivered, that the arms buildup in Cuba would retain its original defensive character and that the Soviet Union had no need or desire to station strategic missiles on the territory of any other nation.

The size of this undertaking makes clear that it has been planned for some months. Yet only last month, after I had made clear the distinction between any introduction of ground-to-ground missiles and the existence of defensive antiaircraft missiles, the Soviet Government publicly stated on September 11 that, and I quote, "The armaments and military equipment sent to Cuba are designed exclusively for defensive purposes," and, and I quote the Soviet Government, "There is no need for the Soviet Government to shift its weapons for a retaliatory blow to any other country, for instance Cuba," and that, and I quote the Government, "The Soviet Union has so powerful rockets to carry these nuclear warheads that there is no need to search for sites for them beyond the boundaries of the Soviet Union." That statement was false.

Only last Thursday, as evidence of this rapid offensive buildup was already in my hand, Soviet Foreign Minister Gromyko told me in my office that he was instructed to make it clear once again, as he said his Government had already done, that Soviet assistance to Cuba, and I quote, "pursued solely the purpose of contributing to the defense capabilities of Cuba," that, and I quote him, "training by Soviet specialists of Cuban nationals in handling defensive armaments was by no means offensive," and that "if it were otherwise," Mr. Gromyko went on, "the Soviet Government would never become involved in rendering such assistance." That statement also was false.

No Room for Deception

Neither the United States of America nor the world community of nations can tolerate deliberate deception and offensive threats on the part of any nation, large or small. We no longer live in a world where only the actual firing of weapons represents a sufficient challenge to a nation's security to constitute maximum peril. Nuclear weapons are so destructive and ballistic missiles are so swift that any substantially increased possibility of their use or any sudden change in their deployment may well be regarded as a definite threat to peace.

For many years both the Soviet Union and the United States, recognizing this fact, have deployed strategic nuclear weapons with great care, never upsetting the precarious *status quo* which insured that these weapons would not be used in the absence of some vital challenge. Our own strategic missiles have never been transferred to the territory of any other nation under a cloak of secrecy and deception; and our history, unlike that of the Soviets since the end of World War II, demonstrates that we have no desire to dominate or conquer any other nation or impose our system upon its people. Nevertheless, American citizens have become adjusted to living daily on the bull's eye of Soviet missiles located inside the U.S.S.R. or in submarines.

In that sense missiles in Cuba add to an already clear and present danger—although it should be noted the nations of Latin America have never previously been subjected to a potential nuclear threat.

But this secret, swift, and extraordinary buildup of Communist missiles —in an area well known to have a special and historical relationship to the United States and the nations of the Western Hemisphere, in violation of Soviet assurances, and in defiance of American and hemispheric policy—this sudden, clandestine decision to station strategic weapons for the first time outside of Soviet soil—is a deliberately provocative and unjustified change in the *status quo* which cannot be accepted by this country if our courage and our commitments are ever to be trusted again by either friend or foe.

The 1930's taught us a clear lesson: Aggressive conduct, if allowed to grow unchecked and unchallenged, ultimately leads to war. This nation is opposed to war. We are also true to our word. Our unswerving objective, therefore, must be to prevent the use of these missiles against this or any other country and to secure their withdrawal or elimination from the Western Hemisphere.

Our policy has been one of patience and restraint, as befits a peaceful and powerful nation, which leads a worldwide alliance. We have been determined not to be diverted from our central concerns by mere irritants and fanatics. But now further action is required—and it is underway; and these actions may only be the beginning. We will not prematurely or unnecessarily risk the costs of worldwide nuclear war in which even the fruits of victory would be ashes in our mouth—but neither will we shrink from that risk at any time it must be faced.

Initial Steps Proposed

Acting, therefore, in the defense of our own security and of the entire Western Hemisphere, and under the authority entrusted to me by the Constitution as endorsed by the resolution of the Congress, I have directed that the following *initial* steps be taken immediately:

First: To halt this offensive buildup, a strict quarantine on all offensive military equipment under shipment to Cuba is being initiated. All ships of any kind bound for Cuba from whatever nation or port will, if found to contain cargoes of offensive weapons, be turned back. This quarantine will be extended, if needed, to other types of cargo and carriers. We are not at this time, however, denying the necessities of life as the Soviets attempted to do in their Berlin blockade of 1948.

Second: I have directed the continued and increased close surveillance of Cuba and its military buildup. The Foreign Ministers of the OAS [Organization of American States] in their communique of October 3 rejected secrecy on such matters in this hemisphere. Should these offensive military preparations continue, thus increasing the threat to the hemisphere, further action will be justified. I have directed the Armed Forces to prepare for any eventualities; and I trust that, in the interest of both the Cuban people and the Soviet technicians at the sites, the hazards to all concerned of continuing this threat will be recognized.

Third: It shall be the policy of this nation to regard any nuclear missile launched from Cuba against any nation in the Western Hemisphere as an attack by the Soviet Union on the United States, requiring a full retaliatory response upon the Soviet Union.

Fourth: As a necessary military precaution I have reinforced our base at Guantanamo, evacuated today the dependents of our personnel there, and ordered additional military units to be on a standby alert basis.

Fifth: We are calling tonight for an immediate meeting of the Organ of Consultation, under the Organization of American States, to consider this threat to hemispheric security and to invoke articles 6 and 8 of the Rio Treaty in support of all necessary action. The United Nations Charter allows for regional security arrangements—and the nations of this hemisphere decided long ago against the military presence of outside powers. Our other allies around the world have also been alerted.

Sixth: Under the Charter of the United Nations, we are asking tonight that an emergency meeting of the Security Council be convoked without delay to take action against this latest Soviet threat to world peace. Our resolution will call for the prompt dismantling and withdrawal of all offensive weapons in Cuba, under the supervision of U.N. observers, before the quarantine can be lifted.

Seventh and finally: I call upon Chairman Khrushchev to halt and eliminate this clandestine, reckless, and provocative threat to world peace and to stable relations between our two nations. I call upon him further to abandon this course of world domination and to join in an historic effort to end the perilous arms race and transform the history of man. He has an opportunity now to move the world back from the abyss of destruction—by returning to his Government's own words that it had no need to station missiles outside its own territory, and withdrawing these weapons from Cuba—by refraining from any action which will widen or deepen the present crisis—and then by participating in a search for peaceful and permanent solutions.

This nation is prepared to present its case against the Soviet threat to peace, and our own proposals for a peaceful world, at any time and in any forum—in the OAS, in the United Nations, or in any other meeting that could be useful—without limiting our freedom of action.

U.S. Wishes Peace with U.S.S.R.

We have in the past made strenuous efforts to limit the spread of nuclear weapons. We have proposed the elimination of all arms and military bases in a fair and effective disarmament treaty. We are prepared to discuss new proposals for the removal of tensions on both sides—including the possibilities of a genuinely independent Cuba, free to determine its own destiny. We have no wish to war with the Soviet Union, for we are a peaceful people who desire to live in peace with all other peoples.

But it is difficult to settle or even discuss these problems in an atmosphere of intimidation. That is why this latest Soviet threat—or any other threat which is made either independently or in response to our actions this week—must and will be met with determination. Any hostile move anywhere in the world against the safety and freedom of peoples to whom we are committed—including in particular the brave people of West Berlin—will be met by whatever action is needed. . . .

U.S. Chooses Difficult Path

My fellow citizens, let no one doubt that this is a difficult and dangerous effort on which we have set out. No one can foresee precisely what course it will take or what costs or casualties will be incurred. Many months of sacrifice and self-discipline lie ahead—months in which both our patience and our will will be tested, months in which many threats and denunciations will keep us aware of our dangers. But the greatest danger of all would be to do nothing.

The path we have chosen for the present is full of hazards, as all paths are; but it is the one most consistent with our character and courage as a nation and our commitments around the world. The cost of freedom is always high—but Americans have always paid it. And one path we shall never choose, and that is the path of surrender or submission.

Our goal is not the victory of might but the vindication of right—not peace at the expense of freedom, but both peace *and* freedom, here in this hemisphere and, we hope, around the world. God willing, that goal will be achieved.

A Republican Criticism of Kennedy's Cuban Policy: Speech of Senator Kenneth B. Keating of New York, February 25, 1963

It would be unfortunate if the debate on Cuba degenerated into a name calling, political brawl.

What the United States does or refrains from doing in regard to the Soviet base in Cuba may determine the peace and security of the whole world. We must consider this issue as Americans, not as Republicans or Democrats. And our goal must be to find solutions, not to develop campaign fodder for the coming elections.

Let it be conceded that the mistakes in Cuba go back many years to periods of Republican as well as Democratic administrations and that both parties bear a heavy responsibility for the tragic conditions which now exist in Cuba. Let it also be conceded that there are men and women in both parties equally dedicated to the task of ridding this hemisphere of its first Communist military base. . . .

My own judgment is that Cuba is now the No. 1 testing ground in the struggle between international communism and the free world. This is not because of any fear of an invasion of the United States from Cuba, as some have said in an effort to belittle concern with the problem of Cuba. Did anyone fear an invasion of the United States from South Korea if it fell to the Chinese Reds? Does anyone now fear an invasion of the United States from South Vietnam if it should fall to the Communists? We have recognized in these areas and in such places as Greece and Turkey and

Lebanon as well as in Berlin, that you cannot appease a tyrant, that the appetite of the Communists is insatiable, and that the only way to prevent the Communists from swallowing up the world piece by piece is to make sure they get indigestion every time they reveal their hunger pains. . . .

No two situations are entirely alike and there are elements in the Cuban situation which certainly are unique. The Soviet takeover of Cuba was accomplished not by an invasion but by subversion. Obviously, this is a more difficult tactic to detect and forestall, but its consequences are no less grave or menacing. Hitler had his Quislings, and the Communists have their Castros not only in Cuba, but in many areas of the world. We cannot blind ourselves to conquest by subversion or covert aggression, anymore than we can to conquest by overt and naked aggression. The same loss of freedom and expansion of communism is involved in both cases and neither can be tolerated without imperiling world peace. If we condone what has happened in Cuba, how can we possibly prevent the same pattern from repeating itself in British Guiana, after it achieves independence, or in Venezuela or Brazil or Mexico, or in any other country in which Communist agents are busily at work?

It seems to me that the first ingredient of any effective policy with regard to Cuba is that we recognize the nature of the threat. There is no possibility of success in efforts to eliminate the Soviets and their military equipment from this hemisphere if we downgrade the implications of the Cuban takeover. Our allies cannot be expected to join in the kind of concerted action which is necessary to deal with this situation, if important figures in our own country portray the problem merely as an irritant or a nuisance, and indicate a readiness to accept the status quo. Our leaders must make clear, not only to all Americans, but to the whole world, that the Soviet takeover in Cuba presents, at the very least, the same threat to the peace, security, and freedom of the world as the attempted Red takeovers of South Korea, South Vietnam, and the Congo.

We have acted boldly and with great determination in all of those areas, and there is no reason for us to respond with any less vigor to a threat in our own hemisphere just off our own shores. I believe that our partners in the struggle against international communism would fully understand our concern with the Soviet base in Cuba if our views were effectively articulated and skillfully conveyed. . . .

The dissatisfaction and uncertainty which are evident throughout the Nation today with regard to what is going on in Cuba and what it really means do not stem from congressional statements on the subject. The real cause for the crisis of confidence, the credibility gap, that exists widely throughout the Nation, lies in the complete failure of our Government leaders to articulate a clear and firm policy toward the Soviet takeover in Cuba. . . .

The present crisis of confidence with respect to Cuba can be traced directly to an increasing disillusionment with the zigzag policy of improvisation which has characterized the executive branch's pronouncements on this subject. At times, the improvisation has been good, as it was last October, when our Government acknowledged that strategic missile systems were in Cuba, and responded with determination and boldness. At other times, such as the Bay of Pigs, our improvisation was disastrous. In the long run, this policy has inevitably tended to undermine national confidence. . .

When the President finally confronted the Nation with the Soviet missile threat in Cuba, the entire country united behind him and applauded his firm action in forcing withdrawal of the missiles and Ilyushin bombers. The country stood 100 percent behind the President's policies in this crisis and the Soviets backed down. . .

Unfortunately, we failed to press our advantage and were unwilling to insist on on-site inspection to make certain that the Soviets were living up to their agreement. As a result of this improvisation of policy, there is doubt again as to just what the Soviets are doing in Cuba. . . .

What we have lacked most in Cuba is a long-term, consistent, and effective policy for ridding this hemisphere of Soviet conquest. When such a policy is enunciated, it will not lack support from either side of the aisle in this Chamber, or from any segment of the American people. Until that time, however, disunity and national concern are unavoidable. . . .

5. *Kennedy Counters De Gaulle's Challenge to Western Unity*

Western Europe by 1963 had outgrown its earlier dependence on the United States. Thanks in large part to the Marshall Plan, the nations of Western Europe were experiencing a phenomenal economic prosperity and with it a resurgence of national pride and confidence. A natural result was an increasing demand for equality and partnership with the United States in directing the affairs of the NATO alliance. President Charles de Gaulle of France especially had challenged the predominant American leadership. After his overture for an Anglo-American-French directorate of the Western alliance was rebuffed in 1959, de Gaulle began to pursue his own vision of a continental European association of "fatherlands," which would counterbalance the Anglo-American influence within NATO and eventually, perhaps, comprise a third force between America and Russia. French cooperation with NATO was reduced, de Gaulle insisted on building a French national nuclear force, and the British application for membership in the European Common Market was vetoed in early 1963. Doubts also were raised by de Gaulle of American readiness to risk destruction of its own cities in a nuclear war in order to defend Western Europe.

President Kennedy acted vigorously to meet the challenge. Fearful lest France disrupt NATO and block a larger European union, Kennedy chose July 4, 1962 to deliver an address at Independence Hall, Philadelphia, in which he strongly advocated further European unity and American interdependence. He seemed thereby to presage a future Atlantic Confederacy which would join Western Europe and America in closer economic and political bonds. A year later he undertook a goodwill tour of West Germany, Great Britain and Italy, obviously in order to counter de Gaulle's divisive tactics and to reassert American leadership. His address at Frankfurt, West Germany answered doubts about the reliability of the American commitment by asserting a readiness to defend Europe even at the risk of all-out nuclear warfare if events should ever necessitate.

The Goal of an Atlantic Partnership: Address by President Kennedy, July 4, 1962

It is high honor for any citizen of the great Republic to speak at this hall of independence on this day of independence. . . .

Because our system is designed to encourage both differences and dissent—because its checks and balances are designed to preserve the rights of the individual and the locality against preeminent central authority—you and I both recognize how dependent we are, one upon the other, for the successful operation of our unique and happy form of government. Our system and our freedom permit the legislative to be pitted upon occasions against the Executive, the State against the Federal Government, the city against the countryside, the party against party, interest against interest, all in competition or in contention one with another. Our task—your task in the statehouse and my task in the White House—is to weave from all these tangled threads a fabric of law and progress. Others may confine themselves to debate, discussion, and that ultimate luxury—free advice. Our responsibility is one of decision, for to govern is to choose.

Thus, in a very real sense you and I are the executors of the testament handed down by those who gathered in this historic hall 186 years ago today. For they gathered to affix their names to a document which was above all else a document not of rhetoric but a bold decision. It was, it is true, a document of protest, but protests had been made before. It set forth their grievances with eloquence, but such eloquence had been heard before. But what distinguished this paper from all the others was the final, irrevocable decision that it took to assert the independence of free States in place of colonies and to commit to that goal their lives, their fortunes, and their sacred honor.

Today, 186 years later, that Declaration—whose yellowing parchment and fading, almost illegible lines I saw in the past week in the National Archives in Washington—is still a revolutionary document. To read it today is to hear a trumpet call. For that Declaration unleashed not merely a revolution against the British but a revolution in human affairs. Its authors were highly conscious of its worldwide implications, and George Washington declared that liberty and self-government were, in his words, "finally staked on the experiment intrusted to the hands of the American people."

This prophecy has been borne out for 186 years. This doctrine of national independence has shaken the globe, and it remains the most powerful force anywhere in the world today. There are those struggling to eke out a bare existence in a barren land who have never heard of free enterprise but who cherish the idea of independence. There are those who are grappling with overpowering problems of illiteracy and ill health and who are ill equipped to hold free elections, but they are determined to hold fast to their national independence. Even those unwilling or unable to take part in any struggle between East and West are strongly on the side of their own national independence. If there is a single issue in the world today which divides the world, it is independence—the independence of Berlin or Laos or Viet-Nam, the longing for independence behind the Iron Curtain, the peaceful transition to independence in those newly emerging areas whose troubles some hope to exploit.

The theory of independence—as old as man himself—was not invented in this hall, but it was in this hall that the theory became a practice—that the word went out to all the world that "The God who gave us life, gave us liberty at the same time."

And today this nation—conceived in revolution, nurtured in liberty, matured in independence—has no intention of abdicating its leadership in the worldwide movement for independence to any nation or society committed to systematic human suppression.

Spirit of European Unity

As apt and applicable as this historic Declaration of Independence is today, we would do well to honor that other historic document drafted in this hall—the Constitution of the United States—for it stressed not independence but interdependence, not the individual liberty of one but the indivisible liberty of all.

In most of the old colonial world the struggle for independence is coming to an end. Even in areas behind the Curtain, that which Jefferson called "the disease of liberty" still appears to be infectious. With the passing of ancient empires, today less than 2 percent of the world's population lives in territories officially termed "dependent." As this effort for independence, inspired by the spirit of the American Declaration of Independence, now approaches a successful close, a great new effort—for interdependence—is transforming the world about us. And the spirit of that new effort is the same spirit which gave birth to the American Constitution.

That spirit is today most clearly seen across the Atlantic Ocean. The nations of Western Europe, long divided by feuds more bitter than any which existed among the Thirteen Colonies, are joining together, seeking, as our forefathers sought, to find freedom in diversity and unity in strength.

The United States looks on this vast new enterprise with hope and admiration. We do not regard a strong and united Europe as a rival but as a partner. To aid its progress has been the basic objective of our foreign policy for 17 years. We believe that a united Europe will be capable of playing a greater role in the common defense, of responding more generously to the needs of poorer nations, of joining with the United States and others in lowering trade barriers, resolving problems of currency and commodities, and developing coordinated policies in all other economic, diplomatic, and political areas. We see in such a Europe a partner with whom we could deal on a basis of full equality in all the great and burdensome tasks of building and defending a community of free nations.

It would be premature at this time to do more than to indicate the high regard with which we view the formation of this partnership. The first order of business is for our European friends to go forward in forming the more perfect union which will some day make this partnership possible.

U.S. Ready for a "Declaration of Interdependence"

A great new edifice is not built overnight. It was 11 years from the Declaration of Independence to the writing of the Constitution. The construction of workable Federal institutions required still another generation. The greatest works of our nation's founders lay not in documents and declarations but in creative, determined action. The building of the new house of Europe has followed this same practical and purposeful course. Building the Atlantic partnership will not be cheaply or easily finished.

But I will say here and now on this day of independence that the United States will be ready for a "Declaration of Interdependence," that we will be prepared to discuss with a United Europe the ways and means of forming a concrete Atlantic partnership, a mutually beneficial partnership between the new union now emerging in Europe and the old American Union founded here 175 years ago.

All this will not be completed in a year, but let the world know it is our goal.

In urging the adoption of the United States Constitution, Alexander Hamilton told his fellow New Yorkers to "think continentally." Today Americans must learn to think intercontinentally.

Acting on our own by ourselves, we cannot establish justice throughout the world. We cannot insure its domestic tranquillity, or provide for its common defense, or promote its general welfare, or secure the blessings of liberty to ourselves and our posterity. But joined with other free nations, we can do all this and more. We can assist the developing nations to throw off the yoke of poverty. We can balance our worldwide trade and payments at the highest possible level of growth. We can mount a deterrent powerful enough to deter any aggression, and ultimately we can help achieve a world of law and free choice, banishing the world of war and coercion.

For the Atlantic partnership of which I speak would not look inward only, preoccupied with its own welfare and advancement. It must look outward to cooperate with all nations in meeting their common concern. It would serve as a nucleus for the eventual union of all free men—those who are now free and those who are avowing that some day they will be free. . . .

Kennedy's Speech at Frankfurt, West Germany, June 25, 1963

. . . We are partners for peace, not in a narrow bilateral context, but in a framework of Atlantic partnership. The ocean divides us less than the Mediterranean divided Greece and Rome. Our constitution is old and yours is young—and our culture is young and yours is old—but in our commitment we can and must speak and act with one voice. Our roles are distinct but complementary—and our goals are the same: Peace and freedom for all men, for all time, in a world of abundance, in a world of justice.

That is why our nations are working together to strengthen NATO, to expand trade, to assist the developing countries, to align our monetary policies and to build the Atlantic Community. I would not diminish the miracle of West Germany's economic achievements. But the true German miracle has been your rejection of the past for the future—your reconciliation with France, your participation in the building of Europe, your leading role in NATO, and your growing support for constructive undertakings throughout the world.

Your economic institutions, your constitutional guarantees, your confidence in civilian authority, are all harmonious with the ideals of older democracies. And they form a firm pillar of the democratic European community. . . .

The future of the West lies in Atlantic partnership—a system of cooperation, interdependence and harmony whose people can jointly meet their burdens and opportunities throughout the world. Some say this is only a dream, but I do not agree. A generation of achievement—the Marshall Plan, NATO, the Schuman Plan, and the Common Market—urges us up the path to greater unity.

There will be difficulties and delays, and doubts and discouragement. There will be differences of approach and opinion. But we have the will and the means to serve three related goals—the heritage of our countries, the unity of our continents and the interdependence of the Western alliance.

Some say that the United States will neither hold to these purposes nor abide by its pledges—that we will revert to a narrow nationalism. But such doubts fly in the face of history. For 18 years the United States has stood its watch for freedom all around the globe. The firmness of American will, and the effectiveness of American strength, have been shown in support of free men and free governments, in Asia, in Africa, in the Americas; and above all, here in Europe we have undertaken, and sustained in honor, relations of mutual trust and obligation with more than 40 allies. We are proud of this record, which more than answers doubts. But, in addition, these proved commitments to the common freedom and safety are assured, in the future as in the past, by one great fundamental fact—that they are deeply rooted in America's own self-interest. Our commitment to Europe is indispensable—in our interest as well as yours.

It is not in our interest to try to dominate the European councils of decision. If that were our objective, we would prefer to see Europe divided and weak, enabling the United States to deal with each fragment individually. Instead we have and now look forward to a Europe united and strong—speaking with a common voice—acting with a common will—a world power capable of meeting world problems as a full and equal partner.

This is in the interest of us all. For war in Europe, as we learned twice in 40 years, destroys peace in America. A threat to the freedom of Europe is a threat to the freedom of America. That is why no administration in Washington can fail to respond to such a threat—not merely from good will but from necessity. And that is why we look forward to a united Europe in an Atlantic partnership—an entity of interdependent parts, sharing equally both burdens and decisions, and linked together in the task of defense as well as the arts of peace.

This is no fantasy. It will be achieved by concrete steps to solve the problems that face us all: military, economic and political. Partnership is not a posture but a process—a continuous process—a continuous process that grows stronger each year as we devote ourselves to common tasks.

The first task of the Atlantic Community was to assure its common defense. That defense was and still is indivisible. The United States will risk its cities to defend yours because we need your freedom to protect ours. Hundreds of thousands of our soldiers serve with yours on this continent, as tangible evidence of this pledge. Those who would doubt our pledge or deny this indivisibility—those who would separate Europe from America or split one ally from another—would only give aid and comfort to the men who make themselves our adversaries and welcome any Western disarray.

The purpose of our common military effort is not war but peace—not the destruction of nations but the protection of freedom. The forces that West Germany contributes to this effort are second to none among the Western European nations. Your nation is in the first line of this defense—and your divisions, side by side with our own, are a source of strength to us all.

These conventional forces are essential, and they are backed by the sanction of thousands of the most modern weapons here on European soil and thousands more, only minutes away, in posts around the world. Together our nations have developed for the forward defense of free Europe a deterrent far surpassing the present or prospective force of any hostile power.

Nevertheless, it is natural that America's nuclear position has raised questions within the alliance. I believe we must confront these questions—not by turning the clock backward to separate nuclear deterrents—but by developing a more closely unified Atlantic deterrent, with genuine European participation.

How this can best be done—and it is not easy—in some ways more difficult to split the atom politically than it was physically—but how this can best be done is under discussion with those who may wish to join in this effort. The proposal before us now is for a new Atlantic force. Such a force would bring strength instead of division. It would belong to all members, not one, with all participating on a basis of full equality. And as Europe moves towards unity, its role and responsibility, here as elsewhere, would and must increase accordingly. Meanwhile, there is much to do. We must work more closely together on strategy, training and planning.

European officers from NATO are being assigned to Strategic Air Command headquarters in Omaha, Neb. Modern weapons are being deployed here in western Europe. And America's strategic deterrent—the most powerful in history—will continue to be at the service of the whole alliance.

Second: Our partnership is not military alone. Economic unity is also imperative—not only among the nations of Europe, but across the wide Atlantic. Indeed, economic cooperation is needed throughout the entire free world. By opening our markets to the developing countries of Africa, Asia and Latin America, by contributing our capital and skills, by stabilizing basic prices, we can help assure them of a favorable climate for freedom and growth. This is the Atlantic responsibility. For the Atlantic nations themselves helped to awaken these peoples. Our merchants and our traders ploughed up their soils—and their societies as well—in search of minerals and oil and rubber and coffee. Now we must help them gain full membership in the 20th century, closing the gap between the rich and the poor.

Another great economic challenge is in the coming round of trade negotiations. Those deliberations are much more important than a technical discussion of trade and commerce. They are an opportunity to build common industrial and agricultural policies across the Atlantic. They are an opportunity to open up new sources of demand, to give new impetus to growth, and make more jobs and prosperity, for our expanding populations. They are an opportunity to recognize the trading needs and aspirations of other free countries, including Japan.

In short, these negotiations are a test of our unity. While each nation must naturally look out for its own interests, each nation must also look out for the common interest—the need to reduce the imbalance between developed and underdeveloped nations—and the need to stimulate the Atlantic economy to higher levels of production rather than stifle it by higher levels of protection.

We must not return to the nineteen-thirties when we exported to each other our own stagnation. We must not return to the discredited view that trade favors some nations at the expense of others. Let no one think that the United States—with only a fraction of its economy dependent on trade and only a small part of that with western Europe—is seeking trade expansion in order to dump its goods on this continent.

Trade expansion will help us all. The experience of the Common Market—like the experience of the German Zollverein—shows an increased rise in business activity and general prosperity resulting for all participants in such trade agreements, with no member profiting at the expense of another. As they say on my own Cape Cod, "A rising tide lifts all the boats." And a partnership, by definition, serves both partners, without domination or unfair advantage. Together we have been partners in adversity—let us also be partners in prosperity.

Beyond development and trade is monetary policy. Here again our interests run together. Indeed there is no field in which the wider interests of all more clearly outweigh the narrow interest of one. We have lived by that principle, as bankers to freedom, for a generation. Now that other nations—including West Germany—have found new economic strength, it is time for common efforts here, too. The great free nations of the world must take control of our monetary problems if these problems are not to take control of us.

And third and finally, our partisanship depends on common political purpose. Against the hazards of division and lassitude, no lesser force will serve. History tells us that disunity and relaxation are the great internal dangers of an alliance. Thucydides reported that the Peloponnesians and their allies were mighty in battle but handicapped by their policy-making body—in which, he related "each presses its own end . . . which generally results in no action at all . . . they devote more time to the prosecution of their own purposes than to the consideration of the general welfare—each supposes that no harm will come of his own neglect, that it is the business of another to do this and that—and so, as each separately entertains the same illusion, the common cause imperceptibly decays."

Is this also to be the story of the grand alliance? Welded in a moment of imminent danger, will it disintegrate into complacency, with each member pressing its own ends to the neglect of the common cause? This must not be the case. Our old dangers are not gone beyond return, and any division among us would bring them back in doubled strength.

Our defenses are now strong—but they must be made stronger. Our economic goals are now clear—but we must get on with that performance. And the greatest of our necessities, the most notable of our omissions, is progress toward unity of political purpose.

For we live in a world in which our own united strength will and must be our first reliance. As I have said before, and will say again, we work toward the day where there may be real peace between us and the Communists. And we will not be second in that effort. But that day is not yet here.

We in the United States and Canada see 200 million people, and here on the European side of the Atlantic alliance 300 million people. The strength and unity of this half-billion human beings are and will continue to be the anchor of all freedom, for all nations. Let us from time to time pledge ourselves again to our common purposes. But let us go on, from words to actions, to intensify our efforts for still greater unity among us, to build new associations and institutions on those already established. Lofty words cannot construct an alliance or maintain it—only concrete deeds can do that.

The great present task of construction is here on this continent where the effort for a unified free Europe is under way. It is not for Americans to prescribe to Europeans how this effort should be carried forward. Nor do I believe that there is any one right course or any single final pattern. It is Europeans who are building Europe.

Yet the reunion of Europe, as Europeans shape it—bringing a permanent end to the civil wars that have repeatedly wracked the world—will continue to have the determined support of the United States. For that reunion is a necessary step in strengthening the community of freedom.

It would strengthen our alliance for defense. And it would be in our national interest as well as yours.

It is only a fully cohesive Europe that can protect us all against fragmentation of our alliance. Only such a Europe will permit full reciprocity of treatment across the ocean, in facing the Atlantic agenda. With only such a Europe can we have a full give-and-take between equals, and equal sharing of responsibilities, and an equal level of sacrifice. I repeat again—so that there may be no misunderstanding—the choice of paths to the unity of Europe is a choice which Europe must make. But as you continue this great effort, undeterred by either difficulty or delay, you should know that this new European greatness will be not an object of fear, but a source of strength, for the United States of America.

There are other political tasks before us. We must all learn to practice more completely the art of consultation on matters stretching well beyond the immediate military and economic questions.

Together, for example, we must explore the possibilities of leashing the tensions of the cold war and reducing the dangers of the arms race. Together we must work to strengthen the spirit of those Europeans who are not now free, to re-establish their old ties to freedom in the West, so that their desire for liberty and their sense of nationhood and their sense of belonging to the Western community over hundreds of years, will survive for future expression.

We ask those who would be our adversaries to understand that in our relations with them we will not bargain one nation's interest against another, and that the commitment to the cause of freedom is common to us all.

All of us in the West must be faithful to our conviction that peace in Europe can never be complete until everywhere in Europe, and that includes Germany, men can choose, in peace and freedom, how their countries shall be governed, and choose, without threat to any neighbor, reunification with their countrymen.

I preach no easy liberation and I make no empty promises, but my countrymen, since our country was founded, believe strongly in the proposition that all men shall be free and all free men shall have this right of choice.

As we look steadily eastward in the hope and purpose of new freedom, we must look—and evermore closely—to our trans-Atlantic ties. The Atlantic Community will not soon become a single overarching superstate. But practical steps toward stronger common purpose are well within our means. As we widen our common effort in defense, and our three-fold cooperation in economics, we shall inevitably strengthen our political ties as well. Just as your current efforts for unity in Europe will produce a stronger voice in the dialogue between us, so in America our current battle for the liberty and prosperity of all our citizens can only deepen the meaning of our common historic purposes. In the far future there may be a great new union for us all. But for the present, there is plenty for all to do in building new and enduring connections.

In short, the words of Thucydides are a warning, not a prediction. We have it in us, as 18 years have shown, to build our defenses, to strengthen our economies, and to tighten our political bonds, both in good weather and bad. We can move forward with the confidence that is born of success and the skill that is born of experience. And as we move, let us take heart from the certainty that we are united not only by danger and necessity, but by hope and purpose as well.

For we know now that freedom is more than the rejection of tyranny—that prosperity is more than an escape from want—that partnership is more than a sharing of power. These are, above all, great human adventures. They must have meaning and conviction and purpose—and because they do, in your country and in mine, in all the nations of the alliance, we are called to a great new mission.

It is not a mission of self-defense alone—for that is a means, not an end. It is not a mission of arbitrary power—for we reject the idea of one nation dominating another. The mission is to create a new social order, founded on liberty and justice, in which men are the masters of their fate, in which states are the servants of their citizens, and in which all men and women can share a better life for themselves and their children. That is the object of our common policy.

To realize this vision, we must seek a world of peace—a world in which peoples dwell together in mutual respect and work together in mutual regard—a world in which peace is not a mere interlude between wars, but an incentive to the creative energies of humanity. We will not find such a peace today, or tomorrow. The obstacles to hope are large and menacing. Yet the goals of a peaceful world—today and tomorrow—must shape our decisions and inspire our purposes.

So we are all idealists. We are all visionaries. Let it not be said of this Atlantic generation that we left ideals and visions to the past, nor purpose and determination to our adversaries. We have come too far, we have sacrificed too much, to disdain the future now. And we shall ever remember what Goethe told us—that the "highest wisdom, the best that mankind ever knew" was the realization that "he only earns his freedom and existence who daily conquers them anew."

Additional Reading

John R. Beal, *John Foster Dulles* (1959).
Marquis Childs, *Eisenhower: Captive Hero* (1958).
David J. Dallin, *Soviet Foreign Policy after Stalin* (1961).
Robert J. Donovan, *Eisenhower: the Inside Story* (1956).
Roscoe Drummond and G. Coblentz, *Duel at the Brink: John Foster Dulles' Command of American Power* (1960).
G. F. Kennan, *Russia, the Atom and the West* (1958).
Hans Morgenthau, "John Foster Dulles," in Norman Graebner, ed., *An Uncertain Tradition: American Secretaries of State in the Twentieth Century* (1961), 289–308.
Hugh Seton-Watson, *Neither War nor Peace* (1960).